Mastering Embedded Linux Development

Fourth Edition

Craft fast and reliable embedded solutions with Linux 6.6 and The Yocto Project 5.0 (Scarthgap)

Frank Vasquez | Chris Simmonds

‹packt›

Mastering Embedded Linux Development
Fourth Edition

Copyright © 2025 Packt Publishing

Portfolio Director: Rohit Rajkumar

Relationship Lead: Kaustubh Manglurkar

Content Engineer: Anuradha Joglekar

Program Manager: Sandip Tadge

Technical Editors: Kushal Sharma and Gaurav Gavas

Copy Editor: SafisEditing

Indexer: Rekha Nair

Proofreader: SafisEditing

Production Designers: Ganesh Bhadwalkar, Gokul Raj ST, and Shantanu Zagade

Marketing Owner: Nivedita Pande

Growth Lead: Namita Velgekar

First edition: December 2015
Second edition: June 2017
Third edition: May 2021
Fourth edition: May 2025

Production reference: 3031225

Published by Packt Publishing Ltd.
Grosvenor House
11 St Paul's Square
Birmingham
B3 1RB, UK.

ISBN 978-1-80323-259-1

www.packt.com

To Chris Simmonds, whose words stand the test of time. And to my wife, Deborah, for encouraging me to do this again. The world still runs on Linux.

— Frank Vasquez

Contributors

About the authors

Frank Vasquez is an independent software consultant specializing in consumer electronics. He has more than a decade of experience designing and building embedded Linux systems. During that time, he has shipped numerous products, including a rackmount DSP audio server, a diver-held sonar camcorder, an IoT hotspot, a home battery, and a grid-scale energy storage system. Since the third edition of this book was published, Frank has also become a frequent speaker at open-source software conferences including The Yocto Project Summit, Embedded Linux Conference, FOSDEM, and All Systems Go! He is passionate about learning new technologies and teaching them to others.

Chris Simmonds is a software consultant and trainer living in southern England. He has almost two decades of experience in designing and building open-source embedded systems. He is the founder and chief consultant at 2net Ltd, which provides professional training and mentoring services in embedded Linux, Linux device drivers, and Android platform development. He has trained engineers at many of the biggest companies in the embedded world, including ARM, Qualcomm, Intel, Ericsson, and General Dynamics. He is a frequent presenter at open-source and embedded conferences, including the Embedded Linux Conference and Embedded World.

About the reviewers

Alex Trifonov is a senior software engineer at Cisco, specializing in embedded systems, Linux, and networking. With a strong background in firmware development, real-time systems, and hardware-software integration, he has contributed to building reliable and scalable embedded solutions for a variety of applications.

Passionate about the intersection of software and hardware, Alex has extensive experience in networking, home automation, and industrial embedded systems. His expertise spans low-level programming, system optimization, and security, making him a valuable contributor to the embedded development community.

As a technical reviewer for *Mastering Embedded Linux Development*, Alex ensures that the book provides accurate, practical, and industry-relevant insights, making it an essential resource for engineers looking to advance their skills.

Khem Raj is an embedded Linux architect and a well-known open-source developer and thought leader. Presently, he works at Comcast on CPE devices and has helped create the RDK stack, which is used on device platforms in millions of devices today. He is a member of The Yocto Project Advisory Committee and serves on the project Technical Steering Council, shaping the project's technical direction. He is a frequent speaker at open-source conferences and has spoken on varied subjects ranging from embedded Linux systems to open-source processes. Along with core toolchains in The Yocto Project, he is also the maintainer of several important Yocto Project layers, notably meta-openembedded, meta-clang, meta-riscv, and meta-raspberrypi, to name a few. He has also been nominated as an RISC-V architecture ambassador. He has reviewed other books, including *Mastering Linux Device Driver Development: Write custom device drivers to support computer peripherals in Linux operating systems*. In his free time, he reads non-fiction, writes programs for fun, likes hiking, and co-hosts the TMPDIR podcast.

I would like to thank my wife, Sweta, and children, Himangi and Vihaan, for always supporting me in my endeavors.

Join our community on Discord

Join our community's Discord space for discussions with the authors and other readers: `https://packt.link/embeddedsystems`

Table of Contents

Chapter 3: All about Bootloaders   47

Chapter 5: Building a Root Filesystem 125

Chapter 8: Yocto under the Hood   237

Part III: System Architecture and Design Decisions   263

Chapter 9: Creating a Storage Strategy   265

Chapter 10: Updating Software in the Field 301

Part IV: Developing Applications   427

Chapter 15: Packaging Python   429

Chapter 16: Deploying Container Images   451

Chapter 17: Learning about Processes and Threads   493

Part V: Debugging and Optimizing Performance   553

Chapter 19: Debugging with GDB   555

Preface

Linux has been the mainstay of embedded computing for many years. And yet, there are remarkably few books that cover the topic as a whole: this book is intended to fill that gap. The term embedded Linux is not well-defined and can be applied to the operating system inside a wide range of devices ranging from thermostats to Wi-Fi routers to industrial control units. However, they are all built on the same basic open source software. Those are the technologies that I describe in this book, based on my experience as an engineer.

Technology does not stand still. The industry based around embedded computing is just as susceptible to Moore's law as mainstream computing. The exponential growth that this implies has meant that a surprisingly large number of things have changed since the first edition of this book was published. This fourth edition is fully revised to use the latest versions of the major open source components, which include Linux 6.6, Yocto Project 5.0 Scarthgap, and Buildroot 2024.02 LTS. In addition to Autotools, the book now covers CMake, a modern build system that has seen increased adoption in recent years.

Who this book is for

This book is written for developers with an interest in embedded computing and Linux, who want to extend their knowledge into the various branches of the subject. In writing the book, I assume a basic understanding of the Linux command line, and in the programming examples, a working knowledge of the C and Python languages. Several chapters focus on the hardware that goes into an embedded target board, so a familiarity with hardware and hardware interfaces will be a definite advantage in these cases.

What this book covers

Chapter 1, Starting Out, sets the scene by describing the embedded Linux ecosystem and the choices available to you as you start your project.

Chapter 2, Learning about Toolchains, describes the components of a toolchain and where to obtain a toolchain for cross-compiling code for your target board.

Chapter 3, All about Bootloaders, explains the role of the bootloader in loading the Linux kernel into memory, and uses U-Boot as an example. It also introduces device trees as the mechanism used to encode the details of hardware in almost all embedded Linux systems.

Chapter 4, Configuring and Building the Kernel, provides information on how to select a Linux kernel for an embedded system and configure it for the hardware within the device. It also covers how to port Linux to the new hardware.

Chapter 5, Building a Root Filesystem, introduces the ideas behind the user space part of an embedded Linux implementation by means of a step-by-step guide on how to configure a root filesystem.

Chapter 6, Selecting a Build System, covers two commonly used embedded Linux build systems, Buildroot and The Yocto Project, which automate the steps described in the previous four chapters.

Chapter 7, Developing with Yocto, demonstrates how to build system images on top of an existing BSP layer, develop onboard software packages with Yocto's extensible SDK, and roll your own embedded Linux distribution complete with runtime package management.

Chapter 8, Yocto under the Hood, is a tour of Yocto's build workflow and architecture, including an explanation of Yocto's unique multi-layer approach. It also breaks down the basics of BitBake syntax and semantics with examples from actual recipe files.

Chapter 9, Creating a Storage Strategy, discusses the challenges created by managing flash memory, including raw flash chips and **embedded MMC (eMMC)** packages. It describes the filesystems that are applicable to each type of technology.

Chapter 10, Updating Software in the Field, examines various ways of updating the software after the device has been deployed, and includes fully managed **Over-the-Air (OTA)** updates. The key topics under discussion are reliability and security.

Chapter 11, Interfacing with Device Drivers, describes how kernel device drivers interact with the hardware by implementing a simple driver. It also describes the various ways of calling device drivers from user space.

Chapter 12, Prototyping with Add-On Boards, demonstrates how to prototype hardware and software quickly using a pre-built Debian image for the BeaglePlay together with MikroElektronika peripheral add-on boards.

Chapter 13, Starting Up – The init Program, explains how the first user space program, `init`, starts the rest of the system. It describes three versions of the `init` program, each suitable for a different group of embedded systems, ranging from the simplicity of the BusyBox `init`, through System V `init`, to the current state-of-the-art, `systemd`.

Chapter 14, Managing Power, considers the various ways that Linux can be tuned to reduce power consumption, including dynamic frequency and voltage scaling, selecting deeper idle states, and system suspend. The aim is to make devices that run longer on a battery charge and also run cooler.

Chapter 15, Packaging Python, explains what choices are available for bundling Python modules together for deployment and when to use one method over another. It covers `pip`, virtual environments, and conda.

Chapter 16, Deploying Container Images, introduces the principles of the DevOps movement and demonstrates how to apply them to embedded Linux. First, we use Docker to bundle a Python application together with its user space environment inside a container image. Then we use GitHub Actions to set up a CI/CD pipeline for our container image. Lastly, we use Docker to perform containerized software updates on a Raspberry Pi 4.

Chapter 17, Learning about Processes and Threads, describes embedded systems from the point of view of the application programmer. This chapter looks at processes and threads, inter-process communications, and scheduling policies.

Chapter 18, Managing Memory, examines the ideas behind virtual memory and how the address space is divided into memory mappings. It also describes how to measure memory usage accurately and how to detect memory leaks.

Chapter 19, Debugging with GDB, shows you how to use the GNU debugger, GDB, together with the debug agent, `gdbserver`, to debug applications running remotely on the target device. It goes on to show how you can extend this model to debug kernel code, making use of the kernel debug stubs, KGDB.

Chapter 20, Profiling and Tracing, covers the techniques available to measure system performance, starting from whole system profiles and then zeroing in on specific areas where bottlenecks are causing poor performance. It also describes how to use Valgrind to check the correctness of an application's use of thread synchronization and memory allocation.

Chapter 21, Real-Time Programming, provides a detailed guide to real-time programming on Linux using the recently merged PREEMPT_RT real-time kernel patch.

To get the most out of this book

The software used in this book is entirely open source. In almost all cases, I have used the latest stable versions available at the time of writing. While I have tried to describe the main features in a manner that is not version-specific, it is inevitable that some of the examples will need adaptation to work with later software. Here is the primary hardware and software used throughout the book:

- QEMU (64-bit Arm)
- Raspberry Pi 4
- BeaglePlay
- Yocto Project 5.0 Scarthgap
- Buildroot 2024.02
- Bootlin aarch64 glibc stable toolchain 2024.02-1
- Arm GNU AArch32 bare-metal target (arm-none-eabi) toolchain 13.2.Rel1
- U-Boot v2024.04
- Linux kernel 6.6

Embedded development involves two systems: the host, which is used for developing the programs, and the target, which runs them. For the host system, I chose Ubuntu 24.04 LTS because of its widespread adoption and long-term maintenance guarantees. You may decide to run Linux on Docker, a virtual machine, or Windows Subsystem for Linux, but be aware that some tasks, such as building a distribution using The Yocto Project, are quite demanding and run better on a native installation of Linux.

For the targets, I chose the QEMU emulator, the Raspberry Pi 4, and the BeaglePlay. Using QEMU means that you can try out most of the examples without having to invest in any additional hardware. On the other hand, some things work better with real hardware. For that, I picked the Raspberry Pi 4 because it is inexpensive, widely available, and has very good community support. The BeaglePlay replaces the BeagleBone Black used in previous editions of the book. Of course, you are not limited to just these three targets. The idea behind the book is to provide you with general solutions to problems so that you can apply them to a wide range of target boards.

Download the example code files

The code bundle for the book is hosted on GitHub at `https://github.com/PacktPublishing/Mastering-Embedded-Linux-Development`. We also have other code bundles from our rich catalog of books and videos available at `https://github.com/PacktPublishing`. Check them out!

Download the color images

We also provide a PDF file that has color images of the screenshots/diagrams used in this book. You can download it here: `https://packt.link/gbp/9781803232591`.

Conventions used

There are a number of text conventions used throughout this book.

`CodeInText`: Indicates code words in text, database table names, folder names, filenames, file extensions, pathnames, dummy URLs, user input, and Twitter handles. For example: "Execute the `make menuconfig` command:"

A block of code is set as follows:

```
require recipes-core/images/core-image-minimal.bb
IMAGE_INSTALL:append = " helloworld strace"
```

Any command-line input or output is written as follows:

```
$ bitbake -c populate_sdk nova-image
```

Bold: Indicates a new term, an important word, or words that you see on the screen. For instance, words in menus or dialog boxes appear in the text like this. For example: "Back out of **External toolchain** and open the **Toolchain** submenu."

Warnings or important notes appear like this.

Tips and tricks appear like this.

Get in touch

Feedback from our readers is always welcome.

General feedback: Email feedback@packtpub.com and mention the book's title in the subject of your message. If you have questions about any aspect of this book, please email us at questions@packtpub.com.

Errata: Although we have taken every care to ensure the accuracy of our content, mistakes do happen. If you have found a mistake in this book, we would be grateful if you reported this to us. Please visit http://www.packtpub.com/submit-errata, click **Submit Errata**, and fill in the form.

Piracy: If you come across any illegal copies of our works in any form on the internet, we would be grateful if you would provide us with the location address or website name. Please contact us at copyright@packtpub.com with a link to the material.

If you are interested in becoming an author: If there is a topic that you have expertise in and you are interested in either writing or contributing to a book, please visit http://authors.packtpub.com/.

Share your thoughts

Once you've read *Mastering Embedded Linux Development, Fourth Edition*, we'd love to hear your thoughts! Scan the QR code below to go straight to the Amazon review page for this book and share your feedback.

https://packt.link/r/1803232595

Your review is important to us and the tech community and will help us make sure we're delivering excellent quality content.

Free Benefits with Your Book

This book comes with free benefits to support your learning. Activate them now for instant access (see the "How to Unlock" section for instructions).

Here's a quick overview of what you get, instantly unlockable with your purchase:

DRM-Free PDF Version

Next-Gen Web-Based Reader

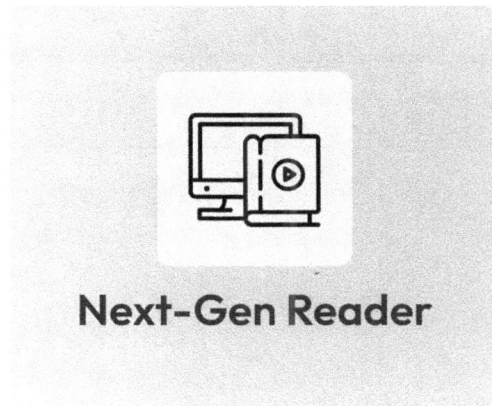

Free PDF and ePub versions

Next-Gen Reader

What you get:

- 📄 Access a DRM-free PDF copy of this book to read anywhere, on any device.
- 📑 Use a DRM-free ePub version with your favorite e-reader.

What you get:

- ☁ **Multi-device progress sync**: Pick up where you left off, on any device.
- 📖 **Highlighting and notetaking**: Capture ideas and turn reading into lasting knowledge.
- 🔖 **Bookmarking**: Save and revisit key sections whenever you need them.
- ☀ **Dark mode**: Reduce eye strain by switching to dark or sepia themes.

How to Unlock

UNLOCK NOW

Scan the QR code (or go to packtpub.com/unlock).
Search for this book by name, confirm the edition, and
then follow the steps on the page.'

*Note: Keep your invoice handy. Purchases made directly from
Packt don't require one.*

Part 1

Elements of Embedded Linux

In this part, you will explore the four key elements of any embedded Linux project. You will learn how to select a toolchain, build the bootloader, and build the kernel for your target device. *Chapter 5* requires you to build a root filesystem step by step from scratch. These manual exercises are difficult, but by the end of this section, you with have a deeper understanding of how embedded Linux works and a greater appreciation for tools that can automate this board bring-up phase.

This part has the following chapters:

- *Chapter 1, Starting Out*
- *Chapter 2, Learning about Toolchains*
- *Chapter 3, All about Bootloaders*
- *Chapter 4, Configuring and Building the Kernel*
- *Chapter 5, Building a Root Filesystem*

1

Starting Out

You are about to begin working on your next project, and this time, it is going to run Linux. What should you think about before you put finger to keyboard? Let's begin with a high-level look at embedded Linux and see why it is popular, what the implications of open source licenses are, and what kind of hardware you need to run it.

Linux first became a viable choice for embedded devices around 1999. That was when AXIS released the 2100 Network Camera and TiVo released their first **Digital Video Recorder (DVR)**. Both were the first Linux-powered devices in their category. Since 1999, Linux has become increasingly popular to the point that today it is the **Operating System (OS)** of choice for many classes of product. In 2024, there were over three billion devices running Linux. That includes all the smartphones running Android, which uses a Linux kernel, and hundreds of millions of set-top boxes, smart TVs, and Wi-Fi routers. We must not forget other devices, such as vehicle diagnostics, industrial equipment, and medical monitoring units, that ship in smaller volumes.

In this chapter, we will cover the following topics:

- Choosing Linux
- When not to choose Linux
- Meeting the players
- Moving through the project life cycle
- Navigating open source
- Selecting hardware for embedded Linux
- Obtaining the hardware for this book
- Provisioning your development environment

Choosing Linux

Why is Linux so pervasive? And why does something as simple as a TV need to run something as complex as Linux just to display streaming video on a screen?

The simple answer is **Moore's law**. Gordon Moore, cofounder of Intel, observed in 1965 that the density of components on a chip doubles approximately every two years. That applies to the devices that we design and use in our everyday lives just as much as it does to desktops, laptops, and servers. At the heart of most embedded devices is a highly integrated chip that contains one or more processor cores and interfaces with main memory, mass storage, and peripherals of many types. This is referred to as a **System on Chip (SoC)**. SoCs are increasing in complexity in accordance with Moore's law. A typical SoC has a technical reference manual that stretches to thousands of pages.

Your TV isn't simply displaying a video stream like the analog sets of old. The stream is digital, possibly encrypted, and needs processing to produce an image. Your TV is (or soon will be) connected to the internet. It can receive content from smartphones, tablets, laptops, desktops, and home media servers. It can be used to play games, stream video, and display live feeds from security cameras. You need a full OS to manage this degree of complexity.

Here are some points that drive the adoption of Linux:

- Linux has the necessary functionality. It has a good scheduler, a good network stack, support for USB, Wi-Fi, Bluetooth, many kinds of storage media, multimedia devices, and so on. It ticks all the boxes.
- Linux has been ported to a wide range of processor architectures, including some that are very commonly found in SoC designs – Arm, RISC-V, x86, PowerPC, and MIPS.
- Linux is open source, so you have the freedom to get the source code and modify it to meet your needs. You or someone working on your behalf can create a board support package for your device. You can add protocols, features, and technologies that may be missing from the mainline source code. You can remove features that you don't need to reduce memory and storage requirements. Linux is flexible.
- Linux has an active community (in the case of the Linux kernel, very active). There is a new release of the kernel every 8 to 10 weeks, and each release contains code from more than 1,000 developers. An active community means that Linux is up to date and supports current hardware, protocols, and standards. The Linux Foundation is a non-profit organization with backing from big tech.

The foundation acts as a steward for several major open source projects besides Linux, including Kubernetes and PyTorch. It also hosts yearly events around the world like the Open Source Summit and Linux Plumbers Conference.

- Open source licenses guarantee that you have access to the source code. There is no vendor lock-in.

For these reasons, Linux is an ideal choice for complex devices. But there are a few caveats I should mention here. Complexity makes it harder to understand. Coupled with the fast-moving development process and the decentralized structures of open source, you need to put some effort into learning how to use it and to keep on re-learning as it changes. I hope that this book helps in the process.

When not to choose Linux

Is Linux suitable for your project? Linux works well where the problem being solved justifies the complexity. It is especially good where connectivity, robustness, and complex user interfaces are required. However, it cannot solve every problem, so here are some things to consider before you jump in:

- Is your hardware up to the job? Compared to a traditional **Real-Time Operating System (RTOS)** such as VxWorks or QNX, Linux requires a lot more resources. It needs at least a 32-bit processor and lots more memory. I will go into more detail in the *Selecting hardware for embedded Linux* section.

- Do you have the right skill set? The early parts of a project, the board bring-up, require detailed knowledge of Linux and how it relates to your hardware. Likewise, when debugging and tuning your application you will need to be able to interpret the results. If you don't have the skills in-house you may want to outsource some of the work. Of course, reading this book helps!

- Is your system real time? Linux can handle many real-time activities as long as you pay attention to certain details, which I cover in depth in *Chapter 21*.

- Will your code require regulatory approval (medical, automotive, aerospace, and so on)? The burden of regulatory verification and validation might make another OS a better choice. Even if you do choose Linux for use in these environments, it may make sense to purchase a commercially available distribution from a company that has supplied Linux for existing products like the one you are building. These commercial Linux vendors include Siemens, Timesys, and Wind River.

Consider these points carefully. Probably the best indicator of success is to look around for similar products that run Linux and see how they did it, and follow best practices.

Meeting the players

Where does open source software come from? Who writes it? In particular, how does it relate to the key components of embedded development – the toolchain, bootloader, kernel, and basic utilities found in the root filesystem?

- **Open source community**: This, after all, is the engine that generates the software you are going to be using. The community is a loose alliance of developers many of whom are funded in some way by a non-profit organization, an academic institution, or a commercial company. They work together to further the aims of the various projects. There are many of them – some small, some large. Some that we will make use of are Linux itself, U-Boot, BusyBox, Buildroot, The Yocto Project, and the many projects under the GNU umbrella.

- **CPU architects**: These are the organizations that design the CPUs we use. The important ones here are Arm/Linaro (Arm Cortex-A), Intel (x86 and x86-64), SiFive (RISC-V), and IBM (PowerPC). They implement or at the very least influence support for the basic CPU architecture.

- **SoC vendors**: These include Broadcom, Intel, Microchip, NXP, Qualcomm, TI, and many others. They take the kernel and toolchain from the CPU architects and modify them to support their chips. They also create reference boards: designs that are used by the next level down to create development boards and working products.

- **Board vendors and OEMs**: These people take the reference designs from SoC vendors and build them into specific products like set-top boxes or cameras. They also create more general-purpose development boards such as those from Advantech and Kontron. An important category is the cheap **Single-Board Computers** (**SBCs**) such as BeagleBoard and Raspberry Pi, which have created their own ecosystems of software and hardware add-ons.

- **Commercial Linux vendors**: Companies such as Siemens, Timesys, and Wind River offer commercial Linux distributions that have undergone strict regulatory verification and validation across multiple industries (medical, automotive, aerospace, and so on).

These form a chain, with your project usually at the end, which means that you do not have a free choice of components. You cannot simply take the latest kernel from kernel.org, except in rare cases, because it does not have support for the chip or board that you are using.

This is an ongoing problem with embedded development. Ideally, the developers at each link in the chain would push their changes upstream but they don't. Developers are under constant time pressure and getting patches accepted into the Linux kernel takes major effort. It is not uncommon to find a kernel that has many thousands of patches that are not merged. In addition, SoC vendors tend to actively develop open source components only for their latest chips, meaning that support for any chip more than a couple of years old will be frozen and not receive any updates.

The consequence is that most embedded designs are based on old versions of software. They do not receive security fixes, performance enhancements, or features that are in newer versions. Problems such as Heartbleed (a bug in the OpenSSL library) and Shellshock (a bug in the Bash shell) go unfixed.

What can you do about it? First, ask questions of your vendors (NXP, TI, and Xilinx to name just a few): what is their update policy, how often do they revise kernel versions, what is the current kernel version, what was the one before that, and what is their policy for merging changes upstream? Some vendors are making great strides in this direction. You should prefer their chips.

Secondly, you can take steps to make yourself more self-sufficient. The chapters in *Part 1* explain the dependencies in more detail and show you where you can help yourself. Don't just take the package offered to you by the SoC or board vendor and use it blindly without considering the alternatives.

Moving through the project life cycle

This book is divided into five sections that reflect the phases of a project. The phases are not necessarily sequential. Usually, they overlap, and you will need to jump back to revisit things that were done previously. However, they are representative of a developer's preoccupations as the project progresses:

- *Elements of Embedded Linux (Chapters 1 to 5)* will help you set up the development environment and create a working platform for the later phases. It is often referred to as the **board bring-up** phase.
- *Building Embedded Linux Images (Chapters 6 to 8)* shows you how to automate the process of building an embedded Linux image by leveraging a build system like Buildroot or The Yocto Project. Automating complex build tasks accelerates the project life cycle so that teams can deliver higher-quality products in less time.
- *System Architecture and Design Choices (Chapters 9 to 14)* will inform some of the design decisions you will have to make concerning the storage of programs and data, how to divide work between kernel device drivers and applications, and how to initialize the system.

- *Developing Applications (Chapters 15 to 18)* shows you how to package and deploy Python applications, make effective use of the Linux process and thread model, and manage memory in a resource-constrained device. What do packaging and deploying Python applications have to do with embedded Linux? The answer is "not much", but bear in mind that the word "development" also happens to be in the title of this book. And *Chapters 15 and 16* have everything to do with modern-day software development.

- *Debugging and Optimizing Performance (Chapters 19 to 21)* describes how to trace, profile, and debug your code in both the application and the kernel. The last chapter explains how to design for real-time behavior when required.

Now, let's focus on the four basic elements of embedded Linux that comprise the first section of the book.

The four elements of embedded Linux

Every project begins by obtaining, customizing, and deploying these four elements: the toolchain, the bootloader, the kernel, and the root filesystem. This is the topic of the first section of this book.

- **Toolchain**: This is the cross compiler and other tools needed to create code for your target device. A cross compiler generates machine code for a target CPU architecture while running on a different host CPU architecture.

- **Bootloader**: This is a bare metal program that initializes the board and the Linux kernel. The term "bare metal" means the program runs directly on the CPU, not on top of an OS.

- **Kernel**: This is the heart of the system, managing system resources and interfacing with the hardware.

- **Root filesystem**: This contains the libraries and programs that are run once the kernel has completed its initialization.

There is also a fifth element not mentioned here. That is the collection of programs specific to your embedded application that make the device do whatever it is supposed to do, be it weighing groceries, displaying movies, controlling a robot, or flying a drone.

Typically, you will be offered some or all of these elements as a package when you buy your SoC or board. But for the reasons mentioned earlier, they may not be the best choices for you. In the first eight chapters, I will give you the background to make the right selection and introduce two tools that automate the whole process for you: Buildroot and The Yocto Project.

Navigating open source

The components of embedded Linux are *open source* so now is a good time to consider what that means, why open source licenses work the way they do, and how this affects the often proprietary embedded device you will be creating from it.

Licenses

When talking about open source the word *free* is often used. People new to the subject often take it to mean *nothing to pay* and open source software licenses do indeed guarantee that you can use the software to develop and deploy systems for no charge. However, the more important meaning here is freedom since you are free to obtain the source code, modify it in any way you see fit, and redeploy it in other systems. Open source licenses give you this right, but some also require you to share these changes with the public.

Compare that with freeware licenses, which allow you to copy the binaries for no cost but do not give you the source code. Other licenses allow you to use the software for free under certain circumstances, for example, for personal use, but not commercial. These are not open source.

I will provide the following comments in the interest of helping you understand the implications of working with open source licenses, but I would like to point out that I am an engineer and not a lawyer. What follows is my understanding of the licenses and how they are interpreted.

Open source licenses fall broadly into two categories:

- *Copyleft* licenses such as the GNU **General Public License (GPL)**
- Permissive licenses such as the **BSD** and **MIT** licenses

The permissive licenses say, in essence, that you may modify the source code and use it in systems of your own choosing as long as you do not modify the terms of the license in any way. In other words, apart from that one restriction, you can do with it what you want, including building it into possibly proprietary systems.

The GPL licenses are similar but have clauses that compel you to pass the rights to obtain and modify the software on to your end users. In other words, you share your source code. One option is to make it completely public by putting it onto a public server. Another is to offer it only to your end users by means of a written offer to provide the code when requested.

The GPL goes further to say that you cannot incorporate GPL code into proprietary programs. Any attempt to do so would make the GPL apply to the whole. In other words, you cannot combine GPL and proprietary code in the same program. Aside from the Linux kernel, the GNU Compiler Collection and GNU Debugger, as well as many other freely available tools associated with the GNU project, fall under the umbrella of the GPL.

So, what about libraries? If they are licensed with the GPL, any program linked with them becomes GPL also. However, most libraries are licensed under the GNU **Lesser General Public License** (**LGPL**). If this is the case, you are allowed to link with them from a proprietary program.

IMPORTANT NOTE

All of the preceding descriptions relate specifically to the GPL v2 and LGPL v2. I should mention the latest versions of the GPL v3 and LGPL v3. These are controversial and I will admit that I don't fully understand the implications. However, the intention is to ensure that the GPL v3 and LGPL v3 components in any system can be replaced by the end user, which is in the spirit of open source software for everyone.

The GPL v3 and LGPL v3 have their problems though. There are security issues. If the owner of a device has access to the system code, then so might an unwelcome intruder. Often the defense is to have kernel images signed by an authority such as the vendor so that unauthorized updates are not possible. Is that an infringement of my right to modify my device? Opinions differ.

IMPORTANT NOTE

The TiVo set-top box is an important part of this debate. It uses a Linux kernel, which is licensed under the GPL v2. TiVo has released the source code of their version of the kernel in compliance with the license. TiVo also has a bootloader that will only load a kernel binary that is signed by them. Consequently, you can build a modified kernel for a TiVo box, but you cannot load it on the hardware.

The **Free Software Foundation (FSF)** takes the position that this is not in the spirit of open source software and refers to this procedure as **tivoization**. The GPL v3 and LGPL v3 were written explicitly to prevent this from happening. Some projects, the Linux kernel in particular, have been reluctant to adopt the GPL version 3 licenses because of the restrictions they place on device manufacturers.

Selecting hardware for embedded Linux

If you are designing or selecting hardware for an embedded Linux project, what do you look out for?

- First, a CPU architecture that is supported by the kernel – unless you plan to add a new architecture yourself of course! Looking at the source code for Linux 5.15 there are 23 architectures each represented by a subdirectory in the arch/ directory. They are all 32-or 64-bit architectures, most with an MMU, but some without. The ones most often found in embedded devices are Arm, RISC-V, PowerPC, MIPS, and x86 each in 32-and 64-bit variants all of which have **Memory Management Units (MMUs)**.

- Most of this book is written with this class of processor in mind. There is another group that doesn't have an MMU and that runs a subset of Linux known as a **microcontroller Linux** or **uClinux**. These processor architectures include **ARC (Argonaut RISC Core)**, Blackfin, MicroBlaze, and Nios. I will mention uClinux from time to time, but I will not go into detail because it is a rather specialized type.

- Second, you will need a reasonable amount of RAM. 16 MB is a good minimum, although it is quite possible to run Linux using half of that. It is even possible to run Linux with 4 MB if you are prepared to go to the trouble of optimizing every part of the system. It may even be possible to get lower, but there comes a point at which it is no longer Linux.

- Third, there is non-volatile storage, usually flash memory. 8 MB is enough for a simple device such as a webcam or basic router. As with RAM, you can create a workable Linux system with less storage if you really want to, but the lower you go the harder it becomes. Linux has extensive support for flash storage devices, including raw NOR and NAND flash chips, and managed flash in the form of SD cards, eMMC chips, USB flash memory, and so on.

- Fourth, a serial port is very useful, preferably a UART-based serial port. It does not have to be fitted on production boards but makes board bring-up, debugging, and development much easier.

- Fifth, you need some means of loading software when starting from scratch. Many microcontroller boards are fitted with a **Joint Test Action Group (JTAG)** interface for this purpose. Modern SoCs can also load boot code directly from the removable media, especially SD and microSD cards, or serial interfaces such as QSPI or USB.

In addition to these basics, there are interfaces to the specific bits of hardware your device needs to get its job done. Mainline Linux comes with open source drivers for many thousands of different devices, and there are drivers available (of variable quality) from the SoC manufacturer and from the OEMs of third-party chips that may be included in the design.

Remember my comments on the commitment and ability of some manufacturers. As a developer of embedded systems, you will find that you spend quite a lot of time evaluating and adapting third-party code, if you have it, or liaising with the manufacturer if you don't. Finally, you will have to write the device support for the interfaces that are unique to the device or find someone to do it for you.

Obtaining the hardware for this book

The examples in this book are intended to be generic. To make them relevant and easy to follow I have had to choose specific hardware. I have chosen three exemplary devices: the Raspberry Pi 4, BeaglePlay, and QEMU. The first is by far the most popular Arm-based SBC on the market. The second is a widely available SBC that can also be used in serious embedded hardware. The third is a machine emulator that can be used to create a range of systems that are typical of embedded hardware.

It was tempting to use QEMU exclusively, but like all emulations, it is not quite the same as the real thing. Using the Raspberry Pi 4 and BeaglePlay, you have the satisfaction of interacting with real hardware and seeing real LEDs flash. The BeaglePlay, like the BeagleBone Black before it, is *open source hardware*, unlike the Raspberry Pi 4. This means that the board design materials are freely available for anyone to build the BeaglePlay or a derivative into their products.

In any case, I encourage you to try out as many of the examples as you can, using either of these three platforms or any embedded hardware you may have on hand.

The Raspberry Pi 4

From June 2019 until October 2023, the Raspberry Pi 4 Model B was the flagship SBC produced by the Raspberry Pi Foundation. The Raspberry Pi 4's technical specs include the following:

- A Broadcom BCM2711 1.5 GHz quad-core Cortex-A72 (Arm v8) 64-bit SoC
- 2, 4, or 8 GB DDR4 RAM
- 2.4 GHz and 5 GHz 802.11ac wireless, Bluetooth 5.0, BLE
- A serial port for debugging and development
- A microSD slot, which can be used as a boot device
- A USB-C connector to power the board
- Two full-size USB 3.0 and two full-size USB 2.0 host ports
- A Gigabit Ethernet port
- Two micro HDMI ports for video and audio output

In addition, there is a 40-pin expansion header for which there are a great variety of daughter boards known as **Hardware Attached on Top (HATs)** that allow you to adapt the board to do many different things. However, you will not need any HATs for the examples in this book.

In addition to the board itself you will require the following:

- A microSD card and a means of writing to it from your development PC or laptop
- A USB-to-TTL serial cable with a 3.3 V logic level
- A 5 V USB-C power supply capable of delivering 3 A
- An Ethernet cable and a router to plug it into as some of the examples require network connectivity

The BeaglePlay

The BeaglePlay is an open source hardware design for an SBC produced by the BeagleBoard.org Foundation. The main points of the specification are:

- A TI AM6254 1.4 GHz Arm quad-core Cortex-A53 (Arm v8) 64-bit Sitara SoC
- 2 GB DDR4 RAM
- 16 GB eMMC on-board flash
- 2.4 GHz and 5 GHz MIMO Wi-Fi, BLE, Zigbee
- A serial port for debugging and development
- A microSD slot, which can be used as a boot device
- A USB-C connector to power the board
- A full-size USB 2.0 host port
- A Gigabit Ethernet port
- A full-size HDMI port for video and audio output

Instead of a large expansion header, the BeaglePlay has mikroBUS, Grove, and Qwiic interfaces for connecting add-on boards.

In addition to the board itself, you will require the following:

- A microSD card and a means of writing to it from your development PC or laptop
- A USB-to-TTL serial cable with a 3.3 V logic level
- A 5 V USB-C power supply capable of delivering 3 A
- An Ethernet cable and a router to plug it into as some of the examples require network connectivity

In addition to the above, *Chapter 12* also requires the following:

- A MikroE-5764 GNSS 7 Click add-on board
- An external active GNSS antenna with an SMA connector
- A MikroE-5546 Environment Click add-on board
- A MikroE-5545 OLED C Click add-on board

QEMU

QEMU is a machine emulator. It comes in different flavors, each of which can emulate a processor architecture and various boards built using that architecture. For example, we have the following:

- qemu-system-arm: 32-bit Arm
- qemu-system-aarch64: 64-bit Arm
- qemu-system-mips: MIPS
- qemu-system-ppc: Power PC
- qemu-system-x86: x86 and x86-64

For each architecture, QEMU emulates a range of hardware that you can see by using the -machine help option. Each architecture emulates most of the hardware that would normally be found on that board. There are options to link hardware to local resources, such as using a local file for the emulated disk drive. Here is a concrete example:

```
$ qemu-system-arm -machine vexpress-a9 -m 256M -drive file=rootfs.
ext4,sd -net nic -net use -kernel zImage -dtb vexpress-v2p-ca9.dtb
-append "console=ttyAMA0,115200 root=/dev/mmcblk0" -serial stdio -net
nic,model=lan9118 -net tap,ifname=tap0
```

IMPORTANT NOTE

The preceding command is not meant to be executed and will fail since qemu-system-arm is not installed and the rootfs.ext4.sd, zImage, and vexpress-v2p-ca9.dtb files do not exist on your host system. It is just an example for us to expand on.

The options used in the preceding command line are as follows:

- `-machine vexpress -a9`: Creates an emulation of an Arm Versatile Express development board with a Cortex-A9 processor.
- `-m 256M`: Populates it with 256 MB of RAM.
- `-drive file=rootfs.ext4,sd`: Connects the SD interface to the local `rootfs.ext4` file, which contains a filesystem image.
- `-kernel zImage`: Loads the Linux kernel from the local file named `zImage`.
- `-dtb vexpress-v2p-ca9.dtb`: Loads the device tree from the local `vexpress-v2p-ca9.dtb` file.
- `-append "…"`: Appends the string in quotes as the kernel command line.
- `-serial stdio`: Connects the serial port to the terminal that launched QEMU so that you can log on to the emulated machine via the serial console.
- `-net nic,model=lan9118`: Creates a network interface.
- `-net tap,ifname=tap0`: Connects the network interface to the virtual network interface `tap0`.

To configure the host side of the network you need the `tunctl` command from the **User Mode Linux (UML)** project. On Debian and Ubuntu, the package is named `uml-utilities`:

```
$ sudo tunctl -u $(whoami) -t tap0
```

This creates a network interface named `tap0` that is connected to the network controller in the emulated QEMU machine. You configure `tap0` the same way as any other network interface.

All these options are described in the following chapters. I will be using Versatile Express for most of my examples, but it should be easy to use a different machine or architecture.

Provisioning your development environment

I have only used open source software for both the development tools and the target OS/applications. I assume you will be using Linux on your development system.

I tested all the host commands using Ubuntu 24.04 LTS, so I recommend using that version throughout the book to prevent any unexpected problems.

Besides Ubuntu, The Yocto Project only supports a select few Linux distributions: Fedora, Debian, openSUSE, AlmaLinux, and Rocky. If you absolutely cannot use Ubuntu, then make sure to choose one of those supported distros for The Yocto Project exercises.

Summary

Embedded hardware continues to get more complex following the trajectory set by Moore's law. Linux has the power and flexibility to make use of hardware in an efficient way. Together, we will learn how to harness that power so we can build robust products that delight our users. This book will take you through the five phases of an embedded project's life cycle, beginning with the four elements of embedded Linux.

The sheer variety of embedded platforms and the fast pace of development lead to isolated pools of software. In many cases, you will become dependent on this software, especially the Linux kernel that is provided by your SoC or board vendor, and to a lesser extent, the toolchain.

Some SoC manufacturers are getting better at pushing their changes upstream and the maintenance of these changes is getting easier. Despite these improvements, selecting the right hardware for your embedded Linux project is still an exercise fraught with peril. Open source license compliance is another topic you need to be aware of when building products atop the embedded Linux ecosystem.

In this chapter, you were introduced to the hardware and some of the software you will use throughout this book (namely QEMU). Later on, we will examine some powerful tools that can help you create and maintain the software for your device. We cover Buildroot and dig deep into The Yocto Project. Before we tackle these build tools, we will deconstruct the four elements of embedded Linux, which you can apply to all embedded Linux projects regardless of how they are built.

Join our community on Discord

Join our community's Discord space for discussions with the authors and other readers: `https://packt.link/embeddedsystems`

2

Learning about Toolchains

The toolchain is the first element of embedded Linux and the starting point of your project. You will use it to compile all the code that will run on your device. The choices you make at this early stage will have a profound impact on the final outcome.

Your toolchain should be capable of making effective use of your hardware by using the optimum instruction set for your processor. It should support the languages that you require and have a solid implementation of the **Portable Operating System Interface (POSIX)** and other system interfaces.

Your toolchain should remain constant throughout the project. In other words, once you have chosen your toolchain, it is important to stick with it. Changing compilers and development libraries inconsistently during a project will lead to subtle bugs. That being said, it is still best to update your toolchain when security flaws or bugs are found.

Obtaining a toolchain can be as simple as downloading and installing a TAR file or it can be as complex as building the whole thing from source code. In this chapter, we take the first approach. Later on, in *Chapter 6*, we will switch to using the toolchain generated by the build system. This is the more usual means of obtaining a toolchain.

In this chapter, we will cover the following topics:

- Introducing toolchains
- Finding a toolchain
- Anatomy of a toolchain
- Linking with libraries – static and dynamic linking
- Art of cross-compiling

Technical requirements

I recommend using Ubuntu 24.04 or a later LTS release since the exercises in this chapter were all tested against that Linux distro at the time of writing.

Here is the command to install all the packages required for this chapter on Ubuntu 24.04 LTS:

```
$ sudo apt-get install autoconf automake bison bzip2 cmake flex g++ gawk
gcc gettext git gperf help2man libstdc++6 libtool libtool-bin make patch
texinfo unzip wget xz-utils
```

The code used in this chapter can be found in the chapter folder in this book's GitHub repository: https://github.com/PacktPublishing/Mastering-Embedded-Linux-Development/tree/main/Chapter02.

Introducing toolchains

A toolchain is a set of tools that compiles source code into executables that can run on your target device. It includes a compiler, a linker, and runtime libraries. You need a toolchain to build the other three elements of an embedded Linux system:

- Bootloader
- Kernel
- Root filesystem

It has to be able to compile code written in C, C++, and an assembly language since these are the languages used in the base open source packages.

Usually, toolchains for Linux are based on components from the GNU project and that is still true at the time of writing. However, over the past few years, the **Clang** compiler and the associated **Low-Level Virtual Machine** (**LLVM**) project have progressed to the point that LLVM is now a viable alternative to a GNU toolchain. One major distinction between LLVM and GNU-based toolchains is the licensing; LLVM has the Apache License v2.0 with LLVM Exceptions while GNU has the GPL.

There are some technical advantages to Clang as well, such as faster compilation, better diagnostics, and more support for the latest C and C++ standards. But **GCC** (**GNU C Compiler**) has the advantage of compatibility with the existing code base and support for a wider range of architectures and **Operating Systems** (**OS**). While it took some years to get there, Clang can now compile all the components needed for embedded Linux and is a viable alternative to GCC. To learn more, see https://docs.kernel.org/kbuild/llvm.html.

There is a good description of how to use Clang for cross-compilation at https://clang.llvm. org/docs/CrossCompilation.html. If you would like to use it as part of an embedded Linux build system, various people are working on using Clang with Buildroot and The Yocto Project. I will cover embedded build systems in *Chapter 6*. Meanwhile, this chapter focuses on the GNU toolchain as it is still the most popular and mature toolchain for Linux.

A standard GNU toolchain consists of three main components:

- **Binutils**: A set of binary utilities including the assembler and the linker.
- **GCC**: Compilers for C and other languages, which include C++, Objective-C, Objective-C++, Java, Fortran, Ada, Go, and D. They all use a common backend that produces assembler code that is fed to the GNU assembler.
- **C library**: A standardized **Application Program Interface (API)** based on the POSIX specification, which is the main interface to the OS kernel for applications. There are several C libraries to consider, as we shall see later in this chapter.

Along with these, you will also need a copy of the Linux kernel headers. The kernel headers contain definitions and constants that are needed when accessing the kernel directly. You need the kernel headers to compile the C library, programs, and libraries. This **user space** code interacts indirectly with Linux devices, for example, to display graphics via the Linux frame buffer driver. This is in stark contrast to kernel modules/drivers inside **kernel space** with direct access to peripheral hardware.

This is not simply a question of making a copy of the header files in the include directory of your kernel source code. Those headers are intended for use in the kernel only and contain definitions that will cause conflicts if used in their raw state to compile regular Linux applications. Instead, you will need to generate a set of sanitized kernel headers, which I have illustrated in *Chapter 5*.

When compiling for user space, the kernel headers do not need to be generated from the exact version of Linux you are going to be running on. Since the kernel interfaces are always backward compatible, it is only necessary that the headers are from a kernel that is the same as or older than the one you are using on the target.

Most people consider the **GNU Debugger (GDB)** to be part of the toolchain as well since it is also normally built at this point. When building a cross compiler, you also need to build a corresponding cross debugger to debug code on the target remotely from your host machine. I will talk about GDB in *Chapter 19*.

Now that we've talked about kernel headers and seen what the components of a toolchain are, let's look at the different types of toolchains.

Types of toolchains

For our purposes, there are two types of toolchains:

- **Native**: A toolchain that runs on the same type of system (or even the actual system) as the programs it generates. This is usually the case for desktops and servers, and it is becoming popular on certain classes of embedded devices. For example, the Raspberry Pi 4 running Debian for ARM has self-hosted native compilers.

- **Cross**: A toolchain that runs on a different type of system than the target allowing development to be done on a fast desktop PC and then loaded onto the embedded target for execution.

Almost all embedded Linux development is done using a cross-development toolchain. This is partly because most embedded devices are not well suited for development since they lack computing power, memory, and storage, but also because it keeps the host and target environments separate. The latter point is especially important when the host and the target are using the same architecture, x86_64, for example. In this case, it is tempting to compile natively on the host and simply copy the binaries to the target.

This works up to a point. However, it is likely that the host distribution will receive updates more often than the target or that different engineers building code for the target will have slightly different versions of the host development libraries. Over time, the development and target systems will diverge. You can upgrade the toolchain if you ensure that the host and the target build environments are in lockstep with each other. However, a much better approach is to keep the host and the target separate, and a cross toolchain is the way to do that.

There is a counterargument in favor of native development. Cross-development creates the burden of having to cross-compile all the libraries and tools that you need for your target. We will see later, in the section titled *Art of cross-compiling*, that cross-development is not always simple because many open source packages are not designed to be built in this way.

Integrated build tools like Buildroot and The Yocto Project help by encapsulating the rules for cross-compiling a range of packages needed by most embedded systems. But if you want to compile lots of additional packages, then it is better to compile them natively. For example, building a Debian distribution for the Raspberry Pi 4 or BeaglePlay using a cross compiler is very hard. Instead, they are natively compiled.

Creating a native build environment from scratch is not easy. You still need a cross compiler at first to create the native build environment on the target, which you then use to build the packages. Then, to perform the native build in a reasonable amount of time, you need a build farm of well-provisioned target boards or **Quick Emulator (QEMU)** to emulate the target.

In this chapter, we will focus on a pre-built cross-compiler environment that is relatively easy to set up and administer. We will start by looking at what distinguishes one target CPU architecture from another.

CPU architectures

The toolchain must be built according to the capabilities of the target CPU, which includes:

- **CPU architecture**: ARM, RISC-V, PowerPC, **Microprocessor without Interlocked Pipelined Stages (MIPS)**, or x86_64.

- **Big- or little-endian operation**: Some CPUs can operate in both modes, but the machine code is different for each.

- **Floating point support**: Not all versions of embedded processors implement a hardware floating point unit. In these cases, the toolchain must be configured to call a software floating point library instead.

- **Application Binary Interface (ABI)**: The calling convention used for passing parameters between function calls.

With many architectures, the ABI is constant across the family of processors. One notable exception is ARM. The ARM architecture transitioned to the **Extended Application Binary Interface (EABI)** in the late 2000s resulting in the previous ABI being named the **Old Application Binary Interface (OABI)**. While the OABI is now obsolete, you continue to see references to EABI. Since then, the EABI has split into three based on the way floating point parameters are passed: softfloat, softfp, and hardfp.

The original EABI uses software emulation (softfloat) or general-purpose integer registers (softfp), while the newer **Extended Application Binary Interface Hard-Float (EABIHF)** uses floating point registers (hardfp). The original EABI's softfloat and softfp modes are ABI-compatible. In **softfloat** mode, the compiler does not generate **Floating Point Unit (FPU)** instructions. All floating point operations are done in software, resulting in suboptimal performance. In **softfp** mode, float values are passed via the stack or integer registers for better performance. EABIHF is significantly faster at floating point operations since **hardfp** mode removes the need for copying between integer and floating point registers.

The downside of EABIHF is that hardfp mode is incompatible with CPUs that do not have a floating point unit. The choice then is between two incompatible ABIs. You cannot mix and match the two, so you must decide at this stage.

GNU adds a prefix to the name of each tool in the toolchain that identifies the various combinations that can be generated. This prefix consists of a tuple of three or four components separated by dashes, as described here:

- **CPU**: The CPU architecture such as ARM, RISC-V, PowerPC, MIPS, or x86_64. If the CPU has both endian modes, they may be differentiated by adding el for little-endian or eb for big-endian. Good examples are little-endian MIPS (mipsel) and big-endian ARM (armeb).
- **Vendor**: Identifies the provider of the toolchain. Examples include buildroot, poky, and just unknown. Sometimes, it is left out altogether.
- **OS**: For our purposes, it is always linux.
- **User space**: A name for the user space component, which might be gnu or musl. The ABI may be appended here as well. So, for ARM toolchains, you may see gnueabi, gnueabihf, musleabi, or musleabihf.

You can find the tuple used when building the toolchain by using the -dumpmachine option of gcc. For example, you may see the following on the host computer:

```
$ gcc -dumpmachine
x86_64-linux-gnu
```

This tuple indicates a CPU of x86_64, a kernel of linux, and a user space of gnu.

IMPORTANT NOTE

When a native compiler is installed on a machine it is normal to create links to each of the tools in the toolchain with no prefixes so that you can call the C compiler with the gcc command.

Here is an example using a cross compiler:

```
$ mipsel-unknown-linux-gnu-gcc -dumpmachine
mipsel-unknown-linux-gnu
```

This tuple indicates a CPU of little-endian MIPS, an unknown vendor, a kernel of linux, and a user space of gnu. Your choice of user space (gnu or musl) determines which C library (glibc or musl) your programs are linked with.

Choosing the C library

The programming interface to the Unix OS is defined in the C language in adherence to POSIX standards. The **C library** is the implementation of that interface. It is the gateway to the kernel for Linux programs. Even if you are writing programs in another language like Go or Python, the respective runtime support libraries will eventually have to call the C library, as shown here:

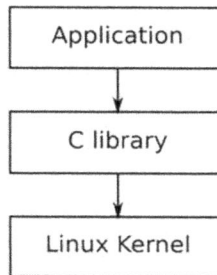

```
┌─────────────────────┐
│     Application      │
└─────────────────────┘
           │
           ▼
┌─────────────────────┐
│      C library       │
└─────────────────────┘
           │
           ▼
┌─────────────────────┐
│     Linux Kernel     │
└─────────────────────┘
```

Figure 2.1 – C library

Whenever the C library needs the services of the kernel, it will use the kernel system call interface to transition between user space and kernel space. It is possible to bypass the C library by making the kernel system calls directly but that is a lot of trouble and almost never necessary.

There are several C libraries to choose from. The main options are as follows:

- **glibc**: This is the standard GNU C library available at `https://gnu.org/software/libc/`. It is big and, until recently, not very configurable, but it is the most complete implementation of the POSIX API. The license is LGPL 2.1.

- **musl libc**: This is comparatively new but has been gaining a lot of attention as a small and standards-compliant alternative to glibc. It is a good choice for systems with a limited amount of RAM and storage. It has an MIT license and is available at `https://musl.libc.org`.

- **uClibc-ng**: *u* is really the Greek *mu* character, indicating that this is the microcontroller C library. uClibc-ng is available at `https://uclibc-ng.org`. It was first developed to work with uClinux (Linux for microcontrollers without a memory management unit) but has since been adapted to be used with full Linux. The uClibc-ng library is a fork of the original uClibc project, which has fallen into disrepair. Both are licensed with LGPL 2.1.

So, which to choose? My advice is to use uClibc-ng only if you are using uClinux. If you have a very limited amount of storage or RAM, then musl libc is a good choice. Otherwise, use glibc, as shown in this flow chart:

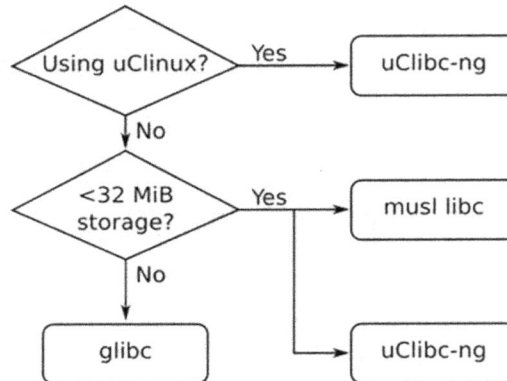

Figure 2.2 – Choosing a C library

Your choice of C library could limit your choice of toolchain since not all pre-built toolchains support all C libraries. Once you know what you need in a toolchain, where do you find one?

Finding a toolchain

You have three choices for your cross-development toolchain: you may find a ready-built toolchain that matches your needs, you can use the one generated by an embedded build tool (which is covered in *Chapter 6*), or you can create one yourself.

A pre-built cross toolchain is an attractive option in that you only have to download and install it. But you are limited to the configuration of that particular toolchain, and you are dependent on the person or organization you got it from. Most likely, it will be one of these:

- An SoC or board vendor. Most vendors offer a Linux toolchain.
- A consortium dedicated to providing system-level support for a given architecture. For example, Linaro (https://www.linaro.org) has pre-built toolchains for the ARM architecture.
- A third-party Linux tool vendor such as Siemens, Timesys, or Wind River.
- The cross-tool packages for your desktop Linux distribution. For example, Debian-based distributions have packages for cross-compiling for ARM, PowerPC, and MIPS targets.

- A binary SDK produced by one of the integrated embedded build tools. The Yocto Project has some available for download at `https://downloads.yoctoproject.org/releases/ yocto/yocto-<version>/toolchain/`. (replace `<version>` with a valid Yocto Project version such as `5.0` in the preceding URL).
- A link from a forum that you can't find anymore.

IMPORTANT NOTE

In all these cases, you must decide whether the pre-built toolchain on offer meets your requirements. Does it use the C library you prefer? Will the provider give you updates for security fixes and bugs? Bear in mind my comments on support and updates from *Chapter 1*. If your answer is no to any of these, then you should consider creating your own.

Unfortunately, building a toolchain is no easy task. If you truly want to do the whole thing yourself, take a look at Cross Linux From Scratch (`https://trac.clfs.org`). There, you will find step-by-step instructions on how to create each component.

A simpler alternative is to use crosstool-NG, which encapsulates the process into a set of scripts and has a menu-driven frontend. You still need a fair degree of knowledge though just to make the right choices.

It is simpler still to use a build system such as Buildroot or The Yocto Project since they generate a toolchain as part of the build process. This is my preferred solution, as we shall see in *Chapter 6*.

You will need a working cross toolchain to complete the exercises in the next section. We will employ a pre-built toolchain from Bootlin. Bootlin's toolchains are built using Buildroot.

To download the pre-built cross toolchain needed for *Chapters 2* through *5*:

```
$ wget https://toolchains.bootlin.com/downloads/releases/toolchains/
aarch64/tarballs/aarch64--glibc--stable-2024.02-1.tar.bz2
```

To download the latest version of this toolchain, visit `https://toolchains.bootlin.com`. Select *aarch64* for architecture and *glibc* for libc. Once these choices have been made, download the stable version of the toolchain.

Install the pre-built toolchain on your Linux host machine by extracting and decompressing it to your home directory:

```
$ bzip2 -d aarch64--glibc--stable-2024.02-1.tar.bz2
$ tar -xvf aarch64--glibc--stable-2024.02-1.tar
<...>
```

You will use this toolchain for the remainder of this chapter. Let's start by looking at its internals.

Anatomy of a toolchain

To get an idea of what is in a typical toolchain, let's examine the toolchain you downloaded from Bootlin. The examples use the aarch64 toolchain, which has the prefix aarch64-buildroot-linux-gnu.

The aarch64 toolchain is in the directory ~/aarch64--glibc--stable-2024.02-1/bin. In there, you will find the cross compiler aarch64-buildroot-linux-gnu-gcc. To make use of it, you need to add the directory to your path using the following command:

```
$ PATH=~/aarch64--glibc--stable-2024.02-1/bin:$PATH
```

If you downloaded a different version, make sure to replace 2024.02-1 with the actual version of the stable toolchain.

Now you can take a simple helloworld program, which, in the C language, looks like this:

```c
#include <stdio.h>
#include <stdlib.h>

int main (int argc, char *argv[])
{
    printf ("Hello, World!\n");
    return 0;
}
```

And compile it like this:

```
$ aarch64-buildroot-linux-gnu-gcc helloworld.c -o helloworld
```

Confirm that it has been cross-compiled by using the file command to print the type of the file:

```
$ file helloworld
helloworld: ELF 64-bit LSB pie executable, ARM aarch64, version 1 (SYSV),
```

```
dynamically linked, interpreter /lib/ld-linux-aarch64.so.1, for GNU/Linux
3.7.0, not stripped
```

Now that you've verified that your cross compiler works, let's take a closer look at it.

Finding out about your cross compiler

Imagine that you have just received a toolchain and that you would like to know more about how it was configured. You can find out a lot by querying gcc. For example, to find the version, you use --version:

```
$ aarch64-buildroot-linux-gnu-gcc --version
aarch64-buildroot-linux-gnu-gcc.br_real (Buildroot 2021.11-11272-ge2962af)
12.3.0
Copyright (C) 2022 Free Software Foundation, Inc.
This is free software; see the source for copying conditions.  There is NO
warranty; not even for MERCHANTABILITY or FITNESS FOR A PARTICULAR
PURPOSE.
```

To find how it was configured, use -v:

```
$ aarch64-buildroot-linux-gnu-gcc -v
Using built-in specs.
COLLECT_GCC=/home/frank/aarch64--glibc--stable-2024.02-1/bin/aarch64-
buildroot-linux-gnu-gcc.br_real
COLLECT_LTO_WRAPPER=/home/frank/aarch64--glibc--stable-2024.02-1/bin/../
libexec/gcc/aarch64-buildroot-linux-gnu/12.3.0/lto-wrapper
Target: aarch64-buildroot-linux-gnu
Configured with: ./configure --prefix=/builds/buildroot.org/toolchains-
builder/build/aarch64--glibc--stable-2024.02-1 --sysconfdir=/builds/
buildroot.org/toolchains-builder/build/aarch64--glibc--stable-2024.02-1/
etc --enable-static --target=aarch64-buildroot-linux-gnu --with-
sysroot=/builds/buildroot.org/toolchains-builder/build/aarch64--glibc--
stable-2024.02-1/aarch64-buildroot-linux-gnu/sysroot --enable-__cxa_atexit
--with-gnu-ld --disable-libssp --disable-multilib --disable-decimal-float
--enable-plugins --enable-lto --with-gmp=/builds/buildroot.org/toolchains-
builder/build/aarch64--glibc--stable-2024.02-1 --with-mpc=/builds/
buildroot.org/toolchains-builder/build/aarch64--glibc--stable-2024.02-1
--with-mpfr=/builds/buildroot.org/toolchains-builder/build/aarch64--glibc-
-stable-2024.02-1 --with-pkgversion='Buildroot 2021.11-11272-ge2962af'
--with-bugurl=http://bugs.buildroot.net/ --without-zstd --disable-
libquadmath --disable-libquadmath-support --enable-tls --enable-threads
```

```
--without-isl --without-cloog --with-abi=lp64 --with-cpu=cortex-a53
--enable-languages=c,c++,fortran --with-build-time-tools=/builds/
buildroot.org/toolchains-builder/build/aarch64--glibc--stable-2024.02-1/
aarch64-buildroot-linux-gnu/bin --enable-shared --enable-libgomp
Thread model: posix
Supported LTO compression algorithms: zlib
gcc version 12.3.0 (Buildroot 2021.11-11272-ge2962af)
<…>
```

There is a lot of output there but the interesting things to note are:

- `--with-sysroot=/builds/buildroot.org/toolchains-builder/build/aarch64--glibc--stable-2024.02-1/aarch64-buildroot-linux-gnu/sysroot`: The location of the `sysroot` directory at build time. See the following section for an explanation.
- `--enable-languages=c,c++,fortran`: Both the C and C++ languages are enabled.
- `--with-cpu=cortex-a53`: Generates code for an ARM Cortex-A53 core.
- `--enable-threads`: Enables POSIX threads.

These are the default settings for the compiler. You can override most of them on the gcc command line. For example, if you want to compile for a different CPU, you can override the configured setting `--with-cpu` by adding `-mcpu=cortex-a72` to the command line, as follows:

```
$ aarch64-buildroot-linux-gnu-gcc -mcpu=cortex-a72 helloworld.c -o
helloworld
```

You can print out the range of architecture-specific options available using `--target-help`, as follows:

```
$ aarch64-buildroot-linux-gnu-gcc --target-help
```

You may be wondering if it matters that you get the configuration exactly right at this point since you can always change it. The answer depends on the way you anticipate using it. If you plan to create a new toolchain for each target, then it makes sense to set everything up at the beginning because it will reduce the risks of getting it wrong later.

I call this the Buildroot philosophy, which we will revisit in *Chapter 6*. If, on the other hand, you want to build a toolchain that is generic, and you are prepared to provide the correct settings when you build for a particular target, then you should make the base toolchain generic, which is the way The Yocto Project handles things.

Now that we've seen the location of the sysroot directory at build time, let's look inside the default sysroot directory installed on your host machine.

sysroot, library, and header files

The toolchain sysroot directory contains subdirectories for libraries, header files, and other configuration files. It can be set when the toolchain is configured through --with-sysroot= or it can be set on the command line using --sysroot=. You can see the location of the default sysroot by using -print-sysroot:

```
$ aarch64-buildroot-linux-gnu-gcc -print-sysroot
/home/frank/aarch64--glibc--stable-2024.02-1/aarch64-buildroot-linux-gnu/
sysroot
```

You will find the following subdirectories in sysroot:

- lib: Contains the shared objects for the C library and the dynamic linker/loader ld-linux
- usr/lib: Contains the static library archive files for the C library and any other libraries that may be subsequently installed
- usr/include: Contains the headers for all the libraries
- usr/bin: Contains the utility programs that run on the target such as the ldd command
- usr/share: Used for localization and internationalization
- sbin: Provides the ldconfig utility that is used to optimize library loading paths

Some of these are needed on the development host to compile programs and others, like the shared libraries and ld-linux, are needed on the target at runtime.

Other tools in the toolchain

Below is a list of commands to invoke the various other components of a GNU toolchain. Like aarch64-buildroot-linux-gnu-gcc, these tools are all located inside the ~/aarch64--glibc--stable-2024.02-1/bin/ directory that you added to your PATH. Here are brief descriptions of these tools:

- addr2line: Converts program addresses into source code filenames and line numbers by reading the debug symbol tables in an executable file. It is very useful when decoding addresses printed out in a system crash report.
- ar: An archive utility used to create static libraries.
- as: GNU assembler.
- c++filt: Demangles C++ and Java symbols.

- cpp: C preprocessor used to expand #define, #include, and other similar directives. You seldom need to use this by itself.
- elfedit: Updates the ELF header of the ELF files.
- g++: GNU C++ frontend, which assumes that source files contain C++ code.
- gcc: GNU C frontend, which assumes that source files contain C code.
- gcov: Code coverage tool.
- gdb: GNU debugger.
- gprof: Program profiling tool.
- ld: GNU linker.
- nm: Lists symbols from object files.
- objcopy: Copies and translates object files.
- objdump: Displays information from object files.
- ranlib: Creates or modifies an index in a static library making the linking stage faster.
- readelf: Displays information about files in ELF object format.
- size: Lists section sizes and the total size.
- strings: Displays strings of printable characters in files.
- strip: Strips an object file of debug symbol tables, making it smaller. Typically, you would strip all the executable code that is put onto the target.

We will now switch gears from command-line tools and return to the topic of the C library.

Looking at the components of the C library

The C library is not a single library file. It is composed of four main parts that together implement the POSIX API:

- libc: The main C library that contains the well-known POSIX functions such as printf, open, close, read, write, and so on
- libm: Contains math functions such as cos, exp, and log
- libpthread: Contains all the POSIX thread functions with names beginning with pthread_
- librt: Has real-time extensions to POSIX including shared memory and asynchronous I/O

The first one, libc, is always linked in but the others must be explicitly linked with the -l option. The parameter to -l is the library name with lib stripped off. For example, a program that calculates a sine function by calling sin() would be linked with libm using -lm:

```
$ aarch64-buildroot-linux-gnu-gcc myprog.c -o myprog -lm
```

You can verify which libraries have been linked in this or any other program by using the `readelf` command:

```
$ aarch64-buildroot-linux-gnu-readelf -a myprog | grep "Shared library"
0x0000000000000001 (NEEDED)           Shared library: [libm.so.6]
0x0000000000000001 (NEEDED)           Shared library: [libc.so.6]
```

Shared libraries need a runtime linker, which you can expose using:

```
$ aarch64-buildroot-linux-gnu-readelf -a myprog | grep "program
interpreter"
      [Requesting program interpreter: /lib/ld-linux-aarch64.so.1]
```

This is so useful that I have a script file named `list-libs`, which you will find in the book code archive in `MELD/list-libs`. It contains the following commands:

```
${CROSS_COMPILE}readelf -a $1 | grep "program interpreter"
${CROSS_COMPILE}readelf -a $1 | grep "Shared library"
```

There are other library files we can link to other than the four components of the C library. We will look at how to do that in the next section.

Linking with libraries — static and dynamic linking

Any application you write for Linux, whether it be in C or C++, will be linked with the C library `libc`. This is so fundamental that you don't even have to tell `gcc` or `g++` to do it because it always links `libc`. Other libraries that you may want to link with have to be explicitly named through the `-l` option.

Library code can be linked in two different ways:

- **Statically**: This means that all the library functions your application calls and their dependencies are pulled from the library archive and bound into your executable.
- **Dynamically**: This means that references to the library files and functions in those files are generated in the code but the actual linking is done dynamically at load time.

You will find the code for the examples that follow in the book code archive in `MELD/Chapter02/library`.

Static libraries

Static linking is useful in a few circumstances. For example, if you are building a small system that consists of only BusyBox and some script files, it is simpler to link BusyBox statically and avoid having to copy the runtime library files and linker. The footprint will also be smaller because you only link in the code that your application uses rather than supplying the entire C library. Static linking is also useful if you need to run a program before the filesystem that holds the runtime libraries is available.

You can link all the libraries statically by adding `-static` to the command line:

```
$ aarch64-buildroot-linux-gnu-gcc -static helloworld.c -o helloworld-
static
```

You will note that the size of the binary increases dramatically:

```
$ ls -l helloworld*
-rwxrwxr-x 1 frank frank   8928 Apr 28 23:34 helloworld
-rw-rw-r-- 1 frank frank    123 Apr 28 23:30 helloworld.c
-rwxrwxr-x 1 frank frank 718472 Apr 28 23:33 helloworld-static
```

Static linking pulls code from a library archive usually named lib<name>.a. In the preceding case, it is libc.a, which is in <sysroot>/usr/lib:

```
$ export SYSROOT=$(aarch64-buildroot-linux-gnu-gcc -print-sysroot)
$ cd $SYSROOT
$  ls -l usr/lib/libc.a
-rw-r--r-- 1 frank frank 5551484 Mar  3  2024 usr/lib/libc.a
```

Note that the syntax export `SYSROOT=$(aarch64-buildroot-linux-gnu-gcc -print-sysroot)` places the path to the `sysroot` in the shell variable `SYSROOT`, which makes the example a little clearer.

Creating a static library is as simple as creating an archive of object files using the `ar` command. If I have two source files named `test1.c` and `test2.c` (this exercise has no Git examples – you are expected to generate your own `test1.c` and `test2.c` files) and I want to create a static library named `libtest.a`, then I would do the following:

```
$ aarch64-buildroot-linux-gnu-gcc -c test1.c
$ aarch64-buildroot-linux-gnu-gcc -c test2.c
$ aarch64-buildroot-linux-gnu-ar rc libtest.a test1.o test2.o
$ ls -l
total 24
```

```
-rw-rw-r-- 1 frank frank 2392 Nov  9 09:28 libtest.a
-rw-rw-r-- 1 frank frank  116 Nov  9 09:26 test1.c
-rw-rw-r-- 1 frank frank 1080 Nov  9 09:27 test1.o
-rw-rw-r-- 1 frank frank  121 Nov  9 09:26 test2.c
-rw-rw-r-- 1 frank frank 1088 Nov  9 09:27 test2.o
```

The book's Git repository contains source and makefiles to assist with the linking exercises that follow:

```
$ cd MELD/Chapter02/library
$ tree
.
├── hello-arm
│   ├── hello-arm.c
│   └── Makefile
├── inc
│   └── testlib.h
├── shared
│   ├── Makefile
│   └── testlib.c
└── static
    ├── Makefile
    └── testlib.c
```

Compile the static `libtest.a` library:

```
$ cd static
$ CC=aarch64-buildroot-linux-gnu-gcc make
aarch64-buildroot-linux-gnu-gcc -Wall -g -I../inc -c testlib.c
ar rc libtest.a testlib.o
```

Compile `hello-arm.c` and link it with `libtest.a` to produce a hello-arm-static executable:

```
$ cd ../hello-arm
$ CC=aarch64-buildroot-linux-gnu-gcc make hello-arm-static
aarch64-buildroot-linux-gnu-gcc -c -Wall -I../inc -o hello-arm.o hello-
arm.c
aarch64-buildroot-linux-gnu-gcc -o hello-arm-static hello-arm.o -L../
static -ltest
```

Now let's rebuild the same program using dynamic linking.

Shared libraries

A more common way to deploy libraries is as shared objects that are linked at runtime, which makes more efficient use of storage and system memory since only one copy of the code needs to be loaded. It also makes it easy to update the library files without having to relink all the programs that use them.

The object code for a shared library must be position independent so that the runtime linker is free to locate it in memory at the next free address. To do this, add the -fPIC parameter to gcc and then link it using the -shared option:

```
$ aarch64-buildroot-linux-gnu-gcc -fPIC -c test1.c
$ aarch64-buildroot-linux-gnu-gcc -fPIC -c test2.c
$ aarch64-buildroot-linux-gnu-gcc -shared -o libtest.so test1.o test2.o
```

This creates the shared library libtest.so. To link an application with this library, you add -ltest just like you did for the static case, but this time, the code is not included in the executable. Instead, there is a reference to the library that the runtime linker will have to resolve.

Compile the shared libtest.so library:

```
$ cd MELD/Chapter02/library
$ cd shared
$ CC=aarch64-buildroot-linux-gnu-gcc make
aarch64-buildroot-linux-gnu-gcc -Wall -g -fPIC -I../inc -c testlib.c
aarch64-buildroot-linux-gnu-gcc -shared -o libtest.so testlib.o
```

Compile hello-arm.c and link it with libtest.so to produce a hello-arm-shared executable:

```
$ cd ../hello-arm
$ CC=aarch64-buildroot-linux-gnu-gcc make hello-arm-shared
aarch64-buildroot-linux-gnu-gcc -c -Wall -I../inc -o hello-arm.o hello-
arm.c
aarch64-buildroot-linux-gnu-gcc -o hello-arm-shared hello-arm.o -L../
shared -ltest
$ ~/MELD/list-libs hello-arm-shared
      [Requesting program interpreter: /lib/ld-linux-aarch64.so.1]
  0x0000000000000001 (NEEDED)                 Shared library: [libtest.so]
  0x0000000000000001 (NEEDED)                 Shared library: [libc.so.6]
```

The runtime linker for this program is /lib/ld-linux-aarch64.so.1, which must be present in the target's filesystem. The linker will look for libtest.so in the default search path: /lib and /usr/lib. If you want it to look for libraries in other directories as well, you can place a colon-separated list of paths in the shell variable LD_LIBRARY_PATH:

```
$ export LD_LIBRARY_PATH=/opt/lib:/opt/usr/lib
```

Because shared libraries are separate from executables, you need to ensure the correct versions of shared libraries are installed on the target so that you don't encounter runtime errors.

Understanding shared library version numbers

One of the benefits of shared libraries is that they can be updated independently of the programs that use them. Library updates are of two types:

- Those that fix bugs or add new functions in a backward-compatible way
- Those that break compatibility with existing applications

GNU/Linux has a versioning scheme to handle both these cases.

Each library has a release version and an interface number. The release version is simply a string that is appended to the library name. For example, the JPEG image library libjpeg is currently at release 8.2.2 and so the library is named libjpeg.so.8.2.2. There is a symbolic link named libjpeg.so to libjpeg.so.8.2.2 so that when you compile a program with -ljpeg, you link with the current version. If you install version 8.2.3, the link is updated, and you will link with that one instead.

Now suppose that version 9.0.0 comes along and that breaks the backward compatibility. The link from libjpeg.so now points to libjpeg.so.9.0.0 so that any new programs are linked with the new version. When the interface to libjpeg changes, the result is compilation errors that a developer can fix.

Any programs on the target that are not recompiled are going to fail in some way because they are still using the old interface. This is where an object known as the **soname** helps. The soname encodes the interface number from when the library was built and is used by the runtime linker when it loads the library. It is formatted as <library name>.so.<interface number>. For libjpeg.so.8.2.2, the soname is libjpeg.so.8 because the interface number when that libjpeg shared library was built is 8:

```
$ readelf -a /usr/lib/x86_64-linux-gnu/libjpeg.so.8.2.2 | grep SONAME
0x000000000000000e (SONAME)     Library soname: [libjpeg.so.8]
```

Any program compiled with it will request libjpeg.so.8 at runtime, which will be a symbolic link on the target to libjpeg.so.8.2.2. When version 9.0.0 of libjpeg is installed, it will have a soname of libjpeg.so.9 and so it is possible to have two incompatible versions of the same library installed on the same system. Programs that were linked with libjpeg.so.8.*.* will load libjpeg.so.8 and those linked with libjpeg.so.9.*.* will load libjpeg.so.9.

This is why, when you look at the directory listing of /usr/lib/x86_64-linux-gnu/libjpeg*, you find these four files:

- libjpeg.a: The library archive used for static linking
- libjpeg.so -> libjpeg.so.8.2.2: A symbolic link used for dynamic linking
- libjpeg.so.8 -> libjpeg.so.8.2.2: A symbolic link used when loading the library at runtime
- libjpeg.so.8.2.2: The actual shared library used at both compile time and runtime

The first two are only needed on the host computer for building and the last two are needed on the target at runtime.

While you can invoke the various GNU cross-compilation tools directly from the command line, this technique does not scale beyond toy examples like helloworld. To really be effective at cross-compiling, we need to combine a cross toolchain with a build system.

Art of cross-compiling

Having a working cross toolchain is the starting point of a journey not the end of it. At some point, you will want to begin cross-compiling the various tools, applications, and libraries that you need for your target. Many of them will be open source packages, each of which has its own method of compiling and its own peculiarities.

Some common build systems include:

- Pure makefiles where the toolchain is usually controlled by the make variable CROSS_ COMPILE
- GNU **Autotools** build system
- **CMake**

Both Autotools and makefiles are needed to build even a basic embedded Linux system. CMake is cross-platform and has seen increased adoption over the years, especially among the C++ community. In this section, we will cover all three build tools.

Simple makefiles

Some important packages are very simple to cross-compile, including the Linux kernel, the U-Boot bootloader, and BusyBox. For each of these, you only need to put the toolchain prefix in the make variable CROSS_COMPILE, for example, aarch64-buildroot-linux-gnu-. Note the trailing hyphen.

To compile BusyBox, you type:

```
$ make CROSS_COMPILE=aarch64-buildroot-linux-gnu-
```

Or you can set it as a shell variable:

```
$ export CROSS_COMPILE=aarch64-buildroot-linux-gnu-
$ make
```

In the case of U-Boot and Linux, you also need to set the make variable ARCH to one of the machine architectures they support, which I will cover in *Chapters 3* and *4*.

Both Autotools and CMake can generate makefiles. Autotools only generates makefiles, whereas CMake supports other ways of building projects depending on which platform(s) you are targeting (strictly Linux in our case). Let's look at cross-compiling with Autotools first.

Autotools

The name Autotools refers to a group of tools that are used as the build system in many open source projects. The components, together with the appropriate project pages, are:

- GNU autoconf (https://www.gnu.org/software/autoconf/)
- GNU automake (https://www.gnu.org/software/automake/)
- GNU libtool (https://www.gnu.org/software/libtool/)
- gnulib (https://www.gnu.org/software/gnulib/)

The role of Autotools is to smooth over the differences between the different types of systems that the package may be compiled for, accounting for different versions of compilers, different versions of libraries, different locations of header files, and dependencies with other packages.

Packages that use Autotools come with a script named configure that checks dependencies and generates makefiles according to what it finds. The configure script may also give you the opportunity to enable or disable certain features. You can find the options on offer by running ./configure --help.

To configure, build, and install a package for the native OS, you would typically run the following three commands:

```
$ ./configure
$ make
$ sudo make install
```

Autotools can handle cross-development as well. You can influence the behavior of the configured script by setting these shell variables:

- CC: C compiler command
- CFLAGS: Additional C compiler flags
- CXX: C++ compiler command
- CXXFLAGS: Additional C++ compiler flags
- LDFLAGS: Additional linker flags; for example, if you have libraries in a non-standard directory, <lib dir>, you would add it to the library search path by adding -L<lib dir>
- LIBS: A list of additional libraries to pass to the linker; for instance, -lm for the math library
- CPPFLAGS: C/C++ preprocessor flags; for example, you would add -I<include dir> to search for headers in a non-standard directory, <include dir>
- CPP: C preprocessor to use

Sometimes, it is sufficient to set only the CC variable, as follows:

```
$ CC=aarch64-buildroot-linux-gnu-gcc ./configure
```

Other times, that will result in an error like this:

```
<...>
checking for suffix of executables...
checking whether we are cross compiling... configure: error: in '/home/
frank/sqlite-autoconf-3440000':
configure: error: cannot run C compiled programs.
If you meant to cross compile, use '--host'.
See 'config.log' for more details
```

The reason for the failure is that configure often tries to discover the capabilities of the toolchain by compiling snippets of code and running them to see what happens, which cannot work if the program has been cross-compiled.

IMPORTANT NOTE

Pass --host=<host> to configure when you are cross-compiling so that configure searches your system for the cross-compiling toolchain targeting the specified <host> platform. That way, configure does not try to run snippets of non-native code as part of the configuration step.

Autotools understands three different types of machines that may be involved when compiling a package:

- **build**: The computer that builds the package, which defaults to the current machine.
- **host**: The computer the program will run on. For a native compile, this is left blank and defaults to the same computer as build. When you are cross-compiling, set it to be the tuple of your toolchain.
- **target**: The computer the program will generate code for. You would set this when building a cross compiler.

To cross-compile, you just need to override the host as follows:

```
$ CC=aarch64-buildroot-linux-gnu-gcc ./configure --host=aarch64-buildroot-
linux-gnu
```

One final thing to note is that the default install directory is <sysroot>/usr/local. You would usually install it in <sysroot>/usr so that the header files and libraries would be picked up from their default locations.

The complete command to configure a typical Autotools package is as follows:

```
$ CC=aarch64-buildroot-linux-gnu-gcc ./configure --host=aarch64-buildroot-
linux-gnu --prefix=/usr
```

Let's dive deeper into Autotools and use it to cross-compile a popular library.

An example: SQLite

The SQLite library implements a simple relational database and is quite popular on embedded devices.

First, begin by getting a copy of SQLite:

```
$ wget http://www.sqlite.org/2023/sqlite-autoconf-3440000.tar.gz
$ tar xf sqlite-autoconf-3440000.tar.gz
$ cd sqlite-autoconf-3440000
```

Version 3.44.0 of SQLite may no longer be available. If so, then download a more up-to-date version of the source code from the SQLite Download page at https://www.sqlite.org/download. html. Modify the preceding tar and cd commands to match the filename of the new tarball.

Next, run the configure script:

```
$ CC=aarch64-buildroot-linux-gnu-gcc ./configure --host=aarch64-buildroot-
linux-gnu --prefix=/usr
```

That seems to work! If it had failed, there would have been error messages printed to the terminal and recorded in config.log. Note that several makefiles have been created so now you can build it:

```
$ make
```

Finally, you install it into the toolchain directory by setting the make variable, DESTDIR. If you don't, it will try to install it into the host computer's /usr directory, which is not what you want:

```
$ make DESTDIR=$(aarch64-buildroot-linux-gnu-gcc -print-sysroot) install
```

You may find that the final command fails with a file permissions error because the toolchain is installed in a system directory such as /opt or /usr/local. In that case, you will need root permissions when running the installation.

After installing, you should find that various files have been added to your toolchain:

- <sysroot>/usr/bin: sqlite3: A command-line interface for SQLite that you can install and run on the target
- <sysroot>/usr/lib: libsqlite3.so.0.8.6, libsqlite3.so.0, libsqlite3.so, libsqlite3.la, libsqlite3.a: The shared and static libraries
- <sysroot>/usr/lib/pkgconfig: sqlite3.pc: The package configuration file, as described in the following section
- <sysroot>/usr/include: sqlite3.h, sqlite3ext.h: The header files
- <sysroot>/usr/share/man/man1: sqlite3.1: The manual page

Now you can compile programs that use sqlite3 by adding -lsqlite3 at the link stage:

```
$ aarch64-buildroot-linux-gnu-gcc -lsqlite3 sqlite-test.c -o sqlite-test
```

Here, `sqlite-test.c` is a hypothetical program that calls SQLite functions. Since `sqlite3` has been installed into the `sysroot`, the compiler will find the header and library files without any problem. If they had been installed elsewhere, you would have had to add -L<lib dir> and -I<include dir>.

Naturally, there will be runtime dependencies as well and you will have to install the appropriate files into the target directory, as described in *Chapter 5*.

To cross-compile a library or package, you first need to cross-compile its dependencies. Autotools relies on a utility called `pkg-config` to gather vital information about packages cross-compiled by Autotools.

Package configuration

Tracking package dependencies is quite complex. The package configuration utility `pkg-config` helps track which packages are installed and which compile flags each package needs by keeping a database of Autotools packages in `<sysroot>/usr/lib/pkgconfig`. For instance, the one for SQLite3 is named `sqlite3.pc` and contains essential information needed by other packages that depend on it:

```
cat $(aarch64-buildroot-linux-gnu-gcc -print-sysroot)/usr/lib/pkgconfig/
sqlite3.pc
# Package Information for pkg-config
prefix=/usr
exec_prefix=${prefix}
libdir=${exec_prefix}/lib
includedir=${prefix}/include

Name: SQLite
Description: SQL database engine
Version: 3.44.0
Libs: -L${libdir} -lsqlite3
Libs.private: -lm -ldl -lpthread
Cflags: -I${includedir}
```

You can use pkg-config to extract information in a form that you can feed straight to gcc. In the case of a library like libsqlite3, you want to know the library name (--libs) and any special C flags (--cflags):

```
$ pkg-config sqlite3 --libs --cflags
Package sqlite3 was not found in the pkg-config search path.
Perhaps you should add the directory containing 'sqlite3.pc' to the PKG_
CONFIG_PATH environment variable
No package 'sqlite3' found
```

Oops! That failed because it was looking in the host's sysroot, and the development package for libsqlite3 has not been installed on the host. You need to point it at the sysroot of the target toolchain by setting the shell variable PKG_CONFIG_LIBDIR:

```
$ export PKG_CONFIG_LIBDIR=$(aarch64-buildroot-linux-gnu-gcc -print-
sysroot)/usr/lib/pkgconfig
$ pkg-config sqlite3 --libs --cflags
-lsqlite3
```

Now the output is -lsqlite3. In this case, you knew that already, but generally, you wouldn't, so this is a valuable technique. The final commands to compile are:

```
$ export PKG_CONFIG_LIBDIR=$(aarch64-buildroot-linux-gnu-gcc -print-
sysroot)/usr/lib/pkgconfig
$ aarch64-buildroot-linux-gnu-gcc $(pkg-config sqlite3 --cflags --libs)
sqlite-test.c -o sqlite-test
```

Many configure scripts read the information generated by pkg-config. This can lead to errors when cross-compiling, as we shall see next.

Problems with cross-compiling

sqlite3 is a well-behaved package that cross-compiles nicely, but not all packages are the same. Typical pain points include:

- Home-grown build systems for libraries like zlib that have a configure script that does not behave like the Autotools configure described in the previous section
- configure scripts that read pkg-config information, headers, and other files from the host disregarding the --host override
- Scripts that insist on trying to run cross-compiled code

Each case requires careful analysis of the error. We can either pass additional parameters to the `configure` script to provide the correct information or apply patches to the code to avoid the problem altogether. Bear in mind that a single package can have many dependencies. This is especially true for programs that have a graphical interface or that handle multimedia content. As an example, MPlayer has dependencies on over 100 libraries. It would take weeks of effort to build them all.

Therefore, I would not recommend manually cross-compiling components for the target in this way, except when there is no alternative or the number of packages to build is small.

A much better approach is to use a build tool such as Buildroot or The Yocto Project or avoid the problem altogether by setting up a native build environment for your target architecture. Now you can see why distributions like Debian are always compiled natively.

CMake

CMake is more of a meta build system in the sense that it relies on an underlying platform's native tools to build software. On Windows, CMake can generate project files for Microsoft Visual Studio, and on macOS, it can generate project files for Xcode. Integrating with the principal IDEs for each of the major platforms is no simple task and explains the success of CMake as the leading cross-platform build system solution. CMake also runs on Linux where it can be used in conjunction with a cross-compiling toolchain of your choice.

To configure, build, and install a package for a native Linux OS, run the following commands:

```
$ cmake .
$ make
$ sudo make install
```

On Linux, the native build tool is GNU make so CMake generates makefiles by default for us to build with. Often, we want to perform out-of-source builds so that object files and other build artifacts remain separate from source files.

To configure an out-of-source build in a subdirectory named build, run the following commands:

```
$ mkdir build
$ cd build
$ cmake ..
```

This will generate the makefiles inside a `build` subdirectory within the project directory where the `CMakeLists.txt` is located. The `CMakeLists.txt` file is the CMake equivalent of the `configure` script for Autotools-based projects.

We can then build the project out of source from inside the `build` directory and install the package just as before:

```
$ make
$ sudo make install
```

CMake uses absolute paths so the `build` subdirectory cannot be copied or moved once the makefiles have been generated or any subsequent make step will likely fail. Note that CMake defaults to installing packages into system directories like `/usr/bin`, even for out-of-source builds.

To generate the makefiles so that CMake installs the package in the `build` subdirectory, replace the previous `cmake` command with the following:

```
$ cmake .. -D CMAKE_INSTALL_PREFIX=../build
```

We no longer need to preface `make install` with `sudo` because we do not need elevated permissions to copy the package files into the `build` directory.

Similarly, we can use another CMake command-line option to generate makefiles for cross-compilation:

```
$ cmake .. -D CMAKE_C_COMPILER="/home/frank/aarch64--glibc--stable-
<version>/bin/aarch64-buildroot-linux-gnu-gcc"
```

But the best practice for cross-compiling with CMake is to create a toolchain file that sets `CMAKE_C_COMPILER` and `CMAKE_CXX_COMPILER` in addition to other relevant variables for targeting embedded Linux.

CMake works best when we design our software in a modular way by enforcing well-defined API boundaries between libraries and components.

Here are some key terms that come up time and time again in CMake:

- `target`: A software component such as a library or executable.
- `properties`: The source files, compiler options, and linked libraries needed to build a target.
- `package`: A CMake file that configures an external target for building just as if it was defined within your `CMakeLists.txt` itself.

For example, if we had a CMake-based executable named dummy that needed to take a dependency on SQLite, we could define the following CMakeLists.txt:

```
cmake_minimum_required (VERSION 3.0)
project (Dummy)
add_executable(dummy dummy.c)
find_package (SQLite3)
target_include_directories(dummy PRIVATE ${SQLITE3_INCLUDE_DIRS})
target_link_libraries (dummy PRIVATE ${SQLITE3_LIBRARIES})
```

The find_package command searches for a package (SQLite3, in this case) and imports it so that the external target can be added as a dependency to the dummy executable's list of target_link_ libraries for linking.

CMake comes with numerous finders for popular C and C++ packages, including OpenSSL, Boost, and protobuf, making native development much more productive than if we were to use just pure makefiles.

The PRIVATE qualifier prevents details like headers and flags from leaking outside of the dummy target. Using PRIVATE makes more sense when the target being built is a library instead of an executable. Think of targets as modules and attempt to minimize their exposed surface areas when using CMake to define your own targets. Only employ the PUBLIC qualifier when absolutely necessary and utilize the INTERFACE qualifier for header-only libraries.

Model your application as a dependency graph with edges between targets. This graph should not only include the libraries that your application links to directly but any transitive dependencies as well. For best results, remove any cycles or other unnecessary independencies seen in the graph. It is often best to perform this exercise before you start coding. A little planning can make the difference between a clean, easily maintainable CMakeLists.txt and an inscrutable mess that nobody wants to touch.

Summary

The toolchain is always your starting point. Everything that follows from that is dependent on having a working, reliable toolchain.

You may start with nothing but a toolchain downloaded from Bootlin or Linaro and use it to compile all the packages that you need on your target. Or you may obtain the toolchain as part of a distribution generated from source code using a build system such as Buildroot or The Yocto Project.

Beware of toolchains or distributions that are offered to you for free as part of a hardware package. They are often poorly configured and not maintained.

Once you have a toolchain, you can use it to build the other components of your embedded Linux system. In the next chapter, you will learn about the bootloader, which brings your device to life and begins the boot process. We will use the toolchain we built in this chapter to build a working bootloader for the BeaglePlay.

Further study

- *Toolchain Options in 2023: What's new in compilers and libcs?* by Bernhard "Bero" Rosenkränzer – `https://www.youtube.com/watch?v=Vgm3GJ2ItDA`
- *Modern CMake for modular design,* by Mathieu Ropert – `https://www.youtube.com/watch?v=eC9-iRN2b04`

Get This Book's PDF Version and Exclusive Extras

UNLOCK NOW

Scan the QR code (or go to `packtpub.com/unlock`). Search for this book by name, confirm the edition, and then follow the steps on the page.

Note: Keep your invoice handy. Purchases made directly from Packt don't require an invoice.

3

All about Bootloaders

The bootloader is the second element of embedded Linux. It is the part that starts the system and loads the operating system kernel. In this chapter, we will look at the role of the bootloader and how it passes control from itself to the kernel using a data structure called a **device tree**, also known as a **flattened device tree** or **FDT**.

I will cover the basics of device trees so that you will be able to follow the connections described in a device tree and relate them to real hardware. I will focus on a popular open source bootloader known as U-Boot and show you how to use it to boot a target device. I will also show you how to customize U-Boot to run on a new device using BeaglePlay as an example.

In this chapter, we will cover the following topics:

- What does a bootloader do?
- Boot sequence
- Moving from the bootloader to the kernel
- Introducing device trees
- U-Boot

Technical requirements

To work through the examples, make sure you have the following:

- An Ubuntu 24.04 or later LTS host system with device-tree-compiler, git, make, patch, and u-boot-tools installed
- A Bootlin toolchain for BeaglePlay from *Chapter 2*

- A microSD card reader and card
- A USB-to-TTL serial cable with a 3.3 V logic level
- BeaglePlay
- A 5 V USB-C power supply capable of delivering 3 A

All of the code for this chapter can be found in the Chapter03 folder from the book's GitHub repository: https://github.com/PacktPublishing/Mastering-Embedded-Linux-Development/tree/main/Chapter03.

What does a bootloader do?

In an embedded Linux system, the bootloader has two main jobs: initializing the system to a basic level and loading the kernel. In fact, the first job is somewhat subsidiary to the second in that it is only necessary to get as much of the system working as is needed to load the kernel.

When the first lines of the bootloader code are executed, following a power-on or reset, the system is in a very minimal state. The **Dynamic Random Access Memory (DRAM)** controller is not set up, so the main memory is not accessible. Likewise, other interfaces are not configured, so storage that's accessed via **NAND (NOT AND) flash** controllers, **MultiMediaCard (MMC)** controllers, and so on is unavailable. Typically, the only resources that are operational at the beginning are a single CPU core, some on-chip **Static Random Access Memory (SRAM)**, and the boot **Read-Only Memory (ROM)**.

A system bootstrap consists of several phases of code, each bringing more of the system into operation. The final act of the bootloader is to load the kernel into RAM and create an execution environment for it. The details of the interface between the bootloader and the kernel are architecture-specific, but in each case, it has to do two things. First, the bootloader has to pass a pointer to a structure containing information about the hardware configuration. Second, it has to pass a pointer to the kernel command line.

The kernel command line is a text string that controls the behavior of Linux. Once the kernel has begun executing, the bootloader is no longer needed and all the memory it was using can be reclaimed.

A subsidiary job of the bootloader is to provide a maintenance mode for updating boot configurations, loading new boot images into memory, and maybe running diagnostics. This is usually controlled by a simple command-line user interface, commonly over a serial console.

Boot sequence

Some years ago, we only needed to place the bootloader in non-volatile memory at the reset vector of the processor. **NOR (NOT OR) flash** memory was common at that time and, since it can be mapped directly into the address space, it was the ideal method of storage. The following diagram shows such a configuration with the **reset vector** at 0xfffffffc at the top end of an area of flash memory:

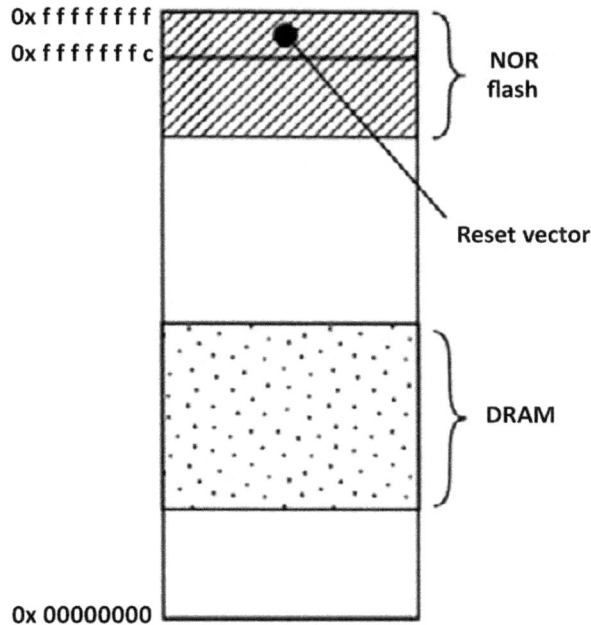

Figure 3.1 – NOR flash

The bootloader is linked so that there is a jump instruction at that location that points to the start of the bootloader code. From that point on, the bootloader code running in NOR flash memory can initialize the DRAM controller so that the main memory – the **DRAM** – becomes available, and then it copies itself into the DRAM. Once fully operational, the bootloader can load the kernel from flash memory into DRAM and transfer control to it.

However, once you move away from a simple linearly addressable storage medium such as NOR flash, the boot sequence becomes a complex, multi-stage procedure. The details are very specific to each SoC, but they generally go through the following phases.

Phase 1 — ROM code

In the absence of reliable external memory, the code that runs immediately after a reset or power-on is stored on-chip in the SoC. This is known as **ROM code**. It is loaded into the chip when it is manufactured, and hence the ROM code is proprietary and cannot be replaced by an open source equivalent.

ROM code does not include code to initialize the memory controller because DRAM configurations are highly device-specific, and so it can only use SRAM, which does not require a memory controller. Most embedded SoC designs have a small amount of SRAM on chip, varying in size from as little as 4 KB to several hundred KB.

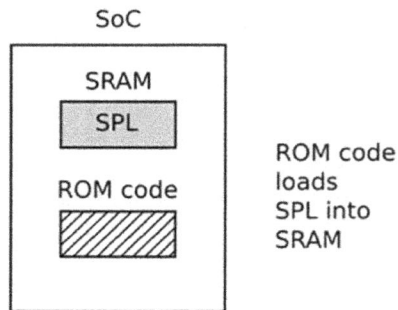

SoC

| SRAM |
| SPL |
| ROM code |

ROM code
loads
SPL into
SRAM

Figure 3.2 – Phase 1 – ROM code

The ROM code can load a small chunk of code from one of several pre-programmed locations into SRAM. As an example, TI Sitara chips try to load code from the first few pages of NAND flash memory, or from flash memory connected through a **Serial Peripheral Interface** (**SPI**). They also try to load code from the first sectors of an MMC device like an eMMC chip or SD card, or from a file named **MLO** (**Memory Loader**) on the first partition of an MMC device. If reading from all these memory devices fails, then it tries reading a byte stream from Ethernet, USB, or UART. The latter is provided mainly as a way to load code into flash memory at production rather than for use in normal operation.

Most embedded SoCs have ROM code that works in a similar way. In SoCs where the SRAM is not large enough to load a full bootloader such as U-Boot, there needs to be an intermediate loader called the **Secondary Program Loader** (**SPL**). At the end of the ROM code phase, the SPL is present in the SRAM and the ROM code jumps to the beginning of that code.

Phase 2 – Secondary Program Loader

The SPL must set up the memory controller and other essential parts of the system in preparation for loading the **Tertiary Program Loader** (TPL) into DRAM. The functionality of the SPL is limited by the size of the SRAM. It can read a program from a list of storage devices, as can the ROM code, once again using pre-programmed offsets from the start of a flash device.

If the SPL has filesystem drivers built into it, it can read well-known filenames such as u-boot. img from a disk partition. The SPL usually doesn't allow any user interaction, but it may print version information and progress messages that you can see on the console. The following diagram displays the phase 2 architecture:

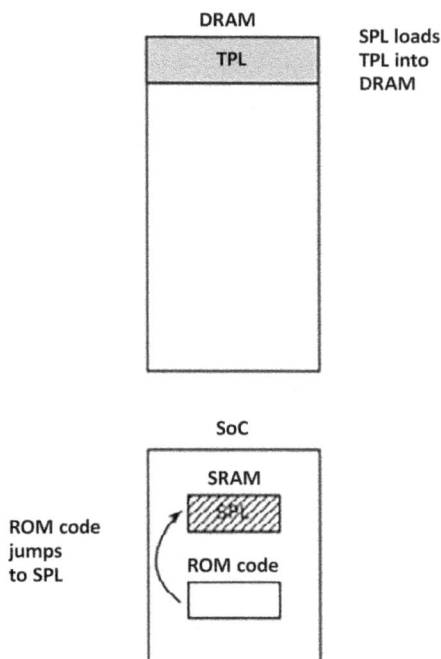

Figure 3.3 – Phase 2 – SPL

The preceding diagram shows the jump from ROM code to SPL. As the SPL executes within SRAM, it loads the TPL into DRAM. At the end of the second phase, the TPL is present in DRAM and the SPL can make a jump to that area.

The SPL may be open source, as is the case with Atmel AT91Bootstrap, but it is quite common for it to contain proprietary code that is supplied by the manufacturer as a binary blob.

Phase 3 — Tertiary Program Loader

At this point, we are running a full bootloader, such as U-Boot, which we will learn about a bit later in this chapter. Usually, there is a simple command-line user interface that lets you perform maintenance tasks such as loading new boot and kernel images into flash storage, as well as a way to load the kernel automatically without user intervention. The following diagram explains the phase 3 architecture:

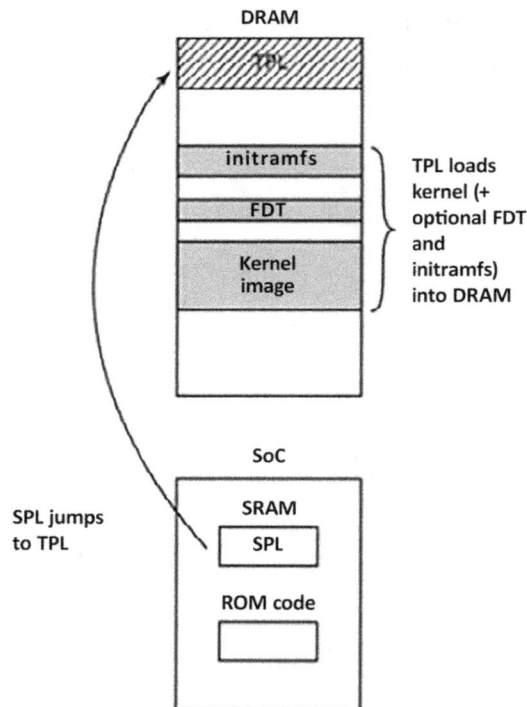

Figure 3.4 – Phase 3 – TPL

The preceding diagram shows the jump from SPL in SRAM to TPL in DRAM. As the TPL executes, it loads the kernel into DRAM. We also have the choice of appending an FDT and/or initial RAM disk to the image in DRAM if we want. Either way, at the end of the third phase, there is a kernel in memory waiting to be started.

Embedded bootloaders usually disappear from memory once the kernel is running and have no further part in the operation of the system. Before that happens, the TPL needs to hand off control of the boot process to the kernel.

Moving from the bootloader to the kernel

When the bootloader passes control to the kernel, it has to pass some basic information, which includes the following:

- The machine number, which is used on PowerPC and Arm platforms without support for a device tree, to identify the type of the SoC
- Basic details of the hardware that's been detected so far, including (at the very least) the size and location of the physical RAM and the CPU's clock speed
- The kernel command line
- Optionally, the location and size of a device tree binary
- Optionally, the location and size of an initial RAM disk, called the **initial RAM file system (initramfs)**

The kernel command line is a plain ASCII string that controls the behavior of Linux by giving it, for example, the name of the device that contains the root filesystem. We will look at the kernel command line in detail in the next chapter. It is common to provide the root filesystem as a RAM disk, in which case it is the responsibility of the bootloader to load the RAM disk image into memory. We will cover how to create initial RAM disks in *Chapter 5*.

The way this information is passed is dependent on the architecture and has changed in recent years. For instance, with PowerPC, the bootloader simply used to pass a pointer to a board information structure, whereas with Arm, it passed a pointer to a list of A tags. There is a good description of the format of A tags in the kernel source tree at `Documentation/arch/arm/booting.rst`. Browse the kernel source tree at `https://github.com/torvalds/linux`.

In both cases, the amount of information being passed is very limited, leaving the bulk to be discovered at runtime or hard-coded into the kernel as **platform data**. The widespread use of platform data meant that each board had to have a kernel configured and modified for that platform. A better way was needed, and that way is the device tree.

In the Arm world, the move away from A tags began in earnest in February 2013 with the release of Linux 3.8. Today, almost all Arm systems use device trees to gather information about the specifics of the hardware platform. This allows a single kernel binary to run on a wide range of Arm platforms.

Now that we've learned what a bootloader does, what the stages of the boot sequence are, and how it passes control to the kernel, let's learn how to configure a bootloader so that it runs on popular embedded SoCs.

Introducing device trees

If you are working with Arm or PowerPC SoCs, you are almost certainly going to encounter device trees at some point. This section aims to give you a quick overview of what they are and how they work. We will revisit the topic of device trees repeatedly throughout the course of this book.

A device tree is a flexible way of defining the hardware components of a computer system. Bear in mind that a device tree is just static data, not executable code. Usually, the device tree is loaded by the bootloader and passed to the kernel, although it is possible to bundle the device tree with the kernel image itself to cater to bootloaders that are not capable of loading them separately.

The format is derived from a Sun Microsystems bootloader known as **OpenBoot**, which was formalized as the Open Firmware specification (IEEE standard IEEE1275-1994). It was used in PowerPC-based Macintosh computers and so was a logical choice for the PowerPC Linux port. Since then, it has been adopted at a large scale by the many Arm Linux implementations and, to a lesser extent, by MIPS, MicroBlaze, ARC, and other architectures.

I recommend visiting https://www.devicetree.org for more information.

Device tree basics

The Linux kernel contains a large number of device tree source files in arch/$ARCH/boot/dts, and this is a good starting point for learning about device trees. Additionally, the U-Boot source code contains a smaller number of sources in arch/$ARCH/dts. If you acquired your hardware from a third party, the dts file forms part of the board support package, so you should expect to receive one along with the other source files.

The device tree represents a computer system as a collection of components joined together in a hierarchy. Every device tree begins with a root node represented by a forward slash, /, which contains subsequent child nodes describing the hardware of the system. Each node has a name and contains several properties in the form name = "value". Here is a simple example:

```
/dts-v1/;
/{
    model = "TI AM335x BeagleBone";
    compatible = "ti,am33xx";
    #address-cells = <1>;
    #size-cells = <1>;
```

```
cpus {
    #address-cells = <1>;
    #size-cells = <0>;
    cpu@0 {
        compatible = "arm,cortex-a8";
        device_type = "cpu";
        reg = <0>;
    };
};
memory@80000000 {
    device_type = "memory";
    reg = <0x80000000 0x20000000>; /* 512 MB */
};
};
```

Here, we have a root node that contains a cpus node and a memory node. The cpus node contains a single CPU node named cpu@0. The names of these nodes often include an @ followed by an address that distinguishes the node from other nodes of the same type. @ is required if the node has a reg property.

Both the root and CPU nodes have a compatible property. The Linux kernel uses this property to find a matching device driver by comparing it with the strings that are exported by each device driver in an of_device_id structure (more on this in *Chapter 11*).

IMPORTANT NOTE

It is a convention that the value of the compatible property is composed of a manufacturer name and a component name to reduce confusion between similar devices made by different manufacturers, hence ti,am33xx and arm,cortex-a8. It is also quite common to have more than one value for the compatible property when there is more than one driver that can handle this device. They are listed with the most suitable mentioned first.

The CPU node and the memory node have a device_type property that describes the class of the device. The node name is often derived from device_type.

reg property

The memory and cpu nodes shown earlier have a reg property, which refers to a range of units in a register space. A reg property consists of two values representing the real physical address and the size (length) of the range. Both are written as zero or more 32-bit integers called cells. Hence, the previous memory node refers to a single bank of memory that begins at 0x80000000 and is 0x20000000 bytes long.

Understanding reg properties becomes more complex when the address or size values cannot be represented in 32 bits. For example, on a device with 64-bit addressing, you need two cells for each:

```
/{
    #address-cells = <2>;
    #size-cells = <2>;
    memory@80000000 {
        device_type = "memory";
        reg = <0x00000000 0x80000000 0 0x80000000>;
    };
};
```

The information about the number of cells required is held in the #address-cells and #size_cells properties in an ancestor node. In other words, to understand a reg property, you have to look backward down the node hierarchy until you find #address-cells and #size_cells. If there are none, the default values are 1 for each – but it is bad practice for device tree writers to depend on defaults. Default values may or may not be obvious, so being explicit prevents any misunderstandings.

Now, let's return to the cpu and cpus nodes. CPUs have addresses as well. In a quadcore device, they might be addressed as 0, 1, 2, and 3. That can be thought of as a one-dimensional array without any depth, so the size is zero. Therefore, you can see that we have #address-cells = <1> and #size-cells = <0> in the cpus node. And in the child node, cpu@0, we assign a single value to the reg property with reg = <0>.

Labels and interrupts

The structure of the device tree described so far assumes that there is a single hierarchy of components when there are, in fact, several. Besides the obvious data connection between a component and other parts of the system, a node might also be connected to an interrupt controller, to a clock source, and to a voltage regulator.

To express these connections, we can add a label to a node and reference the label from other nodes. These labels are sometimes referred to as **phandles** because when the device tree is compiled, nodes with a reference from another node are assigned a unique numerical value in a property called phandle.

You can see phandles if you decompile the device tree binary. Take as an example a system containing an LCD controller that can generate interrupts and an interrupt-controller:

```
/dts-v1/;
{
    intc: interrupt-controller@48200000 {
        compatible = "ti,am33xx-intc";
        interrupt-controller;
        #interrupt-cells = <1>;
        reg = <0x48200000 0x1000>;
    };
    lcdc: lcdc@4830e000 {
        compatible = "ti,am33xx-tilcdc";
        reg = <0x4830e000 0x1000>;
        interrupt-parent = <&intc>;
        interrupts = <36>;
        ti,hwmods = "lcdc";
        status = "disabled";
    };
};
```

Here, we have the interrupt-controller@48200000 node with a label of intc. The interrupt-controller property identifies it as an interrupt controller. Like all interrupt controllers, it has an #interrupt-cells property, which tells us how many cells are needed to represent an interrupt source. In this case, there is only one that represents the **Interrupt Request (IRQ)** number.

Other interrupt controllers may use additional cells to characterize the interrupt, for example, to indicate whether it is edge or level triggered. The number of interrupt cells and their meanings are described in the bindings for each interrupt controller. The device tree bindings can be found in the Linux kernel source in the Documentation/devicetree/bindings directory.

Looking at the lcdc@4830e000 node, it has an interrupt-parent property, which references the interrupt controller it is connected to using the label. It also has an interrupts property, which is 36 in this case. Note that this node has its own label, lcdc, which is used elsewhere. Any node can have a label.

Device tree include files

A lot of hardware is common between SoCs of the same family and between boards using the same SoC. This is reflected in the device tree by splitting out common sections into include files, usually with the .dtsi extension. The Open Firmware standard defines /include/ as the mechanism to be used, as in this snippet from vexpress-v2p-ca9.dts:

```
/include/ "vexpress-v2m.dtsi"
```

Look through the .dts files in the kernel and you will find an alternative include statement that is borrowed from C; for example, this is in am335x-boneblack.dts:

```
#include "am33xx.dtsi"
#include "am335x-bone-common.dtsi"
```

Here is another example from am33xx.dtsi:

```
#include <dt-bindings/gpio/gpio.h>
#include <dt-bindings/pinctrl/am33xx.h>
#include <dt-bindings/clock/am3.h>
```

Lastly, include/dt-bindings/pinctrl/am33xx.h contains normal C macros:

```
#define PULL_DISABLE      (1 << 3)
#define INPUT_EN          (1 << 5)
#define SLEWCTRL_SLOW     (1 << 6)
#define SLEWCTRL_FAST            0
```

All of this is resolved if the device tree sources are built using the Kbuild system, which runs them through the C preprocessor, CPP. CPP processes the #include and #define statements into text that is suitable for the device tree compiler. The motivation is illustrated by the previous example. It means that the device tree sources can use the same definitions of constants as the kernel code.

When we include files using either syntax, the nodes are overlaid on top of one another to create a composite tree in which the outer layers extend or modify the inner ones. For example, am33xx. dtsi, which is general to all am33xx SoCs, defines the first MMC controller interface like this:

```
mmc1: mmc@48060000 {
    compatible = "ti,omap4-hsmmc";
    ti,hwmods = "mmc1";
    ti,dual-volt;
    ti,needs-special-reset;
    ti,needs-special-hs-handling;
```

```
        dmas = <&edma_xbar 24 0 0
                &edma_xbar 25 0 0>;
        dma-names = "tx", "rx";
        interrupts = <64>;
        reg = <0x48060000 0x1000>;
        status = "disabled";
    };
```

Note that status is disabled, meaning that no device driver should be bound to it, and that it has a label of mmc1.

Both BeagleBone and BeagleBone Black have a microSD card interface attached to mmc1. This is why, in am335x-bone-common.dtsi, the same node is referenced by an ampersand and its label, &mmc1:

```
&mmc1 {
    status = "okay";
    bus-width = <0x4>;
    pinctrl-names = "default";
    pinctrl-0 = <&mmc1_pins>;
    cd-gpios = <&gpio0 6 GPIO_ACTIVE_LOW>;
};
```

Referencing a node by an ampersand and its label lets us overwrite properties from previous mmc1 entries. Here, the status property is set to okay, which causes the MMC device driver to bind with this interface at runtime on both variants of BeagleBone. Also, a reference to a label is added to the pin control configuration, mmc1_pins. Alas, there is not sufficient space here to describe pin control and pin multiplexing. The Linux kernel source contains some information in the Documentation/devicetree/bindings/pinctrl directory.

However, the mmc1 interface is connected to a different voltage regulator on BeagleBone Black. This is expressed in am335x-boneblack.dts, where you will see another reference to mmc1, which associates it with the voltage regulator via the vmmcsd_fixed label:

```
&mmc1 {
    vmmc-supply = <&vmmcsd_fixed>;
};
```

So, layering the device tree source files like this gives us flexibility and reduces the need for duplicated code.

Compiling a device tree

The bootloader and kernel require a binary representation of the device tree, so it has to be compiled using the device tree compiler, that is, `dtc`. The result is a file ending with `.dtb`, which is referred to as a device tree binary or a device tree blob.

There is a copy of `dtc` in the Linux source in `scripts/dtc/dtc`, and it is also available as a package on many Linux distributions. You can use it to compile a simple device tree (one that does not use `#include`) like this:

```
$ dtc simpledts-1.dts -o simpledts-1.dtb
DTC: dts->dts on file "simpledts-1.dts"
```

Be wary of the fact that `dtc` does not give helpful error messages and makes no checks other than on the basic syntax of the language. This means that debugging a typing error in a device tree source file can be a lengthy process.

To build more complex examples, you will have to use the Kbuild kernel as shown in *Chapter 4*.

Like the kernel, the bootloader can use a device tree to initialize an embedded SoC and its peripherals. This device tree is critical when you're loading the kernel from a mass storage device such as a QSPI flash. While embedded Linux offers a choice of bootloaders, we will only cover one. Let's dig deep into that bootloader next.

U-Boot

We are going to focus on U-Boot exclusively because it supports a good number of processor architectures and most individual boards and devices. U-Boot, or to give its full name, **Das U-Boot**, began life as an open source bootloader for embedded PowerPC boards. Then, it was ported to Arm-based boards and later to other architectures, including **Microprocessor without Interlocked Pipeline Stages (MIPS)** and **SuperH (SH)**.

U-Boot has been around for a long time and has a good community. The project is hosted and maintained by DENX Software Engineering. There is plenty of information available on it, and a good place to start is `https://u-boot.readthedocs.io`. There is also a mailing list at `u-boot@lists.denx.de` that you can subscribe to by filling out and submitting the form provided at `https://lists.denx.de/listinfo/u-boot`.

Building U-Boot

Begin by getting the source code. As with most projects, the recommended way is to clone the Git repository and check out the tag you intend to use:

```
$ git clone git://git.denx.de/u-boot.git u-boot-mainline
$ cd u-boot-mainline
$ git checkout v2024.04
```

Alternatively, you can download a tarball from `https://ftp.denx.de/pub/u-boot/`.

There are more than 1,000 configuration files for common development boards and devices in the `configs` directory. In most cases, you can take a good guess regarding which to use based on the filename. But you can get more detailed information by looking through the `.rst` files in the `doc/board` directory. Or you can find information in an appropriate web tutorial or forum.

Taking BeaglePlay as an example, we will find that there is a configuration file named `am62x_evm_a53_defconfig` in the `configs` directory. In that same directory, there is another configuration file named `am62x_evm_r5_defconfig` that is for BeaglePlay's Arm Cortex-R5F microcontroller. The ROM code runs on the Arm Cortex-R5F microcontroller and the TPL runs on the main Arm Cortex-A53 CPU. There are two U-Boot SPLs: one that runs on the R5 and another that runs on the main CPU. There is a sequence diagram explaining BeaglePlay's unique boot flow in detail inside `doc/board/beagle/am62x_beagleplay.rst`. Take a close look at this sequence diagram and make sure you understand it. As you progress through the remainder of this chapter, refer to this diagram for clarification.

Building U-Boot for BeaglePlay is a multi-stage process. The Arm Cortex-M4F and Cortex-R5F in BeaglePlay's am62x SoC are 32-bit processors, so they require a 32-bit toolchain. A software component called **TI Foundational Security (TIFS)** runs on the M4. TIFS starts the R5 and asks it to load a firmware image to the TIFS core. That means we need to bundle a TIFS binary firmware image for the M4 together with a U-Boot SPL when generating a bootloader image for the R5. Next, we need to build **Trusted Firmware-A (TF-A)** for the main A53 CPU using a 64-bit toolchain. Lastly, we configure and build a U-Boot SPL and TPL for the main CPU.

Obtaining a 32-bit toolchain

Point your web browser at `https://developer.arm.com/downloads/-/arm-gnu-toolchain-downloads`. Search for **Downloads: 13.2.Rel1** and click on the plus sign in front to expand that section. Then click on the `arm-gnu-toolchain-13.2.rel1-x86_64-arm-none-eabi.tar.xz` file under x86_64 Linux hosted cross toolchains **AArch32 bare-metal target (arm-none-eabi)** to download the toolchain.

The following R5 exercises were successfully performed with that version of the Arm GNU toolchain. I recommend downloading the same version from that web page (if it is still available) to prevent any problems.

Install the 32-bit toolchain in your home directory:

```
$ cd ~
$ tar -xvf ~/Downloads/arm-gnu-toolchain-13.2.rel1-x86_64-arm-none-eabi.
tar.xz
```

Add the 32-bit toolchain to your PATH environment variable:

```
$ export PATH=${HOME}/arm-gnu-toolchain-13.2.Rel1-x86_64-arm-none-eabi/
bin/:$PATH
```

You are now ready to build U-Boot for the R5. Make sure to replace 13.2.rel1 and 13.2.Rel1 in the preceding commands with the actual version of the 32-bit toolchain you downloaded.

Building U-Boot SPL for R5

Support for BeaglePlay in mainline U-Boot was very new back in November 2023 when I wrote this. For this reason, I have instead opted to use BeagleBoard.org's U-Boot fork for BeaglePlay. I suggest building the U-Boot source from the same Git repo (if it is still available) to prevent any problems.

Clone the U-Boot fork to your home directory and check out a stable commit:

```
$ git clone https://github.com/beagleboard/u-boot u-boot-beagleplay
$ cd u-boot-beagleplay
$ git checkout f036fb
```

Install the packages needed to build U-Boot for BeaglePlay:

```
$ sudo apt install bison device-tree-compiler flex libncurses-dev libssl-
dev python3-dev python3-setuptools swig
```

Configure and build U-Boot for the R5:

1. First, create a build directory for the R5 one level up to share build artifacts across builds:

    ```
    $ mkdir -p ../build_uboot/r5
    ```

2. Next, set the ARCH and CROSS_COMPILE environment variables for 32-bit Arm:

```
$ export ARCH=arm
$ export CROSS_COMPILE=arm-none-eabi-
```

3. Select am62x_evm_r5_defconfig for building:

```
$ make am62x_evm_r5_defconfig O=../build_uboot/r5
```

4. Run make menuconfig to configure U-Boot further for building:

```
$ make menuconfig O=../build_uboot/r5
```

-   Drill down into the **Environment** submenu.

-   Select **Environment is in a EXT4 filesystem**.

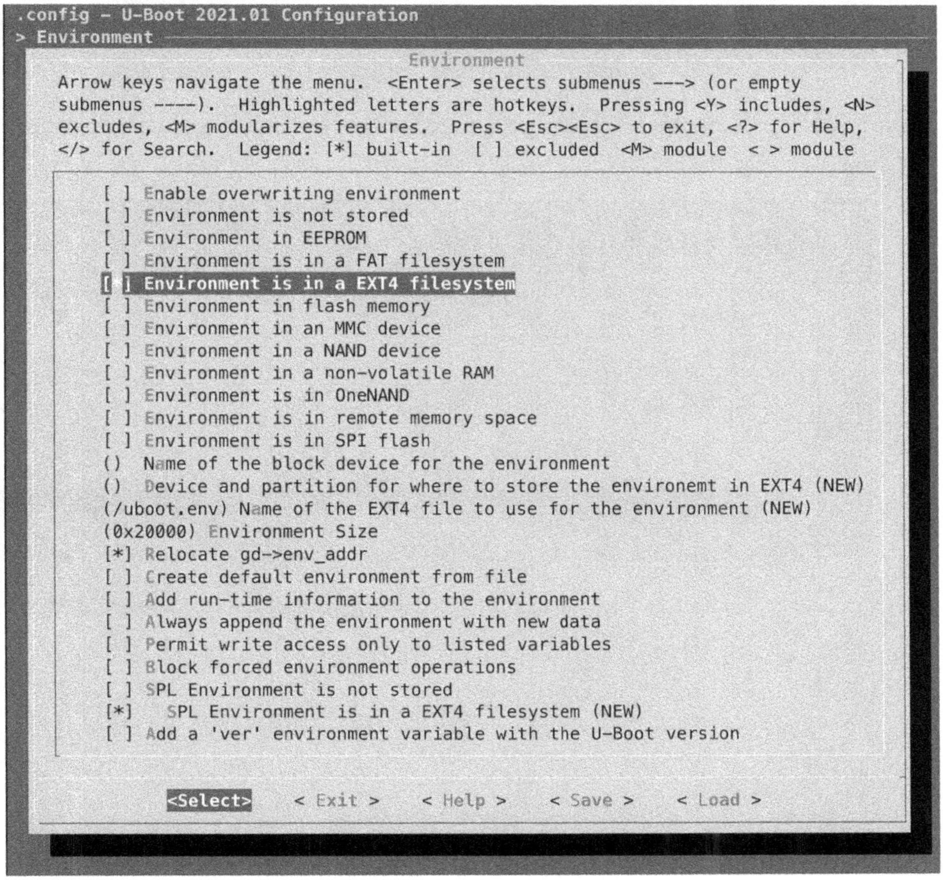

Figure 3.5 – Selecting Environment is in a EXT4 fileystem

5. Deselect any other options (e.g., MMC, NAND, and SPI) for environment storage on that menu page.

6. Enter mmc in the **Name of the block device for the environment** text field.

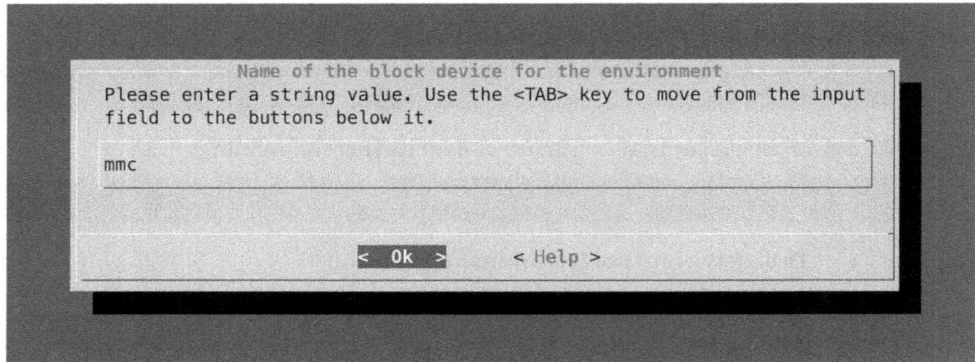

Figure 3.6 – Name of the block device for the environment

7. Enter 1:2 in the **Device and partition for where to store the environment in EXT4** text field.

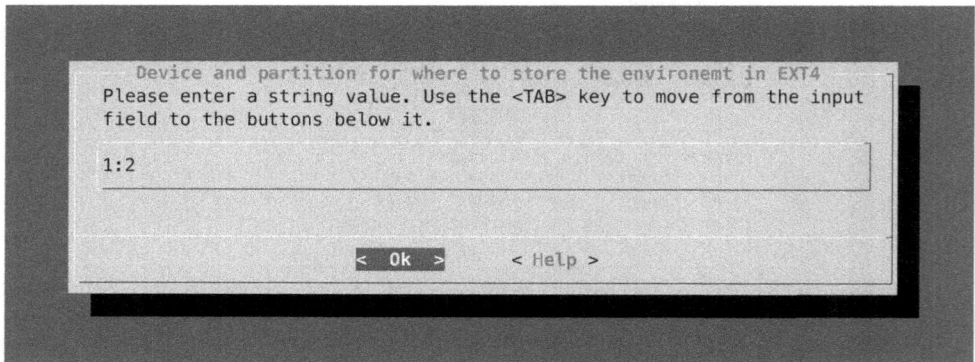

Figure 3.7 – Device and partition for where to store the environment in EXT4

8. Ensure /uboot.env is the **Name of the EXT4 file to use for the environment** text field.

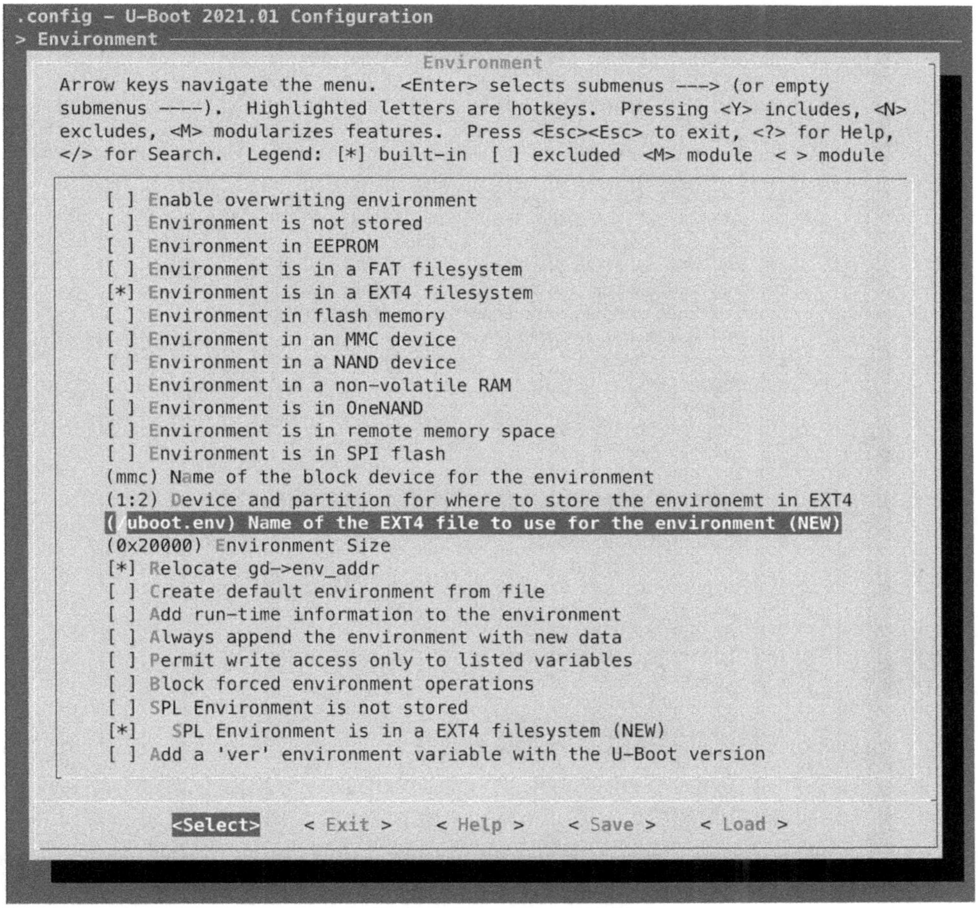

Figure 3.8 – Environment

9. Back out of the **Environment** submenu.

10. Drill down into the **SPL/TPL** submenu.

11. Select **Support EXT filesystems**.

```
.config - U-Boot 2021.01 Configuration
> SPL / TPL
                                 SPL / TPL
     Arrow keys navigate the menu.  <Enter> selects submenus ---> (or empty
     submenus ----).  Highlighted letters are hotkeys.  Pressing <Y> includes, <N>
     excludes, <M> modularizes features.  Press <Esc><Esc> to exit, <?> for Help,
     </> for Search.  Legend: [*] built-in  [ ] excluded  <M> module  < > module

          [*] Enable output of the SPL banner 'U-Boot SPL ...'
          [*] Allows initializing BSS early before entering board_init_f
          [ ] Display a board-specific message in SPL
          [*] MMC raw mode: by sector
          (0x400) Address on the MMC to load U-Boot from
          (0x0) U-Boot main hardware partition image offset
          [ ] MMC Raw mode: by partition
          [ ] Support CRC32
          [ ] Support MD5
          [ ] Support SHA1
          [ ] Support SHA256
          [ ] Support SHA384
          [ ] Support SHA512
          [ ] Remove functionality from SPL FIT loading to reduce size
          [ ] Support CACHE drivers
          [ ] Support CPU drivers
          [ ] Support crypto drivers
          [ ] Support hashing drivers
          [*] Support DMA drivers
          [*] Support misc drivers
          [*] Support an environment
          [ ]    Support save environment
          [ ]    Support Ethernet
          [ ] Support EXT filesystems
          [ ] Support SquashFS filesystems


             <Select>    < Exit >    < Help >    < Save >    < Load >
```

Figure 3.9 – Select Support EXT4 filesystems

12. Back out of the **SPL/TPL** submenu.

13. Drill down into the **Boot Options** submenu.

14. Select **Enable a default value for bootcmd**.

```
.config - U-Boot 2021.01 Configuration
> Boot options
                              Boot options
   Arrow keys navigate the menu.  <Enter> selects submenus ---> (or empty
   submenus ----).  Highlighted letters are hotkeys.  Pressing <Y> includes, <N>
   excludes, <M> modularizes features.  Press <Esc><Esc> to exit, <?> for Help,
   </> for Search.  Legend: [*] built-in  [ ] excluded  <M> module  < > module

            Boot images  --->
            Boot timing  --->
            Boot media  --->
            Autoboot options  --->
      [ ] Enable boot arguments
      [*] Enable a default value for bootcmd
      ()    bootcmd value (NEW)
      [ ] Enable preboot
      ()  Default fdt file
```

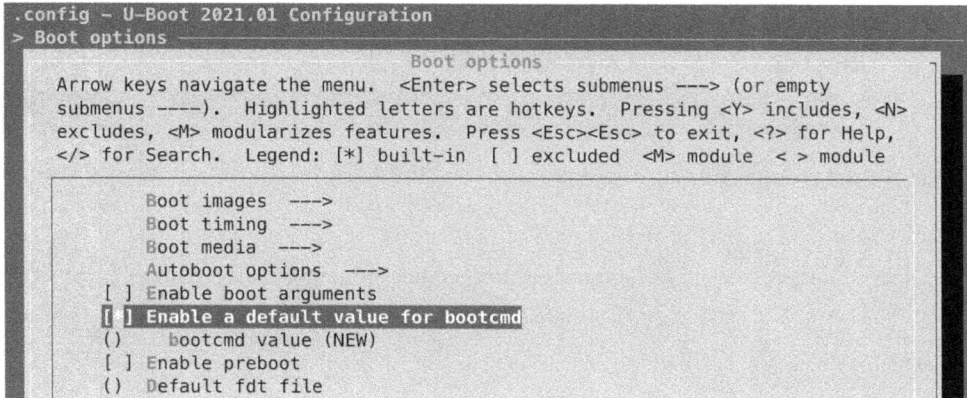

Figure 3.10 – Select Enable a default value for bootcmd

15.   Enter `echo 'no bootcmd yet'` in the **bootcmd value** text field.

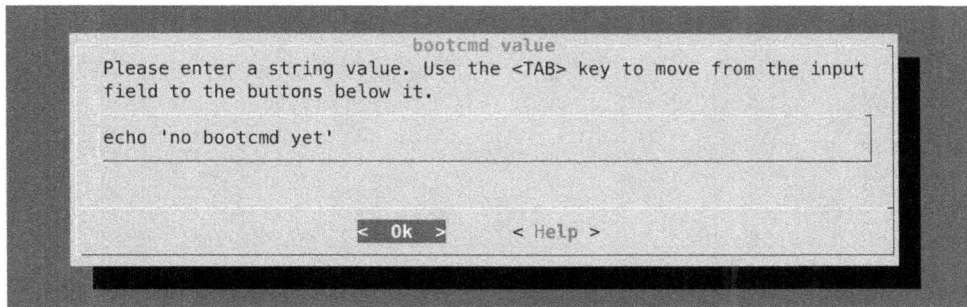

```
                         bootcmd value
   Please enter a string value. Use the <TAB> key to move from the input
   field to the buttons below it.

   echo 'no bootcmd yet'



               <  Ok  >        < Help >
```

Figure 3.11 – bootcmd value

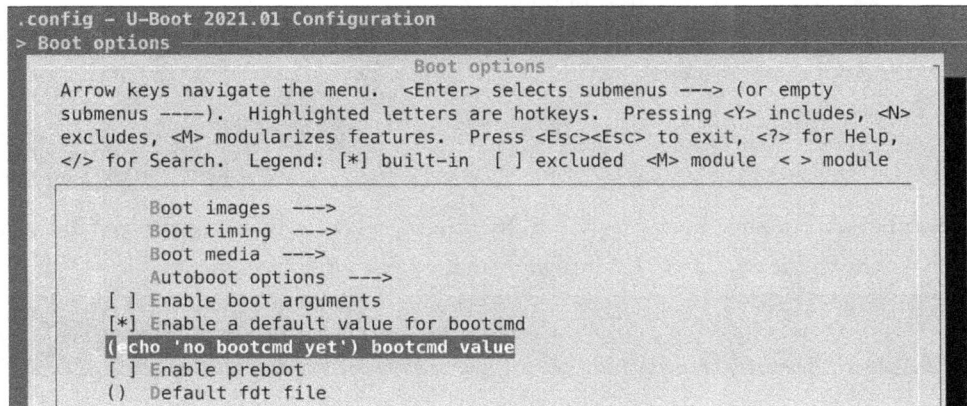

```
.config - U-Boot 2021.01 Configuration
> Boot options
                              Boot options
   Arrow keys navigate the menu.  <Enter> selects submenus ---> (or empty
   submenus ----).  Highlighted letters are hotkeys.  Pressing <Y> includes, <N>
   excludes, <M> modularizes features.  Press <Esc><Esc> to exit, <?> for Help,
   </> for Search.  Legend: [*] built-in  [ ] excluded  <M> module  < > module

            Boot images  --->
            Boot timing  --->
            Boot media  --->
            Autoboot options  --->
      [ ] Enable boot arguments
      [*] Enable a default value for bootcmd
      (echo 'no bootcmd yet') bootcmd value
      [ ] Enable preboot
      ()  Default fdt file
```

Figure 3.12 – Boot options

16. Exit out of menuconfig and choose **Yes** when asked to save your new configuration.

17. Lastly, build the U-Boot for the R5:

```
$ make O=../build_uboot/r5
```

When U-Boot is done building, there should be an SPL binary for the R5 in ../build_uboot/r5/spl.

> Refer to the boot flow sequence diagram in doc/board/beagle/am62x_beagleplay.
> rst.

Generating an image for the R5

Recall that the TIFS firmware image that gets loaded into the M4 needs to be bundled together with the U-Boot SPL for the R5. We obtain the binary TIFS firmware image directly from TI.

Clone the TI firmware repo to your home directory:

```
$ cd ~
$ git clone https://github.com/TexasInstruments-Sandbox/ti-linux-firmware.
git
$ cd ti-linux-firmware
$ git checkout c126d386
```

Bundling the TIFS firmware image for the M4 together with the U-Boot SPL for the R5 requires a tool named k3-image-gen.

Clone the k3-image-gen repo to your home directory:

```
$ cd ~
$ git clone https://github.com/beagleboard/k3-image-gen.git
$ cd k3-image-gen
$ git checkout 150f195
```

Generate the combined image for the R5 by running make in the k3-image-gen directory with paths to the U-Boot SPL and TIFS firmware image passed in as arguments:

```
$ make SOC=am62x SBL=../build_uboot/r5/spl/u-boot-spl.bin SYSFW_PATH=../
ti-linux-firmware/ti-sysfw/ti-fs-firmware-am62x-gp.bin
```

There should now be a tiboot3.bin file in the k3-image-gen directory.

Refer to the boot flow sequence diagram in `doc/board/beagle/am62x_beagleplay.rst`.

Building TF-A for the main A53 CPU

The A53 in BeaglePlay's am62x SoC is a 64-bit CPU, so we must switch to a 64-bit toolchain to cross-compile source code for it. We will use the same 64-bit Bootlin toolchain from *Chapter 2* that you installed in your home directory.

Add that 64-bit Bootlin toolchain to your PATH environment variable:

```
$ export PATH=${HOME}/aarch64--glibc--stable-2024.02-1/bin/:$PATH
```

Make sure to replace 2024.02-1 in the preceding commands with the actual version of the 64-bit toolchain you downloaded.

Clone the TF-A source code to your home directory and check out a stable release tag:

```
$ cd ~
$ git clone https://github.com/ARM-software/arm-trusted-firmware.git
$ cd arm-trusted-firmware
$ git checkout v2.9
```

Configure and build TF-A for the A53:

1. Set the ARCH and CROSS_COMPILE environment variables for 64-bit Arm:

   ```
   $ export ARCH=aarch64
   $ export CROSS_COMPILE=aarch64-buildroot-linux-gnu-
   ```

2. Build TF-A for the A53 specifying k3 as the platform and lite as the target board:

   ```
   $ make PLAT=k3 TARGET_BOARD=lite
   ```

When TF-A is done building, there should be a bl31.bin for the A53 in ./build/k3/lite/release.

Refer to the boot flow sequence diagram in `doc/board/beagle/am62x_beagleplay.rst`.

Building U-Boot for the main A53 CPU

All the build steps performed up until now are unique to the am62x SoC in BeaglePlay. Building U-Boot for most targets only requires compiling an SPL and TPL for the main CPU. We will use the same 64-bit Bootlin toolchain from *Chapter 2* that you installed in your home directory.

Add that 64-bit Bootlin toolchain to your PATH environment variable:

```
$ export PATH=${HOME}/aarch64--glibc--stable-2024.02-1/bin/:$PATH
```

Make sure to replace 2024.02-1 in the preceding commands with the actual version of the 64-bit toolchain you downloaded.

Configure and build U-Boot for the A53:

1. First, navigate back to the u-boot source tree for BeaglePlay:

    ```
    $ cd ~
    $ cd u-boot-beagleplay
    ```

2. Next, create a build directory for the A53 one level up:

    ```
    $ mkdir -p ../build_uboot/a53
    ```

3. Set the ARCH and CROSS_COMPILE environment variables for 64-bit Arm:

    ```
    $ export ARCH=aarch64
    $ export CROSS_COMPILE=aarch64-buildroot-linux-gnu-
    ```

4. Select am62x_evm_a53_defconfig for building:

    ```
    $ make am62x_evm_a53_defconfig O=../build_uboot/a53
    ```

5. Run make menuconfig to configure U-Boot further for building:

    ```
    $ make menuconfig O=../build_uboot/a53
    ```

6. Drill down into the **Environment** submenu.

7. Select **Environment is in a EXT4 filesystem**.

8. Deselect any other options (e.g., MMC, NAND, and SPI) for environment storage on that menu page.

9. Enter mmc in the **Name of the block device for the environment** text field.

10. Enter 1:2 in the **Device and partition for where to store the environment in EXT4** text field.

11. Ensure /uboot.env is entered in the **Name of the EXT4 file to use for the environment** text field.

12. Back out of the **Environment** submenu.

13. Drill down into the **SPL/TPL** submenu.

14. Select **Support EXT filesystems**.

15. Back out of the **SPL/TPL** submenu.

16. Drill down into the **Boot Options** submenu.

17. Select **Enable a default value for bootcmd**.

18. Enter echo 'no bootcmd yet' in the **bootcmd value** text field.

19. Exit out of menuconfig and choose **Yes** when asked to save your new configuration.

20. Lastly, build U-Boot for the A53 passing paths to TI's TF-A and DM firmware as arguments to make:

```
$ make ATF=$HOME/arm-trusted-firmware/build/k3/lite/release/bl131.
bin DM=$HOME/ti-linux-firmware/ti-dm/am62xx/ipc_echo_testb_mcu1_0_
release_strip.xer5f O=../build_uboot/a53
```

IMPORTANT NOTE

Always use absolute paths as opposed to relative ./ paths to point to the ATF and DM firmware in your make command. Otherwise, the resulting SPL and U-Boot binaries will be incorrect in size and content.

The results of the compilation are as follows:

- u-boot: U-Boot in ELF format, suitable for use with a debugger
- u-boot.map: The symbol table
- u-boot.bin: U-Boot in raw binary format, suitable for running on your device
- u-boot.img: u-boot.bin with a U-Boot header added, suitable for uploading to a running copy of U-Boot
- u-boot.srec: U-Boot in Motorola S-record (**SRECORD** or **SRE**) format, suitable for transferring over a serial connection

BeaglePlay also requires an SPL, as described earlier. This is built at the same time and is named tispl.bin (the boot flow sequence diagram in doc/board/beagle/am62x_beagleplay.rst):

```
$ cd ~
$ cd build_uboot/a53
$ ls -l tispl.bin
-rw-rw-r-- 1 frank frank 549508 Jun 29 20:31 tispl.bin
$ ls -l u-boot*
-rwxrwxr-x 1 frank frank 6779128 Jun 29 20:31 u-boot
-rw-rw-r-- 1 frank frank 1098236 Jun 29 20:31 u-boot.bin
-rw-rw-r-- 1 frank frank   18246 Jun 29 20:30 u-boot.cfg
-rw-rw-r-- 1 frank frank   11563 Jun 29 20:31 u-boot.cfg.configs
-rw-rw-r-- 1 frank frank   37485 Jun 29 20:31 u-boot.dtb
-rw-rw-r-- 1 frank frank 1060788 Jun 29 20:31 u-boot-dtb.img
-rw-rw-r-- 1 frank frank 1098236 Jun 29 20:31 u-boot-fit-dtb.bin
-rw-rw-r-- 1 frank frank 1060788 Jun 29 20:31 u-boot.img
-rw-rw-r-- 1 frank frank 1060788 Jun 29 20:31 u-boot.img_HS
-rw-rw-r-- 1 frank frank    1348 Jun 29 20:31 u-boot.lds
-rw-rw-r-- 1 frank frank  765615 Jun 29 20:31 u-boot.map
-rwxrwxr-x 1 frank frank  993104 Jun 29 20:31 u-boot-nodtb.bin
-rwxrwxr-x 1 frank frank  993104 Jun 29 20:31 u-boot-nodtb.bin_HS
-rw-rw-r-- 1 frank frank    1836 Jun 29 20:31 u-boot-spl-k3_HS.its
-rwxrwxr-x 1 frank frank 2979442 Jun 29 20:31 u-boot.srec
-rw-rw-r-- 1 frank frank  342412 Jun 29 20:31 u-boot.sym
```

The procedure is similar for other targets.

Installing U-Boot

Installing a bootloader on a board for the first time requires some manual intervention. If the board has a hardware debug interface, such as a **Joint Test Action Group (JTAG)**, it is usually possible to load a copy of U-Boot directly into RAM and get it running. From that point, you can use U-Boot commands so that it copies itself into flash memory. The details are very board-specific and outside the scope of this book.

Many SoC designs have a boot ROM built in that can be used to read boot code from various external sources, such as SD cards, serial interfaces, or USB mass storage. This is the case with the am62x chip in the Beagle, which makes it easy to try out new software.

You will need a microSD card reader to write the images to a card. There are two types: external readers that plug into a USB port and the internal SD readers that are present on many laptops. A device name is assigned by Linux when a card is plugged into the reader. The lsblk command is a useful tool for finding out which device has been allocated. For example, this is what I see when I plug a nominal 32 GB microSD card into my card reader:

```
$ lsblk
NAME         MAJ:MIN RM   SIZE RO TYPE MOUNTPOINT
sda            8:0    1  29.8G  0 disk
└─sda1         8:1    1  29.8G  0 part /media/frank/6662-6262
nvme0n1      259:0    0 465.8G  0 disk
├─nvme0n1p1  259:1    0   512M  0 part /boot/efi
├─nvme0n1p2  259:2    0    16M  0 part
├─nvme0n1p3  259:3    0 232.9G  0 part
└─nvme0n1p4  259:4    0 232.4G  0 part /
```

In this case, nvme0n1 is my 512 GB hard drive and sda is the microSD card. It has a single partition, sda1, which is mounted as the /media/frank/6662-6262 directory.

If I use the built-in SD card slot, I see this:

```
$ lsblk
NAME          MAJ:MIN RM   SIZE RO TYPE MOUNTPOINT
mmcblk0       179:0    1  29.8G  0 disk
└─mmcblk0p1   179:1    1  29.8G  0 part /media/frank/6662-6262
nvme0n1       259:0    0 465.8G  0 disk
├─nvme0n1p1   259:1    0   512M  0 part /boot/efi
├─nvme0n1p2   259:2    0    16M  0 part
├─nvme0n1p3   259:3    0 232.9G  0 part
└─nvme0n1p4   259:4    0 232.4G  0 part /
```

In this case, the microSD card appears as mmcblk0, and the partition is mmcblk0p1. Note that the microSD card you use may have been formatted differently than this one, so you may see a different number of partitions with different mount points. When formatting an SD card, it is very important to be sure of its device name. You really don't want to mistake your hard drive for an SD card and format that instead.

This has happened to me more than once. So, I have provided a shell script in this book's code repo named MELD/format-sdcard.sh, which has a reasonable number of checks to prevent you (and me) from using the wrong device name. The parameter is the device name of the microSD card, which would be sda in the first example and mmcblk0 in the second. Here is an example of its use:

```
$ MELD/format-sdcard.sh mmcblk0
```

The script creates two partitions. The first is 128 MB and formatted as FAT32, and it will contain the bootloader, while the second is 1 GB and formatted as ext4, which you will use in *Chapter 5*. The script aborts when it's applied to any drive greater than 128 GB so be prepared to modify it if you are using larger microSD cards.

Once you have formatted the microSD card, remove it from the card reader and then reinsert it. Roll over and click on one of the USB stick icons that appears to the left of the Ubuntu desktop so that a window opens for the boot partition. On current versions of Ubuntu, the two partitions are mounted as /media/<user>/boot and /media/<user>/rootfs.

Copy tiboot3.bin, tispl.bin and u-boot.img to the boot partition like this:

```
$ cd ~
$ cd k3-image-gen
$ cp tiboot3.bin /media/$USER/boot/.
$ cd ~
$ cd build_uboot/a53
$ cp tispl.bin u-boot.img /media/$USER/boot/.
```

Right-click on either of the two USB stick icons and select **Eject** to unmount the microSD card. Lastly, remove the microSD card from your host machine's card reader.

To boot BeaglePlay from your newly prepared microSD card:

1. With no power on BeaglePlay, insert the microSD card into BeaglePlay's reader.
2. Plug the USB side of your USB-to-TTL serial cable into your host machine. Make sure your cable has a 3.3 V logic level.
3. The three-pin UART connector is right next to the USB-C connector on BeaglePlay. Do not connect a fourth red wire from your cable. A red wire typically indicates power, which is unnecessary in this instance and could damage the board.
4. Connect the TX wire from the cable to the RX pin on BeaglePlay.
5. Connect the RX wire from the cable to the TX pin on BeaglePlay.
6. Connect the GND (black) wire from the cable to the GND pin on BeaglePlay.

7. A serial port should appear on your PC as /dev/ttyUSB0.

8. Start a suitable terminal program, like gtkterm, minicom, or picocom, and attach it to the port at 115,200 **bits per second (bps)** with no flow control. gtkterm is probably the easiest to set up and use:

```
$ gtkterm -p /dev/ttyUSB0 -s 115200
```

9. If you get a permissions error, then you may need to add yourself to the dialout group to use this port or launch gtkterm with sudo. If garbled or no output appears on the serial console, then swap the wires connected to the RX and TX pins on BeaglePlay.

10. Press and hold the USR button on BeaglePlay.

11. Power up the board using USB-C.

12. Release the button after about 5 seconds.

You should see some output followed by a U-Boot prompt on the serial console:

```
U-Boot SPL 2021.01-gf036fbdc25 (Jun 29 2024 - 18:54:55 -0700)
SYSFW ABI: 3.1 (firmware rev 0x0009 '9.0.4--v09.00.04 (Kool Koala)')
SPL initial stack usage: 13384 bytes
Trying to boot from MMC2
spl_load_fit_image: Skip load 'tee': image size is 0!
Loading Environment from EXT4... ** File not found /uboot.env **

** Unable to read "/uboot.env" from mmc1:2 **
Starting ATF on ARM64 core...

NOTICE:  BL31: v2.9(release):v2.9.0
NOTICE:  BL31: Built : 19:01:43, Jun 29 2024

U-Boot SPL 2021.01-gf036fbdc25 (Jun 29 2024 - 20:30:20 -0700)
SYSFW ABI: 3.1 (firmware rev 0x0009 '9.0.4--v09.00.04 (Kool Koala)')
Trying to boot from MMC2



U-Boot 2021.01-gf036fbdc25 (Jun 29 2024 - 20:30:20 -0700)

SoC:   AM62X SR1.0 GP
Model: BeagleBoard.org BeaglePlay
Board: BEAGLEPLAY-A0- rev 02
```

```
DRAM:  2 GiB
MMC:   mmc@fa10000: 0, mmc@fa00000: 1, mmc@fa20000: 2
Loading Environment from EXT4... ** File not found /uboot.env **

** Unable to read "/uboot.env" from mmc1:2 **
In:    serial@2800000
Out:   serial@2800000
Err:   serial@2800000
Error: Can't set serial# to SSSS
Net:   Could not get PHY for ethernet@8000000port@1: addr 0
am65_cpsw_nuss_port ethernet@8000000port@1: phy_connect() failed
No ethernet found.

Press SPACE to abort autoboot in 2 seconds
no bootcmd yet
=>
```

Hit any key on your keyboard to stop U-Boot from autobooting with the default environment. Now that we have a U-Boot prompt in front of us, let's put U-Boot through its paces.

Using U-Boot

In this section, I describe some of the common tasks that can be performed with U-Boot.

U-Boot provides a command-line interface over a serial port. It provides a command prompt that is customized for each board. In these examples, I use => for the command prompt. Typing help prints out all the commands that have been configured in this version of U-Boot. Typing help <command> prints out more information about a particular command.

The default command interpreter for BeaglePlay is quite simple. You cannot do command-line editing by pressing the left or right keys. There is no command completion by pressing the *Tab* key, and there is no command history by pressing the up arrow key. Pressing any of these keys will disrupt the command you are currently trying to type, and you will have to type *Ctrl + C* and start all over again. The only line editing key you can safely use is the backspace.

As an option, you can configure a different command shell called **Hush**, which has more sophisticated interactive support, including command-line editing.

The default number format is hexadecimal. Consider the following command:

```
=> nand read 82000000 400000 200000
```

This will read `0x200000` bytes from offset `0x400000` from the start of the NAND flash memory into RAM address `0x82000000`.

Environment variables

U-Boot uses environment variables extensively to store and pass information between functions and even to create scripts. Environment variables are simple `name=value` pairs that are stored in an area of memory. The initial population of variables may be coded in the board configuration header file like this:

```
#define CONFIG_EXTRA_ENV_SETTINGS
"myvar1=value1"
"myvar2=value2"
```

You can create and modify variables from the U-Boot command line using `setenv`. For example, `setenv foo bar` creates the `foo` variable with the `bar` value. Note that there is no = sign between the variable name and the value. You can delete a variable by setting it to a null string using `setenv foo`. You can print all the variables to the console using `printenv`, or you can print a single variable using `printenv foo`.

If U-Boot has been configured with space to store the environment, you can use the `saveenv` command to save it. If there is raw NAND or NOR flash, then an erase block can be reserved for this purpose, often with another erase block being used as a redundant copy to guard against corruption. If there is eMMC or SD card storage, it can be stored in a reserved array of sectors, or in a file named uboot.env in a partition of the disk. Other options include storing it in serial **Electrical Erasable Programmable Read Only Memory (EEPROM)** connected via an I2C or SPI interface or non-volatile RAM.

Boot image format

U-Boot doesn't have a filesystem. Instead, it tags blocks of information with a 64-byte header so that it can track the contents. We prepare files for U-Boot using the `mkimage` command-line tool, which comes bundled with the `u-boot-tools` package on Ubuntu. You can also get `mkimage` by running `make tools` from within the U-Boot source tree and then invoke it as `tools/mkimage`. Here is a summary of the command's usage:

```
$ mkimage
Error: Missing output filename
Usage: mkimage -l image
          -l ==> list image header information
```

```
      mkimage [-x] -A arch -O os -T type -C comp -a addr -e ep -n name -d
data_file[:data_file...] image
          -A ==> set architecture to 'arch'
          -O ==> set operating system to 'os'
          -T ==> set image type to 'type'
          -C ==> set compression type 'comp'
          -a ==> set load address to 'addr' (hex)
          -e ==> set entry point to 'ep' (hex)
          -n ==> set image name to 'name'
          -d ==> use image data from 'datafile'
          -x ==> set XIP (execute in place)
      mkimage [-D dtc_options] [-f fit-image.its|-f auto|-F] [-b <dtb>
[-b <dtb>]] [-E] [-B size] [-i <ramdisk.cpio.gz>] fit-image
          <dtb> file is used with -f auto, it may occur multiple times.
          -D => set all options for device tree compiler
          -f => input filename for FIT source
          -i => input filename for ramdisk file
          -E => place data outside of the FIT structure
          -B => align size in hex for FIT structure and header
Signing / verified boot options: [-k keydir] [-K dtb] [ -c <comment>] [-p
addr] [-r] [-N engine]
          -k => set directory containing private keys
          -K => write public keys to this .dtb file
          -G => use this signing key (in lieu of -k)
          -c => add comment in signature node
          -F => re-sign existing FIT image
          -p => place external data at a static position
          -r => mark keys used as 'required' in dtb
          -N => openssl engine to use for signing
      mkimage -V ==> print version information and exit
 Use '-T list' to see a list of available image types
```

For example, to prepare a kernel image for a 32-bit Arm processor, you can use the following command:

```
$ mkimage -A arm -O linux -T kernel -C gzip -a 0x80008000 -e 0x80008000 -n
'Linux' -d zImage uImage
```

In this instance, the architecture is arm, the operating system is linux, and the image type is kernel. Additionally, the compression scheme is gzip, the load address is 0x80008000, and the entry point is the same as the load address. Lastly, the image name is Linux, the image datafile is named zImage, and the image being generated is named uImage.

Loading images

Usually, you load images from removable storage such as an SD card or over a network. SD cards are handled in U-Boot by the MMC driver. Here is an example of loading a file from a microSD card into memory:

```
=> mmc rescan
=> mmc list
mmc@fa10000: 0 (eMMC)
mmc@fa00000: 1 (SD)
mmc@fa20000: 2
=> fatload mmc 1:1 80000000 tiboot3.bin
329021 bytes read in 19 ms (16.5 MiB/s)
```

The mmc rescan command re-initializes the MMC driver, perhaps to detect that an SD card has recently been inserted. Next, fatload is used to read a file from a FAT-formatted partition on the SD card. Note that tiboot3.bin is the firmware image for the R5, not a Linux kernel image, so it cannot be executed at this point in the boot sequence. The format for the fatload command is as follows:

```
fatload <interface> [<dev[:part]> [<addr> [<filename> [bytes [pos]]]]]
```

If <interface> is mmc, as in our case, then <dev:part> is the device number of the MMC interface counting from zero and the partition number counting from one. Hence, <1:1> is the first partition on the second device, which is mmc 1 for the microSD card on BeaglePlay (the onboard eMMC is mmc 0). The chosen memory location of 0x80000000 is in an area of RAM that is not being used at this moment.

To load kernel image files over a network, you must use the **Trivial File Transfer Protocol (TFTP)**. This requires you to install tftpd (a TFTP daemon) on your development system and start running it. You must also configure any firewalls between your PC and the target board to allow the TFTP protocol on UDP port 69 to pass through.

The default configuration of TFTP only allows access to the /var/lib/tftpboot directory. The next step is to copy the files you want to transfer to the target into that directory. Then, assuming that you are using a pair of static IP addresses, which removes the need for further network administration, the sequence of commands to load a kernel image file looks like this:

```
=> setenv ipaddr 192.168.159.42
=> setenv serverip 192.168.159.99
=> tftp 82000000 uImage
link up on port 0, speed 100, full duplex
Using cpsw device
TFTP from server 192.168.159.99; our IP address is 192.168.159.42
Filename 'uImage'.
Load address: 0x82000000
Loading:
#################################################################################
#################################################################################
#################################################################################
#################################################################################
##############
3 MiB/s
done
Bytes transferred = 4605000 (464448 hex)
```

Finally, let's look at how to program images into NAND flash memory and read them back. This is handled by the nand command. This example loads a kernel image via TFTP and programs it into flash:

```
=> tftpboot 82000000 uImage
=> nandecc hw
=> nand erase 280000 400000
NAND erase: device 0 offset 0x280000, size 0x400000
Erasing at 0x660000 -- 100% complete.
OK
=> nand write 82000000 280000 400000

NAND write: device 0 offset 0x280000, size 0x400000
4194304 bytes written: OK
```

Now, you can load the kernel from flash memory using the nand read command:

```
=> nand read 82000000 280000 400000
```

Once the kernel has been loaded into RAM, we can boot it.

Booting Linux

The bootm command starts a kernel image running. The syntax is as follows:

```
bootm <address of kernel> <address of ramdisk> <address of dtb>
```

The address of the kernel image is necessary, but the addresses of the ramdisk and dtb can be omitted if the kernel configuration does not need them. If there is a dtb but no initramfs, then the second address can be replaced with a dash. That would look like this:

```
=> bootm 82000000 - 83000000
```

Typing a long series of commands to boot your board each time it is powered up is clearly not acceptable. Let's look at how to automate the boot process.

Automating the boot with U-Boot scripts

U-Boot stores a sequence of commands in environment variables. If a special variable named bootcmd contains a script, then it is run at power-up after a delay of bootdelay seconds. If you watch this on the serial console, you will see the delay counting down to zero. You can press any key during this period to terminate the countdown and enter an interactive session with U-Boot.

The way that you create scripts is simple, though it's not easy to read. You simply append commands separated by semicolons, which must be preceded by a \ escape character. For example, to load a kernel image from an offset in flash memory and boot it, you might use the following command:

```
setenv bootcmd nand read 82000000 400000 200000\;bootm 82000000
```

We now know how to boot a kernel on BeaglePlay using U-Boot. But how do we port U-Boot to a new board that has no BSP? We'll cover that in the remainder of this chapter.

Porting U-Boot to a new board

Let's assume that your hardware department has created a new board called **Nova** that is based on BeaglePlay and that you need to port U-Boot to it. You will need to understand the layout of the U-Boot code and how the board configuration mechanism works. In this section, I will show you how to create a variant of an existing board – BeaglePlay – which you could go on to use as the basis for further customizations.

There are quite a few files that need to be changed. I have put them together into a patch file at
`MELD/Chapter03/0001-BSP-for-Nova.patch` in the book's code repo. You can simply apply that
patch to a clean copy of the U-Boot fork for BeaglePlay and rebuild it like this:

```
$ cd ~
$ cd u-boot-beagleplay
$ patch -p1 < ~/MELD/Chapter03/0001-BSP-for-Nova.patch
$ rm -rf ../build_uboot/a53
$ mkdir ../build_uboot/a53
$ export PATH=${HOME}/aarch64--glibc--stable-2024.02-1/bin/:$PATH
$ export ARCH=aarch64
$ export CROSS_COMPILE=aarch64-buildroot-linux-gnu-
$ make nova_defconfig O=../build_uboot/a53
$ make ATF=$HOME/arm-trusted-firmware/build/k3/lite/release/bl31.bin
DM=$HOME/ti-linux-firmware/ti-dm/am62xx/ipc_echo_testb_mcu1_0_release_
strip.xer5f O=../build_uboot/a53
```

If you want to use a different version of U-Boot, you will have to regenerate the patch yourself
for it to apply cleanly. The remainder of this section describes how the patch was created. To
skip these details, run the preceding commands and jump to the end of the *Building and testing*
portion of this section. To follow along step by step, you will need a clean copy of the U-Boot
fork for BeaglePlay without the Nova BSP patch applied. The main directories we will be dealing
with are as follows:

- `arch`: Contains code that's specific to each supported architecture in the `arm`, `mips`, and
  `powerpc` directories. Within each architecture, there is a subdirectory for each member of
  the family. For example, in `arch/arm/cpu` there are directories for the various architecture
  variants, including `arm926ejs`, `armv7`, and `armv8`.
- `board`: Contains code that's specific to a board. Where there are several boards from the
  same vendor, they are collected into a subdirectory. Hence, the code for the am62x EVM
  board, which BeaglePlay is based on, is in `board/ti/am62x`.
- `common`: Contains core functions including the command shells and the commands that
  can be called from them each in a file named `cmd_<command name>.c`.
- `doc`: Contains several `.rst` files describing various aspects of U-Boot. If you are wondering
  how to proceed with your U-Boot port, this is a good place to start.
- `include`: In addition to many shared header files, this contains the important `include/
  configs` subdirectory, where you will find the majority of the board configuration settings.

The way that Kconfig extracts configuration information from Kconfig files and stores the total system configuration in a file named .config will be described in some detail in *Chapter 4*. Each board has a default configuration stored in configs/<board name>_defconfig. For the Nova board, we can begin by making a copy of the configuration for the EVM:

```
$ cp configs/am62x_evm_a53_defconfig configs/nova_defconfig
```

Now, edit configs/nova_defconfig and replace CONFIG_TARGET_AM625_A53_EVM=y with CONFIG_TARGET_NOVA=y as shown here:

```
CONFIG_ARM=y
CONFIG_ARCH_K3=y
CONFIG_TI_SECURE_DEVICE=y
CONFIG_TI_COMMON_CMD_OPTIONS=y
CONFIG_SPL_GPIO_SUPPORT=y
CONFIG_SPL_LIBCOMMON_SUPPORT=y
CONFIG_SPL_LIBGENERIC_SUPPORT=y
CONFIG_SYS_MALLOC_F_LEN=0x8000
CONFIG_NR_DRAM_BANKS=2
CONFIG_SOC_K3_AM625=y
CONFIG_K3_ATF_LOAD_ADDR=0x9e780000
CONFIG_TARGET_NOVA=y
CONFIG_ENV_SIZE=0x20000
<...>
```

Note that CONFIG_ARM=y causes the contents of arch/arm/Kconfig to be included.

We are now done modifying configs/nova_defconfig.

Board-specific files

Each board has a subdirectory named board/<board name> or board/<vendor>/<board name> that should contain the following:

- Kconfig: Contains the configuration options for the board.
- MAINTAINERS: Contains a record of whether the board is currently maintained and, if so, by whom.
- Makefile: Used to build the board-specific code.

In addition, there may be source files for board-specific functions.

Our Nova board is based on BeaglePlay, which in turn is based on a TI am62x EVM. So, we should make copies of the am62x board files:

```
$ mkdir board/ti/nova
$ cp -a board/ti/am62x/* board/ti/nova
$ cd board/ti/nova
$ mv evm.c nova.c
```

First, modify board/ti/nova/Makefile so that nova.c is compiled instead of evm.c:

```
<...>
obj-y   += nova.o
```

Duplicating evm.c as nova.c lets you change how U-Boot interacts with your custom board.

Next, edit board/ti/nova/Kconfig:

- Change the "TI K3 AM62x based boards" string under prompt to say "TI K3 AM62x based Nova! board".
- Rename TARGET_AM625_A53_EVM to TARGET_NOVA.
- Delete TARGET_AM625_R5_EVM along with all its items.
- Set SYS_BOARD to "nova" so that it will build the files in board/ti/nova.
- Set SYS_CONFIG_NAME to "nova" so that it will use include/configs/nova.h as the configuration file.

The modified board/ti/nova/Konfig should look as follows:

```
<...>
if TARGET_NOVA

config SYS_BOARD
        default "nova"

config SYS_VENDOR
        default "ti"

config SYS_CONFIG_NAME
        default "nova"

source "board/ti/common/Kconfig"
```

```
endif
<...>
```

Now we need to link the Kconfig file for Nova into the chain of Kconfig files. First, edit arch/arm/Kconfig and insert source "board/ti/nova/Kconfig" after source "board/tcl/sl50/Kconfig", as shown here:

```
<...>
source "board/st/stv0991/Kconfig"
source "board/tcl/sl50/Kconfig"
source "board/ti/nova/Kconfig"
source "board/toradex/colibri_pxa270/Kconfig"
source "board/variscite/dart_6ul/Kconfig"
<...>
```

Now that we have copied and modified the board-specific files for our Nova board, let's move on to the header files.

Configuring header files

Each board has a header file in include/configs that contains most of the configuration information. The file is named by the SYS_CONFIG_NAME identifier in the board's Kconfig file. The format of this file is described in detail in the README file at the top level of the U-Boot source tree. For the purposes of our Nova board, simply copy include/configs/am62x_evm.h into include/configs/nova.h and make a few changes, as shown here:

```
<...>
#ifndef __CONFIG_NOVA_H
#define __CONFIG_NOVA_H

#include <linux/sizes.h>
#include <config_distro_bootcmd.h>
#include <environment/ti/mmc.h>
#include <environment/ti/k3_dfu.h>

#undef CONFIG_SYS_PROMPT
#define CONFIG_SYS_PROMPT          "nova!> "

/* DDR Configuration */
```

```
#define CONFIG_SYS_SDRAM_BASE1              0x880000000
#define CONFIG_SYS_BOOTM_LEN                SZ_64M


#ifdef CONFIG_SYS_K3_SPL_ATF
#define CONFIG_SPL_FS_LOAD_PAYLOAD_NAME "tispl.bin"
#endif


#if defined(CONFIG_TARGET_NOVA)
#define CONFIG_SPL_MAX_SIZE                 SZ_1M
#define CONFIG_SYS_INIT_SP_ADDR             (CONFIG_SPL_TEXT_BASE + SZ_4M)
#else
<...>
#endif /* __CONFIG_NOVA_H */
```

First, replace __CONFIG_AM625_EVM_H with __CONFIG_NOVA_H. Next, redefine CONFIG_SYS_PROMPT so that we can identify this bootloader at runtime. Lastly, replace CONFIG_TARGET_AM625_A53_EVM with CONFIG_TARGET_NOVA so that CONFIG_SPL_MAX_SIZE and CONFIG_SYS_INIT_SP_ADDR are defined correctly.

With the source tree fully modified, we are now ready to build U-Boot for our custom board.

Building and testing

To build U-Boot for the Nova board:

1. First, navigate back to the U-Boot source tree for BeaglePlay:

```
$ cd ~
$ cd u-boot-beagleplay
```

2. Next, set the ARCH and CROSS_COMPILE environment variables for 64-bit Arm:

```
$ export ARCH=aarch64
$ export CROSS_COMPILE=aarch64-buildroot-linux-gnu-
```

3. Clean out any previous build artifacts:

```
$ rm -rf ../build_uboot/a53
$ mkdir ../build_uboot/a53
```

4. Select nova_defconfig for building:

```
$ make nova_defconfig O=../build_uboot/a53
```

5. Run make menuconfig to configure U-Boot further for building:

```
$ make menuconfig O=../build_uboot/a53
```

6. Drill down into the **Environment** submenu.

7. Select **Environment is in a EXT4 filesystem**.

8. Deselect any other options (e.g., MMC, NAND, and SPI) for environment storage on that menu page.

9. Enter mmc in the **Name of the block device for the environment** text field.

10. Enter 1:2 in the **Device and partition for where to store the environment in EXT4** text field.

11. Ensure /uboot.env is entered in the **Name of the EXT4 file to use for the environment** text field.

12. Back out of the **Environment** submenu.

13. Drill down into the **SPL/TPL** submenu.

14. Select **Support EXT filesystems**.

15. Back out of the **SPL/TPL** submenu.

16. Drill down into the **Boot Options** submenu.

17. Select **Enable a default value for bootcmd**.

18. Enter echo 'no bootcmd yet' in the **bootcmd value** text field.

19. Exit out of menuconfig and choose **Yes** when asked to save your new configuration.

20. Save the modified defconfig:

```
$ make savedefconfig O=../build_uboot/a53
```

21. Update nova_defconfig with your changes:

```
$ cp ../build_uboot/a53/defconfig configs/nova_defconfig
```

22. Lastly, build U-Boot for the A53, passing paths to TI's TF-A and DM firmware as arguments to make:

```
$ make ATF=$HOME/arm-trusted-firmware/build/k3/lite/release/bl31.
bin DM=$HOME/ti-linux-firmware/ti-dm/am62xx/ipc_echo_testb_mcu1_0_
release_strip.xer5f O=../build_uboot/a53
```

23. Copy `tispl.bin` and `u-boot.img` to the boot partition of the microSD card you created earlier:

```
$ cd ~
$ cd build_uboot/a53
$ cp tispl.bin u-boot.img /media/$USER/boot/.
```

Reinsert the microSD card into BeaglePlay and reapply power while holding down the USR button. You should see output like this (note the custom command prompt) on the serial console:

```
<…>
U-Boot SPL 2021.01-gf036fbdc25-dirty (Jun 30 2024 - 18:37:39 -0700)
SYSFW ABI: 3.1 (firmware rev 0x0009 '9.0.4--v09.00.04 (Kool Koala)')
Trying to boot from MMC2


U-Boot 2021.01-gf036fbdc25-dirty (Jun 30 2024 - 18:37:39 -0700)

SoC:   AM62X SR1.0 GP
Model: BeagleBoard.org BeaglePlay
Board: BEAGLEPLAY-A0- rev 02
DRAM:  2 GiB
MMC:   mmc@fa10000: 0, mmc@fa00000: 1, mmc@fa20000: 2
Loading Environment from EXT4... ** File not found /uboot.env **

** Unable to read "/uboot.env" from mmc1:2 **
In:    serial@2800000
Out:   serial@2800000
Err:   serial@2800000
Error: Can't set serial# to SSSS
Net:   Could not get PHY for ethernet@8000000port@1: addr 0
am65_cpsw_nuss_port ethernet@8000000port@1: phy_connect() failed
No ethernet found.

Press SPACE to abort autoboot in 2 seconds
no bootcmd yet
nova!>
```

You can create a patch for all these changes by checking them into Git and using the git format-patch command:

```
$ git add .
$ git commit -m "BSP for Nova"
<...>
$ git format-patch -1
0001-BSP-for-Nova.patch
```

Generating this patch concludes our coverage of U-Boot as a TPL. U-Boot can also be configured to bypass the TPL stage of the boot process altogether. Next, let's examine this alternate approach to booting Linux.

Falcon mode

We are used to the idea that booting a modern embedded processor involves the boot ROM loading an SPL, which loads u-boot.bin, which then loads a Linux kernel. You may be wondering if there is a way to reduce the number of steps, thereby simplifying and speeding up the boot process. The answer is U-Boot Falcon mode.

The idea is simple: have the SPL load a kernel image directly skipping over u-boot.bin. There is no user interaction and there are no scripts. It just loads a kernel from a known location in flash memory or eMMC into memory, passes it a pre-prepared parameter block, and starts running it. The details of configuring Falcon mode are beyond the scope of this book.

> **IMPORTANT NOTE**
>
> Falcon mode is named after the peregrine falcon, which is the fastest bird of all, capable of reaching speeds of more than 200 miles per hour in a dive.

Summary

Every system needs a bootloader to bring the hardware to life and to load a kernel. U-Boot has found favor with many developers because it supports a useful range of hardware, and it is fairly easy to port to a new device.

In this chapter, we learned how to inspect and drive U-Boot interactively from the command line over a serial console. These command-line exercises included loading a kernel over a network using TFTP for rapid iteration. Lastly, we learned how to port U-Boot to a new device by generating a patch for our Nova board.

Over the last few years, the complexity and ever-increasing variety of embedded hardware has led to the introduction of the device tree as a way of describing hardware. The device tree is simply a textual representation of a system that is compiled into a device tree binary, which is passed to the kernel when it loads. It is up to the kernel to interpret the device tree and to load and initialize drivers for the devices it finds there.

U-Boot is very flexible, allowing images to be loaded from mass storage, flash memory, or a network and then booted. Having covered some of the intricacies of booting Linux, in the next chapter, we will cover the next stage of the process. This is the third element of your embedded project – the kernel.

4

Configuring and Building the Kernel

The kernel is the third element of embedded Linux. It is the component that is responsible for managing resources and interfacing with hardware. As such, it affects almost every aspect of your final software build. Each finished kernel is usually configured for some specific hardware. However, device trees enable us to employ a generic kernel and tailor it for our custom hardware using the contents of the DTB, as we saw in *Chapter 3*.

In this chapter, we will look at how to get a kernel for a board and how to configure and compile it. We will look again at Bootstrap, this time, focusing on the part the kernel plays. We will also look at device drivers and how they pick up information from the device tree.

In this chapter, we will cover the following topics:

- What does the kernel do?
- Choosing a kernel
- Configuring the kernel
- Compiling with Kbuild
- Building and booting the kernel
- Observing the kernel boot process
- Porting Linux to a new board

Technical requirements

To follow along with the examples, make sure you have the following:

- An Ubuntu 24.04 or later LTS-based host system
- A Bootlin aarch64 toolchain from *Chapter 2*
- A microSD card reader and card
- A microSD card with U-Boot installed from *Chapter 3*
- A USB to TTL serial cable with 3.3V logic level
- The Raspberry Pi 4
- The BeaglePlay
- A 5V USB-C power supply capable of delivering 3A

The code used in this chapter can be found in the chapter folder in this book's GitHub repository: https://github.com/PacktPublishing/Mastering-Embedded-Linux-Development/tree/main/Chapter04.

What does the kernel do?

Linux began in 1991 when Linus Torvalds started writing an operating system for Intel 386- and 486-based personal computers. He was inspired by the MINIX operating system written by Andrew S. Tanenbaum four years earlier. Linux differed in many ways from MINIX; the main differences being that it was a 32-bit virtual memory kernel, and the code was open source, later released under the GPL v2 license. He announced it on 25th August 1991 on the comp.os.minix newsgroup in a famous post that began with:

> *Hello everybody out there using minix—I'm doing a (free) operating system (just a hobby, won't be big and professional like GNU) for 386(486) AT clones. This has been brewing since April, and is starting to get ready. I'd like any feedback on things people like/dislike in minix, as my OS resembles it somewhat (same physical layout of the filesystem (due to practical reasons) among other things).*

To be strictly accurate, Linus did not write an operating system. He wrote a kernel, which is only one component of an operating system. To create a complete operating system with user space commands and a shell command interpreter, he used components from the GNU project, especially the toolchain, the C library, and basic command-line tools. That distinction remains today and gives Linux a lot of flexibility in the way it is used.

Berkeley Software Distribution (BSD) predates Linux by many years. BSD began as a research project at the University of California, Berkeley's renowned Computer Systems Research Group sometime in the late 1970s. Originally known as Berkeley Unix, BSD was based on the original Unix source code developed at Bell Labs. Now a defunct operating system, BSD lives on in the form of its open source descendants including FreeBSD, OpenBSD, and NetBSD. Most notably, the Darwin open source operating system used in Apple's macOS and iOS is a derivative of BSD.

The Linux kernel can be combined with a GNU user space to create a full Linux distribution that runs on desktops and servers, which is sometimes called GNU/Linux. It can be combined with an Android user space to create the well-known mobile operating system, or it can be combined with a small BusyBox-based user space to create a compact embedded system.

Contrast this with the BSD operating systems (FreeBSD, OpenBSD, and NetBSD) in which the kernel, toolchain, and user space are combined into a single code base. By removing the toolchain, you can deploy slimmer runtime images without a compiler or header files. By decoupling user space from the kernel, you gain options in terms of init systems (runit vs systemd), C libraries (musl vs glibc) and package formats (.apk vs .deb).

The kernel has three main jobs – to manage resources, to interface with hardware, and to provide an API that offers a useful level of abstraction to user space programs, as summarized in the following diagram:

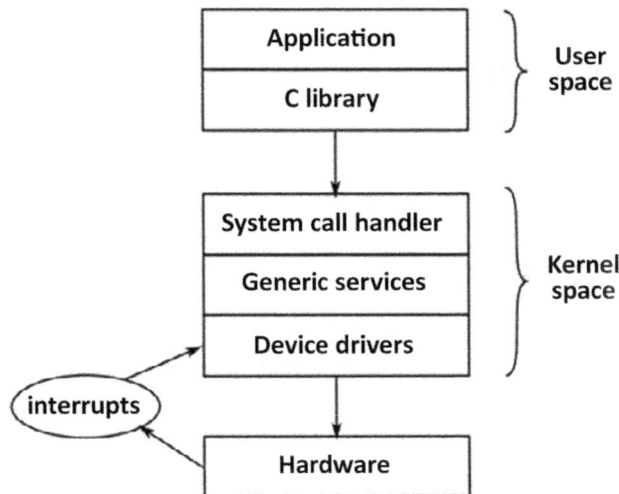

Figure 4.1 – User space, kernel space, and hardware

Applications running in **user space** run at a low CPU privilege level. They can do very little other than make library calls. The primary interface between user space and **kernel space** is the **C library,** which translates user-level functions, such as those defined by POSIX, into kernel system calls. The system call interface uses an architecture-specific method, such as a trap or a software interrupt, to switch the CPU from low-privilege user mode to high-privilege kernel mode. A CPU running in kernel mode has access to all memory addresses and CPU registers.

The system call handler dispatches the call to the appropriate kernel subsystem. Memory allocation calls go to the memory manager, filesystem calls to the filesystem code, and so on. Some of those calls require input from the underlying hardware and will be passed down to a device driver. In some cases, the hardware itself invokes a kernel function by raising an interrupt.

> **IMPORTANT NOTE**
>
> The diagram in *Figure 4.1* shows that there is a second entry point into kernel code: hardware interrupts. Interrupts can only be handled in a device driver, never by a user space application.

In other words, all the useful things that your application does are done through the kernel. The kernel is therefore one of the most important elements in the system. So, it is important to understand how to choose one.

Choosing a kernel

The next step is to choose the kernel for your project. It is important to balance your desire to always use the latest version of software against the need for vendor-specific additions and an interest in the long-term support of the code base.

Kernel development cycle

Linux is developed at a fast pace with a new version being released every 8 to 12 weeks. The way that the version numbers are constructed has changed over the years. Before July 2011, there was a three-number version scheme with version numbers that looked like 2.6.39. The middle number indicated whether it was a developer or stable release. Odd numbers (2.1.x, 2.3.x, 2.5.x) were for developers. Even numbers were for end users.

From version 2.6 onward, the idea of a long-lived development branch (the odd numbers) was dropped, as it slowed down the rate at which new features were made available to the users. The change in numbering from 2.6.39 to 3.0 in July 2011 was purely because Linus felt that the numbers were becoming too large.

There was no huge leap in the features or architecture of Linux between those two versions. He also took the opportunity to drop the middle number. Since then, Linus has bumped the major version three more times: next in April 2015 (3 to 4), again in March 2019 (4 to 5), and most recently, in October 2022 (5 to 6). Each time, he did this purely for neatness, not because of any large architectural shift.

Linus manages the development kernel tree. You can follow him by cloning the Git tree like so:

```
$ git clone git://git.kernel.org/pub/scm/linux/kernel/git/torvalds/linux.
git
```

This will check the source out into a subdirectory named linux. You can keep up to date by running the command git pull in that directory from time to time.

A full cycle of kernel development begins with a merge window of two weeks during which Linus will accept patches for new features. At the end of the merge window, a stabilization phase begins. Once the merge window closes, Linus will produce weekly release candidates with version numbers ending in -rc1, -rc2, and so on, usually up to -rc7 or -rc8. During this time, people test the candidates and submit bug reports and fixes. When all significant bugs have been fixed, the kernel is released.

The code incorporated during the merge window needs to be fairly mature already. Usually, it is pulled from the repositories of the many subsystems and architecture maintainers of the kernel. By keeping to a short development cycle, features can be merged when they are ready. If a feature is deemed not sufficiently stable or well developed by the kernel maintainers, it can simply be delayed until the next release.

Keeping track of what has changed from release to release is not easy. You can read the commit log in Linus' Git repository but, with so many entries, it is not easy to get an overview. Thankfully, there is the Linux **Kernel Newbies** website (https://kernelnewbies.org) where you can find a succinct overview of each version at https://kernelnewbies.org/LinuxVersions.

Stable and long-term support releases

The rapid rate of change of Linux is a good thing in that it brings new features into the mainline code base, but it does not fit very well with the longer life cycle of embedded projects. Kernel developers address this in two ways: stable releases and long-term releases. After the release of a mainline kernel (maintained by Linus Torvalds), it is moved to the **stable** tree (maintained by Greg Kroah-Hartman). Bug fixes are applied to the stable kernel while the mainline kernel begins the next development cycle.

Point releases of the stable kernel are marked by a third number (3.18.1, 3.18.2, and so on). Before version 3, there were four release numbers (2.6.29.1, 2.6.39.2, and so on).

You can get the stable tree by using the following command:

```
$ cd ~
$ git clone git://git.kernel.org/pub/scm/linux/kernel/git/stable/linux-
stable.git
```

You can use `git checkout` to get a particular version like 6.6.46:

```
$ cd linux-stable
$ git checkout v6.6.46
```

The stable kernel is usually updated only until the next mainline release (8 to 12 weeks later) so you will see that there are just one or sometimes two stable kernels at `https://www.kernel.org/`. To cater to those users who would like updates for longer, some kernels are labeled **long-term** and maintained for two or more years. Long-term kernels come with the assurance that any bugs will be found and fixed. There is at least one long-term kernel release each year.

Looking at `https://www.kernel.org/` in August of 2024, there are a total of six long-term kernels: 6.6, 6.1, 5.15, 5.10, 5.4, and 4.19. The oldest has been maintained for nearly six years and is at version 4.19.319. If you are building a product that you will have to maintain for this length of time, then the latest long-term kernel might well be a good choice.

Vendor support

In an ideal world, you would be able to download a kernel from `https://www.kernel.org/` and configure it for any device that claims to support Linux. However, that is not always possible. In fact, mainline Linux has solid support for only a small subset of the many devices that can run Linux. You may find support for your board or SoC from independent open source projects like Linaro (`https://www.linaro.org/`) or The Yocto Project (`https://www.yoctoproject.org/`). There are some companies that offer paid third-party support for embedded Linux. But in many cases, you will be obliged to look to the vendor of your SoC or board for a working kernel.

As we know, some vendors are better at supporting Linux than others. My advice at this point is to choose vendors who give good support or, even better, who take the trouble to get their kernel changes into the mainline. Search the Linux kernel mailing list or commit history for recent activity around a candidate SoC or board. When upstream changes are absent from the mainline kernel, the verdict as to whether a vendor offers good support is largely based on word of mouth. Some vendors are notorious for releasing only one kernel code drop before redirecting all their energies toward their newer SoCs.

Licensing

The Linux source code is licensed under GPL v2. That means you must make the source code of your kernel available in one of the ways specified in the license.

The actual text of the license for the kernel is in the file COPYING. It begins with an addendum written by Linus that states that code calling the kernel from user space via the system call interface is not considered a derivative work of the kernel and so is not covered by the license. Hence, there is no problem with proprietary applications running on top of Linux.

However, there is one area of Linux licensing that causes endless confusion and debate: kernel modules. A **kernel module** is simply a piece of code that is dynamically linked with the kernel at runtime thereby extending the functionality of the kernel. The **General Public License** (**GPL**) makes no distinction between static and dynamic linking, so it would appear that the source for kernel modules is covered by the GPL. In the early days of Linux, there were debates about exceptions to this rule, for example, in connection with the **Andrew File System** (**AFS**). This code predates Linux and, therefore (it was argued), is not a derivative work so the license does not apply.

Similar discussions took place over the years with respect to other pieces of code with the result that it is now accepted practice that the GPL does not necessarily apply to kernel modules. This is codified by the kernel MODULE_LICENSE macro, which may take the value Proprietary to indicate that it is not released under the GPL. If you plan to use the same arguments yourself, you may want to read through an oft-quoted email thread titled *Linux GPL and binary module exception clause?*, which is archived at https://yarchive.net/comp/linux/gpl_modules.html.

The GPL should be considered a good thing because it guarantees that when we are working on embedded projects, we can always get the source code for the kernel. Without it, embedded Linux would be much harder to use and more fragmented.

Best practices

That said, to choose a kernel, you need to weigh the benefits of using the latest version against the need for vendor-specific enhancements and driver stability. Also, the rapid Linux development cycle allows features to be integrated quickly, with stable and long-term support releases available for extended maintenance. The long-term kernels, which receive updates for over two years, are ideal for long-term projects. Vendor support is also crucial, so make sure to choose vendors who actively support Linux and contribute to the mainline kernel. Lastly, licensing under GPL v2 ensures access to the kernel source code, which makes it easier to use and maintain for embedded projects.

Configuring the kernel

Having decided which kernel to base your image on, the next step is configuring the kernel.

Getting the source

All three of the targets used in this book (Raspberry Pi 4, BeaglePlay, and QEMU) are well supported by the mainline kernel. Therefore, it makes sense to use the latest long-term kernel available from https://www.kernel.org/, which, at the time of writing, was 6.6.46. When you come to do this for yourself, you should check to see if there is a later version of the 6.6 kernel and use that instead since it will have fixes for bugs found after 6.6.46 was released.

> **IMPORTANT NOTE**
>
> If there is a later long-term release, you may want to consider using that one. However, be aware that there may have been changes that mean that the following sequence of commands does not work exactly as given.

To fetch and extract a release tarball of the 6.6.46 Linux kernel, use the following:

```
$ cd ~
$ wget https://cdn.kernel.org/pub/linux/kernel/v6.x/linux-6.6.46.tar.xz
$ tar xf linux-6.6.46.tar.xz
$ mv linux-6.6.46 linux-stable
```

To fetch a later version, replace 6.6.46 after linux- with the desired long-term release.

There is a lot of code here. There are over 81,000 files in the 6.6 kernel containing C source code, header files, and assembly code amounting to a total of over 24 million lines of code as measured by the SLOCCount utility. Nevertheless, it is worth knowing the basic layout of the code and approximately where to look for a particular component. The main directories of interest are:

- arch: Contains architecture-specific files. There is one subdirectory per architecture.
- Documentation: Contains kernel documentation. Always look here first if you want to find more information about an aspect of Linux.
- drivers: Contains device drivers, thousands of them. There is a subdirectory for each type of driver.
- fs: Contains filesystem code.

- include: Contains kernel header files including those required when building the toolchain.
- init: Contains the kernel start-up code.
- kernel: Contains core functions including scheduling, locking, timers, power management, and debug/trace code.
- mm: Contains memory management.
- net: Contains network protocols.
- scripts: Contains many useful scripts including the device tree compiler, which I described in *Chapter 3*.
- tools: Contains many useful tools including the Linux performance counters tool (perf), which I will describe in *Chapter 20*.

Over time, you will become familiar with this structure and realize that if you are looking for the serial port code of a particular SoC, you will find it in drivers/tty/serial and not in arch/$ARCH/mach-foo because it is a device driver and not something CPU architecture-specific.

Understanding kernel configuration– Kconfig

One of the strengths of Linux is the degree to which you can configure the kernel to suit different jobs, from a small, dedicated device such as a smart thermostat to a complex mobile handset. In current versions, there are many thousands of configuration options. Getting the configuration right is a task in itself, but before we get into that, I want to show you how it works so that you can better understand what is going on.

The configuration mechanism is called Kconfig, and the build system that it integrates with is called Kbuild. Both are documented in Documentation/kbuild. Kconfig/Kbuild is used in a number of other projects besides the kernel including Crosstool-NG, U-Boot, Barebox, and BusyBox.

The configuration options are declared in a hierarchy of files named Kconfig using a syntax described in Documentation/kbuild/kconfig-language.rst.

In Linux, the top-level Kconfig looks like this:

```
mainmenu "Linux/$(ARCH) $(KERNELVERSION) Kernel Configuration"

comment "Compiler: $(CC_VERSION_TEXT)"

source "scripts/Kconfig.include"
<...>
```

And the first line of arch/Kconfig is:

```
source "arch/$(SRCARCH)/Kconfig"
```

That line includes the architecture-dependent configuration file, which sources other Kconfig files depending on which options are enabled.

Having the architecture play such a prominent role has three implications:

- First, you must specify an architecture when configuring Linux by setting ARCH=<architecture>; otherwise, it will default to the local machine architecture.
- Second, the value you set for ARCH usually determines the value of SRCARCH so you rarely need to set SRCARCH explicitly.
- Third, the layout of the top-level menu is different for each architecture.

The value you put into ARCH is one of the subdirectories you find in the directory arch with the oddity that ARCH=i386 and ARCH=x86_64 both source arch/x86/Kconfig.

The Kconfig files consist largely of menus delineated by the menu and endmenu keywords. Menu items are marked by the keyword config.

Here is an example taken from drivers/char/Kconfig:

```
menu "Character devices"
<...>
config DEVMEM
    bool "/dev/mem virtual device support"
    default y
    help
      Say Y here if you want to support the /dev/mem device.
      The /dev/mem device is used to access areas of physical memory.
      When in doubt, say "Y".
<...>
endmenu
```

The parameter following config names a variable, which, in this case, is DEVMEM. Since this option is a bool (Boolean), it can only have two values: if it is enabled, it is assigned y, and if it is not enabled, the variable is not defined at all. The name of the menu item that is displayed on the screen is the string following the bool keyword.

This configuration item, along with all the others, is stored in a file named .config.

TIP

The leading dot (.) in `.config` means that it is a hidden file that will not be shown by the `ls` command unless you type `ls -a` to show all files.

The line corresponding to this configuration item reads:

```
CONFIG_DEVMEM=y
```

There are several other data types in addition to `bool`. Here is the complete list:

- `bool`: Either y or not defined.
- `tristate`: Used where a feature can be built as a kernel module or built into the main kernel image. The values are m for a module, y to be built in, and not defined if the feature is not enabled.
- `int`: An integer value using decimal notation.
- `hex`: An unsigned integer value using hexadecimal notation.
- `string`: A string value.

There may be dependencies between items expressed by the `depends on` construct, as shown here:

```
config MTD_CMDLINE_PARTS
    tristate "Command line partition table parsing"
    depends on MTD
```

If `CONFIG_MTD` has not been enabled elsewhere, this menu option is not shown and so cannot be selected.

There are also reverse dependencies. The `select` keyword enables other options if this one is enabled. The `Kconfig` file in `arch/$ARCH` has numerous `select` statements that enable features specific to the architecture, as seen here for Arm:

```
config ARM
    bool
    default y
    select ARCH_CLOCKSOURCE_DATA
    select ARCH_HAS_DEVMEM_IS_ALLOWED
<...>
```

By selecting ARCH_CLOCKSOURCE_DATA and ARCH_HAS_DEVMEM_IS_ALLOWED, we are assigning a value of y to these variables so that these features are built statically into the kernel.

There are several configuration utilities that can read the Kconfig files and produce a .config file. Some of them display the menus on the screen and allow you to make choices interactively. menuconfig is probably the one most people are familiar with but there are also xconfig and gconfig.

To use menuconfig, you first need to have ncurses, flex, and bison installed. The following command installs all these prerequisites on Ubuntu:

```
$ sudo apt install libncurses5-dev flex bison
```

You launch menuconfig via the make command, remembering that, in the case of the kernel, you need to supply an architecture, as illustrated here:

```
$ cd ~
$ export PATH=${HOME}/aarch64--glibc--stable-2024.02-1/bin/:$PATH
$ export CROSS_COMPILE=aarch64-buildroot-linux-gnu-
$ cd linux-stable
$ mkdir ../build_arm64
$ make ARCH=arm64 menuconfig O=../build_arm64
```

Make sure that your PATH variable points to the 64-bit toolchain you downloaded back in *Chapter 2*.

Here you can see menuconfig with the DEVMEM config option highlighted previously:

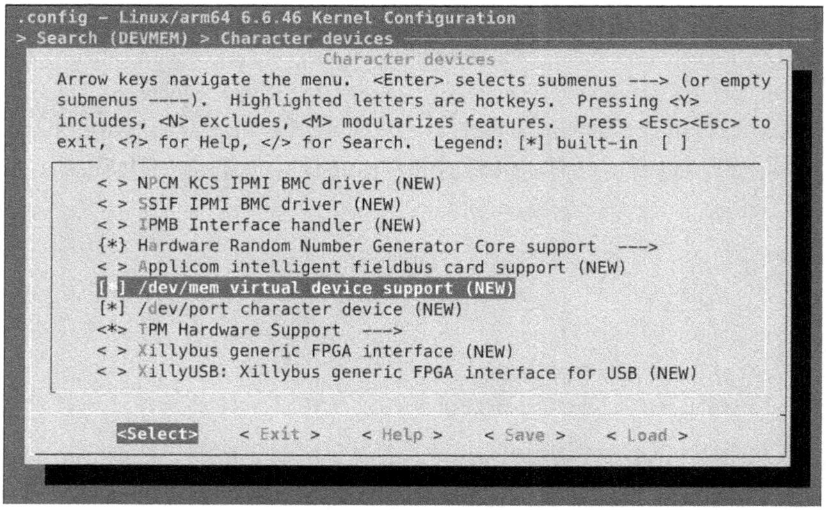

Figure 4.2 – Selecting DEVMEM

The star (*) to the left of an item means that the driver has been selected to be built statically into the kernel. If it is an M, then it has been selected to be built as a kernel module for insertion into the kernel at runtime.

> **TIP**
>
> You often see instructions like enable CONFIG_BLK_DEV_INITRD but, with so many menus to browse through, it can take a while to find the place where that config-uration is set. All configuration editors have a search function. You can access it in menuconfig by pressing the forward slash key /. In xconfig, it is in the **Edit** menu but make sure you leave off the CONFIG_ part of the configuration item you are searching for.

With so many things to configure, it is unreasonable to start with a clean sheet each time you want to build a kernel, so there are a set of known working configuration files in arch/$ARCH/configs, each containing suitable configuration values for a single SoC or a group of SoCs.

You can select one with the make <configuration file name> command. For example, to con-figure Linux to run on a wide range of 64-bit Arm SoCs, you would type:

```
$ make ARCH=arm64 defconfig O=../build_arm64
```

This is a generic kernel that runs on various boards. For a more specialized application, like when using a vendor-supplied kernel, the default configuration file is part of the board support package. You will need to find out which one to use before you can build the kernel.

There is another useful configuration target named oldconfig. You use it when moving a config-uration to a new kernel version. This target takes an existing .config file and prompts you with questions about new configuration options. Copy .config from the old kernel to the new source directory and run the make ARCH=arm64 oldconfig command to bring it up to date.

The oldconfig target can also be used to validate a .config file that you have edited manually (ignoring the text *Automatically generated file; DO NOT EDIT* that occurs at the top).

If you do make changes to the configuration, then the modified .config file becomes part of your board support package and needs to be placed under source code control.

When you start the kernel build, a header file named include/generated/autoconf.h is gener-ated. This header file contains a #define for each configuration value so that it can be included in the kernel source.

Now that we have settled on a kernel and learned how to configure it, we will identify it.

Using LOCALVERSION to identify your kernel

You can discover the kernel version and release that you have built using the make `kernelversion` and make `kernelrelease` targets:

```
$ make ARCH=arm64 kernelversion
6.6.46
$ make ARCH=arm64 kernelrelease O=../build_arm64
6.6.46
```

This is reported at runtime through the uname command and is also used in naming the directory where kernel modules are stored.

If you change the configuration from the default, it is advisable to append your version information, which you can configure by setting CONFIG_LOCALVERSION using menuconfig:

```
$ make ARCH=arm64 menuconfig O=../build_arm64
```

For example, if I wanted to mark the kernel I am building with the identifier meld and version 1.0, then I would define the local version in menuconfig like this:

```
.config - Linux/arm64 6.6.46 Kernel Configuration
> General setup
                          General setup
   Arrow keys navigate the menu.  <Enter> selects submenus ---> (or empty
   submenus ----).  Highlighted letters are hotkeys.  Pressing <Y>
   includes, <N> excludes, <M> modularizes features.  Press <Esc><Esc> to
   exit, <?> for Help, </> for Search.  Legend: [*] built-in  [ ]

       [ ] Compile also drivers which will not load
       [ ] Compile the kernel with warnings as errors
       (-meld-v1.0) Local version - append to kernel release
       [*] Automatically append version information to the version strin
       ()  Build ID Salt
       ()  Default init path
       ((none)) Default hostname
       [*] System V IPC
       [*] POSIX Message Queues
       [ ] General notification queue

            <Select>      < Exit >    < Help >    < Save >    < Load >
```

Figure 4.3 – Appending to kernel release version

Exit out of menuconfig and choose **Yes** when asked to save your new configuration.

Run make prepare to refresh the Makefile with the new kernelrelease version:

```
$ make ARCH=arm64 prepare O=../build_arm64
```

Running make kernelversion produces the same output as before, but if I run make kernelrelease now, I see:

```
$ make ARCH=arm64 kernelrelease O=../build_arm64
6.6.46-meld-v1.0
```

That was a pleasant detour into kernel versioning, but now let's get back to the business of configuring our kernel for compilation.

When to use kernel modules

I have mentioned kernel modules several times already. Desktop Linux distributions use them extensively so that the correct device and kernel functions can be loaded at runtime depending on the hardware detected and features required. Without them, every single driver and feature would have to be statically linked into the kernel, making it infeasibly large.

On the other hand, with embedded devices, the hardware and kernel configuration is usually known at the time the kernel is built; therefore, modules are not so useful. In fact, they cause a problem because they create a version dependency between the kernel and the root filesystem, which can cause boot failures if one is updated but not the other. Consequently, it is quite common for embedded kernels to be built without any modules at all.

Here are a few cases where kernel modules are a good idea in embedded systems:

- When you have proprietary modules, for the licensing reasons given in the preceding section.
- To reduce boot time by deferring the loading of non-essential drivers.
- When there are several drivers to potentially load and it would take up too much memory to compile them statically. For example, you have a USB interface that supports a range of devices. This is essentially the same argument used in desktop distributions.
- Next, let's learn how to compile a kernel image with or without kernel modules using Kbuild.

Compiling with Kbuild

The kernel build system (Kbuild) is a set of make scripts that take the configuration information from the .config file, work out the dependencies, and compile everything necessary to produce a kernel image. This kernel image contains all the statically linked components, an optional device tree binary, and any kernel modules. The dependencies are expressed within Makefiles inside each directory with buildable components. For instance, the following two lines are taken from drivers/char/Makefile:

```
obj-y += mem.o random.o
obj-$(CONFIG_TTY_PRINTK) += ttyprintk.o
```

The obj-y rule unconditionally compiles a file to produce the target, so mem.c and random.c are always part of the kernel. In the second line, ttyprintk.c is dependent on a configuration parameter. If CONFIG_TTY_PRINTK is y, then it is compiled as a built-in. If it is m, then it is built as a module. If the parameter is undefined, then it is not compiled at all.

For most targets, just typing make (with the appropriate ARCH and CROSS_COMPILE) will do the job, but it is instructive to take it one step at a time. See the last section of *Chapter 2* for the meaning of the CROSS_COMPILE make variable.

Finding out which kernel target to build

To build a kernel image, you need to know what your bootloader expects. This is a rough guide:

- **U-Boot**: Can load a compressed Image.gz file for 64-bit Arm. Can also load a self-extracting zImage file for 32-bit Arm using the bootz command.
- **x86 targets**: Require a bzImage file.
- **Most other bootloaders**: Require a zImage file.

Here is an example of building an Image.gz file for 64-bit Arm:

```
$ sudo apt install libssl-dev
$ PATH=~/aarch64--glibc--stable-2024.02-1/bin/:$PATH
$ cd ~
$ cd linux-stable
$ make -j<n> ARCH=arm64 CROSS_COMPILE=aarch64-buildroot-linux-gnu- Image.
gz O=../build_arm64
```

Make sure that your PATH variable points to the 64-bit toolchain you downloaded back in *Chapter 2*.

IMPORTANT NOTE

The first time you run make on the kernel source tree, you may be prompted to include or omit various features, options, and plugins. Most of these features and options offer increased security so there is no harm in adding them. There is one notable exception. When prompted for GCC plugins, make sure to enter n for no as shown:

```
*
* GCC plugins
*
GCC plugins (GCC_PLUGINS) [Y/n/?] (NEW) n
```

Otherwise, the build will fail because make cannot find g++.

Remember to replace <n> after make -j with the number of CPU cores available on your host machine to speed up your build.

TIP

The -j<n> option tells make how many jobs to run in parallel, which reduces the time it takes to build. make -j4 runs four jobs. A rough guide is to run as many jobs as you have CPU cores.

The AArch64 kernel does not currently provide a decompressor and, therefore, requires decompression (gzip, etc.) to be performed by the bootloader if a compressed Image target (e.g., Image.gz) is used.

Regardless of which kernel image format we target, the same two build artifacts (vmlinux and System.map) are first created before the bootable image is generated.

Build artifacts

A kernel build generates two files in the top-level directory: vmlinux and System.map. The first, vmlinux, is the kernel as an ELF binary. If you have compiled your kernel with debug enabled (CONFIG_DEBUG_INFO=y), it will contain debug symbols that can be used with debuggers like kgdb. You can also use other ELF binary tools, such as size to measure the length of each segment (text, data, and bss) that comprises the vmlinux executable:

```
$ cd ~
$ cd build_arm64
```

```
$ aarch64-buildroot-linux-gnu-size vmlinux
   text     data      bss      dec      hex filename
25923719          15631632          620032 42175383          2838b97 vmlinux
```

A program like the kernel is divided into segments in memory. The `text` segment contains executable instructions (code). The `data` segment contains initialized global and static variables. The `bss` segment contains uninitialized global and static variables. The `dec` and `hex` values are the total file size in decimal and hexadecimal, respectively.

`System.map` contains the symbol table in human-readable form.

Most bootloaders cannot handle ELF code directly. There is a further stage of processing that takes `vmlinux` and places binaries that are suitable for the various bootloaders in `arch/$ARCH/boot`:

- `Image`: `vmlinux` converted to raw binary format.
- `zImage`: For the PowerPC architecture, this is just a compressed version of `Image`, implying that the bootloader must do the decompression. For all other architectures, the compressed `Image` is piggybacked onto a stub of code that decompresses and relocates it.
- `uImage`: `zImage` plus a 64-byte U-Boot header.

While the build is running, you will see a summary of the commands being executed:

```
$ make -j<n> ARCH=arm64 CROSS_COMPILE=aarch64-buildroot-linux-gnu- Image.
gz O=../build_arm64
<...>
  CC      scripts/mod/empty.o
  HOSTCC  scripts/mod/mk_elfconfig
  CC      scripts/mod/devicetable-offsets.s
  UPD     scripts/mod/devicetable-offsets.h
  MKELF   scripts/mod/elfconfig.h
  HOSTCC  scripts/mod/modpost.o
  HOSTCC  scripts/mod/file2alias.o
  HOSTCC  scripts/mod/sumversion.o
<...>
```

When the kernel build fails, it is sometimes useful to see the actual commands being executed. To do that, add `V=1` to the command line:

```
$ make -j<n> ARCH=arm64 CROSS_COMPILE=aarch64-buildroot-linux-gnu- V=1
Image.gz O=../build_arm64
```

In this section, we learned how Kbuild takes a precompiled vmlinux ELF binary and converts it into a bootable kernel image. Next, we will look at how we can compile device trees.

Compiling device trees

The next step is to build the device tree, or trees if you have a multi-platform build. The dtbs target builds device trees according to the rules in arch/$ARCH/boot/dts/Makefile using the device tree source files in that directory. The following is a snippet from building the dtbs target for arch/arm64/configs/defconfig:

```
$ make ARCH=arm64 dtbs CROSS_COMPILE=aarch64-buildroot-linux-gnu-  O=../
build_arm64
  <...>
  DTC      arch/arm64/boot/dts/ti/k3-am625-beagleplay.dtb
  DTC      arch/arm64/boot/dts/ti/k3-am625-phyboard-lyra-rdk.dtb
  DTC      arch/arm64/boot/dts/ti/k3-am625-sk.dtb
  DTC      arch/arm64/boot/dts/ti/k3-am625-verdin-nonwifi-dahlia.dtb
  DTC      arch/arm64/boot/dts/ti/k3-am625-verdin-nonwifi-dev.dtb
  DTC      arch/arm64/boot/dts/ti/k3-am625-verdin-nonwifi-yavia.dtb
  DTC      arch/arm64/boot/dts/ti/k3-am625-verdin-wifi-dahlia.dtb
  DTC      arch/arm64/boot/dts/ti/k3-am625-verdin-wifi-dev.dtb
  DTC      arch/arm64/boot/dts/ti/k3-am625-verdin-wifi-yavia.dtb
  <...>
```

The compiled .dtb files are generated in the ../build_arm64 output directory.

Compiling modules

If you have configured some features to be built as modules, then you can build them separately using the modules target:

```
$ make -j<n> ARCH=arm64 CROSS_COMPILE=aarch64-buildroot-linux-gnu- modules
O=../build_arm64
```

Replace <n> after make -j with the number of CPU cores available on your host machine to speed up your build.

The compiled modules have a .ko suffix and are generated in the same directory as the source code, meaning that they are scattered all around the kernel source tree. Finding them is a little tricky, but you can use the modules_install target to install them in the right place.

The default location is /lib/modules in your development system, which is almost certainly not what you want. To install them into the staging area of your root filesystem, provide the path using INSTALL_MOD_PATH:

```
$ mkdir ~/rootfs
$ make -j<n> ARCH=arm64 CROSS_COMPILE=aarch64-buildroot-linux-gnu-
INSTALL_MOD_PATH=$HOME/rootfs modules_install O=../build_arm64
```

Kernel modules are put into the directory /lib/modules/<kernel version> relative to the root of the filesystem.

Cleaning kernel sources

There are three make targets for cleaning the kernel source tree:

- **clean**: Removes object files and most intermediates.
- **mrproper**: Removes all intermediate files including the .config file. Use this target to return the source tree to the state it was in immediately after cloning or extracting the source code. Mr. Proper is a cleaning product common in some parts of the world. The purpose of make mrproper is to give the kernel sources a really good scrub.
- **distclean**: This is the same as mrproper but also deletes editor backup files, patch files, and other artifacts of software development.

Building and booting the kernel

Building and booting Linux is highly device-dependent. In this section, I will show you how it works for the Raspberry Pi 4, BeaglePlay, and QEMU. For other target boards, you must consult the information from the vendor or from the community project if there is one.

Building a kernel for the Raspberry Pi 4

Even though there is support for the Raspberry Pi 4 in the mainline kernel, I prefer to use the Raspberry Pi Foundation's fork of Linux (https://github.com/raspberrypi/linux) for stability. 6.6 was the latest long-term kernel supported by that fork in August 2024, so that is the version we shall build.

Since the Raspberry Pi 4 has a 64-bit quad-core Arm Cortex-A72 CPU, we will use the Bootlin toolchain from *Chapter 2*, to cross-compile a 64-bit kernel for it.

Install a package we need to build the kernel:

```
$ sudo apt install libssl-dev
```

Now that you have the requisite toolchain and packages installed, clone the `6.6.y` branch of the kernel repo one-level deep to a directory named `linux-rpi` and export some prebuilt binaries to a boot subdirectory:

```
$ cd ~
$ git clone --depth=1 -b rpi-6.6.y https://github.com/raspberrypi/linux.
git linux-rpi
$ git clone --depth=1 -b 1.20240529 https://github.com/raspberrypi/
firmware.git firmware-rpi
$ mv firmware-rpi/boot .
$ rm -rf firmware-rpi
$ rm boot/kernel*
$ rm boot/*.dtb
$ rm boot/overlays/*.dtbo
```

The `--depth=n` argument instructs Git to fetch only the last n commits when cloning.

Navigate to the newly cloned `linux-rpi` directory and build the kernel:

```
$ PATH=~/aarch64--glibc--stable-2024.02-1/bin/:$PATH
$ cd ~
$ cd linux-rpi
$ make ARCH=arm64 CROSS_COMPILE=aarch64-buildroot-linux-gnu- bcm2711_
defconfig O=../build_rpi
$ make -j<n> ARCH=arm64 CROSS_COMPILE=aarch64-buildroot-linux-gnu- O=../
build_rpi
```

Replace `<n>` after `make -j` with the number of CPU cores available on your host machine to speed up your build.

When the build finishes, copy the kernel image, device tree blobs, and boot parameters to the boot subdirectory:

```
$ cp ../build_rpi/arch/arm64/boot/Image ../boot/kernel8.img
$ cp ../build_rpi/arch/arm64/boot/dts/overlays/*.dtbo ../boot/overlays/
$ cp ../build_rpi/arch/arm64/boot/dts/broadcom/*.dtb ../boot/
$ cat << EOF > ../boot/config.txt
enable_uart=1
arm_64bit=1
EOF
$ cat << EOF > ../boot/cmdline.txt
console=serial0,115200 console=tty1 root=/dev/mmcblk0p2 rootwait
EOF
```

The preceding commands are all found in the script MELD/Chapter04/build-linux-rpi4.sh. Note that the kernel command line written to cmdline.txt must be all on one line. Let's break these steps down into stages:

1. Clone the rpi-6.6.y branch of the Raspberry Pi Foundation's kernel fork into a linux-rpi directory.

2. Clone the 1.20240529 tag of the Raspberry Pi Foundation's firmware rep into a firmware-rpi directory.

3. Move the boot subdirectory from the Raspberry Pi Foundation's firmware repo to a boot directory.

4. Delete the existing kernel image[s], device tree blobs, and device tree overlays from the boot directory.

5. From the linux-rpi directory, build the 64-bit kernel, modules, and device tree for the Raspberry Pi 4.

6. Copy the newly-built kernel image, device tree blobs, and device tree overlays from ./build_rpi/arch/arm64/boot to the boot directory.

7. Write config.txt and cmdline.txt files out to the boot directory for the Raspberry Pi 4's bootloader to read and pass to the kernel.

Let's look at the settings in config.txt. The enable_uart=1 line enables the serial console during boot, which is disabled by default. The arm_64bit=1 line instructs the Raspberry Pi 4's bootloader to start the CPU in 64-bit mode and load the kernel image from a file named kernel8.img.

Now, let's look at cmdline.txt. The console=serial0,115200 and console=tty1 kernel command-line parameters instruct the kernel to output log messages to the serial console as our kernel boots.

Booting the Raspberry Pi 4

Raspberry Pi devices use a proprietary bootloader provided by Broadcom instead of U-Boot. Unlike previous Raspberry Pi models, the Raspberry Pi 4's bootloader resides on an onboard SPI EEPROM rather than on a microSD card. We still need to put the kernel image and device tree blobs for the Raspberry Pi 4 on a microSD to boot our 64-bit kernel.

Before proceeding, you need a microSD card with a FAT32 boot partition large enough to hold the necessary kernel build artifacts. The boot partition needs to be the first partition on the microSD card. A partition size of 1 GB is sufficient.

For guidance on connecting a USB-to-TTL serial cable to the Raspberry Pi 4, see `https://learn.adafruit.com/adafruits-raspberry-pi-lesson-5-using-a-console-cable/connect-the-lead`.

To prepare a microSD card with your newly built kernel image and boot it on your Raspberry Pi 4:

1. First, navigate one level above the boot directory:

    ```
    $ cd ~
    ```

2. Next, insert the microSD card into your card reader and copy the entire contents of the boot directory to the boot partition.

3. Unmount the card and insert it into the Raspberry Pi 4.

4. Connect your USB-to-TTL serial cable to the GND, TXD, and RXD pins on the 40-pin GPIO header.

5. Start a terminal emulator like gtkterm.

6. Lastly, power on the Raspberry Pi 4.

You should see the following output on the serial console:

```
[    0.000000] Booting Linux on physical CPU 0x0000000000 [0x410fd083]
[    0.000000] Linux version 6.6.45-v8+ (frank@frank-nuc) (aarch64-
buildroot-linux-gnu-gcc.br_real (Buildroot 2021.11-11272-ge2962af) 12.3.0,
GNU ld (GNU Binutils) 2.41) #1 SMP PREEMPT Mon Aug 19 08:51:43 PDT 2024
[    0.000000] KASLR enabled
[    0.000000] random: crng init done
[    0.000000] Machine model: Raspberry Pi 4 Model B Rev 1.1
[    0.000000] efi: UEFI not found.
[    0.000000] Reserved memory: created CMA memory pool at
0x000000002ac00000, size 64 MiB
<...>
```

The sequence will end in a kernel panic because the kernel cannot locate a root filesystem on the microSD card. I'll explain what a kernel panic is later in this chapter.

Building a kernel for the BeaglePlay

Here is the sequence of commands to build a kernel, modules, and device tree for the BeaglePlay:

1. First, add the 64-bit Arm toolchain to your PATH if you haven't already:

    ```
    $ PATH=~/aarch64--glibc--stable-2024.02-1/bin/:$PATH
    ```

2. Next, navigate back to the mainline Linux source tree:

```
$ cd ~
$ cd linux-stable
$ mkdir ../build_beagleplay
```

3. Set the `ARCH` and `CROSS_COMPILE` environment variables for 64-bit Arm:

```
$ export ARCH=arm64
$ export CROSS_COMPILE=aarch64-buildroot-linux-gnu-
```

4. Run `make defconfig` to configure a kernel suitable for most 64-bit Arm SoCs:

```
$ make defconfig O=../build_beagleplay
```

5. Run `make menuconfig` to continue configuring the kernel:

```
$ make menuconfig O=../build_beagleplay
```

6. Drill down into the **General architecture-dependent options** submenu.

7. Deselect **GCC plugins** if it is set.

8. Back out of the **General architecture-dependent options** submenu.

9. Drill down into the **Platform selection** submenu.

10. Deselect support for all SoCs except for **Texas Instruments Inc. K3 multicore SoC architecture**.

11. Back out of the **Platform selection** submenu.

12. Drill down into the **Device drivers | Graphics support** submenu

13. Deselect **Direct Rendering Manager**.

14. Back out of the **Graphics support** and **Device drivers** submenus.

15. Exit out of menuconfig and choose **Yes** when asked to save your new configuration.

16. Lastly, build a kernel, modules, and device tree for the BeaglePlay:

```
$ make -j<n> O=../build_beagleplay
```

Replace `<n>` after `make -j` with the number of CPU cores available on your host machine to speed up your build.

Booting the BeaglePlay

Before proceeding, you need a microSD card with U-Boot installed, as described in the section titled *Installing U-Boot* from *Chapter 3*:

1. First, navigate one level above the build_beagleplay directory:

```
$ cd ~
```

2. Next, insert the microSD card into your card reader and copy the build_beagleplay/arch/ arm64/boot/Image.gz and build_beagleplay/arch/arm64/boot/dts/ti/k3-am625- beagleplay.dtb files to the FAT32 boot partition.

3. Unmount the card and insert it into the BeaglePlay.

4. Start a terminal emulator like gtkterm and be prepared to press the spacebar as soon as you see the U-Boot messages appear.

5. Power on the BeaglePlay while holding down the USR button and press the spacebar.

6. Lastly, enter the following commands at the U-Boot prompt:

```
nova!> setenv bootargs console=ttyS2,115200n8
nova!> fatload mmc 1 0x80000000 Image.gz
nova!> fatload mmc 1 0x82000000 k3-am625-beagleplay.dtb
nova!> setenv kernel_comp_addr_r 0x85000000
nova!> setenv kernel_comp_size 0x2000000
nova!> booti 0x80000000 - 0x82000000
```

You should see the following output on the serial console:

```
Starting kernel ...

[    0.000000] Booting Linux on physical CPU 0x0000000000 [0x410fd034]
[    0.000000] Linux version 6.6.46 (frank@frank-nuc) (aarch64-buildroot-
linux-gnu-gcc.br_real (Buildroot 2021.11-11272-ge2962af)
 12.3.0, GNU ld (GNU Binutils) 2.41) #1 SMP PREEMPT Mon Aug 19 11:24:56
PDT 2024
[    0.000000] KASLR disabled due to lack of seed
[    0.000000] Machine model: BeagleBoard.org BeaglePlay
[    0.000000] efi: UEFI not found.
<...>
```

Note that we set the kernel command line to console=ttyS2. That tells Linux which UART device to use for console output. Without this, we would not see any messages after Starting the kernel... and so would be unable to tell if it was working or not. The sequence ends in a kernel panic, just as it did for the Raspberry Pi 4.

Building a kernel for QEMU

Here is the sequence of commands to build Linux for the `virt` generic virtual platform emulated by QEMU:

1. First, add the 64-bit Arm toolchain to your PATH if you haven't already:

   ```
   $ PATH=~/aarch64--glibc--stable-2024.02-1/bin/:$PATH
   ```

2. Next, navigate back to the mainline Linux source tree:

   ```
   $ cd ~
   $ cd linux-stable
   $ mkdir ../build_qemu
   ```

3. Set the ARCH and CROSS_COMPILE environment variables for 64-bit Arm:

   ```
   $ export ARCH=arm64
   $ export CROSS_COMPILE=aarch64-buildroot-linux-gnu-
   ```

4. Run `make  defconfig` to configure a kernel suitable for most 64-bit Arm SoCs:

   ```
   $ make defconfig O=../build_qemu
   ```

5. Run `make  menuconfig` to continue configuring the kernel:

   ```
   $ make menuconfig O=../build_qemu
   ```

6. Drill down into the **Platform selection** submenu.

7. Deselect support for all SoCs except for **ARMv8 software model (Versatile Express)**.

8. Back out of the **Platform selection** submenu.

9. Select **ACPI (Advanced Configuration and Power Interface) Support**.

10. Exit out of `menuconfig` and choose **Yes** when asked to save your new configuration.

11. Lastly, build a kernel, modules, and device tree for QEMU:

    ```
    $ make -j<n> O=../build_qemu
    ```

Replace <n> after make -j with the number of CPU cores available on your host machine to speed up your build.

Booting QEMU

Assuming that you have already installed qemu-system-aarch64, you can launch QEMU from the mainline kernel source tree as follows:

```
$ qemu-system-aarch64 -M virt -cpu cortex-a53 -nographic -smp 1 -kernel
../build_qemu/arch/arm64/boot/Image -append "console=ttyAMA0"
```

As with the Raspberry Pi 4 and BeaglePlay, this will end with a kernel panic and the system will halt. To exit from QEMU, type *Ctrl + A* and then *x* (two separate keystrokes).

Observing the kernel boot process

At this point, you should have the kernel image files and the device tree blobs for the Raspberry Pi 4, BeaglePlay, and QEMU. Let's start by looking at a kernel panic.

Kernel panic

While things started off well on QEMU, they ended badly:

```
[    0.393978] Kernel panic - not syncing: VFS: Unable to mount root fs on
unknown-block(0,0)
[    0.394269] CPU: 0 PID: 1 Comm: swapper/0 Not tainted 6.6.46 #2
[    0.394443] Hardware name: linux,dummy-virt (DT)
<...>
[    0.396719] ---[ end Kernel panic - not syncing: VFS: Unable to mount
root fs on unknown-block(0,0) ]---
```

This is a good example of a kernel panic. A panic occurs when the kernel encounters an unrecoverable error. By default, it will print out a message to the console and then halt. You can set the panic command-line parameter to allow a few seconds before reboots following a panic. In this case, the unrecoverable error is no root filesystem, illustrating that a kernel is useless without a user space to control it. You can supply a user space by providing a root filesystem, either as a RAM disk or on a mountable mass storage device. We will talk about how to create a root filesystem in the next chapter, but first, I want to describe the sequence of events that leads up to panic.

Early user space

To transition from kernel initialization to user space, the kernel has to mount a root filesystem and execute a program in that root filesystem. This can be achieved via a RAM disk or by mounting a real filesystem on a block device. The code for all of this is in init/main.c starting with the function rest_init(), which creates the first thread with PID 1 and runs the code in kernel_init(). If there is a RAM disk, it will try to execute the program /init, which will take on the task of setting up the user space.

If the kernel fails to find and run /init, it tries to mount a filesystem by calling the function prepare_namespace() in init/do_mounts.c. This requires a root= command line to give the name of the block device to use for mounting usually in the form:

```
root=/dev/<disk name><partition number>
```

Or for SD cards and eMMC:

```
root=/dev/<disk name>p<partition number>
```

For example, for the first partition on an SD card, that would be root=/dev/mmcblk0p1. If the mount succeeds, it will try to execute /sbin/init, followed by /etc/init, /bin/init, and then /bin/sh, stopping at the first one that works. The program can be overridden on the command line. For a RAM disk, use rdinit=. For a filesystem, use init=.

Kernel messages

Kernel developers are fond of printing out useful information through the liberal use of printk() and similar functions. The messages are categorized according to importance, with 0 being the highest:

Level	Value	Meaning
KERN_EMERG	0	The system is unusable
KERN_ALERT	1	Action must be taken immediately
KERN_CRIT	2	Critical conditions
KERN_ERR	3	Error conditions
KERN_WARNING	4	Warning conditions
KERN_NOTICE	5	Normal but significant conditions
KERN_INFO	6	Informational
KERN_DEBUG	7	Debug-level messages

Table 4.1 – List of kernel messages

They are first written to a buffer named __log_buf, the size of which is two to the power of CONFIG_LOG_BUF_SHIFT. For example, if CONFIG_LOG_BUF_SHIFT is 16, then __log_buf is 64 KB. You can dump the entire buffer using the command dmesg.

If the level of a message is less than the console log level, it is displayed on the console as well as placed in __log_buf. The default console log level is 7. This means that messages of level 6 and lower are displayed while filtering out KERN_DEBUG, which is level 7.

You can change the console log level in several ways, including by using the kernel parameter `loglevel=<level>` or the command `dmesg -n <level>`.

Kernel command line

The kernel command line is a string that is passed to the kernel by the bootloader via the `bootargs` variable in the case of U-Boot. It can also be defined in the device tree or set as part of the kernel configuration in `CONFIG_CMDLINE`.

We have seen some examples of the kernel command line already but there are many more. There is a complete list in `Documentation/admin-guide/kernel-parameters.txt`. Here is a smaller list of the most useful ones:

- `debug`: Sets the console log level to the highest level (8) to ensure that you see all the kernel messages on the console.
- `init=`: The `init` program to run from a mounted root filesystem. Defaults to `/sbin/init`.
- `lpj=`: Sets `loops_per_jiffy` to a given constant. There is a description of the significance of this in the paragraph following this list.
- `panic=`: Behavior when the kernel panics. If it is greater than zero, it gives the number of seconds before rebooting; if it is zero, it waits forever (default); or if it is less than zero, it reboots without any delay.
- `quiet`: Sets the console log level to silent, suppressing all but emergency messages. Since most devices have a serial console, it takes time to output all those strings. Consequently, reducing the number of messages using this option reduces boot time.
- `rdinit=`: The init program to run from a RAM disk. Defaults to `/init`.
- `ro`: Mounts the root device as read-only. Has no effect on a RAM disk, which is always read/write.
- `root=`: Device to mount the root filesystem.
- `rootdelay=`: Number of seconds to wait before trying to mount the root device. Defaults to zero. Useful if the device takes time to probe the hardware. Also see `rootwait`.
- `rootfstype=`: Filesystem type for the root device. In many cases, it is auto-detected during mount, although it is required for jffs2 filesystems.
- `rootwait`: Waits indefinitely for the root device to be detected, usually necessary with MMC devices.
- `rw`: Mounts the root device as read-write (default).

The lpj parameter is often mentioned in connection with reducing the kernel boot time. During initialization, the kernel loops for approximately 250 ms to calibrate a delay loop. The value is stored in the variable loops_per_jiffy and reported like this:

```
Calibrating delay loop... 996.14 BogoMIPS (lpj=4980736)
```

If the kernel always runs on the same hardware, it will always calculate the same value. You can shave 250 ms off the boot time by adding lpj=4980736 to the command line.

In the next section, we will learn how to port Linux to a new board based on the BeaglePlay, our hypothetical Nova board.

Porting Linux to a new board

Porting Linux to a new board can be easy or difficult, depending on how similar your board is to an existing development board. In *Chapter 3,* we ported U-Boot to a new board named Nova based on the BeaglePlay. Very few changes need to be made to the kernel code, so it is very easy. If you are porting to completely new and innovative hardware, then there will be more to do. I am only going to consider the simple case. We will delve deeper into the topic of additional hardware peripherals throughout *Chapter 12.*

The organization of architecture-specific code in arch/$ARCH differs from one system to another. The x86 architecture is fairly clean because most hardware details are detected at runtime. The PowerPC architecture organizes SoC- and board-specific files into subdirectories under platforms. The 32-bit Arm architecture, on the other hand, is quite messy because there is a lot of variability between the many Arm-based SoCs. Platform-dependent code is put in directories named mach-*, approximately one per SoC. There are other directories named plat-*, which contain code common to several versions of an SoC.

In the following sections, I am going to explain how to create a device tree for a new 64-bit Arm board.

A new device tree

The first thing to do is create a device tree for the board and modify it to describe the additional or changed hardware of the Nova board. In this simple case, we just copy k3-am625-beagleplay. dts to nova.dts and change the model name to Nova, as shown here:

```
/dts-v1/;

#include <dt-bindings/leds/common.h>
#include <dt-bindings/gpio/gpio.h>
```

```
#include <dt-bindings/input/input.h>
#include "k3-am625.dtsi"

/ {
    compatible = "beagle,am625-beagleplay", "ti,am625";
    model = "Nova";
<...>
```

Complete all the steps from *Building a kernel for the BeaglePlay*.

Add the following dependency to `linux-stable/arch/arm64/boot/dts/ti/Makefile`:

```
dtb-$(CONFIG_ARCH_K3) += nova.dtb
```

This entry ensures that the device tree for Nova is compiled whenever an AM62x target is selected.

Build the Nova device tree binary like this:

```
$ make ARCH=arm64 dtbs O=../build_beagleplay
  DTC      arch/arm64/boot/dts/ti/nova.dtb
```

We can see the effect of using the Nova device tree by booting the BeaglePlay. Follow the same procedure as in *Booting the BeaglePlay*. Insert the same microSD card into your card reader and copy the `build_beagleplay/arch/arm64/boot/dts/ti/nova.dtb` file to the FAT32 boot partition. Use the same `Image.gz` file as before but load `nova.dtb` in place of `k3-am625-beagleplay.dtb`. The following output is the point at which the machine model is printed out:

```
Starting kernel ...

[    0.000000] Booting Linux on physical CPU 0x0000000000 [0x410fd034]
[    0.000000] Linux version 6.6.46 (frank@frank-nuc) (aarch64-buildroot-
linux-gnu-gcc.br_real (Buildroot 2021.11-11272-ge2962af)
 12.3.0, GNU ld (GNU Binutils) 2.41) #1 SMP PREEMPT Mon Aug 19 11:24:56
PDT 2024
[    0.000000] KASLR disabled due to lack of seed
[    0.000000] Machine model: Nova
<...>
```

Now that we have a device tree specifically for the Nova board, we could modify it to describe the hardware differences between Nova and BeaglePlay. There are quite likely to be changes to the kernel configuration as well. In that case, you would create a custom configuration file based on a copy of `arch/arm64/configs/defconfig`.

Summary

What makes Linux so powerful is the ability to configure the kernel however we need to. The definitive place to get the kernel source code is https://www.kernel.org/, but you will probably need to get the source for a particular SoC or board from the vendor of that device or a third party that supports that device. The customization of the kernel for a particular target may consist of changes to the core kernel code, additional drivers for devices that are not in mainline Linux, a default kernel configuration file, and a device tree source file.

Normally, you start with the default configuration for your target board and then tweak it by running one of the configuration tools such as menuconfig. One of the things you should consider at this point is whether the kernel features and drivers should be disabled, compiled as modules, or built-in. Kernel modules are usually no great advantage for embedded systems where the feature set and hardware are usually well defined. However, modules offer a way to import proprietary code into the kernel and reduce boot times by loading non-essential drivers after booting. Disabling unused kernel features and drivers altogether reduces compile times as well as boot times.

Building the kernel produces a compressed kernel image file named zImage, Image.gz, or bzImage, depending on the bootloader you will be using and the target architecture. A kernel build will also generate any kernel modules (.ko files) that you have configured and device tree binaries (.dtb files) if your target requires them.

Porting Linux to a new target board can be quite simple or very difficult, depending on how different the hardware is from that in the mainline or vendor-supplied kernel. If your hardware is based on a well-known reference design, then it may be just a question of making changes to the device tree or the platform data. You may well need to add device drivers, which we'll discuss in *Chapter 11*. However, if the hardware is radically different from a reference design, you may need additional core support, which is outside the scope of this book.

The kernel is the core of a Linux-based system but it cannot work by itself. It requires a root filesystem that contains the user space components. The root filesystem can be a RAM disk or a filesystem accessed via a block device, which will be the subject of the next chapter. As we have seen, booting a kernel without a root filesystem results in kernel panic.

Further study

- *So You Want to Build an Embedded Linux System?* by Jay Carlson – `https://jaycarlson.net/embedded-linux/`

- *Embedded Linux training* – `https://bootlin.com/training/embedded-linux/`

- *Linux Weekly News* – `https://lwn.net/`

- *Raspberry Pi Forums* – `https://forums.raspberrypi.com/`

- *Linux Kernel Development, Third Edition,* by Robert Love

5

Building a Root Filesystem

The root filesystem is the fourth element of embedded Linux. Once you have read this chapter, you will be able to build, boot, and run a simple embedded Linux system.

The techniques described here are broadly known as **roll your own**, or **RYO**. Back in the early days of embedded Linux, this was the only way to create a root filesystem. There are still some use cases where an RYO root filesystem is applicable – for example, when the amount of RAM or storage is very limited, for quick demonstrations, or for any case in which your requirements are not easily covered by the standard build system tools. However, these cases are quite rare.

The purpose of this chapter is educational. It is not meant to be a recipe for building everyday embedded systems. Use the tools described in the next chapter for this.

Our first objective is to create a minimal root filesystem that will give us a shell prompt. Then, using this as a base, we will add scripts to start up other programs and configure a network interface and user permissions. There are examples for both the BeaglePlay and QEMU targets. Knowing how to build the root filesystem from scratch is a useful skill. It will help you to understand what is going on when we look at more complex examples in later chapters.

In this chapter, we will cover the following topics:

- What should be in the root filesystem?
- Transferring the root filesystem to the target
- Creating a boot `initramfs`
- `init` program
- Configuring user accounts

- A better way of managing device nodes
- Configuring the network
- Creating filesystem images with device tables
- Mounting the root filesystem using NFS
- Using TFTP to load the kernel

Technical requirements

To follow along with the examples, make sure you have the following:

- An Ubuntu 24.04 or later LTS host system
- A microSD card reader and card
- A microSD card prepared for the BeaglePlay from *Chapter 4*
- An Image file for QEMU from *Chapter 4*
- A USB to TTL serial cable with a 3.3V logic level
- A BeaglePlay
- A 5V USB-C power supply capable of delivering 3A

The code used in this chapter can be found in the Chapter05 folder in the book's GitHub repository: https://github.com/PacktPublishing/Mastering-Embedded-Linux-Development/tree/main/Chapter05.

What should be in the root filesystem?

The kernel gets a root filesystem either as an initramfs passed as a pointer from the bootloader, or by mounting the block device given on the kernel command line with the root= parameter. Once it has a root filesystem, the kernel executes the first program – by default, named init, as described in the *Early user space* section from *Chapter 4*. Then, as far as the kernel is concerned, its job is complete. It is up to the init program to start other programs and bring the system to life.

To make a minimal root filesystem, you need these components:

- **init**: This is the program that starts everything off, usually by running a series of scripts. I will describe how init works in much more detail in *Chapter 13*.
- **shell**: Gives you a command prompt and (more importantly) runs the shell scripts called by init and other programs.

- **daemons**: These are background programs that provide services to others. Good examples are the system log daemon (`syslogd`) and the secure shell daemon (`sshd`). The `init` program must start the initial population of daemons to support the main system applications. In fact, `init` is itself a daemon. It is the daemon that provides the service of launching other daemons.

- **shared libraries**: Most programs are linked with shared libraries, so they must be present in the root filesystem.

- **configuration files**: These are a series of text files, usually stored in the `/etc` directory, that configure `init` and other daemons.

- **device nodes**: These are the special files that give access to various device drivers.

- **proc and sys**: These are two pseudo filesystems that represent kernel data structures as a hierarchy of directories and files. Many programs and library functions depend on `/proc` and `/sys`.

- **kernel modules**: Need to be installed in the root filesystem, usually in `/lib/modules/<kernel version>`.

Additionally, there are the device-specific applications that make the device do the job it is intended for and the runtime data files that they generate.

> **IMPORTANT NOTE**
>
> In some cases, you could condense most of the above programs into a single statically linked program and start that program instead of `init`. For example, if your program was named `/myprog`, you would add the following command to the kernel command line: `init=/myprog`.
>
> I have come across such a configuration only once in a secure system in which the fork system call had been disabled, thus making it impossible for any other program to be started. The downside of this approach is that you can't make use of the many tools that normally go into an embedded system. You have to do everything yourself.

Directory layout

The Linux kernel does not care about the layout of files and directories beyond the existence of the program named by `init=` or `rdinit=`, so you are free to put things wherever you like. For example, compare the file layout of a device running Android to that of a desktop Linux distribution. They are almost completely different.

However, many programs expect certain files to be in certain places, and it helps us developers if devices use a similar layout. The basic layout of most Linux systems is defined in the **Filesystem Hierarchy Standard (FHS)**, which is available at https://refspecs.linuxfoundation.org/fhs.shtml. The FHS covers all implementations of Linux operating systems, from the largest to the smallest. Embedded devices tend to use a subset based on their needs, but each usually includes the following:

- /bin: Programs essential for all users
- /dev: Device nodes and other special files
- /etc: System configuration files
- /lib: Essential shared libraries, including those that make up the C library
- /proc: Information about processes represented as virtual files
- /sbin: Programs essential to the system administrator
- /sys: Information about devices and their drivers, represented as virtual files
- /tmp: A place to put temporary or volatile files
- /usr: Additional programs, libraries, and system administrator utilities stored in the directories /usr/bin, /usr/lib, and /usr/sbin, respectively

> **IMPORTANT NOTE**
>
> The /usr directory contains all system-wide, read-only files that are installed or provided by the operating system. In the distant past, /bin , /sbin, and /lib only contained executables and libraries required for booting, while /usr/bin, /usr/sbin, and /usr/lib contained all the other executables and binaries. That distinction has since blurred, culminating in a modern movement that merges /bin, /sbin, and /lib into /usr/bin, /usr/sbin, and /usr/lib. Nowadays, the files in /bin, /sbin, and /lib are just symbolic links to their /usr counterparts. The /usr/sbin directory, like the /sbin directory, is for commands that can only be executed by the root user.

- /var: a hierarchy of files and directories that can be modified at runtime, like log messages, some of which must be retained after boot

There are some subtle distinctions here. The difference between /bin and /sbin is simply that the latter need not be included in the search path for non-root users. Users of Red Hat-derived distributions will be familiar with this.

Staging directory

You should begin by creating a **staging** directory on your host computer where you can assemble the files that will eventually be transferred to the target. In the following examples, I have used ~/rootfs. You need to create a skeleton directory structure in it. Look at the following:

```
$ mkdir ~/rootfs
$ cd ~/rootfs
$ mkdir bin dev etc home lib proc sbin sys tmp usr var
$ mkdir usr/bin usr/lib usr/sbin
$ mkdir var/log
$ ln -s lib lib64
```

To see the directory hierarchy more clearly, you can use the handy tree command with the -d option to show only the directories:

```
$ tree -d
.
├── bin
├── dev
├── etc
├── home
├── lib
├── lib64 -> lib
├── proc
├── sbin
├── sys
├── tmp
├── usr
│   ├── bin
│   ├── lib
│   └── sbin
└── var
    └── log
```

Not all directories have the same file permissions, and the individual files inside a directory can have stricter permissions than the directory itself.

POSIX file access permissions

Every process or running program belongs to a user and one or more groups. The user is represented by a 32-bit number called the **user ID** or **UID**. Information about users, including the mapping from a UID to a name, is kept in /etc/passwd. Likewise, groups are represented by a **group ID** or **GID**, with information kept in /etc/group. There is always a root user with a UID of 0 and a root group with a GID of 0. The root user is also called the **superuser** because, in a default configuration, it bypasses most permission checks and can access all the resources in the system. Security in Linux-based systems is mainly about restricting access to the root account.

Each file and directory also has an owner and belongs to exactly one group. The level of access a process has to a file or directory is controlled by a set of access permission flags called the **mode** of the file. There are three collections of three bits: the first collection applies to the *owner* of the file, the second to the *members* of the same group as the file, and the last to *everyone else* – the rest of the world. The bits are for **read** (r), **write** (w), and **execute** (x) permissions on the file. Three bits result in $2^3 = 8$ possible values, represented as octal digits from 0 to 7:

- 0: No permissions
- 1: Execute only (--x)
- 2: Write only (-w-)
- 3: Write and execute (-wx)
- 4: Read only (r--)
- 5: Read and execute (r-x)
- 6: Read and write (rw-)
- 7: Read, write, and execute (rwx)

Since three bits fit neatly into an octal digit, file access permissions are usually represented in octal.

Here are some common file modes:

- 600: Owner - rw-, Group - ---, and Others - ---
- 644: Owner - rw-, Group - r--, and Others - r--
- 666: Owner - rw-, Group - rw-, and Others - rw-
- 700: Owner - rwx, Group - ---, and Others - ---
- 755: Owner - rwx, Group - r-x, and Others - r-x
- 775: Owner - rwx, Group - rwx, and Others - r-x
- 777: Owner - rwx, Group - rwx, and Others - rwx

The first (leftmost) bit of an octal digit is a value of 4, the second (center) bit is a value of 2, and the third (rightmost) bit is a value of 1, as shown below:

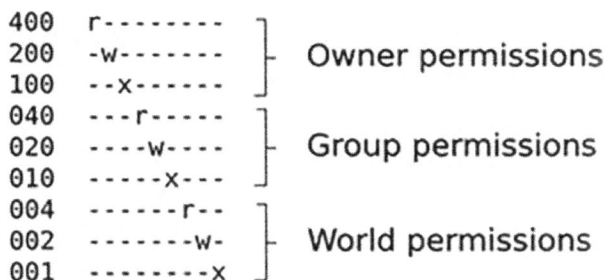

```
400   r--------- ┐
200   -w-------- ├  Owner permissions
100   --x------- ┘
040   ---r------ ┐
020   ----w----- ├  Group permissions
010   -----x---- ┘
004   ------r--- ┐
002   -------w-- ├  World permissions
001   --------x  ┘
```

Figure 5.1 – File access permissions

If all three bits in a collection are set, then the octal value of that collection is 4 + 2 + 1 = 7. Each row in the above diagram comprises 3 collections for a total of 9 bits.

There is a fourth preceding octal digit whose value has special significance:

- **SUID (4)**: If the file is executable, it changes the effective UID of the process to that of the file owner when the program is run.

- **SGID (2)**: Like SUID, this changes the effective GID of the process to that of the group of the file.

- **Sticky (1)**: In a directory, this restricts deletion so that one user cannot delete files that are owned by another user. This is usually set on /tmp and /var/tmp.

The SUID bit is probably used most often. It gives non-root users a temporary privilege escalation to superuser to perform a task. The ping program is a good example: ping opens a raw socket, which is a privileged operation. The ping executable is owned by user root and has the SUID bit set so that when you run ping, it executes with UID 0 regardless of your UID.

To set this leading octal digit, use values of either 4, 2, and 1 with the chmod command. For example, to set SUID on /bin/ping in your staging root directory, you would prepend 4 to a mode of 755 like so:

```
$ cd ~/rootfs
$ ls -l bin/ping
-rwxr-xr-x 1 root root 35712 Feb 6 09:15 bin/ping
$ sudo chmod 4755 bin/ping
$ ls -l bin/ping
-rwsr-xr-x 1 root root 35712 Feb 6 09:15 bin/ping
```

Note that the second `ls` command shows the first three bits of the mode to be `rws`, whereas previously, they had been `rwx`. That `s` indicates that the SUID bit is set.

File ownership permissions in the staging directory

For security and stability reasons, it is important to pay attention to the ownership and permissions of the files that will be placed on the target device. In general, you want to restrict sensitive resources to be accessible only by the root user and run as few programs using non-root users as possible. It is best to run programs using non-root users so that if they are compromised by an outside attack, they offer as few system resources to the attacker as possible.

For example, the device node called /dev/mem gives access to system memory, which is necessary in some programs. But if it is readable and writeable by everyone, then there is no security because everyone can access everything in memory. So /dev/mem should be owned by root, belong to the root group, and have a mode of 600 that denies read and write access to all but the owner.

However, there is a problem with the staging directory. The files you create there will be owned by you. But when they are installed on the device, they should belong to specific owners and groups, mostly the root user. An obvious fix is to change the ownership to root at this stage, with the commands shown here:

```
$ cd ~/rootfs
$ sudo chown -R root:root *
```

> **IMPORTANT NOTE**
>
> Do not run the preceding `sudo chown -R root:root *` command. You could damage your filesystem irreparably.

The problem is that you need root privileges to run the chown command. And from that point onward, you will need to be root to modify any files in the staging directory. Before you know it, you are doing all your development logged in as root, which is not a good idea. This is a problem that we will revisit when creating a standalone `initramfs`.

Programs for the root filesystem

Now, it is time to start populating the root filesystem with the essential programs and the supporting libraries, configuration, and data files they need to operate. I will begin with an overview of the types of programs you will need.

init program

init is the first program to be run, so it is an essential part of the root filesystem. In this chapter, we will use the simple init program provided by BusyBox.

Shell

We need a shell to run scripts and to give us a command prompt so that we can interact with the system. An interactive shell is probably not necessary in a production device, but it is useful for development, debugging, and maintenance. There are various shells in common use on embedded systems:

- bash: This is the big beast that we all know and love from desktop Linux. It is a superset of the Unix Bourne shell with many extensions or bashisms.

- ash: This is also based on the Bourne shell and has a long history with the BSD variants of Unix. BusyBox has a version of ash that has been extended to make it more compatible with bash. It is much smaller than bash, and hence, it is a very popular choice for embedded systems.

- hush: This is a very small shell that we briefly looked at in *Chapter 3*. It is useful on devices with very little memory. There is a version of hush in BusyBox.

> **TIP**
>
> If you are using ash or hush as the shell on the target, make sure that you test your shell scripts on the target. It is very tempting to test them only on the host using bash and then be surprised that they don't work when you copy them to the target.

Utilities

The shell is just a way of launching other programs. A shell script is little more than a list of programs to run with some flow control and a means of passing information between them. To make a shell useful, you need the utility programs that the Unix command line is based on. Even a basic root filesystem needs approximately 50 utilities. This presents two problems. Firstly, tracking down the source code for each one and cross-compiling all of it is a big job. Secondly, the resulting collection of programs takes up several tens of megabytes. This was a real problem in the early days of embedded Linux when a few megabytes were all you had. BusyBox was created expressly to solve this problem.

BusyBox to the rescue!

The genesis of BusyBox had nothing to do with embedded Linux. Bruce Perens started the project in 1996 for the Debian installer so that he could boot Linux from a 1.44 MB floppy disk. Coincidentally, this was about the size of the storage on contemporary devices so the embedded Linux community quickly took it up. BusyBox has been at the heart of embedded Linux ever since.

BusyBox was written from scratch to perform the essential functions of those essential Linux utilities. The developers took advantage of the 80/20 rule: the most useful 80% of a program is implemented in 20% of the code. Hence, BusyBox tools implement a subset of the functionality of their desktop equivalents, but they do enough to be useful in most cases.

Another trick BusyBox employs is to combine all the tools together into a single binary, making it easy to share code between them. It works like this: BusyBox is a collection of applets, each of which exports its main function in the form <applet>_main. For example, the cat command is implemented in coreutils/cat.c and exports cat_main. The main function of BusyBox dispatches the call to the correct applet, based on the command-line arguments.

To read a file, you can launch BusyBox with the name of the applet you want to run, followed by any arguments that the applet expects:

```
$ busybox cat my_file.txt
```

You can also run BusyBox with no arguments to get a list of all the applets that have been compiled.

Using BusyBox in this way is rather clumsy. A better way to get BusyBox to run the cat applet is to create a symbolic link from /bin/cat to /bin/busybox:

```
$ ls -l bin/cat bin/busybox
-rwxr-xr-x 1 root root 1137096 Aug 20 10:31 bin/busybox
lrwxrwxrwx 1 root root       7 Aug 20 10:31 bin/cat -> busybox
```

When you type cat at the command line, BusyBox is the program that actually runs. BusyBox only has to check the path to the executable (/bin/cat) passed in via argv[0], extract the application name (cat), and do a table lookup to match cat with cat_main. All this is expressed in this slightly simplified section of code from libbb/appletlib.c:

```
applet_name = argv[0];
applet_name = bb_basename(applet_name);
run_applet_and_exit(applet_name, argv);
```

BusyBox has over 300 applets, including an `init` program, several shells with varying levels of complexity, and utilities for most admin tasks. There is even a simple version of the `vi` editor so that you can change text files on your device. A typical BusyBox binary will only enable several dozen applets.

In summary, a typical installation of BusyBox consists of a single program, with a symbolic link for each applet but which behaves exactly as if it were a collection of individual applications.

Building BusyBox

BusyBox uses the same `Kconfig` and `Kbuild` system as the kernel, so cross-compiling is straightforward. Get the source by cloning the BusyBox Git repo and checking out the version you want (1_36_1 was the latest in August 2024):

```
$ git clone git://busybox.net/busybox.git
$ cd busybox
$ git checkout 1_36_1
```

You can also download the corresponding TAR file from `https://busybox.net/downloads/`.

Configure BusyBox with the default configuration, which enables pretty much all of the features:

```
$ make distclean
$ make defconfig
```

At this point, you probably want to run `make menuconfig` to fine-tune the configuration. For example, you almost certainly want to set the install path in **Settings | Installation Options ("make install" behavior) | Destination path for 'make install'** to point to the staging directory. Then, you can cross-compile in the usual way. If your intended target is the BeaglePlay, use these commands:

```
$ PATH=~/aarch64--glibc--stable-2024.02-1/bin/:$PATH
$ make ARCH=arm64 CROSS_COMPILE=aarch64-buildroot-linux-gnu-
```

You can cross-compile BusyBox for the 64-bit Arm generic virtual platform emulated by QEMU in the same way.

In either case, the result is the busybox executable. For a default configuration build like this, the size is about 1,100 KB. If this is too big for you, then you can slim it down by changing the configuration to leave out the utilities you don't need.

To install BusyBox in the staging area, use the following command:

```
$ make ARCH=arm64 CROSS_COMPILE=aarch64-buildroot-linux-gnu- install
```

This will copy the binary to the directory configured in **Destination path for 'make install'** and create all the symbolic links to it.

Now, let's look at an alternative to Busybox, known as ToyBox.

ToyBox — an alternative to BusyBox

BusyBox is not the only game in town. There is also ToyBox, which you can find at `https://landley.net/toybox/`. The project was started by Rob Landley, who was previously a maintainer of BusyBox. ToyBox has the same aim as BusyBox but with more emphasis on complying with standards (especially POSIX-2008 and LSB 4.1) and less on compatibility with GNU extensions to those standards. ToyBox is smaller than BusyBox, partly because it implements fewer applets.

The license for ToyBox is BSD rather than GPL v2, making it compatible with operating systems that have a BSD-licensed user space such as Android. Hence, ToyBox ships with all new Android devices. As of the 0.8.3 release, Toybox's `Makefile` can build a full Linux system that boots to a shell prompt when given just the Linux and ToyBox sources.

Libraries for the root filesystem

Programs are linked with libraries. You can link them all statically so that no libraries reside on the target device. This takes up an unnecessarily large amount of storage if you have more than two or three programs. To reduce the size of your programs, you need to copy shared libraries from the toolchain to the staging directory. But how do you know which libraries to copy?

One option is to copy all the `.so` files from the `sysroot` directory of your toolchain. Instead of trying to predict which libraries to include, just assume that your image will eventually need them all. This is certainly logical, and if you are creating a platform to be used by others for a range of applications, it would be the correct approach. However, be aware that a full glibc is quite large. In the case of Buildroot's build of glibc, the libraries, locales, and other supporting files come to 22 MB. You can cut that down considerably by using musl or uClibc-ng.

Another option is to cherry-pick only those libraries that you require. To do that, you need a means of discovering library dependencies. Let's use the `readelf` command from *Chapter 2* for this task:

```
$ PATH=~/aarch64--glibc--stable-2024.02-1/bin/:$PATH
$ cd ~/rootfs
$ aarch64-buildroot-linux-gnu-readelf -a bin/busybox | grep "program
interpreter"
```

```
     [Requesting program interpreter: /lib/ld-linux-aarch64.so.1]
$ aarch64-buildroot-linux-gnu-readelf -a bin/busybox | grep "Shared
library"
 0x0000000000000001 (NEEDED)                 Shared library: [libm.so.6]
 0x0000000000000001 (NEEDED)                 Shared library: [libresolv.so.2]
 0x0000000000000001 (NEEDED)                 Shared library: [libc.so.6]
 0x0000000000000001 (NEEDED)                 Shared library: [ld-linux-
aarch64.so.1]
```

The first readelf command searches the busybox binary for lines containing program interpreter.
The second readelf command searches the busybox binary for lines containing Shared library.
Now, you need to find these files in the toolchain sysroot directory and copy them to the staging
directory. Remember that you can find sysroot like this:

```
$ aarch64-buildroot-linux-gnu-gcc -print-sysroot
/home/frank/aarch64--glibc--stable-2024.02-1/aarch64-buildroot-linux-gnu/
sysroot
```

To reduce typing, keep a copy of the sysroot path in a shell variable:

```
$ export SYSROOT=$(aarch64-buildroot-linux-gnu-gcc -print-sysroot)
```

Let's look at /lib/ld-linux-aarch64.so.1 in sysroot:

```
$ cd $SYSROOT
$ ls -l lib/ld-linux-aarch64.so.1
-rwxr-xr-x 1 frank frank 202248 Mar  3 00:48 lib/ld-linux-aarch64.so.1
```

Repeat the exercise for libc.so.6, libm.so.6 and libresolv.so.2 so that you end up with a list
of four files. Now, copy each one to your rootfs directory:

```
$ cd ~/rootfs
$ cp $SYSROOT/lib/ld-linux-aarch64.so.1 lib
$ cp $SYSROOT/lib/libc.so.6 lib
$ cp $SYSROOT/lib/libm.so.6 lib
$ cp $SYSROOT/lib/libresolv.so.2 lib
```

These are just the shared libraries needed by busybox. Repeat this procedure for each program
you wish to add to your rootfs directory.

Reducing size by stripping

Libraries and programs are often compiled with some information stored in symbol tables to aid with debugging and tracing. You seldom need these in a production system. A quick and easy way to save space is to strip the binaries of symbol tables. This example shows libc before stripping:

```
$ file rootfs/lib/libc.so.6
rootfs/lib/libc.so.6: ELF 64-bit LSB shared object, ARM aarch64, version 1
(GNU/Linux), dynamically linked, interpreter /lib/ld-linux-aarch64.so.1,
for GNU/Linux 3.7.0, with debug_info, not stripped
$ ls -og rootfs/lib/libc.so.6
-rwxr-xr-x 1 1925456 Dec 12 05:43 rootfs/lib/libc.so.6
```

Now, let's see the result of stripping debug information:

```
$ aarch64-buildroot-linux-gnu-strip rootfs/lib/libc.so.6
$ file rootfs/lib/libc.so.6
rootfs/lib/libc.so.6: ELF 64-bit LSB shared object, ARM aarch64, version 1
(GNU/Linux), dynamically linked, interpreter /lib/ld-linux-aarch64.so.1,
for GNU/Linux 3.7.0, stripped
$ ls -og rootfs/lib/libc.so.6
-rwxr-xr-x 1 1392840 Dec 12 05:53 rootfs/lib/libc.so.6
```

In this case, we saved 532,616 bytes, or about 28% of the size of the file, before stripping.

Device nodes

Most devices in Linux are represented by device nodes in accordance with the Unix philosophy that *everything is a file* (except network interfaces, which are sockets). A device node may refer to a block device or a character device. Block devices are mass storage devices such as SD cards or hard drives. A character device is pretty much anything else (again, except for network interfaces).

The conventional place for device nodes is the /dev directory. For example, a serial port can be represented by a device node called /dev/ttyS0.

Device nodes are created using the program named mknod (short for make node):

```
mknod <name> <type> <major> <minor>
```

The parameters for mknod are as follows:

- **name** is the name of the device node that you want to create.
- **type** is either c for character devices or b for a block device.
- **major** and **minor** are a pair of numbers that are used by the kernel to route file requests to the appropriate device driver code. There is a list of standard major and minor numbers in the kernel source file: Documentation/admin-guide/devices.txt.

You will need to create device nodes for all the devices that you want to access on your system. You can do so manually using the mknod command illustrated here, or you can create them automatically at runtime using one of the device managers mentioned later.

In a minimal root filesystem, you need just two nodes to boot with BusyBox: console and null. The console only needs to be accessible to root, the owner of the device node, so the access permissions are 600 (rw-------). The null device should be readable and writable by everyone, so the mode is 666 (rw-rw-rw-). Use the -m option for mknod to set the mode when creating the node. You need to be root to create device nodes:

```
$ cd ~/rootfs
$ sudo mknod -m 666 dev/null c 1 3
$ sudo mknod -m 600 dev/console c 5 1
$ ls -l dev
total 0
crw------- 1 root root 5, 1 Aug 20 11:06 console
crw-rw-rw- 1 root root 1, 3 Aug 20 11:06 null
```

You can delete device nodes using the standard rm command. There is no rmnod command because, once created, they are just files.

Proc and sysfs filesystems

proc and sysfs are two pseudo filesystems that offer a window into the inner workings of the kernel. They both represent kernel data as files in a hierarchy of directories. When you read one of these files, the contents you see do not come from disk storage. Instead, it is formatted on the fly by a function in the kernel. Some files are also writable, meaning that a kernel function is called with the new data you have written. If the data is formatted correctly and you have sufficient permissions, then the function modifies the value stored in the kernel's memory. In other words, proc and sysfs provide another way to interact with device drivers and other kernel code.

> **IMPORTANT NOTE**
>
> The following mount commands are meant to be run on an embedded target device, like the BeaglePlay or Versatile Express (QEMU). Do not run them on your host machine.

The proc and sysfs filesystems should be mounted on the /proc and /sys directories:

```
# mount -t proc proc /proc
# mount -t sysfs sysfs /sys
```

Although very similar in concept, the two perform different functions. proc has been part of Linux since the early days. Its original purpose was to expose information about processes to user space, hence the name. To this end, there is a directory for each process named /proc/<PID>, which contains information about its state. The process list command (ps) reads these files to generate its output.

There are also files that give information about other parts of the kernel. For example, /proc/cpuinfo tells you about the CPU, /proc/interrupts has information about interrupts, and so on. Lastly, /proc/sys contains files that display and control the state and behavior of kernel subsystems, especially scheduling, memory management, and networking. The manual page is the best reference for the files found in the proc directory. You can see this information by typing man 5 proc.

The role of sysfs is to present the kernel **driver model** to user space. It exports a hierarchy of files relating to devices and how they are connected to each other. I will go into more detail on the Linux driver model when I describe the interaction with device drivers in *Chapter 11*.

Mounting filesystems

The mount command allows us to attach one filesystem to a directory within another, forming a hierarchy of filesystems. The one at the top, which was mounted by the kernel when it booted, is called the **root filesystem**. The format of the mount command is as follows:

```
mount [-t vfstype] [-o options] device directory
```

The parameters to mount are as follows:

- **vfstype** is the type of filesystem.
- **options** is a comma-separated list of mount options.
- **device** is the block device node that the filesystem resides on.
- **directory** is the directory that you want to mount the filesystem to.

There are various options you can give after -o. Have a look at the manual page mount(8) for more information. Type the following if you want to mount an SD card containing an ext4 filesystem in the first partition onto the directory named /mnt:

```
# mount -t ext4 /dev/mmcblk0p1 /mnt
```

Assuming that the mount succeeds, you will see the files stored on the SD card in the /mnt directory. In some cases, you can leave out the filesystem type and let the kernel probe the device to find out what is stored there. If mounting fails, you may first need to unmount the partition if your Linux distro is configured to automount all the partitions on an SD card when it is inserted.

Notice something odd in the following examples of mounting the proc filesystem? There is no device node such as /dev/proc, since it is a pseudo filesystem and not a real one. But the mount command requires a device parameter. Consequently, we have to provide a string where a device would go, but it does not matter much what that string is. These two commands achieve exactly the same result:

```
# mount -t proc procfs /proc
# mount -t proc nodevice /proc
```

The procfs and nodevice strings are ignored by the mount command. It is common to use the filesystem type in the place of the device when mounting pseudo filesystems.

Kernel modules

If you have kernel modules, they need to be installed into the root filesystem using the `modules_install` kernel make target, as we saw in *Chapter 4*. This will copy them into the `/lib/modules/<kernel version>` directory, together with the configuration files needed by the `modprobe` command.

Be aware that you have just created a dependency between the kernel and the root filesystem. If you update one, then you will have to update the other.

Now that we know how to mount a filesystem from an SD card, let's look at the different options for mounting a root filesystem. The alternatives (a ramdisk and NFS) may surprise you, especially if you are new to embedded Linux. A ramdisk protects the original source image from corruption and wear. We'll learn more about flash wear in *Chapter 9*. A network filesystem allows for more rapid development because file changes propagate instantly to the target(s).

Transferring the root filesystem to the target

After creating a skeleton root filesystem in your staging directory, the next step is to transfer it to the target. There are three possibilities:

- **initramfs:** This is a filesystem image that is loaded into RAM by the bootloader. Ramdisks are easy to create and have no dependencies on mass storage drivers. They can be used in fallback maintenance mode when the main root filesystem needs updating. They can even be used as the main root filesystem in smaller embedded devices. Ramdisks are also commonly used as the early user space in mainstream Linux distributions. Remember that the contents of a root filesystem on ramdisk are volatile, so any changes made to the root filesystem at runtime are lost when the system reboots. You need another storage type to store permanent data such as configuration parameters.

- **disk image:** A copy of the root filesystem that is formatted and ready to be loaded onto a mass storage device on the target. It can be an image in the ext4 format, ready to be copied onto an SD card, or it can be in jffs2 format, ready to be loaded into flash memory via the bootloader. Creating a disk image is probably the most common option. There is more information about the different types of mass storage in *Chapter 9*.

- **network filesystem:** This is when the staging directory is exported to the network via an NFS server and mounted by the target at boot time. This is often done during development as opposed to repeated cycles of creating a disk image and reloading it onto the mass storage device, which gets tedious quickly.

I will start with `intiramfs` and use it to illustrate a few refinements to the root filesystem, like adding usernames and a device manager to create device nodes automatically. Then, I will show you how to create a disk image and how to use NFS to mount the root filesystem over a network.

Creating a boot initramfs

An initial RAM filesystem or `initramfs` is a compressed cpio archive. cpio is an old Unix archive format like TAR and ZIP, but it is easier to decode and so requires less code in the kernel. You need to configure your kernel with `CONFIG_BLK_DEV_INITRD` to support `initramfs`.

There are three different ways to create a boot ramdisk: as a standalone cpio archive, as a cpio archive embedded in the kernel image, and as a device table that the kernel build system processes as part of the build. The first option gives the most flexibility because we can mix and match kernels and ramdisks to our heart's content. However, it means having to deal with two files instead of one, and not all bootloaders have the facility to load a separate ramdisk.

Standalone initramfs

The following sequence of instructions creates the archive, compresses it, and adds a U-Boot header to load onto the target:

```
$ cd ~/rootfs
$ find . | cpio -H newc -ov --owner root:root > ../initramfs.cpio
$ cd ..
$ gzip initramfs.cpio
$ mkimage -A arm64 -O linux -T ramdisk -d initramfs.cpio.gz uRamdisk
```

Notice that we run cpio with the option `--owner root:root`. This is a quick fix for the file ownership problem mentioned earlier in the *File ownership permissions in the staging directory* section. It makes everything in the cpio archive have a UID and GID of 0.

The final size of the uRamdisk file is about 1.9 MB, with no kernel modules. Add to that 9.8 MB for the kernel Image.gz file and 1,061 KB for U-Boot. This gives us a total of 13 MB of storage needed to boot this board. We are way off from the 1.44 MB floppy that started it all. If size is a real problem, then you can use one of these options:

- Make the kernel smaller by leaving out drivers and functions you don't need.
- Make BusyBox smaller by leaving out utilities you don't need.
- Use musl libc or uClibc-ng in place of glibc.
- Compile BusyBox statically.

Booting an initramfs

The simplest thing we can do is to run a shell on the console so that we can interact with the target. We can do that by adding rdinit=/bin/sh to the kernel command line. The next two sections demonstrate how to do that for both QEMU and the BeaglePlay.

Booting with QEMU

QEMU has a -initrd option to load an initramfs into memory. You should already have an Image file compiled with the aarch64-buildroot-linux-gnu toolchain from *Chapter 4*. From this chapter, you should have created an initramfs, which includes BusyBox compiled with the same toolchain. Now, you can launch QEMU using the script in MELD/Chapter05/run-qemu-initramfs.sh or this command:

```
$ cd ~
$ cd build_qemu
$ qemu-system-aarch64 -M virt -cpu cortex-a53 -nographic -smp 1 -kernel
arch/arm64/boot/Image -append "console=ttyAMA0 rdinit=/bin/sh" -initrd ~/
initramfs.cpio.gz
```

You should get a root shell with a # prompt.

Booting the BeaglePlay

For the BeaglePlay, we need the microSD card prepared in *Chapter 4*, plus a root filesystem built using the aarch64-buildroot-linux-gnu toolchain. Copy the uRamdisk you created earlier in this section to the boot partition on the microSD card. Boot the BeaglePlay to the point where you get a U-Boot prompt. Then, enter these commands:

```
nova!> fatload mmc 1 0x80000000 Image.gz
nova!> fatload mmc 1 0x82000000 k3-am625-beagleplay.dtb
nova!> setenv kernel_comp_addr_r 0x85000000
nova!> setenv kernel_comp_size 0x20000000
nova!> fatload mmc 1 0x83000000 uRamdisk
nova!> setenv bootargs console=ttyS2,115200n8 rdinit=/bin/sh
nova!> booti 0x80000000 0x83000000 0x82000000
```

If all goes well, you will get a root shell with a # prompt on the serial console. After this is done, we will need to mount proc on both platforms.

Mounting proc

You will find that the ps command does not work on either platform. This is because the proc filesystem has not been mounted yet. Try mounting it:

```
# mount -t proc proc /proc
```

Run ps again, and you will see the process listing.

As an improvement, let's write a shell script that mounts proc and anything else that needs to be done at bootup. Then, you can run this script instead of /bin/sh at boot. The following snippet illustrates how this works:

```
#!/bin/sh
/bin/mount -t proc proc /proc
# Other boot-time commands go here
/bin/sh
```

The /bin/sh on the last line launches a new shell that gives you an interactive root shell prompt. Using a shell as init in this way is very handy for quick hacks – for example, when you want to rescue a system with a broken init program. However, in most cases, you would use an init program, which we will cover in the next section of this chapter. Before that, I want to look at two other ways to load initramfs.

Building an initramfs into the kernel image

So far, we have created a compressed initramfs as a separate file and used the bootloader to load it into memory. Some bootloaders do not have the ability to load an initramfs file in this way. To cope with these situations, Linux can be configured to incorporate initramfs into the kernel image. To do this, change the kernel configuration and set CONFIG_INITRAMFS_SOURCE to the full path of the compressed initramfs.cpio.gz archive file you created earlier for your standalone initramfs. If you are using menuconfig, that field can be found in **General setup | Initramfs source file(s)**.

Once these changes have been made, build the kernel. Booting is the same as before, except there is no -initrd option and ramdisk file to pass in.

Enter this command for QEMU:

```
$ qemu-system-aarch64 -M virt -cpu cortex-a53 -nographic -smp 1 -kernel
arch/arm64/boot/Image -append "console=ttyAMA0 rdinit=/bin/sh"
```

For the BeaglePlay, enter these commands at the U-Boot prompt:

```
nova!> fatload mmc 1 0x80000000 Image.gz
nova!> fatload mmc 1 0x82000000 k3-am625-beagleplay.dtb
nova!> setenv kernel_comp_addr_r 0x85000000
nova!> setenv kernel_comp_size 0x20000000
nova!> setenv bootargs console=ttyS2,115200n8 rdinit=/bin/sh
nova!> booti 0x80000000 - 0x82000000
```

Remember to regenerate the `initramfs.cpio` archive, and recompress the `initramfs.cpio.gz` file each time you change the contents of your staging directory and then rebuild the kernel:

> **TIP**
>
> If you experience the following kernel panic on boot:
>
> ```
> [    0.549725] Run /bin/sh as init process
> [    0.573389] Kernel panic - not syncing: Attempted to kill
> init! exitcode=0x00000000
> [    0.573688] CPU: 0 PID: 1 Comm: sh Not tainted 6.6.46 #13
> …
> [    0.576075] ---[ end Kernel panic - not syncing:
> Attempted to kill init! exitcode=0x00000000 ]---
> ```
>
> Make sure that the dev/null and dev/console device nodes exist in your staging directory.

Building an initramfs using a device table

A **device table** is a text file that lists the files, directories, device nodes, and links that go into an archive or filesystem image. The overwhelming advantage is that it allows you to create entries in the archive file that are owned by the root user, or any other UID, without having root privileges yourself. You can even create device nodes without needing to have root privileges. All this is possible because the archive is just a data file. It is only when it is expanded by Linux at boot time that real files and directories get created using the attributes you specified.

The kernel has a feature that allows us to use a device table when creating an `initramfs`. You write the device table file and then point `CONFIG_INITRAMFS_SOURCE` at it. Then, when you build the kernel, it creates the cpio archive from the instructions in the device table. At no point do you need root access.

Here is a device table for our simple root filesystem. To make it manageable, it is missing most of the symbolic links to BusyBox:

```
dir /bin 775 0 0
dir /sys 775 0 0
dir /tmp 775 0 0
dir /dev 775 0 0
nod /dev/null 666 0 0 c 1 3
nod /dev/console 600 0 0 c 5 1
dir /home 775 0 0
dir /proc 775 0 0
dir /lib 775 0 0
file /lib/libm.so.6 /home/frank/rootfs/lib/libm.so.6 755 0 0
file /lib/libresolv.so.2 /home/frank/rootfs/lib/libresolv.so.2 755 0 0
file /lib/libc.so.6 /home/frank/rootfs/lib/libc.so.6 755 0 0
file /lib/ld-linux-aarch64.so.1 /home/frank/rootfs/lib/ld-linux-aarch64.
so.1 755 0 0
```

The syntax is fairly obvious:

- `dir <name> <mode> <uid> <gid>`
- `file <name> <location> <mode> <uid> <gid>`
- `nod <name> <mode> <uid> <gid> <dev_type> <maj> <min>`
- `slink <name> <target> <mode> <uid> <gid>`

The commands `dir`, `nod`, and `slink` create a filesystem object in the cpio archive with the name, mode, user ID, and group ID given. The `file` command copies the file from the source location into the archive and sets the mode, user ID, and group ID.

The task of creating an `initramfs.cpio` archive from scratch is made easier by a script found in the kernel source code, named `gen_initramfs.sh`. First, this script generates a device table from the contents of the input directory. Then, it translates this device table into the finished cpio archive.

To generate an `initramfs.cpio` archive from your `rootfs` directory and change the ownership of all files owned by user ID `1000` and group ID `1000` to user ID `0` and group ID `0`, enter these commands:

```
$ cd ~
$ cp build_qemu/usr/gen_init_cpio linux-stable/usr/.
$ cd linux-stable
$ usr/gen_initramfs.sh -o ~/initramfs.cpio -u 1000 -g 1000 ~/rootfs
```

Old initrd format

There is an older format for a Linux ramdisk known as initrd. It was the only format available before Linux 2.6 and is still needed if you are using uClinux, the MMU-less variant of Linux. It is pretty obscure, so I will not cover it here.

Once our initramfs boots, the system then needs to start running programs. The first program that runs is the init program.

init program

Running a shell or even a shell script at boot time is fine for simple cases, but really, you need something more flexible. Normally, Unix systems run a program called init that starts up and monitors other programs. Over the years, there have been many init programs, some of which I will describe in *Chapter 13*. For now, I will briefly introduce BusyBox init.

The init program begins by reading the /etc/inittab configuration file. Here is a simple example, which is adequate for our needs:

```
::sysinit:/etc/init.d/rcS
::askfirst:-/bin/ash
```

The first line runs a shell script named rcS when init is started. The second line prints the message **Please press Enter to activate this console** to the console and starts a shell when you press *Enter*. The leading - before /bin/ash means that it will become a login shell, which sources /etc/profile and $HOME/.profile before displaying the shell prompt.

One of the advantages of launching the shell like this is that job control is enabled. The most immediate effect is that you can use *Ctrl + C* to terminate the current program. Maybe you didn't notice it before, but wait until you run the ping program and find you can't stop it!

BusyBox init provides a default inittab if none is present in the root filesystem. It is a little more extensive than the preceding one.

The script called /etc/init.d/rcS is the place to put initialization commands that need to be performed at boot, like mounting the proc and sysfs filesystems:

```
#!/bin/sh
mount -t proc proc /proc
mount -t sysfs sysfs /sys
```

Make sure that you make the preceding rcS script executable like this:

```
$ cd ~/rootfs
$ chmod +x etc/init.d/rcS
```

You can try init out on QEMU by changing the -append parameter like this:

```
-append "console=ttyAMA0 rdinit=/sbin/init"
```

For the BeaglePlay, you need to set the bootargs variable in U-Boot as shown here:

```
nova!> setenv bootargs console=ttyS2,115200n8 rdinit=/sbin/init
```

Now, let's take a closer look at the inittab read by init during startup.

Starting a daemon process

Typically, you want to run certain background processes at startup. Take syslogd (the log daemon), for example. The purpose of syslogd is to accumulate log messages from other programs, mostly other daemons. Naturally, BusyBox has an applet for that!

Starting the daemon is as simple as adding a line like this to etc/inittab:

```
::respawn:/sbin/syslogd -n
```

respawn means that if the program terminates, it will be automatically restarted. -n means that it should run as a foreground process. The log is written to /var/log/messages.

> **IMPORTANT NOTE**
>
> You may also want to start klogd in the same way. klogd sends kernel log messages to syslogd so that they can be logged to permanent storage.

So far, all the processes I have mentioned run as root, but that is less than ideal.

Configuring user accounts

As I already said, it is bad practice to run all programs as root because if one program is compromised by an outside attack then the whole system is at risk. It is better to create unprivileged user accounts and use them where full root is not necessary.

Usernames are configured in /etc/passwd. There is one line per user with seven fields of information separated by colons. These are, in order:

- The login name
- The hash code used to verify the password or, more usually, an x to indicate that the password is stored in /etc/shadow
- The UID or user ID
- The GID or group ID
- The comment field (often left blank)
- The user's home directory
- The shell this user will use (optional)

Here is a simple example in which we have the user root with UID 0 and the user daemon with UID 1:

```
root:x:0:0:root:/root:/bin/sh
daemon:x:1:1:daemon:/usr/sbin:/bin/false
```

Setting the shell for the user daemon as /bin/false ensures that any attempt to log on with that name will fail.

Various programs have to read /etc/passwd to look up usernames and UIDs, so the file has to be world-readable. This is a problem if the password hashes are stored in there as well because a malicious program can take a copy and discover the actual passwords, using a variety of cracker programs. To reduce the exposure of this sensitive information, the passwords are stored in /etc/shadow, and x is placed in the password field to indicate that this is the case. The /etc/shadow file only needs to be accessed by root, so as long as the root user is not compromised, the passwords are safe.

The shadow password file consists of one entry per user, made up of nine fields. Here is an example that mirrors the password file shown in the preceding paragraph:

```
root::10933:0:99999:7:::
daemon:*:10933:0:99999:7:::
```

The first two fields are the username and the password hash. The remaining seven fields are related to password aging, which is usually not a concern on embedded devices. If you are curious about the full details, refer to the manual page for shadow(5).

In the example, the password for root is empty meaning that root can log on without providing a password. Having an empty password for root is useful during development but not for production. You can generate or change a password hash by running the passwd command on the target, which will write a new hash to /etc/shadow. If you want all subsequent root filesystems to have this same password, you could copy this file back to the staging directory.

Group names are stored similarly in /etc/group. There is one line per group, consisting of four fields separated by colons. The fields are:

- The name of the group
- The group password or, more usually, an x to indicate that there is no group password
- The GID or group ID
- A comma-separated list of users who belong to this group (optional)

Here is an example:

```
root:x:0:
daemon:x:1:
```

Adding user accounts to the root filesystem

First, add the files etc/passwd, etc/shadow, and etc/group to your staging directory, as shown in the preceding section. Make sure that the permissions of etc/shadow are 0600. Next, initiate the login procedure by starting a program called getty. There is a version of getty in BusyBox. You launch it from your inittab using the keyword respawn, which restarts getty when a login shell is terminated. Your inittab should read like this:

```
::sysinit:/etc/init.d/rcS
::respawn:/sbin/getty 115200 console
```

Then, rebuild the ramdisk, and try it out using QEMU or the BeaglePlay, as before.

Earlier in this chapter, we learned how to create device nodes using the mknod command. Now, let's look at some easier ways to create device nodes.

A better way of managing device nodes

Creating device nodes statically with mknod is hard work and inflexible. However, there are other ways to create device nodes automatically on demand:

- devtmpfs: This is a pseudo filesystem that you mount over /dev at boot time. The kernel populates it with device nodes for all the devices that the kernel currently knows about. The kernel also creates nodes for new devices as they are detected at runtime. The nodes are owned by root and have default permissions of 0600. Some well-known device nodes, such as /dev/null and /dev/random, override the default to 0666. To see exactly how this is done, look at the drivers/char/mem.c file in the Linux source tree and observe how struct memdev is initialized.

- mdev: This is a BusyBox applet that is used to populate a directory with device nodes and create new nodes as needed. There is an /etc/mdev.conf configuration file that contains rules for the ownership and mode of the nodes.

- udev: This is the mainstream equivalent of mdev. You will find it on desktop Linux and in some embedded devices. It is very flexible and a good choice for higher-end embedded devices. It is now part of systemd.

> **IMPORTANT NOTE**
>
> Although both mdev and udev create the device nodes themselves, it is easier to just let devtmpfs do the job and use mdev/udev as a layer on top to implement the policy for setting ownership and permissions. The devtmpfs approach is the only maintainable way to generate device nodes prior to user space startup.

After introducing devtmpfs, I will describe how mdev is used to assign ownership and permissions to device nodes on startup.

Using devtmpfs

Support for the devtmpfs filesystem is controlled by the CONFIG_DEVTMPFS kernel configuration variable. It is not enabled in the default configuration of the 64-bit Arm generic virtual platform, so if you want to try devtmpfs out on QEMU, you will have to go back to your kernel configuration and enable this option.

Enter this command to mount devtmpfs:

```
# mount -t devtmpfs devtmpfs /dev
```

You will notice that there are many more device nodes in /dev afterward. To mount devtmpfs on startup, add the preceding command to /etc/init.d/rcS:

```
#!/bin/sh
mount -t proc proc /proc
mount -t sysfs sysfs /sys
mount -t devtmpfs devtmpfs /dev
```

If you enable CONFIG_DEVTMPFS_MOUNT in your kernel configuration, the kernel will automatically mount devtmpfs just after mounting the root filesystem. However, this option has no effect when booting initramfs, as we are doing here.

Using mdev

While mdev is a bit more complex to set up, it does allow you to modify the permissions of device nodes as they are created. You begin by running mdev with the -s option, which causes it to scan the /sys directory looking for information about current devices. From this information, it populates the /dev directory with the corresponding nodes.

If you want to keep track of new devices coming online and create nodes for them as well, you need to make mdev a hot plug client by writing to /proc/sys/kernel/hotplug. Add two more lines to /etc/init.d/rcS:

```
#!/bin/sh
mount -t proc proc /proc
mount -t sysfs sysfs /sys
mount -t devtmpfs devtmpfs /dev
echo /sbin/mdev > /proc/sys/kernel/hotplug
mdev -s
```

The default mode is 660 and the ownership is root:root. You can change this by adding rules in /etc/mdev.conf. For example, to give the null, random, and urandom devices their correct modes, you would add this to /etc/mdev.conf:

```
null root:root 666
random root:root 444
urandom root:root 444
```

The format is documented in the BusyBox source code in docs/mdev.txt, and there are more examples in the directory named examples.

Are static device nodes so bad after all?

Statically created device nodes have one advantage over running a device manager: they don't take any time to create during boot. If minimizing boot time is a priority, then using statically created device nodes will save a measurable amount of time.

Configuring the network

Next, let's look at some basic network configurations so that we can communicate with the outside world. I assume that there is an Ethernet interface (eth0) and that we only need a simple IPv4 configuration.

These examples use the network utilities that are part of BusyBox, which are sufficient for our simple use case. All we need are the old-but-reliable ifup and ifdown programs. You can read the manual pages for both to get the details. The main network configuration is stored in /etc/network/interfaces. You will need to create these directories in the staging directory:

```
etc/network
etc/network/if-pre-up.d
etc/network/if-up.d
var/run
```

Here is /etc/network/interfaces for a static IP address:

```
auto lo
iface lo inet loopback

auto eth0
iface eth0 inet static
    address 192.168.1.101
    netmask 255.255.255.0
    network 192.168.1.0
```

Here is /etc/network/interfaces for a dynamic IP address, allocated using DHCP:

```
auto lo
iface lo inet loopback

auto eth0
iface eth0 inet dhcp
```

You also need to configure a DHCP client program. BusyBox has one named udchpcd. It requires a shell script that goes in /usr/share/udhcpc/default.script. There is a suitable default at examples/udhcp/simple.script within the BusyBox source code.

Network components for glibc

glibc uses a mechanism known as the **name service switch** (**NSS**) to control the way that names are resolved to numbers for networking and users. Usernames can be resolved to UIDs via the /etc/passwd file, and network services such as HTTP can be resolved to service port numbers via /etc/services. All this is configured by /etc/nsswitch.conf; see the nss(5) manual page for full details. Here is a simple example that will suffice for most embedded Linux implementations:

```
passwd:     files
group:      files
shadow:     files
hosts:      files dns
networks:   files
protocols:  files
services:   files
```

Everything is resolved by the correspondingly named file in /etc, except for host names, which can be resolved by a DNS lookup if they are not in /etc/hosts.

To make this work, you need to populate /etc with those files. Networks, protocols, and services are the same across all Linux systems, so they can be copied from /etc on your development machine. At the very least, /etc/hosts should contain the loopback address:

```
127.0.0.1 localhost
```

The other files (passwd, group, and shadow) were described in the *Configuring user accounts* section earlier.

The last piece of the puzzle is the libraries that perform the name resolution. They are plugins that are loaded as needed, based on the contents of nsswitch.conf. That means they do not show up as dependencies when you use readelf or ldd. You will simply have to copy them from the toolchain's sysroot:

```
$ cd ~/rootfs
$ cp -a $SYSROOT/lib/libnss* lib
$ cp -a $SYSROOT/lib/libresolv* lib
```

At last, our staging directory is complete. Let's generate a filesystem from it.

Creating filesystem images with device tables

We saw in the earlier *Creating a boot initramfs* section that the kernel has the option to create initramfs, using a device table. Device tables are really useful because they allow a non-root user to create device nodes and allocate arbitrary UID and GID values to any file or directory. The same concept has been applied to tools that create other filesystem image formats, as shown in this mapping from the filesystem format to tool:

- **jffs2**: mkfs.jffs2
- **ubifs**: mkfs:ubifs
- **ext2**: genext2fs

We will cover jffs2 and ubifs in *Chapter 9*, when we look at filesystems for flash memory. ext2 is a format commonly used for managed flash memory, including SD cards. The example that follows uses ext2 to create a disk image that can be copied to an SD card.

To begin with, you need to install the genext2fs tool on your host. On Ubuntu, the package to install is named genext2fs:

```
$ sudo apt install genext2fs
```

genext2fs takes a device table file with the format <name> <type> <mode> <uid> <gid> <major> <minor> <start> <inc> <count>. The meanings of the fields are as follows:

- **name**
- **type**: one of the following:
- f: regular file
- d: directory
- c: character device file
- b: block device file
- p: FIFO (named pipe)
- **uid**: UID of the file
- **gid**: GID of the file
- **major** and **minor**: device numbers (device nodes only)
- **start**, **inc**, and **count**: allows you to create a group of device nodes starting from the minor number in start (device nodes only)

You do not have to specify these for every file as you do with the kernel `initramfs` table. You just need to point at a directory—the staging directory—and list the changes and exceptions you need to make in the final filesystem image.

Here is a simple example that populates static device nodes for us:

```
/dev d 755 0 0 - - - - -
/dev/null c 666 0 0 1 3 0 0 -
/dev/console c 600 0 0 5 1 0 0 -
/dev/ttyO0 c 600 0 0 252 0 0 0 -
```

Then, you can use `genext2fs` to generate a filesystem image of 8 MB (8,192 blocks of the default size, 1,024 bytes):

```
$ cd ~
$ genext2fs -b 8192 -d ~/rootfs -D ~/MELD/Chapter05/device-tables.txt -U
rootfs.ext2
```

Now, you can copy the resulting `rootfs.ext2` image to an SD card or similar, as we will do next.

Booting the BeaglePlay

The script named `MELD/format-sdcard.sh` creates two partitions on the microSD card: one for the boot files and one for the root filesystem. Assuming you have created the root filesystem image, as shown in the previous section, you can use the `dd` command to write it to the second partition.

> **IMPORTANT NOTE**
>
> As always, when copying files directly to storage devices like this, make absolutely sure that you know which device is the microSD card.

In this case, I am using a built-in card reader, which is the device called `/dev/mmcblk0`, so the command is:

```
$ sudo dd if=rootfs.ext2 of=/dev/mmcblk0p2
```

Note that the card reader on your host system may have a different name.

Insert the microSD card into the BeaglePlay and set the kernel command line to root=/dev/ mmcblk1p2. Unlike previous Beagles, the eMMC is the mmcblk0 device and the microSD is the mmcblk1 device on the BeaglePlay. Here is the complete sequence of U-Boot commands:

```
nova!> fatload mmc 1 0x80000000 Image.gz
nova!> fatload mmc 1 0x82000000 k3-am625-beagleplay.dtb
nova!> setenv kernel_comp_addr_r 0x85000000
nova!> setenv kernel_comp_size 0x20000000
nova!> setenv bootargs console=ttyS2,115200n8 root=/dev/mmcblk1p2
rootdelay=5 rootwait
nova!> booti 0x80000000 - 0x82000000
```

This is an example of mounting an ext2 filesystem from a normal block device, such as an SD card. The same principles apply to other filesystem types. We will look at these in more detail when we get to *Chapter 9*. Now, let's switch gears and look at how to mount a filesystem over a network.

Mounting the root filesystem using NFS

If your device has a network interface, you can mount the root filesystem over the network for rapid development using **Network File System (NFS)**. This gives you access to almost unlimited storage on your host machine, so you can add debug tools and executables with large symbol tables. As a bonus, updates made to the root filesystem on your development machine are available on the target instantly. You can also access all the target's log files from the host.

To start, you need to install and configure an NFS server on your host machine. The package to install on Ubuntu is named nfs-kernel-server:

```
$ sudo apt install nfs-kernel-server
```

The NFS server needs to be told which directories are being exported to the network. This is controlled by /etc/exports. There is one line for each export. The format is described in the exports(5) manual page. To export the root filesystem, the exports file on my host contains this:

```
/home/frank/rootfs *(rw,sync,no_subtree_check,no_root_squash)
```

* exports the directory to any address on my local network. If you wish, you can specify a single IP address or a range at this point. A list of options enclosed in parentheses follows. There must not be any spaces between * and the opening parenthesis. The options are:

- rw: Exports the directory as read-write.
- sync: Selects the synchronous version of the NFS protocol, which is more robust but a little slower than the async option.

- no_subtree_check: Disables subtree checking, which has mild security implications but can improve reliability in some circumstances.

- no_root_squash: Allows requests from user ID 0 to be processed without squashing to a different user ID. It is necessary for the target to correctly access the files owned by root.

Having made changes to /etc/exports, restart the NFS server to pick them up:

```
$ sudo systemctl restart nfs-kernel-server
```

Now, set up the target to mount the root filesystem over NFS. For this to work, configure your kernel with CONFIG_ROOT_NFS. Then, configure Linux to do the mount at boot time by adding the following to the kernel command line:

```
root=/dev/nfs rw nfsroot=<host-ip>:<root-dir> ip=<target-ip>
```

The options are:

- rw: Mounts the root filesystem read-write.

- nfsroot: Specifies the IP address of the host, followed by the path to the exported root filesystem.

- ip: This is the IP address to be assigned to the target. Usually, network addresses are assigned at runtime, as we saw in the *Configuring the network* section. However, in this case, the interface has to be configured before the root filesystem is mounted and init has started. Hence, it is configured on the kernel command line.

> **IMPORTANT NOTE**
>
> There is more information about NFS root mounts in the kernel source in Documentation/admin-guide/nfs/nfsroot.rst.

Testing with the BeaglePlay

Boot your BeaglePlay from the microSD card and enter these commands at the U-Boot prompt:

```
nova!> setenv serverip 192.168.1.119
nova!> setenv ipaddr 192.168.1.176
nova!> setenv npath <path to staging directory>
nova!> setenv bootargs console=ttyS2,115200n8 root=/dev/nfs
ip=${ipaddr}:::::eth0 nfsroot=${serverip}:${npath},nfsvers=3,tcp rw
nova!> fatload mmc 1 0x80000000 Image.gz
nova!> fatload mmc 1 0x82000000 k3-am625-beagleplay.dtb
```

```
nova!> setenv kernel_comp_addr_r 0x85000000
nova!> setenv kernel_comp_size 0x20000000
nova!> booti 0x80000000 - 0x82000000
```

Replace <path to staging directory> with the full path to your staging directory, and change the serverip and ipaddr values to match the IP addresses of your Linux host and BeaglePlay. Make sure that the BeaglePlay can ping the serverip before attempting this exercise.

Problems with file permissions

The files that you copied into the staging directory will be owned by the UID of the user you are logged on as (typically 1000). However, the target has no knowledge of this user. What's more, any files created by the target will be owned by users configured by the target (often the root user). The whole thing is a mess. Unfortunately, there is no simple way out.

The best solution is to make a copy of the staging directory and change ownership to UID and GID to 0, using the command sudo chown -R 0:0 *. Then, export this directory as the NFS mount. This removes the convenience of having just one copy of the root filesystem shared between development and target systems, but at least the file ownership will be correct.

It's not uncommon in embedded Linux to link device drivers statically to the kernel, rather than load them dynamically from the root filesystem as modules at runtime. So how do we reap the same benefits of rapid iteration provided by NFS when modifying kernel source code or DTBs? The answer is TFTP.

Using TFTP to load the kernel

Now that we know how to mount the root filesystem over a network using NFS, you may be wondering if there is a way to load the kernel, device tree, and initramfs over the network as well. If we can do this, then the only component that needs to be written to storage on the target is the bootloader. Everything else could be loaded from the host machine. This would save time, since you would not need to keep reflashing the target. You could even get work done while the flash storage drivers are still being developed (it happens).

The **Trivial File Transfer Protocol (TFTP)** is the answer. TFTP is a very simple file transfer protocol that is designed for easy implementation with bootloaders such as U-Boot.

To start, you need to install a TFTP daemon on your host machine. The package to install on Ubuntu is named `tftpd-hpa`:

```
$ sudo apt install tftpd-hpa
```

Modify the contents of `/etc/default/tftpd-hpa` as shown:

```
TFTP_USERNAME="tftp"
TFTP_DIRECTORY="/var/lib/tftpboot"
TFTP_ADDRESS="0.0.0.0:69"
TFTP_OPTIONS="--secure"
```

Create the `/var/lib/tftpboot` directory with the necessary ownership and permissions:

```
$ sudo mkdir -p /var/lib/tftpboot
$ sudo chown -R nobody:nogroup /var/lib/tftpboot
$ sudo chmod -R 777 /var/lib/tftpboot
```

Having made changes to `/etc/default/tftpd-hpa`, restart the TFTP server to pick them up:

```
$ sudo systemctl restart tftpd-hpa
```

With `tftpd-hpa` installed and running, copy the files you want loaded on the target to `/var/lib/tftpboot`. For the BeaglePlay, these would be `Image` and `k3-am625-beagleplay.dtb`:

```
$ cd ~
$ cp build_beagleplay/arch/arm64/boot/Image /var/lib/tftpboot/.
$ cp build_beagleplay/arch/arm64/boot/dts/ti/k3-am625-beagleplay.dtb /var/
lib/tftpboot/.
```

Then, enter these commands at the U-Boot prompt:

```
nova!> setenv serverip 192.168.1.119
nova!> setenv ipaddr 192.168.1.176
nova!> setenv npath <path to staging directory>
nova!> tftp 0x80000000 Image
nova!> tftp 0x82000000 k3-am625-beagleplay.dtb
nova!> setenv bootargs console=ttyS2,115200n8 root=/dev/nfs
ip=${ipaddr}:::::eth0 nfsroot=${serverip}:${npath},nfsvers=3,tcp rw
nova!> booti 0x80000000 - 0x82000000
```

Replace <path to staging directory> with the full path to your staging directory, and change the serverip and ipaddr values to match the IP addresses of your Linux host and BeaglePlay. You may find that the tftp command hangs endlessly, printing out the letter T, which means that the TFTP requests time out. There are a number of reasons why this happens. The most common ones are:

- An incorrect IP address for serverip
- The TFTP daemon is not running on the server.
- The firewall on the server is blocking the TFTP protocol. Most firewalls block TFTP port 69 by default.

Once you have resolved the connectivity problem, U-Boot loads the files from the host machine and boots in the usual way.

Summary

One of the strengths of Linux is that it supports a variety of root filesystems, so it can be tailored for a wide range of needs. We have seen how it is possible to construct a simple root filesystem manually with just a small number of components. BusyBox is especially useful in this regard.

By going through the process one step at a time, we gained insight into some of the basic workings of Linux systems, including network configuration and user accounts. However, the task rapidly becomes unmanageable as devices get more complex. Plus, there is the ever-present worry that there may be a security hole in the implementation that we did not notice.

In the next chapter, I will show you how using an embedded build system can make the process of creating an embedded Linux system much easier and more reliable. I will start by looking at Buildroot and then go on to look at the more complex, yet powerful, Yocto Project.

Further study

- *Filesystem Hierarchy Standard, Version 3.0*: https://refspecs.linuxfoundation.org/fhs.shtml
- *Ramfs, rootfs and initramfs*, by Rob Landley, part of the Linux source at Documentation/filesystems/ramfs-rootfs-initramfs.rst

Join our community on Discord

Join our community's Discord space for discussions with the authors and other readers: `https://packt.link/embeddedsystems`

Part 2

Building Embedded Linux Images

This part is meant to help you set up your development environment and create a working platform for the later phases. You will learn how to automate the process of generating a bootable image by leveraging an embedded Linux build system, either Buildroot or The Yocto Project. Automating complex build tasks accelerates the project life cycle so that teams can deliver higher-quality products in less time. The section ends with in-depth coverage of The Yocto Project.

This part has the following chapters:

- *Chapter 6, Selecting a Build System*
- *Chapter 7, Developing with Yocto*
- *Chapter 8, Yocto under the Hood*

6

Selecting a Build System

The preceding chapters covered the first four elements of embedded Linux. You built a bootloader, kernel, and root filesystem step by step before combining them into a basic embedded Linux system. That's a lot of steps! Now it is time to simplify the process by automating as much of it as possible. Embedded Linux build systems can help, and we will look at two in particular: Buildroot and The Yocto Project. Both are complex tools that require an entire book to explain how they work.

In this chapter I will only present the general ideas behind build systems, laying the groundwork for *Chapters 7* and *8*. First, I will show you how to build a simple image to get an overall feel for the system. Then, I will show you how to make some useful modifications to the Nova board and Raspberry Pi 4 examples from the previous chapters. In subsequent chapters, we will dive deeper into The Yocto Project, now the preeminent build system for embedded Linux.

In this chapter we will cover the following topics:

- Comparing build systems
- Distributing binaries
- Introducing Buildroot
- Introducing The Yocto Project

Technical requirements

To follow along with the examples, make sure you have the following:

- An Ubuntu 24.04 or later LTS host system with at least 90 GB of free disk space
- A microSD card reader and card
- balenaEtcher for Linux

- An Ethernet cable and router with an available port for network connectivity
- A USB-to-TTL serial cable with a 3.3 V logic level
- Raspberry Pi 4
- BeaglePlay
- A 5 V USB-C power supply capable of delivering 3A

The code used in this chapter can be found in the chapter folder in this book's GitHub repository: `https://github.com/PacktPublishing/Mastering-Embedded-Linux-Development/tree/main/Chapter06`.

Comparing build systems

In *Chapter 5*, I described the process of creating an image manually as the **Roll Your Own (RYO)** process. This approach gives you complete control over the software so that you can tailor it to do anything you like. If you want to do something truly odd but innovative, or if you want to reduce the memory footprint to the smallest size possible, then RYO is the way to go. But in most situations, building manually is a waste of time and produces inferior, unmaintainable systems.

The idea behind a build system is to automate all the steps described up to this point. A build system should be able to build some or all of the following from upstream source code:

- toolchain
- bootloader
- kernel
- root filesystem

Building from upstream source code is important for several reasons. It gives you the peace of mind that you can rebuild at any time without external dependencies. It also means you can debug at the source level and meet your license requirements to distribute the code to users where necessary.

To do its job, a build system must be able to:

- Download the source code from upstream, either directly from the version control system or as an archive, and cache it locally.
- Apply patches to enable cross-compilation, fix architecture-dependent bugs, apply local configuration policies, and so on.
- Build the various components along with their compile-time and runtime dependencies.
- Create a staging area and assemble a root filesystem.

- Create image files in various formats ready to be loaded onto the target.

Some other useful things are:

- Add your own packages containing applications or kernel changes.

- Select various root filesystem profiles: large or small, with or without graphics, and other features.

- Create a standalone SDK that you can distribute to other developers so they don't have to install the complete build system.

- Track which open source licenses are used by the various packages you selected.

- Have a friendly user interface.

In all cases, build systems encapsulate the components of a system into packages, some for the host and some for the target. Each package defines a set of rules to get the source, build it, and install the results in the correct location. There are dependencies between packages and a mechanism to resolve the dependencies and build the set of packages required.

Open source build systems have matured over the past few years. There are many around, including:

- **Buildroot**: Is an easy-to-use system using GNU Make and Kconfig (`https://buildroot.org/`).

- **OpenEmbedded**: Is a powerful system and a core component of Yocto (`https://openembedded.org`).

- **OpenWrt**: Is a build tool oriented toward building firmware for wireless routers (`https://openwrt.org/`) that supports runtime package management out of the box. It is a derivative of Buildroot.

- **PTXdist**: Is an open source build system sponsored by Pengutronix (`https://www.ptxdist.org/`).

- **Yocto**: Extends the OpenEmbedded core with metadata, tools, and documentation. It is the most popular embedded Linux build system today (`https://www.yoctoproject.org/`).

I will concentrate on two of them: Buildroot and Yocto. They approach the problem in different ways and with different objectives.

Buildroot has the primary aim of building root filesystem images, hence the name. But it can build bootloaders, kernels, and even toolchains as well. It is easy to install and configure. Most importantly, Buildroot generates target images quickly.

Yocto is more general in how it defines the target system, so it can build more complex embedded devices. Every component is generated as a binary package by default using the RPM format. Packages are then combined to make the filesystem image. You can install a package manager in the filesystem image that allows you to update packages at runtime. In other words, when you build with Yocto, you are creating your own custom Linux distribution. Bear in mind that enabling runtime package management also means provisioning and running your own corresponding package feed repository.

Distributing binaries

Mainstream Linux distributions are in most cases constructed from collections of binary (precompiled) packages in either RPM or DEB format. **RPM** stands for **Red Hat Package Manager** and is used in Red Hat, SUSE, Fedora, and other RPM-based distributions. Debian and Debian-derived distributions, including Ubuntu and Mint, use the **Debian package manager (DEB)** format. There is also a lightweight format for embedded devices known as the **Itsy package (IPK)** format, which is based on DEB.

The ability to include a package manager on the device is one of the big differentiators between build systems. Once you have a package manager on the target device, you have an easy path to deploy new packages and to update the existing ones. I will talk about the implications of this in *Chapter 10*.

Now for the main event. We will start with Buildroot. As the simpler of the two build systems, Buildroot is easier to get started with than Yocto and the quickest way of generating a bootable image for all three of our targets.

Introducing Buildroot

The current versions of Buildroot can build a toolchain, a bootloader, a kernel, and a root filesystem. Buildroot uses GNU Make as its principal build tool. There is good online documentation at https://buildroot.org/docs.html along with *The Buildroot user manual* at https://buildroot.org/downloads/manual/manual.html.

Background

Buildroot was one of the first build systems. It began when the uClinux and uClibc projects needed a way to generate a small root filesystem for testing. Buildroot became a separate project in late 2001 and continued to evolve through 2006, after which it went into a dormant phase.

However, since Peter Korsgaard took over stewardship in 2009, it has been developing rapidly, adding support for glibc-based toolchains and a greatly increased number of packages and target boards. Peter is still the lead maintainer of Buildroot and has had a long and illustrious career as a software engineer at Barco in Belgium.

Buildroot is the ancestor of OpenWrt, another popular build system that forked from Buildroot around 2004. The primary focus of OpenWrt is to produce software for wireless routers so the package mix is oriented toward networking infrastructure. It also has a runtime IPK package manager so that a device can be updated or upgraded without a complete reflash of the image. Buildroot and OpenWrt have diverged to such an extent that they are now almost completely different build systems. Packages built with one are not compatible with the other.

Stable releases and long-term support

The Buildroot developers produce stable releases four times a year in February, May, August, and November. They are marked by Git tags of the form `<year>.02`, `<year>.05`, `<year>.08`, and `<year>.11`. Each `<year>.02` release is marked for **Long-Term Support (LTS)**, which means there will be point releases to fix security and other important bugs for 12 months after the initial release. The `2017.02` release is the first to receive the LTS label.

Installing

You install Buildroot either by cloning the repository or downloading an archive. Here is an example of obtaining version `2024.02.6`, which was the latest stable version at the time of writing:

```
$ git clone git://git.buildroot.net/buildroot -b 2024.02.6
```

The equivalent TAR archive is available at `https://buildroot.org/downloads/`.

Read the section titled *System requirements* in *The Buildroot user manual*, available at `https://buildroot.org/downloads/manual/manual.html`, and make sure to install all the packages listed there.

Configuring

Buildroot uses the kernel Kconfig/Kbuild mechanism I described in the *Understanding kernel configuration* section from *Chapter 4*. You can configure Buildroot from scratch directly using `make menuconfig` (`xconfig` or `gconfig`). Or you can choose one of the 100+ configurations for various development boards that you can find stored in the `configs` directory. Typing `make list-defconfigs` lists all the default configurations.

Let's begin by building a default configuration that you can run on the 64-bit Arm QEMU emulator:

```
$ cd buildroot
$ make qemu_aarch64_virt_defconfig
$ make
```

IMPORTANT NOTE

Do not tell GNU Make how many parallel jobs to run with the -j option. Buildroot will make optimum use of your CPU cores all by itself. If you want to limit the number of jobs, then run make menuconfig and look for **Number of jobs to run simultaneously** under **Build options**.

The build can take up to an hour depending on how many CPU cores your host system has and the speed of your internet. It will download approximately 502 MB of code and consume about 12 GB of disk space. When it completes, you will find two new directories have been created:

- dl: Contains archives of the upstream projects that Buildroot has built.
- output: Contains all the intermediate and final compiled artifacts.

Inside output you will find the following subdirectories:

- build: Contains the build directory for each component.
- host: Contains various tools required by Buildroot on the host, including the executables of the toolchain (in output/host/usr/bin).
- images: Contains the finished results of the build. Depending on what you selected when configuring, you will find a bootloader, a kernel, and one or more root filesystem images.
- staging: Is a symbolic link to the sysroot of the toolchain. The name of the link is a little confusing because it does not point to a staging area as defined in *Chapter 5*.
- target: Is the staging area for the root directory. Note that you cannot use it as a root filesystem because the file ownership and permissions are not set correctly. Buildroot uses a device table as described in the previous chapter to set ownership and permissions when the filesystem image is created in the image directory.

Running

Some of the sample targets have a subfolder in the board directory containing custom configuration files and informationon how to install the results.

In the case of the system you just built, the relevant file is board/qemu/aarch64-virt/readme.txt. This readme.txt file tells you how to start QEMU with this target. Assuming you have already installed qemu-system-aarch64 as described in *Chapter 1*, you can run QEMU with this command:

```
$ qemu-system-aarch64 -M virt -cpu cortex-a53 -nographic -smp 1 -kernel
output/images/Image -append "rootwait root=/dev/vda console=ttyAMA0"
-netdev user,id=eth0 -device virtio-net-device,netdev=eth0 -drive
file=output/images/rootfs.ext4,if=none,format=raw,id=hd0 -device virtio-
blk-device,drive=hd0
```

There is a script named start-qemu.sh in output/images that includes the command. When QEMU boots up, you should see the kernel boot messages appear in the same terminal window where you started QEMU followed by a login prompt:

```
Booting Linux on physical CPU 0x0000000000 [0x410fd034]
Linux version 6.1.44 (frank@frank-nuc) (aarch64-buildroot-linux-gnu-gcc.
br_real (Buildroot 2024.02.6) 12.4.0, GNU ld (GNU Binutils) 2.40) #1 SMP
Wed Oct  9 21:24:21 PDT 2024
random: crng init done
Machine model: linux,dummy-virt
efi: UEFI not found.
<...>
VFS: Mounted root (ext4 filesystem) readonly on device 254:0.
devtmpfs: mounted
Freeing unused kernel memory: 1280K
Run /sbin/init as init process
EXT4-fs (vda): re-mounted. Quota mode: disabled.
Saving 256 bits of creditable seed for next boot
Starting syslogd: OK
Starting klogd: OK
Running sysctl: OK
Starting network: udhcpc: started, v1.36.1
udhcpc: broadcasting discover
udhcpc: broadcasting select for 10.0.2.15, server 10.0.2.2
udhcpc: lease of 10.0.2.15 obtained from 10.0.2.2, lease time 86400
deleting routers
adding dns 10.0.2.3
OK
```

```
Welcome to Buildroot
buildroot login:
```

Log in as root with no password.

To exit QEMU type *Ctrl + A* and then *x*.

Targeting real hardware

The steps for configuring and building a bootable image for Raspberry Pi 4 are almost the same as for 64-bit Arm QEMU:

```
$ cd buildroot
$ make clean
$ make raspberrypi4_64_defconfig
$ make
```

The finished image is written to a file named output/images/sdcard.img. The post-image.sh script and the genimage.cfg.in configuration file used to write the image file are both located in the board/raspberrypi4-64 directory. To write sdcard.img onto a microSD card and boot it on your Raspberry Pi 4:

1. Insert a microSD card into your Linux host machine.
2. Launch balenaEtcher.
3. Click **Flash from file** from Etcher.
4. Locate the sdcard.img image that you built for Raspberry Pi 4 and open it.
5. Click **Select target** from Etcher.
6. Select the microSD card that you inserted in *step 1*.
7. Click **Flash** from Etcher to write the image.
8. Eject the microSD card when Etcher is done flashing.
9. Insert the microSD card into your Raspberry Pi 4.
10. Apply power to Raspberry Pi 4 by way of the USB-C port.

Confirm that your Raspberry Pi 4 booted successfully by plugging it into Ethernet and observing that the network activity lights blink. This default image is very minimal and includes little else besides BusyBox. To SSH into your Raspberry Pi 4, you will need to add an SSH server like dropbear or openssh to your Buildroot image configuration.

Creating a custom BSP

Now let's use Buildroot to create a **Board Support Package** (**BSP**) for our Nova board using the same versions of U-Boot and Linux from earlier chapters. You can see the changes I made to Buildroot during this section of the book under MELD/Chapter06/buildroot.

The recommended places to store your changes are:

- board/<organization>/<device>: Contains any patches, blobs, extra build steps, and configuration files for Linux, U-Boot, and other components
- configs/<device>_defconfig: Contains the default configuration for the board
- package/<organization>/<package_name>: Is the place to put any additional packages for this board

Create a directory to store changes to the Nova board:

```
$ mkdir -p board/meld/nova
```

Copy nova_defconfig from MELD/Chapter06/buildroot/configs to buildroot/configs:

```
$ cp ../MELD/Chapter06/buildroot/configs/nova_defconfig configs/.
```

Copy the contents of MELD/Chapter06/buildroot/board/meld/nova to buildroot/board/meld/nova:

```
$ cp ../MELD/Chapter06/buildroot/board/meld/nova/* board/meld/nova/.
```

Clean the artifacts from any previous build (always do this when changing configurations):

```
$ make clean
```

Select the Nova configuration:

```
$ make nova_defconfig
```

The make nova_defconfig command configures Buildroot to build an image targeting the BeaglePlay. This configuration is a good starting point, but we still need to customize it for our Nova board. Let's start by selecting the custom U-Boot patch we created for Nova.

U-Boot

In *Chapter 3*, we created a custom bootloader for Nova based on the f036fb version of TI's U-Boot fork and created a patch file for it saved as MELD/Chapter03/0001-BSP-for-Nova.patch. We can configure Buildroot to select the same version of U-Boot and apply our patch. Running make nova_defconfig already set the U-Boot version to f036fb.

Copy the patch file into board/meld/nova:

```
$ cp ../MELD/Chapter03/0001-BSP-for-Nova.patch board/meld/nova/.
```

Now run make menuconfig and drill down into the **Bootloaders** page. From that page, navigate down to **Custom U-Boot patches** and verify the path to our patch as shown:

```
/home/frank/buildroot/.config - Buildroot 2024.02.6 Configuration
 → Bootloaders
                              Bootloaders
     Arrow keys navigate the menu.  <Enter> selects submenus ---> (or empty
     submenus ----).  Highlighted letters are hotkeys.  Pressing <Y>
     selects a feature, while <N> excludes a feature.  Press <Esc><Esc> to
     exit, <?> for Help, </> for Search.  Legend: [*] feature is selected

         [*] ti-k3-r5-loader
                 U-Boot Version (2022.10)  --->
                 U-Boot Configuration (Using an in-tree board defconfig file
         (am62x_evm_r5) Board defconfig
         [*] U-Boot
                 Build system (Kconfig)  --->
                 U-Boot Version (Custom version)  --->
         (2024.04) U-Boot version
         (board/meld/nova/0001-BSP-for-Nova.patch) Custom U-Boot patches
                 U-Boot configuration (Using an in-tree board defconfig file
         (am62x_evm_a53) Board defconfig
         ()      Additional configuration fragment files
         [*]     U-Boot needs dtc


         <Select>     < Exit >     < Help >     < Save >     < Load >
```

Figure 6.1 – Selecting custom U-Boot patches

Now that we've patched U-Boot for our Nova board, the next step is patching the kernel.

Linux

In *Chapter 4,* we based the kernel on Linux 6.6.46 and supplied a new device tree from MELD/ Chapter04/nova.dts. Running make nova_defconfig already set the kernel version to Linux 6.6.46 and changed the kernel series used for kernel headers to match the kernel being built. Back out of the **Bootloaders** page and drill down into the **Kernel** page. Confirm that the value of **Out-of-tree Device Tree Source file paths** is set to board/meld/nova/nova.dts:

```
/home/frank/buildroot/.config - Buildroot 2024.02.6 Configuration
 → Kernel
                              Kernel
   Arrow keys navigate the menu. <Enter> selects submenus ---> (or empty
   submenus ----).  Highlighted letters are hotkeys.  Pressing <Y> selects a
   feature, while <N> excludes a feature.  Press <Esc><Esc> to exit, <?> for
   Help, </> for Search.  Legend: [*] feature is selected   [ ] feature is

        [*] Linux Kernel
               Kernel version (Custom version)  --->
        (6.6.46) Kernel version
        ()     Custom kernel patches
               Kernel configuration (Using a custom (def)config file)  --->
        (board/meld/nova/linux.config) Configuration file path
        ()     Additional configuration fragment files
        ()     Custom boot logo file path
               Kernel binary format (Image.gz)  --->
               Kernel compression format (gzip compression)  --->
        [*]    Build a Device Tree Blob (DTB)
        [ ]      DTB is built by kernel itself
        (ti/k3-am625-beagleplay) In-tree Device Tree Source file names
        (board/meld/nova/nova.dts) Out-of-tree Device Tree Source file paths
        [ ]      Keep the directory name of the Device Tree
        [ ]      Build Device Tree with overlay support
        [*]    Install kernel image to /boot in target
        [ ]    Needs host OpenSSL

            <Select>    < Exit >    < Help >    < Save >    < Load >
```

Figure 6.2 – Selecting the device tree source

Now that we've defined the device tree, let's build the system image complete with the kernel and root filesystem.

Build

In the last stage of the build, Buildroot uses a tool named genimage to create an image for the microSD that we can copy directly to the card. We need a configuration file to lay out the image in the right way. Modify the existing board/meld/nova/genimage.cfg file by replacing "k3-am625-beagleplay.dtb" with "nova.dtb" as shown:

```
image boot.vfat {
            vfat {
                        files = {
                                    "tiboot3.bin",
                                    "tispl.bin",
```

```
                                                    "u-boot.img",
                                                    "Image.gz",
                                                    "nova.dtb",  // HERE
                                }
                        }

                        size = 16M
        }

image sdcard.img {
                hdimage {
                }

                partition u-boot {
                                partition-type = 0xC
                                bootable = "true"
                                image = "boot.vfat"
                }

                partition rootfs {
                                partition-type = 0x83
                                image = "rootfs.ext4"
                }
        }
```

This will create a file named sdcard.img, which contains two partitions named u-boot and rootfs.
The first contains the boot files listed in boot.vfat and the second contains the root filesystem
image named rootfs.ext4, which will be generated by Buildroot.

Finally, we need a post-image.sh script that will call genimage and create the microSD card
image. See board/meld/nova/post-image.sh:

```
#!/bin/sh
BOARD_DIR="$(dirname $0)"

cp ${BUILD_DIR}/ti-k3-r5-loader-2022.10/tiboot3.bin $BINARIES_DIR/tiboot3.
bin

GENIMAGE_CFG="${BOARD_DIR}/genimage.cfg" GENIMAGE_TMP="${BUILD_DIR}/
```

```
genimage.tmp"

rm -rf "${GENIMAGE_TMP}"

genimage \
    --rootpath "${TARGET_DIR}" \
    --tmppath "${GENIMAGE_TMP}" \
    --inputpath "${BINARIES_DIR}" \
    --outputpath "${BINARIES_DIR}" \
    --config "${GENIMAGE_CFG}"
```

This script copies the R5 firmware image into the output/images directory and runs genimage with our configuration file.

Note that post-image.sh needs to be executable; otherwise the build will fail at the end:

```
$ chmod +x board/meld/nova/post-image.sh
```

Now, run make menuconfig and drill down into the **System configuration** page. From that page, navigate down to **Custom scripts to run before creating filesystem images** and notice the path to our post-image.sh script:

```
/home/frank/buildroot/.config — Buildroot 2024.02.6 Configuration
→ System configuration
                            System configuration
    Arrow keys navigate the menu.  <Enter> selects submenus ---> (or empty
    submenus ----).  Highlighted letters are hotkeys.  Pressing <Y> selects a
    feature, while <N> excludes a feature.  Press <Esc><Esc> to exit, <?> for
    Help, </> for Search.  Legend: [*] feature is selected  [ ] feature is

            () Generate locale data
            [ ] Enable Native Language Support (NLS)
            [ ] Install timezone info
            () Path to the users tables
            () Root filesystem overlay directories
            () Custom scripts to run before commencing the build
            (board/meld/nova/post-image.sh) Custom scripts to run before creatin
            () Custom scripts to run inside the fakeroot environment
            (board/meld/nova/post-image.sh) Custom scripts to run after creating
            (-c board/meld/nova/genimage.cfg) Extra arguments passed to custom s

            <Select>    < Exit >    < Help >    < Save >    < Load >
```

Figure 6.3 – Selecting custom scripts to run after creating filesystem images

Finally, you can build Linux for the Nova board just by typing make. When the build is done, you will see these files in the output/images directory:

```
bl31.bin                rootfs.ext2    tee-header_v2.bin      tispl.bin
boot.vfat               rootfs.ext4    tee-pageable_v2.bin    u-boot.img
Image.gz                rootfs.tar     tee-pager_v2.bin
nova.dtb                sdcard.img     tiboot3.bin
r5-u-boot-spl.bin       tee.bin        ti-connectivity
```

To test it, insert a microSD card into your card reader and use balenaEtcher to write output/images/sdcard.img out to a microSD card like we did for the Raspberry Pi 4. There is no need to format the microSD beforehand like we did in the previous chapter because genimage has created the exact disk layout required.

Having shown that our custom configuration for the Nova board works, it would be nice to save our changes back to the nova_defconfig file so that we and others can use it again. You can do that with this command:

```
$ make savedefconfig BR2_DEFCONFIG=configs/nova_defconfig
```

Now you have a custom Buildroot configuration for the Nova board. You can retrieve this configuration by typing the following command:

```
$ make nova_defconfig
```

With that, we have successfully configured Buildroot. In the next section, we will learn how to add our own code to a Buildroot image.

Adding your own code

Suppose you develop a program and you want to include it in the build. You have two options. Firstly, build it separately using its own build system and then roll the binary into the final build as an overlay. Secondly, create a Buildroot package that can be selected from the menu and build it like any other.

Overlays

An overlay is simply a directory structure that is copied over the top of the Buildroot root filesystem at a later stage in the build process. It can contain executables, libraries, and anything else you may want to include. Note that any compiled code must be compatible with the libraries deployed at runtime, which means that it must be compiled with the same toolchain that Buildroot uses.

Using the Buildroot toolchain is quite easy; just add it to PATH:

```
$ PATH=<path_to_buildroot>/output/host/usr/bin:$PATH
```

The prefix for the toolchain is <ARCH>-linux-. So, to compile a simple program, you would do something like this:

```
$ PATH=/home/frank/buildroot/output/host/usr/bin:$PATH
$ aarch64-linux-gcc helloworld.c -o helloworld
```

Once you have compiled your program with the correct toolchain, install the executables and other supporting files into a staging area and mark it as an overlay for Buildroot. For the helloworld example, you can put it in the board/meld/nova directory:

```
$ mkdir -p board/meld/nova/overlay/usr/bin
$ cp helloworld board/meld/nova/overlay/usr/bin
```

Finally, set BR2_ROOTFS_OVERLAY to the path pointing at the overlay. It can be configured in menuconfig with the **System configuration | Root filesystem overlay directories** option.

Adding a package

Buildroot packages (over 2,000 of them) are stored in the package directory, each in its own subdirectory. A package consists of at least two files: Config.in, containing the snippet of Kconfig code required to make the package visible in the configuration menu, and a makefile named <package_name>.mk.

> **IMPORTANT NOTE**
>
> Note that a Buildroot package does not contain the code, just the instructions to get the code by downloading a tarball, doing git clone, or whatever is necessary to obtain the upstream source.

The makefile is written in a format expected by Buildroot and contains directives that allow Buildroot to download, configure, compile, and install the program. Writing a new package makefile is a complex operation which is covered in detail in *The Buildroot user manual*.

Here is an example that shows you how to create a package for a simple program such as our helloworld program. Begin by creating a package/helloworld subdirectory with a Config.in file that looks like this:

```
config BR2_PACKAGE_HELLOWORLD
    bool "helloworld"
```

```
help
    A friendly program that prints Hello World! every 10s
```

The first line must be of the format `BR2_PACKAGE_<uppercase package name>`. This is followed by `bool` and the package name as it will appear in the configuration menu. The second line is what enables a user to select this package. The `help` section is optional but usually a good idea because it acts as self-documentation.

Link the new package into the **Target Packages** menu by editing `package/Config.in` and sourcing the configuration file as shown below:

```
menu "My programs"
    source "package/helloworld/Config.in"
endmenu
```

You could append this new `helloworld` package to an existing submenu, but it's cleaner to create a new submenu with only our package and insert it before the **Audio and video applications** menu.

After inserting the **My programs** menu into `package/Config.in`, create a `package/helloworld/helloworld.mk` file to supply the data needed by Buildroot:

```
HELLOWORLD_VERSION = 1.0.0

HELLOWORLD_SITE = /home/frank/MELD/Chapter06/helloworld
HELLOWORLD_SITE_METHOD = local

define HELLOWORLD_BUILD_CMDS
    $(MAKE) CC="$(TARGET_CC)" LD="$(TARGET_LD)" -C $(@D) all
endef

define HELLOWORLD_INSTALL_TARGET_CMDS
    $(INSTALL) -D -m 0755 $(@D)/helloworld $(TARGET_DIR)/usr/bin/
helloworld
endef

$(eval $(generic-package))
```

You can find my `helloworld` package in the book's code archive at `MELD/Chapter06/buildroot/package/helloworld` and the source code for the program in `MELD/Chapter06/helloworld`. The location of the code is hardcoded to a local path name.

In a more realistic case, you would get the code from a source code system or from a central server of some kind. There are details on how to do this in *The Buildroot user manual* and plenty of examples in other packages.

License compliance

Buildroot is based on open source software. So are the packages it compiles. At some point during the project, you should check the licenses by running:

```
$ make legal-info
```

The license information is gathered in the output/legal-info directory. There are summaries of the licenses used to compile the host tools in host-manifest.csv and on the target in manifest.csv. There is more information in the README file and in *The Buildroot user manual*.

Now let's switch build systems and start learning about The Yocto Project.

Introducing The Yocto Project

The Yocto Project is a more complex beast than Buildroot. Not only can it build toolchains, boot-loaders, kernels, and root filesystems, but it can generate an entire Linux distribution for you with binary packages that can be installed at runtime. The build process is structured around groups of recipes written using a combination of Python and shell script. The Yocto Project includes a task scheduler called **BitBake** that produces whatever you have configured from the recipes. There is plenty of online documentation at https://www.yoctoproject.org/.

Background

The structure of The Yocto Project makes more sense if you look at the background first. Its roots are in **OpenEmbedded** (https://openembedded.org), which grew out of a number of projects to port Linux to various hand-held computers, including the Sharp Zaurus and the Compaq iPAQ. OpenEmbedded came to life in 2003 as the build system for those hand-held computers. Soon after, other developers began to use it as a general build system for devices running embedded Linux. It was developed and continues to be developed by an enthusiastic community of programmers.

The OpenEmbedded project set out to create a set of binary packages using the compact IPK format. These packages could then be installed on the target at runtime to create a variety of systems. It did this by creating recipes for each package and using BitBake as the task scheduler. OpenEmbedded is very flexible. By supplying the right metadata, you can create an entire Linux distribution according to your specifications.

Back in 2005, Richard Purdie, then a developer at OpenedHand, created a fork of OpenEmbedded that had a more conservative choice of packages and created releases that were stable over a period of time. He named it **Poky** (rhymes with hockey) after the Japanese snack. Although Poky was a fork, OpenEmbedded and Poky continued to track each other, sharing updates and keeping architectures in step. Intel bought OpenedHand in 2008 and transferred Poky to the Linux Foundation in 2010 when they formed The Yocto Project.

Since 2010, the common components of OpenEmbedded and Poky have been combined into a separate project known as **OpenEmbedded Core**, or just **OE-Core**.

The Yocto Project collects together several components, the most important of which are:

- **OE-Core**: Is the core metadata that is shared with OpenEmbedded.
- **BitBake**: Is the task scheduler that is shared with OpenEmbedded and other projects.
- **Poky**: Is the reference distribution. The Git repo for Poky also includes a `meta-yocto-bsp` layer with reference hardware machines.
- **Documentation**: Is the user manuals and developer guides for each component.
- **Toaster**: is a web-based interface to BitBake and its metadata.

Yocto provides a stable base that can be used as-is or extended using **meta layers** which I will discuss later in this chapter. Many SoC vendors provide BSPs for their devices in this way. Meta layers can also be used to create extended or different build systems. Some are open source like Poky and others are commercial like Wind River Linux. Yocto has a branding and compatibility testing scheme to ensure that there is interoperability between components. You will see statements like "Yocto Project compatible" on various web pages.

Consequently, you should think of Yocto as the foundation for a whole sector of embedded Linux in addition to being a complete build system in its own right.

> **IMPORTANT NOTE**
>
> You may be wondering about the name. It turns out *yocto* is the SI prefix for 10^{-24} in the same way that *micro* is 10^{-6}. Why name the project Yocto? The name was chosen partly to indicate that it could build very small Linux systems (although to be fair so can other build systems). It is also a dig at the now defunct Ångström Distribution, which was based on OpenEmbedded. An Ångström is 10^{10}. That's huge compared to a *yocto*!

Stable releases and supports

Routinely, there is a release of Yocto every six months: in April and October. They are principally known by their code names, but it is also useful to know their Yocto and BitBake version numbers. Here is a table of the six most recent releases at the time of writing:

Code Name	Release Date	Yocto Version	BitBake Version
Scarthgap	April 2024	5.0	2.8
Nanbield	November 2023	4.3	2.6
Mickledore	May 2023	4.2	2.4
Langdale	October 2022	4.1	2.2
Kirkstone	May 2022	4.0	2.0
Honister	October 2021	3.4	1.52

Table 6.1 – Six most recent releases of Yocto

The stable releases are supported with security and critical bug fixes for the current release cycle and the next cycle. In other words, each stable version is supported for approximately 12 months after release. In addition to stable releases, Yocto also provides LTS releases. The 3.1 (dunfell) release of Yocto back in April 2020 was the first LTS release. The LTS designation means that the version of Yocto will receive defect fixes and updates for an extended period of two years. Consequently, the plan going forward is to choose an LTS release of Yocto every two years.

As with Buildroot, if you want continued support, you can update to the next stable release or you can backport changes to your version. With Yocto, you also have the option of commercial support for several years from operating system vendors such as Siemens and Wind River.

Installing The Yocto Project

To get a copy of The Yocto Project, clone the repo choosing the code name (scarthgap in this case) as the branch:

```
$ git clone -b scarthgap git://git.yoctoproject.org/poky.git
```

Since we are building images for BeaglePlay, we also need to clone the meta-ti repo:

```
$ git clone -b scarthgap https://github.com/TexasInstruments-Sandbox/meta-ti
```

And since the `meta-ti-bsp` layer depends on the `meta-arm` layer, we must clone that repo well:

```
$ git clone -b scarthgap git://git.yoctoproject.org/meta-arm
```

Note that both the `meta-ti` and `meta-arm` branch names must match the Yocto code name to ensure these additional layers are compatible with the scarthgap version of Yocto. It is also good practice to run `git pull` periodically to grab the latest bug fixes and security patches from all the remote branches.

Read the *Compatible Linux Distribution* and *Build Host Packages* sections in the *Yocto Project Quick Build* guide (`https://docs.yoctoproject.org/brief-yoctoprojectqs/`). Make sure that the essential packages for your Ubuntu host distribution are installed on your host computer. The next step is configuring.

> **IMPORTANT NOTE**
>
> Ubuntu 24.04 LTS (Noble Numbat) was not officially supported by The Yocto Project at the time of writing. Upon Noble Numbat's release, users experienced numerous BitBake errors related to permissions. These errors were a result of increased security restrictions placed on the operating system by AppArmor. To temporarily disable these AppArmor protections:
>
> `$ echo 0 | sudo tee /proc/sys/kernel/apparmor_restrict_unprivileged_userns`
>
> Remember to rerun this command every time you reboot your Ubuntu host before using Yocto.

Configuring

Let's begin by building the 64-bit Arm QEMU emulator. Start by sourcing a script to set up the environment:

```
$ source poky/oe-init-build-env
```

This creates a working directory for you named `build` and makes it the current directory. All the configuration, intermediate, and target image files will be put in this directory. You must source this script each time you want to work on this project.

To choose a different working directory, add it as a parameter to `oe-init-build-env` like so:

```
$ source poky/oe-init-build-env build-qemu-arm64
```

This will put you into the build-qemu-arm64 directory. This way, you can have several build directories, each for a different project. You choose which one you want to work with through the parameter passed to oe-init-build-env.

Initially, the build directory contains only one subdirectory named conf with the configuration files for this project:

- local.conf: Contains a specification of the device you are going to build and the build environment.
- bblayers.conf: Contains paths of the meta layers you are going to use. I will describe layers later.

For now, we just need to set the MACHINE variable in conf/local.conf to qemuarm64 by removing the comment character (#) at the start of this line:

```
MACHINE ?= "qemuarm64"
```

Now we are ready to build our first image with Yocto.

Building

To perform the build, you need to run BitBake and tell it which root filesystem image you want to create. Some common images are:

- core-image-minimal: Is a small console-based system that is useful for tests and as the basis for custom images.
- core-image-minimal-initramfs: Is similar to core-image-minimal but built as a RAM disk.
- core-image-x11: Is a basic image with support for graphics through an X11 server and the XTerminal terminal app.
- core-image-full-cmdline: Is a console-based system that offers a standard CLI experience and full support for the target hardware.

By giving BitBake the final target, it will work backward and build all the dependencies starting with the toolchain. For now, we just want to create a minimal image to see how it works:

```
$ bitbake core-image-minimal
```

The first build will take some time (likely more than an hour) even with several CPU cores and lots of RAM. It will download about 4.9 GB of source code and consume about 49 GB of disk space. When the build completes, you will find several new directories in the build directory.

These include downloads, which contains all the source downloaded for the build, and tmp, which contains most of the build artifacts. Inside tmp you will find the following:

- work: Contains the build directory and the staging area for the root filesystem.
- deploy: Contains the final binaries to be deployed on the target:
- deploy/images/<machine name>: Contains the bootloader, kernel, and root filesystem images for the target.
- deploy/rpm: Contains the RPM packages that make up the images.
- deploy/licenses: Contains the license files extracted from each package.

When the build is done, we can boot the finished image on QEMU.

Running the QEMU target

When you build a QEMU target, an internal version of QEMU is generated. This eliminates the need to install the QEMU package for your distribution. There is a wrapper script named runqemu to run this internal version of QEMU.

To run the QEMU emulation, make sure to first run source oe-init-build-env build-qemu-arm64 and then type:

```
$ runqemu qemuarm64
```

In this case, QEMU has been configured with a graphic console so that the login prompt appears in a black framebuffer. Log in as root without a password. Close the framebuffer window to exit QEMU.

To launch QEMU without the graphic window, add nographic to the command line:

```
$ runqemu qemuarm64 nographic
```

In the nographic case, close QEMU using the key sequence *Ctrl + A* and then *x*.

The runqemu script has many other options. Type runqemu help for more information.

Layers

Yocto metadata is structured as layers. A layer is a directory containing a collection of BitBake metadata in the form of recipe files. Each recipe file is used to build an individual software package. The layers are stacked on top of each other to build or "bake" all the software recipes into a finished Linux image much like baking a cake. By convention, each layer has a name beginning with meta. The core layers are:

- meta: Is the equivalent of an unmodified OpenEmbedded core.
- meta-poky: Is the metadata specific to the Poky distribution.
- meta-yocto-bsp: Contains the BSPs for the reference machines that Yocto regularly tests.

The list of layers in which BitBake searches for recipes is stored in <your build directory>/conf/bblayers.conf and by default includes all three layers from the preceding list.

Structuring the recipes and other configuration data in this way makes it very easy to extend Yocto by adding new layers. Additional layers are available from SoC manufacturers, The Yocto Project itself, and a wide range of people wishing to add value to Yocto and OpenEmbedded. There is a useful list of layers at https://layers.openembedded.org/layerindex/. Here are some examples:

- meta-qt5: Qt 5 libraries and utilities
- meta-intel: BSPs for Intel CPUs and SoCs
- meta-raspberrypi: BSPs for the Raspberry Pi boards
- meta-ti: BSPs for TI Arm-based SoCs

Adding a layer is as simple as copying the meta directory to a suitable location and adding it to bblayers.conf. Make sure that you read the REAMDE file that should accompany each layer to see what dependencies it has on other layers and which versions of Yocto it is compatible with.

To illustrate how layers work, let's create a layer for our Nova board that we can use for the remainder of the chapter as we add features. You can see the complete implementation of the layer under MELD/Chapter06/meta-nova in the code archive.

Each meta layer must have at least one configuration file named conf/layer.conf and should also have a README file and a license.

To create our meta-nova layer, perform the following steps:

```
$ source poky/oe-init-build-env build-nova
$ bitbake-layers create-layer nova
$ mv nova ../meta-nova
```

This will put you in a working directory named build-nova and create a layer named meta-nova with a conf/layer.conf, an outline README, and a COPYING.MIT license under ../meta-nova. The layer.conf file looks like this:

```
# We have a conf and classes directory, add to BBPATH
BBPATH .= ":${LAYERDIR}"
```

```
# We have recipes-* directories, add to BBFILES
BBFILES += "${LAYERDIR}/recipes-*/*/*.bb \
            ${LAYERDIR}/recipes-*/*/*.bbappend"

BBFILE_COLLECTIONS += "nova"
BBFILE_PATTERN_nova = "^${LAYERDIR}/"
BBFILE_PRIORITY_nova = "6"

LAYERDEPENDS_nova = "core"
LAYERSERIES_COMPAT_nova = "scarthgap"
```

The layer adds itself to BBPATH and the recipes it contains to BBFILES. From looking at the code, you can see that the recipes are found in the directories with names beginning with recipes- and have filenames ending in .bb (for normal BitBake recipes) or .bbappend (for recipes that extend existing recipes by overriding or adding to the instructions). This layer has the name nova and is added to the list of layers in BBFILE_COLLECTIONS with a priority of 6. The layer priority is used if the same recipe appears in several layers. The one in the layer with the highest priority wins.

Before adding the Nova layer, we must first add the meta-arm-toolchain, meta-arm, and meta-ti-bsp layers in that precise order:

```
$ bitbake-layers add-layer ../meta-arm/meta-arm-toolchain
$ bitbake-layers add-layer ../meta-arm/meta-arm
$ bitbake-layers add-layer ../meta-ti/meta-ti-bsp
```

Now add the Nova layer to your build configuration:

```
$ bitbake-layers add-layer ../meta-nova
```

Make sure to run all these bitbake-layers add-layer commands from your build-nova working directory after sourcing that environment.

Confirm that your layer structure is set up correctly like this:

```
$ bitbake-layers show-layers
NOTE: Starting bitbake server...
layer                   path                                    priority
=================================================================================
core                    /home/frank/poky/meta                   5
yocto                   /home/frank/poky/meta-poky               5
yoctobsp                /home/frank/poky/meta-yocto-bsp          5
```

```
arm-toolchain        /home/frank/meta-arm/meta-arm-toolchain   5
meta-arm             /home/frank/meta-arm/meta-arm             5
meta-ti-bsp          /home/frank/meta-ti/meta-ti-bsp           6
nova                 /home/frank/meta-nova                     6
```

There you can see the new layer. Because it has a priority of 6, it can override recipes in the other layers that all have a lower priority.

Run a build using this empty layer. The final target will be the Nova board, but for now, build for the BeaglePlay by adding MACHINE ?= "beagleplay-ti" to conf/local.conf. Then build a small image using bitbake core-image-minimal like before.

In addition to recipes, layers may contain BitBake classes, configuration files, distributions, and more. I will look at recipes next and show you how to create a customized image and a package.

BitBake and recipes

BitBake processes metadata of several different types:

- **recipes** (files ending in .bb): Contain information about building a unit of software, including how to get a copy of the source code, the dependencies on other components, and how to build and install it.
- **append** (files ending in .bbappend): Override or extend some details of a recipe. A .bbappend file appends its instructions to the end of a recipe (.bb) file with the same root name.
- **include** (files ending in .inc): Contain information that is common to several recipes allowing information to be shared among them. The files may be included using the **include** or **require** keyword. The difference is that require produces an error if the file does not exist whereas include does not.
- **classes** (files ending in .bbclass): Contain common build information like how to build a kernel or how to build an Autotools project. Classes are inherited by recipes and by other classes using the inherit keyword. The class classes/base.bbclass is implicitly inherited by every recipe.
- **configuration** (files ending in .conf): Define various configuration variables that govern a project's build process.

A **recipe** is a collection of tasks written in a combination of Python and shell script. The tasks have names such as do_fetch, do_unpack, do_patch, do_configure, do_compile, and do_install. You use BitBake to execute these tasks. The default task is do_build, which performs all the subtasks

required to build the recipe. You can list the tasks available in a recipe using `bitbake -c listtasks`
`<recipe>`. For example, to list the tasks in `core-image-minimal`:

```
$ bitbake -c listtasks core-image-minimal
```

> **IMPORTANT NOTE**
>
> The `-c` option tells BitBake to run a specific task from a recipe without having to
> include the `do_` part at the beginning of the task name.

`do_listtasks` is a special task that lists all the tasks defined within a recipe. Here is the `fetch`
task, which downloads the source code for a recipe:

```
$ bitbake -c fetch busybox
```

To get the code for a target and all its dependencies (which is useful when you want to make
sure you have downloaded all the code for the image you are about to build), use the following:

```
$ bitbake core-image-minimal --runall=fetch
```

The recipe files are usually named `<package-name>_<version>.bb`. They may have dependencies
on other recipes, which would allow BitBake to work out all the subtasks that need to be executed
to complete the top-level job.

To create a recipe for our `helloworld` program in `meta-nova`, you would create a directory structure like this:

```
meta-nova/recipes-local/helloworld
├── files
│   └── helloworld.c
└── helloworld_1.0.bb
```

The recipe is `helloworld_1.0.bb` and the source is kept local to the recipe in the `files` subdirectory. The recipe contains these instructions:

```
DESCRIPTION = "A friendly program that prints Hello World!"
SECTION = "examples"

LICENSE = "GPL-2.0-only"
LIC_FILES_CHKSUM = "file://${COMMON_LICENSE_DIR}/GPL-2.0-only;md5=801f8098
0d171dd6425610833a22dbe6"
```

```
SRC_URI = "file://helloworld.c"

S = "${WORKDIR}"

do_compile() {
    ${CC} ${CFLAGS} ${LDFLAGS} helloworld.c -o helloworld
}

do_install() {
    install -d ${D}${bindir}
    install -m 0755 helloworld ${D}${bindir}
}
```

The location of the source code is set by SRC_URI. In this case, the file:// URI means that the code is local to the recipe directory. BitBake will search the files, helloworld, and helloworld-1.0 directories relative to the directory that contains the recipe. The tasks that need to be defined are do_compile and do_install, which compile the source file and install it into the target root filesystem: ${D} expands to the staging area of the recipe and ${bindir} to the default /usr/bin binary directory.

Every recipe has a license defined by LICENSE, which is set to GPL-2.0-only here. The file containing the text of the license and a checksum is defined by LIC_FILES_CHKSUM. BitBake will terminate the build if the checksum does not match, indicating that the license has changed in some way. Note that the MD5 checksum value and COMMON_LICENSE_DIR are on the same line separated by a semicolon. The license file may be part of the package, or it may point to one of the standard license texts in meta/files/common-licenses as is the case here.

Commercial licenses are disallowed by default, but it is easy to enable them. You need to specify the license in the recipe as shown here:

```
LICENSE_FLAGS = "commercial"
```

Then, in your conf/local.conf, explicitly allow this license like so:

```
LICENSE_FLAGS_ACCEPTED = "commercial"
```

To make sure that our helloworld recipe compiles correctly, ask BitBake to build it:

```
$ bitbake helloworld
```

If all goes well, you should see that it has created a working directory for it in `tmp/work/aarch64-poky-linux/helloworld`. You should also see that there is an RPM package for it in `tmp/deploy/rpm/aarch64/helloworld-1.0-r0.aarch64.rpm`.

The package is not part of the target image yet. The list of packages to be installed is held in a variable named `IMAGE_INSTALL`. You can append to the end of that list by adding this line to `conf/local.conf`:

```
IMAGE_INSTALL:append = " helloworld"
```

Note that there needs to be a space between the opening double quote and the first package name. Now the package will be added to any image that you `bitbake`:

```
$ bitbake core-image-minimal
```

If you look in `deploy-ti/images/beagleplay-ti/core-image-minimal-beagleplay-ti.rootfs.tar.xz`, you will see that `/usr/bin/helloworld` has indeed been installed.

Customizing images via local.conf

You often may want to add a package to an image during development or tweak it in other ways. As we've just seen, you can simply append to the list of packages to be installed by adding a statement like:

```
IMAGE_INSTALL:append = " helloworld"
```

You can make more sweeping changes via `EXTRA_IMAGE_FEATURES`. Here is a short list, which should give you an idea of the features you can enable:

- `dbg-pkgs`: Installs debug symbol packages for all the packages installed in the image.
- `debug-tweaks`: Allows root logins without passwords and other changes that make development easier. Never enable `debug-tweaks` in production images.
- `package-management`: Installs package management tools and preserves the package manager database.
- `read-only-rootfs`: Makes the root filesystem read-only. We will cover this in more detail in *Chapter 9*.
- `x11`: Installs the X server.
- `x11-base`: Installs the X server with a minimal environment.

There are many more features you can add in this way. I recommend you look at the *Image Features* section of the *Yocto Project Reference Manual* at `https://docs.yoctoproject.org/ref-manual/` and read through the code in `meta/classes-recipe/core-image.bbclass`.

Writing an image recipe

The problem with making changes to local.conf is that they are, well, local. If you want to create an image that is to be shared with other developers or to be loaded onto a production system, then you should put the changes in an **image recipe**.

An image recipe contains instructions about how to create the image files for a target, including the bootloader, kernel, and root filesystem images. By convention, image recipes are put into a directory named images. You can get a list of all the images that are available by scanning the poky directory and any additional layers that you cloned:

```
$ cd ~
$ ls poky/meta*/recipes*/images/*.bb
$ ls meta*/recipes*/images/*.bb
```

You will find that the recipe for core-image-minimal is in poky/meta/recipes-core/images/core-image-minimal.bb.

A simple approach is to take an existing image recipe and modify it using statements like the ones you used in local.conf.

Imagine that you want an image that is the same as core-image-minimal but includes your helloworld program and the strace utility. You can do that with a two-line recipe file that includes (using the require keyword) the base image and adds the packages you want. It is conventional to put the image in a directory named images, so add the recipe nova-image.bb with this content in meta-nova/recipes-local/images:

```
require recipes-core/images/core-image-minimal.bb

IMAGE_INSTALL:append = " helloworld strace"
```

Now remove the IMAGE_INSTALL:append line from your local.conf and build the image:

```
$ bitbake nova-image
```

This time, the build should proceed much quicker because BitBake reuses the intermediate build objects built during prior runs.

Not only does BitBake build images for running on a target device, but it can also build an SDK for doing cross-development on a host machine.

Creating an SDK

It is very useful to be able to create a standalone toolchain that other developers can install. This avoids the need for everyone on the team to have a full installation of Yocto. Ideally, you want the toolchain to include development libraries and header files for all the libraries installed on the target. You can do that for any image using the `populate_sdk` task, as shown:

```
$ bitbake -c populate_sdk nova-image
```

The result is a self-installing shell script in `deploy-ti/sdk`:

```
poky-<c_library>-<host_machine>-<target_image>-<target_machine>-toolchain-
<version>.sh
```

For the SDK built with the `nova-image` recipe:

```
poky-glibc-x86_64-nova-image-aarch64-beagleplay-toolchain-<version>.sh
```

If you only want a basic toolchain with just C and C++ cross-compilers, the C library, and header files, then run this instead:

```
$ bitbake meta-toolchain
```

To install the SDK, just run the shell script. The default install directory is `/opt/poky` but the install script allows you to change this:

```
$ deploy-ti/sdk/poky-glibc-x86_64-nova-image-aarch64-beagleplay-toolchain-
5.0.3.sh
Poky (Yocto Project Reference Distro) SDK installer version 5.0.3
================================================================
Enter target directory for SDK (default: /opt/poky/5.0.3):
You are about to install the SDK to "/opt/poky/5.0.3". Proceed [Y/n]? Y
[sudo] password for frank:
Extracting SDK.................................................
..............................................done
Setting it up...done
SDK has been successfully set up and is ready to be used.
Each time you wish to use the SDK in a new shell session, you need to
source the environment setup script e.g.
  $ . /opt/poky/5.0.3/environment-setup-aarch64-poky-linux
```

To make use of the toolchain, first source the environment and set up the script:

```
$ source /opt/poky/<version>/environment-setup-aarch64-poky-linux
```

> **TIP**
>
> The environment-setup-* script that sets things up for the SDK is not compatible with the oe-init-build-env script that you source when working in the Yocto build directory. It is a good rule to always start a new terminal session before you source either script.

The toolchain generated by The Yocto Project does not have a valid sysroot directory. We know this to be true because passing the -print-sysroot option to the toolchain's compiler returns /not/exist:

```
$ aarch64-poky-linux-gcc -print-sysroot
/not/exist
```

Consequently, if you try to cross-compile, it will fail like this:

```
$ aarch64-poky-linux-gcc helloworld.c -o helloworld
helloworld.c:1:10: fatal error: stdio.h: No such file or directory
    1 | #include <stdio.h>
      |          ^~~~~~~~~
compilation terminated.
```

This is because the compiler has been configured to work for a wide range of Arm processors and the fine-tuning is done when you launch it using the right set of flags. Instead, you should use the shell variables that are created when you source the environment-setup script for cross-compiling. These include:

- CC: C compiler
- CXX: C++ compiler
- CPP: C preprocessor
- AS: Assembler
- LD: Linker

This is what we find CC has been set to:

```
$ echo $CC
aarch64-poky-linux-gcc -mbranch-protection=standard -fstack-protector-
strong -O2 -D_FORTIFY_SOURCE=2 -Wformat -Wformat-security -Werror=format-
security --sysroot=/opt/poky/5.0.3/sysroots/aarch64-poky-linux
```

As long as you use $CC to compile, everything should work fine:

```
$ $CC -O helloworld.c -o helloworld
```

The license audit

The Yocto Project insists that each package has a license. A copy of the license is placed in tmp/deploy/licenses/<package name> for each package as it is built. In addition, a summary of the packages and licenses used in an image is put into the directory: <image name>-<machine name>.rootfs-<date stamp>. For the nova-image we just built, the directory would be named something like this:

```
tmp/deploy/licenses/beagleplay/nova-image-beagleplay.rootfs-20241012221506
```

This completes our survey of the two leading build systems for embedded Linux. Buildroot is simple and quick, making it a good choice for simple single-purpose devices. Yocto is more complex and flexible. Even though there is good support throughout the community and industry for Yocto, the tool still has a very steep learning curve. You can expect it will take several months for you to become proficient with Yocto, and even then, it will sometimes do things that surprise you.

Summary

In this chapter, you learned how to use both Buildroot and The Yocto Project to configure, customize, and build embedded Linux images. We used Buildroot to create a BSP with a custom U-Boot patch and device tree specification for a hypothetical board based on the BeaglePlay. We then learned how to add our own code to an image in the form of a Buildroot package. You were introduced to The Yocto Project, which we will cover in depth over the next two chapters. In particular, you learned some basic BitBake terminology, how to write an image recipe, and how to create an SDK.

Don't forget that any devices you create using these tools will need to be maintained in the field for a period of time, often over many years. Both Yocto and Buildroot provide point releases for about one year after the initial release, and Yocto now offers long-term support for at least four years. In either case, you will find yourself having to maintain your own releases or paying for commercial support. The third possibility, ignoring the problem, is not an option!

Further study

- *The Buildroot user manual, Buildroot Association* – `https://buildroot.org/downloads/manual/manual.html`

- *Yocto Project Documentation, Yocto Project* – `https://docs.yoctoproject.org/`

7

Developing with Yocto

Bringing up Linux on unsupported hardware can be a painstaking process. Luckily, Yocto provides **Board Support Packages (BSPs)** to bootstrap embedded Linux development on popular single-board computers like BeaglePlay and Raspberry Pi 4. Building on top of an existing BSP layer lets us quickly take advantage of complex built-in peripherals such as Bluetooth and Wi-Fi. In this chapter, we will create a custom application layer to do just that.

Next, we will look at the development workflow enabled by Yocto's extensible SDK. Modifying software running on a target device usually means swapping out the microSD card. Since rebuilding and redeploying full images is too time-consuming, I will show you how to use devtool to quickly automate and iterate over your work. While doing so, you will also learn how to save your work in your own layers so that it does not get lost.

Yocto not only builds Linux images but entire Linux distributions. We will discuss the reasons for doing so before going through the motions of assembling our own Linux distribution. The many choices made include whether or not to add runtime package management for rapid application development on the target device. This comes at the cost of having to maintain a package database and remote package server, which I will touch on last.

In this chapter, we will cover the following topics:

- Building on top of an existing BSP
- Capturing changes with devtool
- Building your own distro
- Provisioning a remote package server

Technical requirements

To follow along with the examples, make sure you have the following:

- An Ubuntu 24.04 or later LTS host system with at least 90 GB of free disk space
- The Yocto 5.0 (scarthgap) LTS release
- A microSD card reader and card
- balenaEtcher for Linux
- An Ethernet cable and router with an available port for network connectivity
- A Wi-Fi router
- A smartphone with Bluetooth
- Raspberry Pi 4
- A 5 V USB-C power supply capable of delivering 3A

You should have already built the 5.0 (scarthgap) LTS release of Yocto in *Chapter 6*. If you have not, then please refer to the *Compatible Linux Distribution* and *Build Host Packages* sections of the *Yocto Project Quick Build* guide (`https://docs.yoctoproject.org/brief-yoctoprojectqs/`) before building Yocto on your Linux host according to the instructions in *Chapter 6*.

The code used in this chapter can be found in the chapter folder in this book's GitHub repository: `https://github.com/PacktPublishing/Mastering-Embedded-Linux-Development`.

Building on top of an existing BSP

A **BSP** layer adds support for a particular hardware device or family of devices to Yocto. This support usually includes the bootloader, device tree blobs, and additional kernel drivers needed to boot Linux on that specific hardware. A BSP may also include any additional user-space software and peripheral firmware needed to fully enable and utilize all the features of the hardware. By convention, BSP layer names start with the `meta-` prefix followed by the machine's name. Locating the best BSP for your target device is the first step toward building a bootable image for it using Yocto.

The OpenEmbedded layer index (`https://layers.openembedded.org/layerindex`) is the best place to start looking for quality BSPs. Your board's manufacturer or silicon vendor may also offer BSP layers. The Yocto Project provides a BSP for all variants of Raspberry Pi. You can find the Git repository for that BSP layer and all the other layers endorsed by The Yocto Project in the project's source repositories (`https://git.yoctoproject.org`).

Building an existing BSP

The following exercises assume you have already cloned or extracted the scarthgap release of Yocto to a directory named poky within your host environment. Before proceeding, we also need to clone the following dependency layers one level up from that poky directory so that the layer and poky directories sit next to each other:

```
$ git clone -b scarthgap git://git.openembedded.org/meta-openembedded
$ git clone -b scarthgap git://git.yoctoproject.org/meta-raspberrypi
```

Notice that the branch name of the dependency layers matches the Yocto release for compatibility. Keep all three clones up to date and in sync with their remotes using periodic git pull commands. The meta-raspberrypi layer is the BSP for all Raspberry Pis. Once these dependencies are in place, you can build an image that's been customized for Raspberry Pi 4. But before we do that, let's explore the recipes for Yocto's generic images:

1. First, navigate to the directory where you cloned Yocto:

```
$ cd poky
```

2. Next, move down into the directory where the recipes for the standard images are:

```
$ cd meta/recipes-core/images
```

3. List the core image recipes:

```
$ ls -1 core*
core-image-base.bb
core-image-initramfs-boot.bb
core-image-minimal.bb
core-image-minimal-dev.bb
core-image-minimal-initramfs.bb
core-image-minimal-mtdutils.bb
core-image-ptest-all.bb
core-image-ptest.bb
core-image-ptest-fast.bb
core-image-tiny-initramfs.bb
```

4. Display the core-image-base recipe:

```
$ cat core-image-base.bb
SUMMARY = "A console-only image that fully supports the target
device \
hardware."

IMAGE_FEATURES += "splash"
```

```
LICENSE = "MIT"

inherit core-image
```

5. Notice that this recipe inherits from core-image so it's importing the contents of core-image.bbclass, which we will look at later.

6. Display the core-image-minimal recipe:

```
$ cat core-image-minimal.bb
SUMMARY = "A small image just capable of allowing a device to boot."

IMAGE_INSTALL = "packagegroup-core-boot ${CORE_IMAGE_EXTRA_INSTALL}"

IMAGE_LINGUAS = " "

LICENSE = "MIT"

inherit core-image

IMAGE_ROOTFS_SIZE ?= "8192"
IMAGE_ROOTFS_EXTRA_SPACE:append = "${@bb.utils.contains("DISTRO_
FEATURES", "systemd", " + 4096", "", d)}"
```

7. Like core-image-base, this recipe also inherits from the core-image class file.

8. Display the core-image-minimal-dev recipe:

```
$ cat core-image-minimal-dev.bb
require core-image-minimal.bb

DESCRIPTION = "A small image just capable of allowing a device to
boot and \
is suitable for development work."

IMAGE_FEATURES += "dev-pkgs"
```

9. Navigate up to the classes directory under poky/meta:

```
$ cd ../../classes-recipe
```

10. Lastly, display the core-image class file:

```
$ cat core-image.bbclass
```

11. Notice the long list of available IMAGE_FEATURES at the top of this class file, including the aforementioned dev-pkgs feature.

Standard images such as core-image-minimal and core-image-minimal-dev are machine-agnostic. In *Chapter 6*, we built core-image-minimal for both the QEMU Arm emulator and BeaglePlay. We could have just as easily built a core-image-minimal image for Raspberry Pi 4. In contrast, a BSP layer includes image recipes intended for a specific board or series of boards.

Now let's take a look at the rpi-test-image recipe inside the meta-rasberrypi BSP layer to see how support for both Wi-Fi and Bluetooth is added to core-image-base for Raspberry Pi 4:

1. First, navigate one level above the directory where you cloned Yocto:

```
$ cd ../../..
```

2. Next, move down into the directory inside the meta-raspberrypi BSP layer where the image recipes for Raspberry Pis are:

```
$ cd meta-raspberrypi/recipes-core/images
```

3. List the Raspberry Pi image recipes:

```
$ ls -1
rpi-test-image.bb
```

4. Display the rpi-test-image recipe:

```
$ cat rpi-test-image.bb
# Base this image on core-image-base
include recipes-core/images/core-image-base.bb

COMPATIBLE_MACHINE = "^rpi$"

IMAGE_INSTALL:append = " packagegroup-rpi-test"
```

5. Notice that the IMAGE_INSTALL variable has been overridden so that it can append packagegroup-rpi-test and include those packages on the image.

6. Navigate to the neighboring packagegroups directory under metaraspberrypi/recipes-core:

```
$ cd ../packagegroups
```

7. Lastly, display the packagegroup-rpi-test recipe:

```
$ cat packagegroup-rpi-test.bb
DESCRIPTION = "RaspberryPi Test Packagegroup"
LICENSE = "MIT"
LIC_FILES_CHKSUM = "file://${COMMON_LICENSE_DIR}/
MIT;md5=0835ade698e0bcf8506ecda2f7b4f302"


PACKAGE_ARCH = "${MACHINE_ARCH}"

inherit packagegroup

COMPATIBLE_MACHINE = "^rpi$"

OMXPLAYER  = "${@bb.utils.contains('MACHINE_FEATURES',
'vc4graphics', '', 'omxplayer', d)}"

RDEPENDS:${PN} = "\
    ${OMXPLAYER} \
    bcm2835-tests \
    raspi-gpio \
    rpio \
    rpi-gpio \
    pi-blaster \
    python3-adafruit-circuitpython-register \
    python3-adafruit-platformdetect \
    python3-adafruit-pureio \
    python3-rtimu \
    connman \
    connman-client \
    wireless-regdb-static \
    bluez5 \
```

```
"
RRECOMMENDS:${PN} = "\
    ${@bb.utils.contains("BBFILE_COLLECTIONS", "meta-multimedia",
"bigbuckbunny-1080p bigbuckbunny-480p bigbuckbunny-720p", "", d)} \
    ${MACHINE_EXTRA_RRECOMMENDS} \
"
```

8. Notice that the `connman`, `connman-client`, and `bluez5` packages are included in the list of runtime dependencies so that Wi-Fi and Bluetooth are fully enabled.

Finally, let's build `rpi-test-image` for Raspberry Pi 4:

1. First, navigate one level above the directory where you cloned Yocto:

```
$ cd ../../..
```

2. Next, set up your BitBake work environment:

```
$ source poky/oe-init-build-env build-rpi
```

3. This sets up a bunch of environment variables and puts you in a newly created `build-rpi` directory.

4. Then, add the following layers to your image:

```
$ bitbake-layers add-layer ../meta-openembedded/meta-oe
$ bitbake-layers add-layer ../meta-openembedded/meta-python
$ bitbake-layers add-layer ../meta-openembedded/meta-networking
$ bitbake-layers add-layer ../meta-openembedded/meta-multimedia
$ bitbake-layers add-layer ../meta-raspberrypi
```

IMPORTANT NOTE

The order in which you add these layers matters because the meta-networking and meta-multimedia layers both depend on the meta-python layer. If `bitbake-layers add-layer` or `bitbake-layers show-layers` starts failing due to parse errors, then delete the `build-rpi` directory and restart this exercise from *step 1*.

5. Verify that all the necessary layers have been added to the image:

```
$ bitbake-layers show-layers
```

6. The output of the command should look like this:

```
layer                path                                              priority
================================================================================
core                 /home/frank/poky/meta                                   5
yocto                /home/frank/poky/meta-poky                              5
yoctobsp             /home/frank/poky/meta-yocto-bsp                         5
openembedded-layer   /home/frank/meta-openembedded/meta-oe                   5
meta-python          /home/frank/meta-openembedded/meta-python               5
networking-layer     /home/frank/meta-openembedded/meta-networking 5
multimedia-layer     /home/frank/meta-openembedded/meta-multimedia 5
raspberrypi          /home/frank/meta-raspberrypi                            9
```

7. Observe the changes that the preceding `bitbake-layers  add-layer` commands made to `bblayers.conf`:

```
$ cat conf/bblayers.conf
```

8. The same eight layers from the previous step should be assigned to the BBLAYERS variable.

9. List the machines supported by the `meta-raspberrypi` BSP layer:

```
$ ls ../meta-raspberrypi/conf/machine
```

10. Notice that there are `raspberrypi4` and `raspberrypi4-64` machine configurations.

11. Add the following line to your `conf/local.conf` file:

```
MACHINE = "raspberrypi4-64"
```

12. This overrides the following default in your `conf/local.conf` file:

```
MACHINE ??= "qemux86-64"
```

13. Setting the MACHINE variable to `raspberrypi4-64` ensures that the image we're about to build works for Raspberry Pi 4.

14. Add the following line to your `conf/local.conf` file:

```
LICENSE_FLAGS_ACCEPTED = "synaptics-killswitch"
```

15. This suppresses the following build error:

```
ERROR: Nothing RPROVIDES 'linux-firmware-rpidistro-bcm43455'
```

16. Now, append `ssh-server-openssh` to the list of `EXTRA_IMAGE_FEATURES` in your `conf/local.conf` file:

```
EXTRA_IMAGE_FEATURES ?= "debug-tweaks ssh-server-openssh"
```

17. This adds an SSH server to our image for local network access.

18. Lastly, build the image:

```
$ bitbake rpi-test-image
```

The first build could take anywhere from minutes to hours to complete depending on how many CPU cores your host environment has available.

`TARGET_SYS` should be `aarch64-poky-linux` and `MACHINE` should be `raspberrypi4-64` since this image is targeting 64-bit for the Arm Cortex-A72 cores in Raspberry Pi 4.

Once the image has finished building, there should be a file named `rpi-test-image-raspberrypi4-64.rootfs.wic.bz2` in the `tmp/deploy/images/raspberrypi4-64` directory:

```
$ ls -l tmp/deploy/images/raspberrypi4-64/rpi-test*wic.bz2
```

Notice that `rpi-test-image-raspberrypi4-64.rootfs.wic.bz2` is a symbolic link pointing to the actual image file in the same directory. An integer denoting the date and time of the build is appended to the image filename before the `wic.bz2` extension.

Now write that image to a microSD card using Etcher and boot it on your Raspberry Pi 4:

1. Insert a microSD card into your host machine.

2. Launch Etcher.

3. Click **Flash from file** from Etcher.

4. Locate the `wic.bz2` image that you built for Raspberry Pi 4 and open it.

5. Click **Select target** from Etcher.

6.   Select the microSD card that you inserted in *step 1*.

7.   Click **Flash** from Etcher to write the image.

8.   Eject the microSD card when Etcher is done flashing.

9.   Insert the microSD card into your Raspberry Pi 4.

10. Apply power to Raspberry Pi 4 by way of its USB-C port.

Confirm that your Raspberry Pi 4 booted successfully by plugging it into your Ethernet and observing that the network activity lights blink.

Controlling Wi-Fi

In the previous exercise, we built a bootable image for Raspberry Pi 4 that includes working Ethernet, Wi-Fi, and Bluetooth. Now that the device has booted and connected to your local network via Ethernet, let's connect to a nearby Wi-Fi network. We will use connman for this exercise since that is what the meta-raspberrypi layer ships with out of the box. Other BSP layers rely on different network interface configuration daemons, such as systemd-networkd and NetworkManager. Follow these steps:

1.   The image we built has a hostname of raspberrypi4-64 so you should be able to SSH into the device as root:

```
$ ssh root@raspberrypi4-64.local
```

2.   Enter yes when asked if you want to continue connecting. You will not be prompted for a password. If no host is found at raspberrypi4-64.local, use a tool such as arp-scan to locate the IP address of your Raspberry Pi 4 and SSH into that instead of doing so by hostname.

3.   Once you are in, verify that the Wi-Fi driver is on board:

```
root@raspberrypi4-64:~# lsmod | grep 80211
cfg80211               753664  1 brcmfmac
rfkill                  32768  6 nfc,bluetooth,cfg80211
```

4.   Start connman-client:

```
root@raspberrypi4-64:~# connmanctl
connmanctl>
```

5. Turn on Wi-Fi:

```
connmanctl> enable wifi
Enabled wifi
```

6. Disregard "Error wifi: Already enabled" if the Wi-Fi is already on.

7. Register connmanctl as the connection agent:

```
connmanctl> agent on
Agent registered
```

8. Scan for Wi-Fi networks:

```
connmanctl> scan wifi
Scan completed for wifi
```

9. List all the available Wi-Fi networks:

```
connmanctl> services
*AO Wired ethernet_dca6320a8ead_cable
 RT-AC66U_B1_38_2G wifi_
dca6320a8eae_52542d41433636555f42315f33385f3247_managed_psk
 RT-AC66U_B1_38_5G wifi_
dca6320a8eae_52542d41433636555f42315f33385f3547_managed_psk
```

10. RT-AC66U_B1_38_2G and RT-AC66U_B1_38_5G are Wi-Fi network SSIDs for an ASUS router. Your list will look different. The *AO before Wired indicates that the device is currently online via Ethernet.

11. Connect to a Wi-Fi network:

```
connmanctl> connect wifi_
dca6320a8eae_52542d41433636555f42315f33385f3547_managed_psk
Agent RequestInput wifi_
dca6320a8eae_52542d41433636555f42315f33385f3547_managed_psk
 Passphrase = [ Type=psk, Requirement=mandatory ]
Passphrase? somepassword
Connected wifi_dca6320a8eae_52542d41433636555f42315f33385f3547_
managed_psk
```

12. Replace the service identifier after connect with your service identifier or target network from the previous step. Substitute your Wi-Fi passphrase for somepassword.

13. List the services again:

```
connmanctl> services
*AO Wired ethernet_dca6320a8ead_cable
*AR RT-AC66U_B1_38_5G wifi_
dca6320a8eae_52542d41433636555f42315f33385f3547_managed_psk
  RT-AC66U_B1_38_2G wifi_
ca6320a8eae_52542d41433636555f42315f33385f3247_managed_psk
```

14. This time, *AR appears before the SSID you just connected to, indicating that this network connection is ready. Ethernet takes precedence over Wi-Fi, so the device remains online over Wired.

15. Exit connman-client:

```
connmanctl> quit
```

16. Unplug your Raspberry Pi 4 from the Ethernet, thereby closing your SSH session:

```
root@raspberrypi4-64:~# client_loop: send disconnect: Broken pipe
```

17. Reconnect to your Raspberry Pi 4:

```
$ ssh root@raspberrypi4-64.local
```

18. Start connman-client again:

```
root@raspberrypi4-64:~# connmanctl
connmanctl>
```

19. List the services again:

```
connmanctl> services
*AO RT-AC66U_B1_38_5G wifi_
dca6320a8eae_52542d41433636555f42315f33385f3547_managed_psk
```

20. Observe that the Wired connection is now gone and that the Wi-Fi SSID you connected to that was previously ready has now been promoted to online.

The connman daemon saves your Wi-Fi credentials to a network profile directory under /var/ lib/connman, which persists on the microSD card. This means that connman will automatically reconnect to your Wi-Fi network when your Raspberry Pi 4 boots up. There is no need to go through these steps again after power cycling. You can leave your Ethernet unplugged if you like.

Controlling Bluetooth

In addition to the connman and connman-client packages, the meta-raspberrypi layer includes bluez5 for its Bluetooth stack. All of these packages as well as the requisite Bluetooth drivers are included in rpi-test-image, which we built for Raspberry Pi 4. Let's get Bluetooth up and running and attempt to pair it with another device:

1. Power up your Raspberry Pi 4 and SSH in:

   ```
   $ ssh root@raspberrypi4-64.local
   ```

2. Verify that the Bluetooth drivers are on board:

   ```
   root@raspberrypi4-64:~# lsmod | grep bluetooth
   bluetooth             643072  29 hci_uart,btbcm,bnep,rfcomm
   ecdh_generic           16384  1 bluetooth
   rfkill                 32768  7 nfc,bluetooth,cfg80211
   libaes                 12288  3 aes_arm64,bluetooth,aes_generic
   ```

3. Initialize the HCI UART driver for Bluetooth connectivity:

   ```
   root@raspberrypi4-64:~# btuart
   ```

4. Start connman-client:

   ```
   root@raspberrypi4-64:~# connmanctl
   connmanctl>
   ```

5. Turn on Bluetooth:

   ```
   connmanctl> enable bluetooth
   Enabled Bluetooth
   ```

6. Disregard "Error bluetooth: Already enabled" if Bluetooth is already on.

7. Exit connman-client:

   ```
   connmanctl> quit
   ```

8. Start the Bluetooth CLI:

```
root@raspberrypi4-64:~# bluetoothctl
Agent registered
[CHG] Controller DC:A6:32:0A:8E:AF Pairable: yes
```

9. Request the default agent:

```
[bluetooth]# default-agent
Default agent request successful
```

10. Power on the controller:

```
[bluetooth]# power on
Changing power on succeeded
```

11. Show information about the controller:

```
[bluetooth]# show
Controller DC:A6:32:0A:8E:AF (public)
Name: BlueZ 5.72
Alias: BlueZ 5.72
Class: 0x00200000
Powered: yes
Discoverable: no
DiscoverableTimeout: 0x000000b4
Pairable: yes
```

12. Start scanning for Bluetooth devices:

```
[bluetooth]# scan on
Discovery started
[CHG] Controller DC:A6:32:0A:8E:AF Discovering: yes
…
[NEW] Device DC:08:0F:03:52:CD Frank's iPhone
…
```

13. If your smartphone is nearby and has Bluetooth enabled, it should appear in the list as a [NEW] device. The DC:08:0F:03:52:CD part next to Frank's iPhone is the Bluetooth MAC address of my smartphone.

14. Stop scanning for Bluetooth devices:

```
[bluetooth]# scan off
…
[CHG] Controller DC:A6:32:0A:8E:AF Discovering: no
Discovery stopped
```

15. If you have an iPhone open, go to **Bluetooth** under **Settings** so that you can accept the pairing request from your Raspberry Pi 4.

16. Attempt to pair with your smartphone:

```
[bluetooth]# pair DC:08:0F:03:52:CD
Attempting to pair with DC:08:0F:03:52:CD
[CHG] Device DC:08:0F:03:52:CD Connected: yes
Request confirmation
[agent] Confirm passkey 936359 (yes/no):
```

17. Substitute your smartphone's Bluetooth MAC address for DC:08:0F:03:52:CD.

18. Before entering yes, accept the pairing request from your smartphone:

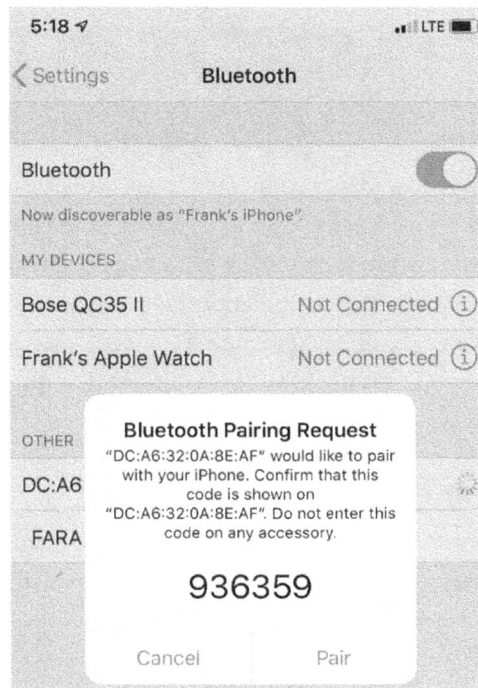

Figure 7.1 – Bluetooth pairing request

19. Enter yes to confirm the passkey:

```
[agent] Confirm passkey 936359 (yes/no): yes
[CHG] Device DC:08:0F:03:52:CD ServicesResolved: yes
[CHG] Device DC:08:0F:03:52:CD Paired: yes
Pairing successful
[CHG] Device DC:08:0F:03:52:CD ServicesResolved: no
[CHG] Device DC:08:0F:03:52:CD Connected: no
```

20. Connect to your smartphone:

```
[bluetooth]# connect DC:08:0F:03:52:CD
Attempting to connect to DC:08:0F:03:52:CD
[CHG] Device DC:08:0F:03:52:CD Connected: yes
Connection successful
[CHG] Device DC:08:0F:03:52:CD ServicesResolved: yes
Authorize service
```

21. Again, substitute your smartphone's Bluetooth MAC address for DC:08:0F:03:52:CD.

22. When prompted to authorize the service, enter yes:

```
[agent] Authorize service 0000110e-0000-1000-8000-
00805f9b34fb (yes/no): yes
[Frank's iPhone]#
```

Your Raspberry Pi 4 is now paired and connected to your smartphone over Bluetooth. It should appear on your smartphone's list of Bluetooth devices as **BlueZ 5.72**. The bluetoothctl program has numerous commands and submenus. We've only just scratched the surface. I recommend entering help and perusing the self-documentation to get an idea of what you can do from the command line. Like connman, the BlueZ Bluetooth stack is a D-Bus service, so you can communicate with it programmatically over D-Bus from Python or other high-level programming languages using D-Bus bindings.

Adding a custom layer

If you are using Raspberry Pi 4 to prototype a new product, then you can quickly generate your own custom images by adding packages to the list that's been assigned to the IMAGE_INSTALL:append variable in conf/local.conf. While this simple technique works, at some point you are going to want to start developing your own embedded application.

How do you build this additional software so that you can include it in your custom images? The answer is to create a custom layer with a new recipe to build your software.

1. First, navigate one level above the directory where you cloned Yocto.

2. Next, set up your BitBake work environment:

```
$ source poky/oe-init-build-env build-rpi
```

3. This sets a bunch of environment variables and puts you back in the build-rpi directory.

4. Create a new layer for your application:

```
$ bitbake-layers create-layer ../meta-gattd
NOTE: Starting bitbake server...
Add your new layer with 'bitbake-layers add-layer ../meta-gattd'
```

5. This layer is named meta-gattd for the GATT daemon. Name your layer whatever you like, but please adhere to the meta- prefix convention.

6. Navigate up to the new layer directory:

```
$ cd ../meta-gattd
```

7. Examine the layer's file structure:

```
$ tree
.
├── conf
│   └── layer.conf
├── COPYING.MIT
├── README
└── recipes-example
    └── example
        └── example_0.1.bb
```

8. Rename the recipes-examples directory:

```
$ mv recipes-example recipes-gattd
```

9. Rename the example directory:

```
$ cd recipes-gattd
$ mv example gattd
```

10. Rename the example recipe file:

```
$ cd gattd
$ mv example_0.1.bb gattd_0.1.bb
```

11. Display the renamed recipe file:

```
$ cat gattd_0.1.bb
```

12. You want to populate this recipe with the metadata that's needed to build your software, including SRC_URI and md5 checksums.

13. For now, just replace gattd_0.1.bb with the finished recipe I have provided for you in MELD/ Chapter07/meta-gattd/recipes-gattd/gattd/gattd_0.1.bb.

14. Create a Git repository for your new layer and push it to GitHub.

15. Create a scarthgap branch in your Git repository and push it to GitHub.

Now that we have a custom layer for our application, let's add it to your working image:

1. First, navigate one level above the directory where you cloned Yocto:

```
$ cd ../../..
```

2. Clone your layer or my meta-gattd layer from GitHub:

```
$ git clone -b scarthgap https://github.com/fvasquez/meta-gattd.git
```

3. Replace fvasquez with your GitHub username and meta-gattd with your layer's repo name.

4. Next, set up your BitBake work environment:

```
$ source poky/oe-init-build-env build-rpi
```

5. This sets a bunch of environment variables and puts you back in the build-rpi directory.

6. Then, add the newly cloned layer to the image:

```
$ bitbake-layers add-layer ../meta-gattd
```

7. Replace meta-gattd with the name of your layer.

8. Verify that all the necessary layers have been added to the image:

```
$ bitbake-layers show-layers
```

9. There should be a total of nine layers in the list, including your new layer.

10. Now, add the extra package to your `conf/local.conf` file:

```
CORE_IMAGE_EXTRA_INSTALL += "gattd"
```

11. `CORE_IMAGE_EXTRA_INSTALL` is a convenience variable that's used to add extra packages to an image that inherits from the `core-image` class like `rpi-test-image` does. `IMAGE_INSTALL` is the variable that controls what packages are included in any image. We cannot use `IMAGE_INSTALL += "gattd"` in `conf/local.conf` because it replaces the default lazy assignment that's done in `core-image.bbclass`. Use `IMAGE_INSTALL:append = " gattd"` or `CORE_IMAGE_EXTRA_INSTALL += " gattd"` instead.

12. Lastly, rebuild the image:

```
$ bitbake rpi-test-image
```

If your software successfully builds and installs, it should be included on the finished `rpi-test-image-raspberrypi4-64.rootfs.wic.bz2` image. Write that image to a microSD card and boot it on your Raspberry Pi 4 to find out. There should be a Python script at `/usr/bin/gatt_server.py`.

Adding packages to `conf/local.conf` makes sense during the earliest stages of development. When you are ready to share the fruits of your labor with the rest of your team, you should create an image recipe and put your packages there. At the end of the previous chapter, we went all the way and wrote a `nova-image` recipe to add a `helloworld` package to `core-image-minimal`.

Now that we've spent a good amount of time testing newly built images on actual hardware, it's time to turn our attention back to software. In the next section, we'll look at a tool that was designed to streamline the tedious compile, test, and debug cycle we've grown accustomed to while developing embedded software.

Capturing changes with devtool

In the previous chapter, you learned how to create a recipe for a `helloworld` program from scratch. A copy-paste approach to packaging recipes may work initially, but it soon becomes very frustrating as your project grows and the number of recipes you need to maintain multiplies. I'm here to show you a better way of working with package recipes – both yours and those that are contributed to upstream by some third party. It is called `devtool` and it is the cornerstone of Yocto's extensible SDK.

Development workflows

Before you get started with devtool, you want to make sure that you're doing your work in a new layer instead of modifying recipes in-tree. Otherwise, you could easily overwrite and lose hours and hours of work:

1. First, navigate one level above the directory where you cloned Yocto.

2. Next, set up your BitBake work environment:

    ```
    $ source poky/oe-init-build-env build-mine
    ```

3. This sets a bunch of environment variables and puts you in a new build-mine directory.

4. Set MACHINE in conf/local.conf for 64-bit Arm:

    ```
    MACHINE ?= "qemuarm64"
    ```

5. Create your new layer:

    ```
    $ bitbake-layers create-layer ../meta-mine
    ```

6. Now, add your new layer:

    ```
    $ bitbake-layers add-layer ../meta-mine
    ```

7. Check that your new layer was created where you want it to be:

    ```
    $ bitbake-layers show-layers
    ```

The output of bitbake-layers show-layers should look like this:

```
layer           path                              priority
========================================================
core            /home/frank/poky/meta                  5
yocto           /home/frank/poky/meta-poky             5
yoctobsp        /home/frank/poky/meta-yocto-bsp        5
meta-mine       /home/frank/meta-mine                  6
```

To get some first-hand experience with development workflows, you are going to need a target to deploy to. That means building an image:

```
$ devtool build-image core-image-full-cmdline
```

Building a full image takes a few hours the first time. When it's complete, go ahead and boot it:

```
$ runqemu qemuarm64 nographic
<...>
Poky (Yocto Project Reference Distro) 5.0.4 qemuarm64 ttyAMA0
qemuarm64 login: root
root@qemuarm64:~#
```

By specifying the `nographic` option, we can run QEMU directly in a separate shell. This makes typing easier than having to cope with the emulated graphics output. Log in as `root`. There is no password. Leave QEMU running for now because we need it for the subsequent exercises. You can SSH into this VM with `ssh root@192.168.7.2`.

`devtool` supports three common development workflows:

- Add a new recipe.
- Patch the source built by an existing recipe.
- Upgrade a recipe to fetch a newer version of the upstream source.

When you initiate any of these workflows, `devtool` creates a temporary workspace for you to make your changes. This sandbox contains the recipe files and fetched source. When you are done with your work, `devtool` integrates your changes back into your layer so that the workspace can be destroyed.

Creating a new recipe

Let's say there is some open source software you want that no one has submitted a BitBake recipe for yet. And let's say that the software in question is the `validator` file-signing, verification, and installation tool. In this instance, you could download a source tarball release of `validator` from GitHub and create a recipe for it. That's exactly what `devtool add` does.

First, `devtool add` creates a workspace with its own local Git repository. Inside this new workspace directory, it creates a `recipes/validator` directory and extracts the tarball contents into a `sources/validator` directory. `devtool` knows about popular build systems such as Autotools and CMake and will do its best to figure out what kind of project this is (Autotools in the case of `validator`). It then uses parsed metadata and built package data cached from previous BitBake builds to figure out the values of `DEPENDS` and `RDEPENDS` as well as what files to inherit and require:

1. First, open another shell and navigate one level above the directory where you cloned Yocto.

2. Next, set up your BitBake environment:

```
$ source poky/oe-init-build-env build-mine
```

3. This sets a bunch of environment variables and puts you back in your build-mine working directory.

4. Then, run devtool add with the URL of the source tarball release:

```
$ devtool add https://github.com/containers/validator/releases/
download/0.2.2/validator-0.2.2.tar.xz
```

5. devtool add will generate a recipe that you can then build.

6. Before you build your new recipe, let's take a look at it:

```
$ devtool edit-recipe validator
```

7. devtool will open recipes/validator/validator_0.2.2.bb in an editor. Notice that devtool has already filled in the MD5 checksums for you.

8. Add this line to the end of validator_0.2.2.bb:

```
FILES:${PN} += "${datadir}"
do_install:append() {
    rm -rf ${D}/usr/lib/dracut
}
```

9. Correct any obvious mistakes, save any changes, and exit your editor.

10. To build your new recipe, use the following command:

```
$ devtool build validator
```

11. Next, deploy the compiled validator executable to the target emulator:

```
$ devtool deploy-target validator root@192.168.7.2
```

12. This installs the necessary build artifacts onto the target emulator.

13. From your QEMU shell, run the validator executable that you just built and deployed:

```
root@qemuarm64:~# validator --help
```

14. If you see a bunch of validator-related self-documentation, then the build and deployment were successful. If you do not, then use devtool to repeat the edit, build, and deploy steps until you are convinced that validator works.

15. Once you are satisfied, clean up your target emulator:

```
$ devtool undeploy-target validator root@192.168.7.2
```

16. Merge all your work back into your layer:

```
$ devtool finish -f validator ../meta-mine
```

17. Delete the leftover sources from the workspace:

```
$ devtool reset validator
```

If you think others might benefit from your new recipe, then submit a patch to Yocto.

Modifying the source built by a recipe

Let's say you find a bug in jq, a command-line JSON preprocessor. You search the Git repository at https://github.com/stedolan/jq and find that no one has reported the issue. Then, you look at the source code. It turns out that the fix requires just a few small code changes, so you decide to patch jq yourself. That's where devtool modify comes in.

This time, when devtool looks at Yocto's cached metadata, it sees that a recipe already exists for jq. Like devtool add, devtool modify creates a new temporary workspace with its own local Git repository where it copies the recipe files and extracts the upstream sources. jq is written in C and located in an existing OpenEmbedded layer named meta-oe. We need to add this layer as well as jq's dependencies to our working image before we can modify the package source:

1. First, delete a couple of layers from your build-mine environment:

```
$ bitbake-layers remove-layer workspace
$ bitbake-layers remove-layer meta-mine
```

2. Next, clone the meta-openembedded repository from GitHub if it does not exist already:

```
$ git clone -b scarthgap https://github.com/openembedded/meta-
openembedded.git ../meta-openembedded
```

3. Then, add the meta-oe and meta-mine layers to your image:

```
$ bitbake-layers add-layer ../meta-openembedded/meta-oe
$ bitbake-layers add-layer ../meta-mine
```

4. Verify that all the necessary layers have been added to the image:

```
$ bitbake-layers show-layers
```

5. The output of the command should look like this:

```
layer                  path                                  priority
=====================================================================
core                   /home/frank/poky/meta                        5
yocto                  /home/frank/poky/meta-poky                   5
yoctobsp               /home/frank/poky/meta-yocto-bsp              5
openembedded-layer /home/frank/meta-openembedded/meta-oe           5
meta-mine              /home/frank/meta-mine                        6
```

6. Add the following line to `conf/local.conf` because the `onig` package is a runtime dependency of `jq`:

```
IMAGE_INSTALL:append = " onig"
```

7. Rebuild your image:

```
$ devtool build-image core-image-full-cmdline
```

8. Exit QEMU with *Ctrl + A* and *x* from your other shell and restart the emulator:

```
$ runqemu qemuarm64 nographic
```

Like many patching tools, `devtool modify` uses your commit messages to generate patch filenames, so keep your commit messages brief and meaningful. It also automatically generates the patch files themselves based on your GitHub history and creates a `.bbappend` file with the new patch filenames. Remember to prune and squash your Git commits so that `devtool` divides your work up into sensible patch files:

1. Run `devtool modify` with the name of the package you wish to modify:

```
$ devtool modify jq
```

2. Make your code changes using your preferred editor. Use the standard Git add and commit workflow to keep track of what you've done.

3. Build the modified sources using the following command:

```
$ devtool build jq
```

4. Next, deploy the compiled jq executable to the target emulator:

```
$ devtool deploy-target jq root@192.168.7.2
```

5. This installs the necessary build artifacts onto the target emulator.

6. If connecting fails, then delete the stale emulator's key as shown here:

```
$ ssh-keygen -f "/home/frank/.ssh/known_hosts" -R "192.168.7.2"
```

7. Replace frank with your username in the path.

8. From your QEMU shell, run the jq executable that you just built and deployed. If you can no longer reproduce the bug, then your changes worked. Otherwise, repeat the edit, build, and deploy steps until you are satisfied.

9. Once you are satisfied, clean up your target emulator:

```
$ devtool undeploy-target jq root@192.168.7.2
```

10. Merge all your work back into your layer:

```
$ devtool finish jq ../meta-mine
```

11. If the merge fails because the Git source tree is dirty, then remove or unstage any leftover jq build artifacts and try devtool finish again.

12. Delete the leftover sources from the workspace:

```
$ devtool reset jq
```

If you think others might benefit from your patch or patches, then submit them to the upstream project maintainers.

Upgrading a recipe to a newer version

Let's say you're using the mypy Python static typechecker to develop on your target device and a new version of mypy has just been released. This latest version of mypy has a new feature that you just can't wait to get your hands on. Instead of waiting for the mypy recipe maintainers to upgrade to the new release version, you decide to upgrade the recipe yourself. You would think that would be as easy as bumping a version number in a recipe file, but there are also source archive checksums involved. Wouldn't it be great if the tedious process could be fully automated? Guess what devtool upgrade is for? mypy is a Python 3 module, so your image needs to include

Python 3, mypy, and mypy's dependencies before you can upgrade it. To obtain all of them, follow these steps:

1. First, delete a couple of layers from your build-mine environment:

    ```
    $ bitbake-layers remove-layer workspace
    $ bitbake-layers remove-layer meta-mine
    ```

2. Next, add the meta-python and meta-mine layers to your image:

    ```
    $ bitbake-layers add-layer ../meta-openembedded/meta-python
    $ bitbake-layers add-layer ../meta-mine
    ```

3. 3. Verify that all the necessary layers have been added to the project:

    ```
    $ bitbake-layers show-layers
    ```

4. The output of the command should look like this:

    ```
    layer                 path                                          priority
    ================================================================
    core                  /home/frank/poky/meta                           5
    yocto                 /home/frank/poky/meta-poky                      5
    yoctobsp              /home/frank/poky/meta-yocto-bsp                 5
    openembedded-layer    /home/frank/meta-openembedded/meta-oe          5
    meta-python           /home/frank/meta-openembedded/meta-python      5
    meta-mine             /home/frank/meta-mine                           6
    ```

5. Now, there should be lots of Python modules available for you to use:

    ```
    $ bitbake -s | grep ^python3
    ```

6. One of those modules is python3-mypy.

7. Make sure python3 and python3-mypy are being built and installed on your image by searching for both of them inside conf/local.conf. If they are not there, then you can include them both by adding the following line to your conf/local.conf:

    ```
    IMAGE_INSTALL:append = " python3 python3-mypy"
    ```

8. Rebuild your image:

    ```
    $ devtool build-image core-image-full-cmdline
    ```

9. Exit QEMU with Ctrl + A and x from your other shell and restart the emulator:

```
$ runqemu qemuarm64 nographic
```

> **IMPORTANT NOTE**
>
> At the time of writing, the version of mypy included with meta-python is 1.9.0 and the latest version of mypy available on PyPI is 1.12.1.

Now that all the pieces are in place, let's do the upgrade:

1. First, run devtool upgrade with the name of the package and the target version to upgrade to:

```
$ devtool upgrade python3-mypy --version 1.12.1
```

2. Before you build your upgraded recipe, let's take a look at it:

```
$ devtool edit-recipe python3-mypy
```

3. devtool will open recipes/python3-mypy/python3-mypy_1.12.1.bb in an editor. There is nothing version-specific to change in this recipe, so save the new file and exit your editor.

4. To build your new recipe, use this command:

```
$ devtool build python3-mypy
```

5. Next, deploy your new mypy module to the target emulator:

```
$ devtool deploy-target python3-mypy root@192.168.7.2
```

This installs the necessary build artifacts onto the target emulator.

6. If connecting fails, then delete the stale emulator's key as shown here:

```
$ ssh-keygen -f "/home/frank/.ssh/known_hosts" -R "192.168.7.2"
```

Replace frank with your username in the path.

7. From your QEMU shell, check what version of mypy was deployed:

```
root@qemuarm64:~# mypy --version
mypy 1.12.1 (compiled: no)
```

8. If entering `mypy --version` returns '1.12.1', then the upgrade worked. If it does not, then use devtool to repeat the edit, build, and deploy steps until you've figured out what went wrong.

9. Once you are satisfied, clean up your target emulator:

    ```
    $ devtool undeploy-target python3-mypy root@192.168.7.2
    ```

10. Clean up your workspace:

    ```
    rm -rf workspace/sources/python3-mypy/build
    rm -rf workspace/sources/python3-mypy/mypy/__pycache__
    ```

11. Commit a change to SOURCES.txt:

    ```
    cd workspace/sources/python3-mypy
    git add mypy.egg-info/SOURCES.txt
    git commit -m "add setup cfg to egg SOURCES"
    ```

12. Merge all your work back into your layer:

    ```
    $ cd ../../..
    $ devtool finish python3-mypy ../meta-mine
    ```

    devtool finish moves the sources to a folder called attic.

13. If the merge fails because the GitHub source tree is dirty, then remove or unstage any leftover `python3-mypy` build artifacts and try devtool finish again.

14. Delete the leftover sources from the workspace:

    ```
    $ devtool reset python3-mypy
    ```

If you think others might also be anxious to upgrade their distros to the latest version of a package, then submit a patch to Yocto.

Finally, we've arrived at the topic of how to build our own distro. This feature is unique to Yocto and notably missing from Buildroot. A **distro layer** is a powerful abstraction that can be shared across multiple projects targeting different hardware.

Building your own distro

At the start of the previous chapter, I told you about distro layers such as meta-poky and the distribution metadata contained in their conf/distro subdirectories. As we have seen, you don't need your own distro layer to build your own custom images. You can go a long way without ever having to modify any of Poky's distribution metadata. But if you want to alter distro policies (e.g., features, C library implementations, choice of package manager, and so on), then you can choose to build your own distro.

Building your own distro is a three-step process:

1. Create a new distro layer.
2. Create a distro configuration file.
3. Add more recipes to your distro.

But before we get into the technical details of how to do that, let's consider when it's the right time to roll your own distro.

When and when not to

Distro settings define the package format (rpm, deb, or ipk), package feed, init system (systemd or sysvinit), and specific package versions. You could create your own distro in a new layer by inheriting from Poky and overriding what needs to change for your distro. However, if you find yourself adding a lot of values to your build directory's local.conf file aside from the obvious local settings (such as relative paths), then it is probably time to create your own distro from scratch.

Creating a new distro layer

You know how to create a layer. Creating a distro layer is no different.

1. First, navigate one level above the directory where you cloned Yocto.
2. Next, set up your BitBake work environment:

    ```
    $ source poky/oe-init-build-env build-rpi
    ```

3. This sets a bunch of environment variables and puts you back in the build-rpi directory from earlier.
4. Delete the meta-gattd layer from your build-rpi environment:

    ```
    $ bitbake-layers remove-layer meta-gattd
    ```

5. Comment out or delete CORE_IMAGE_EXTRA_INSTALL from conf/local.conf:

   ```
   #CORE_IMAGE_EXTRA_INSTALL += "gattd"
   ```

6. Create a new layer for our distro:

   ```
   $ bitbake-layers create-layer ../meta-mackerel
   ```

7. Now, add our new layer to the build-rpi configuration:

   ```
   $ bitbake-layers add-layer ../meta-mackerel
   ```

The name of our distro is mackerel. Creating our own distro layer enables us to keep distro policies separate from package recipes (the implementation).

Configuring your distro

Create the distro configuration file in the conf/distro directory of your meta-mackerel distro layer. Give it the same name as your distro (e.g., mackerel.conf).

Set the required DISTRO_NAME and DISTRO_VERSSION variables in conf/distro/mackerel.conf:

```
DISTRO_NAME = "Mackerel (Mackerel Embedded Linux Distro)"
DISTRO_VERSION = "0.1"
```

The following optional variables can also be set in mackerel.conf:

```
DISTRO_FEATURES: Add software support for these features.
DISTRO_EXTRA_RDEPENDS: Add these packages to all images.
DISTRO_EXTRA_RRECOMMENDS: Add these packages if they exist.
TCLIBC: Select this version of the C standard library.
```

Once you are done with those variables, you can define just about any variable in conf/local. conf that you want for your distro. Look at other distros' conf/distro directories, such as Poky's, to see how they organize things, or copy and use poky/meta/conf/distro/defaultsetup.conf as a template. If you decide to break your distro configuration file up into multiple include files, make sure to place them in the conf/distro/include directory of your layer.

Adding more recipes to your distro

Add more distro-related metadata to your distro layer. You will want to add recipes for additional configuration files. These are configuration files that have yet to be installed by an existing recipe. More importantly, you will also want to add append files to customize existing recipes and add their configuration files to your distro.

Runtime package management

Including a package manager for your distro images is great for enabling secure over-the-air updates and rapid application development. When your team works on software that revs multiple times a day, frequent package updates are one way to keep everybody in sync and moving forward. Full image updates are unnecessary (only one package changes) and disruptive (reboot required). Being able to fetch packages from a remote server and install them on a target device is known as **runtime package management**.

Yocto has support for different package formats (rpm, ipk, and deb) and different package managers (dnf and opkg). The package format you select for your distro determines which package manager you can include on it.

To select a package format for our distro, you can set the PACKAGE_CLASSES variable in your distro's conf file. Add this line to meta-mackerel/conf/distro/mackerel.conf:

```
PACKAGE_CLASSES ?= "package_ipk"
```

Now, let's return to the build-rpi directory:

```
$ source poky/oe-init-build-env build-rpi
```

We are targeting Raspberry Pi 4, so make sure MACHINE is still set accordingly in conf/local.conf:

```
MACHINE = "raspberrypi4-64"
```

Comment out PACKAGE_CLASSES in your build directory's conf/local.conf since our distro already selects package_ipk:

```
#PACKAGE_CLASSES ?= "package_rpm"
```

To enable runtime package management, append package-management to the list of EXTRA_IMAGE_FEATURES in your build directory's conf/local.conf:

```
EXTRA_IMAGE_FEATURES ?= "debug-tweaks ssh-server-openssh package-
management"
```

This will install a package database containing all the packages from your current build onto your distro image. A prepopulated package database is optional because you can always initialize a package database on the target after your distro image has been deployed.

Lastly, set the DISTRO variable in your build directory's conf/local.conf file to the name of our distro:

```
DISTRO = "mackerel"
```

This points your build directory's `conf/local.conf` file at our distro configuration file.

Finally, we are ready to build our distro:

```
$ bitbake -c clean rpi-test-image
$ bitbake rpi-test-image
```

We are rebuilding `rpi-test-image` with a different package format, so this will take a little while. The finished images are placed in a different directory this time around:

```
$ ls tmp-glibc/deploy/images/raspberrypi4-64/rpi-test-image*wic.bz2
```

Write the image to a microSD card using Etcher and boot it on your Raspberry Pi 4. Plug it into your Ethernet and SSH in like you did previously:

```
$ ssh root@raspberrypi4-64.local
```

If connecting fails, then delete Raspberry Pi's stale key, as shown here:

```
$ ssh-keygen -f "/home/frank/.ssh/known_hosts" -R "raspberrypi4-64.local"
```

Replace `frank` with your username in the path.

Once you have logged in, verify that the opkg package manager has been installed:

```
root@raspberrypi4-64:~# which opkg
/usr/bin/opkg
```

A package manager isn't of much use without a remote package server to pull it from.

Provisioning a remote package server

Setting up an HTTP remote package server and pointing your target clients at it is easier than you might think. The client-side server address configuration varies between package managers. We will configure opkg manually on Raspberry Pi 4.

Let's start with the package server:

1. First, navigate one level above the directory where you cloned Yocto.

2. Next, set up your BitBake work environment:

    ```
    $ source poky/oe-init-build-env build-rpi
    ```

3. This sets a bunch of environment variables and puts you back in the `build-rpi` directory.

4. Build the `curl` package:

```
$ bitbake curl
```

5. Populate the package index:

```
$ bitbake package-index
```

6. Locate the package installer files:

```
$ ls tmp-glibc/deploy/ipk
```

7. There should be three directories, named cortexa72, all, and raspberrypi4_64, in ipk. The architecture directory is cortexa72 while the machine directory is raspberrypi4_64. The names of these two directories will vary depending on how your image has been configured for building.

8. Navigate to the `ipk` directory, which is where the package installer files are:

```
$ cd tmp-glibc/deploy/ipk
```

9. Get the IP address of your Linux host machine.

10. Start the HTTP package server:

```
$ sudo python3 -m http.server --bind 192.168.1.69 80
[sudo] password for frank:
Serving HTTP on 192.168.1.69 port 80
(http://192.168.1.69:80/) ...
```

11. Replace `192.168.1.69` with your Linux host machine's IP address.

Now, let's configure the target client:

1. SSH back into your Raspberry Pi 4:

```
$ ssh root@raspberrypi4-64.local
```

2. Edit `/etc/opkg/opkg.conf` so that it looks like this:

```
src/gz all http://192.168.1.69/all
src/gz cortexa72 http://192.168.1.69/cortexa72
src/gz raspberrypi4_64 http://192.168.1.69/raspberrypi4_64
dest root /
option lists_dir /var/lib/opkg/lists
```

3. Replace 192.168.1.69 with your Linux host machine's IP address.

4. Run opkg update:

```
root@raspberrypi4-64:~# opkg update
Downloading http://192.168.1.69/all/Packages.gz.
Updated source 'all'.
Downloading http://192.168.1.69/aarch64/Packages.gz.
Updated source 'aarch64'.
Downloading http://192.168.1.69/raspberrypi4_64/Packages.gz.
Updated source 'raspberrypi4_64'.
```

5. Try to run curl:

```
root@raspberrypi4-64:~# curl
```

6. The command should fail because curl is not installed.

7. Install curl:

```
root@raspberrypi4-64:~# opkg install curl
Installing libcurl4 (7.69.1) on root
Downloading http://192.168.1.69/aarch64/
libcurl4_7.69.1-r0_aarch64.ipk.
Installing curl (7.69.1) on root
Downloading http://192.168.1.69/aarch64/curl_7.69.1-r0_aarch64.ipk.
Configuring libcurl4.
Configuring curl.
```

8. Verify that curl was installed:

```
root@raspberrypi4-64:~# curl
curl: try 'curl --help' for more information
root@raspberrypi4-64:~# which curl
/usr/bin/curl
```

As you continue to work in the build-rpi directory from a Linux host machine, you can check for updates from your Raspberry Pi 4:

```
root@raspberrypi4-64:~# opkg list-upgradable
```

Then, you can apply them:

```
root@raspberrypi4-64:~# opkg upgrade
```

This is faster than rewriting an image, swapping out the microSD card, and rebooting.

Summary

I know that was a lot to absorb. And trust me – this is just the beginning. Yocto certainly has a steep learning curve. Luckily, there is lots of documentation and a friendly community to guide you. There is also devtool to automate much of the tedium and mistakes of copy-paste development. If you use the tools provided for you and continually save your work to your own layers, Yocto doesn't have to be painful. Before you know it, you'll be rolling your own distro layer and running your own remote package server.

A remote package server is just one way to deploy packages and applications. We will learn about a few others later in *Chapter 15*. Despite the title, some of the techniques we'll look at in that chapter (e.g., conda) apply to any programming language. While package managers are great for development, runtime package management is not commonly used on embedded systems running in production. We will look closely at full image and containerized over-the-air update mechanisms in *Chapter 10*.

Further study

- *Transitioning to a custom environment for systems development*, Yocto Project – `https://docs.yoctoproject.org/transitioning-to-a-custom-environment.html`

- *Yocto Project Development Tasks Manual*, Yocto Project – `https://docs.yoctoproject.org/dev-manual/`

- *Using Devtool to Streamline Your Yocto Project Workflow*, by Tim Orling – `https://www.youtube.com/watch?v=CiD7rB35CRE`

8

Yocto under the Hood

In this chapter, we'll dive deeper into **Yocto**, embedded Linux's premier build system. We will begin with a tour of Yocto's architecture, taking you through the entire build workflow step by step. Next, we'll look at Yocto's multi-layer approach and why it is a good idea to separate metadata into different layers. As more and more **BitBake** layers stack up inside your projects, problems will inevitably arise. We will examine a number of ways to debug Yocto build failures, including task logs, devshell, and dependency graphs.

After taking apart the build system, we'll revisit the topic of BitBake from the previous chapter. This time around, we'll cover more of the basic syntax and semantics so that you can write your own recipes from scratch. We'll look at real-world examples of a BitBake shell and Python code from actual recipe, include, and configuration files so that you know what to expect when you begin to venture out into Yocto's ocean of metadata.

In this chapter, we will cover the following topics:

- Decomposing Yocto's architecture and workflow
- Separating metadata into layers
- Troubleshooting build failures
- Understanding BitBake's syntax and semantics

Technical requirements

To follow along with the examples, make sure you have the following:

- A Linux-based host system with at least 90 GB of free disk space
- Yocto 5.0 (scarthgap) LTS release

You should have already built the 5.0 (scarthgap) LTS release of Yocto in *Chapter 6*. If you have not, then please refer to the *Compatible Linux Distribution* and *Build Host Packages* sections of the *Yocto Project Quick Build* guide (`https://docs.yoctoproject.org/brief-yoctoprojectqs/`) before building Yocto on your Linux host according to the instructions in *Chapter 6*.

The code used in this chapter can be found in the chapter folder in this book's GitHub repository: `https://github.com/PacktPublishing/Mastering-Embedded-Linux-Development`.

Decomposing Yocto's architecture and workflow

Yocto is a complex beast. Taking it apart is the first step toward understanding it. The architecture of a build system can be organized in terms of its workflow. Yocto gets its workflow from the **OpenEmbedded** project it is based on. Source materials feed into the system as inputs by way of metadata in the form of BitBake recipes. The build system uses this metadata to fetch, configure, and compile the source code into binary package feeds. These individual output packages are assembled inside a staging area before the finished Linux image and SDK are generated, complete with a manifest that includes a license for each package that's on board:

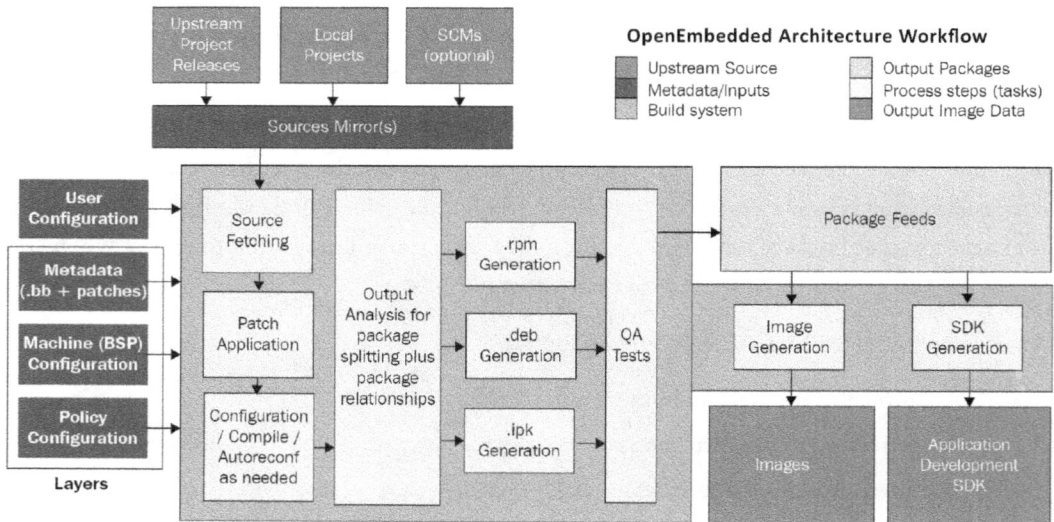

Figure 8.1 – OpenEmbedded architecture workflow

Here are the seven steps of Yocto's build system workflow, as shown in the preceding diagram:

1. Define layers for policy, machine, and software metadata.
2. Fetch sources from the source URI of a software project.
3. Extract the source code, apply any patches, and compile the software.
4. Install the build artifacts into a staging area for packaging.
5. Bundle the installed build artifacts into a package feed for the root filesystem.
6. Run QA checks on a binary package feed before submitting it.
7. Generate the finished Linux image and an SDK in parallel.

Except for the first and last steps, all of the steps in this workflow are performed on a per-package basis. Code linting, sanitizing, and other forms of static analysis may occur before or after compilation. Unit and integration tests can run directly on the build machine, on a QEMU instance acting as a stand-in for the target SoC, or on the target itself. When a build completes, the finished image can then be deployed to a group of dedicated devices for further testing. As the gold standard for embedded Linux build systems, Yocto is a vital component of the software CI/CD pipeline for many products.

The packages Yocto generates can be in either rpm, deb, or ipk format. In addition to the main binary package, the build system attempts to generate all of the following packages for a recipe by default:

*   dbg: Binary files, including debug symbols
*   static-dev: Header files and static libraries
*   dev: Header files and shared library symlinks
*   doc: Documentation, including man pages
*   locale: Language translation information

Packages that would contain no files are not generated unless the ALLOW_EMPTY variable is enabled. The set of packages to be generated by default is determined by the PACKAGES variable. Both variables are defined in meta/classes-recipe/packagegroup.bbclass, but their values can be overridden by package group recipes that inherit from that BitBake class.

Building an SDK enables a whole other development workflow for manipulating individual package recipes. In the *Capturing changes with devtool* section of the previous chapter, we learned how to use devtool to add and modify SDK software packages so that we can integrate them back into an image.

Metadata

Metadata is the input that goes into the build system. It controls what gets built and how. Metadata is more than just recipes. BSPs, policies, patches, and other forms of configuration files are also metadata. Which version of a package to build and where to pull the source code from are certainly forms of metadata. A developer makes all these choices by naming files, setting variables, and running commands. These configuration actions, argument values, and their resulting artifacts are yet another form of metadata. Yocto parses all of these inputs and transforms them into a complete Linux image.

The first choice a developer makes with respect to building with Yocto is what machine architecture to target. You do this by setting the `MACHINE` variable in the `conf/local.conf` file for your project. When targeting QEMU, I like to use `MACHINE ?= "qemuarm64"` to specify `aarch64` as the machine architecture. Yocto ensures that the correct compiler flags propagate from a BSP down to the other build layers.

Architecture-specific settings are defined in files called *tunes*, which are located in Yocto's `meta/conf/machine/include` directory, and the individual BSP layers themselves. A number of BSP layers are included with every Yocto release. We worked extensively with the `meta-raspberrypi` BSP layer in the previous chapter. The source for each BSP resides inside its own Git repository.

To clone Xilinx's BSP layer, which contains support for their Zynq family of SoCs, use the following command:

```
$ git clone git://git.yoctoproject.org/meta-xilinx
```

This is just one example of the many BSP layers that accompany Yocto. You won't need this layer for any of the subsequent exercises, so feel free to discard it.

Metadata needs source code to act upon. BitBake's `do_fetch` task can obtain recipe source files in a number of different ways. Here are the two most prominent methods:

- When someone else develops some software that you need, the easiest way to get it is to tell BitBake to download a tarball release of the project.
- To extend someone else's open source software, simply fork the repository on GitHub. BitBake's `do_fetch` task can then use Git to clone the source files from a given `SRC_URI`.

If your team is responsible for the software, then you can choose to embed it into your work environment as a local project. You can do this either by nesting it as a subdirectory or defining it out-of-tree using the externalsrc class. Embedding means that the sources are tied to your layer repository and can't be easily used somewhere else. Out-of-tree projects that use externalsrc require identical paths on all building instances and sabotage reproducibility. Both of these techniques are merely tools used to expedite development. Neither should be used in production.

Policies are properties that are bundled together as a distribution layer. These include things such as which features (systemd, for example), C library implementation (glibc or musl), and package manager are required by a Linux distribution. Each distro layer has its own conf/distro subdirectory. The .conf files inside that directory define the top-level policies for a distribution or image. See the meta-poky subdirectory for an example of a distro layer. This Poky reference distribution layer includes .conf files for building default, tiny, bleeding-edge, and alternative flavors of Poky for your target device. We covered this in the previous chapter, in the *Building your own distro* section.

Build tasks

We already saw how BitBake's do_fetch task downloads the source for a recipe. The next steps in the build process are extracting, patching, configuring, and compiling said source code: do_unpack, do_patch, do_configure, and do_compile.

The do_patch task uses the FILESPATH variable and a recipe's SRC_URI variable to locate patch files and apply them to the intended source code. The FILESPATH variable, found in meta/classes/base.bbclass, defines the default set of directories that the build system uses to search for patch files (*Yocto Project Reference Manual*, https://docs.yoctoproject.org/ref-manual/index.html). By convention, patch files have names ending in .diff and .patch and reside in a subdirectory below where the corresponding recipe file is located. This default behavior can be extended and overridden by defining a FILESEXTRAPATHS variable and appending file pathnames to the recipe's SRC_URI variable.

After patching the source code, the do_configure and do_compile tasks configure, compile, and link it:

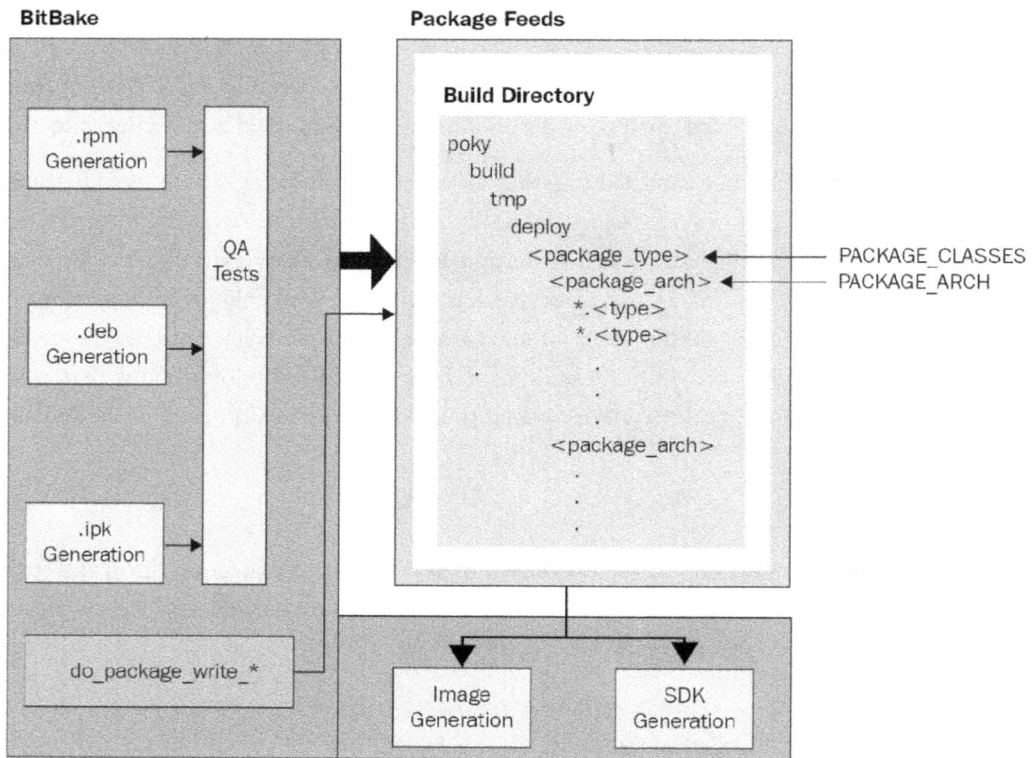

Figure 8.2 – Package feeds

When do_compile is done, the do_install task copies the resulting files to a staging area where they are readied for packaging. There, the do_package task processes the build artifacts and assembles them into one or more packages. Before they are submitted to the package feeds area, the do_package_qa task subjects package artifacts to a battery of QA checks. These autogenerated QA checks are defined in meta/classes-global/insane.bbclass. Lastly, the do_package_write_* tasks create the individual packages and send them to the package feeds area. Once the package feeds area has been populated, BitBake is ready for image and SDK generation.

Image generation

Generating an image is a multi-stage process that relies on several variables to perform a series of tasks. The do_rootfs task creates the root filesystem for an image. These variables determine what packages get installed onto the image:

- IMAGE_INSTALL: Packages to install onto the image
- PACKAGE_EXCLUDE: Packages to omit from the image
- IMAGE_FEATURES: Additional packages to install onto the image
- PACKAGE_CLASSES: Package format (rpm, deb, or ipk) to use
- IMAGE_LINGUAS: Languages (cultures) to include support packages for

Recall that we added packages to the IMAGE_INSTALL variable back in *Chapter 6,* as part of the *Writing an image recipe* section. The list of packages from the IMAGE_INSTALL variable is passed to a package manager (dnf, apt, or opkg) so that they can be installed on the image. Which package manager gets invoked depends on the format of the package feeds: do_package_write_rpm, do_package_write_deb, or do_package_write_ipk. Package installation happens regardless of whether a runtime package manager is included on the target. If there is no package manager onboard, then installation scripts and package metadata get deleted from the image at the end of this phase for hygiene purposes and to save space.

Once package installation is complete, the package's post-installation scripts are run. These post-installation scripts come included with the packages. If all the post-installation scripts run successfully, a manifest is written and optimizations are performed on the root filesystem image. This top-level .manifest file lists all the packages that have been installed on the image. The default library size and executable startup time optimizations are defined by the ROOTFS_ POSTPROCESS_COMMAND variable.

Now that the root filesystem has been fully populated, the do_image task can begin image processing. First, all the pre-processing commands defined by the IMAGE_PREPROCESS_COMMAND variable get executed. Next, the process creates the final image output files. It does this by launching a do_image_* task for every image type (for example, cpio.lz4, ext4, and squashfs-lzo) specified in the IMAGE_FSTYPES variable. The build system then takes the contents of the IMAGE_ROOTFS directory and converts it into one or more image files. These output image files are compressed when the specified filesystem format allows for it. Lastly, the do_image_complete task finishes the image by executing every post-processing command defined by the IMAGE_POSTPROCESS_COMMAND variable.

Now that we have traced through Yocto's entire build workflow from end to end, let's look at some best practices for structuring large projects.

Separating metadata into layers

Yocto metadata is organized around the following concepts:

- **distro**: OS features, including choice of C library, init system, and window manager
- **machine**: CPU architecture, kernel, drivers, and bootloader
- **recipe**: Application binaries and/or scripts
- **image**: Development, manufacturing, or production

These concepts map directly to actual byproducts of the build system, thus offering us guidance when designing our projects. We could rush to assemble everything inside a single layer, but that would likely result in a project that is inflexible and unmaintainable. Hardware inevitably gets revised, and one successful consumer device quickly multiplies into a series of products. For these reasons, it is better to adopt a multi-layered approach early on so that we end up with software components that we can easily modify, swap out, and reuse.

At a minimum, you should create individual distribution, BSP, and application layers for every major project that you start with Yocto. The distribution layer builds the target OS (Linux distro) that your application(s) will run on. Frame buffer and window manager configuration files belong in the distribution layer. The BSP layer specifies the bootloader, kernel, and device tree needed for the hardware to operate. The application layer contains the recipes needed to build all the packages that comprise your custom application(s).

We first encountered the MACHINE variable back in *Chapter 6,* when we performed our first builds with Yocto. We looked at the DISTRO variable toward the end of the previous chapter when we created our own distribution layer. The other Yocto exercises in this book rely on meta-poky for their distro layer. Layers are added to your build by inserting them into the BBLAYERS variable within the conf/bblayers.conf file in your active build directory. Here is an example of Poky's default BBLAYERS definition:

```
BBLAYERS ?= " \
  /home/frank/poky/meta \
  /home/frank/poky/meta-poky \
  /home/frank/poky/meta-yocto-bsp \
  "
```

Rather than edit bblayers.conf directly, use the bitbake-layers command-line tool to work with project layers. Resist the temptation to modify the Poky source tree directly. Always create your own layer (for example, meta-mine) above Poky and make your changes there.

Here is what the BBLAYERS variable should look like within the conf/bblayers.conf file in your active build directory (for example, build-mine) during development:

```
BBLAYERS ?= " \
  /home/frank/poky/meta \
  /home/frank/poky/meta-poky \
  /home/frank/poky/meta-yocto-bsp \
  /home/frank/meta-mine \
  /home/frank/build-mine/workspace \
  "
```

workspace is a special temporary layer we encountered in the previous chapter when we experimented with devtool. Every BitBake layer has the same basic directory structure regardless of what type of layer it is. Layer directory names typically start with the meta prefix by convention. Take the following dummy layer:

```
$ tree meta-example
meta-example
├── classes
│   ├── class-a.bbclass
│   ├── ...
│   └── class-z.bbclass
├── conf
│   └── layer.conf
├── COPYING.MIT
├── README
├── recipes-a
│   ├── package-a
│   │   └── package-a_0.1.bb
│   ├── ...
│   └── package-z
│       └── package-z_0.1.bb
├── recipes-b
│   └── ...
└── recipes-c
    └── ...
```

Every layer must have a conf directory with a `layer.conf` file so that BitBake can set up paths and search patterns for metadata files. We looked closely at the contents of `layer.conf` back in *Chapter 6*, when we created a meta-nova layer for our Nova board. BSP and distribution layers may also have a `machine` or `distro` subdirectory under the `conf` directory with more `.conf` files. We examined the structure of the machine and distro layers in the previous chapter when we built on top of the `meta-raspberrypi` layer and created our own `meta-mackerel` distro layer.

The `classes` subdirectory is only needed for layers that define their own BitBake classes. Recipes are organized by category, such as *connectivity*, so `recipes-a` is actually a placeholder for `recipes-connectivity` and so on. A category can contain one or more packages each with its own set of BitBake recipe files (`.bb`). The recipe files are versioned by package release number. Again, names such as `package-a` and `package-z` are merely placeholders for real packages.

It's very easy to get lost in all these different layers. Even as you become more proficient with Yocto, there will be many times when you find yourself asking how a particular file ended up on your image. Or, more likely, where are the recipe files you need to modify or extend to do what you need to do? Luckily, Yocto provides some command-line tools to help you answer these questions. I recommend that you explore `recipetool`, `oe-pkgdata-util`, and `oe-pkgdata-browser` and familiarize yourself with them. You could save yourself many hours of frustration.

Troubleshooting build failures

In the two preceding chapters, we learned how to build bootable images for QEMU, our Nova board, and Raspberry Pi 4. But what happens when things go wrong? In this section, we will cover a number of useful debugging techniques that should make the prospect of wrangling Yocto build failures less intimidating.

To execute the commands in the subsequent exercises, you need to activate a BitBake environment:

1. First, navigate one level above the directory where you cloned Yocto.
2. Next, set up your BitBake work environment:

    ```
    $ source poky/oe-init-build-env build-rpi
    ```

This sets a bunch of environment variables and puts you back in the `build-rpi` directory that we created in the previous chapter.

Isolating errors

So, your build failed, but where did it fail? You have an error message, but what does it mean and where did it come from? Do not despair. The first step in debugging is reproducing the bug. Once you can reproduce the bug, you can narrow the problem down to a series of known steps. Retracing those steps is how you spot the malfunction:

1. First, look at the BitBake build error message and see if you recognize any package or task names. If you're not sure what packages are in your workspace, you can use the following command to get a list of them:

    ```
    $ bitbake-layers show-recipes
    ```

2. Once you have identified which package failed to build, then search your current layers for any recipe or appends files related to that package like so:

    ```
    $ find ../poky -name "*connman*.bb*"
    ```

3. The package to search for is connman in this instance. The ../poky argument in the preceding find command assumes your build directory is adjacent to poky like build-rpi from the previous chapter.

4. Next, list all the tasks available for the connman recipe:

    ```
    $ bitbake -c listtasks connman
    ```

5. To reproduce the error, you can rebuild connman as follows:

    ```
    $ bitbake -c clean connman && bitbake connman
    ```

Now that you know the recipe and task where your build failed, you are ready to move on to the next stage of debugging.

Dumping the environment

While you are debugging a build failure, you are going to want to see the current values of the variables within BitBake's environment. Let's start from the top and work our way down:

1. First, dump the global environment and search for the value of DISTRO_FEATURES:

    ```
    $ bitbake -e | less
    ```

2. Enter /DISTRO_FEATURES= (note the leading forward slash); less should jump to a line that looks kind of like this:

```
DISTRO_FEATURES="acl alsa argp bluetooth ext2 ipv4 ipv6 largefile
pcmcia usbgadget usbhost wifi xattr nfs zeroconf pci 3g nfc x11 vfat
largefile opengl ptest multiarch wayland vulkan pulseaudio sysvinit
gobject-introspection-data ldconfig"
```

3. To dump BusyBox's package environment and locate its source directory, use the following command:

```
$ bitbake -e busybox | grep ^S=
```

4. To locate ConnMan's working directory, use the following command:

```
$ bitbake-getvar -r connman WORKDIR
```

5. A package's working directory is where its recipe task logs are saved during BitBake builds.

In *step 1*, we could have piped the output from bitbake -e into grep, but less allows us to trace the evaluation of the variable more easily. Enter /DISTRO_FEATURES without the trailing equal sign in less to search for more occurrences of the variable. Hit *n* to jump forward to the next occurrence and *N* to jump back to the previous occurrence.

The same commands work for image as well as package recipes:

```
$ bitbake -e core-image-minimal | grep ^S=
```

In this case, the target environment to dump belongs to core-image-minimal.

Now that you know where the source and task log files are, let's look at some task logs.

Reading the task log

BitBake creates a log file for every shell task and saves it to a temp folder in the package's working directory. In the case of ConnMan, the path to that temp folder looks sort of like this:

```
$ ./tmp-glibc/work/cortexa72-oe-linux/connman/1.42/temp
```

The format of the log filenames is log.do_<task>.<pid>. There are also symlinks with no <pid> at the end of their names, which point to the latest log files for each task. The log files contain the output of the task run, which in most cases is all the information you need to debug the problem. If not, guess what you can do?

Adding more logging

Logging from Python is different from logging from shell in BitBake. To log from Python, you can use BitBake's bb module, which calls out to Python's standard logger module, as shown here:

```
bb.plain -> none; Output: logs console
bb.note -> logger.info; Output: logs
bb.warn -> logger.warning; Output: logs console
bb.error -> logger.error; Output: logs console
bb.fatal -> logger.critical; Output: logs console
bb.debug -> logger.debug; Output: logs console
```

To log from shell, you can use BitBake's logging class, whose source can be found at meta/classes-global/logging.bbclass. All recipes that inherit base.bbclass automatically inherit logging.bbclass. This means that all of the following logging functions should already be available to you from most shell recipe files:

```
bbplain -> Prints exactly what is passed in. Use sparingly.
bbnote -> Prints noteworthy conditions with the NOTE prefix.
bbwarn -> Prints a non-fatal warning with the WARNING prefix.
bberror -> Prints a non-fatal error with the ERROR prefix.
bbfatal -> Prints a fatal error and halts the build.
bbdebug -> Prints debug messages depending on log level.
```

According to the logging.bbclass source, the bbdebug function takes an integer debug log level as its first argument:

```
# Usage: bbdebug 1 "first level debug message"
# bbdebug 2 "second level debug message
bbdebug () {
    USAGE = 'Usage: bbdebug [123] "message"'
    ...
}
```

Depending on the debug log level, a bbdebug message may or may not go to the console.

Running commands from devshell

BitBake provides a development shell so that you can run build commands manually in a more interactive environment. Spawning a `devshell` requires a terminal multiplexer like `tmux`. To install `tmux`, use the following:

```
$ sudo apt install tmux
```

To get into a `devshell` for building ConnMan, use the following command:

```
$ bitbake -c devshell connman
```

First, this command extracts and patches the source code for ConnMan. Next, it opens a new terminal in ConnMan's source directory with the environment correctly set up for building. Once inside a `devshell`, you can run commands such as `./configure` and `make` or invoke the cross-compiler directly using `$CC`. `devshell` is perfect for experimenting with values such as `CFLAGS` or `LDFLAGS`, which get passed to tools such as CMake and Autotools as command-line arguments or environment variables. At the very least, you can increase the verbosity level of build commands if the error messages you are reading aren't meaningful.

Graphing dependencies

Sometimes, the cause of the build error cannot be located inside the package recipe files because the error actually occurred when building one of the package's dependencies. To get a list of dependencies for the ConnMan package, use the following command:

```
$ bitbake -v connman
```

We can use BitBake's built-in task explorer to display and navigate dependencies:

```
$ bitbake -g connman -u taskexp
```

The preceding command launches the task explorer's graphical UI after analyzing ConnMan:

> **IMPORTANT NOTE**
>
> Some larger images like core-image-x11 have complex package dependency trees that will likely crash the task explorer.

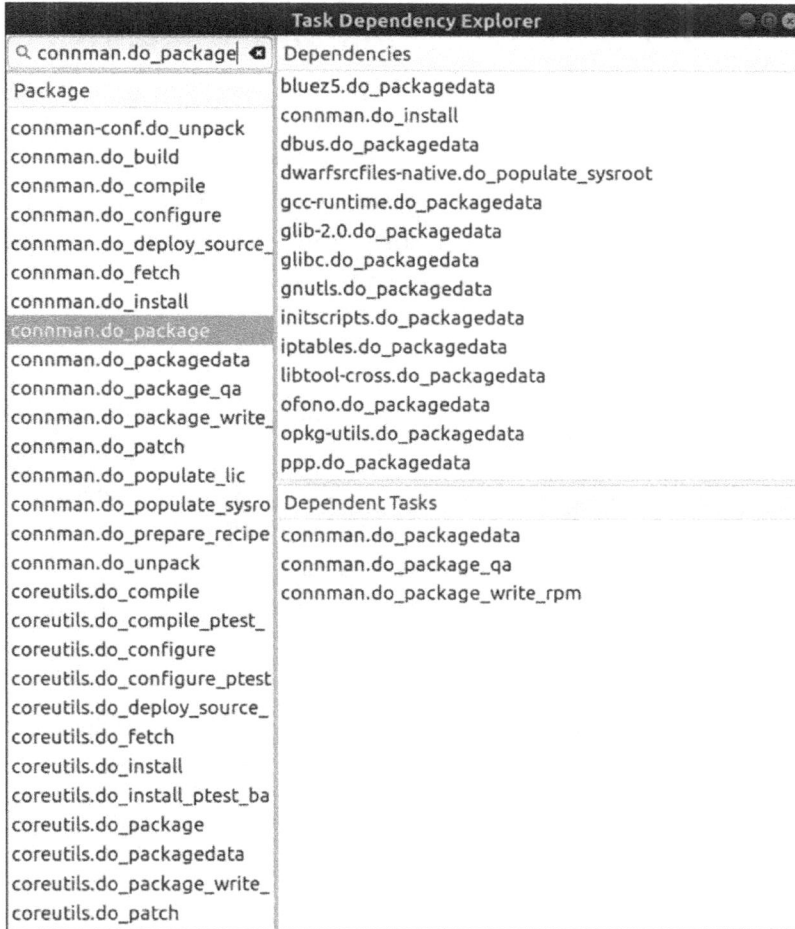

Figure 8.3 – Task explorer

Now, let's move away from the topic of builds and build failures and immerse ourselves in the raw materials of The Yocto Project. I am talking about BitBake metadata.

Understanding BitBake syntax and semantics

BitBake is a task runner. It is similar to GNU Make in that respect, except that it operates on recipes instead of makefiles. The metadata in these recipes defines tasks in shell and Python. BitBake itself is written in Python. The OpenEmbedded project that Yocto is based on consists of BitBake and a large collection of recipes for building embedded Linux distributions. BitBake's power lies in its ability to run tasks in parallel while still satisfying inter-task dependencies. Its layered and inheritance-based approach to metadata enables Yocto to scale in ways Buildroot-based build systems simply cannot.

In *Chapter 6*, we learned about the five types of BitBake metadata files: `.bb`, `.bbappend`, `.inc`, `.bbclass`, and `.conf`. We also wrote BitBake recipes for building a basic helloworld program and nova-image image. Now, we will look more closely at the contents of BitBake metadata files. We know that tasks are written in a mix of shell and Python, but what goes where and why? What language constructs are available to us and what can we do with them? How do we compose metadata to build our applications? Before you can harness the full power of Yocto, you need to learn to read and write BitBake metadata. To do that, you need to learn BitBake's syntax and semantics.

Tasks

Tasks are functions that BitBake needs to run in sequence to execute a recipe. Recall that task names start with the do_ prefix. Here is a task from `recipes-core/systemd`:

```
do_deploy () {
    install ${B}/src/boot/efi/systemd-boot*.efi ${DEPLOYDIR}
}
addtask deploy before do_build after do_compile
```

In this example, a function named do_deploy is defined and immediately elevated to a task using the addtask command. The addtask command also specifies inter-task dependencies. For instance, this do_deploy task depends on the do_compile task completing, while the do_build task depends on the do_deploy task completing. The dependencies expressed by addtask can only be internal to the recipe file.

Tasks can also be deleted using the deltask command. This stops BitBake from executing the task as part of the recipe. To delete the preceding do_deploy task, use the following command:

```
deltask do_deploy
```

This deletes the task from the recipe, but the original do_deploy function definition remains and can still be called.

Dependencies

To ensure efficient parallel processing, BitBake handles dependencies at the task level. We saw just how addtask can be used to express dependencies between tasks within a single recipe file. Dependencies between tasks in different recipes also exist. In fact, these inter-task dependencies are what we usually think of when we consider build-time and runtime dependencies between packages.

Inter-task dependencies

Variable flags (**varflags**) are a means of attaching properties or attributes to variables. They behave like keys in a hash map in the sense that they let you set keys to values and retrieve values by their keys. BitBake defines a large set of varflags for use in recipes and classes. These varflags indicate what the components and dependencies of a task are. Here are some examples of varflags:

```
do_patch[postfuncs] += "copy_sources"
do_package_index[depends] += "signing-keys:do_deploy"
do_rootfs[recrdeptask] += "do_package_write_deb do_package_qa"
```

The value that's assigned to a varflag's key is often one or more other tasks. This means that Bit-Bake varflags offer us another way of expressing inter-task dependencies, different from addtask. The addtask command specifies when a task gets executed (e.g., before do_build after do_compile). Most embedded Linux developers will probably never need to touch varflags in their day-to-day work. I have introduced them here so that we can make sense of the following DEPENDS and RDEPENDS examples.

Build-time dependencies

BitBake uses the DEPENDS variable to manage build-time dependencies. The deptask varflag for a task signifies the task that must be completed for each item in DEPENDS before that task can be executed (*BitBake User Manual*, https://docs.yoctoproject.org/bitbake/bitbake-user-manual/bitbake-user-manual-metadata.html#build-dependencies):

```
do_package[deptask] += "do_packagedata"
```

In this example, the do_packagedata task of each item in DEPENDS must complete before do_package can execute.

Alternatively, you can bypass the DEPENDS variable and define your build-time dependencies explicitly using the depends flag:

```
do_patch[depends] += "quilt-native:do_populate_sysroot"
```

In this example, the do_populate_sysroot task belonging to the quilt-native namespace must be completed before do_patch can execute. A recipe's tasks are often grouped together inside their own namespace to enable this sort of direct access.

Runtime dependencies

BitBake uses the PACKAGES and RDEPENDS variables to manage runtime dependencies. The PACKAGES variable lists all the runtime packages a recipe creates. Each of those packages can have RDEPENDS runtime dependencies. These are packages that must be installed for a given package to run. The rdeptask varflag for a task specifies which tasks must be completed for every runtime dependency before that task can be executed (*BitBake User Manual*, https:// docs.yoctoproject.org/bitbake/bitbake-user-manual/bitbake-user-manual-metadata. html#runtime-dependencies):

```
do_package_qa[rdeptask] = "do_packagedata"
```

In this example, the do_package_data task of each item in RDEPENDS must complete before do_package_qa can execute.

Similarly, the rdepends flag works much like the depends flag by allowing you to bypass the RDEPENDS variable. The only difference is that rdepends is enforced at runtime instead of build time.

Variables

BitBake variable syntax resembles the Make variable syntax. The scope of a variable in BitBake depends on the type of metadata file where a variable was defined. Every variable declared in a recipe file (.bb) is local. Every variable declared in a configuration file (.conf) is global. An image is just a recipe, so an image cannot affect what happens in another recipe.

Assignment and expansion

Variable assignment and expansion work like they do in shell. By default, the assignment occurs as soon as the statement is parsed and is unconditional. The $ character triggers variable expansion. Enclosing braces are optional and serve to protect the variable from being expanded from characters immediately following it. Expanded variables are usually wrapped in double quotes to prevent accidental word splitting and globbing:

```
OLDPKGNAME = "dbus-x11"
PROVIDES:${PN} = "${OLDPKGNAME}"
```

Variables are mutable and normally evaluated at the time of reference, not assignment, like in Make. This means that if a variable is referenced on the right-hand side of an assignment, then that referenced variable is not evaluated until the variable on the left-hand side is expanded. So, if a value on the right-hand side changes over time, then so does the value of the variable on the left-hand side.

Conditional assignment only defines a variable if it is undefined at the time of parsing. This prevents reassignment when you don't want that behavior:

```
PREFERRED_PROVIDER_virtual/kernel ?= "linux-yocto"
```

Conditional assignment is employed at the top of makefiles to prevent variables that may have already been set by the build system (for example, CC, CFLAGS, and LDFLAGS) from being overwritten. Conditional assignment ensures that we don't append or prepend to an undefined variable later on in a recipe.

Lazy assignment using ??= behaves identically to ?= except that the assignment is made at the end of the parsing process rather than immediately (BitBake User Manual, HYPERLINK "https://docs.yoctoproject.org/bitbake/bitbake-user-manual/bitbake-user-manual-metadata.html#setting-a-weak-default-value"):

```
TOOLCHAIN_TEST_HOST ??= "localhost"
```

What that means is that if a variable name is on the left-hand side of multiple lazy assignments, then the last lazy assignment statement wins.

Another form of variable assignment forces the right-hand side of the assignment to be evaluated immediately at the time of parsing:

```
target_datadir := "${datadir}"
```

Note that the := operator for immediate assignment comes from Make not shell.

Appending and prepending

Appending or prepending to a variable or variable flags in BitBake is easy. The following two operators insert a single space in between the value on the left-hand side and the value being appended or prepended from the right-hand side:

```
CXXFLAGS += "-std=c++11"
PACKAGES =+ "gdbserver"
```

Note that the += operator means increment not append when applied to an integer as opposed to string values.

If you wish to omit the single space, there are assignment operators that do that as well:

```
BBPATH .= ":${LAYERDIR}"
FILESEXTRAPATHS =. "${FILE_DIRNAME}/systemd:"
```

The single-space versions of the appending and prepending assignment operators are used throughout BitBake metadata files.

Overrides

BitBake offers an alternative syntax for appending and prepending to variables. This style of concatenating is known as override syntax:

```
CFLAGS:append = " -DSQLITE_ENABLE_COLUMN_METADATA"
PROVIDES:prepend = "${PN}"
```

While it may not be obvious at first glance, the two preceding lines are not defining new variables. The :append and :prepend suffixes modify or override the values of existing variables. They function more like BitBake's .= and =. than the += and =+ operators in the sense that they omit the single space when combining strings. Unlike those operators, overrides are lazy, so assignment does not take place until all parsing has completed.

Finally, let's look at a more advanced form of conditional assignment involving the OVERRIDES variable defined in meta/conf/bitbake.conf. The OVERRIDES variable is a colon-separated list of conditions that you want satisfied. This list is used to select between multiple versions of the same variable, each of which is distinguished by a different suffix. The various suffixes match the names of the conditions. Let's say the OVERRIDES list contains ${TRANSLATED_TARGET_ARCH} as a condition. Now, you can define a version of a variable that is conditional on a target CPU architecture of aarch64, such as the VALGRINDARCH:aarch64 variable:

```
VALGRINDARCH ?= "${TARGET_ARCH}"
VALGRINDARCH:aarch64 = "arm64"
VALGRINDARCH:x86-64 = "amd64"
```

When the TRANSLATED_TARGET_ARCH variable expands to aarch64, the VALGRINDARCH:aarch64 version of the VALGRINDARCH variable is selected over all the other overrides. Selecting variable values based on OVERRIDES is cleaner and less brittle than other methods of conditional assignment, such as #ifdef directives in C.

BitBake also supports appending and prepending operations to variable values based on whether a specific item is listed in OVERRIDES (*BitBake User Manual*, https://docs.yoctoproject.org/bitbake/bitbake-user-manual/bitbake-user-manual-metadata.html#conditional-metadata). Here are various real-world examples:

```
EXTRA_OEMAKE:prepend:task-compile = "${PARALLEL_MAKE} "
EXTRA_OEMAKE:prepend:task-install = "${PARALLEL_MAKEINST} "
DEPENDS = "attr libaio libcap acl openssl zip-native"
DEPENDS:append:libc-musl = " fts "
EXTRA_OECONF:append:libc-musl = " LIBS=-lfts "
EXTRA_OEMAKE:append:libc-musl = " LIBC=musl "
```

Notice how libc-musl is a condition for appending string values to the DEPENDS, EXTRA_OECONF, and EXTRA_OEMAKE variables. Like the earlier unconditional override syntax for appending and prepending to variables, this conditional syntax is also lazy. Assignment does not occur until after the recipes and configuration files have been parsed.

Conditionally appending and prepending to variables based on the contents of OVERRIDES is complicated and can result in unwanted surprises. I recommend getting lots of practice with conditional assignments based on OVERRIDES before adopting these advanced BitBake features.

Inline Python

The @ symbol in BitBake lets us inject and execute Python code inside variables. An inline Python expression gets evaluated each time the variable on the left-hand side of the = operator is expanded. An inline Python expression on the right-hand side of the : = operator is evaluated only once at parse time. Here are some examples of inline Python variable expansion:

```
PV = "${@bb.parse.vars_from_file(d.getVar('FILE', False),d)[1] or '1.0'}"
BOOST_MAJ = "${@"_".join(d.getVar("PV").split(".")[0:2])}"
GO_PARALLEL_BUILD ?= "${@oe.utils.parallel_make_argument(d, '-p %d')}"
```

Notice that bb and oe are aliases for BitBake and OpenEmbedded's Python modules. Also, notice that d.getVar("PV") is used to retrieve the value of the PV variable from the task's runtime environment. The d variable refers to a datastore object that BitBake saves a copy of the original execution environment to. This is largely how a BitBake shell and Python code interoperate.

Functions

Functions are the stuff that BitBake tasks are made of. They are written in either shell or Python and defined inside the .bbclass, .bb, and .inc files.

Shell

Functions written in shell are executed as functions or tasks. Functions that run as tasks usually have names that start with the do_ prefix. This is what a function looks like in shell:

```
meson_do_install() {
    DESTDIR='${D}' ninja -v ${PARALLEL_MAKEINST} install
}
```

Remember to remain shell-agnostic when writing your functions. BitBake executes shell snippets with /bin/sh, which may or may not be a Bash shell, depending on the host distro. Avoid Bashisms by running the scripts/verify-bashisms linter against your shell scripts.

Python

BitBake understands three types of Python functions: pure, BitBake style, and anonymous.

Pure Python functions

A **pure Python function** is written in regular Python and called by other Python code. By pure, I mean that the function lives exclusively within the realm of the Python interpreter's execution environment, not pure in the functional programming sense. Here is an example from meta/recipes-connectivity/bluez5/bluez5.inc:

```
def get_noinst_tools_paths (d, bb, tools):
    s = list()
    bindir = d.getVar("bindir")
    for bdp in tools.split():
        f = os.path.basename(bdp)
        s.append("%s/%s" % (bindir, f))
    return "\n".join(s)
```

Notice that this function takes parameters just like a real Python function. There are a couple more noteworthy things I would also like to point out about this function. First, the datastore object is unavailable, so you need to pass it in as a function parameter (the d variable in this instance). Second, the os module is automatically available, so there is no need to import or pass it in.

Pure Python functions can be called by inline Python assigned to shell variables using the @ symbol. In fact, that is precisely what happens on the next line of this include file:

```
FILES:${PN}-noinst-tools = \
"${@get_noinst_tools_paths(d, bb, d.getVar('NOINST_TOOLS'))}"
```

Notice that both the d datastore object and the bb module are automatically available inside the inline Python scope after the @ symbol.

BitBake-style Python functions

A **BitBake-style Python** function definition is denoted by the python keyword instead of Python's native def keyword. These functions are executed by invoking bb.build.exec_func() from other Python functions, including BitBake's own internal ones. Unlike pure Python functions, Bit-Bake-style functions do not take parameters. The absence of parameters isn't much of a problem since the datastore object is always available as a global variable (d, that is). While not as Pythonic, the BitBake style of defining functions is predominant throughout Yocto. Here is a BitBake-style Python function definition from meta/classes/sign_rpm.bbclass:

```
python sign_rpm () {
    import glob
    from oe.gpg_sign import get_signer

    signer = get_signer(d, d.getVar('RPM_GPG_BACKEND'))
    rpms = glob.glob(d.getVar('RPM_PKGWRITEDIR') + '/*')

    signer.sign_rpms(rpms,
                     d.getVar('RPM_GPG_NAME'),
                     d.getVar('RPM_GPG_PASSPHRASE'),
                     d.getVar('RPM_FILE_CHECKSUM_DIGEST'),
                     int(d.getVar('RPM_GPG_SIGN_CHUNK')),
                     d.getVar('RPM_FSK_PATH'),
                     d.getVar('RPM_FSK_PASSWORD'))
}
```

Anonymous Python functions

An **anonymous Python function** looks much like a BitBake-style Python function, but it executes during parsing. Because they run first, anonymous functions are good for operations that can be done at parse time, such as initializing variables and other forms of setup. Anonymous function definitions can be written with or without the __anonymous function name:

```
python __anonymous () {
    systemd_packages = "${PN} ${PN}-wait-online"
    pkgconfig = d.getVar('PACKAGECONFIG')
    if ('openvpn' or 'vpnc' or 'l2tp' or 'pptp') in pkgconfig.split():
        systemd_packages += " ${PN}-vpn"
    d.setVar('SYSTEMD_PACKAGES', systemd_packages)
}
python () {
    packages = d.getVar('PACKAGES').split()
    if d.getVar('PACKAGEGROUP_DISABLE_COMPLEMENTARY') != '1':
        types = ['', '-dbg', '-dev']
        if bb.utils.contains('DISTRO_FEATURES', 'ptest', True, False, d):
            types.append('-ptest')
        packages = [pkg + suffix for pkg in packages
                    for suffix in types]
        d.setVar('PACKAGES', ' '.join(packages))
    for pkg in packages:
        d.setVar('ALLOW_EMPTY_%s' % pkg, '1')
}
```

The d variable within an anonymous Python function represents the datastore for the entire recipe (*BitBake User Manual*, https://docs.yoctoproject.org/bitbake/bitbake-user-manual/ bitbake-user-manual-metadata.html#anonymous-python-functions). So, when you set a variable inside an anonymous function scope, that value will be available to other functions by way of the global datastore object when they run.

RDEPENDS revisited

Let's return to the subject of runtime dependencies. These are packages that must be installed for a given package to run. This list is defined in the package's RDEPENDS variable. Here is an interesting excerpt from populate_sdk_base.bbclass:

```
do_sdk_depends[rdepends] = "${@get_sdk_ext_rdepends(d)}"
```

And here is the definition of the corresponding inline Python function:

```
def get_sdk_ext_rdepends(d):
    localdata = d.createCopy()
    localdata.appendVar('OVERRIDES', ':task-populate-sdk-ext')
    return localdata.getVarFlag('do_populate_sdk', 'rdepends')
```

There is quite a bit to unpack here. First, the function makes a copy of the datastore object so as not to modify the task runtime environment. Recall that the OVERRIDES variable is a list of conditions used to select between multiple versions of a variable. The next line adds a condition of task-populate-sdk-ext to the OVERRIDES list in the local copy of the datastore. Lastly, the function returns the value of the rdepends varflag for the do_populate_sdk task. The difference now is that rdepends is evaluated using the _task-populate-sdk-ext versions of variables like the following:

```
SDK_EXT:task-populate-sdk-ext = "-ext"
SDK_DIR:task-populate-sdk-ext = "${WORKDIR}/sdk-ext"
```

I find this use of temporary OVERRIDES to be both clever and terrifying.

BitBake syntax and semantics can seem daunting. Combining shell and Python makes for an interesting mix of language features. Not only do we now know how to define variables and functions, but we can also inherit from class files, override variables, and change conditions programmatically. These advanced concepts appear again and again in the .bb, .bbappend, .inc, .bbclass, and .conf files and will become increasingly recognizable over time. As we strive to achieve proficiency in BitBake and begin to stretch our newfound abilities, mistakes are bound to occur.

Summary

Even though you can build just about anything with Yocto, it's not always easy to tell what the build system is doing or how. There is hope for us, though. There are command-line tools to help us find where something came from and how to change it. There are task logs we can read from and write to. There is also devshell, which we can use to configure and compile individual things from the command line. And if we divide our projects into multiple layers from the outset, we are likely to get much more mileage out of the work we do.

BitBake's mix of shell and Python supports some powerful language constructs, such as inheritance, overrides, and conditional variable selection. That's both good and bad. It's good in the sense that layers and recipes are completely composable and customizable.

It's bad in the sense that metadata in different recipe files and different layers can interact in strange and unexpected ways. Combine those powerful language features with the datastore object's ability to act as a portal between the shell and Python execution environments and you have a recipe for countless hours of fun.

This concludes our in-depth exploration of The Yocto Project and the second section of this book, *Building Embedded Linux Images*. In the next section of this book, we switch gears and examine *System Architecture and Design Decisions*, beginning with *Chapter 9*. We will get a chance to use Yocto again in *Chapter 10*, when we evaluate Mender.

Further study

- *Yocto Project Overview and Concepts Manual*, Yocto Project – https://docs.yoctoproject.org/overview-manual/
- *What I wish I'd known about Yocto Project*, Yocto Project – https://docs.yoctoproject.org/what-i-wish-id-known.html
- *BitBake User Manual*, by Richard Purdie, Chris Larson, and Phil Blundell – https://docs.yoctoproject.org/bitbake/
- *Embedded Linux Development Using Yocto Project Cookbook*, by Alex Gonzalez

Join our community on Discord

Join our community's Discord space for discussions with the authors and other readers: https://packt.link/embeddedsystems

Part 3

System Architecture and Design Decisions

This part looks at the various design decisions that need to be made before development can take place in earnest. It covers the topics of filesystems, software updates, device drivers, the init program, and power management. *Chapter 12* demonstrates techniques for rapid prototyping with single-board computers and add-on boards, including how to read schematics and code hardware test scripts in Python.

Each chapter introduces a major area of embedded Linux. It describes the background so that you can learn the general principles, but it also includes detailed working examples that illustrate each of these areas. You can treat this as a book of theory or a book of examples. It works best if you do both: understand the theory and try it out in real life.

This part has the following chapters:

- *Chapter 9, Creating a Storage Strategy*
- *Chapter 10, Updating Software in the Field*
- *Chapter 11, Interfacing with Device Drivers*
- *Chapter 12, Prototyping with Add-On Boards*
- *Chapter 13, Starting Up – The init Program*
- *Chapter 14, Managing Power*

9

Creating a Storage Strategy

The mass storage options for embedded devices have a great impact on the rest of the system in terms of the robustness, speed, and methods used for in-field updates. Most devices employ flash memory in some form or another. Flash memory has become much less expensive over the past few years as storage capacities have increased from tens of megabytes to tens of gigabytes.

In this chapter, we will begin with a detailed look at the technology behind flash memory as well as how different memory organization strategies affect the low-level driver software that has to manage it, including the Linux **memory technology device (MTD)** layer.

For each flash technology, there are different choices when it comes to the filesystem. I will describe those most commonly found on embedded devices and complete the survey by providing a summary of choices for each type of flash memory. Finally, we will consider some techniques that make the best use of flash memory and draw everything together into a coherent storage strategy.

In this chapter, we will cover the following topics:

- Storage options
- Accessing flash memory from the bootloader
- Accessing flash memory from Linux
- Filesystems for flash memory
- Filesystems for NOR and NAND flash memory
- Filesystems for managed flash
- Read-only compressed filesystems
- Temporary filesystems

- Making the root filesystem read-only
- Filesystem choices

Technical requirements

To follow along with the examples, make sure you have the following:

- A Linux-based host system with e2fsprogs, genext2fs, mtd-utils, squashfs-tools, and util-linux or their equivalents installed
- A microSD card reader and card
- balenaEtcher for Linux
- The U-Boot source tree from *Chapter 3*
- The Linux kernel source tree from *Chapter 4*
- A USB to TTL serial cable with 3.3V logic-level pins
- A BeaglePlay
- A 5V USB-C power supply capable of delivering 3A

You should have already downloaded and built U-Boot for the BeaglePlay back in *Chapter 3*. You should have obtained the Linux kernel source tree from *Chapter 4*.

Ubuntu provides packages for most of the tools needed to create and format various filesystems. To install the tools on an Ubuntu 24.04 LTS system, use the following command:

```
$ sudo apt install e2fsprogs genext2fs mtd-utils squashfs-tools util-linux
```

The mtd-utils package includes mtdinfo, mkfs.jffs2, sumtool, nandwrite, and the UBI command-line tools.

Storage options

Embedded devices need storage that takes little power and is physically compact, robust, and reliable over a lifetime of perhaps tens of years. In almost all cases, this means solid-state storage. Solid-state storage was introduced many years ago with **read-only memory (ROM)**, but for the past 20 years, it has been flash memory of some kind. There have been several generations of flash memory in that time, progressing from NOR to NAND to managed flash such as eMMC.

NOR flash is expensive but reliable and can be mapped into the CPU address space, allowing you to execute code directly from flash. NOR flash chips are low capacity, ranging from a few megabytes to a gigabyte or so.

NAND flash memory is much cheaper than NOR and is available in higher capacities from tens of megabytes to tens of gigabytes. However, it needs a lot of hardware and software support to turn it into a useful storage medium.

Managed flash memory consists of one or more NAND flash chips packaged with a controller that handles the complexities of flash memory and presents a hardware interface similar to that of a hard disk. The attraction is that it removes complexity from the driver software and insulates the system designer from the frequent changes in flash technology.

SD cards, eMMC chips, and USB flash drives fit into this category. Almost all the current generations of smartphones and tablets have eMMC storage and this trend is likely to progress with other categories of embedded devices.

Hard drives are seldom found in embedded systems. One exception is digital video recording in set-top boxes and smart TVs where a large amount of storage is needed with fast write times.

In all cases, robustness is of prime importance: you want the device to boot and reach a functional state despite power failures and unexpected resets. You should choose filesystems that behave well under such circumstances. Your choice of storage device technology limits your choice of filesystems.

In this section, we will learn the difference between NOR and NAND flash and consider our options when choosing a managed flash technology.

NOR flash

The memory cells in NOR flash chips are arranged into erase blocks of, for example, 128 KB. Erasing a block sets all the bits to 1. It can be programmed one word at a time (8, 16, or 32 bits depending on the data bus width). Each erase cycle damages the memory cells slightly and after a number of cycles, the erase block becomes unreliable and cannot be used anymore. The maximum number of erase cycles should be given in the data sheet for the chip but is usually in the range of 1 K to 1 M.

The data can be read word by word. The chip is usually mapped into the CPU address space, meaning that you can execute code directly from NOR flash. This makes it a convenient place to put the bootloader code as it needs no initialization beyond hardwiring the address mapping. SoCs that support NOR flash in this way have configurations that provide a default memory mapping so that it encompasses the reset vector of the CPU.

The kernel, and even the root filesystem, can also be located in flash memory, avoiding the need for copying them into RAM and thus creating devices with small memory footprints. This technique is known as **Execute-in-Place** or **XIP**. It is very specialized, and I will not examine it further here. I have included some references at the end of this chapter in the *Further study* section.

There is a standard register-level interface for NOR flash chips called the **Common Flash Interface** or **CFI**, which all modern chips support. The CFI is described in standard JESD68, which you can get from https://www.jedec.org/.

Now that we have learned what NOR flash is, let's look at NAND flash.

NAND flash

NAND flash is much cheaper than NOR flash and has a higher capacity. First-generation NAND chips stored one bit per memory cell in what is now known as a **single-level cell (SLC)** organization. Later generations moved on to two bits per cell in **multi-level cell (MLC)** chips and now to three bits per cell in **tri-level cell (TLC)** chips. As the number of bits per cell increased, the reliability of the storage decreased, requiring more complex controller hardware and software to compensate for this. Where reliability is a concern, you should make sure you are using SLC NAND flash chips.

As with NOR flash, NAND flash is organized into erase blocks ranging in size from 16 KB to 512 KB and, once again, erasing a block sets all the bits to 1. However, the number of erase cycles is lower before the block becomes unreliable. There are typically as few as 1 K cycles for TLC chips and up to 100 K for SLC. NAND flash can only be read and written in pages (usually of 2 or 4 KB). Since they cannot be accessed byte by byte, they cannot be mapped into the address space, so code and data have to be copied into RAM before they can be accessed.

Data transfers to and from the chip are prone to bit flips, which can be detected and corrected using **error-correction codes (ECCs)**. SLC chips generally use a simple **hamming code**, which can be implemented efficiently in software and can correct a single-bit error in a page read. MLC and TLC chips need more sophisticated codes such as **Bose-Chaudhuri-Hocquenghem (BCH)**, which can correct up to 8-bit errors per page. Correcting that many errors requires hardware support inside the flash controller.

The ECCs need to be stored somewhere, so there is an extra area of memory per page known as the **out-of-band (OOB)** area or the spare area. SLC designs usually have 1 byte of OOB per 32 bytes of main storage. So, for a 2 KB page device, the OOB is 64 bytes per page, and for a 4 KB page, it is 128 bytes. MLC and TLC chips have proportionally larger OOB areas to accommodate more complex ECCs. The following diagram shows the organization of a chip with a 128 KB erase block and 2 KB pages:

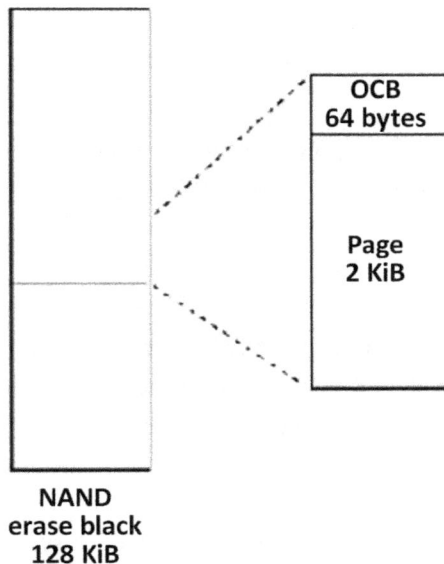

Figure 9.1 – OOB area

During production, the manufacturer tests all the blocks and marks any that fail by setting a flag in the OOB area of each page in the block. It is not uncommon to find that brand-new chips have up to 2% of their blocks marked bad in this way. Saving OOB information for analysis before erasing the area can be useful when there is a problem. Furthermore, it is within the specification for a similar proportion of blocks to give errors on erase before the erase cycle limit is reached. The NAND flash driver should detect this and mark it as bad.

Once space has been made in the OOB area for a bad block flag and ECC bytes, there are still some bytes left. Some flash filesystems make use of these free bytes to store filesystem metadata. Consequently, many parts of the system are interested in the layout of the OOB area: the SoC ROM boot code, the bootloader, the kernel MTD driver, the filesystem code, and the tools to create filesystem images. There is not much standardization, so it is easy to get into a situation in which the bootloader writes data using an OOB format that cannot be read by the kernel MTD driver. It is up to you to make sure that they all agree.

Access to NAND flash chips requires a NAND flash controller, which is usually part of the SoC. You will need the corresponding driver in the bootloader and kernel. The NAND flash controller handles the hardware interface for the chip transferring data to and from pages and may include hardware for error correction.

There is a standard register-level interface for NAND flash chips known as the **Open NAND Flash Interface** or **ONFI**, which most modern chips adhere to. See `https://onfi.org/` for more information.

Modern NAND flash technology is complicated. Pairing NAND flash memory with a controller is no longer enough. We also need an interface to the hardware that abstracts most of the technical details such as error correction away.

Managed flash

The burden of supporting flash memory in the operating system – NAND in particular – becomes smaller if there is a well-defined hardware interface and a standard flash controller that hides the complexities of the memory. This is managed flash memory, and it is becoming more and more common. In essence, it means combining one or more flash chips with a microcontroller that offers an ideal storage device with a small sector size and that is compatible with conventional filesystems. The most important types of chips for embedded systems are **Secure Digital (SD)** cards and the embedded variant known as eMMC.

The MultiMediaCard and Secure Digital cards

The **MultiMediaCard (MMC)** was introduced in 1997 by SanDisk and Siemens as a form of packaged storage using flash memory. Shortly after, in 1999, SanDisk, Matsushita, and Toshiba created the SD card, which is based on MMC but adds encryption and **Digital Rights Management (DRM)**, hence the "secure" part of the name. Both were intended for consumer electronics such as digital cameras, music players, and similar devices. Currently, SD cards are the dominant form of managed flash for consumer and embedded electronics even though the encryption features are seldom used. Newer versions of the SD specification allow smaller packaging (miniSD and microSD) and larger capacities: high capacity SDHC up to 32 GB and extended capacity SDXC up to 2 TB.

The hardware interface for MMC and SD cards is very similar. It is possible to use full-sized MMC cards in full-sized SD card slots (but not the other way around). Early incarnations used a 1-bit **Serial Peripheral Interface (SPI)**. More recent cards use a 4-bit interface.

There is a command set for reading and writing memory in sectors of 512 bytes. Inside the package is a microcontroller and one or more NAND flash chips, as shown in the following diagram:

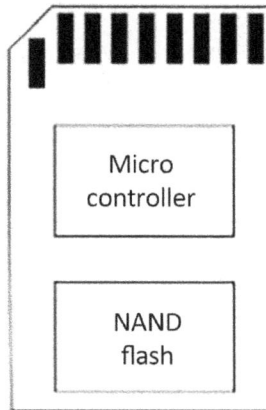

Figure 9.2 – SD card package

The microcontroller implements the command set and manages the flash memory, performing the function of a flash translation layer, as described later in this chapter. They are preformatted with a FAT filesystem: FAT16 on SDSC cards, FAT32 on SDHC, and exFAT on SDXC. The quality of the NAND flash chips and the software on the microcontroller varies greatly between cards. It is questionable whether any of them are sufficiently reliable for deep embedded use. Certainly not with a FAT filesystem, which is prone to file corruption. Remember that the prime use case for MMC and SD cards is for removable storage on cameras, tablets, and phones.

eMMC

Embedded MMC or **eMMC** is simply MMC memory that's been packaged so that it can be soldered onto the motherboard using a 4- or 8-bit interface for data transfer. However, they are intended to be used as storage for an operating system, so the components are capable of performing that task. The chips are usually not preformatted with any filesystem.

Other types of managed flash

One of the first managed flash technologies was **CompactFlash (CF)**, which uses a subset of the **Personal Computer Memory Card International Association (PCMCIA)** hardware interface. CF exposes memory through a **Parallel Advanced Technology Attachment (PATA)** interface and appears to the operating system as a standard hard disk. They were common in x86-based single-board computers and professional video and camera equipment.

One other format that we use every day is the **USB flash drive**. In this case, memory is accessed through a USB interface and the controller implements the USB mass storage specification as well as the flash translation layer and interface to the flash chip or chips. The USB mass storage protocol is based on the SCSI disk command set. As with MMC and SD cards, they are usually preformatted with a FAT filesystem. Their main use case in embedded systems is to exchange data with PCs.

A recent addition to the list of options for managed flash storage is **Universal Flash Storage** (**UFS**). Like eMMC, it is packaged in a chip that is mounted on the motherboard. It has a high-speed serial interface and can achieve data rates greater than eMMC. It supports an SCSI disk command set.

Now that we know what types of flash are available, let's learn how U-Boot loads a kernel image from each of them.

Accessing flash memory from the bootloader

In *Chapter 3* I mentioned the need for the bootloader to load kernel binaries and other images from various flash devices and to perform system maintenance tasks such as erasing and reprogramming flash memory. It follows that the bootloader must have the drivers and infrastructure needed to support read, erase, and write operations on the type of memory you have, whether it be NOR, NAND, or managed. I will use U-Boot in the following examples. Other bootloaders follow a similar pattern.

U-Boot and NOR flash

U-Boot has drivers for NOR CFI chips in `drivers/mtd` and utilizes various `erase` commands to erase memory and `cp.b` to copy data byte by byte onto the flash cells. Suppose that you have NOR flash memory mapped from `0x40000000` to `0x48000000`, of which 4 MB, starting at `0x40040000`, is a kernel image. Here, you would load a new kernel into flash using these U-Boot commands:

```
=> tftpboot 0x100000 uImage
=> erase 0x40040000 0x403fffff
=> cp.b 0x100000 0x40040000 $(filesize)
```

The `filesize` variable in the preceding example is set by the `tftpboot` command to the size of the file just downloaded.

U-Boot and NAND flash

For NAND flash, you need a driver for the NAND flash controller on your SoC, which you can find in the U-Boot source code in the `drivers/mtd/nand` directory.

You can use the nand command to manage memory using its erase, write, and read sub-commands. This example shows a kernel image being loaded into RAM at 0x82000000 and then placed into flash starting at the 0x280000 offset:

```
=> tftpboot 0x82000000 uImage
=> nand erase 0x280000 0x400000
=> nand write 0x82000000 0x280000 $(filesize)
```

U-Boot can also read files stored in the JFFS2, YAFFS2, and UBIFS filesystems. nand write will skip blocks that are marked as bad.

> **IMPORTANT NOTE**
>
> If the data you're writing is for a filesystem, make sure that the filesystem also skips bad blocks.

U-Boot and MMC, SD, and eMMC

U-Boot has drivers for several MMC controllers in drivers/mmc. You can access raw data using mmc read and mmc write at the user interface level, allowing you to handle raw kernel and filesystem images.

U-Boot can also read files from the FAT32 and ext4 filesystems on MMC storage.

U-Boot needs drivers to access NOR, NAND, and managed flash. Which driver you should use depends on your choice of NOR chip or the flash controller on your SoC. Accessing raw NOR and NAND flash from Linux involves additional layers of software.

Accessing flash memory from Linux

Raw NOR and NAND flash memory is handled by the **Memory Technology Device** (MTD) subsystem, which provides you with basic interfaces to read, erase, and write blocks of flash memory. In the case of NAND flash, there are also functions that handle the OOB area and are used to identify bad blocks.

For managed flash, you need drivers to handle a particular hardware interface. MMC/SD cards and eMMC use the mmcblk driver. While CompactFlash and hard drives use the sd SCSI disk driver. USB flash drives use the usb_storage driver together with the sd driver.

Memory technology devices

The MTD subsystem was started by David Woodhouse in 1999 and has been extensively developed over the intervening years. In this section, I will concentrate on the way it handles the two main technologies, NOR and NAND flash.MTD consists of three layers: a core set of functions, a set of drivers for various types of chips, and user-level drivers that present the flash memory as a character device or a block device:

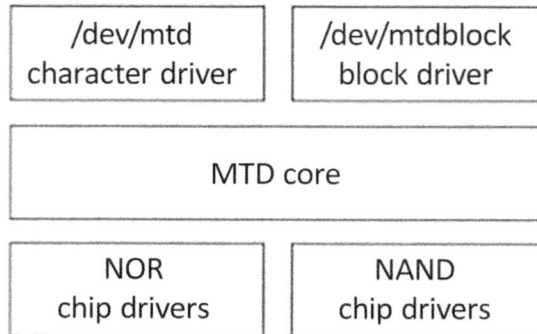

```
+-------------------------+  +-------------------------+
|      /dev/mtd           |  |    /dev/mtdblock        |
|   character driver      |  |     block driver        |
+-------------------------+  +-------------------------+

+-------------------------------------------------------+
|                     MTD core                          |
+-------------------------------------------------------+

+-------------------------+  +-------------------------+
|        NOR              |  |       NAND              |
|     chip drivers        |  |    chip drivers         |
+-------------------------+  +-------------------------+
```

Figure 9.3 – MTD layers

The chip drivers are at the lowest level and interface with flash chips. Only a small number of drivers are needed for NOR flash chips, enough to cover the CFI standard and variations, plus a few non-compliant chips, which are now mostly obsolete. For NAND flash, you will need a driver for the NAND flash controller you are using. This is usually supplied as part of the board support package. There are drivers for about 40 of them in the current mainline kernel in the drivers/ mtd/nand directory.

MTD partitions

In most cases, you will want to partition the flash memory into a number of areas, for example, to provide space for a bootloader, a kernel image, or a root filesystem. In MTD, there are several ways to specify the size and location of partitions, with the main ones being as follows:

- Through the kernel command line using CONFIG_MTD_CMDLINE_PARTS
- Via the device tree using CONFIG_MTD_OF_PARTS
- With a platform-mapping driver

In the case of the first option, the kernel command-line option to use is mtdparts, which is defined within the Linux source code inside drivers/mtd/parsers/cmdlinepart.c:

```
<mtddef>    := <mtd-id>:<partdef>[,<partdef>]
<partdef>   := <size>[@<offset>][<name>][ro][lk][slc]
<mtd-id>    := unique name used in mapping driver/device (mtd->name)
<size>      := standard linux memsize OR "-" to denote all remaining space
               size is automatically truncated at end of device
               if specified or truncated size is 0 the part is skipped
<offset>    := standard linux memsize
               if omitted the part will immediately follow the previous part
               or 0 if the first part
<name>      := '(' NAME ')'
```

Perhaps an example will help. Imagine that you have one flash chip of 128 MB that is to be divided into five partitions. A typical command line would be this:

```
mtdparts=:512k(SPL)ro,780k(U-Boot)ro,128k(U-BootEnv),4m(Kernel),-
(Filesystem)
```

The first element before the colon is mtd-id, which identifies the flash chip either by number or by the name assigned by the board support package. If there is only one chip, as is the case here, it can be left empty. If there is more than one chip, the information for each is separated by a semicolon. Then, for each chip, there is a comma-separated list of partitions each with a size in bytes, KB (k) or MB (m), and a name in parentheses. The ro suffix makes the partition read-only to MTD and is often used to prevent accidental overwriting of the bootloader. The size of the last partition for the chip may be replaced by a dash (-) indicating that it should take up all the remaining space.

You can see a summary of the configuration at runtime by reading /proc/mtd:

```
# cat /proc/mtd
dev: size erasesize name
mtd0: 00080000 00020000 "SPL"
mtd1: 000C3000 00020000 "U-Boot"
mtd2: 00020000 00020000 "U-BootEnv"
mtd3: 00400000 00020000 "Kernel"
mtd4: 07A9D000 00020000 "Filesystem"
```

There is more detailed information for each partition in /sys/class/mtd, including the erase block size and the page size. It is nicely summarized using mtdinfo:

```
# mtdinfo /dev/mtd0
mtd0
Name: SPL
```

```
Type: nand
272 Creating a Storage Strategy
Eraseblock size: 131072 bytes, 128.0 KiB
Amount of eraseblocks: 4 (524288 bytes, 512.0 KiB)
Minimum input/output unit size: 2048 bytes
Sub-page size: 512 bytes
OOB size: 64 bytes
Character device major/minor: 90:0
Bad blocks are allowed: true
Device is writable: false
```

Another way of specifying MTD partitions is through the device tree. Here is an example that creates the same partitions as the command-line example:

```
nand@0,0 {
  #address-cells = <1>;
  #size-cells = <1>;
  partition@0 {
   label = "SPL";
   reg = <0 0x80000>;
  };
  partition@80000 {
   label = "U-Boot";
   reg = <0x80000 0xc3000>;
  };
  partition@143000 {
   label = "U-BootEnv";
   reg = <0x143000 0x20000>;
  };
  partition@163000 {
   label = "Kernel";
   reg = <0x163000 0x400000>;
  };
  partition@563000 {
   label = "Filesystem";
   reg = <0x563000 0x7a9d000>;
  };
};
```

A third alternative is to code the partition information as platform data in an `mtd_partition` structure as shown in this example taken from `arch/arm/mach-omap2/board-omap3beagle.c` (`NAND_BLOCK_SIZE` is defined elsewhere as 128 KB):

```
static struct mtd_partition omap3beagle_nand_partitions[] = {
  {
   .name = "X-Loader",
   .offset = 0,
   .size = 4 * NAND_BLOCK_SIZE,
   .mask_flags = MTD_WRITEABLE, /* force read-only */
  },
  {
   .name = "U-Boot",
   .offset = 0x80000;
   .size = 15 * NAND_BLOCK_SIZE,
   .mask_flags = MTD_WRITEABLE, /* force read-only */
  },
  {
   .name = "U-Boot Env",
   .offset = 0x260000;
   .size = 1 * NAND_BLOCK_SIZE,
  },
  {
   .name = "Kernel",
   .offset = 0x280000;
   .size = 32 * NAND_BLOCK_SIZE,
  },
  {
   .name = "File System",
   .offset = 0x680000;
   .size = MTDPART_SIZ_FULL,
  },
 };
```

Platform data is deprecated: you will only find it used in BSPs for old SoCs that have not been updated to use a device tree.

MTD device drivers

The upper level of the MTD subsystem contains a pair of device drivers:

- A character device with a major number of 90. There are two device nodes per MTD partition number, N: /dev/mtdN (minor number=N*2) and /dev/mtdNro (minor number=(N*2 + 1)). The latter is just a read-only version of the former.

- A block device with a major number of 31 and a minor number of N. The device nodes are in the form /dev/mtdblockN.

Let's look at the character device first since it is the most commonly used of the two. Character devices behave much like files on storage in the sense that you can easily read text from and write text to them.

The MTD character device, mtd

The character devices are the most important: they allow you to access the underlying flash memory as an array of bytes so that you can read and write (program) the flash. It also implements a number of ioctl functions that allow you to erase blocks and manage the OOB area on NAND chips. The following list has been taken from include/uapi/mtd/mtd-abi.h:

- MEMGETINFO: Gets basic MTD characteristic information.
- MEMERASE: Erases blocks in the MTD partition.
- MEMWRITEOOB: Writes out-of-band data for the page.
- MEMREADOOB: Reads out-of-band data for the page.
- MEMLOCK: Locks the chip (if supported).
- MEMUNLOCK: Unlocks the chip (if supported).
- MEMGETREGIONCOUNT: Gets the number of erase regions: non-zero if there are erase blocks of differing sizes in the partition, which is common for NOR flash but rare on NAND.
- MEMGETREGIONINFO: Can be used to get the offset, size, and block count of each region if MEMGETREGIONCOUNT is non-zero.
- MEMGETOOBSEL: Deprecated.
- MEMGETBADBLOCK: Gets the bad block flag.
- MEMSETBADBLOCK: Sets the bad block flag.
- OTPSELECT: Sets OTP (one-time programmable) mode if the chip supports it.
- OTPGETREGIONCOUNT: Gets the number of OTP regions.
- OTPGETREGIONINFO: Gets information about an OTP region.

- ECCGETLAYOUT: Deprecated.

There is a set of utility programs known as mtd-utils for manipulating flash memory that makes use of these ioctl functions. The source can be found at git://git.infradead.org/mtd-utils. git and is available as a package in The Yocto Project and Buildroot. The essential tools are shown in the following list. The package also contains utilities for the JFFS2 and UBI/UBIFS filesystems, which I will cover later. For each of these tools, the MTD character device is one of the following parameters:

- flash_erase: Erases a range of blocks.
- flash_lock: Locks a range of blocks.
- flash_unlock: Unlocks a range of blocks.
- nanddump: Dumps memory from NAND flash, optionally, including the OOB area. Skips bad blocks.
- nandtest: Tests and performs diagnostics for NAND flash.
- nandwrite: Writes (programs) data from a file into NAND flash, skipping bad blocks.

> **TIP**
>
> You must always erase flash memory before writing new content to it.
>
> flash_erase is the command that does this.

To program NOR flash, you simply copy bytes to the MTD device node using a file copy command such as cp.

Unfortunately, this doesn't work with NAND memory as the copy will fail at the first bad block. Instead, use nandwrite, which skips over any bad blocks. To read back NAND memory, you should use nanddump, which also skips bad blocks.

The MTD block device, mtdblock

The mtdblock driver isn't used often. Its purpose is to present flash memory as a block device you can use to format and mount a filesystem. However, it has severe limitations because it does not handle bad blocks in NAND flash, it does not do wear leveling, and it does not handle the mismatch in size between filesystem blocks and flash erase blocks. In other words, it does not have a flash translation layer, which is essential for reliable file storage. The only case where the mtdblock device is useful is for mounting read-only file systems such as SquashFS on top of reliable flash memory such as NOR.

> **TIP**
>
> If you want a read-only filesystem on NAND flash, you should use the UBI driver as described later in this chapter.

Logging kernel oops to MTD

A kernel error or oops is normally logged via the klogd and syslogd daemons to a circular memory buffer or a file. After a reboot, the log will be lost in the case of a ring buffer. Even in the case of a file, it may not have been properly written to before the system crashed. A more reliable method is to write oops and kernel panics to an MTD partition as a circular log buffer. You can enable it with CONFIG_MTD_OOPS and add console=ttyMTDN to the kernel command line with N being the MTD device number to write the messages to.

Simulating NAND memory

The NAND simulator emulates a NAND chip using system RAM. Its main use is to test code that has to be NAND-aware without access to physical NAND memory. The ability to simulate bad blocks, bit flips, and other errors allows you to test code paths that are difficult to exercise using real flash memory. For more information, the best place to look is in the code itself, which provides a comprehensive description of the ways you can configure the driver. The code is in drivers/ mtd/nand/nandsim.c. Enable it with the CONFIG_MTD_NAND_NANDSIM kernel configuration.

The MMC block driver

MMC/SD cards and eMMC chips are accessed using the mmcblk block driver. You need a host controller to match the MMC adapter you are using, which is part of the board support package. The drivers are in the Linux source code under drivers/mmc/host.

MMC storage is partitioned using a partition table in exactly the same way you would for hard disks. That is, by using fdisk or a similar utility.

We now know how Linux accesses each type of flash. Next, we will look at the problems intrinsic to flash memory and how Linux deals with them, either by way of the filesystem or the block device driver.

Filesystems for flash memory

There are several challenges when it comes to making efficient use of flash memory for mass storage: the mismatch between the size of an erase block and a disk sector, the limited number of erase cycles per erase block, and the need for bad block handling on NAND chips. These differences are resolved by a **flash translation layer (FTL)**.

Flash translation layers

A flash translation layer has the following features:

- **Sub allocation:** Filesystems work best with a small allocation unit, traditionally a 512-byte sector. This is much smaller than a flash erase block of 128 KB or more. Therefore, erase blocks need to be subdivided into smaller units to avoid wasting large amounts of space.

- **Garbage collection:** A consequence of sub allocation is that an erase block will contain a mixture of good data and stale data once the filesystem has been in use for a while. Since we can only free up whole erase blocks, the only way to reclaim this free space is to coalesce the good data into one place and then return the now empty erase block to the free list. This is known as garbage collection, and it is usually implemented as a background thread.

- **Wear leveling:** There is a limit on the number of erase cycles for each block. To maximize the lifespan of a chip, it is important to move data around so that each block is erased roughly the same number of times.

- **Bad block handling:** On NAND flash chips, you must avoid using any block marked bad and also mark good blocks as bad if they cannot be erased.

- **Robustness:** Embedded devices may be powered off or reset without warning. Any filesystem should be able to cope without corruption, usually by incorporating a journal or a log of transactions.

There are several ways to deploy the flash translation layer:

- **In the filesystem:** As with JFFS2, YAFFS2, and UBIFS.
- **In the block device driver:** The UBI driver, which UBIFS depends on implements some aspects of a flash translation layer.
- **In the device controller:** As with managed flash devices.

When the flash translation layer is in the filesystem or the block driver, the code is part of the kernel so we can see how it works and expect that it will be improved over time. On the other hand, if the FTL is inside a managed flash device, it is hidden from view, and we cannot verify whether it works as we want. Not only that but putting the FTL into the disk controller means that it misses out on useful information that is held at the filesystem layer, like which sectors belong to files that have been deleted. The latter problem is solved by adding commands that pass this information between the filesystem and the device. I will describe how this works later, in the section on the TRIM command. However, the question of code visibility remains. If you are using managed flash, you just have to choose a manufacturer you can trust.

Now that we know the motivation behind filesystems, let's look at which filesystems are best suited for which types of flash.

Filesystems for NOR and NAND flash memory

To use raw flash chips for mass storage, you have to use a filesystem that understands the peculiarities of the underlying technology. There are three such filesystems:

- **JFFS2 (Journaling Flash File System 2)**: This was the first flash filesystem for Linux and is still in use today. It works for NOR and NAND memory but is notoriously slow during mount.

- **YAFFS2 (Yet Another Flash File System 2)**: This is like JFFS2 but specifically for NAND flash memory. It was adopted by Google as the preferred raw flash filesystem on Android devices.

- **UBIFS (Unsorted Block Image File System)**: This works in conjunction with the UBI block driver to create a reliable flash filesystem. It works well with both NOR and NAND memory. Since it generally offers better performance than JFFS2 or YAFFS2 it should be the preferred solution for new designs.

All of these use MTD as the common interface to flash memory.

JFFS2

The **Journaling Flash File System** had its beginnings in the software for the Axis 2100 network camera back in 1999. For many years, it was the only flash filesystem for Linux and has been deployed on many different types of devices. Today, it is not the best choice, but I will cover it first because it shows the beginning of the evolutionary path.

JFFS2 is a log-structured filesystem that uses MTD to access flash memory. In a log-structured filesystem, changes are written sequentially as nodes to flash memory. A node may contain changes to a directory, such as the names of files created and deleted, or it may contain changes to file data. After a while, a node may be superseded by information contained in subsequent nodes and become an obsolete node. Both NOR and NAND flash are organized as erase blocks. Erasing a block sets all its bits to 1.

JFFS2 categorizes erase blocks into three types:

- **Free**: Contains no nodes at all.
- **Clean**: Only contains valid nodes.
- **Dirty**: Contains at least one obsolete node.

At any one time, there is one block receiving updates, which is called the open block. If power is lost or the system is reset, the only data that can be lost is the last write to the open block. In addition, nodes are compressed as they are written, increasing the effective storage capacity of the flash chip, which is important if you are using expensive NOR flash memory.

When the number of free blocks falls below a certain threshold, a garbage collector kernel thread is started, which scans for dirty blocks, copies the valid nodes into the open block, and then frees up the dirty block.

At the same time, the garbage collector provides a crude form of wear leveling because it cycles valid data from one block to another. The way that the open block is chosen means that each block is erased roughly the same number of times as long as it contains data that changes from time to time. Sometimes, a clean block is chosen for garbage collection to make sure that blocks containing static data that is seldom written are also wear-leveled.

JFFS2 filesystems have a write-through cache, meaning that writes are written to the flash memory synchronously as if they have been mounted with the -o sync option. While improving reliability, this approach increases the time to write data. There is a further problem with small writes: if the length of a write is comparable to the size of the node header (40 bytes), the overhead becomes high. A well-known corner case is log files like those produced by `syslogd`.

Summary nodes

There is one overriding disadvantage to JFFS2: since there is no on-chip index, the directory's structure has to be deduced at mount time by reading the log from start to finish. At the end of the scan, you have a complete picture of the directory structure of the valid nodes, but the mount time taken is proportional to the size of the partition. It is not uncommon to see mount times of the order of one second per megabyte, leading to total mount times of tens or hundreds of seconds.

Summary nodes became an option in Linux 2.6.15 for reducing the time to scan during a mount. A summary node is written at the end of the open erase block, just before it is closed. The summary node contains all of the information needed for the mount-time scan, thereby reducing the amount of data to process during the scan. Summary nodes can reduce mount times by a factor of between two and five at the expense of an overhead of about 5% of the storage space. They are enabled with the `CONFIG_JFFS2_SUMMARY` kernel configuration.

Clean markers

An erased block with all its bits set to 1 is indistinguishable from a block that has been written with 1s, but the latter has not had its memory cells refreshed and cannot be programmed again until it is erased. JFFS2 uses a mechanism called **clean markers** to distinguish between these two situations. After a successful block erase, a clean marker is written either to the beginning of the block or to the OOB area of the first page of the block. If the clean marker exists, then it must be a clean block.

Creating a JFFS2 filesystem

Creating an empty JFFS2 filesystem at runtime is as simple as erasing an MTD partition with clean markers and then mounting it. There is no formatting step because a blank JFFS2 filesystem consists entirely of free blocks. For example, to format MTD partition 6, you would enter these commands on the device:

```
# flash_erase -j /dev/mtd6 0 0
# mount -t jffs2 mtd6 /mnt
```

The -j option to flash_erase adds the clean markers and mounting with the jffs2 type presents the partition as an empty filesystem. Note that the device to be mounted is given as mtd6, not /dev/mtd6. Alternatively, you can give the block the /dev/mtdblock6 device node. This is just a peculiarity of JFFS2. Once mounted, you can treat it like any other filesystem.

You can create a filesystem image directly from the staging area of your development system using mkfs.jffs2 to write out the files in JFFS2 format and sumtool to add the summary nodes. Both of these are part of the mtd-utils package.

As an example, to create an image of the files in rootfs for a NAND flash device with an erase block size of 128 KB (0x20000) and with summary nodes, you would use these two commands:

```
$ mkfs.jffs2 -n -e 0x20000 -p -d ~/rootfs -o ~/rootfs.jffs2
$ sumtool -n -e 0x20000 -p -i ~/rootfs.jffs2 -o ~/rootfs-sum.jffs2
```

The -p option adds padding at the end of the image file to make it a whole number of erase blocks. The -n option suppresses the creation of clean markers in the image, which is normal for NAND devices as the clean marker is in the OOB area. For NOR devices, you would leave out the -n option. You can use a device table with mkfs.jffs2 to set the permissions and the ownership of files by adding -D <device table>. Of course, Buildroot and The Yocto Project will do all this for you.

You can program the image into flash memory from your bootloader. For example, if you have loaded a filesystem image into RAM at address 0x82000000 and you want to load it into a flash partition that begins at 0x163000 bytes from the start of the flash chip and is 0x7a9d000 bytes long, the U-Boot commands for this would be:

```
nand erase clean 163000 7a9d000
nand write 82000000 163000 7a9d000
```

You can do the same thing from Linux using the mtd driver like this:

```
# flash_erase -j /dev/mtd6 0 0
# nandwrite /dev/mtd6 rootfs-sum.jffs2
```

To boot with a JFFS2 root filesystem, you need to pass the mtdblock device on the kernel command line for the partition and a rootfstype since JFFS2 cannot be auto-detected:

```
root=/dev/mtdblock6 rootfstype=jffs2
```

Shortly after JFFS2 was introduced, another log-structured filesystem appeared.

YAFFS2

The YAFFS filesystem was written by Charles Manning starting in 2001 to handle NAND flash chips at a time when JFFS2 did not. Subsequent changes to handle larger (2 KB) page sizes resulted in YAFFS2. The website for YAFFS is https://yaffs.net/.

YAFFS is also a log-structured filesystem that follows the same design principles as JFFS2. The different design decisions mean that it has a faster mount-time scan, simpler and faster garbage collection, and no compression, which speeds up reads and writes at the expense of less efficient use of storage.

YAFFS is not limited to Linux. It has been ported to a wide range of operating systems. It has a dual license: GPLv2 (compatible with Linux) and a commercial license for other operating systems. Unfortunately, the YAFFS code has never been merged into mainline Linux so you will have to patch your kernel.

To get YAFFS2 and patch a kernel, do the following:

```
$ git clone git://www.aleph1.co.uk/yaffs2
$ cd yaffs2
$ ./patch-ker.sh c m <path to your link source>
```

Then, you can configure the kernel with CONFIG_YAFFS_YAFFS2.

Creating a YAFFS2 filesystem

As with JFFS2, to create a YAFFS2 filesystem at runtime, you only need to erase the partition and mount it, but note that in this case, you do not enable clean markers:

```
# flash_erase /dev/mtd/mtd6 0 0
# mount -t yaffs2 /dev/mtdblock6 /mnt
```

To create a filesystem image, the simplest thing to do is use the `mkyaffs2` tool from `https://code.google.com/archive/p/yaffs2utils/`:

```
$ mkyaffs2 -c 2048 -s 64 rootfs rootfs.yaffs2
```

Here, `-c` is the page size and `-s` is the OOB size. There is a tool named `mkyaffs2image` that is part of the YAFFS code, but it has a couple of drawbacks. Firstly, the page and OOB size are hard coded in the source, so you will have to edit and recompile if you have memory that does not match the defaults of 2,048 and 64. Secondly, the OOB layout is incompatible with MTD, which uses the first two bytes as a bad block marker, whereas `mkyaffs2image` uses those bytes to store part of the YAFFS metadata.

To copy the image to the MTD partition from a Linux shell prompt on the target, follow these steps:

```
# flash_erase /dev/mtd6 0 0
# nandwrite -a /dev/mtd6 rootfs.yaffs2
```

To boot with a YAFFS2 root filesystem, add the following to the kernel command line:

```
root=/dev/mtdblock6 rootfstype=yaffs2
```

While we are on the topic of filesystems for raw NOR and NAND flash, let's look at one of the more modern options. This filesystem runs on top of the UBI driver.

UBI and UBIFS

The **Unsorted Block Image** (**UBI**) driver is a volume manager for flash memory that takes care of bad block handling and wear leveling. It was implemented by Artem Bityutskiy and first appeared in Linux 2.6.22. In parallel with that, engineers at Nokia were working on a filesystem that would take advantage of the features of UBI, which they called UBIFS. It appeared in Linux 2.6.27. Splitting the flash translation layer in this way makes the code more modular and also allows other filesystems to take advantage of the UBI driver, as we shall see later on.

UBI

UBI provides an idealized, reliable view of a flash chip by mapping **physical erase blocks (PEBs)** to **logical erase blocks (LEBs)**. Bad blocks are not mapped to LEBs and so are never used. If a block cannot be erased, it is marked as bad and dropped from the mapping. UBI keeps a count of the number of times each PEB has been erased in the header of the LEB and then changes the mapping to ensure that each PEB is erased the same number of times.

UBI accesses the flash memory through the MTD layer. As an extra feature, it can divide an MTD partition into several UBI volumes, which improves wear leveling as follows. Imagine that you have two filesystems: one containing fairly static data, such as a root filesystem, and the other containing data that is constantly changing.

If they are stored in separate MTD partitions, the wear leveling only impacts the second one. Whereas if you choose to store them in two UBI volumes in a single MTD partition, the wear leveling takes place over both areas of the storage, and the lifetime of the flash memory is increased. The following diagram illustrates this situation:

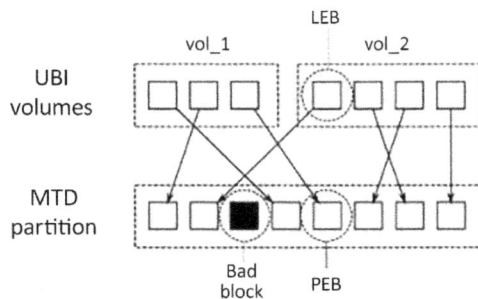

Figure 9.4 – UBI volumes

In this way, UBI fulfills two of the requirements of a flash translation layer: wear leveling and bad-block handling.

To prepare an MTD partition for UBI, you don't use flash_erase as with JFFS2 and YAFFS2. Instead, you use the ubiformat utility, which preserves the erase counts that are stored in the PEB headers. ubiformat needs to know the minimum unit of I/O, which for most NAND flash chips is the page size, but some chips allow reading and writing in subpages that are a half or a quarter of the page size. Consult the chip data sheet for details and, if in doubt, use the page size. This example prepares mtd6 using a page size of 2048 bytes:

```
# ubiformat /dev/mtd6 -s 2048
ubiformat: mtd0 (nand), size 134217728 bytes (128.0 MiB), 1024 eraseblocks
```

```
 of 131072 bytes (128.0 KiB), min. I/O size 2048 bytes
```

Then, you can use the `ubiattach` command to load the UBI driver on an MTD partition that has been prepared in this way:

```
# ubiattach -p /dev/mtd6 -O 2048
UBI device number 0, total 1024 LEBs (130023424 bytes, 124.0 MiB),
available 998 LEBs (126722048 bytes, 120.9 MiB), LEB size 126976 bytes
(124.0 KiB)
```

This creates the `/dev/ubi0` device node through which you can access the UBI volumes. You can use `ubiattach` on several MTD partitions, in which case they can be accessed through `/dev/ubi1`, `/dev/ubi2`, and so on. Note that since each LEB has a header containing the meta information used by UBI, the LEB is smaller than the PEB by two pages. For example, a chip with a PEB size of 128 KB and 2 KB pages would have an LEB of 124 KB. This is important information that you will need when creating a UBIFS image.

The PEB-to-LEB mapping is loaded into memory during the attach phase, a process that takes time proportional to the number of PEBs, typically a few seconds. A new feature was added in Linux 3.7, called the UBI fastmap, which checkpoints the mapping to flash from time to time and so reduces the attach time. The kernel configuration option for this is `CONFIG_MTD_UBI_FASTMAP`.

The first time you attach to an MTD partition after a `ubiformat`, there will be no volumes. You can create volumes using `ubimkvol`. For example, suppose you have a 128 MB MTD partition, and you want to split it into two volumes. The first is to be 32 MB in size and the second will take up the remaining space:

```
# ubimkvol /dev/ubi0 -N vol_1 -s 32MiB
Volume ID 0, size 265 LEBs (33648640 bytes, 32.1 MiB), LEB size 126976
bytes (124.0 KiB), dynamic, name "vol_1", alignment 1
# ubimkvol /dev/ubi0 -N vol_2 -m
Volume ID 1, size 733 LEBs (93073408 bytes, 88.8 MiB), LEB size 126976
bytes (124.0 KiB), dynamic, name "vol_2", alignment 1
```

Now, you have a device with two nodes: `/dev/ubi0_0` and `/dev/ubi0_1`. You can confirm this using `ubinfo`:

```
# ubinfo -a /dev/ubi0
ubi0
Volumes count: 2
Logical eraseblock size: 126976 bytes, 124.0 KiB
```

```
Total amount of logical eraseblocks: 1024 (130023424 bytes, 124.0 MiB)
Amount of available logical eraseblocks: 0 (0 bytes)
Maximum count of volumes 128
Count of bad physical eraseblocks: 0
Count of reserved physical eraseblocks: 20
Current maximum erase counter value: 1
Minimum input/output unit size: 2048 bytes
Character device major/minor: 250:0
Present volumes: 0, 1

Volume ID: 0 (on ubi0)
Type: dynamic
Alignment: 1
Size: 265 LEBs (33648640 bytes, 32.1 MiB)
State: OK
Name: vol_1
Character device major/minor: 250:1
-----------------------------------
Volume ID: 1 (on ubi0)
Type: dynamic
Alignment: 1
Size: 733 LEBs (93073408 bytes, 88.8 MiB)
State: OK
Name: vol_2
Character device major/minor: 250:2
```

At this point, you have a 128 MB MTD partition containing two UBI volumes of sizes 32 MB and 88.8 MB. The total storage available is 32 MB plus 88.8 MB, which equals 120.8 MB. The remaining space, 7.2 MB, is taken up by the UBI headers at the start of each PEB, and space is reserved for mapping out blocks that go bad during the lifetime of the chip.

UBIFS

UBIFS uses a UBI volume to create a robust filesystem. It adds sub-allocation and garbage collection to create a complete flash translation layer. Unlike JFFS2 and YAFFS2, it stores index information on-chip, so mounting is fast, although don't forget that attaching the UBI volume beforehand may take a significant amount of time. It also allows write-back caching as in a normal disk filesystem, so writes are much faster, but data that has not been flushed to flash memory is lost in the event of power down. You can resolve this problem by making careful use of the fsync(2) and fdatasync(2) functions to force a flush of file data at crucial points.

UBIFS has a journal for fast recovery in the event of power down. The minimum size of the journal is 4 MB so UBIFS is not suitable for very small flash devices.

Once you have created the UBI volumes, you can mount them using the device node for the volume, such as /dev/ubi0_0, or by using the device node for the whole partition plus the volume name, as shown here:

```
# mount -t ubifs ubi0:vol_1 /mnt
```

Creating a filesystem image for UBIFS is a two-stage process. First, you create a UBIFS image using mkfs.ubifs, and then embed it into a UBI volume using ubinize. For the first stage, mkfs.ubifs needs to be informed of the page size with -m, the size of the UBI LEB with -e, and the maximum number of erase blocks in the volume with -c. If the first volume is 32 MB and an erase block is 128 KB, then the number of erase blocks is 256. So, to take the contents of the rootfs directory and create a UBIFS image named rootfs.ubi, type the following:

```
$ mkfs.ubifs -r rootfs -m 2048 -e 124KiB -c 256 -o rootfs.ubi
```

The second stage requires you to create a configuration file for ubinize that describes the characteristics of each volume in the image. The help page (ubinize -h) provides details about the format. This example creates two volumes (vol_1 and vol_2):

```
[ubifsi_vol_1]
mode=ubi
image=rootfs.ubi
vol_id=0
vol_name=vol_1
vol_size=32MiB
vol_type=dynamic

[ubifsi_vol_2]
mode=ubi
image=data.ubi
vol_id=1
vol_name=vol_2
vol_type=dynamic
vol_flags=autoresize
```

The second volume has an auto-resize flag and so will expand to fill the remaining space on the MTD partition. Only one volume can have this flag. From this information, ubinize will create an image file named by the -o parameter, with the PEB size as -p, the page size as -m, and the sub-page size as -s:

```
$ ubinize -o ~/ubi.img -p 128KiB -m 2048 -s 512 ubinize.cfg
```

To install this image on the target, you would enter these commands on the target:

```
# ubiformat /dev/mtd6 -s 2048
# nandwrite /dev/mtd6 /ubi.img
# ubiattach -p /dev/mtd6 -O 2048
```

If you want to boot with a UBIFS root filesystem, you will need to provide these kernel command-line parameters:

```
ubi.mtd=6 root=ubi0:vol_1 rootfstype=ubifs
```

UBIFS completes our survey of filesystems for raw NOR and NAND flash memory. Next, we'll look at filesystems for managed flash.

Filesystems for managed flash

As the trend toward managed flash technologies continues, particularly eMMC, we need to consider how to use them effectively. While they appear to have the same characteristics as hard disk drives, the underlying NAND flash chips have the limitations of large erase blocks with limited erase cycles and bad block handling. We also need robustness in the event of power loss.

It is possible to use any of the normal disk filesystems, but we should try to choose one that reduces disk writes and has a fast restart after an unscheduled shutdown.

Flashbench

To make optimum use of the underlying flash memory, you need to know the erase block size and page size. Manufacturers do not publish these numbers as a rule, but it is possible to deduce them by observing the behavior of the chip or card.

Flashbench is one such tool. It was initially written by Arnd Bergman as described in the LWN article available at https://lwn.net/Articles/428584. You can get the code from https://github.com/bradfa/flashbench.

Here is a typical run on a SanDisk 4 GB SDHC card:

```
$ sudo ./flashbench -a /dev/mmcblk0 --blocksize=1024
align 536870912 pre 4.38ms on 4.48ms post 3.92ms diff 332µs
align 268435456 pre 4.86ms on 4.9ms post 4.48ms diff 227µs
align 134217728 pre 4.57ms on 5.99ms post 5.12ms diff 1.15ms
align 67108864 pre 4.95ms on 5.03ms post 4.54ms diff 292µs
align 33554432 pre 5.46ms on 5.48ms post 4.58ms diff 462µs
align 16777216 pre 3.16ms on 3.28ms post 2.52ms diff 446µs
align 8388608 pre 3.89ms on 4.1ms post 3.07ms diff 622µs
align 4194304 pre 4.01ms on 4.89ms post 3.9ms diff 940µs
align 2097152 pre 3.55ms on 4.42ms post 3.46ms diff 917µs
align 1048576 pre 4.19ms on 5.02ms post 4.09ms diff 876µs
align 524288 pre 3.83ms on 4.55ms post 3.65ms diff 805µs
align 262144 pre 3.95ms on 4.25ms post 3.57ms diff 485µs
align 131072 pre 4.2ms on 4.25ms post 3.58ms diff 362µs
align 65536 pre 3.89ms on 4.24ms post 3.57ms diff 511µs
align 32768 pre 3.94ms on 4.28ms post 3.6ms diff 502µs
align 16384 pre 4.82ms on 4.86ms post 4.17ms diff 372µs
align 8192 pre 4.81ms on 4.83ms post 4.16ms diff 349µs
align 4096 pre 4.16ms on 4.21ms post 4.16ms diff 52.4µs
align 2048 pre 4.16ms on 4.16ms post 4.17ms diff 9ns
```

In this case, flashbench reads blocks of 1,024 bytes just before and just after various power-of-two boundaries. As you cross a page or erase a block boundary, the reads after the boundary take longer. The rightmost column shows the difference and is the one that is most interesting. Reading from the bottom, there is a big jump at 4 KB, which is the most likely size of a page. There is a second jump from 52.4µs to 349µs at 8 KB. This is fairly common and indicates that the card can use multi-plane access to read two 4 KB pages at the same time. Beyond that, the differences are less well marked, but there is a clear jump from 485µs to 805µs at 512 KB, which is probably the erase block's size. Given that the card being tested is quite old, these are the sort of numbers you would expect.

Discard and TRIM

Usually, when you delete a file, only the modified directory node is written to storage while the sectors containing the file's contents remain unchanged. When the flash translation layer is in the disk controller, as with managed flash, it does not know that this group of disk sectors no longer contains useful data and so it ends up copying stale data.

In the last few years, the addition of transactions that pass information about deleted sectors down to the disk controller has improved this situation. The SCSI and SATA specifications have a TRIM command, and MMC has a similar command named ERASE. In Linux, this feature is known as **discard**.

To make use of discard, you need a storage device that supports it – most current eMMC chips do – and a Linux device driver to match. You can check this by looking at the block system queue parameters in /sys/block/<block device>/queue/.

The ones of interest are as follows:

- discard_granularity: The size of the internal allocation unit of the device.
- discard_max_bytes: The maximum number of bytes that can be discarded in one go.
- discard_zeroes_data: If this is set to 1, discarded data will be set to 0.

If the device or the device driver does not support discard, these values will all be set to 0. As an example, these are the parameters you will see from the 2 GB eMMC chip on my BeagleBone Black:

```
# grep -s "" /sys/block/mmcblk0/queue/discard_*
/sys/block/mmcblk0/queue/discard_granularity:2097152
/sys/block/mmcblk0/queue/discard_max_bytes:2199023255040
/sys/block/mmcblk0/queue/discard_zeroes_data:1
```

More information can be found in the Documentation/block/queue-sysfs.txt kernel documentation file.

You can enable discard when mounting a filesystem by adding the -o discard option to the mount command. Both ext4 and F2FS support it.

> **Tip**
>
> Make sure that the storage device supports discard before using the -o discard mount option as data loss can occur.

It is also possible to force discard from the command line independently of how the partition is mounted using the fstrim command, which is part of the util-linux package. Typically, you would run this command periodically to free up unused space. fstrim operates on a mounted filesystem so to trim the root filesystem, you would type the following:

```
# sudo fstrim -v /
/: 2061000704 bytes were trimmed
```

The preceding example uses the -v verbose option so that it prints out the number of bytes that have been potentially freed up. In this case, 2,061,000,704 is the approximate amount of free space in the filesystem, so it is the maximum amount of storage that could have been trimmed.

Ext4

The **extended filesystem (ext)** has been the main filesystem for Linux desktops since 1992. The current version (**ext4**) is very stable, well-tested, and has a journal that makes recovering from an unscheduled shutdown fast and mostly painless. It is a good choice for managed flash devices, and you will find that it is the preferred filesystem for Android devices that have eMMC storage. If the device supports discard, you can mount an ext4 filesystem on it with the -o discard option.

To format and create an ext4 filesystem at runtime, type the following:

```
# mkfs.ext4 /dev/mmcblk0p2
# mount -t ext4 -o discard /dev/mmcblk0p1 /mnt
```

To create a filesystem image at build time, you can use the genext2fs utility available from https://github.com/bestouff/genext2fs. In this example, I have specified the block size with -B and the number of blocks in the image with -b:

```
$ genext2fs -B 1024 -b 10000 -d rootfs rootfs.ext4
```

genext2fs can make use of a device table to set the file permissions and ownership as described in *Chapter 5* with -D <file table>.

As the name implies, this will generate an image in ext2 format. You can upgrade to ext4 using tune2fs as follows (details of the command's options can be found on the tune2fs(8) manual page):

```
$ tune2fs -j -J size=1 -O filetype,extents,uninit_bg,dir_index rootfs.ext4
$ e2fsck -pDf rootfs.ext4
```

Both The Yocto Project and Buildroot use exactly these steps when creating images in ext4 format.

While a journal is an asset for devices that may power down without warning, it does add extra write cycles to each write transaction, wearing out the flash memory. If the device is battery-powered, especially if the battery is not removable, the chances of an unscheduled power down are small, so you may want to leave the journal out.

Even with journaling, filesystem corruption can occur on unexpected power loss. In many devices, holding down the power button, unplugging the power cord, or pulling out the battery can result in immediate shutdown.

Due to the nature of buffered I/O, data being written out to flash may be lost if the power goes out before the write is done flushing to storage. For these reasons, it is good to run `fsck` non-interactively on a user partition to check for and repair any filesystem corruption before mounting. Otherwise, the corruption can compound over time until it becomes a serious issue.

F2FS

The **Flash-Friendly File System (F2FS)** is a log-structured filesystem designed for managed flash devices, especially eMMC chips and SD cards. It was written by Samsung and was merged into mainline Linux in 3.8. It is marked as experimental, indicating that it has not been extensively deployed yet, but it seems that some Android devices are using it.

F2FS takes into account the page and erase block sizes and then tries to align data on these boundaries. The log format provides resilience in the face of power down and also provides good write performance. In some tests, F2FS shows a twofold improvement over ext4. There is a good description of the design of F2FS in the `Documentation/filesystems/f2fs.txt` kernel documentation file and there are references at the end of this chapter in the *Further study* section.

The `mkfs.f2fs` utility creates an empty F2FS filesystem with the -l label:

```
# mkfs.f2fs -l rootfs /dev/mmcblock0p1
# mount -t f2fs /dev/mmcblock0p1 /mnt
```

There isn't a tool you can use to create F2FS filesystem images offline yet.

FAT16/32

The old Microsoft filesystems (FAT16 and FAT32) continue to be important as a common format understood by most operating systems. When you buy an SD card or USB flash drive, it is almost certain to be formatted as FAT32, and, in some cases, the on-card microcontroller is optimized for FAT32 access patterns. Also, some boot ROMs require a FAT partition for the second-stage bootloader. However, FAT formats are definitely not suitable for storing critical files because they are prone to corruption and make poor use of the storage space.

Linux supports FAT16 through both the `msdos` and `vfat` filesystems, but FAT32 is only supported through the `vfat` filesystem. To mount a device, say an SD card, on the second MMC hardware adapter, type this:

```
# mount -t vfat /dev/mmcblock1p1 /mnt
```

> **IMPORTANT NOTE**
>
> In the past, there have been licensing issues with the vfat driver, which may (or
> may not) infringe a patent held by Microsoft.

FAT32 has a limitation of 32 GB on the device's size. Devices of a larger capacity may be formatted using the Microsoft exFAT format and it is a requirement for SDXC cards. There is no kernel driver for exFAT, but it can be supported by means of a user space FUSE driver. Since exFAT is proprietary to Microsoft, there are bound to be licensing implications if you support this format on your device.

That does it for read-write filesystems geared toward managed flash. What about space-saving read-only filesystems? The choice is simple: SquashFS.

Read-only compressed filesystems

Compressing data is useful if you don't have quite enough storage to fit everything in. Both JFFS2 and UBIFS do on-the-fly data compression by default. However, if the files are never going to be written, as is usually the case with the root filesystem, you can achieve better compression ratios by using a read-only compressed filesystem. Linux supports several of these: romfs, cramfs, and squashfs. The first two are obsolete now, so I will only describe SquashFS.

SquashFS

The SquashFS filesystem was written by Phillip Lougher in 2002 as a replacement for cramfs. It existed as a kernel patch for a long time, eventually being merged into mainline Linux in version 2.6.29 in 2009. It is very easy to use. You create a filesystem image using mksquashfs and install it to the flash memory:

```
$ mksquashfs rootfs rootfs.squashfs
```

The resulting filesystem is read-only so there is no mechanism for modifying any of the files at runtime. The only way to update a SquashFS filesystem is to erase the whole partition and program in a new image.

SquashFS is not bad-block aware so it must be used with reliable flash memory such as NOR flash. However, it can be used on NAND flash as long as you use UBI to create an emulated, reliable MTD. You have to enable the CONFIG_MTD_UBI_BLOCK kernel configuration, which will create a read-only MTD block device for each UBI volume. The following diagram shows two MTD partitions, each with accompanying mtdblock devices. The second partition is also used to create a UBI volume that is exposed as a third, reliable mtdblock device, which you can use for any read-only filesystem that is not bad-block aware:

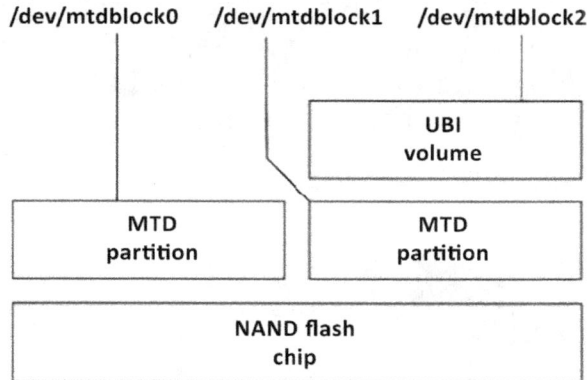

Figure 9.5 – UBI volume

A read-only filesystem is great for immutable contents, but what about temporary files that don't need to persist across reboots? This is where a RAM disk comes in handy.

Temporary filesystems

There are always some files that have a short lifetime or have no significance after a reboot. Many such files are put into /tmp, so it makes sense to keep these files from reaching permanent storage.

The temporary filesystem (tmpfs) is ideal for this purpose. You can create a temporary RAM-based filesystem by simply mounting tmpfs:

```
# mount -t tmpfs tmp_files /tmp
```

As with procfs and sysfs, there is no device node associated with tmpfs, so you have to supply a placekeeper string, which is tmp_files in the preceding example.

The amount of memory used will grow and shrink as files are created and deleted. The default maximum size is half the physical RAM. In most cases, it would be a disaster if tmpfs grew to be that large, so it is a very good idea to cap it with the -o size parameter. The parameter can be given in bytes, KB (k), MB (m), or GB (g) like this for example:

```
# mount -t tmpfs -o size=1m tmp_files /tmp
```

In addition to /tmp, some subdirectories of /var contain volatile data and it is good practice to use tmpfs for them as well, either by creating a separate filesystem for each or, more economically, using symbolic links. Buildroot does this like so:

```
/var/cache -> /tmp
/var/lock -> /tmp
```

```
/var/log -> /tmp
/var/run -> /tmp
/var/spool -> /tmp
/var/tmp -> /tmp
```

In The Yocto Project, `/run` and `/var/volatile` are `tmpfs` mounts with symbolic links pointing to them as shown:

```
/tmp -> /var/tmp
/var/lock -> /run/lock
/var/log -> /var/volatile/log
/var/run -> /run
/var/tmp -> /var/volatile/tmp
```

It is not uncommon to load the root filesystem into RAM on embedded Linux systems. That way, any damage to its contents that may occur at runtime is not permanent. The root filesystem does not need to reside on SquashFS or `tmpfs` to be protected. You just need to make sure the root filesystem is read-only.

Making the root filesystem read-only

You need to make your target device able to survive unexpected events, including file corruption, and still be able to boot and achieve at least a minimum level of functionality. Making the root filesystem read-only is a key part of achieving this ambition because it eliminates accidental overwrites. Making it read-only is easy. Replace `rw` with `ro` on the kernel command line or use an inherently read-only filesystem such as SquashFS. However, you will find that there are a few files and directories that are traditionally writable:

- `/etc/resolv.conf`: This file is written by network configuration scripts to record the addresses of DNS name servers. The information is volatile so you simply have to make it a symlink to a temporary directory like `/etc/resolv.conf -> /var/run/resolv.conf`.

- `/etc/passwd`: This file, along with `/etc/group`, `/etc/shadow`, and `/etc/gshadow`, stores user and group names and passwords. They need to be symbolically linked to an area of persistent storage.

- `/var/lib`: Many applications expect to be able to write to this directory and to keep permanent data here as well. One solution is to copy a base set of files to a `tmpfs` filesystem at boot time and then bind mount `/var/lib` to the new location. You can do this by putting a sequence of commands such as these into one of the boot scripts:

```
$ mkdir -p /var/volatile/lib
$ cp -a /var/lib/* /var/volatile/lib
$ mount --bind /var/volatile/lib /var/lib
```

- `/var/log`: This is the place where `syslogd` and other daemons keep their logs. Generally, logging to flash memory is not desirable because of the many small write cycles it generates. A simple solution is to mount `/var/log` using `tmpfs` making all log messages volatile. In the case of `syslogd`, BusyBox has a version that can log to a circular ring buffer.

If you are using The Yocto Project, you can create a read-only root filesystem by adding `IMAGE_FEATURES = "read-only-rootfs"` to `conf/local.conf` or to your image recipe.

Filesystem choices

So far, we have looked at the technology behind solid-state memory and at the many types of filesystems. Now it is time to summarize the options that are available. In most cases, you will be able to divide your storage requirements into these three categories:

- **Permanent, read-write data**: Runtime configuration, network parameters, passwords, data logs, and user data
- **Permanent, read-only data**: Programs, libraries, and configurations files that are constant; for example, the root filesystem
- **Volatile data**: Temporary storage; for example, `/tmp`

The choices for read-write storage are as follows:

- **NOR**: UBIFS or JFFS2
- **NAND**: UBIFS, JFFS2, or YAFFS2
- **eMMC**: ext4 or F2FS

For read-only storage, you can use any of these mounted with the `ro` attribute. Additionally, if you want to save space, you could use SquashFS. Finally, for volatile storage, there is only one choice: `tmpfs`.

Summary

Flash memory has been the storage technology of choice for embedded Linux from the beginning. Over the years, Linux has gained very good flash memory support from low-level drivers up to flash-aware filesystems, with the latest being UBIFS.

As the rate at which new flash technologies are introduced increases, it is becoming harder to keep pace with the changes at the top end. System designers are increasingly turning to managed flash in the form of eMMC to provide a stable hardware and software interface that is independent of the memory chips inside. Embedded Linux developers are beginning to get to grips with these new chips. Support for TRIM in ext4 and F2FS is well-established, and it is slowly finding its way into the chips themselves. Also, the appearance of new filesystems that have been optimized to manage flash, such as F2FS, is a welcome step forward.

However, the fact remains that flash memory is not the same as a hard disk drive. You have to be careful when you're minimizing the number of filesystem writes – especially as the higher density TLC chips may be able to support as few as 1,000 erase cycles.

In the next chapter, we will continue with the theme of storage options as we consider different ways to keep software up to date on devices that may be deployed to remote locations.

Further study

- *XIP: The past, the present… the future?*, by Vitaly Wool – https://archive.fosdem.org/2007/slides/devrooms/embedded/Vitaly_Wool_XIP.pdf

- *Optimizing Linux with cheap flash drives*, by Arnd Bergmann – https://lwn.net/Articles/428584/

- *eMMC/SSD File System Tuning Methodology*, Cogent Embedded, Inc. – https://elinux.org/images/b/b6/EMMC-SSD_File_System_Tuning_Methodology_v1.0.pdf

- *Flash-Friendly File System (F2FS)*, by Joo-Young Hwang – https://elinux.org/images/1/12/Elc2013_Hwang.pdf

- *An F2FS teardown*, by Neil Brown – https://lwn.net/Articles/518988/

10
Updating Software in the Field

In previous chapters, we discussed various ways to build software for a Linux device and how to create system images for various types of mass storage. When you go into production, you just need to copy the system image to the flash memory, and it is ready to be deployed. Now I want to consider the life of the device beyond the first shipment.

As we move into the era of the *Internet of Things*, the devices that we create are very likely to be connected to the internet. At the same time, software is becoming exponentially more complex. More software means more bugs. Connection to the internet means those bugs can be exploited from afar. Consequentially, we have a common requirement to be able to update software *in the field*. By "in the field," we mean "outside of the factory." Software updates bring more advantages than fixing bugs. They open the door to adding value to existing hardware by enabling new features and improving system performance over time.

In this chapter, we will cover the following topics:

- From where do updates originate?
- What to update
- Basics of software updates
- Types of update mechanism
- OTA updates
- Using Mender for local updates
- Using Mender for OTA updates

Technical requirements

To follow along with the examples, make sure you have the following:

- An Ubuntu 24.04 or later LTS host system with at least 90 GB of free disk space
- Yocto 5.0 (scarthgap) LTS release

You should have already built the 5.0 (scarthgap) LTS release of Yocto in *Chapter 6*. If you have not, then please refer to the *Compatible Linux Distributions* and *Build Host Packages* sections of the *Yocto Project Quick Build* guide (https://docs.yoctoproject.org/brief-yoctoprojectqs/) before building Yocto on your Linux host according to the instructions in *Chapter 6*.

The code used in this chapter can be found in the chapter folder in this book's GitHub repository: https://github.com/PacktPublishing/Mastering-Embedded-Linux-Development/tree/main/Chapter10.

From where do updates originate?

There are many approaches to software updates. Broadly, I characterize them as the following:

- **Local updates**: Performed by a technician who carries the update on a portable medium such as a USB flash drive or an SD card and has to access each system individually.
- **Remote updates**: Initiated by the user or a technician locally, but downloaded from a remote server.
- **Over-the-air (OTA) updates**: Pushed and managed entirely remotely without any need for local input.

I will begin by describing several approaches to software updates, then I will show an example using Mender.

What to update

Embedded Linux devices are very diverse in their design and implementation. However, they all have these basic components:

- Bootloader
- Kernel
- Root filesystem
- System applications
- Device-specific data

Some components are harder to update than others, as summarized in this diagram:

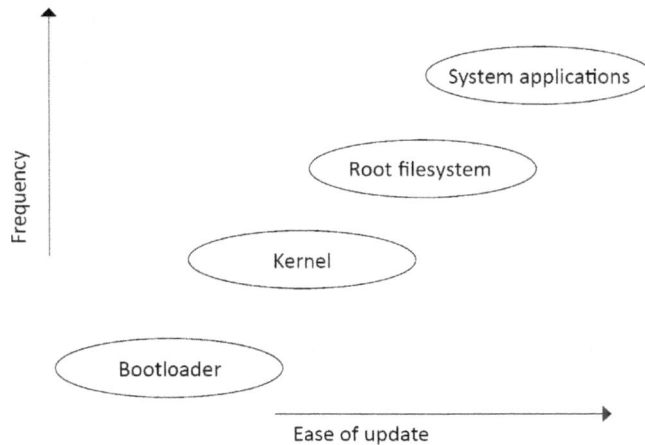

Figure 10.1 – Components of an update

Let's look at each component in turn.

Bootloader

The bootloader is the first piece of code to run when the processor is powered up. The way the processor locates the bootloader is very device-specific, but in most cases, there is only one such location, so there can only be one bootloader. If there is no backup, then updating the bootloader is risky: what happens if the system powers down midway? Consequently, most update solutions leave the bootloader alone. This is not a big problem, because the bootloader only runs for a short time at power-on and is not normally a great source of runtime bugs.

Kernel

The Linux kernel is a critical component that will certainly need updating from time to time.

There are several parts to the kernel:

- A binary image loaded by the bootloader, often stored in the root filesystem.
- Many devices also have a **device tree binary (DTB)** that describes hardware to the kernel, and so must be updated in tandem. The DTB is usually stored alongside the kernel binary.
- There may be kernel modules in the root filesystem.

The kernel and DTB may be stored in the root filesystem if the bootloader can read the filesystem format, or it may be in a dedicated partition. In either case, it is possible and safer to have redundant copies.

Root filesystem

The root filesystem contains the essential system libraries, utilities, and scripts needed to make the system work. It is very desirable to be able to replace and upgrade all of these. The mechanism depends on the filesystem implementation.

Common formats for embedded root filesystems are the following:

- **RAM disk**: Loaded from raw flash memory or a disk image at boot. To update it, simply overwrite the RAM disk image and reboot.

- **Read-only compressed filesystems (squashfs)**: Stored in a flash partition. Since these filesystems don't have a write function, the only way to update them is to write a complete filesystem image to the partition.

- **Normal filesystem types**: JFFS2 and UBIFS formats are common for raw flash memory. For managed flash memory such as eMMC and SD cards, the format is likely to be ext4 or F2FS. Since these are writable at runtime, it is possible to update them file by file.

System applications

The system applications are the main payload of the device; they implement its primary function. As such, they are likely to be updated frequently to fix bugs and add features. They may be bundled with the root filesystem, but it is also common for them to be placed in a separate filesystem to make updating easier and to maintain separation between the system files, which are usually open source, and the application files, which are often proprietary.

Device-specific data

This is the combination of files that are modified at runtime. Device-specific data includes configuration settings, logs, user-supplied data, and similar files. It is not often that they need to be updated, but they do need to be preserved during an update. Such data needs to be stored in a partition of its own.

Components that need to be updated

In summary, an update may include new versions of the kernel, root filesystem, and system applications. The device will have other partitions that should not be disturbed by an update, as is the case with the device runtime data.

The cost of software updates failing can be catastrophic. Secure software updates are also a major concern within both enterprise and home internet environments. Before we can ship any hardware, we need to be able to update the software with confidence.

Basics of software updates

Updating software seems, at first sight, to be a simple task: you just need to overwrite some files with new copies. But then your engineer training kicks in as you begin to realize all the things that could go wrong. What if the power goes down during the update? What if a bug missed during testing of the update renders a percentage of the devices unbootable? What if a third party sends a fake update that enlists your device as part of a botnet? At the very least, the software update mechanism must be:

- **Robust** so that an update does not render the device unusable.
- **Fail-safe** so that there is a fallback mode if all else fails.
- **Secure** to prevent the device from being hijacked by people installing unauthorized updates.

In other words, we need a system that is not susceptible to Murphy's law. Murphy's law states that if something can go wrong, then it eventually will go wrong. Some of these problems are non-trivial. Deploying software to a device in the field is different from deploying software to the cloud. Embedded Linux systems need to detect and respond to mishaps like kernel panics or boot loops without any human intervention.

Making updates robust

You might think that the problem of updating Linux systems was solved a long time ago – we all have Linux desktops that we update regularly (don't we?). Also, there are vast numbers of Linux servers running in data centers that are similarly kept up to date. However, there is a difference between a server and a device. The former operates in a protected environment. It is unlikely to suffer a sudden loss of power or network connectivity. In the unlikely event that an update does fail, it is always possible to get access to the server and use external mechanisms to repeat the installation.

Devices, on the other hand, are often deployed at remote sites with intermittent power and a poor network connection, making it much more likely that an update will be interrupted. Therefore, consider that it may be very expensive to get access to a device to take remedial action over a failed update. What if, for example, the device is an environmental monitoring station at the top of a mountain or controlling the valves of an oil well at the bottom of the sea? In consequence, it is much more important for embedded devices to have a robust update mechanism that will not result in the system becoming unusable.

The key word here is **atomicity**. To be atomic, there should be no stage of the update where only part of the system is updated. There must be a single, uninterruptible change to the system that switches to the new version of the software.

This removes the most obvious update mechanism from consideration: that of simply updating individual files by extracting an archive over parts of the filesystem. There is just no way to ensure that there will be a consistent set of files if the system is reset during the update. Even using a package manager such as apt, dnf, or pacman does not help. If you look at the internals of all these package managers, you will see that they do indeed work by extracting an archive over the filesystem and running scripts to configure the package both before and after the update. Package managers are fine for the protected world of the data center, or even your desktop, but not for a device.

To achieve atomicity, the update must be installed alongside the running system, and then a switch is thrown to move from the old to the new. In later sections, we will describe two different approaches to achieving atomicity. The first is to have two copies of the root filesystem and other major components. One copy is live, while the other can receive updates. When the update is complete, the switch is thrown so that, on reboot, the bootloader selects the updated copy. This is known as a **symmetric image update** or an **A/B image update**. A variant of this theme is to use a special **recovery mode** operating system that is responsible for updating the main operating system. The guarantee of atomicity is shared between the bootloader and the recovery operating system. This is known as an **asymmetric image update**. It is the approach taken by Android prior to the Nougat 7.x version. The second approach is to have two or more copies of the root filesystem in different subdirectories of the system partition, and then use chroot(8) at boot time to select one of them. Once Linux is running, the update client can install updates into the other root filesystem, and then when everything is complete and checked, it can throw the switch and reboot. This is known as an **atomic file update** and is exemplified by **OSTree**.

Making updates fail-safe

The next problem to consider is that of recovering from an update that was installed correctly but that contains code that stops the system from booting. Ideally, we want the system to detect this case and revert to a previous working image.

There are several failure modes that can lead to a non-operational system. The first is a kernel panic, typically caused by a bug in a kernel device driver or being unable to run the init program. A sensible place to start is by configuring the kernel to reboot a number of seconds after a panic.

You can do this either when you build the kernel by setting CONFIG_PANIC_TIMEOUT or by setting the kernel command line to panic. For example, to reboot 5 seconds after a panic, you would add panic=5 to the kernel command line.

You may want to go further and configure the kernel to panic on an Oops. Remember that an Oops is generated when the kernel encounters a fatal error. In some cases, it will be able to recover from the error, in other cases not. But in all cases, something has gone wrong and the system is not working as it should. To enable panic on Oops in the kernel configuration, set CONFIG_PANIC_ON_OOPS=y or, on the kernel command line, oops=panic.

A second failure mode occurs when the kernel launches init successfully but for some reason the main application fails to run. For this, you need a watchdog. A **watchdog** is a hardware or software timer that restarts the system if the timer is not reset before it expires. If you are using systemd, you can use the built-in watchdog function, which I'll describe in *Chapter 13*. If not, then you may want to enable the watchdog support built into Linux as described in Documentation/watchdog from the kernel source code.

Both failures result in **boot loops**: either a kernel panic or a watchdog timeout causes the system to reboot. If the problem is persistent, the system will reboot continually. To break out of the boot loop, we need some code in the bootloader to detect the case and to revert to the previously known good version. A typical approach is to use a **boot count** that is incremented by the bootloader on each boot and that is reset to zero in user space once the system is up and running. If the system enters a boot loop, the counter is not reset and so continues to increase. The bootloader is then configured to take remedial action if the counter exceeds a threshold.

In U-Boot this is handled by three variables:

- bootcount: Incremented each time the processor boots.
- bootlimit: If bootcount exceeds bootlimit, U-Boot runs the commands in altbootcmd instead of bootcmd.
- altbootcmd: Contains the alternative boot commands, for example, to roll back to a previous version of the software or to start the recovery-mode operating system.

For this to work, there must be a way for a user-space program to reset the boot count. We can do that using U-Boot utilities that allow the U-Boot environment to be accessed at runtime:

- fw_printenv: Prints the value of a U-Boot variable
- fw_setenv: Sets the value of a U-Boot variable

These two commands need to know where the U-Boot environment block is stored, for which there is a configuration file in /etc/fw_env.config. For example, if the U-Boot environment is stored at offset 0x800000 from the start of the eMMC memory with a backup copy at 0x1000000, then the configuration would look like this:

```
# cat /etc/fw_env.config
/dev/mmcblk0 0x800000 0x40000
/dev/mmcblk0 0x1000000 0x40000
```

There is one final thing to cover in this section. Incrementing the boot count on each boot and then resetting it when the application starts leads to unnecessary writes to the environment block that wear out the flash memory. To prevent this from happening on all reboots, U-Boot has an additional variable named upgrade_available. If upgrade_available is 0, then bootcount is not incremented since there is no unproven upgrade to guard against. upgrade_available is set to 1 after an update has been installed so that the boot count protection is only enabled when needed.

Making updates secure

The final problem relates to the potential misuse of the update mechanism itself. Your prime intention when implementing an update mechanism is to provide a reliable automated or semi-automated method to install security patches and new features. However, others may use the same mechanism to install unauthorized versions of software and hijack the device. We need to ensure that this does not happen.

The biggest vulnerability is that of a fake remote update. To prevent this, we need to authenticate the update server before starting the download. We also need a secure transfer channel, such as HTTPS, to guard against tampering with the download stream. Checksums offer a second line of defense. A checksum is generated for each update and published on the server. The update only gets applied if the checksum validates against the download. I will return to the topic of server authenticity when I describe OTA updates.

There is also the question of image authenticity. One way to detect a bogus update is to use a Secure Boot protocol in the bootloader. If the kernel image is signed at the factory with a digital key, the bootloader can check the signature before it loads the kernel and refuse to load it if verification fails. As long as the keys are kept private by the manufacturer, it will not be possible to load a kernel that is not authorized. U-Boot implements such a mechanism, which is described in the online documentation at https://docs.u-boot.org/en/latest/usage/fit/verified-boot.html.

IMPORTANT NOTE

Secure Boot: good or bad?

If I have purchased a device that has a software update feature, then I am trusting the vendor of that device to deliver useful updates. I definitely do not want a malicious third party to install software without my knowledge. But should I be allowed to install the software myself? If I own the device outright, should I not be entitled to modify it, including loading new software? Recall the TiVo set-top box, which ultimately led to the creation of the GPL v3 license. Remember the Linksys WRT54G Wi-Fi router. When access to the hardware became easy, it spawned a whole new industry, including the OpenWrt project. This is a complex issue that sits at the crossroads between freedom and control. It is my opinion that some device manufacturers use security as an excuse to protect their (sometimes shoddy) software.

Updating software may seem mundane but a bad update can do catastrophic damage to your business. The CrowdStrike outage of July 2024 is a perfect example. For that reason, it is important to roll out updates incrementally using safe techniques like blue-green deployments. That way, if something goes bad, you can roll back a software release without impacting many of your users. Now that we know what is required, how do we go about updating software on embedded Linux systems?

Types of update mechanism

In this section, I will describe three approaches to applying software updates: symmetric, or A/B, image update; asymmetric image update, also known as *recovery mode update*; and finally, atomic file update.

Symmetric image update

In this scheme, there are two copies of the operating system, each comprising the Linux kernel, root filesystem, and system applications. They are labeled as **A** and **B** in the following diagram:

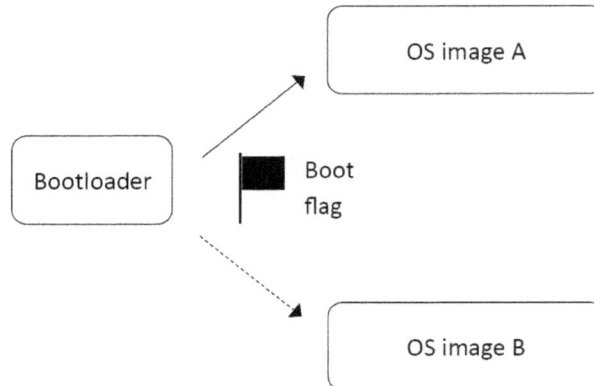

Figure 10.2 – Symmetric image update

Symmetric image updates work as follows:

1. The bootloader has a flag that indicates which image it should load. Initially, the flag is set to **A**, so the bootloader loads OS image **A**.

2. To install an update, the updater application, which is part of the operating system, overwrites OS image **B**.

3. When complete, the updater changes the boot flag to **B** and reboots.

4. Now the bootloader will load the new operating system.

5. When a further update is installed, the updater overwrites image **A** and changes the boot flag to **A**, so you ping-pong between the two copies.

6. If an update fails before the boot flag is changed, the bootloader continues to load the good operating system.

There are several open-source projects that implement symmetric image updates. One is the **Mender** client operating in standalone mode, which I will describe in the *Using Mender for local updates* section. Another is **SWUpdate** (https://github.com/sbabic/swupdate), which can receive multiple image updates in a CPIO format package and then deploy those updates to different parts of the system. It allows you to write plugins in the Lua language to do custom processing.

SWUpdate also has filesystem support for raw flash memory that is accessed as MTD flash partitions, for storage organized into UBI volumes, and for SD/eMMC storage with a disk partition table. A third example is **RAUC**, the **Robust Auto-Update Controller** (https://github.com/rauc/rauc). It too has support for raw flash storage, UBI volumes, and SD/eMMC devices. The images can be signed and verified using OpenSSL keys. A fourth example is **fwup** (https://github.com/fwup-home/fwup) by long-time Buildroot contributor Frank Hunleth.

There are some drawbacks to this scheme. One is that by updating an entire filesystem image, the size of the update package is large, which can put a strain on the network infrastructure connecting the devices. This can be mitigated by sending only the filesystem blocks that have changed by performing a binary diff of the new filesystem with the previous version. SWUpdate, RAUC, and fwup all have support for such **delta updates**. So does the commercial edition of Mender.

A second drawback is the need to keep storage space for a redundant copy of the root filesystem and other components. If the root filesystem is the largest component, it comes close to doubling the amount of flash memory you need to fit both copies. It is for this reason that the asymmetric update scheme is used.

Asymmetric image update

You can reduce storage requirements by keeping a minimal recovery operating system purely for updating the main one as shown here:

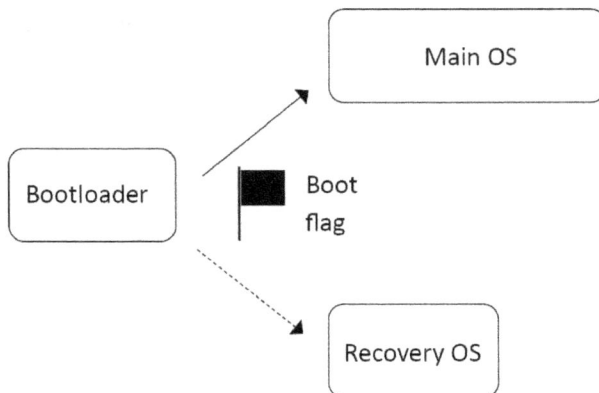

Figure 10.3 – Asymmetric image update

To install an asymmetric update, do the following:

1. Set the boot flag to point to the recovery OS and reboot.
2. Once the recovery OS is running, it can stream updates to the main operating system image.

3. If the update is interrupted, the bootloader will again boot into the recovery OS, which can resume the update.

4. Only when the update is complete and verified will the recovery OS clear the boot flag and reboot again—this time, loading the new main operating system.

5. The fallback in the case of a correct but buggy update is to drop the system back into recovery mode, which can attempt remedial actions, possibly by requesting an earlier update version.

The recovery OS is usually a lot smaller than the main operating system, maybe only a few megabytes, and so the storage overhead is not great. As a matter of interest, this is the scheme that was adopted by Android prior to the Nougat release. For open-source implementations of an asymmetric image update, consider SWUpdate or RAUC.

A major drawback of this scheme is that while the recovery OS is running, the device is not operational. Such a scheme also does not allow for updates of the recovery OS itself. That would require something like A/B image updates, thus defeating the whole purpose.

Atomic file updates

Another approach is to have redundant copies of a root filesystem present in multiple directories of a single filesystem and then use the chroot(8) command to choose one of them at boot time. This allows one directory tree to be updated while another is mounted as the root directory. Furthermore, rather than making copies of files that have not changed between versions of the root filesystem, you could use links. That would save a lot of disk space and reduce the amount of data to be downloaded in an update package. These are the basic ideas behind atomic file updates.

> **IMPORTANT NOTE**
>
> The chroot command runs a program in an existing directory. The program sees this directory as its root directory and so cannot access any files or directories at a higher level. It is often used to run a program in a constrained environment, which is sometimes referred to as **chroot jail**.

The **libostree** project (https://github.com/ostreedev/ostree), formerly **OSTree**, is the most popular implementation of this idea. OSTree started around 2011 as a means of deploying updates to the GNOME desktop developers and improving their continuous integration testing.

It has since been adopted as an update solution for embedded devices. It is one of the update methods available in **Automotive Grade Linux** (**AGL**), and it is available in The Yocto Project through the `meta-updater` layer, which is supported by **Advanced Telematic Systems** (**ATS**).

With OSTree, the files are stored on the target in the `/ostree/repo/objects` directory. They are given names such that several versions of the same file can exist in the repository. Then, a given set of files is linked into a deployment directory which has a name such as `/ostree/deploy/os/29ff9…/`. This is referred to as *checking out* since it has some similarities to the way a branch is checked out of a Git repository. Each deployment directory contains the files that make up a root filesystem. There can be any number of them, but by default there are only two. For example, here are two `deploy` directories, each with links back into the `repo` directory:

```
/ostree/repo/objects/...
/ostree/deploy/os/a3c83.../
 /usr/bin/bash
 /usr/bin/echo
/ostree/deploy/os/29ff9.../
 /usr/bin/bash
 /usr/bin/echo
```

To boot from an OSTree directory:

1. The bootloader boots the kernel with an `initramfs` passing on the kernel command line the path of the deployment to use:

    ```
    bootargs=ostree=/ostree/deploy/os/deploy/29ff9...
    ```

2. The `initramfs` contains an `init` program named `ostree-init` that reads the command line and executes the `chroot` to the path given.

3. When a system update is installed, the files that have changed are downloaded into the repo directory by the OSTree install agent.

4. When complete, a new `deploy` directory is created with links to the collection of files that will make up the new root filesystem. Some of these will be new files. Some will be the same as before.

5. Finally, the OSTree install agent will change the bootloader's boot flag so that on the next reboot, it will `chroot` to the new `deploy` directory.

6. The bootloader implements the check on the boot count and falls back to the previous root if a boot loop is detected.

Even though a developer can operate the updater or install the client manually on a target device, eventually software updates need to happen automatically OTA.

OTA updates

Updating **OTA** means having the ability to push software to a device or group of devices via a network, usually without any end user interaction with the device. For this to happen, we need a central server to control the update process and a protocol for downloading the update to the update client. In a typical implementation, the client polls the update server from time to time to check if there are any updates pending. The polling interval needs to be long enough that the poll traffic does not take a significant portion of the network bandwidth, but short enough that the updates can be delivered in a timely fashion. An interval of tens of minutes to several hours is often a good compromise. The poll messages from the device contain some sort of unique identifier, such as a serial number or MAC address, and the current software version. From this the update server can see if an update is needed. The poll messages may also contain other status information such as uptime, environmental parameters, or anything that would be useful for the central management of the devices.

The update server is usually linked to a management system that will assign new versions of software to the various populations of devices under its control. If the device population is large, it may send updates in batches to avoid overloading the network. There will be some sort of status display where the current state of the devices can be shown and problems highlighted.

Of course, the update mechanism must be secure so that fake updates cannot be sent to the end devices. This involves the client and server being able to authenticate each other by an exchange of certificates. Then the client can validate that the packages downloaded are signed by the key that is expected.

Here are three examples of open-source projects that you can use for OTA updates:

- Mender in managed mode
- balena
- Eclipse hawkBit (`https://github.com/eclipse/hawkbit`) in conjunction with an updater client such as SWUpdate or RAUC

We will walk through Mender in detail.

Using Mender for local updates

So much for the theory. In the remaining sections of this chapter, I will demonstrate how these principles work in practice. The first set of examples involves Mender. Mender uses a symmetric A/B image update mechanism with a fallback in the event of a failed update. It can operate in *standalone mode* for local updates or in *managed mode* for OTA updates. I will begin with stand-alone mode.

Mender is written and supported by Northern.tech. There is much more information about the software in the **Documentation** section of the website (`https://mender.io`). I will not delve deeply into the configuration of the software here since my aim is to illustrate the principles of software updates. Let's begin with the Mender client.

Building the Mender client

The Mender client is available as a Yocto meta layer. These examples use the scarthgap release of The Yocto Project, which is the same one that we used in *Chapter 6*.

Start by fetching the `meta-mender` layer as follows:

```
$ git clone -b scarthgap https://github.com/mendersoftware/meta-mender
```

You want to navigate one level above the poky directory before cloning the `meta-mender` layer so that the two directories are located next to each other at the same level.

The Mender client requires some changes to the configuration of U-Boot to handle the boot flag and boot count variables. The stock Mender client layer has sub-layers for sample implementations of this U-Boot integration that we can use straight out of the box, such as `meta-mender-qemu` and `meta-mender-raspberrypi`. We will use QEMU.

The next step is to create a build directory and add the layers for this configuration:

```
$ source poky/oe-init-build-env build-mender-qemu
$ bitbake-layers add-layer ../meta-openembedded/meta-oe
$ bitbake-layers add-layer ../meta-mender/meta-mender-core
$ bitbake-layers add-layer ../meta-mender/meta-mender-demo
$ bitbake-layers add-layer ../meta-mender/meta-mender-qemu
```

Then, we need to set up the environment by adding some settings to `conf/local.conf`:

```
1 MENDER_ARTIFACT_NAME = "release-1"
2 INHERIT += "mender-full"
```

```
3 MACHINE = "vexpress-qemu"
4 INIT_MANAGER = "systemd"
5 IMAGE_FSTYPES = "ext4"
```

Omit the line numbers (*1* to *5*) from conf/local.conf. *Line 2* includes a BitBake class named mender-full, which is responsible for the special processing of the image required to create the A/B image format. *Line 3* selects a machine named vexpress-qemu, which uses QEMU to emulate an Arm Versatile Express board instead of the Versatile PB that is the default for The Yocto Project. *Line 4* selects systemd as the init daemon in place of the default System V init. I describe init daemons in more detail in *Chapter 13*. *Line 5* causes the root filesystem images to be generated in ext4 format.

Now we can build an image:

```
$ bitbake core-image-full-cmdline
```

As usual, the results of the build are in tmp/deploy/images/vexpress-qemu. You will notice some new things here compared to The Yocto Project builds we have done in the past. There is a file named core-image-full-cmdline-vexpress-qemu-grub-<timestamp>.mender and another similarly named file that ends with .uefiimg. The .mender file is required for the next subsection: *Installing an update with Mender*. The .uefiimg file is created using a tool from The Yocto Project known as wic. The output is an image that contains a partition table and that is ready to be copied directly to an SD card or eMMC chip.

We can run the QEMU target using the script provided by the Mender layer, which will first boot U-Boot and then load the Linux kernel:

```
$ ../meta-mender/meta-mender-qemu/scripts/mender-qemu
<...>
[  OK  ] Started Boot script to demo Mender OTA updates.
[  OK  ] Started Periodic Command Scheduler.
         Starting D-Bus System Message Bus...
[  OK  ] Started Getty on tty1.
         Starting IPv6 Packet Filtering Framework...
         Starting IPv4 Packet Filtering Framework...
         Starting Mender-configure device configuration...
[  OK  ] Started Serial Getty on ttyAMA0.
<...>
[  OK  ] Finished Wait for Network to be Configured.
[  OK  ] Started Time & Date Service.
```

```
[  OK  ] Finished Mender-configure device configuration.

Poky (Yocto Project Reference Distro) 5.0.7 vexpress-qemu ttyAMA0

vexpress-qemu login:
```

If, instead of a login prompt, you see an error like this:

```
mender-qemu: 117: qemu-system-arm: not found
```

Then install qemu-system-arm on your system and rerun the script:

```
$ sudo apt install qemu-system-arm
```

Log on as root with no password. Looking at the layout of the partitions on the target, we can see this:

```
# fdisk -l /dev/mmcblk0
Disk /dev/mmcblk0: 1 GiB, 1073741824 bytes, 2097152 sectors
Units: sectors of 1 * 512 = 512 bytes
Sector size (logical/physical): 512 bytes / 512 bytes
I/O size (minimum/optimal): 512 bytes / 512 bytes
Disklabel type: gpt
Disk identifier: 00000000-0000-0000-0000-00004D9B9EF0

Device           Start     End Sectors  Size Type
/dev/mmcblk0p1   16384   49151   32768   16M EFI System
/dev/mmcblk0p2   49152  933887  884736  432M Linux filesystem
/dev/mmcblk0p3  933888 1818623  884736  432M Linux filesystem
/dev/mmcblk0p4 1818624 2097118  278495  136M Linux filesystem
```

There are four partitions in all:

- **Partition 1** contains the U-Boot boot files.
- **Partitions 2 and 3** contain the A/B root filesystems (identical at this stage).
- **Partition 4** is just an extension partition that contains the remaining space.

Running the mount command shows that the second partition is being used as the root filesystem, leaving the third to receive updates:

```
# mount | head -1
/dev/mmcblk0p2 on / type ext4 (rw,relatime)
```

With the Mender client now on board, we can begin installing updates.

Installing an update with Mender

Now we want to make a change to the root filesystem and then install it as an update:

1. Open another shell and put yourself back in the working build directory:

```
$ source poky/oe-init-build-env build-mender-qemu
```

2. Make a copy of the image we just built. This will be the live image that we are going to update:

```
$ cd tmp/deploy/images/vexpress-qemu
$ cp core-image-full-cmdline-vexpress-qemu-grub.uefiimg \
core-image-live-vexpress-qemu-grub.uefiimg
$ cd -
```

If we don't do this, the QEMU script will just load the latest image generated by BitBake including updates, which defeats the object of the demonstration.

3. Next, change the hostname of the target, which will be easy to see when it is installed. To do this, edit conf/local.conf and add this line:

```
hostname:pn-base-files = "vexpress-qemu-release2"
```

4. Now we can build the image in the same way as before:

```
$ bitbake core-image-full-cmdline
```

This time we are not interested in the .uefiimg file, which contains a completely new image. Instead, we want to take only the new root filesystem, which is in core-image-full-cmdline-vexpress-qemu-grub.mender. The .mender file is in a format that is recognizesssd by the Mender client. The .mender file format consists of version information, a header, and the root filesystem image bundled together in a compressed .tar archive.

5. The next step is to deploy the new artifact to the target, initiating the update locally on the device, but receiving the update from a server. Stop the emulator you started in the previous Terminal session by pressing *Ctrl + A* then *x* to terminate it. This extra step ensures that QEMU boots with the previous image rather than the latest image. To boot QEMU with the previous image:

```
$ ../meta-mender/meta-mender-qemu/scripts/mender-qemu \
core-image-live
```

6. Check that the network is configured with QEMU at 10.0.2.15 and the host at 10.0.2.2:

```
# ping 10.0.2.2
PING 10.0.2.2 (10.0.2.2) 56(84) bytes of data.
64 bytes from 10.0.2.2: icmp_seq=1 ttl=255 time=0.842 ms
^C
--- 10.0.2.2 ping statistics ---
1 packets transmitted, 1 received, 0% packet loss, time 0ms
rtt min/avg/max/mdev = 0.842/0.842/0.842/0.000 ms
```

7. Now, in another Terminal session, start a web server on the host that can serve up the update:

```
$ cd tmp/deploy/images/vexpress-qemu
$ python3 -m http.server
Serving HTTP on 0.0.0.0 port 8000 (http://0.0.0.0:8000/) ...
```

8. It is listening on port 8000. When you are done with the web server, press *Ctrl + C* to terminate it.

9. Back on the target, issue this command to get the update:

```
# mender-update --log-level info install \
> http://10.0.2.2:8000/core-image-full-cmdline-vexpress-qemu-grub.
mender
Installing artifact...
100%
<...>
Installed, but not committed.
Use 'commit' to update, or 'rollback' to roll back the update.
At least one payload requested a reboot of the device it updated.
```

The update was written to the third partition (/dev/mmcblk0p3) while our root filesystem is still on the second partition (/dev/mmcblk0p2).

10. Reboot QEMU by entering reboot from the QEMU command line. Note that now the root filesystem is mounted on partition 3 and that the hostname has changed:

```
# mount
/dev/mmcblk0p3 on / type ext4 (rw,relatime)
<...>
# hostname
vexpress-qemu-release2
```

Success!

11. There is one more thing to do. We need to consider the issue of boot loops. Use grub-mender-grubenv-print to look at the relevant U-Boot variables:

```
# grub-mender-grubenv-print upgrade_available
upgrade_available=1
# grub-mender-grubenv-print bootcount
bootcount=1
```

If the system reboots without clearing bootcount, U-Boot should detect it and fall back to the previous installation.

Let's test U-Boot's fallback behavior:

1. Reboot the QEMU target immediately.

   When the target comes up again, we see that U-Boot has reverted to the previous installation:

```
# mount
/dev/mmcblk0p2 on / type ext4 (rw,relatime)
<...>
# hostname
vexpress-qemu
```

2. Now, let's repeat the update procedure:

```
# mender-update rollback
Rolled back.
# mender-update --log-level info install \
> http://10.0.2.2:8000/core-image-full-cmdline-vexpress-qemu-grub.
mender
# reboot
```

3. This time, after the reboot, commit the change:

```
# mender-update commit
Committed.
# grub-mender-grubenv-print upgrade_available
upgrade_available=0
# grub-mender-grubenv-print bootcount
bootcount=1
```

Once `upgrade_available` is cleared, U-Boot will no longer check `bootcount`, and so the device will continue to mount this updated root filesystem. When a further update is loaded, the Mender client will clear `bootcount` and set `upgrade_available` once again.

This example uses the Mender client from the command line to initiate an update locally. The update itself came from a server but could just as easily have been provided on a USB flash drive or an SD card. In place of Mender we could have used one of the other image update clients mentioned: SWUpdate, RAUC, or fwup. They each have their advantages, but the basic technique is the same.

Using Mender for OTA updates

Once again, we will be using the Mender client on the device, but this time operating it in managed mode. In addition, we will be configuring a server to deploy the update so that no local interaction is needed. Mender provides an open-source server for this. For documentation on how to set up this demo server, see `https://docs.mender.io/2.4/getting-started/on-premise-installation`.

The installation requires Docker Engine version 19.03 or later. It also requires Docker Compose version 1.25 or later. Refer to the Docker website at `https://docs.docker.com/engine/install/` and `https://docs.docker.com/compose/install/` for each.

To verify which versions of Docker and Docker Compose you have on your system, use these commands:

```
$ docker --version
Docker version 26.1.3, build 26.1.3-0ubuntu1~24.04.1
$ docker-compose --version
docker-compose version 1.29.2, build unknown
```

Docker Compose started being bundled with Docker in 2022. If the second command fails, try invoking Docker Compose without the hyphen:

```
$ docker compose
```

The Mender server also requires a command-line JSON parser called `jq`:

```
$ sudo apt install jq
```

Once all three are installed, install the Mender integration environment as shown:

```
$ git clone -b \
3.7.9 https://github.com/mendersoftware/integration.git integration-3.7.9
$ cd integration-3.7.9
$ ./demo up
Starting the Mender demo environment...
<...>
Creating a new user...
*****************************************


Username: mender-demo@example.com
Login password: F26E0B14587A


*****************************************
Please keep the password available, it will not be cached by the login
script.
Mender demo server ready and running in the background. Copy credentials
above and log in at https://localhost
Press Enter to show the logs.
Press Ctrl-C to stop the backend and quit.
```

When you run `./demo up`, you will see that the script downloads several hundred megabytes of Docker images, which may take some time depending on your internet connection speed. After a while, you will see that it creates a new demo user and password. This means that the server is up and running.

With the Mender web interface now running on `https://localhost/`, point a web browser at that URL and accept the certificate warning that pops up. The warning appears because the web service is using a self-signed certificate that the browser will not recognize. Enter the username and password generated by the Mender server into the login page.

We now need to make a change to the configuration of the target so that it will poll our local server for updates. For this demonstration, we map the `docker.mender.io` and `s3.docker.mender.io` server URLs to the `10.0.2.2` localhost address by appending a line to the `hosts` file. To make this change with The Yocto Project, do the following:

1. First, navigate one level above the directory where you cloned Yocto.

2. Next, create a layer with a file that appends to the recipe that creates the `hosts` file, which is `recipes-core/base-files/base-files_%.bbappend`.

3. There is already a suitable layer in `MELD/Chapter10/meta-ota` that you can copy:

```
$ cp -a MELD/Chapter10/meta-ota .
```

4. Source the working build directory:

```
$ source poky/oe-init-build-env build-mender-qemu
```

5. Add the `meta-ota` layer:

```
$ bitbake-layers add-layer ../meta-ota
```

Your layer structure should now contain eight layers including `meta-oe`, `meta-mender-core`, `meta-mender-demo`, `meta-mender-qemu`, and `meta-ota`.

6. Build the new image using the following command:

```
$ bitbake core-image-full-cmdline
```

7. Then, make a copy. This will be our live image for the session:

```
$ cd tmp/deploy/images/vexpress-qemu
$ cp core-image-full-cmdline-vexpress-qemu-grub.uefiimg \
core-image-live-ota-vexpress-qemu-grub.uefiimg
$ cd -
```

8. Stop any emulator you may have started by pressing *Ctrl + A* then *x* in that Terminal session.

9. Boot up the live image:

```
$ ../meta-mender/meta-mender-qemu/scripts/mender-qemu \
core-image-live-ota
```

10. After a few seconds, you will see a new device appear on the dashboard of the web interface. This happens so quickly because the Mender client has been configured to poll the server every 5 seconds for the purpose of demonstrating the system. A much longer polling interval would be used in production—30 minutes is recommended.

11. See how this polling interval is configured by looking at the `/etc/mender/mender.conf` file on the target:

```
# cat /etc/mender/mender.conf
{
  "InventoryPollIntervalSeconds": 5,
  "RetryPollIntervalSeconds": 30,
  "ServerURL": "https://docker.mender.io",
```

```
  "TenantToken": "dummy",
  "UpdatePollIntervalSeconds": 5
}
```

Notice the server URL in there as well.

12. Back in the web UI, click on the green checkmark to authorize the new device:

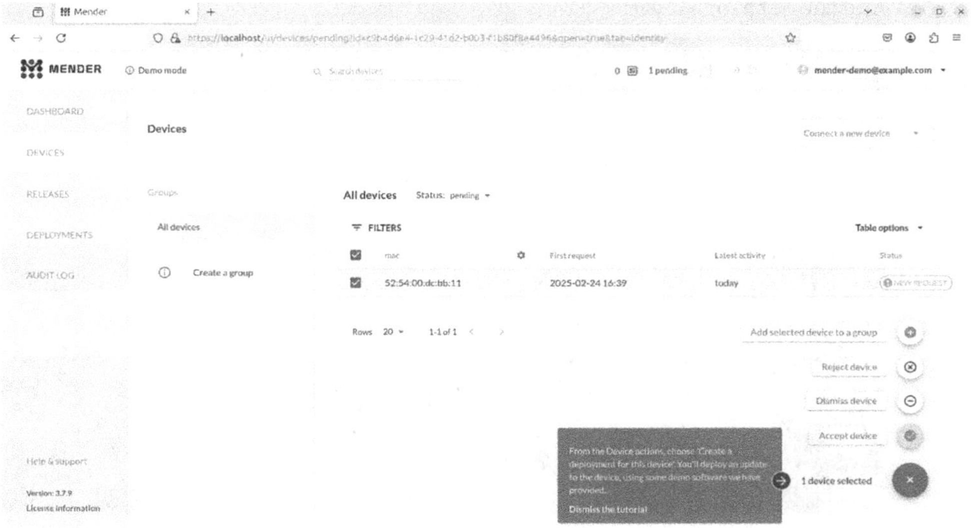

Figure 10.4 – Accept device

13. Then, click on the entry for the device to see the details.

Once again, we can create an update and deploy it – this time OTA:

1. Update the following line in conf/local.conf:

```
MENDER_ARTIFACT_NAME = "OTA-update1"
```

2. Build the image once again:

```
$ bitbake core-image-full-cmdline
```

This will produce a new core-image-full-cmdline-vexpress-qemu-grub.mender file in tmp/deploy/images/vexpress-qemu.

3. Import this into the web interface by opening the **Releases** tab and clicking on the purple **Upload** button.

4. Browse for the `core-image-full-cmdline-vexpress-qemu-grub.mender` file in `tmp/deploy/images/vexpress-qemu` and upload it:

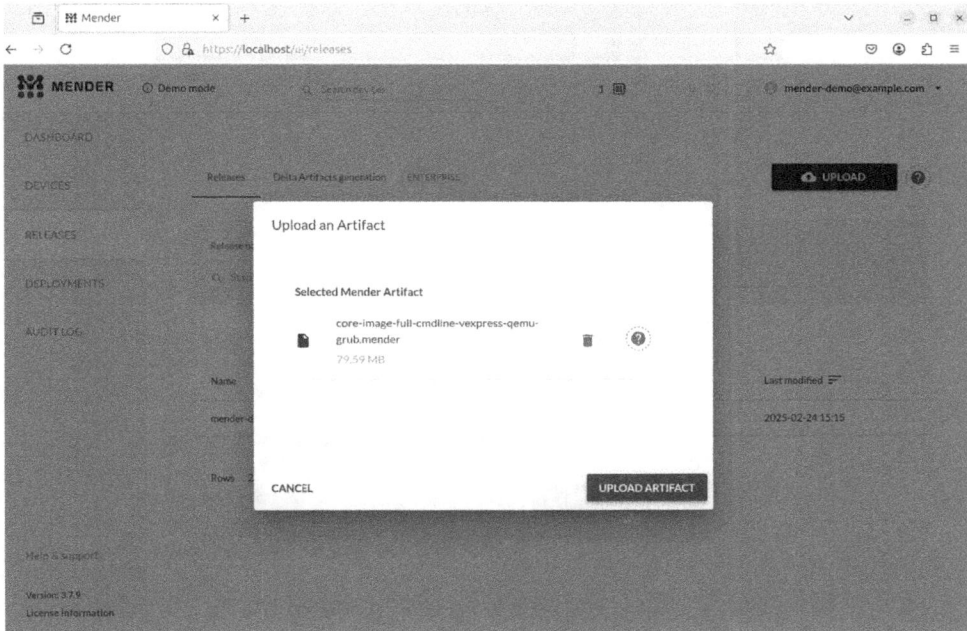

Figure 10.5 – Upload an Artifact

The Mender server should copy the file into the server data store, and a new artifact with the name **OTA-update1** should appear under **Releases**.

To deploy the update to our QEMU device, do the following:

1. Click on the **Devices** tab and select the device.

2. Click on the **Create deployment for this device** option at the bottom right of the device information.

3.   Select the **OTA-update1** artifact and click on the **CREATE DEPLOYMENT** button:

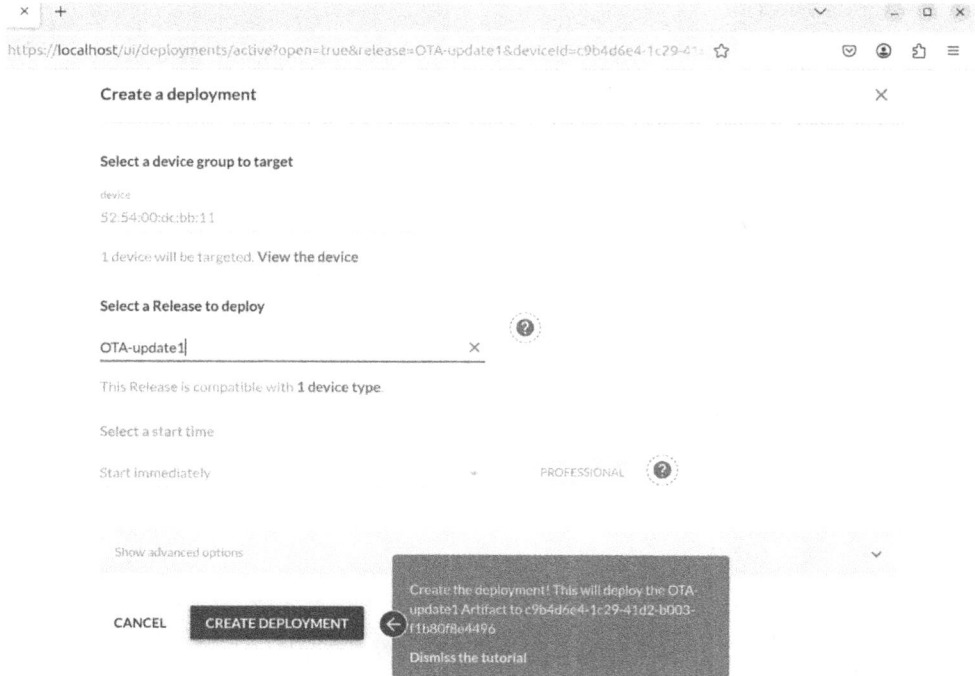

Figure 10.6 – Create a deployment

The deployment should shortly transition from **Pending** to **In Progress**.

4. Click on the **View details** button.

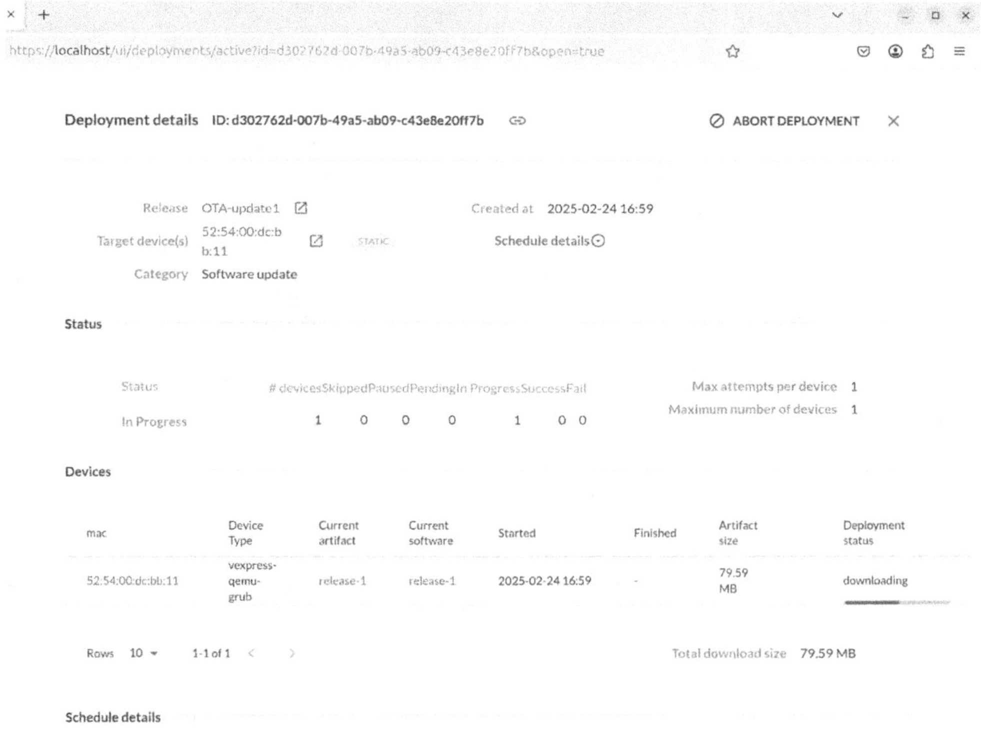

Figure 10.7 – In Progress

5. After about 13 minutes, the Mender client should finish writing the update to the spare filesystem image. At that point, QEMU will reboot and commit the update. The web UI should report **Finished** and now the client is running **OTA-update1**.

Mender is neat and is used in many commercial products, but sometimes we just want to deploy a software project to a small fleet of popular dev boards as quickly as possible.

> **TIP**
>
> After a few experiments with the Mender server, you may want to clear the state and start all over again. You can do that with these two commands from the `integration-3.7.9` directory:

```
./demo down
./demo up
```

Containers are the quickest way to deploy software to edge devices. We will revisit containerized software updates in *Chapter 16*.

Using SWUpdate for local updates

Like Mender, SWUpdate uses a symmetric A/B image update mechanism with a fallback in the event of a failed update. SWUpdate can receive multiple image updates in a CPIO format package and then deploy those updates to different parts of the system. It allows you to write plugins in the Lua language to do custom processing. Lua is a powerful scripting language that is easy to embed in applications. SWUpdate is a client-only solution, so unlike Mender there is no corresponding enterprise hosting plan to pay for. Instead, you deploy your own OTA server using something like hawkBit.

The SWUpdate project (`https://github.com/sbabic/swupdate`) was started and is still maintained by Stefano Babic, an employee of DENX Software Engineering, the same folks behind U-Boot. There is extensive documentation (`https://sbabic.github.io/swupdate/`) beginning with motives for robust and fail-safe updates followed by clear explanations of various update strategies.

Summary

Being able to update the software on devices in the field is at the very least a useful attribute. If the device is connected to the internet, then updating software in the field is an absolute must. And yet, all too often it is a feature that is left until the last part of a project, on the assumption that it is not a hard problem to solve. In this chapter, I hope that I have illustrated the various problems associated with designing an effective and robust update mechanism. There are also several open-source options readily available. You do not have to reinvent the wheel anymore.

The two approaches used most often are the symmetric image (A/B) update or its cousin, the asymmetric (recovery) image update. Here, you have the choice of SWUpdate, RAUC, Mender, and fwup. A more recent innovation is the atomic file update in the form of OSTree. Atomic file update reduces the amount of data that needs to be downloaded and the amount of redundant storage that needs to be fitted on the target. Lastly, with the proliferation of Docker came the desire for containerized software updates. This is the approach that balena takes.

It is quite common to deploy updates on a small scale by visiting each site and applying the update from a USB memory stick or SD card. However, if you want to deploy to remote locations, or deploy at scale, an OTA update option will be needed.

The next chapter describes how you control the hardware components of your system with device drivers, both in the conventional sense of drivers that are part of the kernel and the extent to which you can control hardware from user space.

Get This Book's PDF Version and Exclusive Extras

UNLOCK NOW

Scan the QR code (or go to `packtpub.com/unlock`). Search for this book by name, confirm the edition, and then follow the steps on the page.

Note: Keep your invoice handy. Purchases made directly from Packt don't require an invoice.

11

Interfacing with Device Drivers

Kernel device drivers are the mechanism by which the underlying hardware is exposed to the rest of the system. As a developer of embedded systems, you need to know how these device drivers fit into the overall architecture and how to access them from user space programs. Your system will probably have some novel pieces of hardware and you will have to work out a way of accessing them. In many cases, you will find that there are device drivers provided for you and you can achieve everything you want without writing any kernel code. For example, you can manipulate GPIO pins and LEDs using files in sysfs, and there are libraries you can use to access serial buses including **SPI (Serial Peripheral Interface)** and **I2C (Inter-Integrated Circuit)**.

There are many places to find out how to write a device driver, but few tell you why you would want to and the choices you have in doing so. This is what I want to cover here. However, remember that this is not a book dedicated to writing kernel device drivers and that the information given here is to help you navigate the territory but not necessarily set up home there. There are many good books and blog posts that will help you write device drivers, some of which are listed at the end of this chapter in the *Further study* section.

In this chapter, we will cover the following topics:

- Role of device drivers
- Character devices
- Block devices
- Network devices
- Finding out about drivers at runtime
- Finding the right device driver

- Device drivers in user space
- Writing a kernel device driver
- Discovering the hardware configuration

Technical requirements

To follow along with the examples, make sure you have the following:

- A Linux-based host system
- A microSD card reader and card
- A BeaglePlay
- A 5V USB-C power supply capable of delivering 3A
- An Ethernet cable and router with an available port for network connectivity

The code used in this chapter can be found in the chapter folder in this book's GitHub repository: `https://github.com/PacktPublishing/Mastering-Embedded-Linux-Development/tree/main/Chapter11`.

Role of device drivers

As I mentioned in *Chapter 4*, one of the functions of the kernel is to encapsulate the many hardware interfaces of a computer system and present them in a consistent manner to user space programs. The kernel has frameworks designed to make it easy to write a device driver, which is the piece of code that mediates between the kernel above and the hardware below. A device driver may be written to control physical devices such as a UART or an MMC controller, or it may represent a virtual device such as the null device (`/dev/null`) or a RAMdisk. One driver may control multiple devices of the same kind.

Kernel device driver code runs at a high privilege level, as does the rest of the kernel. It has full access to the processor address space and hardware registers. It can handle interrupts and DMA transfers. It can also make use of the sophisticated kernel infrastructure for synchronization and memory management. However, you should be aware that there is a downside to this; if something goes wrong in a buggy driver, it can go really wrong and bring the system down.

Consequently, there is a principle that device drivers should be as simple as possible by just providing information to applications (where the real decisions are made). You often hear this being expressed as *no policy in the kernel*. It is the responsibility of user space to set the policy that governs the overall behavior of the system. For example, loading kernel modules in response to external events, such as plugging in a new USB device, is the responsibility of the udev user space program, not the kernel. The kernel just supplies a means of loading a kernel module.

In Linux, there are three main types of device drivers:

- **Character:** This is for unbuffered I/O with a rich range of functions and a thin layer between the application code and the driver. It is the first choice when implementing custom device drivers.

- **Block:** This has an interface tailored for block I/O to and from mass storage devices. There is a thick layer of buffering designed to make disk reads and writes as fast as possible, which makes it unsuitable for anything else.

- **Network:** This is similar to a block device but is used for transmitting and receiving network packets rather than disk blocks.

There is also a fourth type that presents itself as a group of files in one of the pseudo filesystems. For example, you might access the GPIO driver through a group of files in /sys/class/gpio, as I will describe later in this chapter. Let's begin by looking at these three basic device types in more detail.

Character devices

Character devices are identified in user space by a special file called a **device node**. This filename is mapped to a device driver using the major and minor numbers associated with it. Broadly speaking, the **major number** maps the device node to a particular device driver, while the **minor number** tells the driver which interface is being accessed. For example, the device node of the first serial port on the Arm Versatile PB is named /dev/ttyAMA0 and has a major number of 204 and a minor number of 64. The device node for the second serial port has the same major number but the minor number is 65. We can see the numbers for all four serial ports in the directory listing:

```
# ls -l /dev/ttyAMA*
crw-rw---- 1 root root 204, 64    Jan  1 1970 /dev/ttyAMA0
crw-rw---- 1 root root 204, 65    Jan  1 1970 /dev/ttyAMA1
crw-rw---- 1 root root 204, 66    Jan  1 1970 /dev/ttyAMA2
crw-rw---- 1 root root 204, 67    Jan  1 1970 /dev/ttyAMA3
```

The list of standard major and minor numbers can be found in the kernel documentation in Documentation/admin-guide/devices.txt. The list does not get updated very often and does not include the ttyAMA device described in the preceding paragraph. Nevertheless, if you look at the kernel source code in drivers/tty/serial/amba-pl011.c, you will see where the major and minor numbers are declared:

```
#define SERIAL_AMBA_MAJOR 204
#define SERIAL_AMBA_MINOR 64
```

Where there is more than one instance of a device, as with the ttyAMA driver, the convention for forming the name of the device node is to take a base name (ttyAMA) and append the instance number from 0 to 3.

As I mentioned in *Chapter 5*, device nodes can be created in several ways:

- devtmpfs: The device node is created when the device driver registers a new device interface using a base name supplied by the driver (ttyAMA) and an instance number.
- udev or mdev (without devtmpfs): These are essentially the same as devtmpfs, except that a user space daemon program has to extract the device name from sysfs and create the node.
- mknod: If you are using static device nodes, they are created manually using mknod.

You may have gotten the impression from the numbers I used here that both major and minor numbers are 8-bit numbers in the range of 0 to 255. In fact, the major number is 12 bits long, which gives valid major numbers from 1 to 4,095, and the minor number is 20 bits long, from 0 to 1,048,575.

When you open a character device node, the kernel checks whether the major and minor numbers fall into a range registered by a character device driver. If so, it passes the call to the driver; otherwise, the open(2) call fails. The device driver can extract the minor number to find out which hardware interface to use.

To write a program that accesses a device driver, you need to have some knowledge of how it works. In other words, a device driver is not the same as a file: the things you do with it change the state of the device. A simple example is the urandom pseudorandom number generator, which returns bytes of random data every time you read it.

Here is a program that does just this:

```
#include <stdio.h>
#include <sys/types.h>
#include <sys/stat.h>
#include <fcntl.h>
#include <unistd.h>

int main(void)
{
    int f;
    unsigned int rnd;
    int n;
```

```
    f = open("/dev/urandom", O_RDONLY);

        if (f < 0) {
            perror("Failed to open urandom");
            return 1;
        }

        n = read(f, &rnd, sizeof(rnd));

        if (n != sizeof(rnd)) {
            perror("Problem reading urandom");
            return 1;
        }

        printf("Random number = 0x%x\n", rnd);
        close(f);
        return 0;
    }
```

You can find the full source code and a BitBake recipe for this program in the MELD/Chapter11/ meta-device-drivers/recipes-local/read-urandom directory.

The nice thing about the Unix driver model is that once we know that there is a device named urandom, then every time we read from it, it returns a fresh set of pseudorandom data, so we don't need to know anything else about it. We can just use standard functions such as open(2), read(2), and close(2).

> **TIP**
>
> You could use the stream I/O functions known as fopen(3), fread(3), and fclose(3) instead, but the buffering implicit in these functions often causes unexpected behavior. For example, fwrite(3) usually only writes to the user space buffer, not to the device. You need to call fflush(3) to force the buffer to be written out. Therefore, it is best to not use stream I/O functions when calling device drivers.

Most device drivers employ a character interface. Mass storage devices are a notable exception. Reading and writing to disk requires a block interface for maximum speed.

Block devices

Block devices are also associated with a device node that also has major and minor numbers.

> **TIP**
>
> Although character and block devices are identified using major and minor numbers, they are in different namespaces. A character driver with a major number of 4 is in no way related to a block driver with a major number of 4.

With block devices, the major number is used to identify the device driver, and the minor number is used to identify the partition. Let's look at the MMC driver on the BeaglePlay:

```
# ls -l /dev/mmcblk*
brw-rw---- 1 root disk 179,   0 Aug  7 13:25 /dev/mmcblk0
brw-rw---- 1 root disk 179, 256 Aug  7 13:25 /dev/mmcblk0boot0
brw-rw---- 1 root disk 179, 512 Aug  7 13:25 /dev/mmcblk0boot1
brw-rw---- 1 root disk 179,   1 Aug  7 13:25 /dev/mmcblk0p1
brw-rw---- 1 root disk 179,   2 Aug  7 13:25 /dev/mmcblk0p2
brw-rw---- 1 root disk 236,   0 Aug  7 13:25 /dev/mmcblk0rpmb
brw-rw---- 1 root disk 179, 768 Feb  4 09:42 /dev/mmcblk1
brw-rw---- 1 root disk 179, 769 Feb  4 09:42 /dev/mmcblk1p1
brw-rw---- 1 root disk 179, 770 Feb  4 09:42 /dev/mmcblk1p2
```

Here, mmcblk0 is the eMMC chip, which has two partitions, and mmcblk1 is the microSD card slot, which has a card also with two partitions. The major number for the MMC block driver is 179 (you can look it up in devices.txt). The minor numbers are used in ranges to identify different physical MMC devices and the partitions of the storage medium that are on that device. In the case of the MMC driver, the ranges are eight minor numbers per device: the minor numbers from 0 to 7 are for the first device, the numbers from 8 to 15 are for the second, and so on. Within each range, the first minor number represents the entire device as raw sectors, and the others represent up to seven partitions. On the BeaglePlay's eMMC chip, there are two 4 MB areas of memory reserved for use by a bootloader. These are represented as two devices known as mmcblk0boot0 and mmcblk0boot1, and they have minor numbers of 256 and 512, respectively.

As another example, you are probably aware of the SCSI disk driver known as sd, which is used to control a range of disks that use the SCSI command set, including SCSI, SATA, USB mass storage, and **Universal Flash Storage (UFS)**. It has the major number 8 and ranges of 16 minor numbers per interface or disk.

The minor numbers from 0 to 15 are for the first interface with device nodes named sda up to sda15; the numbers from 16 to 31 are for the second disk with device nodes sdb up to sdb15; and so on. This continues up to the 16th disk from 240 to 255 with the node name sdp. There are other major numbers reserved for them because SCSI disks are so popular, but we needn't worry about that here.

Both the MMC and SCSI block drivers expect to find a partition table at the start of the disk. The partition table is created using utilities such as fdisk, sfidsk, and parted.

A user space program can open and interact with a block device directly via the device node. This is not a common thing to do, though. It is usually only done to perform administrative operations such as creating partitions, formatting a partition with a filesystem, and mounting. Once the filesystem has been mounted, you interact with the block device indirectly through the files in that filesystem.

Most block devices will have a kernel driver that works, so we rarely need to write our own. The same goes for network devices. Just like a filesystem abstracts the details of a block device, the network stack eliminates the need to interact directly with a network device.

Network devices

Network devices are not accessed through device nodes, and they do not have major and minor numbers. Instead, a network device is allocated a name by the kernel based on a string and an instance number. Here is an example of the way a network driver registers an interface:

```
my_netdev = alloc_netdev(0, "net%d", NET_NAME_UNKNOWN, netdev_setup);
ret = register_netdev(my_netdev);
```

This creates a network device named net0 the first time it is called, net1 the second time, and so on. More common names include lo, eth0, enp2s0, wlan0, and wlp1s0. Note that this is the name it starts off with; device managers such as udev may change it to something different later.

Usually, the network interface name is only used when configuring the network using utilities such as ip to establish a network address and route. Thereafter, you interact with the network driver indirectly by opening sockets and letting the network layer decide how to route them to the right interface.

However, it is possible to access network devices directly from the user space by creating a socket and using the ioctl commands listed in include/linux/sockios.h. Here is a program that uses SIOCGIFHWADDR to query the network driver for a hardware (MAC) address:

```
#include <stdio.h>
#include <stdlib.h>
#include <string.h>
#include <unistd.h>
#include <sys/ioctl.h>
#include <linux/sockios.h>
#include <net/if.h>

int main(int argc, char *argv[])
{
    int s;
    int ret;
    struct ifreq ifr;

    if (argc != 2) {
        printf("Usage %s [network interface]\n", argv[0]);
        return 1;
    }

    s = socket(PF_INET, SOCK_DGRAM, 0);

    if (s < 0) {
        perror("socket");
        return 1;
    }

    strcpy(ifr.ifr_name, argv[1]);
    ret = ioctl(s, SIOCGIFHWADDR, &ifr);

    if (ret < 0) {
        perror("ioctl");
        return 1;
    }
```

```
for (int i = 0; i < 6; i++) {
    printf("%02x:", (unsigned char)ifr.ifr_hwaddr.sa_data[i]);
}

printf("\n");
close(s);
return 0;
}
```

You will find the full source code and a BitBake recipe for this program in the `MELD/Chapter11/ meta-device-drivers/recipes-local/show-mac-address` directory. The `show-mac-address` program takes a network interface name as an argument. After opening a socket, we copy the interface name to a struct and pass that struct into the `ioctl` call on the socket before printing out the resulting MAC address.

Now that we know what the three categories of device drivers are, how do we list the different drivers that are in use on our system?

Finding out about drivers at runtime

Once you have a running Linux system, it is useful to know which device drivers have been loaded and what state they are in. You can find out a lot by reading the files in `/proc` and `/sys`.

List the character and block device drivers that are currently loaded and active by reading `/proc/ devices`:

```
$ cat /proc/devices
Character devices:
  1 mem
  4 /dev/vc/0
  4 tty
  4 ttyS
  5 /dev/tty
  5 /dev/console
<...>
```

For each driver, you can see the major number and the base name. However, this does not tell you how many devices each driver is attached to. It only shows `ttyAMA` but it gives you no clue as to whether it is attached to four real serial ports. I will come back to that later when we look at `sysfs`.

Network devices do not appear in this list because they do not have device nodes. Instead, you can use the `ip` tool to get a list of network devices:

```
# ip link show
1: lo: <LOOPBACK,UP,LOWER_UP> mtu 65536 qdisc noqueue qlen 1000
    link/loopback 00:00:00:00:00:00 brd 00:00:00:00:00:00
2: eth0: <BROADCAST,MULTICAST,UP,LOWER_UP> mtu 1500 qdisc mq qlen 1000
    link/ether 34:08:e1:85:07:d9 brd ff:ff:ff:ff:ff:ff
3: eth1: <BROADCAST,MULTICAST> mtu 1500 qdisc noop qlen 1000
    link/ether 7a:1f:d8:46:36:b1 brd ff:ff:ff:ff:ff:ff
```

You can also find out about devices attached to USB or PCI buses using the well-known `lsusb` and `lspci` commands, respectively. There is information about them in the respective manual pages and plenty of online guides, so I will not describe them any further here.

The really interesting information is in `sysfs`, which is the next topic we'll cover.

Getting information from sysfs

You can define `sysfs` in a pedantic way as a representation of kernel objects, attributes, and relationships. A kernel object is a **directory**, an attribute is a **file**, and a relationship is a **symbolic link** from one object to another. From a more practical point of view, since the Linux device driver model represents all devices and drivers as kernel objects, you can see the kernel's view of the system laid out before you by looking in `/sys`:

```
# ls /sys
block      class      devices    fs         module
bus        dev        firmware   kernel     power
```

In the context of discovering information about devices and drivers, I will look at three of these directories: `devices`, `class`, and `block`.

Devices — /sys/devices

This is the kernel's view of the devices that have been discovered since boot and how they are connected to each other. It is organized at the top level by the system bus, so what you see varies from one system to another. Here is the QEMU emulation of the Arm Versatile board:

```
# ls /sys/devices
platform  software  system   tracepoint virtual
```

There are three directories that are present on all systems:

- `system/`: This contains devices at the heart of the system including CPUs and clocks.
- `virtual/`: This contains devices that are memory-based. You will find the memory devices that appear as `/dev/null`, `/dev/random`, and `/dev/zero` in `virtual/mem`. You will also find the lo loopback device in `virtual/net`.
- `platform/`: This is a catch-all for devices that are not connected via a conventional hardware bus. This may be almost everything on an embedded device.

The other devices appear in directories that correspond to actual system buses. For example, the PCI root bus, if there is one, appears as `pci0000:00`.

Navigating this hierarchy is quite hard because it requires some knowledge of the topology of your system and the pathnames become quite long and hard to remember. To make life easier, `/sys/class` and `/sys/block` offer two different views of the devices.

Drivers — /sys/class

This is a view of the device drivers presented by their type. In other words, it is a software view rather than a hardware view. Each of the subdirectories represents a class of drivers and is implemented by a component of the driver framework. For example, UART devices are managed by the tty layer, so you will find them in `/sys/class/tty`. Likewise, you will find network devices in `/sys/class/net`, input devices such as keyboard, touchscreen, and mouse in `/sys/class/input`, and so on.

There is a symbolic link in each subdirectory for each instance of that type of device pointing to its representation in `/sys/device`.

Let's look at the serial ports on the Versatile PB. We can see that there are four of them:

```
# ls -d /sys/class/tty/ttyAMA*
/sys/class/tty/ttyAMA0    /sys/class/tty/ttyAMA2
/sys/class/tty/ttyAMA1    /sys/class/tty/ttyAMA3
```

Each directory is a representation of the kernel object that is associated with an instance of a device interface. Looking within one of these directories, we can see the attributes of the object, represented as files, and the relationships with other objects, represented by links:

```
# ls /sys/class/tty/ttyAMA0
close_delay     flags     line     uartclk
closing_wait    io_type   port     uevent
```

custom_divisor	iomem_base	power	xmit_fifo_size
dev	iomem_reg_shift	subsystem	
device	irq	type	

The link called device points to the hardware object for the device. The link called subsystem points back to the parent subsystem at /sys/class/tty. The remaining directory entries are attributes. Some are specific to a serial port, such as xmit_fifo_size, while others apply to many types of devices, such as irq for the interrupt number and dev for the device number. Some attribute files are writable and allow you to tune parameters in the driver at runtime.

The dev attribute is particularly interesting. If you look at its value, you will find the following:

```
# cat /sys/class/tty/ttyAMA0/dev
204:64
```

These are the major and minor numbers of the device. This attribute is created when the driver registers the interface. It is from this file that udev and mdev find the major and minor numbers of the device driver.

Block drivers — /sys/block

There is one more view of the device model that is important to this discussion: the block driver view that you will find in /sys/block. There is a subdirectory for each block device. This listing is from a BeaglePlay:

```
# ls /sys/block
loop0   loop4   mmcblk0        ram0    ram12   ram2    ram6
loop1   loop5   mmcblk1        ram1    ram13   ram3    ram7
loop2   loop6   mmcblk0boot0   ram10   ram14   ram4    ram8
loop3   loop7   mmcblk0boot1   ram11   ram15   ram5    ram9
```

If you look inside mmcblk0, which is the eMMC chip on this board, you will see the attributes of the interface and the partitions within it:

```
# ls /sys/block/mmcblk0
alignment_offset    events              holders        mmcblk0p2   ro
bdi                 events_async        inflight       mq          size
capability          events_poll_msecs   integrity      power       slaves
dev                 ext_range           mmcblk0boot0   queue       stat
device              force_ro            mmcblk0boot1   range       subsystem
discard_alignment   hidden              mmcblk0p1      removable   uevent
```

In conclusion, you can learn a lot about the devices (the hardware) and the drivers (the software) that are present on a system by reading `sysfs`.

Finding the right device driver

A typical embedded board is based on a reference design from the manufacturer with changes to make it suitable for a particular application. The BSP that comes with the reference board should support all the peripherals on that board. Then you customize the design, perhaps by adding a temperature sensor attached via I2C, some lights and buttons connected via GPIO pins, a display panel via a MIPI interface, or many other things. Your job is to create a custom kernel to control all of these, but where do you start looking for device drivers that support all these peripherals?

The most obvious place to look is the driver support page on the manufacturer's website, or you could ask them directly. In my experience, this seldom gets you the result you want. Hardware manufacturers are not particularly Linux-savvy, and they often give you misleading information. They may have proprietary drivers as binary blobs or source code for a different version of the kernel than the one you have. So, by all means, try this route. Personally, I will always try to find an open-source driver for the task at hand.

There may be support in your kernel already: there are many thousands of drivers in mainline Linux and there are many vendor-specific drivers in the vendor kernels. Begin by running `make menuconfig` (or `xconfig`) and search for the product name or number. If you do not find an exact match, try more generic searches allowing for the fact that most drivers handle a range of products from the same family. Next, try searching through the code in the `drivers` directory (`grep` is your friend here).

If you still don't have a driver, you can try searching online and asking in the relevant forums to see if there is a driver for a later version of Linux. If you find one, you should seriously consider updating the BSP to use the later kernel. Sometimes, this is not practical, so you may have to think about backporting the driver to your kernel. If the kernel versions are similar, it may be easy, but if they are more than 12 to 18 months apart, then chances are that the code will have changed to the extent that you will have to rewrite a chunk of the driver to integrate it with your kernel. If all these options fail, you will have to find a solution yourself by writing the missing kernel driver. However, this is not always necessary. We will look at an alternative in the next section.

Device drivers in user space

Before you start writing a device driver, pause for a moment to consider whether it is really necessary. There are generic device drivers for many common types of devices that allow you to interact with hardware directly from user space, without having to write a line of kernel code. User space code is certainly easier to write and debug. It is also not covered by the GPL, although I don't feel that is a good reason to do it this way.

These drivers fall into two broad categories: those that you control through files in sysfs, including GPIO and LEDs, and serial buses that expose a generic interface through a device node, such as I2C.

Let's build a Yocto image for the BeaglePlay with some examples installed:

1. Navigate one level above the directory where you cloned Yocto:

    ```
    $ cd ~
    ```

2. Copy the meta-device-driver layers from the book's Git repo:

    ```
    $ cp -a MELD/Chapter11/meta-device-drivers .
    ```

3. Set up your BitBake work environment for the BeaglePlay:

    ```
    $ source poky/oe-init-build-env build-beagleplay
    ```

4. This sets up a bunch of environment variables and puts you back in the build-beagleplay directory you populated during the *Layers* section from *Chapter 6*. Repeat the exercise where you add your own meta-nova layer and build core-image-minimal for the Beagle-Play if you have since deleted that work.

5. Remove the meta-nova layer:

    ```
    $ bitbake-layers remove-layer ../meta-nova
    ```

6. Add the meta-device-drivers layer:

    ```
    $ bitbake-layers add-layer ../meta-device-drivers
    ```

7. Confirm that your layer structure is set up correctly:

    ```
    $ bitbake-layers show-layers
    NOTE: Starting bitbake server...
    layer                 path
    priority
    ================================================================
    ======
    ```

core	/home/frank/poky/meta	5
yocto	/home/frank/poky/meta-poky	5
yoctobsp	/home/frank/poky/meta-yocto-bsp	5
arm-toolchain	/home/frank/meta-arm/meta-arm-toolchain	5
meta-arm	/home/frank/meta-arm/meta-arm	5
meta-ti-bsp	/home/frank/meta-ti/meta-ti-bsp	6
device-drivers	/home/frank/meta-device-drivers	6

8. Modify conf/local.conf so that the example programs and dummy driver are installed:

```
IMAGE_INSTALL:append = " read-urandom show-mac-address gpio-int i2c-
eeprom-read dummy-driver"
```

9. Enable the legacy /sys/class/gpio interface in the kernel:

```
$ bitbake -c menuconfig virtual/kernel
```

10. Ensure that the CONFIG_EXPERT, CONFIG_GPIO_SYSFS, CONFIG_DEBUG_FS, and CONFIG_
    DEBUG_FS_ALLOW_ALL options are enabled. Ensure that the CONFIG_KEYBOARD_GPIO option
    is disabled.

11. Enable the /sys/class/leds interface in the kernel by ensuring that the CONFIG_LEDS_
    CLASS, CONFIG_LEDS_GPIO, and CONFIG_LEDS_TRIGGER_TIMER options are enabled.

12. Save the modified kernel .config and exit menuconfig.

13. Build core-image-minimal:

```
$ bitbake core-image-minimal
```

Write the finished image to a microSD using balenaEtcher, insert the microSD into your BeaglePlay, and boot it as described in the *Running the BeaglePlay target* section from *Chapter 6*.

GPIO

General-Purpose Input/Output (GPIO) is the simplest form of digital interface since it gives you direct access to individual hardware pins, each of which can be in one of two states: either high or low. In most cases, you can configure the GPIO pin to be either an input or an output. You can even use a group of GPIO pins to create higher-level interfaces such as I2C or SPI by manipulating each bit in software, a technique that is called **bit banging**. The main limitation is the speed and accuracy of the software loops and the number of CPU cycles you want to dedicate to them. Generally, it is hard to achieve timer accuracy better than a millisecond unless you configure a real-time kernel, as we shall see in *Chapter 21*. More common use cases for GPIO are for reading push buttons and digital sensors and controlling LEDs, motors, and relays.

Most SoCs have a lot of GPIO bits grouped together in GPIO registers, usually 32 bits per register. On-chip GPIO bits are routed through to GPIO pins on the chip package via a multiplexer known as a **pin mux**. There may be additional GPIO pins available off-chip in the power management chip and in dedicated GPIO extenders connected through I2C or SPI buses. All this diversity is handled by a kernel subsystem known as gpiolib, which is not actually a library, but the infrastructure GPIO drivers use to expose I/O in a consistent way. There are details about the implementation of gpiolib in the kernel source under Documentation/driver-api/gpio/, and the code for the drivers themselves is in drivers/gpio/.

Applications can interact with gpiolib through files in the /sys/class/gpio/ directory. Here is what you would see on a typical embedded board like a BeaglePlay:

```
# ls /sys/class/gpio
export        gpiochip512  gpiochip515  gpiochip539  gpiochip631  unexport
```

The directories named gpiochip512 through to gpiochip631 represent four GPIO registers, each with a variable number of GPIO bits. If you look in one of the gpiochip directories, you will see the following:

```
# ls /sys/class/gpio/gpiochip512
base        device      label      ngpio       power       subsystem  uevent
```

The file named base contains the number of the first GPIO pin in the register, while ngpio contains the number of bits in the register. In this case, gpiochip512/base is 512 and gpiochip512/ngpio is 3, which tells you that it contains GPIO bits 512 to 514. It is possible for there to be a gap between the last GPIO in one register and the first GPIO in the next.

To control a GPIO bit from user space, you first need to export it from kernel space, which you can do by writing the GPIO number to /sys/class/gpio/export. This example shows the process for GPIO 640, which is wired to the INT pin of the mikroBUS connector on the BeaglePlay:

```
# echo 640 > /sys/class/gpio/export
# ls /sys/class/gpio
export        gpiochip512  gpiochip539  unexport
gpio640       gpiochip515  gpiochip631
```

Now, there is a new gpio640 directory containing the files you need to control the pin.

> **IMPORTANT NOTE**
>
> If the GPIO bit is already claimed by the kernel, you will not be able to export it in this way:
>
> ```
> # echo 640 > /sys/class/gpio/export
> bash: echo: write error: Device or resource busy
> ```

The gpio640 directory contains these files:

```
# ls /sys/class/gpio/gpio640
active_low  direction  power      uevent
device      edge       subsystem  value
```

The pin begins as an input that is valid for the INT (interrupt) pin of the mikroBUS connector. To convert a GPIO to an output, write out to the direction file. The value file contains the current state of the pin, which is 0 for low and 1 for high. If it is an output, you can change the state by writing 0 or 1 to value. Sometimes the meaning of low and high is reversed in hardware (hardware engineers enjoy doing that sort of thing), so writing 1 to active_low inverts the meaning of value so that a low voltage is reported as 1 and a high voltage is reported as 0.

Conversely, you can remove a GPIO from user space control by writing the GPIO number to /sys/class/gpio/unexport, as you did for export.

Handling interrupts from GPIO

In many cases, a GPIO input can be configured to generate an interrupt when it changes state. This allows you to wait for the interrupt rather than polling in an inefficient software loop. If the GPIO bit can generate interrupts, a file called edge exists. Initially, it has the value called none, meaning that it does not generate interrupts. To enable interrupts, you can set it to one of these values:

- rising: Interrupt on the rising edge.
- falling: Interrupt on the falling edge.
- both: Interrupt on both rising and falling edges.
- none: No interrupts (default).

To determine which GPIO the USR button on the BeaglePlay is assigned to:

```
# cat /sys/kernel/debug/gpio | grep USR_BUTTON
 gpio-557 (USR_BUTTON          |sysfs               ) in  hi  IRQ
```

If you want to wait for a falling edge on GPIO 557 (USR button), you must first enable interrupts:

```
# echo 557 > /sys/class/gpio/export
# echo falling > /sys/class/gpio/gpio557/edge
```

Here is a program that waits for an interrupt from the GPIO:

```c
#include <stdio.h>
#include <fcntl.h>
#include <unistd.h>
#include <sys/epoll.h>
#include <sys/types.h>

int main(int argc, char *argv[])
{
    int ep;
    int f;
    struct epoll_event ev, events;
    char value[4];
    int ret;
    int n;

    ep = epoll_create(1);

    if (ep == -1) {
        perror("Can't create epoll");
        return 1;
    }

    f = open("/sys/class/gpio/gpio557/value", O_RDONLY | O_NONBLOCK);

    if (f == -1) {
        perror("Can't open gpio557");
        return 1;
    }

    n = read(f, &value, sizeof(value));

    if (n > 0) {
```

```
            printf("Initial value value=%c\n", value[0]);
            lseek(f, 0, SEEK_SET);
    }

    ev.events = EPOLLPRI;
    ev.data.fd = f;
    ret = epoll_ctl(ep, EPOLL_CTL_ADD, f, &ev);

    while (1) {
        printf("Waiting\n");
        ret = epoll_wait(ep, &events, 1, -1);
        if (ret > 0) {
            n = read(f, &value, sizeof(value));
            printf("Button pressed: value=%c\n", value[0]);
            lseek(f, 0, SEEK_SET);
        }
    }

    return 0;
}
```

Here is how the code for the gpio-int program works. First, call epoll_create to create the epoll notification facility. Next, open the GPIO and read out its initial value. Call epoll_ctl to register the GPIO's file descriptor with POLLPRI as the event. Lastly, wait for an interrupt using the epoll_wait function. When you press the USR button on the BeaglePlay, the program will print Button pressed: followed by the number of bytes and value read from the GPIO.

While we could have used select and poll to handle interrupts, unlike those other two system calls, the performance of epoll does not degrade rapidly as the number of file descriptors being monitored increases.

The complete source code for this program, as well as a BitBake recipe and GPIO configuration script, can be found inside the MELD/Chapter11/meta-device-drivers/recipes-local/gpio-int directory.

Like GPIOs, LEDs are accessible from sysfs. The interface, however, is noticeably different.

LEDs

LEDs are often controlled through a GPIO pin, but there is another kernel subsystem that offers more specialized control specifically for this purpose. The leds kernel subsystem adds the ability to set brightness, should the LED have that ability, and it can handle LEDs connected in other ways than a simple GPIO pin. It can be configured to trigger the LED on an event, such as block device access or a heartbeat, to show that the device is working. You will have to configure your kernel with the CONFIG_LEDS_CLASS option and with the LED trigger actions that are appropriate to you. There is more information in Documentation/leds/ and the drivers are in drivers/leds/.

As with GPIOs, LEDs are controlled through a sysfs interface in the /sys/class/leds/ directory. In the case of the BeaglePlay, the user LED names are encoded in the device tree in the form of :function, as shown here:

```
# ls /sys/class/leds
:cpu               :heartbeat      :wlan         mmc1::
:disk-activity    :lan            mmc0::        mmc2::
```

Now, we can look at the attributes of one of the LEDs:

```
# cd /sys/class/leds/\:heartbeat
# ls
brightness      invert          power         trigger
device          max_brightness  subsystem     uevent
```

Note that leading backslashes are required by the shell to escape any colons in the path.

The brightness file controls the brightness of the LED and can be a number between 0 (off) and max_brightness (fully on). If the LED doesn't support intermediate brightness, any non-zero value turns it on. The file called trigger lists the events that trigger the LED to turn on. The list of triggers is implementation-dependent. Here is an example:

```
# cat trigger
none kbd-scrolllock kbd-numlock <...> disk-write [heartbeat] cpu <...>
```

The trigger currently selected is shown in square brackets. You can change it by writing one of the other triggers to the file. If you want to control the LED entirely through brightness, select none. If you set trigger to timer, two extra files will appear that allow you to set the on and off times in milliseconds:

```
# echo timer > trigger
# ls
brightness       delay_on        max_brightness  subsystem       uevent
delay_off        device          power           trigger
# cat delay_on
500
# cat delay_off
500
```

If the LED has on-chip timer hardware, the blinking takes place without interrupting the CPU.

I2C

I2C is a simple low-speed 2-wire bus that is common on embedded boards. It is typically used to access peripherals that are not on the SoC such as display controllers, camera sensors, GPIO extenders, and so on. There is a related standard known as **system management bus (SMBus)** that is found on PCs and is used to access temperature and voltage sensors. SMBus is a subset of I2C.

I2C is a master-slave protocol with the master being one or more host controllers on the SoC. Slaves have a 7-bit address assigned by the manufacturer (read the data sheet) allowing up to 128 nodes per bus, but 16 are reserved, so only 112 nodes are allowed in practice. The master may initiate read or write transactions with one of the slaves. Frequently, the first byte is used to specify a register on the slave, while the remaining bytes are the data that's read from or written to that register.

There is one device node for each host controller. This SoC has five:

```
# ls -l /dev/i2c*
crw-rw---- 1 root gpio 89, 0 Aug  7 13:25 /dev/i2c-0
crw-rw---- 1 root gpio 89, 1 Aug  7 13:25 /dev/i2c-1
crw-rw---- 1 root gpio 89, 2 Aug  7 13:25 /dev/i2c-2
crw-rw---- 1 root gpio 89, 3 Aug  7 13:25 /dev/i2c-3
crw-rw---- 1 root gpio 89, 5 Aug  7 13:25 /dev/i2c-5
```

The device interface provides a series of ioctl commands that query the host controller and send the read and write commands to I2C slaves. There is a package named i2c-tools that uses this interface to provide basic command-line tools to interact with I2C devices. The tools are as follows:

- i2cdetect: Lists the I2C adapters and probes the bus.
- i2cdump: Dumps data from all the registers of an I2C peripheral.
- i2cget: Reads data from an I2C slave.
- i2cset: Writes data to an I2C slave.

The i2c-tools package is available in Buildroot and The Yocto Project as well as most mainstream distributions. Writing a user space program to talk to the device is straightforward as long as you know the address and protocol of the slave. The example that follows shows how to read the first four bytes from the FT24C32A-ELR-T EEPROM, which is mounted on the BeaglePlay on I2C bus 0. The EEPROM has a slave address of 0x50.

Here is the code for a program that reads the first four bytes from an I2C address:

```c
#include <stdio.h>
#include <unistd.h>
#include <fcntl.h>
#include <sys/ioctl.h>
#include <linux/i2c-dev.h>

#define I2C_ADDRESS 0x50

int main(void)
{
    int f;
    int n;
    char buf[10];
    /* Open the adapter and set the address of the I2C device */
    f = open("/dev/i2c-0", O_RDWR);

    /* Set the address of the i2c slave device */
    ioctl(f, I2C_SLAVE, I2C_ADDRESS);

    /* Set the 16-bit address to read from to 0 */
    buf[0] = 0; /* address byte 1 */
    buf[1] = 0; /* address byte 2 */
    n = write(f, buf, 2);

/* Now read 4 bytes from that address */
    n = read(f, buf, 4);
    printf("0x%x 0x%x 0x%x 0x%x\n", buf[0], buf[1], buf[2], buf[3]);

    close(f);
    return 0;
}
```

This `i2c-eeprom-read` program prints `0xaa` `0x55` `0x33` `0x33` when executed on a BeaglePlay. That four-byte sequence is the magic number for the EEPROM. The complete source and a Bit-Bake recipe for this program can be found inside the `MELD/Chapter11/meta-device-drivers/recipes-local/i2c-eeprom-read` directory.

Note that a device on the other end of the I2C bus can be little-endian or big-endian. Little-endian and big-endian refer to the order of bytes within a data word. A 32-bit word contains four bytes. Little-endian means that the least significant byte is at index 0 and the most significant byte is at index 3. In contrast, big-endian means that the most significant byte is at index 0 and the least significant byte is at index 3. Big-endian is also referred to as *network order* corresponding to the order in which the bytes are transmitted over the wire in network protocols.

This program is like `i2cget` except that the address and register bytes being read from are both hardcoded rather than passed in as arguments. We can use `i2cdetect` to discover the addresses of any peripherals on an I2C bus. `i2cdetect` can leave I2C peripherals in a bad state or lock up the bus, so it's good practice to reboot after using it. A peripheral's data sheet tells us what the registers map to. With that information, we can then use `i2cset` to write to its registers over I2C. These I2C commands can easily be converted into a library of C functions for interfacing with the peripheral.

> **IMPORTANT NOTE**
>
> There is more information about the Linux implementation of I2C in `Documentation/i2c/dev-interface.rst`. The host controller drivers are in `drivers/i2c/busses/`.

Another popular communication protocol is the **SPI**, which utilizes a 4-wire bus.

SPI

The SPI bus is similar to I2C but is a lot faster by up to tens of MHz. The interface uses four wires with separate send and receive lines, which allow it to operate in full duplex. Each chip on the bus is selected with a dedicated chip select line. It is commonly used to connect to touchscreen sensors, display controllers, and serial NOR flash devices.

As with I2C, it is a master-slave protocol, with most SoCs implementing one or more master host controllers. There is a generic SPI device driver that you can enable through the `CONFIG_SPI_SPIDEV` kernel configuration. This creates a device node for each SPI controller, which allows you to access SPI chips from user space. The device nodes are named `spidev<bus>.<chip select>`:

```
# ls -l /dev/spi*
crw-rw---- 1 root root 153, 0  Jan  1 00:29 /dev/spidev1.0
```

For examples of using the spidev interface, please refer to the example code in Documentation/spi/.

So far, the device drivers we've seen all have longstanding upstream support within the Linux kernel. Because all these device drivers are generic (GPIO, LEDs, I2C, and SPI), accessing them from user space is straightforward. At some point, you will encounter a piece of hardware that lacks a compatible kernel device driver. That hardware may be the centerpiece of your product (LiDAR, SDR, and so on). There may also be an FPGA in between the SoC and this hardware. Under these circumstances, you may have no other recourse than to write your own kernel module(s).

Writing a kernel device driver

Eventually, when you have exhausted all the previous user space options, you will find yourself having to write a device driver to access a piece of hardware attached to your device. Character drivers are the most flexible and should cover 90% of all your needs; network drivers apply if you are working with a network interface; and block drivers are for mass storage. The task of writing a kernel driver is complex and beyond the scope of this book. There are some references at the end that will help you on your way. In this section, I want to outline the options available for interacting with a driver – a topic not normally covered – and show you the bare bones of a character device driver.

Designing a character driver interface

The main character driver interface is based on a stream of bytes, as you would have with a serial port. However, many devices don't fit this description: a controller for a robot arm needs functions to move and rotate each joint, for example. Luckily, there are other ways to communicate with device drivers than just read and write:

- ioctl: The ioctl function allows you to pass two arguments to your driver. These arguments can have any meaning you like. By convention, the first argument is a command that selects one of several functions in your driver, while the second is a pointer to a structure that serves as a container for the input and output parameters. This is a blank canvas that allows you to design any program interface you like. It is pretty common when the driver and application are closely linked and written by the same team. However, ioctl is deprecated in the kernel, and you will find it hard to get any drivers with new uses of ioctl accepted upstream. The kernel maintainers dislike ioctl because it makes kernel code and application code too interdependent, and it is hard to keep both of them in step across kernel versions and architectures.

- sysfs: This is the preferred way to do things now, with a good example being the LED interface described earlier. The advantage is that it is somewhat self-documenting, so long as you choose descriptive names for the files. It is also scriptable because the file's content is usually text strings. On the other hand, the requirement for each file to contain a single value makes it hard to achieve atomicity if you need to change more than one value at a time. Conversely, ioctl passes all its arguments in a structure, via a single function call.

- mmap: You can get direct access to kernel buffers and hardware registers by mapping kernel memory into user space, thus bypassing the kernel. You may still need some kernel code to handle interrupts and DMA. There is a subsystem that encapsulates this idea known as uio, which is short for **user I/O**. There is more documentation in Documentation/driver-api/uio-howto.rst and there are example drivers in drivers/uio/.

- sigio: You can send a signal from a driver using the kernel function named kill_fasync() to notify applications of an event such as input becoming ready or an interrupt being received. By convention, the signal called SIGIO is used, but it could be any. You can see some examples in drivers/uio/uio.c and drivers/char/rtc.c. The main problem is that it is difficult to write reliable signal handlers in user space, so it remains a little-used facility.

- debugfs: This is another pseudo filesystem that represents kernel data as files and directories, like proc and sysfs. The main distinction is that debugfs must not contain information that is needed for the normal operation of the system; it is for debug and trace information only. It is mounted via mount -t debugfs debug /sys/kernel/debug. There is a good description of debugfs in Documentation/filesystems/debugfs.rst.

- proc: The proc filesystem is deprecated for all new code unless it relates to processes, which was what the filesystem was originally intended for. However, you can use proc to publish any information you choose. And, unlike sysfs and debugfs, it is available to non-GPL modules.

- netlink: This is a socket protocol family. AF_NETLINK creates a socket that links kernel space to user space. It was originally created so that network tools could communicate with the Linux network code to access the routing tables and other details. It is also used by udev to pass events from the kernel to the udev daemon. It is very rarely used in general device drivers.

There are many examples of all the preceding filesystems in the kernel source code, and you can design really interesting interfaces to your driver code. The only universal rule is the *principle of least astonishment*. In other words, application writers who are using your driver should find that everything works in a logical way without any quirks or oddities.

Anatomy of a device driver

It's time to draw some threads together by looking at the code for a simple device driver.

Here is the start of a device driver named dummy, which creates four devices that can be accessed through /dev/dummy0 to /dev/dummy3:

```
#include <linux/kernel.h>
#include <linux/module.h>
#include <linux/init.h>
#include <linux/fs.h>
#include <linux/device.h>

#define DEVICE_NAME "dummy"
#define MAJOR_NUM 42
#define NUM_DEVICES 4

static struct class *dummy_class;
```

Next, we will define the dummy_open(), dummy_release(), dummy_read(), and dummy_write() functions for the character device interface:

```
static int dummy_open(struct inode *inode, struct file *file)
{
    pr_info("%s\n", __func__);
    return 0;
}

static int dummy_release(struct inode *inode, struct file *file)
{
    pr_info("%s\n", __func__);
    return 0;
}

static ssize_t dummy_read(struct file *file, char *buffer, size_t length,
loff_t * offset)
{
    pr_info("%s %u\n", __func__, length);
    return 0;
}
```

```
static ssize_t dummy_write(struct file *file, const char *buffer, size_t
length, loff_t * offset)
{
    pr_info("%s %u\n", __func__, length);
    return length;
}
```

After that, we need to initialize a file_operations structure and define the dummy_init() and dummy_exit() functions, which are called when the driver is loaded and unloaded:

```
struct file_operations dummy_fops = {
    .open = dummy_open,
    .release = dummy_release,
    .read = dummy_read,
    .write = dummy_write,
};

int __init dummy_init(void)
{
    int ret;
    int i;

    printk("Dummy loaded\n");
    ret = register_chrdev(MAJOR_NUM, DEVICE_NAME, &dummy_fops);

    if (ret != 0){
        return ret;
    }

    dummy_class = class_create(DEVICE_NAME);

    for (int i = 0; i < NUM_DEVICES; i++) {
        device_create(dummy_class, NULL, MKDEV(MAJOR_NUM, i), NULL,
"dummy%d", i);
    }

    return 0;
}
```

```
void __exit dummy_exit(void)
{
    int i;
    for (int i = 0; i < NUM_DEVICES; i++) {
        device_destroy(dummy_class, MKDEV(MAJOR_NUM, i));
    }

    class_destroy(dummy_class);

    unregister_chrdev(MAJOR_NUM, DEVICE_NAME);
    printk("Dummy unloaded\n");
}
```

At the end of the code, the macros called module_init and module_exit specify the functions to be called when the module is loaded and unloaded:

```
module_init(dummy_init);
module_exit(dummy_exit);
```

The closing three macros, named MODULE_*, add some basic information about the module:

```
MODULE_LICENSE("GPL");
MODULE_AUTHOR("Chris Simmonds");
MODULE_DESCRIPTION("A dummy driver");
```

This information can be retrieved from the compiled kernel module using the modinfo command. The complete source code, as well as a Makefile for this driver, can be found inside the MELD/ Chapter11/meta-device-drivers/recipes-kernel/dummy-driver directory.

When the module is loaded, the dummy_init() function is called. The point at which it becomes a character device is when it makes the call to register_chrdev passing a pointer to struct file_operations containing pointers to the four functions that the driver implements. While register_chrdev tells the kernel that there is a driver with a major number of 42, it doesn't say anything about the class of the driver, so it will not create an entry in /sys/class/.

Without an entry in /sys/class/, the device manager cannot create device nodes. So, the next few lines of code create a device class named dummy and four devices of that class called dummy0 to dummy3. The result is that the /sys/class/dummy/ directory is created containing subdirectories dummy0 to dummy3 when the driver is initialized. Each of the subdirectories contains a dev file that contains the major and minor numbers of the device. This is all that a device manager needs to create device nodes /dev/dummy0 to /dev/dummy3.

The `dummy_exit()` function has to release the resources claimed by `dummy_init()` by freeing up the device class and major number.

The file operations for this driver are implemented by `dummy_open()`, `dummy_read()`, `dummy_write()`, and `dummy_release()`. They are called when a user space program calls `open(2)`, `read(2)`, `write(2)`, and `close(2)`, respectively. They just print a kernel message so that you can see that they were called. You can demonstrate this from the command line using the `echo` command:

```
# echo hello > /dev/dummy0
dummy_open
dummy_write 6
dummy_release
```

In this case, the messages appear because I was logged on to the console, and kernel messages are printed to the console by default. If you are not logged on to the console, you can still see the kernel messages by using the `dmesg` command.

The full source code for this driver is less than 100 lines, but it is enough to illustrate how the linkage between a device node and driver code works, how the device class is created, and how the data is moved between the user and kernel spaces. Next, you need to build it.

Compiling kernel modules

At this point, you have some driver code that you want to compile and test on your target system. You can copy it into the kernel source tree and modify makefiles to build it, or you can compile it as a module out of tree. Let's start by building out of tree.

You will need a simple `Makefile` that uses the kernel build system to do all the hard work:

```
obj-m := dummy.o

SRC := $(shell pwd)

all:
        $(MAKE) -C $(KERNEL_SRC) M=$(SRC)

modules_install:
        $(MAKE) -C $(KERNEL_SRC) M=$(SRC) modules_install
```

```
clean:
        rm -f *.o *~ core .depend .*.cmd *.ko *.mod.c
        rm -f Module.markers Module.symvers modules.order
        rm -rf .tmp_versions Modules.symvers
```

Yocto sets `KERNEL_SRC` to the directory of the kernel for your target device that you will be running the module on. The `obj-m := dummy.o` code will invoke the kernel build rule to take the `dummy.c` source file and create a `dummy.ko` kernel module. I will show you how to load kernel modules in the next section.

> **IMPORTANT NOTE**
>
> Kernel modules are not binary compatible between kernel releases and configurations: the module will only load on the kernel it was compiled with.

If you want to build a driver in the kernel source tree, the procedure is quite simple. Choose a directory appropriate to the type of driver you have. The driver is a basic character device, so I would put `dummy.c` in `drivers/char/`. Then, edit the makefile in the directory and add a line to build the driver unconditionally as a module, like so:

```
obj-m += dummy.o
```

Alternatively, you can add the following line to build it unconditionally as a built-in:

```
obj-y += dummy.o
```

If you want to make the driver optional, you can add a menu option to the `Kconfig` file and make the compilation conditional on the configuration option, as I described in the *Understanding kernel configuration* section of *Chapter 4*.

Loading kernel modules

You can load, list, and unload modules using the simple `modprobe`, `lsmod`, and `rmmod` commands. Here, they are loading and unloading the dummy driver:

```
# modprobe dummy
# lsmod
Module                  Size  Used by
dummy                  12288  0
# rmmod dummy
```

If the module is placed in a subdirectory in /lib/modules/<kernel release>, you can create a modules dependency database using the depmod -a command, like so:

```
# depmod -a
# ls /lib/modules/6.12.9-ti-g8906665ace32
modules.alias              modules.builtin.modinfo    modules.softdep
modules.alias.bin          modules.dep                modules.symbols
modules.builtin            modules.dep.bin            modules.symbols.bin
modules.builtin.alias.bin  modules.devname            updates
modules.builtin.bin        modules.order
```

The information in the modules.* files is used by the modprobe command to locate a module by name rather than its full path. modprobe has many other features, all of which are described on the modprobe(8) manual page.

Now that we have written and loaded our dummy kernel module, how do we get it to talk to some real piece of hardware? We need to bind our driver to that hardware either by way of the device tree or platform data. Discovering hardware and linking that hardware to a device driver is the topic of the next section.

Discovering the hardware configuration

The dummy driver demonstrates the structure of a device driver, but it lacks interaction with real hardware since it only manipulates memory structures. Device drivers are usually written to interact with hardware. Part of that is being able to discover the hardware in the first place, bearing in mind that it may be at different addresses in different configurations.

In some cases, the hardware provides the information itself. Devices on a discoverable bus such as PCI or USB have a query mode that returns resource requirements and a unique identifier. The kernel matches the identifier and possibly other characteristics with the device drivers and marries them up.

However, most of the hardware blocks on an embedded board do not have such identifiers. You have to provide the information yourself in the form of a **device tree** or as C structures known as **platform data**.

In the standard driver model for Linux, device drivers register themselves with the appropriate subsystem: PCI, USB, open firmware (device tree), platform device, and so on. The registration includes an identifier and a callback function called a probe function that is called if there is a match between the ID of the hardware and the ID of the driver. For PCI and USB, the ID is based on the vendor and the product IDs of the devices. For device trees and platform devices, it is a name (a text string).

Device trees

I gave you an introduction to device trees in *Chapter 3*. Here, I want to show you how the Linux device drivers hook up with this information.

As an example, I will use the Arm Versatile board (`arch/arm/boot/dts/versatile-ab.dts`) for which the Ethernet adapter is defined here:

```
net@10010000 {
    compatible = "smsc,lan91c111";
    reg = <0x10010000 0x10000>;
    interrupts = <25>;
};
```

Pay special attention to the `compatible` property of this node. This string value will reappear later in the source code for the Ethernet adapter. We will learn more about device trees in *Chapter 12*.

Platform data

In the absence of device tree support, there is a fallback method of describing hardware using C structures, known as the platform data.

Each piece of hardware is described by `struct platform_device`, which has a name and a pointer to an array of resources. The resource's type is determined by flags, which include the following:

- `IORESOURCE_MEM`: This is the physical address of a region of memory.
- `IORESOURCE_IO`: This is the physical address or port number of I/O registers.
- `IORESOURCE_IRQ`: This is the interrupt number.

Here is an example of the platform data for an Ethernet controller taken from `arch/arm/machversatile/core.c`, which has been edited for clarity:

```
#define VERSATILE_ETH_BASE 0x10010000
#define IRQ_ETH 25

static struct resource smc91x_resources[] = {
[0] = {
    .start = VERSATILE_ETH_BASE,
    .end = VERSATILE_ETH_BASE + SZ_64K - 1,
```

```
      .flags = IORESOURCE_MEM,
  },
  [1] = {
    .start = IRQ_ETH,
    .end = IRQ_ETH,
    .flags = IORESOURCE_IRQ,
  },
};

static struct platform_device smc91x_device = {
  .name = "smc91x",
  .id = 0,
  .num_resources = ARRAY_SIZE(smc91x_resources),
  .resource = smc91x_resources,
};
```

It has a memory area of 64 KB and an interrupt. The platform data is usually registered with the kernel when the board is initialized:

```
void __init versatile_init(void)
{
    platform_device_register(&versatile_flash_device);
    platform_device_register(&versatile_i2c_device);
    platform_device_register(&smc91x_device);
<…>
```

The platform data shown here is functionally equivalent to the previous device tree source except for the name field, which takes the place of the compatible property.

Linking hardware with device drivers

In the preceding section, you saw how an Ethernet adapter is described using a device tree or platform data. The corresponding driver code is in drivers/net/ethernet/smsc/smc91x.c and it works with both the device tree and platform data.

Here is the initialization code, once again edited for clarity:

```
static const struct of_device_id smc91x_match[] = {
    { .compatible = "smsc,lan91c94", },
    { .compatible = "smsc,lan91c111", },
```

```
    {},
};


MODULE_DEVICE_TABLE(of, smc91x_match);

static struct platform_driver smc_driver = {
    .probe = smc_drv_probe,
    .remove = smc_drv_remove,
    .driver = {
        .name = "smc91x",
        .of_match_table = of_match_ptr(smc91x_match),
},
};

static int __init smc_driver_init(void)
{
    return platform_driver_register(&smc_driver);
}

static void __exit smc_driver_exit(void)
{
    platform_driver_unregister(&smc_driver);
}

module_init(smc_driver_init);
module_exit(smc_driver_exit);
```

When the driver is initialized, it calls platform_driver_register() pointing to struct platform_driver, in which there is a callback to a probe function, a driver name of smc91x, and a pointer to struct of_device_id.

If this driver has been configured by the device tree, the kernel will look for a match between the compatible property in the device tree node and the string being pointed to by the compatible structure element. For each match, it calls the probe function.

On the other hand, if it was configured through platform data, the probe function will be called for each match on the string pointed to by driver.name.

The probe function extracts information about the interface:

```
static int smc_drv_probe(struct platform_device *pdev)
{
    struct smc91x_platdata *pd = dev_get_platdata(&pdev->dev);
    const struct of_device_id *match = NULL;
    struct resource *res, *ires;
    int irq;

    res = platform_get_resource(pdev, IORESOURCE_MEM, 0);
    ires = platform_get_resource(pdev, IORESOURCE_IRQ, 0);
    <...>
    addr = ioremap(res->start, SMC_IO_EXTENT);
    irq = ires->start;
    <...>
}
```

The calls to platform_get_resource() extract the memory and irq information from either the device tree or the platform data. It is up to the driver to map the memory and install the interrupt handler. The third parameter (0 in both of the previous cases) comes into play if there is more than one resource of that particular type.

Device trees allow you to configure more than just basic memory ranges and interrupts. There is a section of code in the probe function that extracts optional parameters from the device tree. In this snippet, it gets the register-io-width property:

```
match = of_match_device(of_match_ptr(smc91x_match), &pdev->dev);

if (match) {
    struct device_node *np = pdev->dev.of_node;
    u32 val;
    <...>
    of_property_read_u32(np, "reg-io-width", &val);
    <...>
}
```

For most drivers, specific bindings are documented in Documentation/devicetree/bindings/. For this particular driver, the information is in Documentation/devicetree/bindings/net/ smsc,lan9115.yaml.

The main thing to remember here is that drivers should register a probe function and enough information for the kernel to call probe as it finds matches with the hardware it knows about. The linkage between the hardware described by the device tree and the device driver is done through the compatible property. The linkage between platform data and a driver is done through the name.

Summary

Device drivers have the job of handling devices, usually physical hardware but sometimes virtual interfaces, and presenting them to the user space in a consistent and useful way. Linux device drivers fall into three broad categories: character, block, and network. Of the three, the character driver interface is the most flexible and, therefore, the most common. Linux drivers fit into a framework known as the driver model, which is exposed through sysfs. Pretty much the entire state of the devices and drivers is visible in /sys/.

Each embedded system has its own unique set of hardware interfaces and requirements. Linux provides drivers for most standard interfaces, and by selecting the right kernel configuration, you can get a working target board very quickly. This leaves you with the non-standard components for which you will have to add your own device support.

In some cases, you can sidestep the issue by using generic drivers for GPIO, I2C, and SPI, and instead, write user space code to do the work. I recommend this as a starting point as it gives you the chance to become familiar with the hardware without writing kernel code. Writing kernel drivers is not particularly difficult, but you do need to code carefully so as not to compromise the stability of the system.

I have talked about writing the kernel driver code: if you go down this route, you will inevitably want to know how to check whether it is working correctly and detect any bugs. I will cover that topic in *Chapter 19*.

The next chapter demonstrates techniques for rapid prototyping with single board computers and add-on boards.

Further study

- *Linux Kernel Development, 3rd Edition*, by Robert Love
- *Linux Weekly News* – https://lwn.net/Kernel
- *Async IO on Linux: select, poll, and epoll*, by Julia Evans – https://jvns.ca/blog/2017/06/03/async-io-on-linux--select--poll--and-epoll/
- *Essential Linux Device Drivers, 1st Edition*, by Sreekrishnan Venkateswaran

Join our community on Discord

Join our community's Discord space for discussions with the authors and other readers: `https://packt.link/embeddedsystems`

12

Prototyping with Add-On Boards

Custom board bring-up is what embedded Linux engineers are called on to do time and time again. Say a consumer electronics manufacturer wants to build a new device and that device needs to run Linux. The process of assembling the Linux image starts before the hardware is ready and is done with prototypes pieced together from SBCs and add-on boards. Once a proof of concept has been validated then an initial run of prototype PCBs is fabricated with peripherals on board. There is no more satisfying experience than seeing a custom board boot into Linux for the very first time.

The BeaglePlay is unique among SBCs in that it has a mikroBUS socket for quick plug and play peripheral expansion. There is a MikroE Click add-on board for just about any hardware peripheral you can think of. In this chapter, we will integrate a GNSS receiver, environmental sensor module, and OLED display with the BeaglePlay. Leveraging mikroBUS eliminates the need to read schematics and wire up breadboards so that you spend less time troubleshooting hardware and more time coding your application.

Rapid prototyping with real hardware involves lots of trial and error. With a full Debian Linux distribution at our disposal, we can use mainstream tools such as git, pip3, and python3 to develop software directly on the BeaglePlay.

In this chapter, we will cover the following topics:

- Mapping schematics to pins
- Prototyping with add-on boards
- Testing hardware peripherals

Technical requirements

To follow along with the examples, make sure you have the following:

- An Ubuntu 24.04 or later LTS host system
- A microSD card reader and card
- balenaEtcher for Linux
- A BeaglePlay
- A 5V USB-C power supply capable of delivering 3A
- A USB to TTL serial cable with 3.3V logic level
- An Ethernet cable and router with an available port for network connectivity
- A MikroE-5764 GNSS 7 Click add-on board
- An external active GNSS antenna
- A MikroE-5546 Environment Click add-on board
- A MikroE-5545 OLED C Click add-on board

The code used in this chapter can be found in the chapter folder in this book's GitHub repository: `https://github.com/PacktPublishing/Mastering-Embedded-Linux-Development/tree/main/Chapter12`.

Mapping schematics to pins

Because the BeaglePlay's **Bill Of Materials** (**BOM**), PCB design files, and schematics are all open source, anyone can manufacture a BeaglePlay as part of their consumer product. Since the BeaglePlay is intended for development, it contains several components that may not be needed for production, such as Ethernet ports, USB ports, and a microSD slot. As a dev board, the BeaglePlay may also be missing one or more peripherals needed for your application such as sensors, an LTE modem, or an OLED display.

The BeaglePlay is built around Texas Instruments' AM6254, a quad-core 64-bit Arm Cortex-A53 SoC with **Programmable Real-Time Unit** (**PRU**) and M4 microcontrollers. Like the Raspberry Pi 4, the BeaglePlay has built-in Wi-Fi and Bluetooth. Unlike other SBCs, it also has a programmable radio capable of sub-GHz and 2.4 GHz low-power wireless communication. While the BeaglePlay is extremely versatile, at some point you may want to design your own custom PCB around the AM6254 to reduce the cost of your finished product.

In *Chapter 11*, we looked at an example of how to bind an Ethernet adapter to a Linux device driver. Binding peripherals is done with device tree source or C structs known as platform data. Over the years, device tree source has become the preferred means of binding to Linux device drivers, especially on Arm SoCs. As with U-Boot, compiling device tree source into DTBs is also part of the Linux kernel build process.

If you need to transfer lots of packets from a local network to and from the cloud, then running Linux is a sensible choice since it has an extremely mature TCP/IP network stack. The Beagle-Play's Arm Cortex-A53 CPU meets the requirements (enough addressable RAM and a memory management unit) for running mainstream Linux. This means your product can benefit from security and bug fixes that have been done to the Linux kernel.

Now that we have selected our SBC let's look at the BeaglePlay's schematic.

Reading schematics

The BeaglePlay has a mikroBUS socket as well as Grove and QWIIC connectors for add-on boards. Of the three standards, mikroBUS is the only one with UART, I2C, and SPI communications ports as well as **Analog to Digital Converter (ADC)**, **Pulse Width Modulation (PWM)**, and GPIO functionality. Consider I/O expansion options when selecting an SBC for development. More options mean more peripheral modules to choose from when prototyping.

When given the choice, I usually pick SPI over UART and I2C for production. UARTs are scarce on many SoCs and reserved for things such as Bluetooth and/or a serial console. I2C drivers and hardware can have serious bugs. Some I2C kernel drivers are so poorly implemented that the bus locks up when there are too many connected peripherals talking at once. Other times the bugs are in hardware. The I2C controllers found in Broadcom SoCs such as the one in the Raspberry Pi 4 are notorious for glitching when peripherals attempt to perform **clock stretching**. Clock stretching is when an I2C subnode device temporarily slows down or stops the bus clock.

Every mikroBUS socket consists of two pairs of 1x8 female headers. We can find both header strips on page 22 of the BeaglePlay's schematic (`https://github.com/beagleboard/beagleplay/blob/main/BeaglePlay_sch.pdf`).

Here is the right header strip of the BeaglePlay's mikroBUS socket:

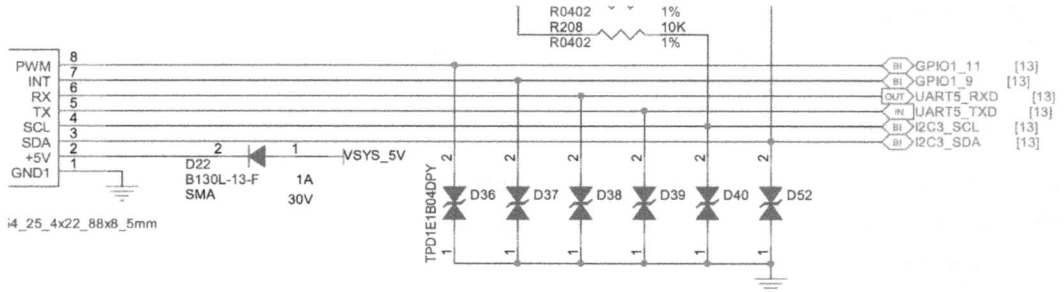

Figure 12.1 – mikroBUS socket (right header strip)

Pin 1 is tied to ground and pin 2 outputs 5V. Pins 3 (I2C3_SDA) and 4 (I2C3_CL) are connected to the BeaglePlay's I2C3 bus. Pins 5 (UART5_TXD) and 6 (UART5_RXD) are connected to UART5 on the BeaglePlay. Pins 7 (GPIO1_9) and 8 (GPIO1_11) are GPIOs, with pin 7 acting as an interrupt and pin 8 functioning as a PWM.

Here is the left header strip of the BeaglePlay's mikroBUS socket:

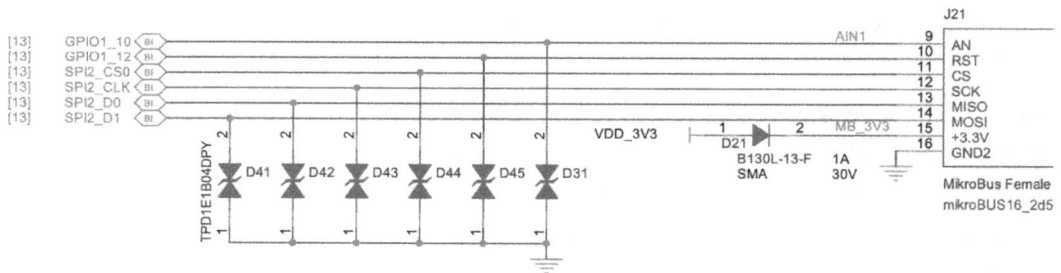

Figure 12.2 – mikroBUS socket (left header strip)

Pins 9 (GPIO1_10) and 10 (GPIO1_12) are GPIOs, with pin 9 acting as an analog input and pin 10 functioning as a reset. Pins 11 (SPI2_CS0), 12 (SPI2_CLK), 13 (SPI2_D0), and 14 (SPI2_D1) are connected to the BeaglePlay's SPI2 bus. Lastly, pin 15 outputs 3.3V, and pin 16 is tied to ground.

Notice that the SPI2 bus has CS0, CLK, D0, and D1 lines. CS stands for chip select. Since each SPI bus is a main-subnode interface, pulling a CS signal line low typically selects which peripheral to transmit to on the bus. This kind of negative logic is known as **active low**. CLK stands for clock and is always generated by the bus main, which is the AM6254 in this case. Data transmitted over the SPI bus is synchronized to this CLK signal. SPI supports much higher clock frequencies than I2C. The D0 data line corresponds to main in, subnode out (MISO).

The D1 data line corresponds to main out, subnode in (MOSI). SPI is a full-duplex interface, which means that both the main and selected subnode can send data at the same time.

Here is a block diagram showing the directions of all four SPI signals:

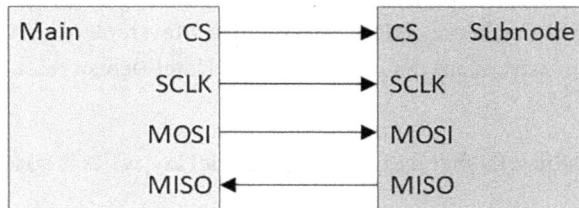

Figure 12.3 – SPI signals

Now let's enable mikroBUS on the BeaglePlay. The quickest way to do this is to install a prebuilt Debian image from BeagleBoard.org.

Installing Debian on the BeaglePlay

BeagleBoard.org provides Debian images for their various dev boards. Debian is a popular Linux distribution that includes a comprehensive set of open source software packages. It is a massive effort, with contributors from all over the world. Building Debian for the various BeagleBoards is unconventional by embedded Linux standards because the process does not rely on cross-compilation. Rather than attempting to build Debian for the BeaglePlay yourself, simply download a finished image directly from BeagleBoard.org.

To download and decompress the Debian Bookworm minimal eMMC flasher image for the BeaglePlay, use the following command::

```
$ wget https://files.beagle.cc/file/beagleboard-public-2021/images/
beagleplay-emmc-flasher-debian-12.7-minimal-arm64-2024-09-04-8gb.img.xz
$ xz -d beagleplay-emmc-flasher-debian-12.7-minimal-arm64-2024-09-04-8gb.
img.xz
```

If the above link is broken, visit https://beagleboard.org/distros for a current list of Debian images available for download. BeagleBoard.org can decide to delete links to Debian images as those images age out. Long-term maintenance of Debian releases is costly and labor-intensive.

At the time of writing, 12.7 was the latest Debian image for AM6254-based BeaglePlay boards. The major version number of 12 indicates that 12.7 is a Bookworm LTS release of Debian. Since Debian 12.0 was originally released on June 10, 2023, Bookworm should receive updates for up to 5 years from that date.

IMPORTANT NOTE

If possible, download version 12.7 (also known as Bookworm) rather than the latest Debian image from `BeagleBoard.org` for the exercises in this chapter. The Beagle-Play bootloader, kernel, DTBs, and command-line tools are in constant flux, so the following instructions may not work with a later Debian release.

Now that you have a Debian flasher image for the BeaglePlay, write it out to a microSD card:

1. Insert a microSD card into your Linux host machine.
2. Launch balenaEtcher.
3. Click **Flash from file** from **Etcher**.
4. Locate the `img` file that you downloaded from BeagleBoard.org and open it.
5. Click **Select target** from **Etcher**.
6. Select the microSD card that you inserted in *step 1*.
7. Click **Flash from Etcher** to write the image.
8. Eject the microSD card when Etcher is done flashing.

Next, boot the flasher image from the microSD and flash Debian onto the BeaglePlay's eMMC. Before proceeding, make sure that your USB to TTL serial cable has a 3.3 V logic level. The three-pin UART connector is right next to the USB-C connector on the BeaglePlay. Do not connect any fourth red wire from your cable. A red wire typically indicates power, which is unnecessary in this instance and could damage the board.

To copy the Debian image from the microSD to the BeaglePlay's eMMC:

1. Unplug the BeaglePlay from USB-C power.
2. Plug the USB side of your serial cable into your host machine.
3. Connect the TX wire from the serial cable to the RX pin on the BeaglePlay.
4. Connect the RX wire from the serial cable to the TX pin on the BeaglePlay.
5. Connect the GND (black) wire from the serial cable to the GND pin on the BeaglePlay.
6. Start a suitable terminal program such as `gtkterm`, `minicom`, or `picocom`, and attach it to the port at 115,200 bits per second (bps) with no flow control. `gtkterm` is probably the easiest to set up and use:

```
$ sudo gtkterm -p /dev/ttyUSB0 -s 115200
```

7. Insert the microSD card into the BeaglePlay.

8. Press and hold the USR button on the BeaglePlay.

9. Apply power to the BeaglePlay by way of the USB-C port.

10. Release the USR button once the BeaglePlay begins to boot from the microSD card.

11. Wait for the following prompt:

```
BeaglePlay microSD (extlinux.conf) (swap enabled)
1:       microSD disable BCFSERIAL
2:       copy microSD to eMMC (default)
3:       microSD (debug)
4:       microSD
Enter choice: 2
```

12. Enter 2.

It takes several minutes for the image to copy. Progress is reported on the serial console. If garbled or no output appears on the serial console, then swap the wires connected to the RX and TX pins on the BeaglePlay. Once the eMMC is done flashing, power off the BeaglePlay and remove the microSD card. Apply power to the BeaglePlay by way of the USB-C port. Plug an Ethernet cable from the BeaglePlay into a free port on your router. When the onboard Ethernet lights start blinking, the BeaglePlay should be online. Internet access allows us to install packages and fetch code from Git repos from within Debian.

To SSH into the BeaglePlay from your Linux host:

```
$ ssh debian@beaglebone.local
```

Enter temppwd at the debian user's password prompt. Change the password when prompted. SSH and log in again with your new password when the connection closes.

Now that Debian is running on your target, let's downgrade the Linux kernel to a version with the necessary mikroBUS driver.

Prototyping with add-on boards

ClickID is MikroE's plug and play solution for MikroE Click add-on boards. ClickID enables Linux to automatically identify a Click add-on board and instructs the mikroBUS driver to load the correct interface driver (UART, I2C, SPI, ADC, or PWM) for communicating with the peripheral. All the information about a peripheral is located on an EEPROM chip soldered to the bottom right of the add-on board. Linux talks to this EEPROM via 1-Wire at startup to perform the plug and play process. Not all Click add-on boards have this EEPROM so only some support ClickID.

Debian automatically upgrades packages including the Linux kernel without prompting the user. This is problematic because we will use an older Linux 5.10 kernel to talk to MikroE Click add-on boards.

To disable auto-upgrades in Debian:

```
debian@BeagleBone:~$ sudo apt remove unattended-upgrades
```

To downgrade the Linux kernel from 6.6 to 5.10:

```
debian@BeagleBone:~$ sudo apt update
debian@BeagleBone:~$ sudo apt install bbb.io-kernel-5.10-ti-k3-am62
debian@BeagleBone:~$ sudo apt remove bbb.io-kernel-6.6-ti
debian@BeagleBone:~$ sudo shutdown -r now
```

SSH back into the BeaglePlay once it is back online.

To confirm that the Linux kernel on the BeaglePlay was built with the necessary mikroBUS driver:

```
debian@BeagleBone:~$ dmesg | grep mikrobus
[    1.952311] mikrobus:mikrobus_port_register: registering port
mikrobus-0
[    1.952373] mikrobus mikrobus-0: mikrobus port 0 eeprom empty probing
default eeprom
```

Every ClickID EEPROM has a manifest section containing board specifics like pinout, interfaces, or Linux driver. Even if your Click add-on board does not have ClickID, a manifest may already exist for it.

To install the latest manifests on the BeaglePlay:

```
debian@BeagleBone:~$ sudo apt update
debian@BeagleBone:~$ sudo apt install bbb.io-clickid-manifests
```

To view the complete list of manifest files installed on the BeaglePlay:

```
debian@BeagleBone:~$ ls /lib/firmware/mikrobus/
```

To load a manifest with the mikroBUS driver, write that manifest to the mikrobus-0/new_device entry:

```
debian@BeagleBone:~$ sudo su root
# cd /lib/firmware/mikrobus
# cat GNSS-7-CLICK.mnfb > /sys/bus/mikrobus/devices/mikrobus-0/new_device
# exit
```

The manifest doesn't stick so you must reload it every time you reboot the BeaglePlay.

Even if you can't find a manifest for your Click add-on board, not all is lost. BeagleBoard.org has created a simple Python tool for creating new Click add-on manifests called Manifesto (`https://github.com/beagleboard/manifesto`).

> **IMPORTANT NOTE**
>
> Loading the GNSS Click 7 manifest manually as shown is completely unnecessary because the GNSS Click 7 has a ClickID EEPROM built in.

Many Click add-on boards appear as Linux **Industrial I/O (IIO)** devices. The `iio_info` tool can be used to discover IIO driver-enabled devices.

To install the `iio_info` tool:

```
debian@BeaglePlay:~$ sudo apt install libiio-utils
```

There are peripheral test scripts in the book's code repository. Debian comes with Git installed, so you can clone the book's repository to fetch the code:

```
debian@BeagleBone:~$ cd ~
debian@BeagleBone:~$ git clone https://github.com/PacktPublishing/
Mastering-Embedded-Linux-Development MELD
```

Now we are ready to test each Click add-on board.

Testing hardware peripherals

We will incorporate three peripherals into the BeaglePlay: a u-blox NEO-M9N GNSS receiver, a Bosch BME680 environmental sensor, and a Shenzhen Boxing World Technology PSP27801 OLED display. There are three test programs under *Chapter12* in the book's code repository. The `parse_nmea.py` program tests the NEO-M9N; the `sensors.py` program tests the BME680; and the `display.py` program tests the PSP27801. While it is possible to stack multiple Click add-on boards on a single mikroBUS socket, we will test each peripheral individually one at a time.

Attaching the GNSS Click 7 add-on board

Global Navigation Satellite System (GNSS) receivers send **National Marine Electronics Association (NMEA)** data over UART (serial port), I2C, or SPI. Many GNSS user space tools like `gpsd` only work with modules connected via serial port.

Download the NEO-M9N series data sheet from u-blox's product page at https://www.u-blox.com/en/product/neo-m9n-module. Jump to the section describing SPI. It says that SPI is disabled by default because its pins are shared with the UART and I2C interfaces. To enable SPI on the NEO-M9N, we must connect the D_SEL pin to GND. Pulling down D_SEL converts the two UART and two 12C pins into four SPI pins. This explains why the GNSS 7 Click add-on board defaults to operating over I2C and UART. To select SPI communication on the GNSS 7 Click, you need to insert a jumper.

To attach your GNSS Click 7 add-on board to the BeaglePlay:

1. Unplug the BeaglePlay from USB-C power.
2. Insert the GNSS Click 7 add-on board into the mikroBUS socket on the BeaglePlay.
3. Screw the external active GNSS antenna onto the GNSS SMA connector.
4. Apply power to the BeaglePlay by way of the USB-C port.
5. Reconnect the Ethernet cable from the BeaglePlay to a free port on your router if disconnected.

SSH back into the BeaglePlay once it is back online.

To confirm that your GNSS Click 7 add-on board was correctly attached and recognized:

```
debian@BeagleBone:~$ dmesg | grep mikrobus
[    1.969019] mikrobus:mikrobus_port_register: registering port
mikrobus-0
[    1.969093] mikrobus mikrobus-0: mikrobus port 0 eeprom empty probing
default eeprom
[    2.734524] mikrobus_manifest:mikrobus_manifest_attach_device: parsed
device 1, driver=neo-8, protocol=4, reg=0
[    2.739995] mikrobus_manifest:mikrobus_manifest_attach_device: device
1, number of properties=1
[    2.740005] mikrobus_manifest:mikrobus_manifest_parse:  GNSS 7 Click
manifest parsed with 1 devices
[    2.740073] mikrobus mikrobus-0: registering device : neo-8
```

If the output from dmesg looks like what's above, then you have successfully attached your add-on board to the BeaglePlay.

To examine your newly attached GNSS device:

```
debian@BeagleBone:~$ ls /sys/class/gnss/gnss0/
dev  device  power  subsystem  type  uevent
```

This means that a GNSS device is now available for use at /dev/gnss0.

Receiving NMEA messages

Lastly, we will install the Python test program and run it on the target. This program simply outputs the live message stream from the GNSS module to the console.

NMEA is a data message format supported by most GNSS receivers. The NEO-M9N outputs NMEA sentences by default. These sentences are ASCII text starting with the $ character followed by comma-separated fields. What we want to do first is read the stream of NMEA sentences from the NEO-M9N out of the /dev/gnss0 interface. Raw NMEA messages are not always easy to read, so we will use a parser to add helpful annotations to the data fields.

To stream the ASCII input from the GNSS module to stdout:

```
debian@BeagleBone:~$ sudo cat /dev/gnss0
$GNRMC,201929.00,A,3723.40927,N,12204.29313,W,0.159,,181224,,,A,V*04
$GNVTG,,T,,M,0.159,N,0.294,K,A*3F
$GNGGA,201929.00,3723.40927,N,12204.29313,W,1,09,1.16,43.4,M,-30.0,M,,*41
$GNGSA,A,3,30,08,14,07,20,,,,,,,,2.10,1.16,1.75,1*0C
$GNGSA,A,3,,,,,,,,,,,,,2.10,1.16,1.75,2*04
$GNGSA,A,3,03,,,,,,,,,,,,2.10,1.16,1.75,3*06
$GNGSA,A,3,36,20,19,,,,,,,,,,2.10,1.16,1.75,4*0D
$GPGSV,3,1,11,04,13,142,,07,63,045,35,08,36,068,25,09,39,150,,1*61
$GPGSV,3,2,11,13,11,316,07,14,46,233,21,17,04,184,,20,19,269,19,1*62
$GPGSV,3,3,11,22,25,228,32,27,13,041,,30,60,318,28,1*5D
$GLGSV,1,1,00,1*78
$GAGSV,1,1,04,02,22,228,23,03,60,310,30,05,63,148,,16,77,040,33,7*76
$GBGSV,1,1,03,19,47,204,31,20,10,168,25,36,62,293,35,1*4E
$GNGLL,3723.40927,N,12204.29313,W,201929.00,A,A*66
<...>
```

You should see a spurt of NMEA sentences once every second. Hit *Ctrl + C* to cancel the stream and return to the command-line prompt.

An NMEA parser script is included in the GitHub repo. That parse_nmea.py script depends on the pynmea2 library.

To install `pynmea2` on the BeaglePlay:

```
debian@BeagleBone:~$ sudo apt install python3.11-venv
debian@BeagleBone:~$ python3 -m venv gnss-click
debian@BeagleBone:~$ source gnss-click/bin/activate
(gnss-click) $ pip3 install pynmea2
```

To pipe the output from `/dev/gnss0` into the NMEA parser:

```
(gnss-click) $ cd ~/MELD/Chapter12
(gnss-click) $ sudo cat /dev/gnss0 | ./parse_nmea.py
```

The parsed NMEA output looks like this:

```
<RMC(timestamp=datetime.time(20, 33, 31, tzinfo=datetime.timezone.utc),
status='A', lat='3723.40678', lat_dir='N', lon='12204.28976', lon_dir='W',
spd_over_grnd=0.389, true_course=None, datestamp=datetime.date(2024,
12, 18), mag_variation='', mag_var_dir='', mode_indicator='A', nav_
status='V')>
<VTG(true_track=None, true_track_sym='T', mag_track=None, mag_track_
sym='M', spd_over_grnd_kts=Decimal('0.389'), spd_over_grnd_kts_sym='N',
spd_over_grnd_kmph=0.72, spd_over_grnd_kmph_sym='K', faa_mode='A')>
<GGA(timestamp=datetime.time(20, 33, 31, tzinfo=datetime.timezone.utc),
lat='3723.40678', lat_dir='N', lon='12204.28976', lon_dir='W', gps_qual=1,
num_sats='11', horizontal_dil='1.10', altitude=50.1, altitude_units='M',
geo_sep='-30.0', geo_sep_units='M', age_gps_data='', ref_station_id='')>
<...>
```

Don't be discouraged if your GNSS module can't see any satellites or acquire a fixed position. This could be due to any number of reasons, such as choosing the wrong GNSS antenna or no clear line of sight to the sky. RF is complicated and the goal of this chapter was only to prove we could get communications with the GNSS module working. Now we can experiment with alternate GNSS antennas and more of the NEO-M9N's advanced features, like the much richer UBX message protocol.

With NMEA data now streaming out to the terminal, our first project is finished. We succeeded in verifying that the AM6254 can communicate with the NEO-M9N via a combination of I2C and UART.

Attaching the Environment Click add-on board

The BME680 environmental sensor measures temperature, relative humidity, pressure, and gas. It communicates with the AM6254 SoC over SPI or I2C from the Environment Click add-on board. Like the GNSS 7 Click, the Environment Click defaults to I2C. To select SPI communication on the Environment Click, you need to insert a jumper.

To attach your Environment Click add-on board to the BeaglePlay:

1. Unplug the BeaglePay from USB-C power.
2. Insert the Environment Click add-on board into the mikroBUS socket on the BeaglePlay.
3. Apply power to the BeaglePlay by way of the USB-C port.
4. Reconnect the Ethernet cable from the BeaglePlay to a free port on your router if disconnected.

SSH back into the BeaglePlay once it is back online.

To confirm that your Environment Click add-on board was correctly attached and recognized:

```
debian@BeagleBone:~$ dmesg | grep mikrobus
[    1.962765] mikrobus:mikrobus_port_register: registering port
mikrobus-0
[    1.962829] mikrobus mikrobus-0: mikrobus port 0 eeprom empty probing
default eeprom
[    2.413200] mikrobus_manifest:mikrobus_manifest_attach_device: parsed
device 1, driver=bme680, protocol=3, reg=77
[    2.413212] mikrobus_manifest:mikrobus_manifest_parse:  Environment
Click manifest parsed with 1 devices
[    2.413281] mikrobus mikrobus-0: registering device : bme680
```

If the output from dmesg looks like what's above, then you have successfully attached your add-on board to the BeaglePlay.

To examine your newly attached environmental sensor:

```
debian@BeagleBone:~$ iio_info
Library version: 0.24 (git tag: v0.24)
Compiled with backends: local xml ip usb
IIO context created with local backend.
Backend version: 0.24 (git tag: v0.24)
Backend description string: Linux BeagleBone 5.10.168-ti-arm64-r118
```

```
#1bookworm SMP Thu Feb 6 01:00:48 UTC 2025 aarch64
IIO context has 2 attributes:
        local,kernel: 5.10.168-ti-arm64-r118
        uri: local:
IIO context has 2 devices:
        iio:device0: bme680
                4 channels found:
                        temp:  (input)
                        2 channel-specific attributes found:
                                attr  0: input value: 25020
                                attr  1: oversampling_ratio value: 8
                        pressure:  (input)
                        2 channel-specific attributes found:
                                attr  0: input value: 1014.370000000
                                attr  1: oversampling_ratio value: 4
                        resistance:  (input)
                        1 channel-specific attributes found:
                                attr  0: input value: 1183
                        humidityrelative:  (input)
                        2 channel-specific attributes found:
                                attr  0: input value: 42.810000000
                                attr  1: oversampling_ratio value: 2
                1 device-specific attributes found:
                                attr  0: oversampling_ratio_available
 value: 1 2 4 8 16
                No trigger on this device
<…>
```

Notice that the bme680 appears as iio:device0.

Reading sensor values

Like other Linux IIO devices, the BME680's register values are accessible from sysfs.

To read the humidity, pressure, gas, and temperature values from the BME680:

```
$ cd /sys/bus/iio/devices/iio\:device0
$ cat in_humidityrelative_input
41.074000000
$ cat in_pressure_input
```

```
1014.350000000
$ cat in_resistance_input
3966
$ cat in_temp_input
24540
```

A script to continually poll all four channels is included in the GitHub repo. That `sensors.py` script has no dependencies outside of the Python standard library.

To run the script:

```
$ cd ~/MELD/Chapter12
$ ./sensors.py
```

With sensor values now streaming out to the terminal, our second project is finished. We succeeded in verifying that the AM6254 can communicate with the BME680 via I2C.

Attaching the OLED C Click add-on board

The OLED C Click comes with a Solomon Systech SSD1351 controller to drive the PSP27801 OLED display. You write to the 128x128 pixel SRAM display buffer inside the SSD1351 over SPI. The SSD1351 supports two color modes: 65K (6:5:6) and 262K (6:6:6). An (r:g:b) triplet indicates how many bits are used to represent the individual RGB components of a pixel. The PSP27801 has a resolution of 96x96 pixels, noticeably less than that of the SD1351's display buffer.

To attach your OLED C Click add-on board to the BeaglePlay:

1. Unplug the BeaglePay from USB-C power.
2. Insert the OLED C Click add-on board into the mikroBUS socket on the BeaglePlay.
3. Apply power to the BeaglePlay by way of the USB-C port.
4. Reconnect the Ethernet cable from the BeaglePlay to a free port on your router if disconnected.

SSH back into the BeaglePlay once it is back online.

To confirm that your OLED C Click add-on board was correctly attached and recognized:

```
debian@BeagleBone:~$ dmesg | grep mikrobus
[    1.946050] mikrobus:mikrobus_port_register: registering port
mikrobus-0
[    1.946117] mikrobus mikrobus-0: mikrobus port 0 eeprom empty probing
default eeprom
```

```
[    3.553403] mikrobus_manifest:mikrobus_manifest_attach_device: parsed
device 1, driver=fb_ssd1351, protocol=11, reg=0
[    3.553416] mikrobus_manifest:mikrobus_manifest_attach_device: device
1, number of properties=7
[    3.553430] mikrobus_manifest:mikrobus_manifest_attach_device: device
1, number of gpio resource=2
[    3.553437] mikrobus_manifest:mikrobus_manifest_parse:  OLEDC Click
manifest parsed with 1 devices
[    3.553513] mikrobus mikrobus-0: registering device : fb_ssd1351
[    3.553520] mikrobus mikrobus-0:  adding lookup table : spi1.0
```

If the output from dmesg looks like what's above, then you have successfully attached your add-on board to the BeaglePlay.

To examine your newly attached OLED display:

```
$ ls /sys/class/graphics/fb0
bits_per_pixel  console   dev      mode    pan     state      uevent
bl_curve                  coursor  device  modes   power      stride      virtual_size
blank                     debug    gamma   name    rotate     subsystem
$ cd /sys/class/graphics/fb0
$ cat name
fb_ssd1351
$ cat bits_per_pixel
16
$ cat virtual_size
128,128
```

Exposing the SSD1351 as a Linux framebuffer greatly simplifies how we interact with the OLED display. You do not need to link a mikroSDK library and deal with its clumsy C API. Just write directly to the fb0 device any way you like.

Displaying an animation

A test script for the OLED display is included in the GitHub repo. That display.py script depends on the luma.core and numpy libraries:

To install luma.core and numpy on the BeaglePlay:

```
debian@BeagleBone:~$ python3 -m venv ./oledc-click
debian@BeagleBone:~$ source ./oledc-click/bin/activate
(oledc-click) $ pip install luma.core numpy
```

To run the test script:

```
(oledc-click) $ cd ~/MELD/Chapter12
(oledc-click) $ ./display.py
```

A continuous animation involving a red, a green, and a blue square appears on the OLED display. As the three squares move towards each other, they overlap to form a white square in the center. The squares then separate and move back to their starting places so that the animation repeats itself.

Our third and final project is now done. We succeeded in verifying that the AM6254 can display moving images on the PSP27801 via SPI.

Summary

In this chapter, we learned how to integrate peripherals with an SoC. To do that, we first had to glean knowledge from schematics and data sheets. Without finished hardware in hand, we also had to select and plug in add-on boards. Lastly, we coded simple test programs in Python and ran them to verify peripheral functionality. Now that we have working hardware, we can begin to develop our embedded application.

The next two chapters are all about system startup and the different options you have for the init program, from the simple BusyBox init to more complex systems such as System V init and systemd. Your choice of init program can have a big impact on the user experience of your product, both in terms of boot times and fault tolerance.

Further study

- *Introduction to SPI Interface*, by Piyu Dhaker – https://www.analog.com/en/analog-dialogue/articles/introduction-to-spi-interface.html
- *Soldering is Easy*, by Mitch Altman, Andie Nordgren, and Jeff Keyzer – https://mightyohm.com/blog/2011/04/soldering-is-easy-comic-book

Get This Book's PDF Version and Exclusive Extras

Scan the QR code (or go to packtpub.com/unlock). Search for this book by name, confirm the edition, and then follow the steps on the page.

Note: Keep your invoice handy. Purchases made directly from Packt don't require an invoice.

13

Starting Up – The init Program

We looked at how the kernel boots up to the point where it launches the first program, init, in *Chapter 4*. In *Chapters 5* and *6*, we looked at creating root filesystems of varying complexity, all of which contained an init program. Now, it is time to look at the init program itself in more detail and discover why it is so important to the rest of the system.

There are many implementations of init. In this chapter, I will describe the three main ones: BusyBox init, System V init, and systemd. I will explain how they work and what types of systems are best suited for each. Part of this is balancing the tradeoff between size, complexity, and flexibility. We will learn how to launch a daemon using both BusyBox init and System V init. We will also learn how to add a service to systemd.

In this chapter, we will cover the following topics:

- After the kernel has booted
- Introducing the init programs
- BusyBox init
- System V init
- systemd

Technical requirements

To follow along with the examples, make sure you have the following:

- An Ubuntu 24.04 or later LTS host system with at least 90 GB of free disk space
- Buildroot 2024.02.6 LTS release
- Yocto 5.0 (scarthgap) LTS release

You should have already installed the 2024.02.6 LTS release of Buildroot for *Chapter 6*. If you have not, then refer to the *System requirements* section of *The Buildroot user manual* (https://buildroot. org/downloads/manual/manual.html) before installing Buildroot on your Linux host according to the instructions from *Chapter 6*.

You should have already built the 5.0 (scarthgap) LTS release of Yocto in *Chapter 6*. If you have not, then please refer to the *Compatible Linux Distribution* and *Build Host Packages* sections of the *Yocto Project Quick Build* guide (https://docs.yoctoproject.org/brief-yoctoprojectqs/) before building Yocto on your Linux host according to the instructions in *Chapter 6*.

The code used in this chapter can be found in the chapter folder in this book's GitHub repository: https://github.com/PacktPublishing/Mastering-Embedded-Linux-Development.

After the kernel has booted

In *Chapter 4*, we saw how the kernel bootstrap code looks for a root filesystem, either initramfs or a filesystem specified by root= on the kernel command line. The kernel bootstrap code then executes a program, which, by default, is /init for initramfs and /sbin/init for a regular filesystem. The init program has root privilege, and since it is the first process to run, it has a **process ID (PID)** of 1. If, for some reason, init cannot be started, the kernel will panic and the system will fail to boot.

The init program is the ancestor of all other processes, as shown here by the pstree command running on a simple embedded Linux system:

```
# pstree -gn
init(1)-+-syslogd(63)
        |-klogd(66)
        |-dropbear(99)
        `-sh(100)---pstree(109)
```

The job of the init program is to take control of the boot process in user space and set it running. It may be as simple as a shell command running a shell script—there is an example of this at the start of *Chapter 5*—but in most cases, you will use a dedicated init daemon to perform the following tasks:

- Start other daemons and configure system parameters and other things needed to get the system into a working state.
- Optionally, launch a login daemon, such as getty, on terminals that allow a login shell.

- Adopt processes that become orphaned due to their immediate parent terminating and there being no other processes in the thread group.

- Respond to any of its immediate children terminating by catching the SIGCHLD signal and collecting the return value to prevent them from becoming zombie processes. I will talk more about zombies in *Chapter 17*.

- Optionally, restart other daemons that have terminated.

- Handle system shutdown.

In other words, init manages the life cycle of the system from bootup to shutdown. There is a school of thought that says init is well placed to handle other runtime events such as new hardware and the loading and unloading of modules. This is what systemd does.

Introducing the init programs

The three init programs you are most likely to encounter in embedded devices are BusyBox init, System V init, and systemd. Buildroot offers all three with BusyBox init as the default. The Yocto Project lets you choose between System V init and systemd with System V init as the default. While Yocto's tiny distribution ships with BusyBox init, most other distro layers do not.

The following table gives some metrics to compare the three:

Metric	BusyBox init	System V init	systemd
Complexity	Low	Medium	High
Bootup speed	Fast	Slow	Medium
Required shell	ash	dash or bash	None
Number of executables	1(*)	4	50
libc	Any	Any	glibc
Size (MB)	< 0.1(*)	0.1	34(**)

Table 13.1 – Comparison of BusyBox init, System V init, and systemd

(*) BusyBox init is part of BusyBox's single executable, which is optimized for size on disk.

(**) Based on the Buildroot configuration of systemd.

Broadly speaking, there is an increase in flexibility and complexity as you go from BusyBox init to systemd.

BusyBox init

BusyBox has a minimal init program that uses an /etc/inittab configuration file to start programs at bootup and stop them at shutdown. The actual work is done by shell scripts, which, by convention, are placed in the /etc/init.d directory.

init begins by reading /etc/inittab. This file contains a list of programs to run, one per line, in this format:

```
<id>::<action>:<program>
```

The roles of these parameters are:

- id: The controlling terminal for the command
- action: When and how to run the program
- program: The program to run along with all its command-line arguments

The actions are:

- sysinit: Runs the program when init starts before any of the other types of actions.
- respawn: Runs the program and restarts it if it terminates. It is used to run a program as a daemon.
- askfirst: The same as respawn, but it prints the message **Please press Enter to activate this console** to the console and runs the program after *Enter* has been pressed. It is used to start an interactive shell on a terminal without prompting for a username or password.
- once: Runs the program once but does not attempt to restart it if it terminates.
- wait: Runs the program and waits for it to complete.
- restart: Runs the program when init receives the SIGHUP signal, indicating that it should reload the inittab file.
- ctrlaltdel: Runs the program when init receives the SIGINT signal, usually as a result of pressing *Ctrl + Alt + Del* on the console.
- shutdown: Runs the program when init shuts down.

Here is a small example that mounts proc and sysfs and then runs a shell on a serial interface:

```
null::sysinit:/bin/mount -t proc proc /proc
null::sysinit:/bin/mount -t sysfs sysfs /sys
console::askfirst:-/bin/sh
```

For simple projects in which you want to launch a small number of daemons and start a login shell on a serial terminal, it is easy to write the scripts manually. This is appropriate if you are creating a **roll-your-own (RYO)** embedded Linux. However, you will find that handwritten init scripts rapidly become unmaintainable as the number of things to be configured increases. They are not very modular and need updating each time a new component is added or removed.

Buildroot init scripts

Buildroot has been making effective use of BusyBox init for many years. Buildroot has two scripts in /etc/init.d/ named rcS and rcK (rc stands for "run commands"). The rcS script runs at bootup. It iterates over all the scripts in /etc/init.d/ with names that begin with a capital S followed by two digits and runs them in numerical order. These are the start scripts. The rcK script is run at shutdown. It iterates over all the scripts beginning with a capital K followed by two digits and runs them in numerical order. These are the kill scripts.

With this structure in place, it becomes easy for Buildroot packages to supply their own start and kill scripts so that the system becomes extensible. The two-digit number controls the order in which the init scripts are run. If you are using Buildroot, this structure is transparent. If not, then you can use it as a model for writing your own BusyBox init scripts.

Like BusyBox init, System V init relies on shell scripts inside /etc/init.d and an /etc/inittab configuration file. While the two init systems are similar in many ways, System V init has more features and a much longer history.

System V init

This init program was inspired by the one from Unix System V and dates back to the mid-1980s. The version most often found in Linux distributions was written initially by Miquel van Smoorenburg. Until recently, it was the init daemon for almost all desktop and server distributions and a fair number of embedded systems as well. However, in recent years it has been replaced by systemd, which we will describe in the next section.

The BusyBox init daemon is just a trimmed-down version of System V init. System V init has two advantages compared to BusyBox init:

- Firstly, the boot scripts are written in a well-known modular format making it easy to add new packages at build time or runtime.
- Secondly, it has the concept of **runlevels**, which allow a collection of programs to be started or stopped in one go when switching from one runlevel to another.

There are eight runlevels numbered from 0 to 6 plus S:

- S: Runs startup tasks
- 0: Halts the system
- 1 to 5: Available for general use
- 6: Reboots the system

Levels 1 to 5 can be used as desired. On most desktop Linux distributions, they are assigned as:

- 1: Single user
- 2: Multi-user without network configuration
- 3: Multi-user with network configuration
- 4: Not used
- 5: Multi-user with graphical login

The init program starts the default runlevel given by the initdefault line in /etc/inittab:

```
id:3:initdefault:
```

You can change the runlevel at runtime using the telinit <runlevel> command, which sends a message to init. You can find the current runlevel and the previous one using the runlevel command. Here is an example:

```
# runlevel
N 5
# telinit 3
INIT: Switching to runlevel: 3
# runlevel
5 3
```

The initial output from the runlevel command is N 5. An N indicates that there is no previous runlevel because the runlevel has not changed since booting. The current runlevel is 5. After changing the runlevel, the output is 5 3, indicating that there has been a transition from 5 to 3.

The halt and reboot commands switch to runlevels 0 and 6, respectively. You can override the default runlevel by giving a different one (a single digit from 0 to 6) on the kernel command line. For example, to force the default runlevel to be single user, you append 1 to the kernel command line like this:

```
console=ttyAMA0 root=/dev/mmcblk1p2 1
```

Each runlevel has a number of kill scripts that stop things, and another group of start scripts to get them going. When entering a new runlevel, init first runs the kill scripts followed by the start scripts from the new level. Daemons that are currently running and have neither a start script nor a kill script in the new runlevel are sent a SIGTERM signal. In other words, the default action when switching runlevels is to terminate daemons unless told otherwise.

In truth, runlevels are not used much in embedded Linux. Most devices simply boot to the default runlevel and stay there. I have a feeling this is partly because most people are not aware of them.

> **TIP**
>
> Runlevels are a simple and convenient way to switch between modes, for example, from production to maintenance mode.

System V init is an option in Buildroot and The Yocto Project. In both cases, the init scripts have been stripped of any bash shell specifics, so they will work with the BusyBox ash shell. However, Buildroot cheats somewhat by replacing the BusyBox init program with System V init and adding an inittab that mimics the behavior of BusyBox. Buildroot does not implement runlevels except for 0 and 6, which halt or reboot the system.

Next, let's look at some of the details. The following examples are taken from The Yocto Project 5.0 release. Other Linux distributions may implement init scripts a little differently.

inittab

The init program begins by reading entries that define what happens at each runlevel from an /etc/inittab configuration file. The format is an extended version of the BusyBox inittab described in the preceding section. This is no surprise since BusyBox borrowed it from System V in the first place.

The format of each entry in the inittab is:

```
<id>:<runlevels>:<action>:<process>
```

The fields are:

- id: A unique identifier of up to four characters
- runlevels: The runlevels this entry belongs to
- action: When and how to run the command
- process: The command to run

The actions are the same as for BusyBox init: sysinit, respawn, once, wait, restart, ctrlaltdel, and shutdown. However, System V init does not have askfirst, which is specific to BusyBox.

Here is the complete inittab supplied by The Yocto Project when building core-image-minimal for the qemuarm machine:

```
# /etc/inittab: init(8) configuration.
# $Id: inittab,v 1.91 2002/01/25 13:35:21 miquels Exp $

# The default runlevel.
id:5:initdefault:

# Boot-time system configuration/initialization script.
# This is run first except when booting in emergency (-b) mode.
si::sysinit:/etc/init.d/rcS

# What to do in single-user mode.
~~:S:wait:/sbin/sulogin
# /etc/init.d executes the S and K scripts upon change
# of runlevel.
#
# Runlevel 0 is halt.
# Runlevel 1 is single-user.
# Runlevels 2-5 are multi-user.
# Runlevel 6 is reboot.

l0:0:wait:/etc/init.d/rc 0
l1:1:wait:/etc/init.d/rc 1
l2:2:wait:/etc/init.d/rc 2
l3:3:wait:/etc/init.d/rc 3
l4:4:wait:/etc/init.d/rc 4
l5:5:wait:/etc/init.d/rc 5
l6:6:wait:/etc/init.d/rc 6

# Normally not reached, but fallthrough in case of emergency.
z6:6:respawn:/sbin/sulogin
AMA0:12345:respawn:/sbin/getty 115200 ttyAMA0
```

```
# /sbin/getty invocations for the runlevels
#
# The "id" field MUST be the same as the last
# characters of the device (after "tty").
#
# Format:
# <id>:<runlevels>:<action>:<process>
#

1:2345:respawn:/sbin/getty 38400 tty1
```

The first id:5:initdefault entry sets the default runlevel to 5. The next si::sysinit entry runs the /etc/init.d/rcS script at bootup. All the rcS script does is enter the S runlevel:

```
#!/bin/sh
<...>
exec /etc/init.d/rc S
```

Hence, the first runlevel entered is S, followed by the default runlevel of 5. Note that runlevel S is not recorded and is never displayed as a prior runlevel by the runlevel command.

The seven entries beginning with 10 to 16 run the /etc/init.d/rc script whenever there is a change to the runlevel. The rc script is responsible for processing the start and kill scripts.

Scan down a bit further for an entry that runs a getty daemon:

```
AMA0:12345:respawn:/sbin/getty 115200 ttyAMA0
```

This entry generates a login prompt on /dev/ttyAMA0 when entering runlevels 1 through 5 allowing you to log in and get an interactive shell. The ttyAMA0 device is the serial console on the Arm Versatile board emulated by QEMU. The device name may be different for serial consoles on other development boards.

The last entry runs another getty daemon on /dev/tty1:

```
1:2345:respawn:/sbin/getty 38400 tty1
```

This entry is triggered when entering runlevels 2 through 5. The tty1 device is a virtual console that is mapped to a graphical screen when you build your kernel with CONFIG_FRAMEBUFFER_CONSOLE or VGA_CONSOLE.

Desktop Linux distributions usually spawn six getty daemons on virtual terminals 1 to 6, with tty7 reserved for the graphical screen. Ubuntu and Arch Linux are notable exceptions since they use tty1 for graphics. You can switch between virtual terminals with key combinations *Ctrl + Alt + F1* through *Ctrl + Alt + F6*. Virtual terminals are seldom used on embedded devices.

The init.d scripts

Each component that needs to respond to a runlevel change has a script in /etc/init.d to perform the change. The script should expect two parameters: start and stop. I will give an example of each in the *Adding a new daemon* section.

The /etc/init.d/rc runlevel-handling script takes the runlevel it is switching to as a parameter. There is a directory named rc<runlevel>.d for each runlevel:

```
# ls -d /etc/rc*
/etc/rc0.d   /etc/rc2.d   /etc/rc4.d   /etc/rc6.d
/etc/rc1.d   /etc/rc3.d   /etc/rc5.d   /etc/rcS.d
```

There you will find a set of scripts beginning with a capital S followed by two digits. You may also find scripts beginning with a capital K. These are the start and kill scripts. Here is an example of the scripts for runlevel 5:

```
# ls /etc/rc5.d
S01networking    S20hwclock.sh   S99rmnologin.sh   S99stop-bootlogd
S15mountnfs.sh   S20syslog
```

These are, in fact, symbolic links back to their corresponding scripts in init.d. The rc script first runs all the scripts beginning with a K passing in the stop parameter. Then it runs all the scripts beginning with an S passing in the start parameter. Once again, the two-digit codes are there to impart the order in which to execute the scripts.

Adding a new daemon

Imagine that you have a program named simpleserver that is written as a traditional Unix daemon; in other words, it forks and runs in the background. The code for this program is in MELD/Chapter13/simpleserver. The corresponding init.d script (see below) is in MELD/Chapter13/simpleserver-sysvinit/init.d:

```
#! /bin/sh

case "$1" in
```

```
    start)
      echo "Starting simpelserver"
      start-stop-daemon -S -n simpleserver -a /usr/bin/simpleserver
      ;;
    stop)
      echo "Stopping simpleserver"
      start-stop-daemon -K -n simpleserver
      ;;
    *)
      echo "Usage: $0 {start|stop}"
      exit 1
  esac

  exit 0
```

start-stop-daemon is a program that makes it easier to manipulate background processes. It originally came from the Debian installer package (dpkg) but most embedded systems use the one from BusyBox. Running start-stop-daemon with the -S parameter starts the daemon, making sure that there is never more than one instance running at any one time. Running start-stop-daemon with the -K parameter stops the daemon by sending it a signal, SIGTERM by default, to indicate to the daemon that it is time to terminate.

To make simpleserver operational, copy the init.d script to /etc/init.d and make it executable. Then, add links from each of the runlevels that you want to run this program from—in this case, only the default runlevel of 5:

```
# cd /etc/init.d/rc5.d
# ln -s ../init.d/simpleserver S99simpleserver
```

The number 99 means that this will be one of the last programs to start.

> **IMPORTANT NOTE**
>
> Bear in mind that there may be other links beginning with S99, in which case the rc script will just run them in lexical order.

It is rare in embedded devices to have to worry too much about shutdown operations, but if there is something that needs to be done, add kill links to levels 0 and 6:

```
# cd /etc/init.d/rc0.d
# ln -s ../init.d/simpleserver K01simpleserver
# cd /etc/init.d/rc6.d
# ln -s ../init.d/simpleserver K01simpleserver
```

We can circumvent runlevels and ordering for more immediate testing and debugging of init.d scripts.

Starting and stopping services

You can interact with the scripts in /etc/init.d by calling them directly. Here is an example using the syslog script that controls the syslogd and klogd daemons:

```
# /etc/init.d/syslog --help
Usage: syslog { start | stop | restart }

# /etc/init.d/syslog stop
Stopping syslogd/klogd: stopped syslogd (pid 198)
stopped klogd (pid 201)
done

# /etc/init.d/syslog start
Starting syslogd/klogd: done
```

All scripts implement start and stop, and they should also implement help. Some implement status as well, which will tell you whether the service is running or not. Mainstream distributions that still use System V init have a command named service to start and stop services, which hides the details of calling the scripts directly.

System V init is a simple init daemon that has served Linux admins for decades. While runlevels offer a greater degree of sophistication than BusyBox init, System V init still lacks the ability to monitor services and restart them if needed. As System V init starts to show its age, most popular Linux distributions have moved on to systemd.

systemd

systemd (https://systemd.io/) defines itself as a *system and service manager*. The project was initiated in 2010 by Lennart Poettering and Kay Sievers to create an integrated set of tools for managing a Linux system based around an init daemon. It also includes device management (udev) and logging, among many other things. systemd is state of the art and is still evolving rapidly. It is common on desktop and server Linux distributions and is becoming increasingly popular on embedded Linux systems. So, how is it better than System V init?

- Configuration is simpler and more logical (once you understand it). Instead of convoluted shell scripts, systemd has unit configuration files that are written in a well-defined format.
- There are explicit dependencies between services. This is a huge improvement over two-digit numbers that only control the order in which scripts are executed.
- It is easy to set the permissions and resource limits for each service in the interest of security.
- It can monitor services and restart them if needed.
- Services are started in parallel, reducing boot time.

A complete description of systemd is not possible here. As with System V init, I will focus on the embedded use cases with examples based on The Yocto Project 5.0 release with systemd version 255.

Building systemd with The Yocto Project and Buildroot

The default init daemon in The Yocto Project is System V. To select systemd, add this line to your conf/local.conf:

```
INIT_MANAGER = "systemd"
```

Buildroot uses BusyBox init by default. You can select systemd through menuconfig by looking in the **System configuration | Init system** menu. You will also have to configure the toolchain to use glibc for the C library since systemd does not officially support uClibc-ng or musl. In addition, there are restrictions on the version and configuration of the kernel. There is a complete list of library and kernel dependencies in the README file at the top level of the systemd source code.

Introducing targets, services, and units

Before I describe how systemd works, I need to introduce three key concepts:

- **Unit**: A configuration file that describes a target, a service, or several other things. Units are text files that contain properties and values.

- **Service**: A daemon that can be started and stopped, much like a System V init service.
- **Target**: A group of services, similar to a System V init runlevel. There is a default target consisting of all the services that are started at boot time.

You can change states and find out what is going on using the systemctl command.

Units

The basic item of configuration is the **unit** file. Unit files are found in four different places:

- /etc/systemd/system: Local configuration
- /run/systemd/system: Runtime configuration
- /usr/lib/systemd/system: Distribution-wide configuration (default location)
- /lib/systemd/system: Distribution-wide configuration (legacy default location)

When looking for a unit, systemd searches these directories in the preceding order, stopping as soon as it finds a match. You can override the behavior of a distribution-wide unit by placing a unit of the same name in /etc/systemd/system. You can also disable a unit completely by creating a local file that is empty or linked to /dev/null.

All unit files begin with a section marked [Unit] that contains basic information and dependencies. For example, here is the Unit section of the D-Bus service /lib/systemd/system/dbus.service:

```
[Unit]
Description=D-Bus System Message Bus
Documentation=man:dbus-daemon(1)
Requires=dbus.socket
```

In addition to the description and a reference to the documentation, there is a dependency on the dbus.socket unit expressed through the Requires keyword. This tells systemd to create a local socket when the D-Bus service is started.

Dependencies are expressed by the Requires, Wants, and Conflicts keywords:

- Requires: A list of units that this unit depends on; these are started when this unit is started.
- Wants: A weaker form of Requires; this unit continues even when any of these dependencies fails to start.
- Conflicts: A negative dependency; these units are stopped when this one is started, and conversely, if one of them is subsequently restarted, then this one is stopped.

These three keywords define **outgoing dependencies**. They are used to create dependencies between *targets*. There is another set of dependencies called **incoming dependencies**, which are used to create links between *services* and *targets*. In other words, outgoing dependencies are used to create the list of targets that need to be started as the system goes from one state to another, and incoming dependencies are used to determine the services that should be started or stopped when entering any state. Incoming dependencies are created by the WantedBy keyword, which I will describe in the upcoming section, *Adding your own service*.

Processing the dependencies produces a list of units that should be started or stopped. The Before and After keywords determine the order in which they are started. The stop order is simply the reverse of the start order:

- Before: Start this unit before the units listed.
- After: Start this unit after the units listed.

For example, the After directive ensures that the following web server is started after the network subsystem is started:

```
[Unit]
Description=Lighttpd Web Server
After=network.target
```

In the absence of a Before or After directive, the units are started or stopped in parallel with no ordering.

Services

A **service** is a daemon that can be started and stopped like a System V init service. A service has a unit file with a name ending in .service.

A service unit has a [Service] section that describes how the service should be run. Here is the [Service] section from lighttpd.service:

```
[Service]
ExecStart=/usr/sbin/lighttpd -f /etc/lighttpd/lighttpd.conf -D
ExecReload=/bin/kill -HUP $MAINPID
```

These are the commands to run when starting and restarting the service. There are many more configuration points you can add here so refer to the manual page for systemd.service(5).

Targets

A **target** is a unit that groups services or other types of units together. A target is a metaservice in that respect and serves as a synchronization point. A target only has dependencies. Targets have names ending in .target like multi-user.target. A target is a desired state that performs the same role as System V init runlevels. Here is the complete multi-user.target:

```
[Unit]
Description=Multi-User System
Documentation=man:systemd.special(7)
Requires=basic.target
Conflicts=rescue.service rescue.target
After=basic.target rescue.service rescue.target
AllowIsolate=yes
```

This says that the basic target must be started before the multi-user target. This also says that since it conflicts with the rescue target, starting the rescue target will cause the multi-user target to be stopped first. The rescue and multi-user targets cannot run simultaneously because the rescue target boots into single-user mode. Activating the rescue target only makes sense during system recovery.

How systemd boots the system

Let's see how systemd implements the bootstrap. The kernel starts systemd because /sbin/init is symbolically linked to /lib/systemd/systemd. systemd runs default.target, which is always a link to the desired target: either multi-user.target for a text login or graphical.target for a graphical environment. If the default target is multi-user.target, you will see this symbolic link:

```
/etc/systemd/system/default.target -> /lib/systemd/system/multi-user.
target
```

Override the default target by passing system.unit=<new target> on the kernel command line.

To discover the default target:

```
# systemctl get-default
multi-user.target
```

Starting a target like multi-user.target creates a tree of dependencies that bring the system into a working state. In a typical system, multi-user.target depends on basic.target, which depends on sysinit.target, which depends on the services that need to be started early.

To print a text graph of system dependencies:

```
# systemctl list-dependencies
```

To list all services and their current states:

```
# systemctl list-units --type service
```

To list all targets:

```
# systemctl list-units --type target
```

Now that we've seen the dependency tree for the system, how do we insert an additional service?

Adding your own service

Here is a unit for our `simpleserver` service:

```
[Unit]
Description=Simple server

[Service]
Type=forking
ExecStart=/usr/bin/simpleserver

[Install]
WantedBy=multi-user.target
```

You will find this `simpleserver.service` file in `MELD/Chapter13/simpleserver-systemd`.

The `[Unit]` section only contains a description that shows up under `systemctl`. There are no dependencies since this service is very simple.

The `[Service]` section points to the executable and has a flag to indicate that it forks. If `simpleserver` was even simpler and ran in the foreground, `systemd` would do the daemonizing for us and `Type=forking` would not be needed.

The `[Install]` section creates an incoming dependency on `multi-user.target` so that our server is started when the system enters multi-user mode.

Once you place the `simpleserver.service` file in the `/etc/systemd/system` directory, you can start and stop the service using the `systemctl start simpleserver` and `sytemctl stop simpleserver` commands. You can also use `systemctl` to get its current status:

```
# systemctl status simpleserver
simpleserver.service - Simple server
   Loaded: loaded (/etc/systemd/system/simpleserver.service; disabled)
   Active: active (running) since Thu 1970-01-01 02:20:50 UTC; 8s ago
 Main PID: 180 (simpleserver)
   CGroup: /system.slice/simpleserver.service
           └─180 /usr/bin/simpleserver -n


Jan 01 02:20:50 qemuarm systemd[1]: Started Simple server.
```

At this point, the service only starts and stops on command. To make it persistent, you need to add a permanent dependency to a target. The [Install] section says that when this service is enabled, it becomes dependent on `multi-user.target` so that it starts at boot time.

To enable the service:

```
# systemctl enable simpleserver
Created symlink from /etc/systemd/system/multiuser.target.wants/
simpleserver.service to /etc/systemd/system/simpleserver.service.
```

To update the `systemd` dependency tree without rebooting:

```
# systemctl daemon-reload
```

You can also add dependencies to services without having to edit target unit files. A target can have a directory named `<target_name>.target.wants` with links to services. Creating a link inside this directory is the same as adding a unit to the [Wants] list in the target. The `systemctl enable simpleserver` command created the following link:

```
/etc/systemd/system/multi-user.target.wants/simpleserver.service -> /etc/
systemd/system/simpleserver.service
```

You might want to restart an important service if it crashes. To achieve that, add the following flag to the [Service] section:

```
Restart=on-abort
```

The other `Restart` options are `on-success`, `on-failure`, `on-abnormal`, `on-watchdog`, and `always`.

Adding a watchdog

Many embedded systems require a watchdog: you need to act if a critical service stops. This usually means rebooting the system. Most embedded SoCs have a hardware watchdog that can be accessed via the /dev/watchdog device node. The **watchdog** is initialized with a timeout at boot. If this timer is not reset within the timeout period, the watchdog is triggered and the system reboots. The interface with the watchdog driver is described in the kernel source under Documentation/watchdog/ and the code for the drivers is in drivers/watchdog/.

A problem arises when there are two or more critical services that need to be protected by a watchdog. systemd has a useful feature that distributes the watchdog between multiple services. systemd can be configured to expect a regular keepalive call from a service and act when no keepalive is received, creating a software watchdog. For this to work, you need to add code to the daemon to send the keepalive messages. The daemon reads the value of the WATCHDOG_USEC environment variable and calls sd_notify(false, "WATCHDOG=1") within this time period. The period should be set to about half the watchdog timeout. There are examples in the systemd source code.

To enable the software watchdog in a service unit, add something like this to the [Service] section:

```
WatchdogSec=30s
Restart=on-watchdog
StartLimitInterval=5min
StartLimitBurst=4
StartLimitAction=reboot-force
```

In this example, the service expects a keepalive call every 30 seconds. If the keepalive fails to be delivered, the service is restarted, but if it is restarted more than four times in 5 minutes, systemd immediately reboots the entire system. There is a full description of these settings in the systemd.service(5) manual page.

A software watchdog takes care of individual services, but what if systemd itself fails, the kernel crashes, or the hardware locks up? In those cases, we need to tell systemd to use the hardware watchdog. Add RuntimeWatchdogSec=<N> to /etc/systemd/system.conf. This will reset the watchdog within the given N period so that the system reboots if systemd fails for some reason. This will be an immediate hard reboot or "reset" of the system without any graceful shutdown.

Implications for embedded Linux

systemd has a lot of features that are useful for embedded Linux. This chapter only mentions some of them. The others include resource control (described in the manual pages for systemd. slice(5) and systemd.resource-control(5)), device management (udev(7)), system logging facilities (journald(5)), mount units for auto-mounting filesystems, and timer units for cron jobs.

You need to balance these features with systemd's size. Even a minimal build of just the core components (systemd, udevd, and journald) approaches 10 MB of storage including shared libraries.

You also need to keep in mind that systemd development follows the kernel and glibc closely, so a systemd release won't work on a kernel and glibc more than a year or two older than itself.

Summary

Every Linux device needs an init program of some kind. If you are designing a system that only needs to launch a small number of daemons at startup, then BusyBox init is sufficient. BusyBox init is also usually a good choice if you are using Buildroot as your build system.

On the other hand, if you have a system with complex dependencies between services at boot time or runtime, then systemd is the best choice. Even without such complexity, systemd has some useful features like watchdogs, remote logging, and so on. If you have the storage space, you should seriously consider systemd.

Meanwhile, System V init lives on. It is well understood and there are already init scripts for every component that is important to us. System V remains the default init for The Yocto Project reference distribution (Poky). In terms of boot time, systemd is faster for similar workloads. However, if you are looking for the fastest boot, neither beats simple BusyBox init with minimal boot scripts.

Further study

*   *systemd System and Service Manager* – https://systemd.io/

14

Managing Power

For devices operating on battery power, power management is critical. Anything we can do to reduce power usage will increase battery life. Even for devices running on mains power, reducing power usage lowers energy costs and decreases the need for cooling. In this chapter, I will introduce the four principles of power management:

- Don't rush if you don't have to.
- Don't be ashamed of being idle.
- Turn off things you are not using.
- Sleep when there is nothing else to do.

In more technical terms, the power management system should reduce the CPU clock frequency. During idle periods, it should choose the deepest sleep state possible; it should reduce the load by powering down unused peripherals; and it should put the whole system into a suspended state while ensuring power state transitions are quick.

Linux has features that address each of these points. I will describe each one in turn with examples and advice on how to apply them to an embedded system.

Some of the terms, such as **C-states** and **P-states**, are taken from the **Advanced Configuration and Power Interface (ACPI)** specification. I will describe these as we get to them. The full reference to the specification is given in the *Further study* section.

In this chapter, we will cover the following topics:

- Measuring power usage
- Scaling the clock frequency

- Selecting the best idle state
- Powering down peripherals
- Putting the system to sleep

Technical requirements

To follow along with the examples, make sure you have the following:

- An Ubuntu 24.04 or later LTS host system
- A microSD card reader and card
- balenaEtcher for Linux
- An Ethernet cable and router with an available port for network connectivity
- A USB-to-TTL serial cable with 3.3 V logic level
- BeaglePlay
- A 5 V USB-C power supply capable of delivering 3 A

The code used in this chapter can be found in the chapter folder in this book's GitHub repository: https://github.com/PacktPublishing/Mastering-Embedded-Linux-Development.

Measuring power usage

For the examples in this chapter, we need to use real hardware rather than virtual. This means that we need a BeaglePlay with working power management. The necessary firmware for BeaglePlay's **Power Management Integrated Circuit (PMIC)** might exist in the meta-ti layer but I did not investigate that. We will use a pre-built Debian image instead.

The procedure for installing Debian on BeaglePlay is the same as in *Chapter 12*. Revisit the *Installing Debian on BeaglePlay* section and flash the eMMC with Debian Bookworm if you have not already. Remove any microSD from your BeaglePlay and boot from the eMMC. SSH to beaglebone.local and log in as the debian user.

Verify that the correct version of Debian is running:

```
debian@BeagleBone:~$ cat /etc/os-release
PRETTY_NAME="Debian GNU/Linux 12 (bookworm)"
NAME="Debian GNU/Linux"
VERSION_ID="12"
VERSION="12 (bookworm)"
VERSION_CODENAME=bookworm
```

```
ID=debian
HOME_URL="https://www.debian.org/"
SUPPORT_URL="https://www.debian.org/support"
BUG_REPORT_URL="https://bugs.debian.org/"
```

Now check whether the power management is working:

```
debian@BeagleBone:~$ cat /sys/power/state
freeze mem disk
```

If you see all three states, then everything is working fine. If you see only `freeze`, then the power management subsystem is not working. Go back and double-check the previous steps.

Now we can move on to measuring power usage. There are two approaches: *external* and *internal*. To measure power externally, we need an ammeter to measure the current and a voltmeter to measure the voltage, then multiply the two together to get the wattage. You can use basic meters that give a readout that you then jot down, or they can be much more sophisticated and integrate data logging so that you can see the change in power as the load fluctuates millisecond by millisecond. For the purposes of this chapter, I powered the BeaglePlay from the USB-C port and used a cheap USB-C power monitor of the type that costs a few dollars.

The other approach is to use the monitoring systems that are built into Linux. You will find that plenty of information is reported to you via `sysfs`. There is also a very useful program called **PowerTOP**, which gathers information together from various sources and presents it in a single place. PowerTOP is a package for both The Yocto Project and Buildroot. It is also available for installation on Debian.

To install PowerTOP on BeaglePlay from Debian Bookworm, run the following:

```
debian@BeagleBone:~$ sudo apt update
<...>
debian@BeagleBone:~$ sudo apt install powertop
[sudo] password for debian:
Reading package lists... Done
Building dependency tree... Done
Reading state information... Done
Suggested packages:
  cpufrequtils laptop-mode-tools
The following NEW packages will be installed:
  powertop
```

```
0 upgraded, 1 newly installed, 0 to remove and 39 not upgraded.
Need to get 183 kB of archives.
After this operation, 649 kB of additional disk space will be used.
Get:1 http://deb.debian.org/debian bookworm/main arm64 powertop arm64
2.14-1+b2 [183 kB]
Fetched 183 kB in 0s (1279 kB/s)
Selecting previously unselected package powertop.
(Reading database ... 72376 files and directories currently installed.)
Preparing to unpack .../powertop_2.14-1+b2_arm64.deb ...
Unpacking powertop (2.14-1+b2) ...
Setting up powertop (2.14-1+b2) ...
```

Don't forget to plug your BeaglePlay into Ethernet before updating the list of available packages and installing PowerTOP.

Here is an example of PowerTOP running on BeaglePlay:

```
PowerTOP 2.14       Overview   Idle stats   Frequency stats   Device stats   Tunables   WakeUp

Summary: 26.3 wakeups/second,  0.0 GPU ops/seconds, 0.0 VFS ops/sec and 2.7% CPU use

            Usage       Events/s    Category      Description
        380.9 us/s        6.6       Timer         tick_sched_timer
         12.0 ms/s        0.10      Process       [PID 45] [khugepaged]
        167.5 us/s        4.3       Interrupt     [2] IPI
          5.4 ms/s        0.3       Process       [PID 728] powertop
        189.3 us/s        2.1       Process       [PID 17] [rcu_preempt]
        107.1 us/s        1.9       kWork         thermal_zone_device_check
        102.6 us/s        1.9       Process       [PID 43] [kcompactd0]
         88.3 us/s        1.6       kWork         psi_avgs_work
          1.4 ms/s        1.0       kWork         phy_state_machine
        293.3 us/s        1.0       Interrupt     [3] net_rx(softirq)
        552.9 us/s        0.8       Interrupt     [7] sched(softirq)
         48.6 us/s        1.0       Timer         watchdog_timer_fn
         25.0 us/s        1.0       kWork         pm_runtime_work
          0.9 ms/s        0.4       Process       [PID 257] /lib/systemd/systemd-network
          0.9 ms/s        0.4       Process       [PID 340] avahi-daemon: running [Beagl
          1.8 ms/s        0.00      Interrupt     [11] arch_timer
         99.6 us/s        0.4       kWork         flush_memcg_stats_dwork
         31.4 us/s        0.4       kWork         vmstat_shepherd

<ESC> Exit | <TAB> / <Shift + TAB> Navigate |
```

Figure 14.1 – PowerTOP overview

In this screenshot, we can see that the system is quiet, with only 2.7% of CPU used. I will show more interesting examples later in the *Using CPUFreq* and *CPUIdle driver* subsections of this chapter.

Now that we have a way to measure power consumption, let's look at one of the biggest knobs for managing power in an embedded Linux system: the clock frequency.

Scaling the clock frequency

If running for a kilometer takes more energy than walking, then maybe running the CPU at a lower frequency can save energy. Let's see.

The power consumption of a CPU when executing code is the sum of a static component, caused primarily by gate leakage current, and a dynamic component, caused by the gate switching:

$P_{cpu} = P_{static} + P_{dyn}$

The dynamic power component is dependent on the total capacitance of the logic gates being switched, the clock frequency, and the square of the voltage:

$P_{dyn} = CFV_2$

Changing the frequency by itself does not save energy because the same number of CPU cycles need to be completed for a given task. If we reduce the frequency by half while keeping the voltage constant, then it will take twice as long to complete the task, even though the total amount of energy expended is the same. In fact, reducing the frequency may actually increase the power budget because it takes longer for the CPU to enter an idle state. This is especially the case when there are no other competing tasks to run, and the CPU's idle state is extremely energy efficient. So, under these conditions, it is best to use the highest frequency possible so that the CPU can go back to idle quickly. This is called the **race to idle**.

> **IMPORTANT NOTE**
>
> There is another motivation to reduce frequency: **thermal management**. It may become necessary to operate at a lower frequency just to keep the temperature of the package within bounds. But that is not our focus here.

Therefore, if we want to reduce power consumption, we must be able to change the voltage that the CPU core operates at. But for any given voltage, there is a maximum frequency beyond which the switching of the gates becomes unreliable. Higher frequencies need higher voltages, and so the two need to be adjusted together. Many SoCs implement such a feature. It is called **Dynamic Voltage and Frequency Scaling (DVFS)**. Manufacturers calculate optimum combinations of core frequency and voltage. Each combination is called an **Operating Performance Point (OPP)**. The ACPI specification refers to them as **P-states**, with P0 being the OPP with the highest frequency. Although an OPP is a combination of a frequency and a voltage, it is most often referred to by the frequency component alone.

A kernel driver is needed to switch between P-states. Next, we will look at that driver and the governors that control it.

CPUFreq driver

Linux has a component named **CPUFreq** that manages the transitions between OPPs. It is part of the board support for the package for each SoC. CPUFreq consists of drivers that make the transition from one OPP to another and a set of governors that implement the policy of when to switch. It is controlled per CPU via the /sys/devices/system/cpu/cpuN/cpufreq directory, with N being the CPU number. In there, we find a number of files, the most interesting of which are:

- cpuinfo_cur_freq, cpuinfo_max_freq, and cpuinfo_min_freq: These are the current frequencies for this CPU, together with the maximum and minimum in KHz.
- cpuinfo_transition_latency: This is the time in nanoseconds to switch from one OPP to another. If the value is unknown, it is set to -1.
- scaling_available_frequencies: This is a list of OPP frequencies available on this CPU.
- scaling_available_governors: This is a list of governors available on this CPU.
- scaling_governor: This is the CPUFreq governor currently being used.
- scaling_min_freq and scaling_max_freq: This is the range of frequencies available to the governor in KHz.
- scaling_setspeed: This is a file that allows you to manually set the frequency when the governor is userspace, which I will describe at the end of this subsection.

The governor sets the policy to change the OPP. It can set the frequency between the limits of scaling_min_freq and scaling_max_freq. The governors are named:

- performance: This always selects the highest frequency.
- powersave: This always selects the lowest frequency.
- userspace: This is where the frequency is set by a user-space program.
- ondemand: This changes the frequency based on the CPU utilization. If the CPU is idle less than 20% of the time, it sets the frequency to the maximum. If the CPU is idle more than 30% of the time, it lowers the frequency as idle time increases.
- conservative: This is like ondemand except it switches to higher frequencies in 5% steps rather than going immediately to the maximum.
- schedutil: This aims at better integration with the Linux scheduler.

The default governor when Debian Bookworm starts up is performance:

```
$ cd /sys/devices/system/cpu/cpu0/cpufreq
$ cat scaling_governor
performance
```

The TI Linux kernel for BeaglePlay comes with only two governors built-in:

```
$ cat scaling_available_governors
performance schedutil
```

The other governors can be loaded dynamically using cpupower or modprobe:

```
debian@BeagleBone:~$ sudo modprobe cpufreq_userspace
```

To install cpupower on BeaglePlay from Debian Bookworm, run the following:

```
debian@BeagleBone:~$ sudo apt install linux-cpupower
Reading package lists... Done
Building dependency tree... Done
Reading state information... Done
The following additional packages will be installed:
  libcpupower1
The following NEW packages will be installed:
  libcpupower1 linux-cpupower
0 upgraded, 2 newly installed, 0 to remove and 39 not upgraded.
Need to get 1953 kB of archives.
After this operation, 2174 kB of additional disk space will be used.
Do you want to continue? [Y/n] Y
Get:1 http://deb.debian.org/debian bookworm-updates/main arm64
libcpupower1 arm64 6.1.124-1 [960 kB]
Get:2 http://deb.debian.org/debian bookworm-updates/main arm64 linux-
cpupower arm64 6.1.124-1 [992 kB]
Fetched 1953 kB in 0s (8989 kB/s)
Selecting previously unselected package libcpupower1.
(Reading database ... 72409 files and directories currently installed.)
Preparing to unpack .../libcpupower1_6.1.124-1_arm64.deb ...
Unpacking libcpupower1 (6.1.124-1) ...
Selecting previously unselected package linux-cpupower.
Preparing to unpack .../linux-cpupower_6.1.124-1_arm64.deb ...
Unpacking linux-cpupower (6.1.124-1) ...
```

```
Setting up libcpupower1 (6.1.124-1) ...
Setting up linux-cpupower (6.1.124-1) ...
Processing triggers for libc-bin (2.36-9+deb12u9) ...
```

To switch to the ondemand governor, run the following:

```
debian@BeagleBone:~$ sudo cpupower frequency-set -g ondemand
Setting cpu: 0
Setting cpu: 1
Setting cpu: 2
Setting cpu: 3
```

The parameters that the ondemand governor uses to decide when to change OPP can be found and set in /sys/devices/system/cpu/cpufreq/ondemand/.

Both the ondemand and conservative governors take into account the effort required to change frequency and voltage. This CPUFreq value is cpuinfo_transition_latency. This calculation only applies to threads with a normal scheduling policy. If a thread is being scheduled in real time, both governors will immediately select the highest OPP so that the thread can meet its scheduling deadline.

The userspace governor allows the logic of selecting the OPP to be performed by a user-space daemon. Examples include cpudyn and powernowd, although both are orientated toward x86-based laptops rather than embedded devices.

Now that we know where the runtime details about the CPUFreq driver are located, let's look at how to define the OPPs at compile time.

Using CPUFreq

Looking at BeaglePlay, we find that the OPPs are coded in the device tree. Here is an extract from k3-am625.dtsi:

```
a53_opp_table: opp-table {
    compatible = "operating-points-v2-ti-cpu";
    opp-shared;
    syscon = <&wkup_conf>;

    opp-200000000 {
        opp-hz = /bits/ 64 <200000000>;
        opp-supported-hw = <0x01 0x0007>;
```

```
                    clock-latency-ns = <6000000>;
        };

        opp-400000000 {
                opp-hz = /bits/ 64 <400000000>;
                opp-supported-hw = <0x01 0x0007>;
                clock-latency-ns = <6000000>;
        };

        opp-600000000 {
                opp-hz = /bits/ 64 <600000000>;
                opp-supported-hw = <0x01 0x0007>;
                clock-latency-ns = <6000000>;
        };

        opp-800000000 {
                opp-hz = /bits/ 64 <800000000>;
                opp-supported-hw = <0x01 0x0007>;
                clock-latency-ns = <6000000>;
        };

        opp-1000000000 {
                opp-hz = /bits/ 64 <1000000000>;
                opp-supported-hw = <0x01 0x0006>;
                clock-latency-ns = <6000000>;
        };

        opp-1250000000 {
                opp-hz = /bits/ 64 <1250000000>;
                opp-supported-hw = <0x01 0x0004>;
                clock-latency-ns = <6000000>;
                opp-suspend;
        };
};
```

We can confirm that these are the OPPs in use at runtime by viewing the available frequencies:

```
$ cd /sys/devices/system/cpu/cpu0/cpufreq
$ cat scaling_available_frequencies
200000 400000 600000 800000 1000000 1250000 1400000
```

Select the `userspace` governor:

```
debian@BeagleBone:~$ sudo cpupower frequency-set -g userspace
Setting cpu: 0
Setting cpu: 1
Setting cpu: 2
Setting cpu: 3
```

List the available frequency steps:

```
debian@BeagleBone:~$ sudo cpupower frequency-info
analyzing CPU 0:
  driver: cpufreq-dt
  CPUs which run at the same hardware frequency: 0 1 2 3
  CPUs which need to have their frequency coordinated by software: 0 1 2 3
  maximum transition latency: 6.00 ms
  hardware limits: 200 MHz - 1.40 GHz
  available frequency steps:  200 MHz, 400 MHz, 600 MHz, 800 MHz, 1000
MHz, 1.25 GHz, 1.40 GHz
  available cpufreq governors: ondemand userspace performance schedutil
  current policy: frequency should be within 200 MHz and 1.40 GHz.
                  The governor "userspace" may decide which speed to use
                  within this range.
  current CPU frequency: 1.25 GHz (asserted by call to hardware)
```

Now we can measure the power consumed at each OPP with a USB-C power monitor. These measurements are not very accurate, so do not take them too seriously.

Set the frequency by writing to `scaling_setspeed`:

```
# echo 200000 > /sys/devices/system/cpu/cpufreq/policy0/scaling_setspeed
```

Build and run the `MELD/Chapter14/do-work` program on BeaglePlay:

```
$ cd MELD/Chapter15/do-work
$ make
$ ./do-work -l 80828
```

If we run this constant load while varying the frequency, then we observe the following:

Frequency (MHz)	CPU utilization (%)	Power (mW)
200	88	1,160
400	44	1,160
600	29	1,160
800	22	1,210
1,000	18	1,210
1,250	14	1,210
1,400	13	1,210

Table 14.1 – Power consumed at different frequencies

This shows power savings of about 4% at the lower frequencies.

In most cases, the ondemand governor is the best one to use since it switches between OPPs based on CPU load. To select a particular governor, you can either configure the kernel with a default governor like CPU_FREQ_DEFAULT_GOV_ONDEMAND, or you can use an init script to change the governor at boot time. See MELD/Chapter14/cpufrequtils for an example of how Debian does this with SysVinit.

For more information on the CPUFreq driver, look at the files in the Documentation/cpu-freq directory of the Linux kernel source tree.

In this section, we were concerned about the power used when the CPU is busy. In the next section, we will look at how to save power when the CPU is idle.

Selecting the best idle state

When a processor has no more work to do, it executes a **halt instruction** and enters an idle state. While idle, the CPU uses less power. It exits the idle state when an event such as a hardware interrupt occurs. Most CPUs have multiple idle states that use varying amounts of power. Usually, there is a trade-off between the power usage and the latency, or the length of time, it takes to exit the state. In the ACPI specification, they are called **C-states**.

In the deeper C-states, more circuitry is turned off at the expense of losing some state, so it takes longer to return to normal operation. For example, in some C-states, the CPU caches may be powered off, and so when the CPU runs again, it may have to reload some information from the main memory. This is expensive, so you only want to do this if there is a good chance that the CPU will remain in this state for some time. The number of states varies from one system to another. Each takes some time to recover from sleeping to being fully active.

The key to selecting the right idle state is to have a good idea of how long the CPU is going to be inactive. Predicting the future is always tricky, but there are some things that can help. One is the current CPU load: if it is high now, it is likely to continue to be so in the immediate future, so a deep sleep would not be beneficial. Even if the load is low, it is worth looking to see whether there is a timer event that expires soon. If there is no load and no timer, then a deeper idle state is justified.

The part of Linux that selects the best idle state is the CPUIdle driver. There is a good deal of information about it available in the `Documentation/driver-api/pm/cpuidle.rst` file inside the Linux kernel source tree.

CPUIdle driver

Like the CPUFreq subsystem, **CPUIdle** consists of a driver that is part of the BSP and a governor that determines the policy. Unlike CPUFreq, the governor cannot be changed at runtime and there is no interface for user-space governors. There was no CPUIdle support in Debian Bookworm for BeaglePlay at the time of writing, so I can only describe it here.

CPUIdle exposes information about each of the idle states in the `/sys/devices/system/cpu/cpu0/cpuidle` directory. Inside that directory, there is a subdirectory for each of the sleep states named `state0` to `stateN`. `state0` is the lightest sleep and `stateN` is the deepest. Note that the numbering does not match that of the C-states and that CPUIdle does not have a state equivalent to `C0` (running). Each state has these files:

- `desc`: A short description of the state
- `disable`: An option to disable this state by writing 1 to this file
- `latency`: The time in microseconds that the CPU core takes to resume normal operation when exiting this state
- `name`: The name of this state
- `power`: The power in milliwatts consumed while in this idle state
- `time`: The total time in microseconds spent in this idle state
- `usage`: The count of the number of times this state was entered

CPUIdle has two governors:

- `ladder`: Steps idle states down or up, one at a time, depending on the time spent in the last idle period. It works well with a regular timer tick but not with a dynamic tick.
- `menu`: Selects an idle state based on the expected idle time. It works well with dynamic tick systems.

You should choose one or the other depending on your configuration of NO_HZ, which I will describe at the end of this section.

Once again, user interaction is via the sysfs filesystem. In the /sys/devices/system/cpu/cpuidle directory, you will find two files:

- current_driver: This is the name of the CPUIdle driver.
- current_governor_ro: This is the name of the governor.

These show which driver and which governor are being used.

Even with the CPU fully idling, most Linux systems are still configured to wake up periodically on receipt of a system timer interrupt. To save more power, we need to configure the Linux kernel for tickless operation.

Tickless operation

A related topic is the tickless, or NO_HZ, option. If the system is truly idle, the most likely source of interruptions will be the system timer, which is programmed to generate a regular time tick at a rate of HZ per second, where HZ is typically 100. Historically, Linux uses the timer tick as the main time base for measuring timeouts.

And yet it is plainly wasteful to wake the CPU up to process a timer interrupt if no timer events are registered for that given moment. The dynamic tick kernel configuration option, CONFIG_NO_HZ_ IDLE, looks at the timer queue at the end of the timer processing routine and schedules the next interruption at the time of the next event. This avoids unnecessary wakeups and allows the CPU to be idle for long periods. In any power-sensitive application, the kernel should be configured with this option enabled.

While the CPU consumes much of the power in an embedded Linux system, there are other components of the system that can also be powered down for energy savings.

Powering down peripherals

The discussion up to now has been about CPUs and how to reduce power consumption when they are running or idling. Now it is time to focus on other parts of the system and see whether we can achieve power savings here.

In the Linux kernel, this is managed by the **runtime power management system**, or **runtime pm** for short. It works with drivers that support runtime pm by shutting down those that are not in use and waking them again when they are next needed.

It is dynamic and should be transparent to user space. It is up to the device driver to decide how to power down the hardware. Typically, runtime pm includes turning off the clock to the subsystem, also known as clock gating, and turning off core circuitry where possible.

Runtime power management is exposed via a sysfs interface. Each device has a subdirectory named power where you will find these files:

- control: This allows user space to determine whether runtime pm is used on this device. If it is set to auto, then runtime pm is enabled, but by setting it to on, the device is always on and does not use runtime pm.

- runtime_enabled: This reports that runtime pm is enabled or disabled, or, if control is on, it reports forbidden.

- runtime_status: This reports the current state of the device. It may be active, suspended, or unsupported.

- autosuspend_delay_ms: This is the time before the device is suspended. -1 means wait forever. Some drivers implement this if there is a significant cost to suspending the device hardware since it prevents rapid suspend/resume cycles.

For a concrete example, let's look at the MMC driver on BeaglePlay:

```
# cd /sys/devices/platform/bus@f0000/fa00000.mmc/mmc_host/mmc1/power
# grep "" *
async:enabled
grep: autosuspend_delay_ms: Input/output error
control:auto
runtime_active_kids:0
runtime_active_time:0
runtime_enabled:disabled
runtime_status:unsupported
runtime_suspended_time:0
runtime_usage:0
```

So, runtime pm is disabled, the device is currently unsupported, and we cannot determine how much delay there will be when it is suspended again.

For more information on runtime pm, look in the Linux kernel source code at Documentation/power/runtime_pm.rst.

Now that we know what the runtime pm is and what it does, let's see it in action.

Putting the system to sleep

There is one more power management technique to consider: putting the whole system into sleep mode with the expectation that it will not be used again for a while. In the Linux kernel, this is known as **system sleep**. It is usually user-initiated: the user decides that the device should be shut down for a while. For example, I shut the lid of my laptop and put it in my bag when it is time to go home. Much of the support for system sleep in Linux comes from the support for laptops. In the laptop world, there are usually two options:

- Suspend
- Hibernate

The first, also known as **suspend to RAM,** shuts everything down except the system memory, so the machine is still consuming a little power. When the system wakes up, the memory retains all the previous state, and my laptop is operational within a few seconds.

If I select the **hibernate** option, the contents of the memory are saved to the hard drive. The system consumes no power at all, and so it can stay in this state indefinitely. On wake up, it takes some time to restore the memory from disk. Hibernate is very seldom used in embedded systems, mostly because the flash storage tends to be quite slow on read/write, but also because it is intrusive to the flow of work.

For more information, look at the Documentation/power directory in the kernel source tree.

The suspend to RAM and hibernate options map to two of the four sleep states supported by Linux. We'll look at these two types of system sleep and the rest of the ACPI power states next.

Power states

In the ACPI specification, the sleep states are called **S-states**. Linux supports four sleep states (**freeze, standby, mem,** and **disk**), which are shown in the following list along with the corresponding ACPI S-state ([S0], S1, S3, and S4):

- freeze ([S0]): This stops (freezes) all activity in user space while the CPU and memory continue to operate as normal.

  The power savings result from the fact that no user-space code is being run. ACPI does not have an equivalent state so S0 is the closest match. S0 is the state for a running system.

- standby (S1): This is like freeze except that, in addition, it takes all CPUs offline except for the boot CPU.

- `mem` (S3): This powers down the system and puts the memory in self-refresh mode. Also known as **suspend to RAM**.
- `disk` (S4): This saves the memory to the hard disk and powers the system down. Also known as **suspend to disk**.

Not all systems have support for all states. To find out which are available, read the `/sys/power/state` file as shown:

```
debian@BeaglePlay:~$ cat /sys/power/state
freeze mem disk
```

To enter one of the system sleep states, just write the desired state to `/sys/power/state`.

For embedded devices, the most common need is to suspend to RAM using the `mem` option. For example, I can suspend BeaglePlay like this:

```
# echo mem > /sys/power/state
```

The device powers down in less than a second and then power usage drops down to 10 milliwatts, as measured by my basic multimeter. But how do I wake it up again? That is the next topic.

Wakeup events

Before you suspend a device, you must have some way of waking it up again. The kernel tries to help you here. If there is not at least one wakeup source, the system will refuse to suspend and will return the following message:

```
No sources enabled to wake-up! Sleep abort.
```

Of course, this means that some parts of the system have to remain powered on even during the deepest sleep. This usually involves the **power management IC (PMIC)** and the **real-time clock (RTC)**, and may additionally include interfaces such as GPIO, UART, Ethernet, and Wi-Fi.

Wakeup events are controlled through `sysfs`. Each device in `/sys/device` has a subdirectory named power containing a wakeup file with one of these strings:

- `enabled`: Means this device will generate wakeup events
- `disabled`: Means this device will not generate wakeup events
- (empty): Means this device is not capable of generating wakeup events

To get a list of devices that can generate wakeups, search for all devices where wakeup contains either enabled or disabled:

```
$ find /sys/devices/ -name wakeup | xargs grep "abled"
```

We've seen how to put a device to sleep and then wake it up with an event from a peripheral interface like a UART. What if we want a device to wake itself up without any outside interaction? This is where the RTC comes into play.

Timed wakeups from the real-time clock

BeaglePlay has an RTC that can generate alarm interrupts up to 24 hours in the future. If so, the /sys/class/rtc/rtc1 directory will exist. It should contain the wakealarm file. Writing a number to wakealarm will cause it to generate an alarm that number of seconds later. If you also enable wakeup events from rtc1, the RTC will resume a suspended device.

For example, the following rtcwake command puts the system in freeze with the RTC waking it up after 5 seconds:

```
debian@BeagleBone:~$ sudo su -
root@BeagleBone:~# rtcwake -d /dev/rtc1 -m freeze -s 5
rtcwake: assuming RTC uses UTC ...
rtcwake: wakeup from "freeze" using /dev/rtc1 at Thu Jan  1 00:06:21 1970
```

The corresponding journalctl output looks like this:

```
Feb 08 01:21:53 BeagleBone kernel: PM: suspend entry (s2idle)
Feb 08 01:21:59 BeagleBone kernel: Filesystems sync: 0.000 seconds
Feb 08 01:21:59 BeagleBone kernel: Freezing user space processes
Feb 08 01:21:59 BeagleBone kernel: Freezing user space processes completed
(elapsed 0.001 seconds)
Feb 08 01:21:59 BeagleBone kernel: OOM killer disabled.
Feb 08 01:21:59 BeagleBone kernel: Freezing remaining freezable tasks
Feb 08 01:21:59 BeagleBone kernel: Freezing remaining freezable tasks
completed (elapsed 0.001 seconds)
Feb 08 01:21:59 BeagleBone kernel: printk: Suspending console(s) (use no_
console_suspend to debug)
Feb 08 01:21:59 BeagleBone kernel: wlcore: down
Feb 08 01:21:59 BeagleBone kernel: wlcore: down
Feb 08 01:21:59 BeagleBone kernel: am65-cpsw-nuss 8000000.ethernet eth0:
Link is Down
```

```
Feb 08 01:21:59 BeagleBone kernel: ti-sci 44043000.system-controller: ti_
sci_resume: wakeup source: 0xFF
Feb 08 01:21:59 BeagleBone kernel: am65-cpsw-nuss 8000000.ethernet: set
new flow-id-base 19
Feb 08 01:21:59 BeagleBone kernel: am65-cpsw-nuss 8000000.ethernet eth0:
PHY [8000f00.mdio:00] driver [RTL8211F-VD Gigabit Ethernet]>
Feb 08 01:21:59 BeagleBone kernel: am65-cpsw-nuss 8000000.ethernet eth0:
configuring for phy/rgmii-rxid link mode
Feb 08 01:21:59 BeagleBone kernel: wlcore: using inverted interrupt logic:
2
Feb 08 01:21:59 BeagleBone kernel: wlcore: PHY firmware version: Rev
8.2.0.0.243
Feb 08 01:21:59 BeagleBone kernel: wlcore: firmware booted (Rev
8.9.0.0.83)
Feb 08 01:21:59 BeagleBone kernel: OOM killer enabled.
Feb 08 01:21:59 BeagleBone kernel: Restarting tasks ... done.
Feb 08 01:21:59 BeagleBone kernel: PM: suspend exit
```

The **Power** button on BeaglePlay is also a wakeup source so you can use that to resume from freeze in the absence of a serial console. Make sure to press the **Power** button and not the **Reset** button, which is next to it; otherwise, the board will reboot.

This concludes our coverage of the four Linux system sleep modes. We learned how to suspend a device to the mem or freeze power state and then wake it up via an event from an RTC or the **Power** button. While the runtime pm in Linux was created mostly for laptops, we can leverage this support for embedded systems that also run on battery power.

Summary

Linux has sophisticated power management functions. In this chapter, I described four main components:

- **CPUFreq** changes the OPP of each processor core to reduce power on those that are busy but have some bandwidth to spare, thereby allowing us to scale the frequency back. OPPs are known as P-states in the ACPI specification.
- **CPUIdle** selects deeper idle states when the CPU is not expected to be woken up for a while. Idle states are known as C-states in the ACPI specification.
- **Runtime pm** will shut down peripherals that are not needed.

- **System sleep** modes will put the whole system into a low-power state. They are usually under end user control, for example, by pressing a standby button. System sleep states are known as S-states in the ACPI specification.

Most of the power management is done for you by the BSP. Your main task is to make sure that it is configured correctly for your intended use cases. Only the last component, selecting a system sleep state, requires you to write some code that will allow the end user to enter and exit the state.

The next part of the book is about writing embedded applications. We will start with packaging and deploying Python code and then explore containerization techniques.

Further study

- *Advanced Configuration and Power Interface Specification*, UEFI Forum, Inc. – `https://uefi.org/sites/default/files/resources/ACPI_Spec_6_5_Aug29.pdf`

Join our community on Discord

Join our community's Discord space for discussions with the authors and other readers: `https://packt.link/embeddedsystems`

Part 4

Developing Applications

This part will help you with the implementation phase of the project. We will start with Python packaging and dependency management, a topic of growing importance as machine learning applications continue to take the world by storm. *Chapter 16* is a new chapter on DevOps that explains how to continuously build and deploy Python applications inside containers with Docker. Next, we will move on to various forms of inter-process communication and multithreaded programming. The section concludes with a careful examination of how Linux manages memory and demonstrates how to measure memory usage and detect memory leaks using the various tools that are available.

This part has the following chapters:

15

Packaging Python

Python is the most popular programming language for **machine learning (ML)**. Combine that with the proliferation of ML in our day-to-day lives and it is no surprise that the desire to run Python on edge devices is intensifying. Even in this era of transpilers and WebAssembly, packaging Python applications for deployment remains an unsolved problem. In this chapter, you will learn what choices are out there for bundling Python modules together and when to use one method over another.

We start with a look back at the origins of today's Python packaging solutions, from the built-in standard distutils to its successor, setuptools. Next, we examine the pip package manager, before moving on to venv for Python virtual environments, followed by conda, the reigning general-purpose cross-platform solution.

Since Python is an interpreted language, you cannot compile a program into a standalone executable like you can with a language such as Go. This makes deploying Python applications complicated. Running a Python application requires installing a Python interpreter and several runtime dependencies. These requirements need to be code-compatible for the application to work. That requires the precise versioning of software components. Solving these deployment problems is what Python packaging is all about.

In this chapter, we will cover the following topics:

- Retracing the origins of Python packaging
- Installing Python packages with pip
- Managing Python virtual environments with venv
- Installing precompiled binaries with conda

Technical requirements

To follow along with the examples, make sure you have the following software installed on your Linux host system:

- Python: Python 3 interpreter and standard library
- pip: Package installer for Python 3
- venv: Python module for creating and managing lightweight virtual environments
- Miniconda: Minimal installer for the conda package and virtual environment manager

I recommend using Ubuntu 24.04 LTS or later for this chapter. Even though Ubuntu 24.04 LTS runs on the Raspberry Pi 4, I still prefer to develop on an x86-64 desktop PC or laptop. Ubuntu also comes with Python 3 and pip already installed since Python is used extensively throughout the system. Do not uninstall python3 or you will render Ubuntu unusable. To install venv on Ubuntu, enter the following:

```
$ sudo apt install python3-venv
```

> **IMPORTANT NOTE**
>
> Do not install Miniconda until you get to the section on conda because it interferes with the earlier pip exercises that rely on the system Python installation.

Retracing the origins of Python packaging

The Python packaging landscape is a vast graveyard of failed attempts and abandoned tools. Best practices around dependency management change often within the Python community, and the recommended solution one year may be a broken nonstarter the next. As you research this topic, remember to look at when the information was published and do not trust any advice that may be out of date.

Most Python libraries are distributed using setuptools, including all the packages found on the **Python Package Index (PyPI)**. This distribution method relies on a setup.py project specification file that the **package installer for Python (pip)** uses to install a package. pip can also generate or *freeze* a precise list of dependencies after a project is installed. This optional requirements.txt file is used by pip in conjunction with setup.py to ensure that project installations are repeatable.

distutils

distutils is the original packaging system for Python. It was included in the Python standard library from Python 2.0 until its removal in Python 3.12. distutils provided a Python package of the same name that could be imported by your setup.py script. Now that distutils is deprecated, direct usage of the package is no longer supported. setuptools has become its preferred replacement.

While distutils may continue to work for simple projects, the community has moved on. Today, distutils survives only for legacy reasons. Many Python libraries were first published back when distutils was the only game in town. Porting them to setuptools now would take considerable effort and could break existing users.

setuptools

setuptools extends distutils by adding support for complex constructs that make larger applications based on web frameworks like Flask and FastAPI easier to distribute. It has become the de facto packaging system within the Python community. Like distutils, setuptools offers a Python package of the same name that you can import into your setup.py script. distribute was an ambitious fork of setuptools that eventually merged back into setuptools 0.7, cementing the status of setuptools as the definitive choice for Python packaging.

setuptools introduced a command-line utility known as easy_install (now deprecated) and a Python package called pkg_resources for runtime package discovery and access to resource files. setuptools can also produce packages that act as plugins for other extensible packages (for example, frameworks and applications). You do this by registering entry points in your setup.py script for the other overarching package to import.

The term *distribution* means something different in the context of Python. A distribution is a versioned archive of packages, modules, and other resource files used to distribute a release. A *release* is a versioned snapshot of a Python project taken at a given point in time. To make matters worse, the terms *package* and *distribution* are overloaded and often used interchangeably by Pythonistas. For our purposes, let's say that a distribution is what you download, and a package is the module that gets installed and imported.

Cutting a release can result in multiple distributions, such as a source distribution and one or more built distributions. There can be different built distributions for different platforms, such as one that includes a Windows installer. The term *built distribution* means that no build step is required before installation. It does not necessarily mean precompiled. Some built distribution formats such as **Wheel** (.whl) exclude compiled Python files, for example. A built distribution containing compiled extensions is known as a *binary distribution*.

An **extension module** is a Python module that is written in C or C++. Every extension module compiles down to a single dynamically loaded library, such as a shared object (.so) on Linux and a dynamic link library (.pyd) on Windows. Contrast this with pure modules, which must be written entirely in Python. The Egg (.egg) built distribution format introduced by setuptools supports both pure and extension modules. Since a Python source code (.py) file compiles down to a bytecode (.pyc) file when the Python interpreter imports a module at runtime, you can see how a built distribution format such as Wheel might exclude precompiled Python files.

setup.py

Say you are developing a small program in Python, maybe something that queries a remote REST API and saves response data to a local SQL database. How do you package your program together with its dependencies for deployment? You start by defining a setup.py script that setuptools can use to install your program. Deploying with setuptools is the first step toward more elaborate automated deployment schemes.

Even if your program is small enough to fit comfortably inside a single module, chances are it won't stay that way for long. Let's say that your program consists of a single file named follower. py, like so:

```
$ tree follower
follower
└── follower.py
```

You could then convert this module into a package by splitting follower.py up into three separate modules and placing them inside a nested directory, also named follower:

```
$ tree follower/
follower/
└── follower
    ├── fetch.py
    ├── __main__.py
    └── store.py
```

The __main__.py module is where your program starts, so it contains mostly top-level, user-facing functionality. The fetch.py module contains functions for sending HTTP requests to the remote REST API and the store.py module contains functions for saving response data to the local SQL database. To run this package as a script, you need to pass the -m option to the Python interpreter as follows:

```
$ PYTHONPATH=follower python -m follower
```

The PYTHONPATH environment variable points to the directory where a target project's package directories are located. The follower argument after the -m option tells Python to run the __main__. py module belonging to the follower package. Nesting package directories inside a project directory like this paves the way for your program to grow into a larger application made up of multiple packages each with its own namespace.

With the pieces of your project all in their right place, we are now ready to create a minimal setup. py script that setuptools can use to package and deploy it:

```
from setuptools import setup
    setup(
    name='follower',
    version='0.1',
    packages=['follower'],
    include_package_data=True,
    install_requires=['requests', 'sqlalchemy']
)
```

The install_requires argument is a list of external dependencies that need to be installed automatically for a project to work at runtime. Notice that I did not specify what versions of these dependencies are needed or where to fetch them from in my example. I only asked for libraries that look and act like requests and sqlalchemy. Separating policy from implementation like this allows you to easily swap out the official PyPI version of a dependency with your own in case you need to fix a bug or add a feature.

> **Information note**
>
> Adding optional version specifiers to your dependency declarations is fine, but hardcoding distribution URLs within setup.py as dependency_links is wrong in principle.

The packages argument tells setuptools what in-tree packages to distribute with a project release. Since every package is defined inside its own subdirectory of the parent project directory, the only package being shipped in this case is follower. I am including data files along with my Python code in this distribution. To do that, you need to set the include_package_data argument to True so that setuptools looks for a MANIFEST.in file and installs all the files listed there. Here are the contents of the MANIFEST.in file:

```
include data/events.db
```

If the data directory contained nested directories of data we wanted to include, we could glob all of them along with their contents using `recursive-include`:

```
recursive-include data *
```

Here is the final directory layout:

```
$ tree follower
follower
├── data
│   └── events.db
├── follower
│   ├── fetch.py
│   ├── __init__.py
│   └── store.py
├── MANIFEST.in
└── setup.py
```

setuptools excels at building and distributing Python packages that depend on other packages. It can do this thanks to features such as entry points and dependency declarations, which are simply absent from distutils. setuptools works well with pip and new releases of setuptools arrive on a regular basis. The Wheel build distribution format was created to replace the Egg format that setuptools introduced. That effort has largely succeeded with the addition of a popular setuptools extension for building wheels and pip's great support for installing wheels.

Installing Python packages with pip

You now know how to define your project's dependencies in a setup.py script. But how do you install those dependencies? How do you upgrade a dependency or replace it when you find a better one? How do you decide when it is safe to delete a dependency you no longer need?

Managing project dependencies is a tricky business. Luckily, Python comes with a tool called **pip** that can help, especially in the early stages of your project. The name stands for **pip installs Python**, which is a recursive acronym. pip is the official package manager for Python.

The initial 1.0 release of pip arrived on April 4, 2011, around the same time that Node.js and npm were taking off. Before it became pip, the tool was named pyinstall. pyinstall was created in 2008 as an alternative to easy_install, which came bundled with setuptools at the time. easy_install is now deprecated and setuptools recommends using pip instead.

Since `pip` is included with the Python installer and you can have multiple versions of Python installed on your system (for example, 2.7 and 3.13), it helps to know which version of `pip` you are running:

```
$ pip --version
```

If no `pip` executable is found on your system, that probably means you are on Ubuntu 20.04 LTS or later and do not have Python 2.7 installed. That is fine. We will merely substitute `pip3` for `pip` and `python3` for `python` throughout the rest of this section:

```
$ pip3 --version
```

If there is `python3` but no `pip3` executable, then install it as shown on Debian-based distributions such as Ubuntu:

```
$ sudo apt install python3-pip
```

`pip` installs packages to a directory called `site-packages`. To find the location of your `site-packages` directory, run the following command:

```
$ python3 -m site | grep ^USER_SITE
```

> **IMPORTANT NOTE**
>
> Now that Python 2 has been deprecated, `pip3` and `python3` commands are available on popular Linux distributions like Ubuntu. If your Linux distribution does not have the `pip3` and `python3` commands, then use the `pip` and `python` commands instead.

To get a list of packages already installed on your system, use this command:

```
$ pip3 list
```

The list shows that `pip` is just another Python package, so you could use `pip` to upgrade itself, but I would advise you not to do that, at least not in the long term. I'll explain why in the next section when I introduce virtual environments.

To get a list of packages installed in your `site-packages` directory, use the following:

```
$ pip3 list --user
```

This list should be empty or much shorter than the list of system packages.

Go back to the example project from the last section. cd into the parent follower directory where setup.py is located. Then run the following command:

```
$ pip3 install --ignore-installed --user --break-system-packages .
```

pip will use setup.py to fetch and install the packages declared by install_requires to your site-packages directory. The --user option instructs pip to install packages to your site-packages directory rather than globally. The --ignore-installed option forces pip to re-install any required packages already present on the system to site-packages so that no dependencies go missing. The --break-system-packages option is required on Debian-based Linux distributions like Ubuntu, which discourages users from installing non-Debian-packaged packages system-wide.

Now list all the packages in your site-packages directory again:

```
$ pip3 list --user
Package             Version
------------------  ---------
certifi             2025.1.31
charset-normalizer  3.4.1
follower            0.1
greenlet            3.1.1
idna                3.10
requests            2.32.3
SQLAlchemy          2.0.38
typing_extensions   4.12.2
urllib3             2.3.0
```

This time, you should see that both requests and SQLAlchemy are in the package list.

To view details on the SQLAlchemy package you just installed, issue the following:

```
$ pip3 show sqlalchemy
```

The details shown contain the Requires and Required-by fields. Both are lists of related packages. You could use the values in these fields and successive calls to pip show to trace the dependency tree of your project. But it's probably easier to pip install a command-line tool called pipdeptree and use that instead.

When a `Required-by` field becomes empty, that is a good indicator that it is now safe to uninstall a package from your system. If no other packages depend on the packages in the deleted package's `Requires` field, then it's safe to uninstall those as well. This is how you uninstall `sqlalchemy` using `pip`:

```
$ pip3 uninstall sqlalchemy -y --break-system-packages
```

The trailing `-y` suppresses the confirmation prompt. To uninstall more than one package at a time, simply add more package names before the `-y`. The `--user` option is omitted here because `pip` is smart enough to uninstall from `site-packages` first when a package is also installed globally.

> **TIP**
>
> Uninstall the `follower` package and all its dependencies from your `site-packages` directory so that you do not pollute your Python installation or Linux distribution with non-Debian-packaged packages.

Sometimes you need a package that serves some purpose or utilizes a particular technology, but you don't know the name of it. You can use `pip` to perform a keyword search against PyPI from the command line, but that approach often yields too many results. It is much easier to search for packages on the PyPI website (`https://pypi.org/search/`), which allows you to filter results by various classifiers.

requirements.txt

`pip install` will install the latest published version of a package, but often you want to install a specific version of a package that you know works with your project's code. Eventually, you will want to upgrade your project's dependencies. But before I show you how to do that, I first need to show you how to use `pip freeze` to fix your dependencies.

Requirements files allow you to specify exactly which packages and versions `pip` should install for your project. By convention, project **requirements files** are always named `requirements.txt`. The contents of a requirements file are just a list of `pip install` arguments enumerating your project's dependencies. These dependencies are precisely versioned so that there are no surprises when someone attempts to rebuild and deploy your project. It is good practice to add a `requirements.txt` file to your project's repo to ensure reproducible builds.

Returning to our follower project, now that we have installed all our dependencies and verified that the code works as expected, we are now ready to freeze the latest versions of the packages that pip installed for us. pip has a freeze command that outputs the installed packages along with their versions. You redirect the output from this command to a requirements.txt file:

```
$ pip3 freeze --user > requirements.txt
```

Now that you have a requirements.txt file, people who clone your project can install all its dependencies using the -r option and the name of the requirements file:

```
$ pip3 install --user -r requirements.txt
```

The autogenerated requirements file format defaults to exact version matching (==). For example, a line such as requests==2.32.3 tells pip that the version of requests to install must be exactly 2.32.3. There are other version specifiers you can utilize in a requirements file, such as minimum version (>=), version exclusion (!=), and maximum version (<=). Minimum version (>=) matches any version greater than or equal to the right-hand side. Version exclusion (!=) matches any version except the right-hand side. Maximum version (<=) matches any version less than or equal to the right-hand side.

You can combine multiple version specifiers in a single line using commas to separate them:

```
requests >=2.32.3,<3.0
```

The default behavior when pip installs the packages specified in a requirements file is to fetch them all from PyPI. You can override PyPI's URL (https://pypi.org/simple/) with that of an alternate Python package index by adding a line such as the following to the top of your requirements.txt file:

```
--index-url http://pypi.mydomain.com/mirror
```

The effort required to stand up and maintain your own private PyPI mirror is not insubstantial. When all you need to do is fix a bug or add a feature to a project dependency, it makes more sense to override the package source instead of the entire package index.

I mentioned earlier how hardcoding distribution URLs inside setup.py is wrong. You can use the -e argument form in a requirements file to override individual package sources:

```
-e git+https://github.com/myteam/flask.git#egg=flask
```

In this example, I am instructing pip to fetch the flask package sources from my team's GitHub fork of pallets/flask.git. The -e argument form also takes a Git branch name, commit hash, or tag name:

```
-e git+https://github.com/myteam/flask.git@master
-e git+https://github.com/myteam/flask.
git@5142930ef57e2f0ada00248bdaeb95406d18eb7c
-e git+https://github.com/myteam/flask.git@v1.0
```

Using pip to upgrade a project's dependencies to the latest versions published on PyPI is straight-forward:

```
pip3 install --user --upgrade -r requirements.txt
```

After you have verified that installing the latest versions of your dependencies does not break your project, you can then write them back out to the requirements file:

```
$ pip3 freeze --user > requirements.txt
```

Make sure that freezing did not overwrite any of the overrides or special version handling in your requirements file. Undo any mistakes and commit the updated requirements.txt file to version control.

At some point, upgrading your project dependencies will result in your code breaking. A new package release may introduce a regression or incompatibility with your project. The requirements file format provides syntax to deal with these situations. Let's say you have been using version 2.32.3 of requests in your project and version 3.0 is released. According to the practice of semantic versioning, incrementing the major version number indicates that version 3.0 of requests includes breaking changes to that library's API.

You can express the new version requirements like this:

```
requests ~= 2.32.3
```

The compatible release specifier (~=) relies on semantic versioning. Compatible means greater than or equal to the right-hand side and less than the next version's major number (for example, >= 1.1 and == 1.*). You have already seen me express these same version requirements for requests less ambiguously as follows:

```
requests >=2.32.3,<3.0
```

These `pip` dependency management techniques work fine if you only develop a single Python project at a time. But chances are you use the same machine to work on several Python projects at once, each potentially requiring a different version of the Python interpreter. The biggest problem with using only `pip` for multiple projects is that it installs all packages to the same user `site-packages` directory for a particular version of Python. This makes it very hard to isolate dependencies from one project to the next.

As we'll see in the next chapter, `pip` combines well with Docker for deploying Python applications. You can add `pip` to a Buildroot or Yocto-based Linux image but that only enables quick on-device experimentation. A Python runtime package installer such as `pip` is ill-suited for Buildroot and Yocto environments where you want to define the entire contents of your embedded Linux image at build time. `pip` works great inside containerized environments such as Docker where the line between build time and runtime is often blurry.

In *Chapter 7*, you learned about the Python modules available to you in the `meta-python` layer and how to define a custom layer for your own application. You can use the `requirements.txt` files generated by `pip freeze` to inform the selection of dependencies from `meta-python` for your own layer recipes. Buildroot and Yocto both install Python packages in a system-wide manner, so the virtual environment techniques we are going to discuss next do not apply to embedded Linux builds per se. They do, however, help you assemble a complete list of dependencies for your embedded Python applications.

Managing Python virtual environments with venv

A **virtual environment** is a self-contained directory tree containing a Python interpreter for a particular version of Python, a `pip` executable for managing project dependencies, and a local `site-packages` directory. Switching between virtual environments tricks the shell into thinking that the only Python and `pip` executables available are the ones present in the active virtual environment. Best practice dictates that you create a different virtual environment for each of your projects. This form of isolation solves the problem of two projects depending on different versions of the same package.

Virtual environments are not new to Python. The system-wide nature of Python installations necessitates them. Besides enabling you to install different versions of the same package, virtual environments also provide an easy way for you to run multiple versions of the Python interpreter. Several options exist for managing Python virtual environments. A tool that was immensely popular circa 2019 (`pipenv`) has since languished. The popular conda package manager has supported Python virtual environments since late 2014. Meanwhile, Python 3's built-in support for virtual environments (`venv`) introduced back in 2012 has slowly matured and is now widely adopted.

venv has been shipping with Python since version 3.3. Because it only comes bundled with Python 3 installations, venv is incompatible with projects that require Python 2.7. As support for Python 2.7 officially ended on January 1, 2020, this Python 3 limitation is less of a concern. venv is based on the popular virtualenv tool, which is still maintained and available on PyPI. If you have one or more projects that still require Python 2.7, then you can use virtualenv instead of venv to work on those.

By default, venv installs the most recent version of Python found on your system. If you have multiple versions of Python on your system, you can select a specific Python version by running python3 or whichever version you want when creating each virtual environment (*The Python Tutorial*, https://docs.python.org/3/tutorial/venv.html). Developing with the most recent version of Python is usually fine for greenfield projects but unacceptable for most legacy and enterprise software. We will use the version of Python 3 that came with your Ubuntu system to create and work with a virtual environment.

To create a virtual environment, first, decide where you want to put it, and then run the venv module as a script with the target directory path:

1. Ensure venv is installed on your Ubuntu system:

```
$ sudo apt install python3-venv
```

2. Create a new directory for your project:

```
$ mkdir myproject
```

3. Switch to that new directory:

```
$ cd myproject
```

4. Create the virtual environment inside a subdirectory named venv:

```
$ python3 -m venv ./venv
```

Now that you have created a virtual environment, here is how you activate and verify it:

1. Switch to your project directory if you haven't already:

```
$ cd myproject
```

2. Check where your system's pip3 executable is installed:

```
$ which pip3
/usr/bin/pip3
```

3. Activate the project's virtual environment:

```
$ source ./venv/bin/activate
```

4. Check where your project's pip3 executable is installed:

```
(venv) $ which pip3
/home/frank/myproject/venv/bin/pip3
```

5. List the packages that came installed with the virtual environment:

```
(venv) $ pip3 list
Package Version
------- -------
pip     24.0
```

If you enter the which pip command from within your virtual environment, you will see that pip now points to an executable. You can now omit the 3 when running either pip or python from within your virtual environment.

Next, let's install a property-based testing library named hypothesis into our existing virtual environment:

1. Switch to your project directory if you haven't already:

```
$ cd myproject
```

2. Reactivate the project's virtual environment if it is not already active:

```
$ source ./venv/bin/activate
```

3. Install the hypothesis package:

```
(venv) $ pip install hypothesis
```

4. List the packages now installed inside the virtual environment:

```
(venv) $ pip list
Package          Version
---------------- -------
attrs            25.1.0
hypothesis       6.125.2
pip              24.0
sortedcontainers 2.4.0
```

Notice that two new packages (`attrs` and `sortedcontainers`) were added to the list besides `hypothesis`. `hypothesis` depends on these two packages. Let's say you had another Python project that depended on version 1.5.10 instead of version 2.4.0 of `sortedcontainers`. Those two versions would be incompatible and thus conflict with each other. Virtual environments allow you to install both versions of the same package, a different version for each of the two projects.

You may have noticed that switching out of a project directory does not deactivate its virtual environment. Don't worry. Deactivating a virtual environment is as easy as this:

```
(venv) $ deactivate
$
```

This puts you back in the global system environment where you have to enter `python3` and `pip3` again. You have now seen everything you need to know to get started with Python virtual environments. Creating and switching between virtual environments is common practice now when developing in Python. Isolated environments make it easier to keep track of and manage your dependencies across multiple projects.

Installing precompiled binaries with conda

conda is a package and virtual environment management system used by the **Anaconda** distribution of software for the PyData community. The Anaconda distribution includes Python as well as binaries for several hard-to-build open source projects such as PyTorch and TensorFlow. conda can be installed without the full Anaconda distribution, which is very large, or the minimal **Miniconda** distribution, which is still over 256 MB.

Even though it was created for Python shortly after `pip`, conda has evolved into a general-purpose package manager like APT or Homebrew. Now, it can be used to package and distribute software for any language. Because conda downloads precompiled binaries, installing Python extension modules is a breeze. Another one of conda's big selling points is that it is cross-platform, with full support for Linux, macOS, and Windows.

Besides package management, conda is also a full-blown virtual environment manager. conda virtual environments have all the benefits we have come to expect from Python venv environments and more. Like venv, conda lets you use `pip` to install packages from PyPI into a project's local `site-packages` directory. If you prefer, you can use conda's own package management capabilities to install packages from different channels. Channels are package feeds provided by Anaconda and other software distributions.

Environment management

Unlike venv, conda's virtual environment manager can easily juggle multiple versions of Python, including Python 2.7. You will need to have Miniconda installed on your Ubuntu system to do the following exercises. You want to use Miniconda instead of Anaconda for your virtual environments because Anaconda environments come with lots of preinstalled packages, many of which you will never need. Miniconda environments are stripped down and allow you to easily install any of Anaconda's packages should you have to.

To install and update Miniconda on Ubuntu 24.04 LTS:

1. Download Miniconda:

    ```
    $ wget https://repo.anaconda.com/miniconda/Miniconda3-latest-
    Linux-x86_64.sh
    ```

2. Install Miniconda:

    ```
    $ bash Miniconda3-latest-Linux-x86_64.sh
    ```

3. Update all the installed packages in the root environment:

    ```
    (base) $ conda update --all
    ```

Your fresh Miniconda installation comes with conda and a root environment with a Python interpreter and some basic packages installed. By default, the python and pip executables of conda's root environment are installed in your home directory. The conda root environment is known as base. You can view its location, along with the locations of any other available conda environments, by issuing the following command:

```
(base) $ conda env list
```

Verify this root environment before creating your own conda environment:

1. Open a new shell after installing Miniconda.

2. Check where the root environment's python executable is installed:

    ```
    (base) $ which python
    ```

3. Check the version of Python:

    ```
    (base) $ python --version
    ```

4. Check where the root environment's `pip` executable is installed:

```
(base) $ which pip
```

5. Check the version of `pip`:

```
(base) $ pip --version
```

6. List the packages installed in the root environment:

```
(base) $ conda list
```

Next, create and work with your own `conda` environment named py311:

1. Create a new virtual environment named py311:

```
(base) $ conda create --name py311 python=3.11.9
```

2. Activate your new virtual environment:

```
(base) $ source activate py311
```

3. Check where your environment's `python` executable is installed:

```
(py311) $ which python
```

4. Check that the version of Python is 3.11.9:

```
(py311) $ python --version
```

5. List the packages installed in your environment:

```
(py311) $ conda list
```

6. Deactivate your environment:

```
(py311) $ conda deactivate
```

Using conda to create a virtual environment with Python 2.7 installed is as simple as the following:

```
(base) $ conda create --name py27 python=2.7.18
```

View your conda environments again to see whether py311 and py27 now appear in the list:

```
(base) $ conda env list
```

Lastly, let's delete the py27 environment since we won't be using it:

```
(base) $ conda remove --name py27 --all
```

Now that you know how to use conda to manage virtual environments, let's use it to manage packages within those environments.

Package management

Since conda supports virtual environments, we can use pip to manage Python dependencies from one project to another in an isolated manner, just like we did with venv. As a general-purpose package manager, conda has its own facilities for managing dependencies. We know that conda list lists all the packages that conda has installed in the active virtual environment. I also mentioned conda's use of package feeds, which are called channels:

1. You can get the list of channel URLs conda is configured to fetch from by entering this command:

    ```
    (base) $ conda info
    ```

2. Before proceeding any further, let's reactivate the py311 virtual environment you created during the last exercise:

    ```
    (base) $ source activate py311
    (py311) $
    ```

3. Most Python development nowadays happens inside a Jupyter notebook, so let's install those packages first:

    ```
    (py311) $ conda install jupyter notebook
    ```

4. Enter *y* when prompted. This will install the jupyter and notebook packages along with all their dependencies. When you enter conda list, you'll see that the list of installed packages is much longer than before. Now, let's install some more Python packages that we would need for a computer vision project:

    ```
    (py311) $ conda install opencv matplotlib
    ```

5. Again, enter *y* when prompted. This time, the number of dependencies installed is smaller. Both opencv and matplotlib depend on numpy, so conda installs that package automatically without you having to specify it. If you want to specify an older version of opencv, you can install the desired version of the package this way:

    ```
    (py311) $ conda install opencv=4.6.0
    ```

6. conda will then attempt to *solve* the active environment for this dependency. Since no other packages installed in this active virtual environment depend on opencv, the target version is easy to solve for. If they did, then you might encounter a package conflict and the reinstallation would fail. After solving, conda will prompt you before downgrading opencv and its dependencies. Enter *y* to downgrade opencv to version 4.6.0.

7. Now let's say you change your mind or a newer version of opencv is released that addresses your previous concern. This is how you would upgrade opencv to the latest version provided by the Anaconda distribution:

```
(py311) $ conda update opencv
```

8. This time, conda will prompt you to ask whether you want to update opencv and its dependencies for the latest version. This time, enter *n* to cancel the package update. Instead of updating packages individually, it's often easier to update all the packages installed in an active virtual environment at once:

```
(py311) $ conda update --all
```

9. Removing installed packages is also straightforward:

```
(py311) $ conda remove jupyter notebook
```

When conda removes jupyter and notebook, it removes all of their dangling dependencies as well. A dangling dependency is an installed package that no other installed packages depend on. Like most general-purpose package managers, conda will not remove any dependencies that other installed packages still depend on.

10. Sometimes you may not know the exact name of a package you want to install. Amazon offers an AWS SDK for Python called Boto. Like many Python libraries, there is a version of Boto for Python 2 and a newer version (Boto3) for Python 3. To search Anaconda for packages with the word boto in their names, enter the following command:

```
(py311) $ conda search '*boto*'
```

11. You should see boto3 and botocore in the search results. At the time of writing, the most recent version of boto3 available on Anaconda is 1.36.3. To view details on that specific version of boto3, enter the following command:

```
(py311) $ conda search boto3=1.36.3 --info
```

The package details reveal that boto3 version 1.36.3 depends on botocore (botocore >=1.36.3,<1.37.0), so installing boto3 gets you both.

Now let's say you've installed all the packages you need to develop an OpenCV project inside a Jupyter notebook. How do you share these project requirements with someone else so that they can recreate your work environment? The answer may surprise you:

1.   You export your active virtual environment to a YAML file:

```
(py311) $ conda env export > my-environment.yaml
```

2.   Much like the list of requirements that pip freeze generates, the YAML that conda exports is a list of all the packages installed in your virtual environment together with their pinned versions. Creating a conda virtual environment from an environment file requires the -f option and the filename:

```
$ conda env create -f my-environment.yaml
```

3.   The environment name is included in the exported YAML, so no --name option is necessary to create the environment. Whoever creates a virtual environment from my-environment.yaml will now see py311 in their list of environments when they issue conda env list.

conda is a very powerful tool in a developer's arsenal. By combining general-purpose package installation with virtual environments, it offers a compelling deployment story. conda achieves many of the same goals Docker (up next) does, but without the use of containers. It has an edge over Docker with respect to Python due to its focus on the data science community. Because the leading ML frameworks (such as PyTorch and TensorFlow) are largely CUDA-based, finding GPU-accelerated binaries is often difficult. conda solves this problem by providing multiple pre-compiled binary versions of packages.

Exporting conda virtual environments to YAML files for installation on other machines offers another deployment option. This solution is popular among the data science community, but it does not work in production for embedded Linux. conda is not one of the three package managers that Yocto supports. Even if conda was an option, the storage needed to accommodate Miniconda on a Linux image is not a good fit for most embedded systems due to resource constraints.

If your dev board has an NVIDIA GPU such as the NVIDIA Jetson series, then you really want to use conda for on-device development. Luckily, there is a conda installer named **Miniforge** (https://github.com/conda-forge/miniforge) that is known to work on 64-bit ARM machines like the Jetsons. With conda on the device, you can then install jupyter, numpy, pandas, scikit-learn, and most of the other popular Python data science libraries out there.

Summary

By now, you're probably asking yourself, "What does any of this Python packaging stuff have to do with embedded Linux?" The answer is "not much" but bear in mind that the word *development* also happens to be in the title of this book, and this chapter has everything to do with modern-day software development. To succeed as a developer, you need to be able to deploy your code to production fast, frequently, and in a repeatable manner. That means managing your dependencies carefully and automating as much of the process as possible. You now know how to do that with Python.

Further study

- *Python Packaging User Guide*, PyPA – `https://packaging.python.org`
- *setup.py vs requirements.txt*, by Donald Stufft – `https://caremad.io/posts/2013/07/setup-vs-requirement`
- *pip User Guide*, PyPA – `https://pip.pypa.io/en/latest/user_guide/`
- *Conda User Guide*, Anaconda, Inc. – `https://docs.conda.io/projects/conda/en/latest/user-guide`

Get This Book's PDF Version and Exclusive Extras

UNLOCK NOW

Scan the QR code (or go to `packtpub.com/unlock`). Search for this book by name, confirm the edition, and then follow the steps on the page.

Note: Keep your invoice handy. Purchases made directly from Packt don't require an invoice.

16

Deploying Container Images

In this chapter, I will introduce the principles of the DevOps movement and demonstrate how to apply them to embedded Linux. First, we will learn how to use Docker to bundle a Python application together with its user-space environment inside a container image. Next, we will set up a Docker-based **continuous integration and continuous delivery (CI/CD)** pipeline for a Python Bluetooth server application. Then I will demonstrate how to quickly add Docker to a Yocto image for the Raspberry Pi 4. Lastly, we will deploy a containerized software update to a Raspberry Pi 4 running Docker.

In this chapter, we will cover the following topics:

- What is DevOps?
- DevOps and embedded Linux
- Deploying Python applications with Docker
- Setting up a CI/CD pipeline for a Python application
- Adding Docker to a Yocto image
- Updating software with Docker

Technical requirements

To follow along with the examples, make sure you have the following:

- An Ubuntu 24.04 or later LTS host system with at least 90 GB of free disk space
- A user account with admin or sudo privileges on the host system
- Yocto 5.0 (Scarthgap) LTS release
- A microSD card reader and card

- `balenaEtcher` for Linux
- An Ethernet cable and router with an available port for network connectivity
- A Raspberry Pi 4
- A 5 V USB-C power supply capable of delivering 3 A

You should have already built the 5.0 (Scarthgap) LTS release of Yocto in *Chapter 6*. If you have not, then please refer to the *Compatible Linux Distribution* and *Build Host Packages* sections of the *Yocto Project Quick Build* guide (https://docs.yoctoproject.org/brief-yoctoprojectqs/) before building Yocto on your Linux host according to the instructions in *Chapter 6*.

The code used in this chapter can be found in the chapter folder in this book's GitHub repository: https://github.com/PacktPublishing/Mastering-Embedded-Linux-Development/tree/main/Chapter16.

Getting Docker

To install Docker on Ubuntu 24.04 LTS:

1. Update the package repositories:

```
$ sudo apt update
```

2. Install Docker:

```
$ sudo apt install docker.io
```

3. Start the Docker daemon and enable it to start at boot time:

```
$ sudo systemctl enable --now docker
```

4. Add yourself to the docker group:

```
$ sudo usermod -aG docker <username>
```

5. Restart the Docker daemon:

```
$ sudo systemctl restart docker
```

Replace <username> in *step 4* with your username. I recommend creating your own Ubuntu user account rather than using the default ubuntu user account, which is supposed to be reserved for administrative tasks.

What is DevOps?

Since its inception in 2009, the **DevOps movement** has taken the software industry by storm. Patrick Debois coined the term **DevOps** after seeing the 2009 Velocity Conference presentation *10 Deploys per Day*. Patrick is one of the four co-authors of *The DevOps Handbook* along with Gene Kim, Jez Humble, and John Willis. The *DevOps Handbook* was first published in 2016 and codifies the principles of the movement. These ideas originate from the Lean manufacturing and Agile software development communities. DevOps practices are closely aligned with Agile methodologies like Scrum and Kanban. The goal of all these approaches is always to ship quality products to customers faster.

DevOps strives to integrate the development and operations teams within an organization. Historically, the people who operate software at a company are separate from the people who develop that same software. Sometimes there is a dedicated team of system administrators (IT) responsible for provisioning servers and deploying scheduled software releases. This separation of concerns combined with big bang deployments inevitably leads to lengthy delays and outages. The relationship between development and operations becomes adversarial as finger-pointing ensues amid failures. By contrast, DevOps encourages close collaboration, rapid iteration, and experimentation. Mistakes are how we learn.

Continuous integration and continuous deployment

Two core concepts of Lean manufacturing are the notions of a **value stream** and the **lead time** associated with that. The Lean philosophy comes from the automotive industry, specifically the Toyota Production System. If a value stream is a factory assembly line, then the lead time is the time from when a customer request is submitted to when it is fulfilled. Lead time is one of the metrics by which the performance of a value stream is measured. Reducing lead time enables factories to build cars faster. The same idea applies to software.

In software, we can think of lead time as the time from when a feature request is submitted to when that finished feature is deployed to production. Every time a developer commits and pushes a change to the software an automated build is kicked off. A suite of unit tests is run against this newly changed code as part of the automated build. A code change can only be merged to the main branch if the build succeeds and the test suite passes. All these checks are scripted and performed automatically. The longer it takes to build the software and execute the tests, the longer the lead time is.

Integrating code is only part of the value stream. To deliver value to customers, software must be deployed to production. That typically means tagging a release, spinning up servers in the cloud, and installing the new release onto those servers. There are several techniques to ensure deployments go smoothly. Run integration tests first. Roll releases out incrementally across your fleet of servers. Roll back to a prior release in the event of a bad software update. Maximum developer productivity can only be achieved when software is deployed to production multiple times a day. The value stream is the **CI/CD** pipeline.

Infrastructure as code

We need more than source code to build and deploy most software. Today, most modern software development involves Docker. An application typically requires a Dockerfile, makefile, and shell scripts to build and bundle the software for release. These items are invoked by a YAML file at different stages of the CI/CD pipeline. Since they aren't part of the actual software, we may not think of these items as code per se. Still, they reside inside version control along with the source code and likewise need to be reviewed and maintained. Because the building and bundling of the software is entirely scripted, the task is easily repeatable.

The amount of YAML involved increases during deployment. Cloud-native tools like Terraform and CloudFormation are YAML-based. We provision cloud infrastructure and deploy software release artifacts onto it with these tools by applying declarative YAML files. Deployment is driven by the same top-level YAML file used for building and bundling. That way, the whole process is automated from end to end. While they may not look like it, YAML files are indeed code and should adhere to the same standards of quality as code written in high-level programming languages like Python.

Security is a shared responsibility

When time to market is everything, security takes a back seat. Like deployments, security is often relegated to operations. High-profile incidents like the Log4j vulnerability of 2022 and the xz backdoor of 2024 demonstrate how critical security is to day-to-day business. DevOps argues that security is a concern at every stage of development, not an afterthought. Intellectual property and customer data are always encrypted. Secrets like keys and passphrases are stored safely outside of version control. Security best practices are everyone's responsibility and need to be enforced from the outset.

Monitoring and observability

Gathering telemetry in the form of system stats, logs, and traces provides us with visibility into the health and performance of our applications. Once we have telemetry, it can be displayed on a Grafana dashboard for analysis. That way, we can detect performance regressions, resource leaks, and other systemic problems before they result in a costly service outage. Real-time insights trigger rapid incident responses and resolutions. More importantly, telemetry gives us quick unfiltered feedback on how we are doing as developers so that we can learn and improve.

Continuous improvement

Lean manufacturing espouses short lead times, small changes, and rapid iteration. *The Lean Startup* by Eric Ries popularized the notion of a **minimum viable product** (**MVP**). An MVP is a version of a product with just enough functionality that initial customers can offer feedback on said product. This feedback is reviewed, and improvements are made to the next version in rapid succession. A software CI/CD pipeline cranks out MVPs faster than a factory assembly line.

Continuous feedback incentivizes developers to ship small incremental improvements with greater frequency. An MVP approach enables teams to see what works and what doesn't before committing more time and resources. This way, adjustments can be made so that more value is delivered to users. DevOps argues that integrating small changes sooner results in better outcomes. This is in stark contrast to having a lone developer toil away on a long-lived feature branch without any feedback from users.

Transparency

Collaboration is unlikely if an organization's culture discourages it. Fear pervades dysfunctional organizations. Individuals act strategically by hiding information away from others who could benefit from it. This behavior leads to silos where all communication happens in private meetings and chats on a need-to-know basis. Mistakes are hidden for fear of punishment (e.g., leadership "shoots the messenger"). The DevOps mindset is one of openness. Successes, failures, and ideas are shared across the organization to promote best practices. If you are struggling with a task, then you ask your team for help.

DevOps and Embedded Linux

Hardware is hard. PCB layout, contract manufacturing, and board revisions cost time and money. The risks are bigger than with software. Lead times are longer, and mistakes can be catastrophic. Embedded Linux forms the bridge between hardware and software.

Embedded Linux engineers work closely with electrical engineers during board bring-up, troubleshooting issues as they arise. It's not uncommon to ask an electrical engineer to rewire a component or add a pull-up resistor. PCB layout is extremely complex. Nobody is perfect, so a new board rarely ever boots the first time around.

With such high stakes, it might seem like DevOps principles are a bad fit for hardware products. Industry trends like **test-driven development** (**TDD**) are often dismissed as impractical by experienced embedded developers. Automated testing is harder when dealing with real hardware but not impossible. Investing time and energy in establishing a CI/CD pipeline pays dividends once features begin landing in rapid succession. Management may question why you are doing so much process work up front, but their tune will change when new products begin to be delivered ahead of schedule.

Continuous integration and cross-compilation

Linux and much of the middleware on top of it is written mostly in C. This means it must be compiled natively for the target's **instruction set architecture** (**ISA**). In the cloud, that ISA is usually x86-64 running on Intel or AMD CPUs. On embedded devices capable of running Linux, it is increasingly 64-bit Arm. Since most cloud infrastructure runs on Intel and AMD CPUs, building software for embedded Linux requires a cross-compiling toolchain. However, cross-compilation is not a common use case for cloud-based CI/CD services like GitHub Actions or GitLab CI.

Buildroot and Yocto are both designed to cross-compile embedded Linux images, but running these tools in the cloud can be challenging. They require lots of disk space and the extended build times are prohibitive. Build times can be improved by employing incremental builds and intelligent caching (e.g., Yocto's shared `sstate-cache`). Alternatively, you can use Docker in conjunction with QEMU to cross-compile container images for 64-bit Arm. This containerized approach works great for user space but emulating the target architecture slows down compilation.

Automated testing on real hardware

One of the biggest challenges involved in shipping hardware is implementing **hardware-in-the-loop** (**HIL**) testing. Like cross-compilation, automated testing can be done easily in the cloud with QEMU, but there is no substitute for testing software on its intended hardware. When safety is a concern, HIL testing is an obligation, not a cautionary measure. The challenge is in how to automate it. This is why HIL testing often requires as much effort as coding the software.

The most effective form of HIL testing is to simulate the real world. Hardware interacts with the real world through sensors and actuators. It receives input from sensors and sends output to actuators via communications interfaces like I2C, SPI, and CAN. We simulate the real world by modeling it with software. This software model runs on a separate Linux machine. It sends and receives messages over the various comms interfaces just like the sensors and actuators in the actual system. For example, to test an EV charger we would connect a PCB on a test bench to a mock battery running our model.

Continuous delivery and OTA updates

When a deployment fails in the cloud, we simply delete the problem servers and spin up new instances. We don't need to worry about bricking servers because we can always just start over from scratch. Reprovisioning servers is relatively quick and painless to do in the cloud. The same cannot be said for consumer devices out in the field. If a device cannot boot, then it is useless. Similarly, if a connected device suddenly becomes disconnected from the internet, then it cannot receive critical OTA updates.

OTA updates are how the continuous delivery of software happens in embedded systems. OTA updates need to be fail-safe in the face of accidental power loss. A failed OTA update cannot result in a partial or unknown flash image. Otherwise, the device may be rendered unbootable. Buildroot and Yocto support fail-safe OTA update solutions like Mender, RAUC, and SWUpdate. Even though these tools will save you from bricking your fleet, you should still test your software releases thoroughly before a full rollout. Nothing sinks a new product launch quicker than a bad user experience.

Infrastructure as code and build systems

Buildroot relies on makefiles. Yocto consists of BitBake recipes. Like the YAML files that define your cloud infrastructure, this build metadata also qualifies as code and should be kept in version control. That includes board defconfigs and package definitions for Buildroot. For Yocto, the build metadata is comprised of BSP and distro layers. It also pays to containerize your embedded Linux build environment by defining a Dockerfile for it. This makes it easier to spin up a CI/CD pipeline to build images for your target device. It also makes it easier for others to reproduce your build environment so that they can develop locally on their machines.

Securing edge devices

The internet is full of danger. The infamous Mirai botnet was started by kids wanting to knock out rival Minecraft servers. The idea evolved into large-scale **distributed denial-of-service (DDoS)** attacks. Mirai hijacks consumer IoT devices like webcams and home routers and points them at selected websites. Securing the boot and OTA update processes prevents malware like Mirai from running on users' devices. The mechanisms for securing the boot and OTA update processes are described in *Chapter 10*. Security is table stakes at the edge because once your fleet is hijacked, you can't get it back.

Secure boot means that a device will only boot from an image that has been cryptographically signed by the device manufacturer. A signature verification step is inserted at boot time to ensure the authenticity of the latest image applied by an OTA update. Users also expect all data to be encrypted on their devices for privacy. Auto-unlocking an encrypted volume requires a passphrase on startup. Any keys or passphrases needed by a device at runtime should be stored safely inside a TPM or secure element.

Monitoring and observability of edge devices

Gathering telemetry from consumer devices is difficult because they are deployed in people's homes and offices. Like all other devices connected to the internet, any new product that wants to stream telemetry up to the cloud will need to get past the firewall. This typically requires a user to open an outgoing port on their Wi-Fi router. Users may not be network savvy enough or object to doing this for privacy. While standard IoT protocols for telemetry like MQTT exist, they are not always a good fit for every application. There is still much room for innovation in this space by startups like Golioth and Memfault.

Enough theory and rationale. Let's put these principles into practice. We'll start by performing a containerized software deployment. You should have already installed Docker on your Linux host according to the instructions in the *Getting Docker* section.

Deploying Python applications with Docker

Docker offers another way to bundle Python code with software written in other languages. The idea behind Docker is that instead of packaging and installing your application onto a precon-figured server environment, you build and ship a container image with your application and all its runtime dependencies. A container image is more like a virtual environment than a virtual machine. A virtual machine is a complete system image including a kernel and an operating system. A container image is a minimal user-space environment that only comes with the binaries needed to run your application.

Virtual machines run on top of a hypervisor that emulates hardware. Containers run directly on top of the host operating system. Unlike virtual machines, containers are able to share the same operating system and kernel without the use of hardware emulation. Instead, they rely on two special features of the Linux kernel for isolation: namespaces and cgroups. Docker did not invent container technology, but they were the first to build tooling that made them easy to use. The tired excuse of "works on my machine" no longer flies now that Docker makes it so simple to build and deploy container images.

Anatomy of a Dockerfile

A **Dockerfile** describes the contents of a Docker image. Every Dockerfile contains a set of instructions specifying what environment to use and which commands to run. Instead of writing a Dockerfile from scratch, we will use an existing Dockerfile for a project template. This Dockerfile generates a Docker image for a very simple Flask web application that you can extend to fit your needs. The Docker image is built on top of Debian Bookworm. Besides Flask, the Docker image also includes uWSGI and Nginx for better performance.

Start by pointing your web browser at the uwsgi-nginx-flask-docker project on GitHub (https://github.com/tiangolo/uwsgi-nginx-flask-docker). Then, click on the link to the python-3.12 Dockerfile from the README.md file.

Now, look at the first line in that Dockerfile:

```
FROM tiangolo/uwsgi-nginx:python3.12
```

This FROM command tells Docker to pull an image named uwsgi-nginx from the tiangolo namespace with python3.12 from Docker Hub. Docker Hub is a public registry where people publish their Docker images for others to fetch and deploy. You can set up your own image registry using a service such as AWS ECR or Quay if you prefer. You will need to insert the name of your registry service in front of your namespace like this:

```
FROM quay.io/my-org/my-app:my-tag
```

Otherwise, Docker defaults to fetching images from Docker Hub. FROM is like an include statement in a Dockerfile. It inserts the contents of another Dockerfile into yours so that you have something to build on top of. I like to think of this approach as layering images. Debian Bookworm is the base layer, followed by Python 3.12, then uWSGI plus Nginx, and finally your Flask application. You can learn more about how image layering works by digging into the python3.12 Dockerfile at https://hub.docker.com/r/tiangolo/uwsgi-nginx.

Here is the next line of interest in the Dockerfile:

```
RUN pip install --no-cache-dir -r /tmp/requirements.txt
```

A RUN instruction runs a command. Docker executes the RUN instructions contained in the Dockerfile sequentially in order to build the resulting Docker image. If you look at the requirements. txt file in the Git repo, you will see that this RUN instruction installs Flask in the system site-packages directory. We know that pip is available because the uwsgi-nginx base image also includes Python 3.12.

Let's skip over Nginx's environment variables and go straight to copying:

```
COPY ./app /app
```

This particular Dockerfile is located inside a Git repo along with several other files and subdirectories. The COPY instruction copies a directory from the host Docker runtime environment (usually a Git clone of a repo) into the container being built.

The python3.12.dockerfile file you are looking at resides in a docker-images subdirectory of the tiangolo/uwsgi-nginx-flask-docker repo. Inside that docker-images directory is an app subdirectory containing a Hello World Flask web application. This COPY instruction copies the app directory from the example repo into the root directory of the Docker image:

```
WORKDIR /app
```

The WORKDIR instruction tells Docker which directory to work from inside the container. In this example, the /app directory that it just copied becomes the working directory. If the target working directory does not exist, then WORKDIR creates it. Any subsequent non-absolute paths that appear in this Dockerfile are hence relative to the /app directory.

Now let's see how an environment variable gets set inside the container:

```
ENV PYTHONPATH=/app
```

ENV tells Docker that what follows is an environment variable definition. PYTHONPATH is an environment variable that expands into a list of colon-delimited paths where the Python interpreter looks for modules and packages.

Next, let's jump a few lines down to the second RUN instruction:

```
RUN chmod +x /entrypoint.sh
```

The RUN instruction tells Docker to run a command from the shell. In this case, the command being run is chmod, which changes file permissions. Here, it renders the /entrypoint.sh executable.

The next line in this Dockerfile is optional:

```
ENTRYPOINT ["/entrypoint.sh"]
```

ENTRYPOINT is the most interesting instruction in this Dockerfile. It exposes an executable to the Docker host command line when starting the container. This lets you pass arguments from the command line down to the executable inside the container. You can append these arguments after docker run <image> on the command line. If there is more than one ENTRYPOINT instruction in a Dockerfile, then only the last ENTRYPOINT is executed.

The last line in the Dockerfile is:

```
CMD ["/start.sh"]
```

Like ENTRYPOINT instructions, CMD instructions execute at container start time rather than build time. When an ENTRYPOINT instruction is defined in a Dockerfile, a CMD instruction defines default arguments to be passed to that ENTRYPOINT. In this instance, the /start.sh path is the argument passed to /entrypoint.sh. The last line in /entrypoint.sh executes /start.sh:

```
#! /usr/bin/env sh
set -e

# If there's a prestart.sh script in the /app directory, run it before
# starting
PRE_START_PATH=/app/prestart.sh
echo "Checking for script in $PRE_START_PATH"
if [ -f $PRE_START_PATH ] ; then
    echo "Running script $PRE_START_PATH"
    . $PRE_START_PATH
else
    echo "There is no script $PRE_START_PATH"
fi

# Start Supervisor, with Nginx and uWSGI
exec /usr/bin/supervisord
```

The /start.sh script comes from the uwsgi-nginx base image. /start.sh starts Nginx and uWSGI after /entrypoint.sh has configured the container runtime environment for them. When CMD is used in conjunction with ENTRYPOINT, the default arguments set by CMD can be overridden from the Docker host command line.

Most Dockerfiles do not have an ENTRYPOINT instruction, so the last line of a Dockerfile is usually a CMD instruction that runs in the foreground instead of default arguments. You can use this Dockerfile trick to keep a general-purpose Docker container running for development:

```
CMD tail -f /dev/null
```

Except for ENTRYPOINT and CMD, all of the instructions in this example python-3.12 Dockerfile only execute when the container is being built.

Building a Docker image

Before we can build a Docker image, we need a Dockerfile. You may already have some Docker images on your system.

To see a list of Docker images:

```
$ docker images
```

Now, let's fetch and build the Dockerfile we just dissected:

1. Clone the repo containing the Dockerfile:

    ```
    $ git clone https://github.com/tiangolo/uwsgi-nginx-flask-docker.git
    ```

2. Switch to the docker-images subdirectory inside the repo:

    ```
    $ cd uwsgi-nginx-flask-docker/docker-images
    ```

3. Copy python3.12.dockerfile to a file named Dockerfile:

    ```
    $ cp python3.12.dockerfile Dockerfile
    ```

4. Build an image from the Dockerfile:

    ```
    $ docker build -t my-image .
    ```

Once the image is done building, it will appear in your list of local Docker images:

```
$ docker images
```

The newly built my-image should appear in the list.

Running a Docker image

We now have a Docker image built that we can run as a container.

To get a list of running containers on your system:

```
$ docker ps
```

To run a container based on my-image:

```
$ docker run -d --name my-container -p 80:80 my-image
```

If the preceding command fails because port 80 is busy, then substitute port 8080 for 80. Now observe the status of your running container:

```
$ docker ps
```

You should see a container named my-container based on an image named my-image in the list. The -p option in the docker run command maps a container port to a host port. So, container port 80 maps to host port 80 in this example. This port mapping allows the Flask web server running inside the container to service HTTP requests.

To stop my-container:

```
$ docker stop my-container
```

Now check the status of your running container again:

```
$ docker ps
```

my-container should no longer appear in the list of running containers. Is the container gone? No, it is only stopped. You can still see my-container and its status by adding the -a option to the docker ps command:

```
$ docker ps -a
```

We'll look at how to delete containers we no longer need a bit later.

Fetching a Docker image

Earlier in this section, I touched on image registries such as Docker Hub, AWS ECR, and Quay. As it turns out, the Docker image that we built locally from a cloned Git repo is already published on Docker Hub. It is much quicker to fetch the prebuilt image from Docker Hub than to build it yourself on your system. The Docker images for the project can be found at https://hub.docker.com/r/tiangolo/uwsgi-nginx-flask.

To pull the same Docker image that we built as my-image from Docker Hub:

```
$ docker pull tiangolo/uwsgi-nginx-flask:python3.12
```

Now look at your list of Docker images again:

```
$ docker images
```

You should see a new uwsgi-nginx-flask image in the list.

To run this newly fetched image:

```
$ docker run -d --name flask-container -p 80:80 tiangolo/uwsgi-nginx-
flask:python3.12
```

You can substitute the full image name (repo:tag) in the preceding docker run command with the corresponding image ID (hash) from docker images if you prefer not to type out the full image name.

Publishing a Docker image

To publish a Docker image to Docker Hub, you must first have an account and log in to it. You can create an account on Docker Hub by going to the https://hub.docker.com website and signing up. Once you have an account, then you can push an existing image to your Docker Hub repository:

1. Log in to the Docker Hub image registry from the command line:

    ```
    $ docker login
    ```

2. Enter your Docker Hub username and password when prompted.

3. Tag an existing image with a new name that starts with the name of your repository:

    ```
    $ docker tag my-image:latest <repository>/my-image:latest
    ```

4. Replace <repository> in the preceding command with the name of your repository (the same as your username) on Docker Hub. You can also substitute the name of another existing image you wish to push for my-image:latest.

5. Push the image to the Docker Hub image registry:

    ```
    $ docker push <repository>/my-image:latest
    ```

6. Again, make the same replacements as you did for *step 3*.

Images pushed to Docker Hub are publicly available by default. To visit the web page for your newly published image, go to `https://hub.docker.com/repository/docker/<repository>/my-image`. Replace `<repository>` in the preceding URL with the name of your repository (the same as your username) on Docker Hub. You can also substitute the name of the actual image you pushed for `my-image:latest` if different. If you click on the **Tags** tab on that web page, you should see the `docker pull` command for fetching that image.

Cleaning up

We know that `docker images` lists images and `docker ps` lists containers. Before we can delete a Docker image, we must first delete any containers that reference it. To delete a Docker container, you first need to know the container's name or ID:

1. Find the target Docker container's name:

   ```
   $ docker ps -a
   ```

2. Stop the container if it is running:

   ```
   $ docker stop flask-container
   ```

3. Delete the Docker container:

   ```
   $ docker rm flask-container
   ```

Replace `flask-container` in the two preceding commands with the container name or ID from *step 1*. Every container that appears under `docker ps` also has an image name or ID associated with it. Once you have deleted all the containers that reference an image, you can then delete the image.

Docker image names (`repo:tag`) can get quite long (for example, `tiangolo/uwsgi-nginx-flask:python3.12`). For that reason, I find it easier to just copy and paste an image's ID (hash) when deleting:

1. Find the Docker image's ID:

   ```
   $ docker images
   ```

2. Delete the Docker image:

   ```
   $ docker rmi <image-ID>
   ```

Replace `<image-ID>` in the preceding command with the image ID from *step 1*.

If you simply want to blow away all the containers and images that you are no longer using on your system:

```
$ docker system prune -a
```

docker system prune deletes all stopped containers and dangling images.

We've seen how pip can be used to install a Python application's dependencies. You simply add a RUN instruction that calls pip install to your Dockerfile. Because containers are sandboxed environments, they offer many of the same benefits that virtual environments do. But unlike conda and venv virtual environments, Buildroot and Yocto both have support for Docker containers. Buildroot has the docker-engine and docker-cli packages. Yocto has the meta-virtualization layer. If your device needs isolation because of Python package conflicts, then you can achieve that with Docker.

The docker run command provides options for exposing operating system resources to containers. Specifying a bind mount allows a file or directory on the host machine to be mounted inside a container for reading and writing. By default, containers publish no ports to the outside world. When you ran your my-container image, you used the -p option to publish port 80 from the container to port 80 on the host. The --device option adds a host device file under /dev to an unprivileged container. If you wish to grant access to all devices on the host, then use the --privileged option.

What containers excel at is deployment. Being able to push a Docker image that can then be easily pulled and run on any of the major cloud platforms has revolutionized the DevOps movement. Docker is also making inroads in the embedded Linux space thanks to OTA update solutions such as balena. One of the downsides of Docker is the storage footprint and memory overhead of the runtime. The Go binaries are a bit bloated, but Docker runs on quad-core 64-bit Arm SBCs like the Raspberry Pi 4 and BeaglePlay just fine. If your target device has enough power, then run Docker on it. Your software development team will thank you.

IMPORTANT NOTE

Podman is an alternative to Docker that offers a lighter, daemonless architecture. Unlike Docker, Podman does not require a service to be continuously running in the background, making it more resource-efficient. Its support for rootless containers enhances security and its compatibility with OCI standards ensures flexibility.

Setting up a CI/CD pipeline for a Python application

Docker is not just for deploying software to the cloud. Cloud-based CI/CD services can build and publish 64-bit Arm container images for deploying to edge devices. Containerized software updates are less disruptive than full A/B image updates because they don't require a reboot. Users get nervous when they see their devices fall offline even if just for a moment.

Containerized software updates are also less risky than full A/B image updates because they don't include a Linux kernel. An edge device may fail to boot because of a bad kernel update. Unless there is a fail-safe mechanism in place, the device is effectively bricked. Upstream kernel modules fall into disrepair as hardware ages out. Kernel upgrades are especially dangerous because they can introduce kernel panics.

Back in the *Building on top of an existing BSP* section of *Chapter 7*, we added a custom layer for a Python Bluetooth server application to a Yocto image for the Raspberry Pi 4. We can deploy the same application to a fleet of Raspberry Pi 4s using Docker.

The source code for the Python Bluetooth server resides in a public Git repo (https://github.com/fvasquez/gattd). GitHub Actions can attempt to build and publish a container image every time a commit is pushed to the repo.

Creating a Dockerfile

To run gattd inside a container, we first need a Dockerfile. Since gattd is a **Bluetooth Low Energy (BLE)** GATT server, it depends on working Bluetooth hardware and software being available at runtime. Fortunately, the Raspberry Pi 4 comes with Bluetooth built in, so there is robust kernel support for BLE already in place. Our gattd container image needs to include the BlueZ software stack to take advantage of all this Bluetooth support. BlueZ in turn requires D-Bus so that must be included in our image as well. **D-Bus** is message-based middleware that enables communication between multiple processes running on the same computer. The *D* in D-Bus stands for *desktop* but servers also rely on it for inter-process communication. D-Bus supports both request-response and publish/subscribe messaging and is deeply integrated into systemd.

Since gattd is a Python application, the Dockerfile does not have a compilation step. The Python distribution is not compiled by Yocto. It is part of the underlying Linux distribution or base layer specified at the top of the Dockerfile. I chose Ubuntu as my base layer because Ubuntu LTS releases are tested thoroughly against real hardware like the Raspberry Pi 4.

Relying on Ubuntu for user space eliminates the need to build your own distro and perform all the testing that goes along with that. Why go through all the trouble of maintaining a Linux distro layer when Canonical already does that for you? Choosing Ubuntu saves precious development time. The rest of your software team does not need to get up to speed on Yocto or install the eSDK. Ubuntu is a known entity.

Here is the Dockerfile I committed to the root level of the gattd repo:

```
# Dockerfile
FROM arm64v8/ubuntu:24.04
LABEL maintainer="fvasquez@gmail.com"
RUN apt update && apt-get install -y \
    bluez \
    dbus \
    python3-dbus \
    python3-gi

# Your app code, binaries, or other instructions
COPY . /app
WORKDIR /app

# Example app run
CMD ./entrypoint.sh
```

Docker Official Images (DOI) are hosted on Docker Hub. One of the primary goals of the DOI program is to publish container images for architectures other than amd64. One of the architectures DOI supports is arm64v8, which is the ISA for the Raspberry Pi 4. The Docker Hub arm64v8 organization publishes and maintains scores of container images on behalf of the DOI program. These include official arm64v8 container images for Debian, Ubuntu, and Python. 24.04 was the most recent LTS release of Ubuntu when I wrote this Dockerfile.

The gattd application relies primarily on the Python standard library. The only other Python package dependencies are bindings for D-Bus and bindings for the GObject introspection libraries. These two packages do not justify an additional pip install step since there are Ubuntu packages readily available for both. Unlike JavaScript, which has a very limited standard library, Python ships with "batteries included" so your application may not need another package manager besides apt.

Remember that the COPY instruction copies source files from the Git repo into the container being built. I will talk about the entrypoint.sh script after I explain how container images are published for gattd.

Creating a GitHub Actions workflow

GitHub Actions is the free CI/CD service offered by GitHub. GitHub Actions can build a container image and publish it to **GitHub Container Registry (GHCR)** whenever a change is pushed to the gattd repo. **GitHub Packages** is GitHub's software package hosting service for software releases. GHCR is part of GitHub Packages so no additional steps are needed to access GHCR other than using a repo owned by you or your organization. I own the gattd repo, which I forked from https://github.com/Jumperr-labs/python-gatt-server. The Python code was written by Dan Shemesh and dates back to 2017.

Like most CI/CD services, GitHub Actions workflows are defined as YAML files. The default workflow file is named main.yml. Changes to workflow files are committed to the .github/workflows directory of the repo. Since these files reside in version control along with the source code they build and deploy, workflow files constitute infrastructure as code.

Here are the contents of the main.yml workflow file I defined for the gattd repo:

```yaml
name: Publish Docker Image to GHCR

on:
  push:
    branches: [ "master" ]

permissions:
  contents: read
  packages: write

jobs:
  build-and-push:
    runs-on: ubuntu-24.04-arm

    steps:
      # 1) Check out the code
      - name: Check out code
        uses: actions/checkout@v4

      # 2) Log in to GitHub Container Registry
      - name: Log in to GHCR
        uses: docker/login-action@v2
```

```
      with:
        registry: ghcr.io
        username: ${{ github.repository_owner }}
        password: ${{ secrets.GITHUB_TOKEN }}

    # 3) Build and Push the Docker image
    - name: Build and push Docker image
      uses: docker/build-push-action@v4
      with:
        context: .
        file: ./Dockerfile
        platforms: linux/arm64
        push: true
        tags: |
          ghcr.io/${{ github.repository_owner }}/${{ github.event.
repository.name }}:latest
```

This `main.yml` file is also included in the `Chapter16` folder of the book's Git repo.

A simple three-step workflow is all that is needed to publish a container image to GHCR. The workflow is triggered every time a commit is pushed to the `master` branch of the repo.

IMPORTANT NOTE

Make sure to replace `master` with `main` in the branches list of your `main.yml` file when creating a GitHub Actions workflow for one of your own repos. Otherwise, the workflow will fail if no branch named `master` exists. Even though `main` is now the name of the default branch on GitHub, `master` is still the name of the default branch in Git when you create a new repository.

Another point of interest is `runs-on: ubuntu-24.04-arm`, which instructs GitHub Actions to leverage arm64-hosted runners for this workflow. This means that any hosted runners GitHub spins up for this workflow will run on real 64-bit Arm CPU cores, eliminating the need for cross-compilation or emulation.

Step 3 of the workflow builds and pushes the container image defined by the repo's Dockerfile. Notice that only `linux/arm64` is specified for `platforms`. The `platforms` element is for building multi-platform container images using Docker `buildx`. Docker `buildx` leverages QEMU to compile container images for non-native architectures, aka "platforms." Since gattd is targeted at the Raspberry Pi 4, a container image only needs to be built for the native linux/arm64 platform. Docker buildx is under active development. Learn more about the plugin and building multi-platform images at https://github.com/docker/buildx.

To create a GitHub Actions workflow:

1. From your repo, click on the **Actions** icon in the top bar.
2. Below **Get started with GitHub Actions**, click **Skip this and set up a workflow yourself.**
3. Paste the contents of main.yml into the **Edit** window.
4. Click the green **Commit changes…** button.
5. From the **Commit changes** dialog, click the green **Commit changes** button.

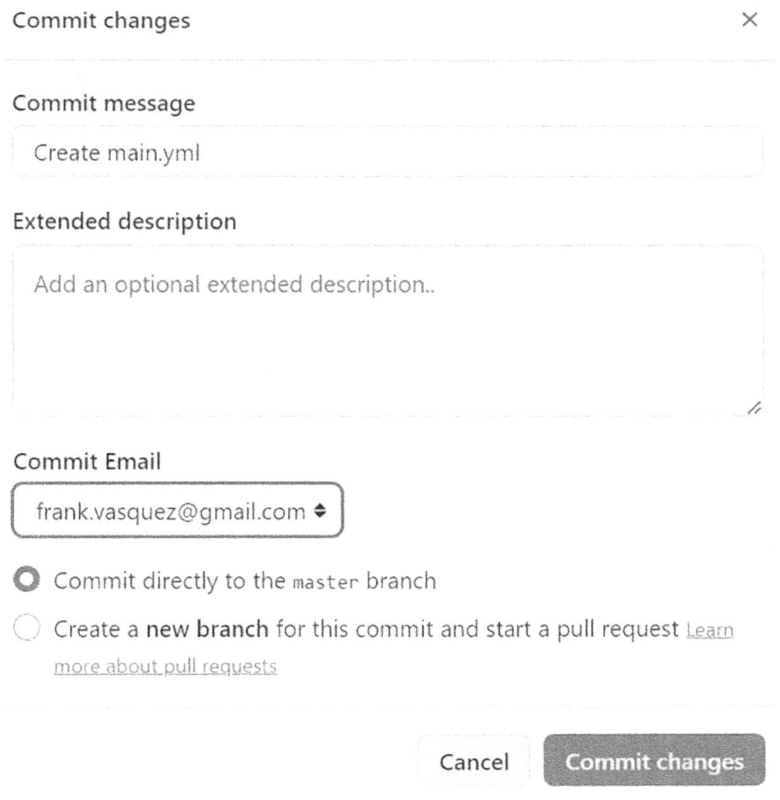

Figure 16.1 – Commit changes

Clicking the green **Commit changes** button triggers the GitHub Actions workflow. GitHub then spins up a hosted runner to build the repo's Dockerfile and push any resulting container image to GHCR. If everything goes as planned, you will see a status of **Success** for the commit and a white check mark inside of a green circle next to the **build-and-push** job. This workflow took 58 seconds to complete the first time I ran it and now triggers every time a commit is pushed to the `master` branch.

Pulling and running the latest image

Docker needs space to write the container images that it pulls. Most embedded Linux filesystems are either read-only or too small to store container images like `gattd:latest`. That is why you want to install a general-purpose Linux distribution like Ubuntu Server on your Raspberry Pi 4 for this exercise. The easiest way to do that is with the official Raspberry Pi Imager available from raspberrypi.org.

First, download and install the Raspberry Pi Imager onto your Linux host. Directions on how to do that can be found online at raspberrypi.com.

To download and install Ubuntu Server onto a microSD card:

1.   Insert a microSD card into your Linux host machine.

2.   Launch Raspberry Pi Imager.

3.   Select **Raspberry Pi 4** as your **Raspberry Pi Device**.

4.   Select **Other general-purpose OS** as your operating system.

5.   From the **Operating System** menu, select **Ubuntu**.

6.   Then select **Ubuntu Server 24.04.1 LTS** (64-bit) or the closest available equivalent.

7.   Click the **Edit Settings** button when asked **Would you like to apply OS customization settings?**

8. Enter a username and password on the **GENERAL** page as shown:

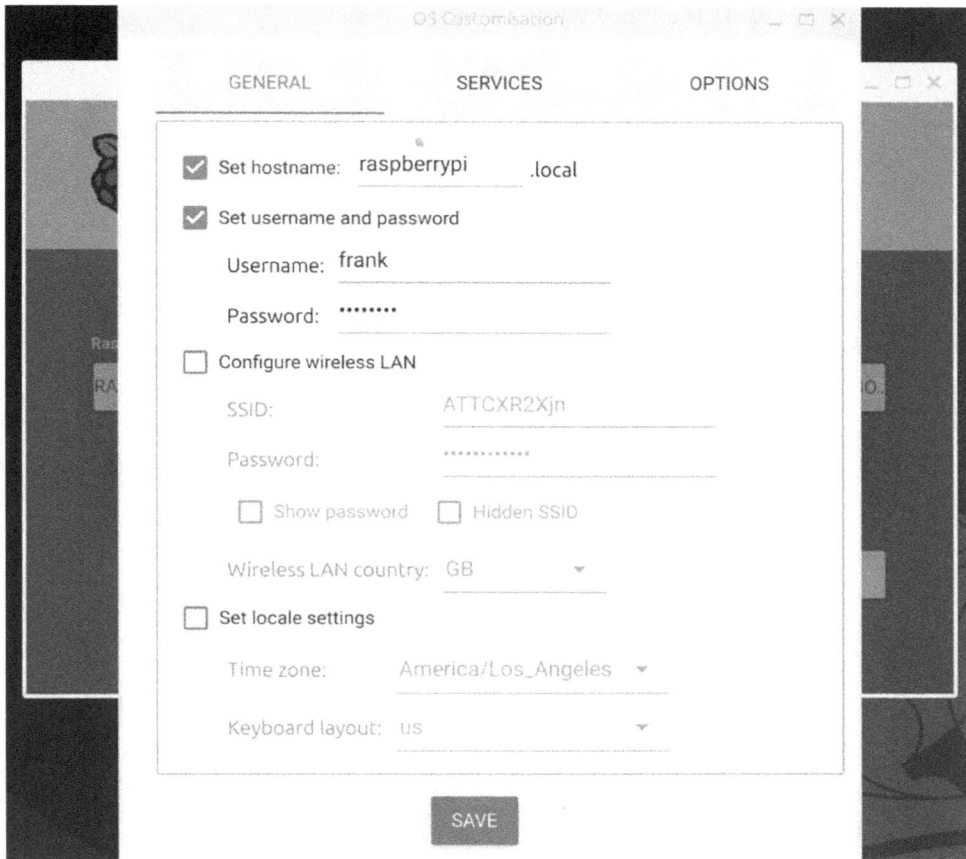

Figure 16.2 – GENERAL

9. Replace `frank` with your desired username.

10. Check **Enable SSH** on the **SERVICES** page as shown:

OS Customisation   _ ▢ ✕

GENERAL   SERVICES   OPTIONS

☑ Enable SSH

⦿ Use password authentication

◯ Allow public-key authentication only
Set authorized_keys for 'frank':

RUN SSH-KEYGEN

SAVE

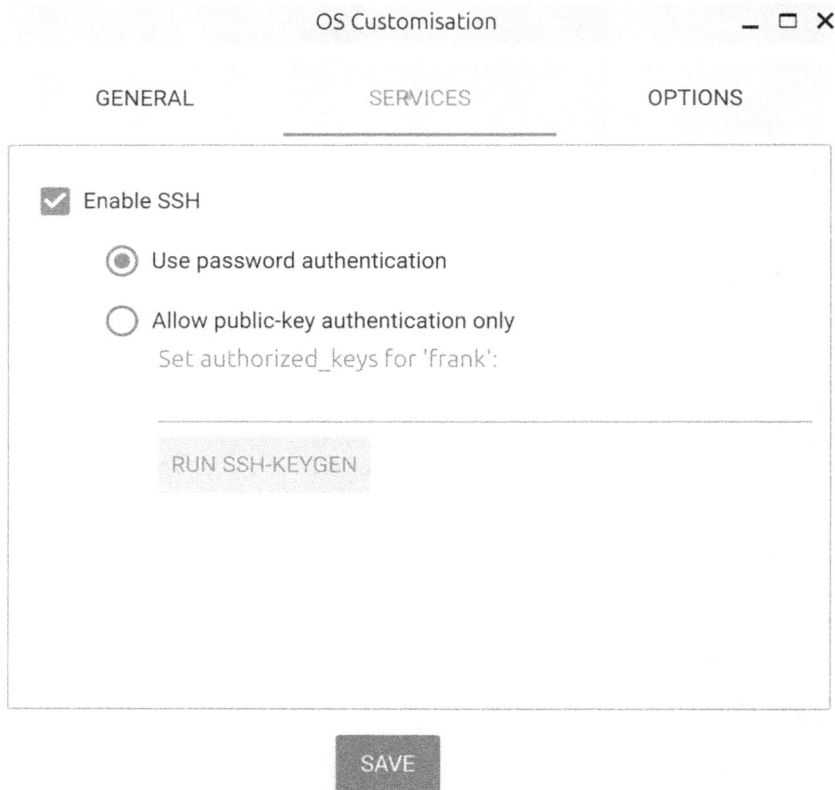

Figure 16.3 – SERVICES

11. Click the red **SAVE** button.

12. Select the microSD card as your storage.

13. Write the Ubuntu Server image to the microSD card. This takes several minutes because
    Raspberry Pi Imager formats all the available space on the microSD card.

14. Eject the microSD card when Raspberry Pi Imager is done writing.

15. Insert the microSD card into your Raspberry Pi 4.

16. Apply power to the Raspberry Pi 4 by way of its USB-C port.

To SSH into the Raspberry Pi 4:

```
$ ssh <username>@raspberrypi.local
```

Replace <username> with the username for the account you created when installing Ubuntu Server. Log in with the password you created with that account when prompted.

To install and configure Docker on the Raspberry Pi 4:

1. Update the package metadata:

    ```
    $ sudo apt update
    ```

2. Install the Docker daemon:

    ```
    $ sudo apt install docker.io
    ```

3. Configure the system to start the Docker daemon on power up:

    ```
    $ sudo systemctl enable --now docker
    ```

4. Add the user to the Docker group:

    ```
    $ sudo usermod -aG docker <frank>
    ```

5. Replace <frank> with the username for the account you created when installing Ubuntu Server.

6. Restart the Docker daemon:

    ```
    $ sudo systemctl restart docker
    ```

7. Close the session:

    ```
    $ exit
    ```

SSH into the Raspberry Pi 4 again.

To pull the latest gattd container image from GHCR:

```
frank@raspberrypi:~$ docker pull ghcr.io/fvasquez/gattd:latest
latest: Pulling from fvasquez/gattd
820619057a1c: Pull complete
84a50057c1f4: Pull complete
b6caffbfe56a: Pull complete
4f4fb700ef54: Pull complete
Digest:
sha256:85ad5878bda3a390fe33d7474d88c2e921f51a7df314351be9d2e00a4c3ba8f1
Status: Downloaded newer image for ghcr.io/fvasquez/gattd:latest
ghcr.io/fvasquez/gattd:latest
```

To run the latest gattd container image:

```
frank@raspberrypi:~$ docker run --net=host --privileged -t ghcr.io/
fvasquez/gattd:latest
 * Starting system message bus dbus
[ OK ]
 * Starting bluetooth
[ OK ]
Waiting for services to start... done! (in 2 s)
/app/gatt_server_example.py:25: PyGIDeprecationWarning: GObject.MainLoop
is deprecated; use GLib.MainLoop instead
  mainloop = GObject.MainLoop()
checking adapter /org/bluez, keys: dict_keys([dbus.String('org.
freedesktop.DBus.Introspectable'), dbus.String('org.bluez.AgentManager1'),
dbus.String('org.bluez.ProfileManager1'), dbus.String('org.bluez.
HealthManager1')])
checking adapter /org/bluez/hci0, keys: dict_keys([dbus.String('org.
freedesktop.DBus.Introspectable'), dbus.String('org.bluez.Adapter1'),
dbus.String('org.freedesktop.DBus.Properties'), dbus.String('org.bluez.
BatteryProviderManager1'), dbus.String('org.bluez.GattManager1'), dbus.
String('org.bluez.Media1'), dbus.String('org.bluez.NetworkServer1'), dbus.
String('org.bluez.LEAdvertisingManager1')])
found adapter /org/bluez/hci0
returning adapter /org/bluez/hci0
adapter: /org/bluez/hci0
checking adapter /org/bluez, keys: dict_keys([dbus.String('org.
freedesktop.DBus.Introspectable'), dbus.String('org.bluez.AgentManager1'),
dbus.String('org.bluez.ProfileManager1'), dbus.String('org.bluez.
HealthManager1')])
checking adapter /org/bluez/hci0, keys: dict_keys([dbus.String('org.
freedesktop.DBus.Introspectable'), dbus.String('org.bluez.Adapter1'),
dbus.String('org.freedesktop.DBus.Properties'), dbus.String('org.bluez.
BatteryProviderManager1'), dbus.String('org.bluez.GattManager1'), dbus.
String('org.bluez.Media1'), dbus.String('org.bluez.NetworkServer1'), dbus.
String('org.bluez.LEAdvertisingManager1')])
found adapter /org/bluez/hci0
returning adapter /org/bluez/hci0
Registering GATT application...
GetManagedObjects
GetAll
```

```
returning props
GATT application registered
Advertisement registered
Battery level: 98
Battery level: 96
Battery level: 94
Battery level: 92
Battery level: 90
Battery level: 88
```

Here is the entrypoint.sh script that executes when the gattd container image is run:

```bash
#!/bin/bash

# Start services
systemctl start dbus
systemctl start bluetooth

# Wait for services to start
msg="Waiting for services to start..."
time=0
echo -n $msg
while [[ "$(pidof start-stop-daemon)" != "" ]]; do
    sleep 1
    time=$((time + 1))
    echo -en "\r$msg $time s"
done
echo -e "\r$msg done! (in $time s)"

# Reset Bluetooth adapter by restarting it
hciconfig hci0 down
hciconfig hci0 up

# Start application
python3 /app/gatt_server_example.py
```

This entrypoint.sh file comes from a Medium blog post that Thomas Huffert wrote on how to run containerized Bluetooth applications with BlueZ. A link to his original post is included in the *Further study* section at the end of the chapter.

Adding Docker to a Yocto image

We don't need to install Ubuntu on a Raspberry Pi 4 to take advantage of Docker. Buildroot and Yocto are both able to build Docker for embedded targets. Adding Docker to a Yocto image is straightforward. Simply append the package to an existing image. We will leverage the rpi-test-image from the *Building on top of an existing BSP* section of *Chapter 7*.

Adding the meta-virtualization layer

Yocto's meta-virtualization layer contains recipes to enable support for cloud tooling. Over time, the project's emphasis has moved away from virtualization technologies like Xen, KVM, and libvirt to more popular containerization tools. Bruce Ashfield has led the maintenance of meta-virtualization for more than a decade, working tirelessly to stay abreast of the latest innovations in cloud computing.

There are so many competing containerization tools to choose from, it's hard to know where to start. The meta-virtualization layer is agnostic with respect to the choice of container runtime in that Docker, Podman, containerd, and Kubernetes are all fully supported. I made the conscious decision to focus on Docker because it remains the most popular tool for deploying container images.

The following exercises assume you have already completed the *Building an existing BSP* exercise from *Chapter 7* and the directory where poky was cloned is in your home directory.

To add the meta-virtualization layer:

1. First, navigate one level above the directory where you cloned poky:

    ```
    $ cd ~
    ```

2. Next, set up your BitBake work environment:

    ```
    $ source poky/oe-init-build-env build-rpi
    ```

3. This sets up a bunch of environment variables and puts you back in the build-rpi directory where you previously built rpi-test-image.

4. Then, add the meta-virtualization layer to your image:

    ```
    $ bitbake-layers layerindex-fetch --branch scarthgap --fetchdir ~
    meta-virtualization
    ```

5. This command will clone the `meta-virtualization` layer and all its dependency layers into your home directory.

6. Verify that all the necessary layers have been added to the image:

```
$ bitbake-layers show-layers
```

7. The output of the command should look like this:

```
layer                 path                                                priority

==================================================================================
core                  /home/frank/poky/meta                               5
yocto                 /home/frank/poky/meta-poky                          5
yoctobsp              /home/frank/poky/meta-yocto-bsp                     5
openembedded-layer    /home/frank/meta-openembedded/meta-oe              5
meta-python           /home/frank/meta-openembedded/meta-python          5
networking-layer      /home/frank/meta-openembedded/meta-networking      5
multimedia-layer      /home/frank/meta-openembedded/meta-multimedia      5
raspberrypi           /home/frank/meta-raspberrypi                        9
filesystems-layer     /home/frank/meta-openembedded/meta-filesystems     5
selinux               /home/frank/meta-selinux                            5
webserver             /home/frank/meta-openembedded/meta-webserver       5
virtualization-layer  /home/frank/meta-virtualization                    8
```

If your output is missing layers from `meta-raspberrypi` upwards, then return to *Chapter 7* and repeat the *Building an existing BSP* exercise before reattempting to add the `meta-virtualization` layer.

Installing Docker

The `meta-virtualization` layer contains the recipes needed to build and install Docker. Once the layer has been added, we can then append the `docker` package to a Yocto image. There are several ways to achieve this goal, including creating a custom image recipe or distro layer. I chose to piggyback on top of `rpi-test-image` and modify the `conf/local.conf` file in the `build-rpi` directory. I did this solely for expediency. Changing `conf/local.conf` is not maintainable.

The Docker daemon relies on SSL certificates to verify the authenticity of image registries. SSL certificates have set lifespans, so some measure of accurate time is needed. Most computers update their system clocks on startup according to time received from the internet via **Network Time Protocol (NTP)**. So, not only do you need to install Docker on your target, but you also need some way to synchronize the system clock before you can pull a container image.

To install Docker on `rpi-test-image`:

1. Add the following line to your `conf/local.conf` file:

```
IMAGE_INSTALL:append = " ntp-utils docker"
```

2. Add the following lines to your `conf/local.conf` file:

```
EXTRA_USERS_PARAMS = "\
    groupadd -r docker; \
    usermod -a -G docker root; \
"
```

3. Build the image:

```
$ bitbake rpi-test-image
```

4. *Step 2* creates a group named `docker` and adds the `root` user to that group. This allows us to run Docker commands when we log in as `root`. The `rpi-test-image` permits `root` logins via SSH. There is no password required. This image is for demonstration only.

Once the image has finished building, there should be a file named `rpi-test-image-raspberrypi4-64.rootfs.wic.bz2` in the `tmp/deploy/images/raspberrypi4-64` directory. Write that image to a microSD card using Etcher and boot it on your Raspberry Pi 4:

1. Insert a microSD card into your host machine.
2. Launch Etcher.
3. Click **Flash from file** from Etcher.
4. Locate the `wic.bz2` image that you built for the Raspberry Pi 4 and open it.
5. Click **Select target** from Etcher.
6. Select the microSD card that you inserted in *step 1*.
7. Click **Flash** from Etcher to write the image.
8. Eject the microSD card when Etcher is done flashing.
9. Insert the microSD card into your Raspberry Pi 4.
10. Apply power to the Raspberry Pi 4 by way of its USB-C port.

Confirm that your Pi 4 booted successfully by plugging it into your Ethernet and observing that the network activity lights blink.

Verifying the Docker daemon is running

In the previous exercise, we built a bootable image for the Raspberry Pi 4 that includes Docker. Now that the device has booted and connected to your local network via Ethernet, let's verify the Docker daemon is running. Follow these steps:

1. The image we built has a hostname of `raspberrypi4-64`, so you should be able to SSH into the device as `root`:

```
$ ssh root@raspberrypi4-64.local
```

2. Enter yes when asked if you want to continue connecting. You will not be prompted for a password. If no host is found at `raspberrypi4-64.local`, use a tool such as `arp-scan` to locate the IP address of your Raspberry Pi 4 and SSH into that instead of doing so by hostname.

3. To list information about the version of Docker that is running:

```
# docker info
Client:
 Version:    25.0.3
 Context:    default
 Debug Mode: false
<...>
WARNING: No memory limit support
WARNING: No swap limit support
WARNING: No kernel memory TCP limit support
WARNING: No oom kill disable support
```

4. To update the system clock:

```
# ntpdate pool.ntp.org
14 Jan 04:22:49 ntpdate[783]: step time server 45.33.53.84 offset
+216229384.417735 sec
```

5. To pull and run a `hello-world` container image:

```
# docker run hello-world
Unable to find image 'hello-world:latest' locally
latest: Pulling from library/hello-world
```

```
478afc919002: Pull complete
Digest:
sha256:5b3cc85e16e3058003c13b7821318369dad01dac3dbb877aac3c28182255c724
Status: Downloaded newer image for hello-world:latest

Hello from Docker!
This message shows that your installation appears to be working
correctly.
```

Most modern Linux distributions rely on systemd-timesyncd to update the system clock automatically. This eliminates the need to install and run ntp-utils. Yocto's Poky reference distro defaults to SysVinit as its init system. To take advantage of systemd-timesyncd, we need to switch from SysVinit to systemd for startup. If you want to use systemd with Poky, then select "poky-altcfg" as your distro in conf/local.conf.

There are more reasons to switch from SysVinit to systemd than just time synchronization. Since it was designed for process supervision, systemd is well-suited to monitoring microservices. A microservice is typically deployed as a container. It makes sense to use systemd together with Docker to start, stop, and restart containers on a Linux system. Alternatively, you can also use Docker Compose to run multi-container applications, but that requires adding another tool to your Yocto image.

Updating software with Docker

Balena uses Docker containers to deploy software updates. Devices run balenaOS, a Yocto-based Linux distribution that comes with balenaEngine, balena's Docker-compatible container engine. OTA updates occur automatically by way of releases pushed from balenaCloud, a hosted service for managing fleets of devices. Balena can also operate in **local mode** so that updates originate from a server running on your local host machine rather than the cloud. We will stick to local mode for the following exercises.

Balena is written and supported by balena.io (https://balena.io). Like Mender, balenaCloud is a paid OTA update service. Your first ten devices are free, but you must adopt a monthly or yearly billing plan for anything beyond that. There is much more information about the software in the **Reference** section of the online docs at balena.io. We won't dig into how balena works since our goal is to deploy and automatically update software on a small fleet of devices for fast development.

Balena provides prebuilt balenaOS images for popular dev boards such as the Raspberry Pi 4 and BeaglePlay. Downloading these images requires a balenaCloud account.

Creating an account

The first thing you need to do even if you only intend to operate in local mode is to sign up for a balenaCloud account. You do this by visiting https://dashboard.balenacloud.com/signup and entering your email address and a password, as shown:

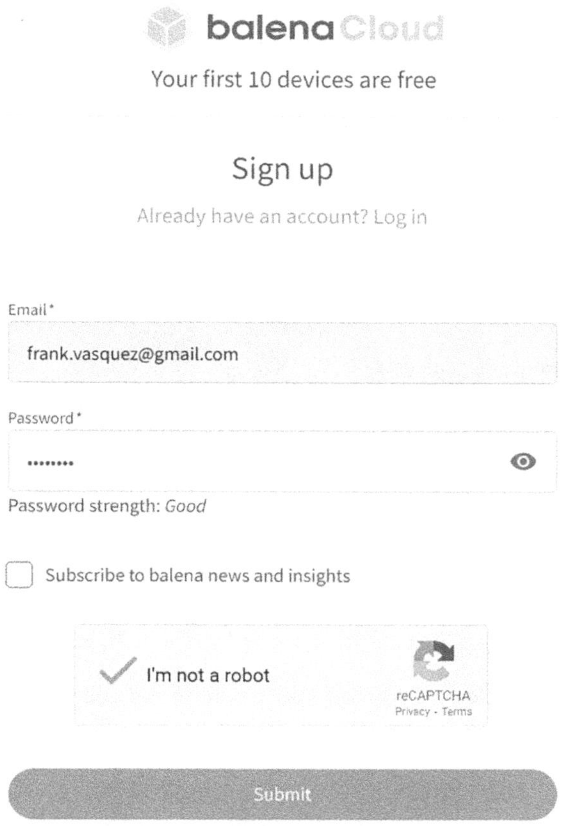

Figure 16.4 – balenaCloud signup

Click the **Submit** button to submit the form and once it is done processing, you will be prompted to enter your profile details. You may choose to skip this form, at which point you will enter the **balenaCloud** dashboard under your new account.

If you sign out or your session expires, you can log back in to the dashboard by navigating to https://dashboard.balena-cloud.com/login and entering the email address and password you signed up with.

Creating an application

Before we can add a Raspberry Pi 4 to a balenaCloud account, we first need to create a fleet.

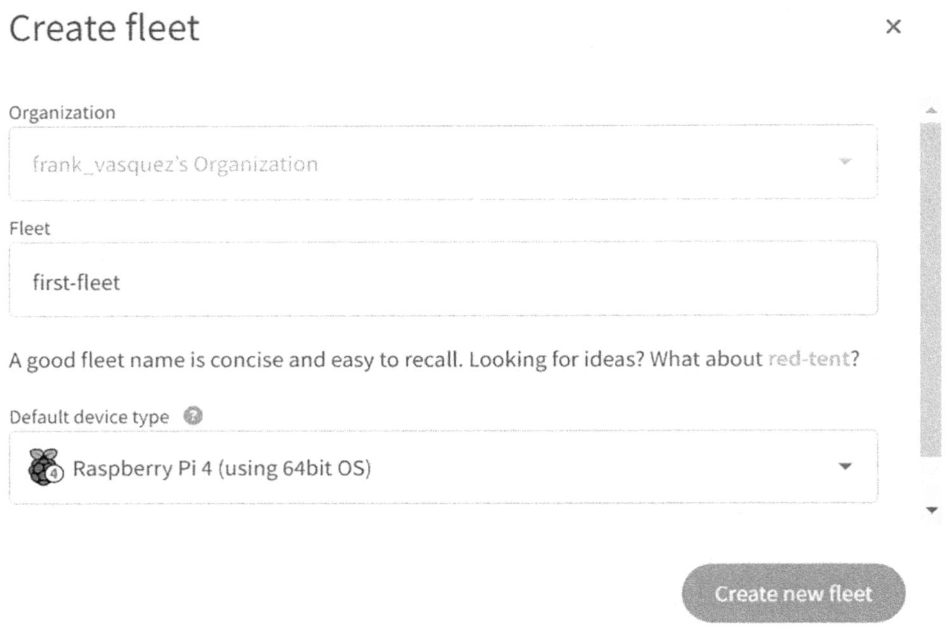

Create fleet   ×

Organization

frank_vasquez's Organization   ▾

Fleet

first-fleet

A good fleet name is concise and easy to recall. Looking for ideas? What about red-tent?

Default device type ❓

🍓 Raspberry Pi 4 (using 64bit OS)   ▾

Create new fleet

Figure 16.5 – Create fleet

Here are the steps for creating a fleet for the Raspberry Pi 4 on balenaCloud:

1. Log in to the **balenaCloud** dashboard with your email address and password.
2. Click on the **Create fleet** button in the upper-left corner, next to **Fleets**, to open the **Create fleet** dialog.
3. Enter a name for your new fleet and select **Raspberry Pi 4 (using 64bit OS)** for **Default device type**.
4. Click on the **Create new fleet** button in the **Create fleet** dialog to submit the form.

Your new fleet should appear in the **balenaCloud** dashboard on the **Fleets** page.

Adding a device

Now that we have a fleet on balenaCloud, let's add a Raspberry Pi 4 to it:

1. Log in to the **balenaCloud** dashboard with your email address and password.
2. Click on the new fleet we created.

3. Click on the **Add device** button from the fleet **Summary** page.

4. Clicking on the button will bring up the **Add new device** dialog.

5. Ensure that **Raspberry Pi 4 (using 64bit OS)** is the selected device type. That option should already be selected since you created the application with **Raspberry Pi 4 (using 64bit OS)** as the default device type.

6. Ensure that **balenaOS** is the selected OS.

7. Ensure that the selected version of balenaOS is the latest. That option should already be selected since **Add new device** defaults to the latest available version of balenaOS, which it designates as **RECOMMENDED**.

8. Select **Development** as the edition of balenaOS. A development image is required to enable local mode for better testing and troubleshooting.

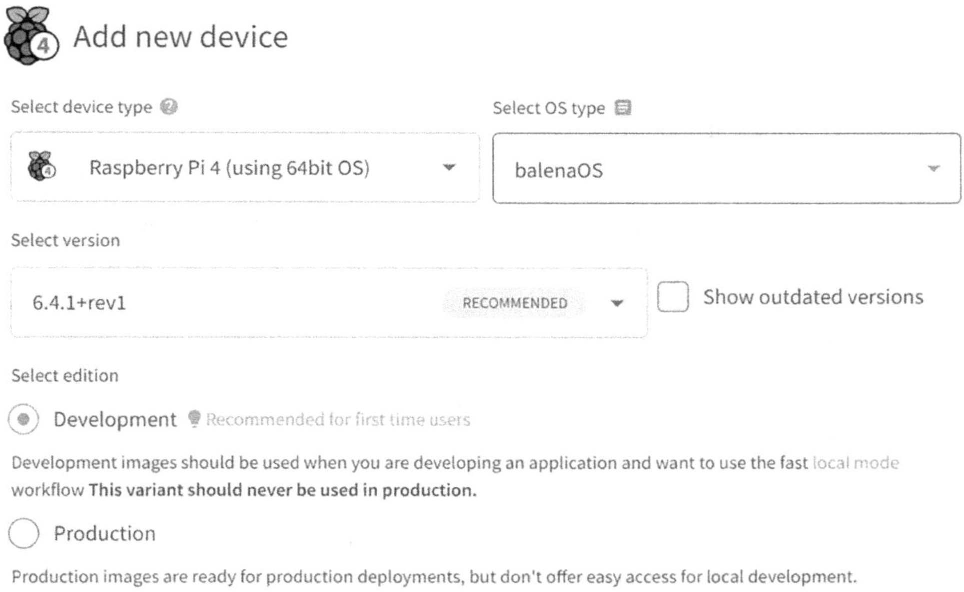

Figure 16.6 – Add new device

9. Select **Wifi + Ethernet** for **Network**. You could choose **Ethernet only** but auto-connecting to Wi-Fi is a very convenient feature.

10. Enter your Wi-Fi router's SSID and passphrase in their respective fields. Replace **ATTCX-R2Xjn** in the following screenshot with your Wi-Fi router's SSID:

Network

○ Ethernet only

◉ Wifi + Ethernet

WiFi SSID

ATTCXR2Xjn

Wifi Passphrase

••••••••••••

Figure 16.7 – Wifi + Ethernet

11. Click the down arrow on the **Flash** button.

12. Save the zipped image file to your host machine.

We now have a microSD card image we can use to provision any number of Raspberry Pi 4s for your test fleet.

The steps for provisioning a Raspberry Pi 4 from your host machine should be familiar by now. Locate the balenaOS img.zip file that you downloaded from balenaCloud and use Etcher to write it to a microSD card. Insert the microSD card into your Raspberry Pi 4 and power it up by way of the USB-C port.

It will take a minute or two for the Raspberry Pi 4 to appear on the **Devices** page of your balenaCloud dashboard:

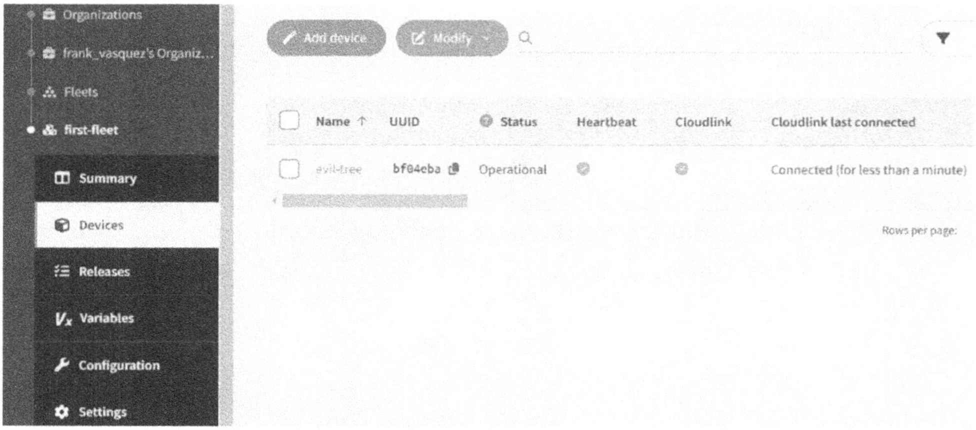

Figure 16.8 – Devices

Now that we have connected a Raspberry Pi 4 to a balena application, we need to enable local mode so that we can deploy OTA updates to it from a nearby host machine rather than the cloud:

1. Click on your target Raspberry Pi 4 from the **Devices** page of your balenaCloud dashboard. My device is named **evil-tree**. Yours will have a different name.
2. Click on **Settings** for your Raspberry Pi 4.
3. Enable **Local mode** from the **Settings** page:

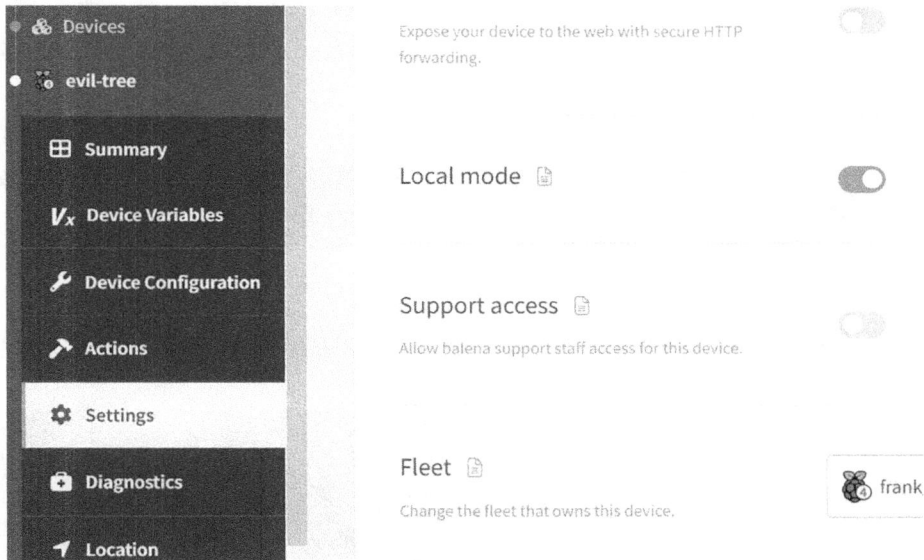

Figure 16.9 – Enable local mode

Once local mode is enabled, the **Logs** panel is no longer available on the device **Summary** page.

With local mode now enabled on our target device, we are almost ready to deploy some code to it. Before we can do that, we need to install the balena CLI.

Installing the CLI

Here are the instructions for installing the balena CLI on a Linux host machine:

1. Open a web browser and navigate to the latest balena CLI release page at `https://github.com/balena-io/balena-cli/releases/latest`.
2. Click on the latest ZIP file for Linux to download it. Look for a filename of the form `balena-cli-vX.Y.Z-linux-x64-standalone.zip`, substituting major, minor, and patch version numbers for X, Y, and Z.

3. Extract the ZIP file contents to your home directory:

```
$ cd ~
$ unzip Downloads/balena-cli-v20.2.9-linux-x64-standalone.zip
```

4. The extracted contents are enclosed in a `balena-cli` directory.

5. Add the `balena-cli` directory to your `PATH` environment variable:

```
$ export PATH=$PATH:~/balena-cli
```

6. Add a line like this to the `.bashrc` file in your home directory if you want these changes to your `PATH` variable to persist.

7. Verify that the installation was successful:

```
$ balena version
20.2.9
```

8. The latest version of the balena CLI at the time of writing was 20.2.9.

Now that we have a working balena CLI, let's scan the local network for the Raspberry Pi 4 we provisioned:

```
$ sudo env "PATH=$PATH" balena device detect
Scanning for local balenaOS devices... Reporting scan results
-
  host:          bf04eba.local
  address:       192.168.1.183
  osVariant:     development
  dockerInfo:
    Containers:        1
    ContainersRunning: 1
    ContainersPaused:  0
    ContainersStopped: 0
    Images:            1
    Driver:            overlay2
    SystemTime:        2025-03-06T05:10:40.708637573Z
    KernelVersion:     6.1.77-v8
    OperatingSystem:   balenaOS 6.4.1+rev1
    Architecture:      aarch64
```

```
dockerVersion:
    Version:    v20.10.43
    ApiVersion: 1.41
```

Notice the hostname of bf04eba.local and the IP address of 192.168.1.83 in the scan output. The hostname and IP address of your Raspberry Pi 4 will vary. Record these two pieces of information because we will need them for the remaining exercises.

Pushing a project

Let's push a Python project to the Raspberry Pi over the local network:

1. Clone a project for a simple "Hello World!" Python web server:

    ```
    $ git clone https://github.com/balena-io-examples/balena-python-
    hello-world.git
    ```

2. Navigate into the project directory:

    ```
    $ cd balena-python-hello-world
    ```

3. Push the code to your Raspberry Pi 4:

    ```
    $ balena push 192.168.1.183
    ```

4. Substitute your device's IP address for the 192.168.1.183 argument.

5. Wait for the Docker image to finish building and starting and let the application run in the foreground so that it logs to stdout.

6. Issue a request to the web server at http://192.168.1.183 from a web browser. Substitute your device's IP address for 192.168.1.183.

The web server running on the Raspberry Pi 4 should display a splash page with **Welcome to balena** and a line like the following should appear in the live output from balena push:

```
[Logs]    [2025-03-06T05:16:46.546Z] [balena-hello-world] 192.168.1.177 -
- [06/Mar/2025 05:16:46] "GET / HTTP/1.1" 200 -
```

The IP address in the log entry should be that of the machine from which you issued the web request. A new log entry should appear every time you refresh the web page. To stop tailing the logs and return to the shell, enter *Ctrl + C*. The container will continue running on the target device and the web server will continue to service requests.

We can restart tailing the logs at any time by issuing the following command:

```
$ balena device logs 192.168.1.183
```

Substitute your device's IP address for the `192.168.1.183` argument.

The HTML for this simple web server can be found in a file named `index.html` within the project directory:

```
tree
.

├── balena.yml
├── CHANGELOG.md
├── docker-compose.yml
├── Dockerfile.template
├── license.md
├── logo.png
├── README.md
├── repo.yml
├── requirements.txt
├── src
│   └── app.py
├── VERSION
└── views
    ├── index.html
    └── public
        ├── bootstrap.min.css
        ├── confetti.js
        ├── favicon.ico
        ├── logo.svg
        └── main.css
```

Now let's make a slight modification to the project source code and redeploy:

1. Open `views/index.html` in your favorite editor.
2. Replace `Welcome to balena!` with `Welcome to banana!` and save your changes.

3. The following `git diff` output captures the changes:

```
$ git diff

diff --git a/views/index.html b/views/index.html
index c5fcddd..7796f5a 100644
--- a/views/index.html
+++ b/views/index.html
@@ -26,7 +26,7 @@
      <div class="container mt-5 mb-5 p-0 pb-5">

        <div class="row d-flex flex-column align-items-center">
-          <h1>Welcome to balena!</h1>
+          <h1>Welcome to banana!</h1>
          <p class="text-center pl-5 pr-5 pt-0 pb-0">Now that you've
deployed code to your device,<br /> explore the resources below to
continue on your journey!</p>
        </div>
```

4. Push the new code to your Raspberry Pi 4:

```
$ balena push 192.168.1.183
```

5. Substitute your device's IP address for the 192.168.1.183 argument.

6. Wait for the Docker image to update. The process should be much quicker this time around because of an intelligent caching feature called **Livepush** that is unique to local mode.

7. Issue a request to the web server at http://192.168.1.183 from a web browser. Substitute your device's IP address for 192.168.1.183.

The web server running on the Raspberry Pi 4 should display **Welcome to banana!**

We can SSH into a local target device by IP address:

```
$ balena device ssh 192.168.1.183

Last login: Thu Mar  6 05:59:21 2025 from 192.168.1.124
root@bf04eba:~#
```

Substitute your device's IP address for 192.168.1.183. This is not especially useful because the application is running inside a Docker container.

To SSH into the container where the Python web server is running and observe what it's doing, we need to include the service name in the `balena ssh` command:

```
$ balena device ssh 192.168.1.183 balena-hello-world
root@6a4ef89e6f10:/usr/src/app# ls
CHANGELOG.md          VERSION              logo.png              views
Dockerfile            balena.yml           repo.yml
Dockerfile.template   docker-compose.yml   requirements.txt
README.md             license.md           src
```

The service name for this starter application is `balena-hello-world` as seen in the live logs output.

Congratulations! You have successfully created a balenaOS image and host development environment that you and your team can use to iterate on project code and quickly redeploy to a target device. This is no small feat. Pushing code changes in the form of a Docker container is a common development workflow that full-stack engineers are very accustomed to. With balena, they can now use the techniques they are familiar with to develop embedded Linux applications on actual hardware.

Summary

We accomplished a lot in this chapter. You now know how to create Dockerfiles and YAML workflows for your software projects. CI/CD pipelines use this infrastructure as code to automatically build and push containerized software updates out to edge devices. You also leveraged containers to develop locally on real hardware before pushing your changes out to the rest of the world. Modern DevOps practices like these enable software teams to move faster without breaking things.

In the next chapter, we will look in detail at the Linux process model and describe what a process really is, how it relates to threads, how they cooperate, and how they are scheduled. Understanding these things is important if you want to create a robust and maintainable embedded system.

Further study

- *The DevOps Handbook, Second Edition,* by Gene Kim, Jez Humble, Patrick Debois, and John Willis
- *Docker Docs,* Docker Inc. – https://docs.docker.com/reference/cli/docker/
- *How to run containerized Bluetooth applications with BlueZ,* by Thomas Huffert – https://medium.com/omi-uulm/how-to-run-containerized-bluetooth-applications-with-bluez-dced9ab767f6

17

Learning about Processes and Threads

In the preceding chapters, we considered the various aspects of creating an embedded Linux platform. Now, it is time to start looking at how you can use the platform to create a working device. In this chapter, I will talk about the implications of the Linux process model and how it encompasses multithreaded programs. I will look at the pros and cons of using single-threaded and multithreaded processes, as well as asynchronous message passing between processes and coroutines. Lastly, I will look at scheduling and differentiate between timeshare and real-time scheduling policies.

While these topics are not specific to embedded computing, it is important for a designer of any embedded device to have an overview of these topics. There are many good references on the subject, some of which I will list at the end of this chapter, but in general, they do not consider the embedded use cases. Due to this, I will be concentrating on the concepts and design decisions rather than on the function calls and code.

In this chapter, we will cover the following topics:

- Process or thread?
- Processes
- Threads
- ZeroMQ
- Scheduling

Technical requirements

To follow along with the examples, make sure you have the following:

- Python: Python 3 interpreter and standard library
- Miniconda: Minimal installer for the conda package and virtual environment manager

See the section on conda in *Chapter 15* for directions on how to install Miniconda if you haven't already. The GCC C compiler and GNU Make are also needed for this chapter's exercises, but these tools already come with most Linux distributions.

The code used in this chapter can be found in the Chapter17 folder in this book's GitHub repository: https://github.com/PacktPublishing/Mastering-Embedded-Linux-Development/tree/main/Chapter17.

Process or thread?

Many embedded developers who are familiar with **real-time operating systems (RTOSs)** consider the Unix process model to be cumbersome. On the other hand, they see a similarity between an RTOS task and a Linux thread, and they have a tendency to transfer an existing design using a one-to-one mapping of RTOS tasks to threads. I have, on several occasions, seen designs in which the entire application is implemented with one process containing 40 or more threads. I want to spend some time considering whether this is a good idea or not. Let's begin with some definitions.

A **process** is a memory address space and a thread of execution, as shown in the following diagram. The address space is private to the process, so threads running in different processes cannot access it. This **memory separation** is created by the memory management subsystem in the kernel, which keeps a memory page mapping for each process and reprograms the memory management unit on each context switch. I will describe how this works in detail in *Chapter 18*. Part of the address space is mapped to a file that contains the code and static data that the program is running, as shown here:

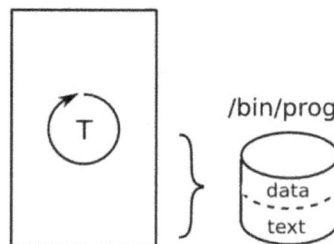

Figure 17.1 – Process

As the program runs, it will allocate resources such as stack space, heap memory, references to files, and so on. When the process terminates, these resources are reclaimed by the system: all the memory is freed up and all the file descriptors are closed.

Processes can communicate with each other using **inter-process communication (IPC)**, such as local sockets. I will talk about IPC later on.

A **thread** is a thread of execution within a process. All processes begin with one thread that runs the main() function and is called the main thread. You can create additional threads, for example, using the pthread_create(3) POSIX function, which results in multiple threads executing in the same address space, as shown in the following diagram:

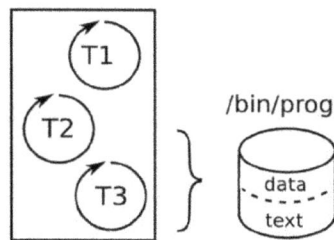

Figure 17.2 – Multiple threads

Being in the same process, the threads share resources with each other. They can read and write the same memory and use the same file descriptors. Communication between threads is easy, as long as you take care of the synchronization and locking issues.

So, based on these brief details, you can imagine two extreme designs for a hypothetical system with 40 RTOS tasks being ported to Linux.

You could map tasks to processes and have 40 individual programs communicating through IPC, for example, with messages being sent through sockets. You would greatly reduce memory corruption problems since the main thread running in each process is protected from the others, and you would reduce resource leakage since each process is cleaned up after it exits. However, the message interface between processes is quite complex and, where there is tight cooperation between a group of processes, the number of messages might be large and become a limiting factor regarding the performance of the system. Furthermore, any one of those 40 processes may terminate, perhaps because of a bug causing it to crash, leaving the other 39 to carry on. Each process would have to handle the fact that its neighbors are no longer running and recover gracefully.

At the other extreme, you could map tasks to threads and implement the system as a single process containing 40 threads. Cooperation becomes much easier because they share the same address space and file descriptors. The overhead of sending messages is reduced or eliminated, and context switches between threads are faster than between processes. The downside is that you have introduced the possibility of one task corrupting the heap or the stack of another. If any of the threads encounters a fatal bug, the whole process will terminate, taking all the threads with it. Finally, debugging a complex multithreaded process can be a nightmare.

The conclusion you should draw is that neither design is ideal and that there is a better way to do things. But before we get to that point, I will delve a little more deeply into the APIs and the behavior of processes and threads.

Processes

A process holds the environment in which threads can run: it holds the memory mappings, the file descriptors, the user and group IDs, and more. The first process is the init process, which is created by the kernel during boot and has a PID of 1. Thereafter, processes are created by duplication in an operation known as **forking**.

Creating a new process

The POSIX function to create a process is fork(2). It is an odd function because, for each successful call, there are two returns: one in the process that made the call, known as the **parent**, and one in the newly created process, known as the **child**, as shown in the following diagram:

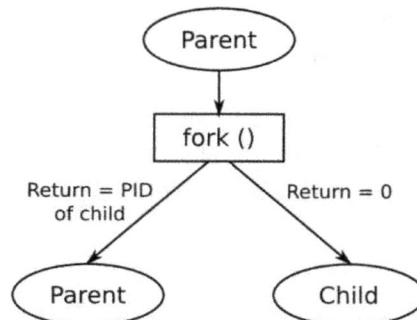

Figure 17.3 – Forking

Immediately after the call, the child is an exact copy of the parent: it has the same stack, the same heap, and the same file descriptors, and it executes the same line of code – the one following fork.

The only way the programmer can tell them apart is by looking at the return value of fork: it is *zero* for the child and *greater than zero* for the parent. Actually, the value that's returned to the parent is the PID of the newly created child process. There is a third possibility, which is that the return value is negative, which means that the fork call failed and there is still only one process.

Although the two processes are mostly identical, they are in separate address spaces. Changes that are made to a variable by one will not be seen by the other. Under the hood, the kernel does not make a physical copy of the parent's memory, which would be quite a slow operation and consume memory unnecessarily. Instead, the memory is shared but marked with a **copy-on-write** (**CoW**) flag. If either parent or child modifies this memory, the kernel makes a copy and then writes to the copy. This makes it an efficient fork function that also retains the logical separation of process address spaces. I will discuss CoW in *Chapter 18*.

Terminating a process

A process may be stopped voluntarily by calling the exit(3) function or, involuntarily, by receiving a signal that is not handled. One signal in particular, SIGKILL, cannot be handled, so it will always kill a process. In all cases, terminating the process will stop all threads, close all file descriptors, and release all memory. The system sends a signal, SIGCHLD, to the parent so that it knows this has happened.

Processes have a return value that is composed of either the argument to exit, if it terminated normally, or the signal number if it was killed. The chief use for this is in shell scripts: it allows you to test the return value from a program. By convention, 0 indicates success and any other values indicate a failure of some sort.

The parent can collect the return value with the wait(2) or waitpid(2) function. This causes a problem: there will be a delay between a child terminating and its parent collecting the return value. In that period, the return value must be stored somewhere, and the PID number of the now-dead process cannot be reused. A process in this state is known as a **zombie**, which is displayed as state Z in the ps and top commands. As long as the parent calls wait or waitpid whenever it is notified of a child's termination (by means of the SIGCHLD signal; refer to *Linux System Programming*, by Robert Love and O'Reilly Media, or *The Linux Programming Interface*, by Michael Kerrisk, No Starch Press, for details on handling signals). Usually, zombies exist for too short a time to show up in process listings. They will become a problem if the parent fails to collect the return value because, eventually, there will not be enough resources to create any more processes.

The program in MELD/Chapter17/fork-demo illustrates process creation and termination:

```c
#include <stdio.h>
#include <stdlib.h>
#include <unistd.h>
#include <sys/types.h>
#include <sys/wait.h>

int main(void)
{
    int pid;
    int status;

    pid = fork();

    if (pid == 0) {
        printf("I am the child, PID %d\n", getpid());
        sleep(10);
        exit(42);
    } else if (pid > 0) {
        printf("I am the parent, PID %d\n", getpid());
        wait(&status);
        printf("Child terminated, status %d\n", WEXITSTATUS(status));
    } else {
        perror("fork:");
    }

    return 0;
}
```

The wait function blocks until a child process exits and stores the exit status. When you run it, you will see something like this:

```
I am the parent, PID 13851
I am the child, PID 13852
Child terminated with status 42
```

The child process inherits most of the attributes of the parent, including the user and group IDs, all open file descriptors, signal handling, and scheduling characteristics.

Running a different program

The fork function creates a copy of a running program, but it does not run a different program. For that, you need one of the exec functions:

```
int execl(const char *path, const char *arg, ...);
int execlp(const char *file, const char *arg, ...);
int execle(const char *path, const char *arg, ..., char * const envp[]);
int execv(const char *path, char *const argv[]);
int execvp(const char *file, char *const argv[]);
int execvpe(const char *file, char *const argv[], ..., char *const
envp[]);
```

Each takes a path to the program file to load and run. If the function succeeds, the kernel discards all the resources of the current process, including memory and file descriptors, and allocates memory to the new program being loaded. When the thread that called exec* returns, it returns not to the line of code after the call but to the main() function of the new program. There is an example of a command launcher in MELD/Chapter17/exec-demo: it prompts for a command, such as /bin/ls, and forks and executes the string you enter. Here is the code:

```c
#include <stdio.h>
#include <stdlib.h>
#include <string.h>
#include <unistd.h>
#include <sys/types.h>
#include <sys/wait.h>

int main(int argc, char *argv[])
{
    char command_str[128];
    int pid;
    int child_status;
    int wait_for = 1;

    while (1) {
        printf("sh> ");
        scanf("%s", command_str);
        pid = fork();
        if (pid == 0) {
```

```
                /* child */
                printf("cmd '%s'\n", command_str);
                execl(command_str, command_str, (char *)NULL);
                /* We should not return from execl, so only get
                   to this line if it failed */
                perror("exec");
                exit(1);
        }
        if (wait_for) {
                waitpid(pid, &child_status, 0);
                printf("Done, status %d\n", child_status);
        }
    }

    return 0;
}
```

This is what you will see when you run it:

```
# ./exec-demo
sh> /bin/ls
cmd '/bin/ls'
bin etc lost+found proc sys var
boot home media run tmp
dev lib mnt sbin usr
Done, status 0
sh>
```

You can terminate the program by typing *Ctrl + C*.

It might seem odd to have one function that duplicates an existing process and another that discards its resources and loads a different program into memory, especially since it is common for a fork to be followed almost immediately by one of the exec functions. Most operating systems combine the two actions into a single call.

There are distinct advantages to this, however. For example, it makes it very easy to implement redirection and pipes in the shell. Imagine that you want to get a directory listing. This is the sequence of events:

1. You type ls in the shell prompt.

2. The shell forks a child copy of itself.

3. The shell waits for the child process to finish.

4. The child execs /bin/ls.

5. The ls program prints the directory listing to stdout (file descriptor 1), which is attached to the terminal. You will see the directory listing.

6. The ls program terminates, and the shell regains control.

Now, imagine that you want the directory listing to be written to a file by redirecting the output using the > character. Now, the sequence is as follows:

1. You type ls > listing.txt.

2. The shell forks a child copy of itself.

3. The shell waits for the child process to finish.

4. The child opens and truncates the listing.txt file and uses dup2(2) to copy the file descriptor of the file over file descriptor 1 (stdout).

5. The child execs /bin/ls.

6. The program prints the listing as it did previously, but this time, it is writing to listing.txt.

7. The ls program terminates, and the shell regains control.

> **IMPORTANT NOTE**
>
> There was an opportunity in *step 4* to modify the environment of the child process before executing the program. The ls program does not need to know that it is writing to a file rather than a terminal. Instead of a file, stdout could be connected to a pipe so that the ls program, still unchanged, can send output to another program. This is part of the Unix philosophy of combining many small components that each do a job well, as described in *The Art of Unix Programming*, by Eric Steven Raymond and Addison Wesley, especially in the *Pipes, Redirection, and Filters* section.

So far, the programs we've looked at in this section all run in the foreground. But what about programs that run in the background, waiting for things to happen? Let's take a look.

Daemons

We have encountered daemons in several places already. A **daemon** is a process that runs in the background, is owned by the init process, and is not connected to a controlling terminal. The steps to create a daemon are as follows:

1. Call fork to create a new process, after which the parent should exit, thus creating an orphan that will be re-parented to init.

2. The child process calls setsid(2), creating a new session and process group that it is the sole member of. The exact details do not matter here; you can simply consider this a way of isolating the process from any controlling terminal.

3. Change the working directory to the root directory.

4. Close all file descriptors and redirect stdin, stdout, and stderr (descriptors 0, 1, and 2) to /dev/null so that there is no input, and all output is hidden.

Thankfully, all of the preceding steps can be achieved with a single function call, daemon(3).

Inter-process communication

Each process is an island of memory. You can pass information from one to another in two ways. Firstly, you can move it from one address space to the other. Secondly, you can create an area of memory that both can access and share the data.

The first is usually combined with a queue or buffer so that there is a sequence of messages passing between processes. This implies copying the message twice: first to a holding area and then to the destination. Some examples of this are sockets, pipes, and message queues.

The second way requires not only a method of creating memory that is mapped to two (or more) address spaces at once, but it is also a means of synchronizing access to that memory, for example, using semaphores or mutexes.

POSIX has functions for all of these. There is an older set of APIs known as **System V IPC**, which provides message queues, shared memory, and semaphores, but it is not as flexible as the POSIX equivalents, so I will not describe them here. The manual page on svipc(7) gives an overview of these facilities, and there are more details in *The Linux Programming Interface*, by Michael Kerrisk, and *Unix Network Programming, Volume 2*, by W. Richard Stevens.

Message-based protocols are usually easier to program and debug than shared memory, but are slow if the messages are large or there are many of them.

Message-based IPC

There are several options for message-based IPC, all of which I will summarize as follows. The attributes that differentiate one from the other are as follows:

- Whether the message flow is uni- or bi-directorial.

- Whether the data flow is a byte stream with no message boundary or discrete messages with boundaries preserved. In the latter case, the maximum size of a message is important.

- Whether messages are tagged with a priority.

The following table summarizes these properties for FIFOs, sockets, and message queues:

Property	FIFO	Unix socket: stream	Unix socket: datagram	POSIX message queue
Message boundary	Byte stream	Byte stream	Discrete	Discrete
Uni/bi-directional	Uni	Bi	Uni	Uni
Max message size	Unlimited	Unlimited	In the range of 100 KB to 200 KB	Fefault: 8 KB absolute maximum: 1 MB
Priority levels	None	None	None	0 to 32767

Table 17.1 – Properties for FIFOs, sockets, and message queues

The first form of message-based IPC we will look at is Unix sockets.

Unix (or local) sockets

Unix sockets fulfill most requirements and, coupled with the familiarity of the sockets API, are by far the most common mechanism.

Unix sockets are created with the AF_UNIX address family and bound to a pathname. Access to the socket is determined by the access permission of the socket file. As with internet sockets, the socket type can be SOCK_STREAM or SOCK_DGRAM, the former giving a bidirectional byte stream and the latter providing discrete messages with preserved boundaries. Unix socket datagrams are reliable, which means that they will not be dropped or reordered. The maximum size for a datagram is system-dependent and is available via /proc/sys/net/core/wmem_max. It is typically 100 KB or more.

Unix sockets do not have a mechanism to indicate the priority of a message.

FIFOs and named pipes

FIFO and **named pipe** are just different terms for the same thing. They are an extension of the anonymous pipe that is used to communicate between parent and child processes when implementing pipes in the shell.

A FIFO is a special sort of file, created by the mkfifo(1) command. As with Unix sockets, the file access permissions determine who can read and write. They are unidirectional, which means that there is one reader and usually one writer, though there may be several. The data is a pure byte stream but guarantees the atomicity of messages that are smaller than the buffer associated with the pipe. In other words, writes less than this size will not be split into several smaller writes, so you will read the whole message in one go as long as the size of the buffer on your end is large enough. The default size of the FIFO buffer is 64 KB on modern kernels and can be increased using fcntl(2) with F_SETPIPE_SZ, up to the value in /proc/sys/fs/pipe-max-size, which is typically 1 MB. There is no concept of priority.

POSIX message queues

Message queues are identified by a name beginning with a forward slash and containing only one / character. Message queues are kept in a pseudo filesystem of the mqueue type. You create a queue and get a reference to an existing queue through mq_open(3), which returns a file descriptor. Each message has a priority, and messages are read from the queue based on priority and then on the age order. Messages can be up to /proc/sys/kernel/msgmax bytes long.

The default value is 8 KB, but you can set it to be any size in the range of 128 bytes to 1 MB by writing the value to /proc/sys/kernel/msgmax. Since the reference is a file descriptor, you can use select(2), poll(2), and other similar functions to wait for activity in the queue.

Refer to the Linux mq_overview(7) man page for more details.

Summary of message-based IPC

Unix sockets are used the most often because they offer all that is needed, except perhaps message priority. They are implemented on most operating systems, so they confer maximum portability.

FIFOs are less frequently used, mostly because they lack an equivalent to a **datagram**. On the other hand, the API is very simple, since it provides the normal open(2), close(2), read(2), and write(2) file calls.

Message queues are the least commonly used of this group. The code paths in the kernel are not optimized in the way that socket (network) and FIFO (filesystem) calls are.

There are also higher-level abstractions such as D-Bus, which are moving from mainstream Linux to embedded devices. D-Bus uses Unix sockets and shared memory under the surface.

Shared memory-based IPC

Sharing memory removes the need to copy data between address spaces but introduces the problem of synchronizing accesses to it. Synchronization between processes is commonly achieved using semaphores.

POSIX shared memory

To share memory between processes, you must create a new area of memory and then map it to the address space of each process that wants access to it, as shown in the following diagram:

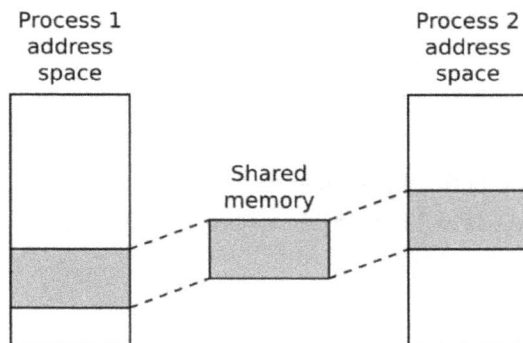

Figure 17.4 – POSIX shared memory

Naming POSIX shared memory segments follows the pattern we encountered with message queues. The segments are identified by names that begin with a / character and have exactly one such character:

```
#define SHM_SEGMENT_NAME "/demo-shm"
```

The shm_open(3) function takes the name and returns a file descriptor for it. If it does not exist already and the O_CREAT flag is set, then a new segment is created. Initially, it has a size of zero. You can use the (misleadingly named) ftruncate(2) function to expand it to the desired size:

```
int shm_fd;
struct shared_data *shm_p;
```

```
/* Attempt to create the shared memory segment */
shm_fd = shm_open(SHM_SEGMENT_NAME, O_CREAT | O_EXCL | O_RDWR, 0666);

if (shm_fd > 0) {
    /* succeeded: expand it to the desired size (Note: dont't
       do this every time because ftruncate fills it with zeros) */
    printf("Creating shared memory and setting size=%d\n",
    SHM_SEGMENT_SIZE);
    if (ftruncate(shm_fd, SHM_SEGMENT_SIZE) < 0) {
        perror("ftruncate");
        exit(1);
    }
    <...>
} else if (shm_fd == -1 && errno == EEXIST) {
    /* Already exists: open again without O_CREAT */
    Shm_fd = shm_open(SHM_SEGMENT_NAME, O_RDWR, 0);
    <...>
}
```

Once you have a descriptor for the shared memory, you map it to the address space of the process using mmap(2) so that threads in different processes can access the memory:

```
/* Map the shared memory */
shm_p = mmap(NULL, SHM_SEGMENT_SIZE, PROT_READ | PROT_WRITE, MAP_SHARED,
shm_fd, 0);
```

The program in MELD/Chapter17/shared-mem-demo provides an example of using a shared memory segment to communicate between processes. Here is the main function:

```
static sem_t *demo_sem;
<...>
int main(int argc, char *argv[])
{
    char *shm_p;

    printf("%s PID=%d\n", argv[0], getpid());
    shm_p = get_shared_memory();

    while (1) {
```

```
            printf("Press enter to see the current contents of shm\n");
            getchar();
            sem_wait(demo_sem);
            printf("%s\n", shm_p);
            /* Write our signature to the shared memory */
            sprintf(shm_p, "Hello from process %d\n", getpid());
            sem_post(demo_sem);
        }

    return 0;
}
```

The program uses a shared memory segment to communicate a message from one process to another. The message is Hello from process string, followed by its PID. The get_shared_ memory function is responsible for creating the memory segment, if it does not exist, or getting the file descriptor for it if it does. It returns a pointer to the memory segment. Notice that there is a semaphore to synchronize access to the memory so that one process does not overwrite a message from another.

To try it out, you need two instances of the program running in separate terminal sessions. In the first terminal, you will see something like this:

```
# ./shared-mem-demo
./shared-mem-demo PID=271
Creating shared memory and setting size=65536
Press enter to see the current contents of shm


Press enter to see the current contents of shm


Hello from process 271
```

Because this is the first time the program is being run, it creates the memory segment. Initially, the message area is empty, but after one run through the loop, it contains the PID of this process, which is 271. Now, you can run a second instance in another terminal:

```
# ./shared-mem-demo
./shared-mem-demo PID=279
Press enter to see the current contents of shm

Hello from process 271
```

```
Press enter to see the current contents of shm

Hello from process 279
```

It does not create the shared memory segment because it exists already, and it displays the message that it contains already, which is the PID of the other program. Pressing *Enter* causes it to write its own PID, which the first program would be able to see. By doing this, the two programs can communicate with each other.

The POSIX IPC functions are part of the POSIX real-time extensions, so you need to link them with librt. Oddly, the POSIX semaphores are implemented in the POSIX threads library, so you need to link to the pthreads library as well. Hence, the compilation arguments are as follows when you're targeting 64-bit Arm SoCs:

```
$ aarch64-buildroot-linux-gnu-gcc shared-mem-demo.c -lrt -pthread -o
shared-mem-demo
```

This concludes our survey of IPC methods. We will revisit message-based IPC when we cover ZeroMQ. Now, it is time to look at multithreaded processes.

Threads

The programming interface for threads is the POSIX threads API, which was first defined in the *IEEE POSIX 1003.1c standard (1995)* and is commonly known as **pthreads**. It is implemented as an additional part of the libpthread.so.0 C library. There have been two implementations of pthreads over the last 20 years or so: **LinuxThreads** and **Native POSIX Thread Library (NPTL)**. The latter is much more compliant with the specification, especially in regard to the handling of signals and process IDs. NPTL is dominant now. If you happen to come across any C standard library that still employs LinuxThreads, I would refrain from using it.

Creating a new thread

The function you can use to create a thread is pthread_create(3):

```
int pthread_create(pthread_t *restrict thread, const pthread_attr_t
*restrict attr, typeof(void *(void *)) *start_routine, void *restrict
arg);
```

It creates a new thread of execution that begins in the start_routine function and places a descriptor in pthread_t, which is pointed to by thread. It inherits the scheduling parameters of the calling thread, but these can be overridden by passing a pointer to the thread attributes in attr. The thread will start executing immediately.

pthread_t is the main way to refer to the thread within the program, but the thread can also be seen from outside using a command such as ps -eLf:

```
UID PID PPID LWP C NLWP STIME TTY TIME CMD
<...>
chris 6072 5648 6072 0 3 21:18 pts/0 00:00:00 ./thread-demo
chris 6072 5648 6073 0 3 21:18 pts/0 00:00:00 ./thread-demo
```

The BusyBox ps applet does not support the -eLf option so make sure to install the full procps package on embedded targets.

In the preceding output, the thread-demo program has two threads. The PID and PPID columns show that they all belong to the same process and have the same parent, as you would expect. The column marked LWP is interesting, though. **LWP** stands for **Light Weight Process**, which, in this context, is another name for a thread. The numbers in that column are also known as **Thread IDs** or **TIDs**. In the main thread, the TID is the same as the PID, but for the others, it is a different (higher) value. You can use a TID in places where the documentation states that you must give a PID, but be aware that this behavior is specific to Linux and is not portable. Here is a simple program that illustrates the life cycle of a thread (the code is in MELD/Chapter17/thread-demo):

```
#include <stdio.h>
#include <unistd.h>
#include <pthread.h>
#include <sys/syscall.h>

static void *thread_fn(void *arg)
{
    printf("New thread started, PID %d TID %d\n",
        getpid(), (pid_t)syscall(SYS_gettid));
    sleep(10);
    printf("New thread terminating\n");
    return NULL;
}
```

```
int main(int argc, char *argv[])
{
    pthread_t t;
    printf("Main thread, PID %d TID %d\n",
        getpid(), (pid_t)syscall(SYS_gettid));
    pthread_create(&t, NULL, thread_fn, NULL);
    pthread_join(t, NULL);
    return 0;
}
```

Note that, in the thread_fn function, I am retrieving the TID using syscall(SYS_gettid). Prior to glibc 2.30, you had to call Linux directly through a syscall because there was no C library wrapper for gettid().

There is a limit to the total number of threads that a given kernel can schedule. The limit scales according to the size of the system, from around 1,000 on small devices up to tens of thousands on larger embedded devices. The actual number is available in /proc/sys/kernel/threads-max. Once you reach this limit, fork and pthread_create will fail.

Terminating a thread

A thread terminates when any of the following occurs:

- It reaches the end of its start_routine.
- It calls pthread_exit(3).
- It is canceled by another thread calling pthread_cancel(3).
- The process that contains the thread terminates, for example, because of a thread calling exit(3), or the process receiving a signal that is not handled, masked, or ignored.

Note that if a multithreaded program calls fork, only the thread that made the call will exist in the new child process. Forking does not replicate all threads.

A thread has a return value, which is a void pointer. One thread can wait for another to terminate and collect its return value by calling pthread_join(2). There is an example of this in the code for thread-demo, as we mentioned in the preceding section. This produces a problem that is very similar to the zombie problem among processes: the resources of the thread, such as the stack, cannot be freed up until another thread has joined with it. If threads remain *unjoined*, there is a resource leak in the program.

Compiling a program with threads

The support for POSIX threads is part of the C library in the `libpthread.so.0` library. However, there is more to building programs with threads than linking the library: there must be changes to the way the compiler generates code to make sure that certain global variables, such as `errno`, have one instance per thread rather than one for the whole process.

> **TIP**
>
> When building a threaded program, add the `-pthread` switch. Adding `-pthread` will automatically add `-lpthread` to the linker command from the compiler driver.

Inter-thread communication

The big advantage of threads is that they share the address space and can share memory variables. This is also a big disadvantage because it requires synchronization to preserve data consistency in a manner similar to memory segments shared between processes but with the provision that, with threads, all memory is shared. In fact, threads can create private memory using **thread local storage (TLS)**, but I will not cover that here.

The `pthreads` interface provides the basics necessary to achieve synchronization: mutexes and condition variables. If you want more complex structures, you will have to build them yourself.

It is worth noting that all the IPC methods we described earlier – that is, sockets, pipes, and message queues – work equally well between threads in the same process.

Mutual exclusion

To write robust programs, you need to protect each shared resource with a mutex lock and make sure that every code path that reads or writes the resource has locked the mutex first. If you apply this rule consistently, most of the problems should be solved. The ones that remain are associated with the fundamental behavior of mutexes. I will list them briefly here but will not go into too much detail:

- **Deadlock:** This occurs when mutexes become permanently locked. A classic situation is the **deadly embrace**, in which two threads each require two mutexes and have managed to lock one of them but not the other. Each thread blocks, waiting for the lock the other has, and so they remain as they are. One simple rule for avoiding the deadly embrace problem is to make sure that mutexes are always locked in the same order. Other solutions involve timeouts and back-off periods.

- **Priority inversion**: The delays caused by waiting for a mutex can cause a real-time thread to miss deadlines. The specific case of priority inversion happens when a high-priority thread becomes blocked, waiting for a mutex locked by a low-priority thread. If the low-priority thread is preempted by other threads of intermediate priority, the high-priority thread is forced to wait for an unbounded length of time. There are mutex protocols called **priority inheritance** and **priority ceiling** that resolve the problem at the expense of greater processing overhead in the kernel for each lock and unlock call.

- **Poor performance**: Mutexes introduce minimal overhead to the code, as long as threads don't have to block on them most of the time. If your design has a resource that is needed by a lot of threads, however, the contention ratio becomes significant. This is usually a design issue that can be resolved using finer-grained locking or a different algorithm.

Mutexes are not the only way to synchronize between threads. We witnessed how two processes can use a semaphore to notify each other back when we covered POSIX shared memory. Threads have a similar construct.

Changing conditions

Cooperating threads need to be able to alert one another that something has changed and needs attention. This is called a **condition**, and the alert is sent through a **condition variable**, or **condvar**.

A condition is just something that you can test to give a true or false result. A simple example is a buffer that contains either zero or some items. One thread takes items from the buffer and sleeps when it is empty. Another thread places items into the buffer and signals to the other thread that it has done so because the condition that the other thread is waiting on has changed. If it is sleeping, it needs to wake up and do something. The only complexity is that the condition is, by definition, a shared resource, so it must be protected by a mutex.

Here is a simple program with two threads. The first is the producer: it wakes every second and puts some data into a global variable before signaling that there has been a change. The second thread is the consumer: it waits on the condition variable and tests the condition (that there is a string in the buffer of nonzero length) each time it wakes up. You can find the code in `MELD/Chapter17/condvar-demo`:

```
#include <stdio.h>
#include <stdlib.h>
#include <pthread.h>
#include <unistd.h>
#include <string.h>
```

```c
char g_data[128];
pthread_cond_t cv = PTHREAD_COND_INITIALIZER;
pthread_mutex_t mutx = PTHREAD_MUTEX_INITIALIZER;

void *consumer(void *arg)
{
    while (1) {
        pthread_mutex_lock(&mutx);
        while (strlen(g_data) == 0)
            pthread_cond_wait(&cv, &mutx);

        /* Got data */
        printf("%s\n", g_data);
        /* Truncate to null string again */
        g_data[0] = 0;
        pthread_mutex_unlock(&mutx);
    }

    return NULL;
}

void *producer(void *arg)
{
    int i = 0;

    while (1) {
        sleep(1);
        pthread_mutex_lock(&mutx);
        sprintf(g_data, "Data item %d", i);
        pthread_mutex_unlock(&mutx);
        pthread_cond_signal(&cv);
        i++;
    }

    return NULL;
}
```

Note that when the consumer thread blocks on the condvar, it does so while holding a locked mutex, which would seem to be a recipe for deadlock the next time the producer thread tries to update the condition. To avoid this, pthread_cond_wait(3) unlocks the mutex after the thread is blocked and then locks it again before waking it and returning from the wait.

Partitioning the problem

Now that we have covered the basics of processes and threads and the ways in which they communicate, it is time to see what we can do with them.

Here are some of the rules I use when building systems:

- **Rule 1**: Keep tasks that have a lot of interaction together: It is important to minimize overheads by keeping closely inter-operating threads together in one process.

- **Rule 2**: Don't put all your threads in one basket: On the other hand, try and keep components with limited interaction in separate processes, in the interests of resilience and modularity.

- **Rule 3**: Don't mix critical and noncritical threads in the same process: This is an amplification of *Rule 2*: the critical part of the system, which might be a machine control program, should be kept as simple as possible and written in a more rigorous way than other parts. It must be able to continue, even if other processes fail. If you have real-time threads, by definition, they must be critical and should go into a process by themselves.

- **Rule 4**: Threads shouldn't get too intimate: One of the temptations when writing a multithreaded program is to intermingle the code and variables between threads because it is an all-in-one program and easy to do. Keep the threads modular, with well-defined interactions.

- **Rule 5**: Don't think that threads are free: It is very easy to create additional threads, but there is a high cost in terms of the additional complexity needed to coordinate their activities.

- **Rule 6**: Threads can work in parallel: Threads can run simultaneously on a multicore processor, giving higher throughput. If you have a large computing job, you can create one thread per core and make maximum use of the hardware. There are libraries to help you do this, such as OpenMP. You should probably not be coding parallel programming algorithms from scratch.

The Android design is a good illustration. Each application is a separate Linux process that helps modularize memory management and ensures that one app crashing does not affect the whole system. The process model is also used for access control: a process can only access the files and resources that its UID and GIDs allow it to. There is a group of threads in each process. There is one to manage and update the user interface, one to handle signals from the operating system, several to manage dynamic memory allocation and freeing up Java objects, and a worker pool of at least two threads for receiving messages from other parts of the system using the Binder protocol.

To summarize, processes provide resilience because each process has a protected memory space, and when the process terminates, all resources, including memory and file descriptors, are freed up, reducing resource leaks. On the other hand, threads share resources, can communicate easily through shared variables, and can cooperate by sharing access to files and other resources. Threads give parallelism through worker pools and other abstractions, which is useful in multicore processors.

ZeroMQ

Sockets, named pipes, and shared memory are the means by which inter-process communication takes place. They act as the transport layers for the message-passing process that makes up most non-trivial applications. Concurrency primitives such as mutexes and condition variables are used to manage shared access and coordinate work between threads running inside the same process. Multithreaded programming is notoriously difficult, and sockets and named pipes come with their own set of gotchas. A higher-level API is needed to abstract the complex details of asynchronous message passing. Enter ZeroMQ.

ZeroMQ is an asynchronous messaging library that acts like a concurrency framework. It has facilities for in-process, inter-process, TCP, and multicast transports, as well as bindings for various programming languages, including C, C++, Go, and Python. Those bindings, along with ZeroMQ's socket-based abstractions, allow teams to easily mix programming languages within the same distributed application. Support for common messaging patterns such as request/reply, publish/subscribe, and parallel pipeline is also built into the library. The *zero* in ZeroMQ stands for *zero cost*, while the *MQ* part stands for *message queue*.

We will explore both inter-process and in-process message-based communication using ZeroMQ. Let's start by installing ZeroMQ for Python.

Getting pyzmq

We are going to use ZeroMQ's official Python binding for the following exercises. I recommend installing this pyzmq package inside a new virtual environment. Creating a Python virtual environment is easy if you already have conda on your system. Here are the steps for provisioning the necessary virtual environment using conda:

1. Navigate to the zeromq directory containing the examples:

    ```
    (base) $ cd MELD/Chapter17/zeromq
    ```

2. Create a new virtual environment named zeromq:

    ```
    (base) $ conda create --name zeromq python=3.12 pyzmq
    ```

3. Activate your new virtual environment:

    ```
    (base) $ conda activate zeromq
    ```

4. Check that the version of Python is 3.12:

    ```
    (zeromq) $ python --version
    ```

5. List the packages that have been installed in your environment:

    ```
    (zeromq) $ conda list
    ```

If you see pyzmq and its dependencies in the list of packages, then you are now ready to run the following exercises.

Messaging between processes

We will begin our exploration of ZeroMQ with a simple echo server. The server expects a name in the form of a string from a client and replies with Hello <name>. The code is in MELD/Chapter17/zeromq/server.py:

```
    time
    zmq

context = zmq.Context()
socket = context.socket(zmq.REP)
socket.bind("tcp://*:5555")

    True:
```

```
    # Wait     next request from client
    message = socket.recv_pyobj()
    print(f"Received request: {message}")

    # Do some 'work'
    time.sleep(1)

    # Send reply back to client
    socket.send_pyobj(f"Hello {message}")
```

The server process creates a socket of the REP type for its response, binds that socket to port 5555, and waits for messages. A 1-second sleep is used to simulate some work being done in between the time when a request is received and a reply is sent back.

The code for the echo client is in MELD/Chapter17/zeromq/client.py:

```
        zmq

def main(who):
    context = zmq.Context()

    # Socket to talk to server
    print("Connecting to echo server...")
    socket = context.socket(zmq.REQ)
    socket.connect("tcp://localhost:5555")

    # Do 5 requests, waiting each time     a response
        request in range(5):
        print(f"Sending request {request} ...")
        socket.send_pyobj(who)

        # Get the reply.
        message = socket.recv_pyobj()
        print(f"Received reply {request} [ {message} ]")

__name__ == '__main__':
        sys
    len(sys.argv) != 2:
        print("usage: client.py <username>")
```

```
        raise SystemExit
    main(sys.argv[1])
```

The client process takes a username as a command-line argument. The client creates a socket of the REQ type for requests, connects to the server process listening on port 5555, and begins sending messages containing the username that was passed in. Like socket.recv() in the server, socket.recv() in the client blocks until a message arrives in the queue.

To see the echo server and client code in action, activate your zeromq virtual environment and run the planets.sh script from the MELD/Chapter17/zeromq directory:

```
(zeromq) $ ./planets.sh
```

The planets.sh script spawns three client processes called Mars, Jupiter, and Venus. We can see that the requests from the three clients are interleaved because each client waits for a reply from the server before sending its next request. Since each client sends five requests, we should receive a total of 15 replies from the server. Message-based IPC is remarkably easy with ZeroMQ. Now, let's use Python's built-in asyncio module, along with ZeroMQ, to do in-process messaging.

Messaging within processes

The asyncio module was introduced in version 3.4 of Python. It adds a pluggable event loop for executing single-threaded concurrent code using coroutines. **Coroutines** (also known as *green threads*) in Python are declared with the async/await syntax, which has been adopted from C#. They are much lighter weight than POSIX threads and work more like resumable functions. Because coroutines operate in the single-threaded context of an event loop, we can use pyzmq in conjunction with asyncio for in-process socket-based messaging.

Here is a slightly modified version of an example of coroutines taken from the https://github.com/zeromq/pyzmq repository:

```
import asyncio
import time
import zmq
from zmq.asyncio import Context, Poller

url = 'inproc://#1'
ctx = Context.instance()

async def ping() -> None:
```

```python
        """print dots to indicate idleness"""
        while True:
            await asyncio.sleep(0.5)
            print('.')


async def receiver() -> None:
    """receive messages with polling"""
    pull = ctx.socket(zmq.PAIR)
    pull.connect(url)
    poller = Poller()
    poller.register(pull, zmq.POLLIN)
    while True:
        events = await poller.poll()
        if pull in dict(events):
            print("recving", events)
            msg = await pull.recv_multipart()
            print('recvd', msg)


async def sender() -> None:
    """send a message every second"""
    tic = time.time()
    push = ctx.socket(zmq.PAIR)
    push.bind(url)
    while True:
        print("sending")
        await push.send_multipart([str(time.time() - tic).
encode('ascii')])
        await asyncio.sleep(1)


async def main() -> None:
    tasks = [asyncio.create_task(coroutine()) for coroutine in [ping,
receiver, sender]]
    await asyncio.wait(tasks)


if __name__ == "__main__":
    asyncio.run(main())
```

Notice that the receiver() and sender() coroutines share the same context. The inproc transport method specified in the url part of the socket is meant for inter-thread communications and is much faster than the tcp transport we used in the previous example. The PAIR pattern connects two sockets exclusively. Like the inproc transport, this messaging pattern only works in-process and is intended for signaling between threads. Neither the receiver() or sender() coroutines returns. The asyncio event loop alternates between the two coroutines, suspending and resuming each on blocking or completing I/O.

To run the coroutines example from your active zeromq virtual environment, use the following command:

```
(zeromq) $ python coroutines.py
```

sender() sends timestamps to receiver(), which displays them. Use *Ctrl + C* to terminate the process. Congratulations! You have just witnessed in-process asynchronous messaging without the use of explicit threads. There is much more to say and learn about coroutines and asyncio. This example was only meant to give you a taste of what is now possible with Python when paired with ZeroMQ. Let's leave single-threaded event loops behind for the time being and get back to the subject of Linux.

Scheduling

The second big topic I want to cover in this chapter is scheduling. The Linux scheduler has a queue of threads that are ready to run, and its job is to schedule them on CPUs as they become available. Each thread has a scheduling policy that may be time-shared or real-time. The time-shared threads have a **niceness** value that increases or reduces their entitlement to CPU time. The real-time threads have **priority** in that a higher-priority thread will preempt a lower one. The scheduler works with threads, not processes. Each thread is scheduled regardless of which process it is running in.

The scheduler runs when any of the following occurs:

- A thread is blocked by calling sleep() or another blocking system call.
- A time-shared thread exhausts its time slice.
- An interruption causes a thread to be unblocked, for example, because of I/O completing.

For background information on the Linux scheduler, I recommend that you read the chapter on process scheduling in *Linux Kernel Development, 3rd Edition*, by Robert Love.

Fairness versus determinism

I have grouped the scheduling policies into two categories: time-shared and real-time. Time-shared policies are based on the principle of *fairness*. They are designed to make sure that each thread gets a fair amount of processor time and that no thread can hog the system. If a thread runs for too long, it is put to the back of the queue so that others can have a go. At the same time, a fairness policy needs to adjust to threads that are doing a lot of work and give them the resources to get the job done. Time-shared scheduling is good because of the way it automatically adjusts to a wide range of workloads.

On the other hand, if you have a real-time program, fairness is not helpful. In this case, you want a policy that is **deterministic**, which will give you at least minimal guarantees that your real-time threads will be scheduled at the right time so that they don't miss their deadlines. This means that a real-time thread must preempt time-shared threads. Real-time threads also have a static priority that the scheduler can use to choose between them when there are several of them to run at once. The Linux real-time scheduler implements a fairly standard algorithm that runs the highest-priority real-time thread. Most RTOS schedulers are also written in this way.

Both types of thread can coexist. Those requiring deterministic scheduling are scheduled first, and any remaining time is divided between the time-shared threads.

Time-shared policies

Time-shared policies are designed for fairness. From Linux 2.6.23 onward, the scheduler that's been used has been the **completely fair scheduler (CFS)**. It does not use time slices in the normal sense of the word. Instead, it calculates a running tally of the length of time a thread would be entitled to run if it had its fair share of CPU time, and it balances that with the actual amount of time it has run for. If it exceeds its entitlement and there are other time-shared threads waiting to run, the scheduler will suspend the thread and run a waiting thread instead.

The time-shared policies are as follows:

- SCHED_NORMAL (also known as SCHED_OTHER): This is the default policy. The vast majority of Linux threads use this policy.
- SCHED_BATCH: This is similar to SCHED_NORMAL, except that threads are scheduled with a larger granularity; that is, they run for longer but have to wait longer until they are scheduled again. The intention is to reduce the number of context switches for background processing (batch jobs) and reduce the amount of CPU cache churn.

- SCHED_IDLE: These threads are run only when there are no threads from any other policy that are ready to run. It is the lowest possible priority.

There are two pairs of functions you can use to get and set the policy and priority of a thread. The first pair takes a PID as a parameter and affects the main thread in a process:

```
struct sched_param {
    <...>
    int sched_priority;
    <...>
};

int sched_setscheduler(pid_t pid, int policy,
    const struct sched_param *param);
int sched_getscheduler(pid_t pid);
```

The second pair operates on pthread_t and can change the parameters of the other threads in a process:

```
int pthread_setschedparam(pthread_t thread, int policy,
    const struct sched_param *param);
int pthread_getschedparam(pthread_t thread, int *policy,
    struct sched_param *param);
```

See the sched(7) man page for more on thread policies and priorities. Now that we know what time-shared policies and priorities are, let's talk about niceness.

Niceness

Some time-shared threads are more important than others. You can indicate this with the nice value, which multiplies a thread's CPU entitlement by a scaling factor. The name comes from the function call, nice(2), which has been part of Unix since the early days. A thread becomes nice by reducing its load on the system or moving in the opposite direction by increasing it. The range of values is from 19, which is really nice, to -20, which is really not nice. The default value is 0, which is averagely nice, or so-so.

The nice value can be changed for SCHED_NORMAL and SCHED_BATCH threads. To reduce niceness, which increases the CPU load, you need the CAP_SYS_NICE capability, which is available to the root user. See the capabilities(7) man page for more information on capabilities.

Almost all the documentation for functions and commands that change the nice value (nice(2) and the nice and renice commands) talk in terms of processes. However, it really relates to threads. As we mentioned in the preceding section, you can use a TID in place of a PID to change the nice value of an individual thread. One other discrepancy in the standard descriptions of nice is this: the nice value is referred to as the priority of a thread (or sometimes, mistakenly, a process). I believe this is misleading and confuses the concept with real-time priority, which is a completely different thing.

Real-time policies

Real-time policies are intended for determinism. The real-time scheduler will always run the highest-priority real-time thread that is ready to run. Real-time threads always preempt time-share threads. In essence, by selecting a real-time policy over a timeshare policy, you are saying that you have inside knowledge of the expected scheduling of this thread and wish to override the scheduler's built-in assumptions.

There are two real-time policies:

- SCHED_FIFO: This is a **run-to-completion** algorithm, which means that once the thread starts to run, it will continue until it is preempted by a higher-priority real-time thread, it is blocked in a system call, or until it terminates (completes).

- SCHED_RR: This a **round-robin** algorithm that will cycle between threads of the same priority if they exceed their time slice, which is 100 ms by default. Since Linux 3.9, it has been possible to control the timeslice value through /proc/sys/kernel/sched_rr_timeslice_ms. Apart from this, it behaves in the same way as SCHED_FIFO.

Each real-time thread has a priority in the range of 1 to 99, with 99 being the highest.

To give a thread a real-time policy, you need CAP_SYS_NICE, which is given only to the root user by default.

One problem with real-time scheduling, both in terms of Linux and elsewhere, is that a thread that becomes compute-bound, often because a bug has caused it to loop indefinitely, will prevent real-time threads of a lower priority from running along with all the timeshare threads. In this case, the system becomes erratic and may lock up completely. There are a couple of ways to guard against this possibility.

First, since Linux 2.6.25, the scheduler has, by default, reserved 5% of its CPU time for non-real-time threads so that even a runaway real-time thread cannot completely halt the system. It is configured via two kernel controls:

- `/proc/sys/kernel/sched_rt_period_us`
- `/proc/sys/kernel/sched_rt_runtime_us`

They have default values of 1,000,000 (1 second) and 950,000 (950 ms), respectively, which means that every second, 50 ms is reserved for non-real-time processing. If you want real-time threads to be able to take 100%, then set `sched_rt_runtime_us` to `-1`.

The second option is to use a watchdog, either hardware or software, to monitor the execution of key threads and take action when they begin to miss deadlines. I mentioned watchdogs in *Chapter 13*.

Choosing a policy

In practice, time-shared policies satisfy the majority of computing workloads. Threads that are I/O-bound spend a lot of time blocked and always have some spare entitlement in hand. When they are unblocked, they will be scheduled almost immediately. Meanwhile, CPU-bound threads will naturally take up any CPU cycles left over. Positive nice values can be applied to the less important threads and negative values to the more important ones.

Of course, this is only average behavior; there are no guarantees that this will always be the case. If more deterministic behavior is needed, then real-time policies will be required. The things that mark out a thread as being real-time are as follows:

- It has a deadline by which it must generate an output.
- Missing the deadline would compromise the effectiveness of the system.
- It is event-driven.
- It is not compute-bound.

Examples of real-time tasks include the classic robot arm servo controller, multimedia processing, and communication processing. I will discuss real-time system design later, in *Chapter 21*.

Choosing a real-time priority

Choosing real-time priorities that work for all expected workloads is a tricky business and a good reason to avoid real-time policies in the first place.

The most widely used procedure for choosing priorities is known as **rate monotonic analysis (RMA)**, after the 1973 paper by Liu and Layland. It applies to real-time systems with periodic threads, which is a very important class. Each thread has a period and a utilization, which is the proportion of the period it will be executing. The goal is to balance the load so that all the threads can complete their execution phase before the next period. RMA states that this can be achieved if the following occurs:

- The highest priorities are given to the threads with the shortest periods.
- The total utilization is less than 69%.

The total utilization is the sum of all the individual utilizations. It also makes the assumption that the interaction between threads or the time spent blocked on mutexes and the like is negligible.

Summary

The long Unix heritage that is built into Linux and the accompanying C libraries provides almost everything you need in order to write stable and resilient embedded applications. The issue is that for every job, there are at least two ways to achieve the end you desire.

In this chapter, I focused on two aspects of system design: partitioning into separate processes, each with one or more threads to get the job done, and scheduling those threads. I hope that I shed some light on this and have given you the basis to study them further.

In the next chapter, I will examine another important aspect of system design: memory management.

Further study

- *The Art of Unix Programming,* by Eric Steven Raymond
- *Linux System Programming, 2nd Edition,* by Robert Love
- *Linux Kernel Development, 3rd Edition,* by Robert Love
- *The Linux Programming Interface,* by Michael Kerrisk
- *UNIX Network Programming, Volume 2: Interprocess Communications, 2nd Edition,* by W. Richard Stevens
- *Programming with POSIX Threads,* by David R. Butenhof
- *Scheduling Algorithms for Multiprogramming in a Hard-Real-Time Environment,* by C. L. Liu and James W. Layland, Journal of ACM, 1973, vol 20, no 1, pp. 46-61

Join our community on Discord

Join our community's Discord space for discussions with the authors and other readers: `https://packt.link/embeddedsystems`

18

Managing Memory

This chapter covers issues related to memory management, which is an important topic for any Linux system but especially for embedded Linux, where system memory is usually in limited supply. After a brief refresher on virtual memory, I will show you how to measure memory usage and how to detect problems with memory allocation, including memory leaks, as well as what happens when you run out of memory. You will have to understand the tools that are available, from simple tools such as free and top to complex ones such as mtrace and Valgrind.

We will learn the difference between kernel- and user-space memory, and how the kernel maps physical pages of memory to the address space of a process. Then we will locate and read the memory maps for individual processes under the proc filesystem. We will see how the mmap system call can be used to map a program's memory to a file, so that it can allocate memory in bulk or share it with another process. In the second half of this chapter, we will use ps to measure per-process memory usage before moving on to more accurate tools such as smem and ps_mem.

In this chapter, we will cover the following topics:

- Virtual memory basics
- Kernel-space memory layout
- User-space memory layout
- Process memory map
- Managing memory
- Swapping
- Mapping memory with mmap
- How much memory does my application use?

- Per-process memory usage
- Identifying memory leaks
- Running out of memory

Technical requirements

To follow along with the examples, make sure you have a Linux-based host system with gcc, make, top, procps, valgrind, and smem installed.

All of these tools are available on most popular Linux distributions (such as Ubuntu, Arch, and so on).

The code used in this chapter can be found in the chapter folder in this book's GitHub repository: https://github.com/PacktPublishing/Mastering-Embedded-Linux-Development/tree/main/Chapter18.

Virtual memory basics

To recap, Linux configures the **Memory Management Unit (MMU)** of the CPU to present a virtual address space to a running program that begins at zero and ends at the highest address, 0xffffffff, on a 32-bit processor. This address space is divided into pages of 4 KB by default. If 4 KB pages are too small for your application, then you can configure the kernel to use **HugePages**, reducing the amount of system resources needed to access page table entries and increasing the **Translation Lookaside Buffer (TLB)** hit ratio.

Linux divides this virtual address space into an area for applications, called **user space**, and an area for the kernel, called **kernel space**. The split between the two is set by a kernel configuration parameter named PAGE_OFFSET. In a typical 32-bit embedded system, PAGE_OFFSET is 0xc0000000, giving the lower 3 gigabytes to user space and the top gigabyte to kernel space. The user address space is allocated per process so that each process runs in a sandbox, separated from the others. The kernel address space is the same for all processes, as there is only one kernel.

Pages in this virtual address space are mapped to physical addresses by the MMU, which uses page tables to perform the mapping.

Each page of virtual memory may be unmapped or mapped as follows:

- Unmapped so that trying to access these addresses will result in a SIGSEGV.
- Mapped to a page of physical memory that is private to the process.
- Mapped to a page of physical memory that is shared with other processes.

- Mapped and shared with a **copy-on-write (CoW)** flag set: a write is trapped in the kernel, which makes a copy of the page and maps it to the process in place of the original page before allowing the write to take place.
- Mapped to a page of physical memory that is used by the kernel.

The kernel may additionally map pages to reserved memory regions, for example, to access registers and memory buffers in device drivers.

An obvious question is this: why do we do it this way instead of simply referencing physical memory directly, as a typical RTOS would?

There are numerous advantages to virtual memory, some of which are described here:

- Invalid memory accesses are trapped and applications are alerted by SIGSEGV.
- Processes run in their own memory space, isolated from other processes.
- Efficient use of memory through the sharing of common code and data, for example, in libraries.
- The possibility of increasing the apparent amount of physical memory by adding swap files, although swapping on embedded targets is rare.

These are powerful arguments, but I have to admit that there are some disadvantages as well. It is difficult to determine the actual memory budget of an application, which is one of the main concerns of this chapter. The default allocation strategy is to overcommit, which leads to tricky out-of-memory situations, which I will also discuss later, in the *Running out of memory* section. Finally, the delays introduced by the memory management code in handling exceptions—page faults—make the system less deterministic, which is important for real-time programs. I will cover this in *Chapter 21*.

Memory management is different for kernel space and user space. The upcoming sections describe the essential differences and the things you need to know.

Kernel-space memory layout

Kernel memory is managed in a straightforward way. It is not demand-paged, which means that for every allocation using kmalloc() or a similar function, there is real physical memory. Kernel memory is never discarded or paged out.

Some architectures show a summary of the memory mapping at boot time in the kernel log messages. This trace is taken from a 32-bit Arm device (a BeagleBone Black):

```
Memory: 511MB = 511MB total
Memory: 505980k/505980k available, 18308k reserved, 0K highmem
Virtual kernel memory layout:
    vector  : 0xffff0000 - 0xffff1000   ( 4 kB)
    fixmap  : 0xfff00000 - 0xfffe0000   ( 896 kB)
    vmalloc : 0xe0800000 - 0xff000000   ( 488 MB)
    lowmem  : 0xc0000000 - 0xe0000000   ( 512 MB)
    pkmap   : 0xbfe00000 - 0xc0000000   ( 2 MB)
    modules : 0xbf800000 - 0xbfe00000   ( 6 MB)
     .text  : 0xc0008000 - 0xc0763c90   (7536 kB)
     .init  : 0xc0764000 - 0xc079f700   ( 238 kB)
     .data  : 0xc07a0000 - 0xc0827240   ( 541 kB)
     .bss   : 0xc0827240 - 0xc089e940   ( 478 kB)
```

The figure of 505,980 KB available is the amount of free memory the kernel sees when it begins execution but before it begins making dynamic allocations.

Consumers of kernel-space memory include the following:

- The kernel itself, in other words, the code and data loaded from the kernel image file at boot time. This is shown in the preceding kernel log in the .text, .init, .data, and .bss segments. The .init segment is freed once the kernel has completed initialization.

- Memory allocated through the slab allocator, which is used for kernel data structures of various kinds. This includes allocations made using kmalloc(). They come from the region marked **lowmem**.

- Memory allocated via vmalloc(), usually for larger chunks of memory than is available through kmalloc(). These are in the **vmalloc** area.

- A mapping for device drivers to access registers and memory belonging to various bits of hardware, which you can see by reading /proc/iomem. These also come from the **vmalloc** area, but since they are mapped to physical memory that is outside of the main system memory, they do not take up any real memory.

- Kernel modules which are loaded into the area marked **modules**.

- Other low-level allocations that are not tracked anywhere else.

Now that we know the layout of memory in kernel space, let's find out how much memory the kernel is using.

How much memory does the kernel use?

Unfortunately, there isn't a precise answer to the question of how much memory the kernel uses, but what follows is as close as we can get.

Firstly, you can see the memory taken up by the kernel code and data in the kernel log shown previously, or you can use the `size` command:

```
$ cd ~
$ cd build_arm64
$ aarch64-buildroot-linux-gnu-size vmlinux
    text     data      bss      dec  hex        filename
26412819 15636144   620032 42668995 28b13c3 vmlinux
```

Usually, the amount of memory taken by the kernel for the static code and data segments shown here is small when compared to the total amount of memory. If that is not the case, you need to look through the kernel configuration and remove the components that you don't need. An effort to allow building small kernels known as **Linux Kernel Tinification** had been making good progress until the project stalled, and Josh Triplett's patches were eventually removed from the `linux-next` tree in 2016. Now, your best bet at reducing the kernel's in-memory size is **Execute-in-Place (XIP)** where you trade RAM for flash (`https://lwn.net/Articles/748198/`).

You can get more information about memory usage by reading /proc/meminfo:

```
# cat /proc/meminfo
MemTotal:       1996796 kB
MemFree:        1917020 kB
MemAvailable:   1894044 kB
Buffers:           2444 kB
Cached:           11976 kB
SwapCached:           0 kB
Active:            9440 kB
Inactive:          8964 kB
Active(anon):        92 kB
Inactive(anon):    4096 kB
Active(file):      9348 kB
```

```
    Inactive(file):      4868 kB
    Unevictable:            0 kB
    Mlocked:                0 kB
    SwapTotal:              0 kB
    SwapFree:               0 kB
    Dirty:                  8 kB
    Writeback:              0 kB
    AnonPages:           4008 kB
    Mapped:              6864 kB
    Shmem:                200 kB
    KReclaimable:        7412 kB
    Slab:               20924 kB
    SReclaimable:        7412 kB
    SUnreclaim:         13512 kB
    KernelStack:         1552 kB
    PageTables:           540 kB
    SecPageTables:          0 kB
    NFS_Unstable:           0 kB
    Bounce:                 0 kB
    WritebackTmp:           0 kB
    CommitLimit:       998396 kB
    Committed_AS:        7396 kB
    VmallocTotal:  135288315904 kB
    VmallocUsed:         4072 kB
    VmallocChunk:           0 kB
    <…>
```

There is a description of each of these fields on the manual page proc(5). The kernel memory usage is the sum of the following:

- Slab: the total memory allocated by the slab allocator
- KernelStack: the stack space used when executing kernel code
- PageTables: the memory used to store page tables
- VmallocUsed: the memory allocated by vmalloc()

In the case of slab allocations, you can get more information by reading /proc/slabinfo. Similarly, there is a breakdown of allocations in /proc/vmallocinfo for the **vmalloc** area. In both cases, you need detailed knowledge of the kernel and its subsystems in order to see exactly which subsystem is making the allocations and why, which is beyond the scope of this discussion.

With modules, you can use lsmod to find out the memory space taken up by the code and data:

```
# lsmod
Module          Size   Used by
g_multi         47670  2
libcomposite    14299  1 g_multi
mt7601Usta      601404 0
```

This leaves the low-level allocations, of which there is no record, and that prevents us from generating an accurate account of kernel-space memory usage. This will appear as missing memory when we add up all the kernel- and user-space allocations that we know about.

Measuring kernel-space memory usage is complicated. The information in /proc/meminfo is somewhat limited and the additional information provided by /proc/slabinfo and /proc/vmallocinfo is difficult to interpret. User space offers better visibility into memory usage by way of the process memory map.

User-space memory layout

Linux employs a lazy allocation strategy for user space, only mapping physical pages of memory when the program accesses it. For example, allocating a buffer of 1 MB using malloc(3) returns a pointer to a block of memory addresses but no actual physical memory. A flag is set in the page table entries such that any read or write access is trapped by the kernel. This is known as a **page fault**. Only at this point does the kernel attempt to find a page of physical memory and add it to the page table mapping for the process. Let's demonstrate this with a simple program from MELD/Chapter18/pagefault-demo:

```
#include <stdio.h>
#include <stdlib.h>
#include <string.h>
#include <sys/resource.h>

#define BUFFER_SIZE (1024 * 1024)

void print_pgfaults(void)
```

```
{
    int ret;
    struct rusage usage;

    ret = getrusage(RUSAGE_SELF, &usage);

    if (ret == -1) {
        perror("getrusage");
    } else {
        printf("Major page faults %ld\n", usage.ru_majflt);
        printf("Minor page faults %ld\n", usage.ru_minflt);
    }
}

int main(int argc, char *argv[])
{
    unsigned char *p;

    printf("Initial state\n");
    print_pgfaults();

    p = malloc(BUFFER_SIZE);
    printf("After malloc\n");
    print_pgfaults();

    memset(p, 0x42, BUFFER_SIZE);
    printf("After memset\n");
    print_pgfaults();

    memset(p, 0x42, BUFFER_SIZE);
    printf("After 2nd memset\n");
    print_pgfaults();

    return 0;
}
```

When you run it, you will see output like this:

```
Initial state
Major page faults 0
```

```
Minor page faults 172
After malloc
Major page faults 0
Minor page faults 186
After memset
Major page faults 0
Minor page faults 442
After 2nd memset
Major page faults 0
Minor page faults 442
```

There were 172 minor page faults encountered after initializing the program's environment and a further 14 when calling getrusage(2) (these numbers will vary depending on the architecture and the version of the C library you are using). The important part is the increase when filling the memory with data: 442 - 186 = 256. The buffer is 1 MB, which is 256 pages. The second call to memset(3) makes no difference because all the pages are now mapped.

As you can see, a page fault is generated when the kernel traps access to a page that has not been mapped yet. In fact, there are two kinds of page faults: minor and major. With a minor fault, the kernel just has to find a page of physical memory and map it to the process address space, as shown in the preceding code. A major page fault occurs when the virtual memory is mapped to a file, for example, using mmap(2), which I will describe shortly. Reading from this memory means that the kernel not only has to find a page of memory and map it in but also has to fill it with data from the file. Consequently, major faults are much more expensive in terms of time and system resources.

While getrusage(2) offers useful metrics on minor and major page faults within a process, sometimes what we really want to see is an overall memory map of a process.

Process memory map

Each running process in user space has a process map that we can inspect. These memory maps tell us how a program's memory is allocated and what shared libraries it is linked to. You can see the memory map for a process through the proc filesystem. Here is the map for the init process (PID 1):

```
# cat /proc/1/maps
aaaaaf830000-aaaaaf83a000 r-xp 00000000 b3:62 397    /sbin/init.sysvinit
aaaaaf84f000-aaaaaf850000 r--p 0000f000 b3:62 397    /sbin/init.sysvinit
aaaaaf850000-aaaaaf851000 rw-p 00010000 b3:62 397    /sbin/init.sysvinit
```

```
aaaae9d63000-aaaae9d84000 rw-p 00000000 00:00 0          [heap]
ffff7ffb0000-ffff8013b000 r-xp 00000000 b3:62 309        /lib/libc.so.6
ffff8013b000-ffff8014d000 ---p 0018b000 b3:62 309        /lib/libc.so.6
ffff8014d000-ffff80150000 r--p 0018d000 b3:62 309        /lib/libc.so.6
ffff80150000-ffff80152000 rw-p 00190000 b3:62 309        /lib/libc.so.6
ffff80152000-ffff8015e000 rw-p 00000000 00:00 0
ffff8016c000-ffff80193000 r-xp 00000000 b3:62 304        /lib/ld-linux-aarch64.so.1
ffff801a4000-ffff801a6000 rw-p 00000000 00:00 0
ffff801a6000-ffff801a8000 r--p 00000000 00:00 0          [vvar]
ffff801a8000-ffff801aa000 r-xp 00000000 00:00 0          [vdso]
ffff801aa000-ffff801ac000 r--p 0002e000 b3:62 304        /lib/ld-linux-aarch64.so.1
ffff801ac000-ffff801ae000 rw-p 00030000 b3:62 304        /lib/ld-linux-aarch64.so.1
ffffd73ca000-ffffd73eb000 rw-p 00000000 00:00 0          [stack]
```

The first two columns show the start and end virtual addresses and the permissions for each mapping. The permissions are shown here:

- r: read
- w: write
- x: execute
- s: shared
- p: private (copy-on-write)

If the mapping is associated with a file, the filename appears in the final column, and columns three, four, and five contain the offset from the start of the file, the block device number, and the inode of the file. Most of the mappings are to the program itself and the libraries it is linked with. There are two areas where the program can allocate memory, marked [heap] and [stack]. Memory allocated using malloc comes from the former (except for very large allocations, which we will come to later); allocations on the stack come from the latter. The maximum size of both areas is controlled by the process's ulimit:

- **heap**: ulimit -d, default unlimited
- **stack**: ulimit -s, default 8 MB

Allocations that exceed the limit are rejected by SIGSEGV.

When running out of memory, the kernel may decide to discard pages that are mapped to a file and are read-only. If that page is accessed again, it will cause a major page fault and be read back in from the file.

Swapping

The idea of swapping is to reserve some storage where the kernel can place pages of memory that are not mapped to a file, freeing up the memory for other uses. It increases the effective size of physical memory by the size of the swap file. It is not a panacea: there is a cost to copying pages to and from a swap file, which becomes apparent on a system that has too little real memory for the workload it is carrying and so swapping becomes the main activity. This is sometimes known as **disk thrashing**.

Swapping is seldom used on embedded devices because it does not work well with flash storage, where constant writing would wear it out quickly. However, you may want to consider swapping to compressed RAM (zram).

Swapping to compressed memory (zram)

The **zram** driver creates RAM-based block devices named /dev/zram0, /dev/zram1, and so on. Pages written to these devices are compressed before being stored. With compression ratios in the range of 30% to 50%, you can expect an overall increase in free memory of about 10% at the expense of more processing and a corresponding increase in power usage.

To enable zram, configure the kernel with these options:

```
CONFIG_SWAP
CONFIG_CGROUP_MEM_RES_CTLR
CONFIG_CGROUP_MEM_RES_CTLR_SWAP
CONFIG_ZRAM
```

Then, mount zram at boot time by adding the following to /etc/fstab:

```
/dev/zram0 none swap defaults zramsize=<size in bytes>, swapprio=<swap
partition priority>
```

You can turn swapping on and off using the following commands:

```
# swapon /dev/zram0
# swapoff /dev/zram0
```

Swapping memory out to zram is better than swapping out to flash storage, but neither technique is a substitute for adequate physical memory.

User-space processes depend on the kernel to manage virtual memory for them. Sometimes a program wants greater control over its memory map than the kernel can offer. There is a system call that lets us map memory to a file for more direct access from user space.

Mapping memory with mmap

A process begins life with a certain amount of memory mapped to the **text** (the code) and **data** segments of the program file, together with the shared libraries that it is linked with. It can allocate memory on its heap at runtime using malloc(3) and on the stack through locally scoped variables and memory allocated through alloca(3). It may also load libraries dynamically at runtime using dlopen(3). All of these mappings are taken care of by the kernel. However, a process can also manipulate its memory map in an explicit way using mmap(2):

```
void *mmap(void *addr, size_t length, int prot, int flags,int fd, off_t
offset);
```

This function maps length bytes of memory from the file with the fd descriptor, starting at offset in the file, and returns a pointer to the mapping, assuming it is successful. Since the underlying hardware works in pages, length is rounded up to the nearest whole number of pages. The protection parameter, prot, is a combination of read, write, and execute permissions and the flags parameter contains at least MAP_SHARED or MAP_PRIVATE. There are many other flags, which are described in the mmap manpage.

There are many things you can do with mmap. I will show some of them in the upcoming sections.

Using mmap to allocate private memory

You can use mmap to allocate an area of private memory by setting MAP_ANONYMOUS in the flags parameter and setting the file descriptor fd to -1. This is similar to allocating memory from the heap using malloc, except that the memory is page-aligned and in multiples of pages. The memory is allocated in the same area as that used for libraries. In fact, this area is referred to by some as the mmap area for this reason.

Anonymous mappings are better for large allocations because they do not pin down the heap with chunks of memory, which would make fragmentation more likely. Interestingly, you will find that malloc (in glibc at least) stops allocating memory from the heap for requests over 128 KB and uses mmap in this way, so in most cases, just using malloc is the right thing to do. The system will choose the best way of satisfying the request.

Using mmap to share memory

As we saw in *Chapter 17*, POSIX shared memory requires mmap to access the memory segment. In this case, you set the MAP_SHARED flag and use the file descriptor from shm_open():

```
int shm_fd;
char *shm_p;

shm_fd = shm_open("/myshm", O_CREAT | O_RDWR, 0666);
ftruncate(shm_fd, 65536);
shm_p = mmap(NULL, 65536, PROT_READ | PROT_WRITE, MAP_SHARED, shm_fd, 0);
```

Another process uses the same calls, filename, length, and flags to map to that memory region for sharing. Subsequent calls to msync(2) control when updates to memory are carried through to the underlying file.

Sharing memory via mmap also offers a straightforward way to read from and write to device memory.

Using mmap to access device memory

As I mentioned in *Chapter 11*, it is possible for a driver to allow its device node to be memory mapped and share some of the device memory with an application. The exact implementation is dependent on the driver.

One example is the Linux framebuffer, /dev/fb0. FPGAs such as the Xilinx Zynq series are also accessed as memory via mmap from Linux. The framebuffer interface is defined in /usr/include/linux/fb.h, including an ioctl function to get the size of the display and the bits per pixel. You can then use mmap to ask the video driver to share the framebuffer with the application and read and write pixels:

```
int f;
int fb_size;
unsigned char *fb_mem;

f = open("/dev/fb0", O_RDWR);
/* Use ioctl FBIOGET_VSCREENINFO to find the display
   dimensions and calculate fb_size */
fb_mem = mmap(0, fb_size, PROT_READ | PROT_WRITE, MAP_SHARED, fd, 0);
/* read and write pixels through pointer fb_mem */
```

A second example is the streaming video interface, **Video 4 Linux 2 (V4L2)**, which is defined in /usr/include/linux/videodev2.h. Each video device has a node named /dev/video<N>, starting with /dev/video0. There is an ioctl function to ask the driver to allocate a number of video buffers that you can mmap into user space. Then, it is just a question of cycling the buffers and filling or emptying them with video data, depending on whether you are playing back or capturing a video stream.

Now that we have covered memory layout and mapping, let's look at memory usage, starting with how to measure it.

How much memory does my application use?

As with kernel space, the different ways of allocating, mapping, and sharing user-space memory make it quite difficult to answer this seemingly simple question.

To begin, you can ask the kernel how much memory it thinks is available, which you can do using the free command. Here is a typical example of the output:

```
            total        used    free shared buffers cached
   Mem:     509016      504312    4704 0       26456   363860
   -/+ buffers/cache: 113996 395020
   Swap:         0           0       0
```

At first sight, this looks like a system that is almost out of memory, with only 4,704 KB free out of 509,016 KB: less than 1%. However, note that 26,456 KB is in buffers and a whopping 363,860 KB is in caches. Linux believes that free memory is wasted memory; the kernel uses free memory for buffers and caches with the knowledge that they can be shrunk when the need arises. Removing buffers and cache from the measurement provides true free memory, which is 395,020 KSB: 77% of the total. When using free, the numbers on the second line marked -/+ buffers/cache are the important ones.

You can force the kernel to free up caches by writing a number between 1 and 3 to /proc/sys/vm/drop_caches:

```
# echo 3 > /proc/sys/vm/drop_caches
```

The number is actually a bitmask that determines which of the two broad types of caches you want to free: 1 for the page cache and 2 for the dentry and inode caches combined. Since 1 and 2 are different bits, writing a 3 frees both types of caches.

The exact roles of these caches are not particularly important here, only that there is memory that the kernel is using but that can be reclaimed at short notice.

The `free` command tells us how much memory is being used and how much is left. It neither tells us which processes are using the unavailable memory nor in what proportions. To measure that, we need other tools.

Per-process memory usage

There are several metrics to measure the amount of memory a process is using. I will begin with the two that are easiest to obtain: the **virtual set size (VSS)** and the **resident memory size (RSS)**, both of which are available in most implementations of the `ps` and `top` commands:

- **VSS**: Called `VSZ` in the `ps` command and `VIRT` in `top`, this is the total amount of memory mapped by a process. It is the sum of all the regions shown in `/proc/<PID>/map`. This number is of limited interest since only part of the virtual memory is committed to physical memory at any time.

- **RSS**: Called `RSS` in `ps` and `RES` in `top`, this is the sum of memory that is mapped to physical pages of memory. This gets closer to the actual memory budget of the process, but there is a problem: if you add the RSS of all the processes, you will get an overestimate of the memory in use because some pages will be shared.

Let's learn more about the `top` and `ps` commands.

Using top and ps

The versions of `top` and `ps` from BusyBox provide very limited information. The examples that follow use the full versions from the `procps` package.

Here is the output from a `ps` command with a custom format that includes `vsz` and `rss`:

```
# ps -eo pid,tid,class,rtprio,stat,vsz,rss,comm
   PID    TID CLS RTPRIO STAT    VSZ    RSS COMMAND
     1      1 TS       -  Ss     4496   2652 systemd
  <...>
   205    205 TS       -  Ss     4076   1296 systemd-journal
   228    228 TS       -  Ss     2524   1396 udevd
   581    581 TS       -  Ss     2880   1508 avahi-daemon
   584    584 TS       -  Ss     2848   1512 dbus-daemon
   590    590 TS       -  Ss     1332    680 acpid
   594    594 TS       -  Ss     4600   1564 wpa_supplicant
```

Likewise, top shows a summary of the free memory and memory usage per process:

```
top - 21:17:52 up 10:04, 1 user, load average: 0.00, 0.01, 0.05
Tasks: 96 total, 1 running, 95 sleeping, 0 stopped, 0 zombie
%Cpu(s):  1.7 us,  2.2 sy,  0.0 ni, 95.9 id,  0.0 wa,  0.0 hi
KiB Mem : 509016 total, 278524 used, 230492 free,  25572 buffers
KiB Swap:      0 total,      0 used,      0 free, 170920 cached
PID USER PR NI   VIRT   RES   SHR S  %CPU  %MEM    TIME+ COMMAND
595 root 20  0  64920  9.8m  4048 S   0.0   2.0  0:01.09 node
866 root 20  0  28892  9152  3660 S   0.2   1.8  0:36.38 Xorg
<...>
```

These simple commands give you a feel for the memory usage and provide the first indication that you have a memory leak when you see that the RSS of a process keeps on increasing. However, they are not very accurate in the absolute measurements of memory usage.

Using smem

In 2009, Matt Mackall began looking at the problem of accounting for shared pages in process memory measurement and added two new metrics called **unique set size (USS)** and **proportional set size (PSS)**:

- **USS**: This is the amount of memory that is committed to physical memory and is unique to a process; it is not shared with any others. It is the amount of memory that would be freed if the process were to terminate.

- **PSS**: This splits the accounting of shared pages that are committed to physical memory between all the processes that have them mapped. For example, if an area of library code is 12 pages long and is shared by six processes, each will accumulate two pages in PSS. Thus, if you add the PSS numbers for all processes, you will get the actual amount of memory being used by those processes. In other words, PSS is the number we have been looking for.

Information about PSS is available in /proc/<PID>/smaps, which contains additional information for each of the mappings shown in /proc/<PID>/maps. Here is a section from such a file that provides information on the mapping for the libc code segment:

```
ffffbd080000-ffffbd20b000 r-xp 00000000 b3:62 309 /lib/libc.so.6
Size:               1580 kB
KernelPageSize:        4 kB
MMUPageSize:           4 kB
Rss:                1132 kB
Pss:                 112 kB
Pss_Dirty:             0 kB
Shared_Clean:       1132 kB
Shared_Dirty:          0 kB
Private_Clean:         0 kB
Private_Dirty:         0 kB
Referenced:         1132 kB
Anonymous:             0 kB
KSM:                   0 kB
LazyFree:              0 kB
AnonHugePages:         0 kB
ShmemPmdMapped:        0 kB
FilePmdMapped:         0 kB
Shared_Hugetlb:        0 kB
Private_Hugetlb:       0 kB
Swap:                  0 kB
SwapPss:               0 kB
Locked:                0 kB
THPeligible:           0
VmFlags: rd ex mr mw me
```

Note that the Rss is 1132 kB, but because it is shared between many other processes, the Pss is only 112 kB.

There is a tool named **smem** that collates information from the smaps files and presents it in various ways, including as pie or bar charts. The project page for smem is https://www.selenic.com/smem/. It is available as a package in most desktop distributions. However, since it is written in Python, installing it on an embedded target requires a Python environment, which may be too much trouble for just one tool. To help with this, there is a small program named **smemcap** that captures the state from /proc on the target and saves it to a TAR file that can be analyzed later on the host computer. smemcap is part of BusyBox, but it can also be compiled from source.

If you run smem natively, as root, you will see these results:

```
# smem -t
PID User Command                          Swap    USS   PSS    RSS
  1 root init [5]                            0    136   267   1532
361 root /sbin/klogd -n                      0    104   273   1708
367 root /sbin/getty 38400 tty1              0    108   278   1788
369 root /sbin/getty -L 115200 ttyS2         0    108   278   1788
358 root /sbin/syslogd -n -O /var/lo         0    108   279   1728
306 root udhcpc -R -b -p /var/run/ud         0    168   284   1372
366 root /bin/sh /bin/start_getty 11         0    116   315   1736
383 root -sh                                 0    220   506   2184
129 root /sbin/udevd -d                      0   1436  1517   2380
351 root sshd: /usr/sbin/sshd [liste         0    928  1893   3764
380 root sshd: root@pts/0                    0   3816  4900   7160
387 root python3 /usr/bin/smem -t            0  11968 12136  13456
-------------------------------------------------------------------
 12 1                                        0  19216 22926  40596
```

You can see from the last line of the output that, in this case, the total PSS is about half of the RSS.

If you don't have or don't want to install Python on your target, you can capture the state using smemcap, again as root:

```
# smemcap > smem-beagleplay-cap.tar
```

Then, copy the TAR file to the host and read it using smem -t -S, although this time there is no need to run the command as root:

```
$ smem -t -S smem-beagleplay-cap.tar
```

The output is identical to the output we get when running smem natively.

Other tools to consider

Another way to display PSS is via **ps_mem** (https://github.com/pixelb/ps_mem), which prints much the same information but in a simpler format. It is also written in Python.

Android also has a tool that displays a summary of USS and PSS for each process, named **procrank**, which can be cross-compiled for embedded Linux with a few small changes. You can get the code from https://github.com/csimmonds/procrank_linux.

We now know how to measure per-process memory usage. Let's say we use the tools just shown to find the process that is the memory hog in our system. How do we then drill down into that process to figure out where it is going wrong? That is the topic of the next section.

Identifying memory leaks

A memory leak occurs when memory is allocated but not freed when it is no longer needed. Memory leakage is by no means unique to embedded systems, but it becomes an issue partly because targets don't have much memory in the first place and partly because they often run for long periods of time without rebooting, allowing the leaks to become a large puddle.

You will realize that there is a leak when you run free or top and see that free memory is continually going down even if you drop caches, as shown in the preceding section. You will be able to identify the culprit (or culprits) by looking at the USS and RSS per process.

There are several tools to identify memory leaks in a program. I will look at two: mtrace and valgrind.

mtrace

mtrace is a component of glibc that traces calls to malloc, free, and related functions, and identifies areas of memory not freed when the program exits. You need to call the mtrace() function from within the program to begin tracing and then, at runtime, write a path name to the MALLOC_TRACE environment variable in which the trace information is written. If MALLOC_TRACE does not exist or if the file cannot be opened, the mtrace hooks are not installed.

While the trace information is written in ASCII, it is usual to use the mtrace command to view it. Here is an example of a program that uses mtrace from MELD/Chapter18/mtrace-example:

```
#include <mcheck.h>
#include <stdlib.h>
#include <stdio.h>

int main(int argc, char *argv[])
{
    int j;

    mtrace();
```

```
    for (j = 0; j < 2; j++)
        malloc(100); /* Never freed:a memory leak */

    calloc(16, 16); /* Never freed:a memory leak */
    exit(EXIT_SUCCESS);
}
```

Here is what you might see when running the program and looking at the trace:

```
$ export MALLOC_TRACE=mtrace.log
$ ./mtrace-example
$ mtrace mtrace-example mtrace.log


Memory not freed:
-----------------
            Address    Size      Caller
0x0000000001479460     0x64  at /home/chris/mtrace-example.c:12
0x00000000014794d0     0x64  at /home/chris/mtrace-example.c:12
0x0000000001479540    0x100  at /home/chris/mtrace-example.c:14
```

Unfortunately, mtrace does not tell you about leaked memory while the program runs. It has to terminate first.

Valgrind

Valgrind is a very powerful tool used to discover memory problems including leaks and other things. One advantage is that you don't have to recompile the programs and libraries that you want to check, although it works better if they have been compiled with the -g option so that they include debug symbol tables. It works by running the program in an emulated environment and trapping execution at various points. This leads to the big downside of Valgrind, which is that the program runs at a fraction of normal speed, which makes it less useful for testing anything with real-time constraints.

> **TIP**
>
> Incidentally, the name is often mispronounced: it says in the Valgrind FAQ that the grind part is pronounced with a short *i*, as in grinned (rhymes with tinned) rather than grind (rhymes with find). The FAQ, documentation, and downloads are available at https://valgrind.org.

Valgrind contains several diagnostic tools:

- memcheck: This is the default tool, and it detects memory leaks and general misuse of memory.

- cachegrind: This calculates the processor cache hit rate.

- callgrind: This calculates the cost of each function call.

- helgrind: This highlights the misuse of the Pthread API, including potential deadlocks, and race conditions.

- DRD: This is another Pthread analysis tool.

- massif: This profiles the usage of the heap and stack.

You can select the tool you want with the -tool option. Valgrind runs on the major embedded platforms: Arm (Cortex-A), PowerPC, MIPS, and x86 in 32-bit and 64-bit variants. It is available as a package in both The Yocto Project and Buildroot.

To find our memory leak, we need to use the default memcheck tool, with the --leak-check=full option to print the lines where the leak was found:

```
$ valgrind --leak-check=full ./mtrace-example
==3384686== Memcheck, a memory error detector
==3384686== Copyright (C) 2002-2022, and GNU GPL'd, by Julian Seward et
al.
==3384686== Using Valgrind-3.22.0 and LibVEX; rerun with -h for copyright
info
==3384686== Command: ./mtrace-example
==3384686==
==3384686==
==3384686== HEAP SUMMARY:
==3384686==     in use at exit: 456 bytes in 3 blocks
==3384686==   total heap usage: 3 allocs, 0 frees, 456 bytes allocated
==3384686==
==3384686== 200 bytes in 2 blocks are definitely lost in loss record 1 of
2
==3384686==    at 0x4846828: malloc (in /usr/libexec/valgrind/vgpreload_
memcheck-amd64-linux.so)
==3384686==    by 0x1091D3: main (mtrace-example.c:12)
==3384686==
==3384686== 256 bytes in 1 blocks are definitely lost in loss record 2 of
2
```

```
==3384686==     at 0x484D953: calloc (in /usr/libexec/valgrind/vgpreload_
memcheck-amd64-linux.so)
==3384686==     by 0x1091EC: main (mtrace-example.c:14)
==3384686==
==3384686== LEAK SUMMARY:
==3384686==    definitely lost: 456 bytes in 3 blocks
==3384686==    indirectly lost: 0 bytes in 0 blocks
==3384686==      possibly lost: 0 bytes in 0 blocks
==3384686==    still reachable: 0 bytes in 0 blocks
==3384686==         suppressed: 0 bytes in 0 blocks
==3384686==
==3384686== For lists of detected and suppressed errors, rerun with: -s
==3384686== ERROR SUMMARY: 2 errors from 2 contexts (suppressed: 0 from 0)
```

The output from Valgrind shows that two memory leaks were found in `mtrace-example.c`: a
`malloc` at line 12 and a `calloc` at line 14. The subsequent calls to `free` that are supposed to accompany these two memory allocations are missing from the program. Left unchecked, memory
leaks in a long-running process may eventually result in the system running out of memory.

Running out of memory

The standard memory allocation policy is to **overcommit**, which means that the kernel will
allow more memory to be allocated by applications than there is physical memory. Most of the
time, this works fine because it is common for applications to request more memory than they
really need. This also helps in the implementation of `fork(2)`: it is safe to make a copy of a large
program because the pages of memory are shared with the copy-on-write flag set. In the majority
of cases, `fork` is followed by an exec function call, which unshares the memory and then loads
a new program.

However, there is always the possibility that a particular workload will cause a group of processes to try to cash in on the allocations they have been promised simultaneously and so demand
more than there really is. This is an **out-of-memory**, or **OOM**, situation. At this point, there is
no other alternative but to kill off processes until the problem goes away. This is the job of the
out-of-memory killer.

Before we get to that, there is a tuning parameter for kernel allocations in `/proc/sys/vm/overcommit_memory`, which you can set to the following:

- `0`: heuristic overcommit
- `1`: always overcommit; never check
- `2`: always check; never overcommit

Option `0` is the default and is the best choice in the majority of cases.

Option 1 is only useful if you run programs that work with large sparse arrays and allocate large areas of memory but write to a small proportion of them. Such programs are rare in the context of embedded systems.

Option 2 seems to be a good choice if you are worried about running out of memory, perhaps in a mission or safety-critical application. It will fail allocations that are greater than the commit limit, which is the size of swap space plus the total memory multiplied by the overcommit ratio. The overcommit ratio is controlled by /proc/sys/vm/overcommit_ratio and has a default value of 50%.

As an example, suppose you have a device with 2 GB of system RAM and you set a really conservative ratio of 25%:

```
# echo 25 > /proc/sys/vm/overcommit_ratio
# grep -e MemTotal -e CommitLimit /proc/meminfo
MemTotal:        1996796 kB
CommitLimit:      499196 kB
```

There is no swap, so the commit limit is 25% of `MemTotal`, as expected.

There is another important variable in `/proc/meminfo`, called `Committed_AS`. This is the total amount of memory that is needed to fulfill all the allocations made so far. I found the following on one system:

```
# grep -e MemTotal -e Committed_AS /proc/meminfo
MemTotal:        1996796 kB
Committed_AS:    2907335 kB
```

In other words, the kernel had already promised more memory than the available memory. Consequently, setting overcommit_memory to 2 would mean that all allocations would fail regardless of overcommit_ratio. To get to a working system, I would have to either install double the amount of RAM or severely reduce the number of running processes, of which there were about 40.

In all cases, the final defense is `oom-killer`. It uses a heuristic method to calculate a badness score between 0 and 1,000 for each process and then terminates those with the highest score until there is enough free memory. You should see something like this in the kernel log:

```
[44510.490320] eatmem invoked oom-killer: gfp_mask=0x200da, order=0, oom_
score_adj=0
```

You can force an OOM event using `echo f > /proc/sysrq-trigger`.

You can influence the badness score for a process by writing an adjustment value to `/proc/<PID>/oom_score_adj`. A value of `-1000` means that the badness score can never be greater than zero and so it will never be killed; a value of `+1000` means that it will always be greater than 1,000 and so it will always be killed.

Summary

Accounting for every byte of memory used in a virtual memory system is just not possible. However, you can find a fairly accurate figure for the total amount of free memory, excluding that taken by buffers and the cache, using the `free` command. By monitoring it over a period of time and with different workloads, you should become confident that it will remain within a given limit.

When you want to tune memory usage or identify sources of unexpected allocations, there are resources that give more detailed information. For kernel space, the most useful information is in `/proc`: `meminfo`, `slabinfo`, and `vmallocinfo`.

When it comes to getting accurate measurements for user space, the best metric is PSS, as shown by `smem` and other tools. For memory debugging, you can get help from simple tracers such as `mtrace`, or you have the heavyweight option of the Valgrind `memcheck` tool.

If you have concerns about the consequence of an OOM situation, you can fine-tune the allocation mechanism via `/proc/sys/vm/overcommit_memory` and you can control the likelihood of particular processes being killed though the `oom_score_adj` parameter.

The next chapter is all about debugging user-space and kernel code using the GNU Debugger and the insights you can gain from watching code as it runs, including the memory management functions I have described here.

Further study

- *Linux Kernel Development, 3rd edition,* by Robert Love
- *Linux System Programming, 2nd Edition,* by Robert Love
- *Understanding the Linux Virtual Memory Manager,* by Mel Gorman — https://www.kernel.org/doc/gorman/pdf/understand.pdf
- *Valgrind 3.3: Advanced Debugging and Profiling for GNU/Linux Applications,* by Julian Seward, Nicholas Nethercote, and Josef Weidendorfer

Part 5

Debugging and Optimizing Performance

This last part shows you how to make effective use of the many debug and profiling tools that Linux has to offer to detect problems and identify bottlenecks. *Chapter 19* describes how to set up GDB for remote debugging on the target device. *Chapter 20* includes coverage of eBPF, a new technology that enables advanced programmatic tracing inside the Linux kernel. The final chapter brings together several threads to explain how Linux can be used in real-time applications.

This part has the following chapters:

- *Chapter 19, Debugging with GDB*
- *Chapter 20, Profiling and Tracing*
- *Chapter 21, Real-Time Programming*

19

Debugging with GDB

Bugs happen. Identifying and fixing them is part of the development process. There are many different techniques for finding and characterizing program defects, including static and dynamic analysis, code review, tracing, profiling, and interactive debugging. We will look at tracers and profilers in the next chapter, but here I want to concentrate on the traditional approach of watching code execution through a debugger, which in our case is the **GNU Debugger (GDB)**. GDB is a powerful and flexible tool. You can use it to debug applications, examine the postmortem files (core files) that are created after a program crash, and even step through kernel code.

In this chapter, we will cover the following topics:

- GNU debugger
- Preparing to debug
- Debugging applications
- Just-in-time debugging
- Debugging forks and threads
- Core files
- GDB user interfaces
- Debugging kernel code

Technical requirements

To follow along with the examples, make sure you have the following:

- An Ubuntu 24.04 or later LTS host system with at least 90 GB of free disk space
- Buildroot 2024.02.6 LTS release

- Yocto 5.0 (Scarthgap) LTS release

- A microSD card reader and card

- balenaEtcher for Linux

- An Ethernet cable and router with an available port for network connectivity

- A USB to TTL serial cable with a 3.3 V level

- A Raspberry Pi 4

- A 5 V USB-C power supply capable of delivering 3 A

You should have already installed the 2024.02.6 LTS release of Buildroot for *Chapter 6*. If you have not, then refer to the *System requirements section* of *The Buildroot user manual* (`https://buildroot.org/downloads/manual/manual.html`) before installing Buildroot on your Linux host according to the instructions from *Chapter 6*.

You should have already built the 5.0 (Scarthgap) LTS release of Yocto in *Chapter 6*. If you have not, then please refer to the *Compatible Linux Distribution* and *Build Host Packages* sections of the *Yocto Project Quick Build* guide (`https://docs.yoctoproject.org/brief-yoctoprojectqs/`) before building Yocto on your Linux host according to the instructions in *Chapter 6*.

The code used in this chapter can be found in the chapter folder in this book's GitHub repository: `https://github.com/PacktPublishing/Mastering-Embedded-Linux-Development/tree/main/Chapter19`.

GNU debugger

GDB is a source-level debugger for compiled languages, primarily C and C++, although there is also support for a variety of other languages, such as Go and Objective-C. You should read the notes for the version of GDB you are using to find out the status of support for the various languages.

The project website is `https://www.gnu.org/software/gdb/` and it contains a lot of useful information, including the GDB user manual, *Debugging with GDB*.

Out of the box, GDB has a command-line user interface that some people find off-putting, although, in reality, it is easy to use with a little practice. If command-line interfaces are not to your liking, there are plenty of frontend user interfaces to GDB, and I will describe three of them later in this chapter.

Preparing to debug

You need to compile the code you want to debug with debug symbols. GCC offers two options for this: -g and -ggdb. The latter adds debug information that is specific to GDB, whereas the former generates information in an appropriate format for whichever target operating system you are using, making it the more portable option. Since GDB is the default debugger on Linux, it is best to use -ggdb. Both options allow you to specify the level of debug information, from 0 to 3:

- 0: This produces no debug information at all and is equivalent to omitting the -g or -ggdb switch.

- 1: This produces minimal information but includes function names and external variables, which is enough to generate a backtrace.

- 2: This is the default and includes information about local variables and line numbers so that you can perform source-level debugging and single-step through the code.

- 3: This includes extra information which, among other things, means that GDB can handle macro expansions correctly.

In most cases, -g suffices: reserve -g3 or -ggdb3 for if you are having problems stepping through code, especially if it contains macros.

The next issue to consider is the level of code optimization. Compiler optimization tends to destroy the relationship between lines of source code and machine code, which makes stepping through the source unpredictable. If you experience problems such as this, you will most likely need to compile without optimization, leaving out the -O compile switch, or using -Og, which enables optimizations that do not interfere with debugging.

A related issue is that of stack-frame pointers, which are required by GDB to generate a backtrace of function calls up to the current one. On some architectures, GCC will not generate stack-frame pointers with higher levels of optimization (-O2 and above). If you find yourself in a situation where you really have to compile with -O2 but still want backtraces, you can override the default behavior with -fno-omit-frame-pointer. Also, look out for code that has been hand-optimized to leave out frame pointers through the addition of -fomit-frame-pointer: you may want to temporarily remove those bits.

Debugging applications

You can use GDB to debug applications in one of two ways: if you are developing code to run on desktops and servers, or indeed any environment where you compile and run the code on the same machine, it is natural to run GDB natively. However, most embedded development is done using a cross toolchain, and hence you want to debug code running on the device but control it from the cross-development environment, where you have the source code and the tools. I will focus on the latter case, since it is the most likely scenario for embedded developers, but I will also show you how to set up a system for native debugging. I am not going to describe the basics of using GDB here since there are many good references on that topic already, including the GDB user manual and the suggested *Further study* section at the end of the chapter.

Remote debugging using gdbserver

The key component for remote debugging is the debug agent, **gdbserver**, which runs on the target and controls the execution of the program being debugged. gdbserver connects to a copy of GDB running on the host machine via a network connection or a serial interface.

Debugging through gdbserver is almost, but not quite, the same as debugging natively. The differences are mostly centered around the fact that there are two computers involved, and they have to be in the right state for debugging to take place. Here are some things to look out for:

- At the start of a debug session, you need to load the program you want to debug on the target using gdbserver and then separately load GDB from your cross toolchain on the host.

- GDB and gdbserver need to connect to each other before a debug session can begin.

- GDB needs to be told where on the host to look for debug symbols and source code, especially for shared libraries.

- The GDB run command is not supported.

- gdbserver will terminate when the debug session ends, and you will need to restart it if you want another debug session.

- You need debug symbols and source code for the binaries you want to debug on the host, but not on the target. Often, there is not enough storage space for them on the target, and they will need to be stripped before deploying to the target.

- The GDB/gdbserver combination does not support all the features of natively running GDB: for example, gdbserver cannot follow the child process after a fork, whereas native GDB can.

- Odd things can happen if GDB and gdbserver are from different versions of GDB or are the same version but configured differently. Ideally, they should be built from the same source using your favorite build tool.

Debug symbols increase the size of executables dramatically, sometimes by a factor of 10. As mentioned in *Chapter 5*, it can be useful to remove debug symbols without recompiling everything. The tool for the job is strip from the binutils package in your cross toolchain. You can control the strip level with these switches:

- --strip-all: This removes all symbols (default).
- --strip-unneeded: This removes symbols not required for relocation processing.
- --strip-debug: This removes only debug symbols.

> **IMPORTANT NOTE**
>
> For applications and shared libraries, --strip-all (the default) is fine, but when it comes to kernel modules, you will find that it will stop the module from loading. Use --strip-unneeded instead. I am still working on a use case for --strip-debug.

With that in mind, let's look at the specifics involved in debugging with The Yocto Project and Buildroot.

Setting up The Yocto Project for remote debugging

There are two things to be done to debug applications remotely when using The Yocto Project: you need to add gdbserver to the target image, and you need to create an SDK that includes GDB and has debug symbols for the executables that you plan to debug. There is detailed documentation on setting up Yocto for remote debugging at https://docs.yoctoproject.org/dev-manual/debugging.html#using-the-gdbserver-method.

First, to include gdbserver in the target image, you can add the package explicitly by adding this to conf/local.conf:

```
IMAGE_INSTALL:append = " gdbserver"
```

In the absence of a serial console, an SSH daemon also needs to be added so that you have some way to start gdbserver on the target:

```
EXTRA_IMAGE_FEATURES:append = " ssh-server-openssh"
```

Alternatively, you can add `tools-debug` to `EXTRA_IMAGE_FEATURES`, which will add gdbserver, native gdb, and `strace` to the target image (I will talk about `strace` in the next chapter):

```
EXTRA_IMAGE_FEATURES:append = " tools-debug ssh-server-openssh"
```

Then rebuild the target image:

```
$ bitbake core-image-minimal-dev
```

For the second part, you just need to build an SDK as I described in *Chapter 6*:

```
$ bitbake -c populate_sdk core-image-minimal-dev
```

The SDK contains a copy of GDB. It also contains a sysroot for thetarget with debug symbols for all the programs and libraries that are part of the target image. Lastly, the SDK contains the source code for the executables. Instead of the SDK, you can use the sysroots inside of the Yocto build directly (`https://docs.yoctoproject.org/sdk-manual/extensible.html#when-using-the-extensible-sdk-directly-in-a-yocto-build`).

The SDK built for the Raspberry Pi 4 for version 5.0.<n> of The Yocto Project is installed by default in `/opt/poky/5.0.<n>/`. The sysroot for the target is `/opt/poky/5.0.<n>/sysroots/cortexa72-poky-linux/`. The programs are in `/bin/`, `/sbin/`, `/usr/bin/`, and `/usr/sbin/`, relative to the sysroot, and the libraries are in `/lib/` and `/usr/lib/`. In each of these directories, you will find a subdirectory named `.debug/` that contains the symbols for each program and library. GDB knows to look in .debug/ when searching for symbol information. The source code for the executables is stored in `/usr/src/debug/` relative to the sysroot.

Setting up Buildroot for remote debugging

Buildroot does not make a distinction between the environment used to build and the environment used for application development: there is no SDK. Assuming that you are using the Buildroot internal toolchain, you need to enable these options to copy GDB to the host and copy gdbserver to the target:

- BR2_TOOLCHAIN_EXTERNAL, in **Toolchain** | **Toolchain type** | **External toolchain**
- BR2_TOOLCHAIN_EXTERNAL_GDB_SERVER_COPY, in **Toolchain** | **Copy gdb server to the Target**
- BR2_PACKAGE_GDB, in **Target packages** | **Debugging, profiling and benchmark** | **gdb**

An external toolchain is needed because the toolchain that Buildroot 2024.02.6 builds cannot compile gdbserver.

You also need to build executables with debug symbols, for which you need to enable BR2_ENABLE_ DEBUG, in **Build options | build packages with debugging symbols**.

This will create libraries with debug symbols in output/host/<arch>/sysroot.

Starting to debug

Now that you have gdbserver installed on the target and a cross GDB on the host, you can start a debug session.

Connecting GDB and gdbserver

The connection between GDB and gdbserver can be through a network or serial interface. In the case of a network connection, you launch gdbserver with the TCP port number to listen on and, optionally, an IP address to accept connections from. In most cases, you don't care which IP address is going to connect, so you can just provide the port number. In this example, gdbserver waits for a connection on port 10000 from any host:

```
# gdbserver :10000 /usr/bin/helloworld
Process /usr/bin/helloworld created; pid = 581
Listening on port 10000
```

Next, start the copy of GDB from your toolchain, pointing it at an unstripped copy of the program so that GDB can load the symbol table:

```
$ aarch64-poky-linux-gdb helloworld
```

In GDB, use the target remote command to make the connection to gdbserver, giving it the IP address or hostname of the target and the port it is waiting on:

```
(gdb) target remote raspberrypi4-64:10000
```

When gdbserver sees the connection from the host, it prints the following:

```
Remote debugging from host 192.168.1.123, port 50696
```

The procedure is similar for a serial connection. On the target, you tell gdbserver which serial port to use:

```
# gdbserver /dev/ttyAMA0 /usr/bin/helloworld
```

You may need to configure the port baud rate beforehand using stty(1) or a similar program. A simple example would be as follows:

```
# stty -F /dev/ttyAMA0 115200
```

There are many other options to `stty`, so read the manual page for more details. It is worthwhile noting that the port must not be used for anything else. For example, you can't use a port that is being used as the system console.

On the host, you make the connection to `gdbserver` using `target remote` plus the serial device at the host end of the cable. In most cases, you will want to set the baud rate of the host serial port first, using the GDB command `set serial baud`:

```
(gdb) set serial baud 115200
(gdb) target remote /dev/ttyUSB0
```

Even though GDB and `gdbserver` are now connected, we are not ready to set breakpoints and start stepping through the source code yet.

Setting the sysroot

GDB needs to know where to find debug information and source code for the program and shared libraries you are debugging. When debugging natively, the paths are well known and built into GDB. But when using a cross toolchain, GDB has no way to guess where the root of the target filesystem is. You have to provide this information.

If you built your application using The Yocto Project SDK, the `sysroot` is within the SDK, and so you can set it in GDB like this:

```
(gdb) set sysroot /opt/poky/5.0.<n>/sysroots/cortexa72-poky-linux
```

If you are using Buildroot, you will find that the `sysroot` is in `output/host/<toolchain>/sysroot`, and that `output/staging` is a symbolic link to it. So, for Buildroot, you would set the `sysroot` like this:

```
(gdb) set sysroot /home/frank/buildroot/output/staging
```

GDB also needs to find the source code for the files you are debugging. GDB has a search path for source files, which you can see using the `show directories` command:

```
(gdb) show directories
Source directories searched: $cdir:$cwd
```

These are the defaults: `$cwd` is the current working directory of the GDB instance running on the host; `$cdir` is the directory where the source was compiled. The latter is encoded into the object files with the tag `DW_AT_comp_dir`. You can see these tags using `objdump --dwarf` like this:

```
$ aarch64-poky-linux-objdump --dwarf helloworld | grep DW_AT_comp_dir
<...>
<23a> DW_AT_comp_dir : (indirect line string, offset: 0xfc): /home/frank/
helloworld
<...>
```

In most cases, the defaults, $cdir and $cwd, are sufficient, but problems arise if the directories have been moved between compilation and debugging. One such case occurs with The Yocto Project. Taking a deeper look at the DW_AT_comp_dir tags for a program compiled using The Yocto Project SDK, you may notice this:

```
$ aarch64-poky-linux-objdump --dwarf helloworld | grep DW_AT_comp_dir
<1e> DW_AT_comp_dir : (indirect string, offset: 0x1b): /usr/src/debug/
glibc/2.39+git/csu
<4f> DW_AT_comp_dir : (indirect line string, offset: 0): /usr/src/debug/
glibc/2.39+git/csu
<1c5> DW_AT_comp_dir : (indirect line string, offset: 0): /usr/src/debug/
glibc/2.39+git/csu
<209> DW_AT_comp_dir : (indirect string, offset: 0x1b): /usr/src/debug/
glibc/2.39+git/csu
<23a> DW_AT_comp_dir : (indirect line string, offset: 0xfc): /usr/src/
debug/helloworld/1.0
<3e0> DW_AT_comp_dir : (indirect string, offset: 0x1b): /usr/src/debug/
glibc/2.39+git/csu
<...>
```

Here, you can see multiple references to the directory /usr/src/debug/glibc/2.39+git, but where is it? The answer is that it is in the sysroot for the SDK, so the full path is /opt/poky/5.0.6/sysroots/cortexa72-poky-linux/usr/src/debug/glibc/2.39+git. The SDK contains source code for all of the programs and libraries in the target image. GDB has a simple way to cope with an entire directory tree being moved like this: substitute-path. So, when debugging with The Yocto Project SDK, you need to use these commands:

```
(gdb) set sysroot /opt/poky/5.0.<n>/sysroots/cortexa72-poky-linux
(gdb) set substitute-path /usr/src/debug /opt/poky/5.0.<n>/sysroots/
cortexa72-poky-linux/usr/src/debug
```

You may have additional shared libraries that are stored outside the sysroot. In that case, you can use set solib-search-path, which can contain a colon-separated list of directories to search for shared libraries. GDB searches solib-search-path only if it cannot find the binary in the sysroot.

A third way of telling GDB where to look for source code, for both libraries and programs, is to use the `directory` command:

```
(gdb) directory /home/frank//lib_mylib
Source directories searched: /home/frank//lib_mylib:$cdir:$cwd
```

Paths added in this way take precedence because they are searched *before* those from `sysroot` or `solib-search-path`.

GDB command files

There are some things that you need to do each time you run GDB, like setting the `sysroot`. It is convenient to put such commands into a command file and run them each time GDB is started. GDB reads commands from `$HOME/.gdbinit`, then from `.gdbinit` in the current directory, and then from files specified on the command line with the `-x` parameter. However, recent versions of GDB will refuse to load `.gdbinit` from the current directory for security reasons. You can override that behavior by adding a line such as this to `$HOME/.gdbinit`:

```
set auto-load safe-path /
```

Alternatively, if you don't want to enable auto-loading globally, you can specify a particular directory like this:

```
add-auto-load-safe-path /home/frank/myprog
```

My personal preference is to use the `-x` parameter to point to the command file, which exposes the location of the file so that I don't forget about it.

To help you set up GDB, Buildroot creates a GDB command file containing the correct `sysroot` command in `output/staging/usr/share/buildroot/gdbinit`. It will contain a line like this one:

```
set sysroot /home/frank/buildroot/output/host/aarch64-buildroot-linux-gnu/
sysroot
```

Now that GDB is running and can find the information it needs, let's look at some of the commands we can perform with it.

Overview of GDB commands

GDB has many more commands, which are described in the online manual and in the resources mentioned in the *Further study* section. To help you get going as quickly as possible, here is a list of the most commonly used commands. In most cases, there is a short form for commands, which are listed in the following tables.

Breakpoints

These are the commands for managing breakpoints:

Command	Short-form command	Use
`break <location>`	`b <location>`	Set a breakpoint on a function name, line number, or line. Examples of locations are main, 5, and `sortbug.c:42`.
`info breakpoints`	`i b`	List breakpoints.
`delete breakpoint <N>`	`d b <N>`	Delete the breakpoint <N>.

Running and stepping

These are commands for controlling the execution of a program:

Command	Short-form command	Use
`run`	`r`	Load a fresh copy of the program into memory and start running it. *This does not work for remote debugging using gdbserver.*
`continue`	`c`	Continue execution from a breakpoint.
Ctrl + C	-	Stop the program from being debugged.
`step`	`s`	Step one line of code, stepping *into* any function that is called.
`next`	`n`	Step one line of code, stepping *over* a function call.
`finish`	-	Run until the current function returns.

Getting information

These are commands for getting information regarding the debugger:

Command	Short-form command	Use
`backtrace`	`bt`	List the call stack.
`info threads`	`i th`	Display information about the threads executing in the program.
`info sharedlibrary`	`i share`	Display information about shared libraries currently loaded by the program.
`print <variable>`	`p <variable>`	Print the value of the variable. For example, `print foo`.
`list`	`l`	List lines of code around the current program counter.

Before we can begin stepping through a program inside a debug session, we first need to set an initial breakpoint.

Running to a breakpoint

gdbserver loads the program into memory and sets a breakpoint at the first instruction. Then it waits for a connection from GDB. When the connection is made, you enter into a debug session. However, you will find that if you try to single-step immediately, you will get this message:

```
Cannot find bounds of current function
```

This is because the program has halted at code written in assembly, which creates the runtime environment for C/C++ programs. The first line of C/C++ code is the main() function. To stop at main(), you would set a breakpoint there and then use the continue command (abbreviation c) to tell gdbserver to continue from the start of the program and stop at main():

```
(gdb) break main
Breakpoint 1, main (argc=1, argv=0xbefffe24) at helloworld.c:8
printf("Hello, world!\n");
(gdb) c
```

At this point, you may see the following:

```
Reading /lib/ld-linux.so.3 from remote target...
warning: File transfers from remote targets can be slow. Use "set sysroot"
to access files locally instead.
```

With older versions of GDB, you may instead see this:

```
warning: Could not load shared library symbols for 2 libraries, e.g. /lib/
libc.so.6.
```

In both cases, the problem is that you have forgotten to set the sysroot! Take another look at the earlier section on sysroot.

This is all very different from starting a program natively, where you just type run. In fact, if you try typing run in a remote debug session, you will either see a message saying that the remote target does not support the run command, or, in older versions of GDB, it will just hang without any explanation.

Extending GDB with Python

We can embed a full Python interpreter into GDB to extend its functionality. This is done by configuring GDB using the --with-python option prior to building. GDB has an API that exposes much of its internal state as Python objects. This API allows us to define our own custom GDB commands as scripts written in Python. These extra commands may include useful debugging aids such as tracepoints and pretty printers that are not built into GDB.

Building GDB with Python support

We have already covered *Setting up Buildroot for remote debugging*. There are some additional steps needed to enable Python support inside GDB. We cannot use a toolchain generated by Buildroot to build GDB with Python support because it is missing some necessary thread support.

To build cross GDB for the host with Python support, perform the following steps:

1. Navigate to the directory where you installed Buildroot:

    ```
    $ cd buildroot
    ```

2. Copy the configuration file for the board you wish to build an image for:

    ```
    $ cd configs
    $ cp raspberrypi4_64_defconfig rpi4_64_gdb_defconfig
    $ cd ..
    ```

3. Clean previous build artifacts from the output directory:

```
$ make clean
```

4. Activate your configuration file:

```
$ make rpi4_64_gdb_defconfig
```

5. Begin customizing your image:

```
$ make menuconfig
```

6. Enable the use of an external toolchain by navigating to **Toolchain | Toolchain type | External toolchain** and selecting that option.

7. Back out of **External toolchain** and open the **Toolchain** submenu. Select a known working toolchain, such as **Linaro AArch64 2018.05**, as your external toolchain.

8. Select **Build cross gdb for the host** from the Toolchain page and enable both **TUI support** and **Python support**.

9. Drill down into the **GDB debugger Version** submenu from the **Toolchain** page and select the newest version of GDB available in Buildroot.

10. Back out of the **Toolchain** page and drill down into **Build options**. Select **Build packages with debugging symbols**.

11. Back out of the **Build options** page, drill down into **System Configuration**, and select **Enable root login with password**. Open **Root password** and enter a non-empty password in the text field.

12. Back out of the **System Configuration** page and drill down into **Target packages | Debugging, profiling and benchmark**. Select the **gdb** package to add gdbserver to the target image.

13. Back out of **Debugging, profiling and benchmark** and drill down into **Target packages | Networking applications**. Select the **dropbear** package to enable scp and ssh access to the target. Note that dropbear does not allow root scp and ssh access without a password.

14. Add the **haveged** entropy daemon, which can be found under **Target packages | Miscellaneous** so that SSH is available quicker upon booting.

15. Add another package to your image so you have something to debug. I chose the bsdiff binary patch/diff tool, which is written in C and can be found under **Target packages | Development tools**.

16. Save your changes and exit Buildroot's menuconfig.

17. Save your changes to your configuration file:

```
$ make savedefconfig
```

18. Build the image for the target:

```
$ make
```

A readymade rpi4_64_gdb_defconfig file for the Raspberry Pi 4 can be found in the code archive for this chapter if you wish to skip the previous menuconfig steps. Copy that file from MELD/ Chapter19/buildroot/configs/ to your buildroot/configs directory and run make on that if you prefer.

When the build is done, there should be a bootable sdcard.img file in output/images/ that you can write to a microSD card using Etcher. Insert that microSD into your target device and boot it. Connect the target device to your local network with an Ethernet cable and locate its IP address using arp-scan --localnet. SSH into the device as root and enter the password that you set when configuring your image. I specified temppwd as the root password for my rpi4_64_gdb_ defconfig image.

Now, let's debug bsdiff remotely using GDB:

1. First, navigate to the /usr/bin directory on the target:

```
# cd /usr/bin
```

2. Then, start bdiff with gdbserver, as we did with helloworld earlier:

```
# gdbserver :10000 ./bsdiff /usr/bin/bzless /usr/bin/bzmore ~/
patchfile
Process ./bsdiff created; pid = 197
Listening on port 10000
```

3. On your Linux host, copy tp.py to your home directory:

```
$ cd ~
$ cp MELD/Chapter19/tp.py .
```

4. Next, start the copy of GDB from your toolchain, pointing it at an unstripped copy of the program so that GDB can load the symbol table:

```
$ cd ~/buildroot/output/build/bsdiff-4.3
$ ~/buildroot/output/host/bin/aarch64-linux-gdb bsdiff
```

5. In GDB, set the `sysroot` like this:

    ```
    (gdb) set sysroot ~/buildroot/output/staging
    ```

6. Then, use the command target remote to make the connection to gdbserver, giving it the IP address or hostname of the target and the port it is waiting on:

    ```
    (gdb) target remote 192.168.1.127:10000
    ```

7. When gdbserver sees the connection from the host, it prints the following:

    ```
    Remote debugging from host 192.168.1.123, port 36980
    ```

8. We can now load Python command scripts such as tp.py into GDB and invoke these commands like so:

    ```
    (gdb) source ~/tp.py
    (gdb) tp search
    Breakpoint 1 at 0x555b7b9154: file /home/frank/buildroot/output/
    build/bsdiff-4.3/bsdiff.c, line 170.
    ```

    In this case, tp is the name of the *tracepoint* command and search is the name of a recursive function in bsdiff.

9. Set a breakpoint at main():

    ```
    (gdb) break main
    Breakpoint 2 at 0x555b7b8e50: file /home/frank/buildroot/output/
    build/bsdiff-4.3/bsdiff.c, line 216.
    ```

10. Continue:

    ```
    (gdb) c
    Continuing.
    Breakpoint 2, main (argc=4, argv=0x7ff2c99ec8) at /home/frank/
    buildroot/output/build/bsdiff-4.3/bsdiff.c:216
    216             if(argc!=4) errx(1,"usage: %s oldfile newfile
    patchfile\n",argv[0]);
    ```

11. Continue again:

    ```
    (gdb) c
    Continuing.
    search @ /home/frank/buildroot/output/build/bsdiff-4.3/bsdiff.c:170
    ```

```
        x(off_t: <optimized out>) [8]
        y(off_t: <optimized out>) [8]
<...>
search @ /home/frank/buildroot/output/build/bsdiff-4.3/bsdiff.c:170
        x(off_t: <optimized out>) [8]
        y(off_t: <optimized out>) [8]
[Inferior 1 (process 251) exited normally]
Tracepoint 'search' Count: 10
(gdb)
```

The bsdiff program performs binary diffs and takes three arguments: oldfile, newfile, and patchfile. The patchfile that bsdiff generates serves as input to the bspatch program for patching binaries. We start the bsdiff program on the target with /usr/bin/bzless, /usr/bin/bzmore, and ~/patchfile as arguments. The output from the GDB *tracepoint* command indicates that the search function at *line 170* of bsdiff.c was called 10 times over the course of the process.

The Python support in GDB can also be used to debug Python programs. GDB has visibility into CPython's internals that the standard pdb debugger for Python does not. It can even inject Python code into a running Python process. This enables the creation of powerful Python debugging tools like memory analyzers that would otherwise be impossible.

Native debugging

Running a native copy of GDB on the target is not as common as doing it remotely, but it is possible. In addition to installing GDB onto the target image, you will also need to install unstripped copies of the executables you wish to debug and their corresponding source code. Both The Yocto Project and Buildroot allow you to do this.

> **IMPORTANT NOTE**
>
> While native debugging is not a common activity for embedded developers, running profile and trace tools on the target is very common. These tools usually work best if you have unstripped binaries and source code on the target, which is half of the story I am telling here. I will return to this topic in the next chapter.

The Yocto Project

To begin with, add gdb to the target image by adding this to conf/local.conf:

```
EXTRA_IMAGE_FEATURES:append = "tools-debug dbg-pkgs src-pkgs"
```

You need the debug information for the packages you want to debug. The Yocto Project builds debug variants of packages, which contain the debug info and symbols stripped from the binaries. You can add these debug packages selectively to your target image by adding `<package name>-dbg` to your `conf/local.conf`. Or, you can simply install all debug packages by adding `dbg-pkgs` to `EXTRA_IMAGE_FEATURES` as just shown. Be warned that this will increase the size of the target image dramatically, perhaps by several hundreds of megabytes.

Similarly, you can add source packages to your target image by adding `<package name>-src` to your `conf/local.conf`. Or, you can simply install all source packages by adding `src-pkgs` to `EXTRA_IMAGE_FEATURES`. Again, this will dramatically increase the size of the target image. The source code is installed in `/usr/src/debug/<package name>` in the target image. This means that GDB will pick it up without needing to run `set substitute-path`.

Buildroot

With Buildroot, you can tell it to install a native copy of GDB in the target image by enabling this option:

- `BR2_PACKAGE_GDB_DEBUGGER` in **Target packages | Debugging, profiling and benchmark | Full debugger**

Then, to build binaries with debug information and install them in the target image without stripping, enable the first and disable the second of these two options:

- `BR2_ENABLE_DEBUG` in **Build options | Build packages with debugging symbols**
- `BR2_STRIP_strip` in **Build options | Strip target binaries**

That's all I have to say about native debugging. Again, the practice is uncommon on embedded devices because the extra source code and debug symbols add bloat to the target image. Next, let's look at another form of remote debugging.

Just-in-time debugging

Sometimes, a program will start to misbehave after it has been running for a while, and you would like to know what it is doing. The GDB `attach` feature does exactly this. I call it just-in-time debugging. It is available with both native and remote debug sessions.

In the case of remote debugging, you need to find the PID of the process to be debugged and pass it to gdbserver with the `--attach` option. For example, if the PID is 109, you would type this:

```
# gdbserver --attach :10000 109
Attached; pid = 109
Listening on port 10000
```

This forces the process to stop as if it were at a breakpoint, allowing you to start your cross GDB in the normal way and connect to gdbserver. When you are done, you can detach, allowing the program to continue running without the debugger:

```
(gdb) detach
Detaching from program: /home/frank/helloworld, process 109
Ending remote debugging.
```

Attaching to a running process by PID is certainly handy, but what about multi-process or multi-threaded programs? There are techniques for debugging those types of programs with GDB as well.

Debugging forks and threads

What happens when the program you are debugging forks? Does the debug session follow the parent process or the child? This behavior is controlled by follow-fork-mode, which may be parent or child, with parent being the default. Unfortunately, current versions of gdbserver do not support this option, so it only works for native debugging. If you really need to debug the child process while using gdbserver, a workaround is to modify the code so that the child loops on a variable immediately after the fork, giving you the opportunity to attach a new gdbserver session to it and then to set the variable so that it drops out of the loop.

When a thread in a multithreaded process hits a breakpoint, the default behavior is for all threads to halt. In most cases, this is the best thing to do as it allows you to look at static variables without them being changed by the other threads. When you resume execution of the thread, all the stopped threads start up, even if you are single-stepping, and it is especially this last case that can cause problems. There is a way to modify the way in which GDB handles stopped threads, through a parameter called scheduler-locking. Normally it is off, but if you set it to on, only the thread that was stopped at the breakpoint is resumed and the others remain stopped, giving you a chance to see what the thread alone does without interference. This continues to be the case until you turn scheduler-locking off. gdbserver supports this feature.

Core files

Core files capture the state of a failing program at the point that it terminates. You don't even have to be in the room with a debugger when the bug manifests itself. So, when you see Segmentation fault (core dumped), don't shrug; investigate the **core file** and extract the goldmine of information in there.

The first observation is that core files are not created by default, but only when the core file resource limit for the process is non-zero. You can change it for the current shell using ulimit -c. To remove all limits on the size of core files, type the following command:

```
$ ulimit -c unlimited
```

By default, the core file is named core and is placed in the current working directory of the process, which is the one pointed to by /proc/<PID>/cwd. There are a number of problems with this scheme. Firstly, when looking at a device with several files named core, it is not obvious which program generated each one. Secondly, the current working directory of the process may well be in a read-only filesystem, there may not be enough space to store the core file, or the process may not have permissions to write to the current working directory.

There are two files that control the naming and placement of core files. The first is /proc/sys/kernel/core_uses_pid. Writing a 1 to it causes the PID number of the dying process to be appended to the filename, which is somewhat useful as long as you can associate the PID number with a program name from log files.

Much more useful is /proc/sys/kernel/core_pattern, which gives you a lot more control over core files. The default pattern is core, but you can change it to a pattern composed of these meta characters:

- %p: PID
- %u: Real UID of the dumped process
- %g: Real GID of the dumped process
- %s: Number of the signal causing the dump
- %t: Time of dump expressed as seconds since the Epoch, 1970-01-01 00:00:00 +0000 (UTC)
- %h: Hostname
- %e: Executable filename
- %E: Path name of executable with slashes (/) replaced by exclamation marks (!)
- %c: Core file size soft resource limit of the dumped process

You can also use a pattern that begins with an absolute directory name so that all core files are gathered together in one place. As an example, the following pattern puts all core files into the /corefiles directory and names them with the program name and the time of the crash:

```
# echo /corefiles/core.%e.%t > /proc/sys/kernel/core_pattern
```

Following a core dump, you would find something like this:

```
# ls /corefiles
core.sort-debug.1431425613
```

For more information, refer to the core(5) manual page.

Using GDB to look at core files

Here is a sample GDB session looking at a core file:

```
$ arm-poky-linux-gnueabi-gdb sort-debug /home/chris/rootfs/corefiles/core.
sort-debug.1431425613
<...>
Core was generated by './sort-debug'.
Program terminated with signal SIGSEGV, Segmentation fault.
#0  0x000085c8 in addtree (p=0x0, w=0xbeac4c60 "the") at sort-debug.c:41
41  p->word = strdup (w);
```

This shows that the program stopped at *line 41*. The list command shows the code in the vicinity:

```
(gdb) list
37 static struct tnode *addtree (struct tnode *p, char *w)
38 {
39     int cond;
40
41     p->word = strdup (w);
42     p->count = 1;
43     p->left = NULL;
44     p->right = NULL;
45
```

The backtrace command (shortened to bt) shows how we got to this point:

```
(gdb) bt
#0  0x000085c8 in addtree (p=0x0, w=0xbeac4c60 "the") at sort-debug.c:41
#1  0x00008798 in main (argc=1, argv=0xbeac4e24) at sort-debug.c:89
```

This is an obvious mistake: addtree() was called with a null pointer.

GDB began as a command-line debugger and many people still use it this way. Even though the LLVM Project's LLDB debugger is gaining in popularity, GCC and GDB remain the prominent compiler and debugger for Linux. So far, we have focused exclusively on GDB's command-line interface. Now we will look at some frontends to GDB with progressively more modern user interfaces.

GDB user interfaces

GDB is controlled at a low level through the GDB machine interface, GDB/MI, which can be used to wrap GDB in a user interface or as part of a larger program, and it considerably extends the range of options available to you.

In this section, I will describe three that are well suited to debugging embedded targets: the **Terminal User Interface (TUI)**, **Data Display Debugger (DDD)**, and **Visual Studio Code**.

Terminal User Interface

The **Terminal User Interface (TUI)** is an optional part of the standard GDB package. The main feature is a code window that shows the line of code about to be executed, together with any breakpoints. It is a definite improvement on the `list` command in command-line mode GDB.

The attraction of the TUI is that it just works without any extra setup, and since it is in text mode, it is possible to use over an SSH terminal session, for example, when running gdb natively on a target. Most cross toolchains configure GDB with the TUI. Simply add `-tui` to the command line and you will see the following:

```
         ┌─ frank@franktop: ~/umoria/umoria ─────────────────────  Q  ≡  _  □  ⊗
         ┌─/home/frank/umoria/src/main.cpp──────────────────────────────────────
            102               startMoria(seed, new_game);
            103
            104         return 0;
            105    }
            106
            107         static bool parseGameSeed(const char *argv, uint32_t &seed) {
            108             int value;
            109
         b+ 110             if (!stringToNumber(argv, value)) {
            111                 return false;
            112             }
            113             if (value <= 0 || value > INT_MAX) {
            114                 return false;
         ─────────────────────────────────────────────────────────────────────
         exec No process In:                                       L??    PC: ??

         For help, type "help".
         --Type <RET> for more, q to quit, c to continue without paging--
         Type "apropos word" to search for commands related to "word"...
         Reading symbols from umoria...
         (gdb) b 110
         Breakpoint 1 at 0x100c7: file /home/frank/umoria/src/main.cpp, line 110.
         (gdb) run
```

Figure 19.1 – TUI

If you still find the TUI lacking and prefer a truly graphical frontend to GDB, the GNU project also offers one of those (https://www.gnu.org/software/ddd).

Data Display Debugger

Data Display Debugger (DDD) is a simple standalone program that gives you a graphical user interface to GDB with minimal fuss and bother, and although the UI controls look dated, it does everything that is necessary.

The --debugger option tells DDD to use GDB from your toolchain, and you can use the -x argument to give the path to a GDB command file:

```
$ ddd --debugger aarch64-poky-linux-gdb -x gdbinit sort-debug
```

The following screenshot shows off one of the nicest features: the data window, which contains items in a grid that you can rearrange as you wish. If you double-click on a pointer, it is expanded into a new data item and the link is shown with an arrow:

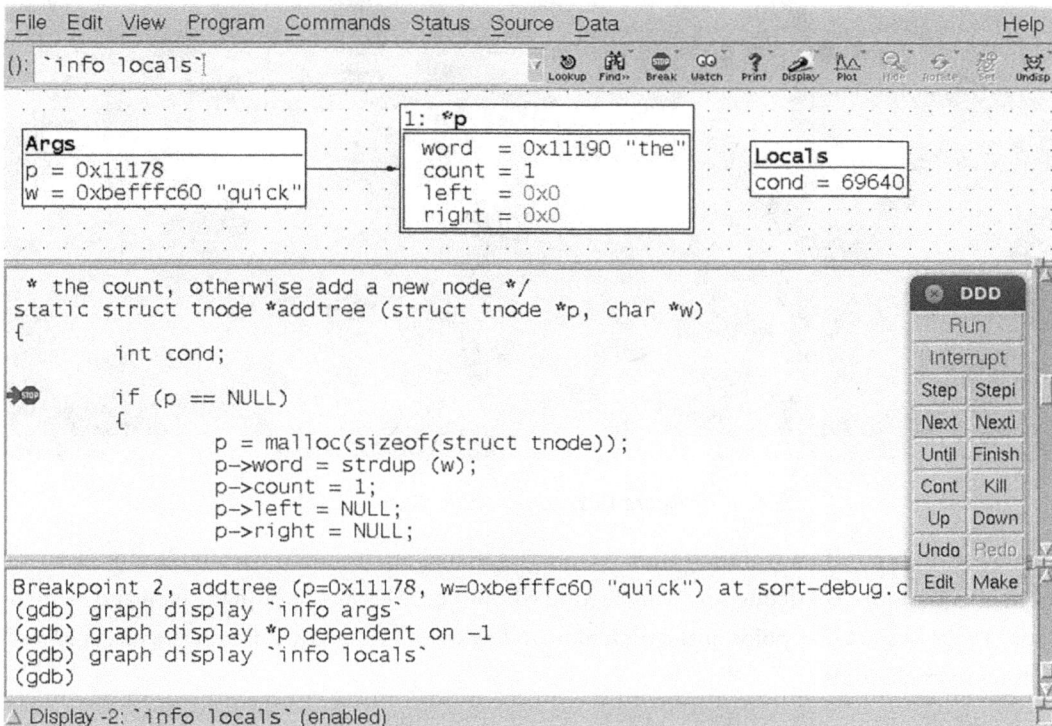

Figure 19.2 – DDD

If neither of these two GDB frontends is acceptable because you are a full stack web developer accustomed to working with the latest tools in your industry, then we still have you covered.

Visual Studio Code

Visual Studio Code is a very popular open-source code editor from Microsoft. Because it is an Electron application written in TypeScript, Visual Studio Code feels more lightweight and responsive than full-blown IDEs such as Eclipse. There is rich language support (code completion, go to definition, etc.) for many languages by way of extensions contributed by its large community of users. Remote cross GDB debugging can be integrated into Visual Studio Code using extensions for C/C++.

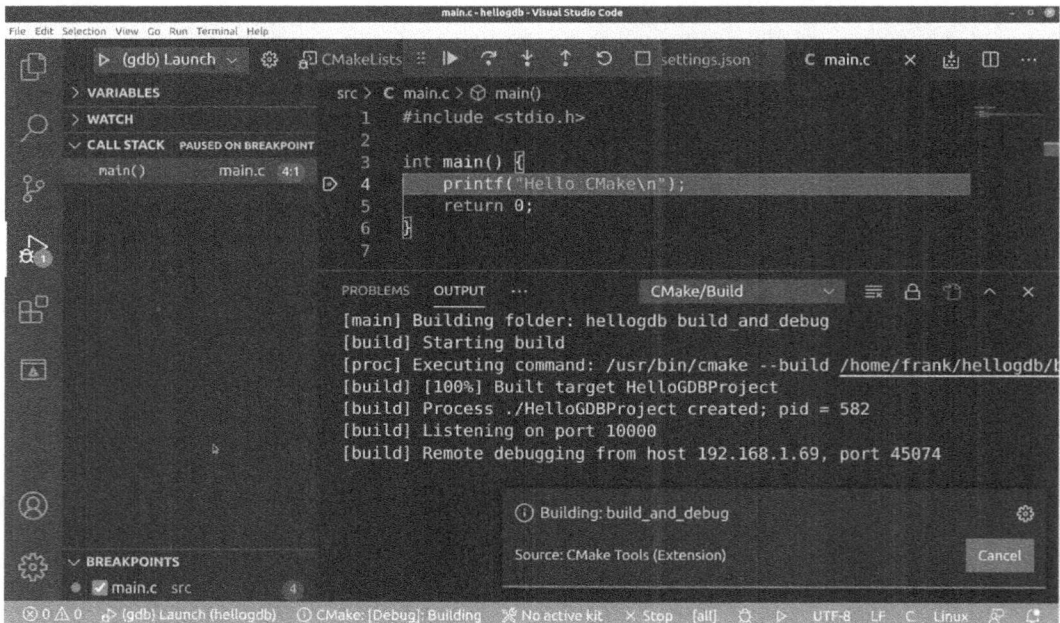

Figure 19.3 – Visual Studio Code

There are no prescribed workflows for integrating Visual Studio Code with Buildroot or Yocto. To enable remote GDB debugging, you need to edit project files like settings.json and launch. json. These project files point at the toolchain and sysroot. They also contain the target IP and SSH login credentials.

Debugging kernel code

You can use `kgdb` for source-level debugging, in a manner similar to remote debugging with `gdbserver`. There is also a self-hosted kernel debugger, `kdb`, that is handy for lighter-weight tasks such as seeing whether an instruction is executed and getting the backtrace to find out how it got there. Finally, there are kernel *Oops* messages and panics, which tell you a lot about the cause of a kernel exception.

Debugging kernel code with kgdb

When looking at kernel code using a source debugger, you must remember that the kernel is a complex system, with real-time behaviors. Don't expect debugging to be as easy as it is for applications. Stepping through code that changes the memory mapping or switches context is likely to produce odd results.

kgdb is the name given to the kernel GDB stubs that have been part of mainline Linux for many years now. There is a user manual in the kernel DocBook, and you can find an online version at `https://kernel.org/doc/html/v6.6/dev-tools/kgdb.html`.

In most cases, you will connect to `kgdb` over the serial interface, which is usually shared with the serial console. Hence, this implementation is called **kgdboc**, which is short for **kgdb over console**. To work, it requires a platform `tty` driver that supports I/O polling instead of interrupts, since `kgdb` has to disable interrupts when communicating with GDB. A few platforms support `kgdb` over USB, and there have been versions that work over Ethernet but, unfortunately, none of them have found their way into mainline Linux.

The same caveats regarding optimization and stack frames apply to the kernel, with the limitation that the kernel is written to assume an optimization level of at least -O1. You can override the kernel compile flags by setting `KCFLAGS` before running `make`.

These, then, are the kernel configuration options you will need for kernel debugging:

- `CONFIG_DEBUG_INFO` is in the **Kernel hacking | Compile-time checks and compiler options | Debug information | Rely on the toolchain's implicit default DWARF version** menu.

- `CONFIG_FRAME_POINTER` may be an option for your architecture and is in the **Kernel hacking | Compile-time checks and compiler options | Compile the kernel with frame pointers** menu.

- `CONFIG_KGDB` is in the **Kernel hacking | Generic Kernel Debugging Instruments | KGDB: kernel debugger** menu.

- `CONFIG_KGDB_SERIAL_CONSOLE` is in the **Kernel hacking | Generic Kernel Debugging Instruments | KGDB: kernel debugger | KGDB: use kgdb over the serial console** menu.

The kernel image must be in ELF object format so that GDB can load the symbols into memory. This is the file called `vmlinux` that is generated in the directory where Linux is built. In Yocto, you can request that a copy be included in the target image and SDK. It is built as a package named `kernel-vmlinux`, which you can install like any other, for example, by adding it to the `IMAGE_INSTALL` list.

The file is put into the `sysroot` boot directory, with a name like this:

```
/opt/poky/5.0.<n>/sysroots/cortexa72-poky-linux/boot/vmlinux-<version
string>-v8
```

In Buildroot, you will find `vmlinux` in the directory where the kernel was built, which is in `output/build/linux-<version string>/vmlinux`.

You need to tell `kgdb` which serial port to use, either through the kernel command line or at run-time via `sysfs`. For the first option, add `kgdboc=<tty>,<baud rate>` to the kernel command line:

```
kgdboc=ttyS0,115200
```

A sample debug session

The best way to show you how kgdb works is with a simple example. But before you can use kgdb, you first need to build it. To build kgdb and kdb, complete *Building GDB with Python support*, then perform these steps:

1. Navigate to the directory where you installed Buildroot:

```
$ cd buildroot
```

2. Clean previous build artifacts from the output directory:

```
$ make clean
```

3. Comment out the `miniuart-bt` dtoverlay from `board/raspberrypi4-64/config_4_64bit.txt`:

```
#dtoverlay=miniuart-bt
```

4. Append the following lines to board/raspberrypi4-64/config_4_64bit.txt:

```
enable_uart=1
dtoverlay=uart
```

5. Activate your saved configuration file:

```
$ make rpi4_64_gdb_defconfig
```

6. Build your saved configuration:

```
$ make
```

7. Begin customizing your kernel:

```
$ make linux-menuconfig
```

8. Enable kernel debugging by navigating to **Kernel hacking | Compile-time checks and compiler options | Debug information** and selecting **Rely on the toolchain's implicit default DWARF version.**

9. Deselect **Reduce debugging information.**

10. Back out of **Debug information** and select the **Compile the kernel with frame pointers** menu.

11. Back out of **Compile-time checks and compiler options** and drill down into **Generic Kernel Debugging Instruments | KGDB: kernel debugger.**

12. Select both **KGDB: use kgdb over the serial console** and **KGDB_KDB: include kdb frontend for kgdb.**

13. Back out of **Kernel hacking** and drill down into **Kernel Features.**

14. Deselect **Randomize the address of the kernel image.**

15. Save your changes and exit linux-menuconfig.

16. Rebuild the kernel:

```
$ make linux-rebuild
```

17. Delete the microSD card image:

```
$ rm output/images/sdcard.img
```

18. Regenerate the microSD card image:

```
$ make
```

When the build is done, there should be a bootable `sdcard.img` file in `output/images/` that you can write to a microSD card using Etcher. Insert that microSD into your target device. Connect a USB-to-TTL serial cable to the Raspberry Pi 4 (`https://learn.adafruit.com/adafruits-raspberry-pi-lesson-5-using-a-console-cable/connect-the-lead`). Boot the device.

Connect the target device to your local network with an Ethernet cable and locate its IP address using `arp-scan --localnet`. SSH into the device as `root` and enter the password that you set when configuring your image. I specified `temppwd` as the root password for my `rpi4_64_gdb_defconfig` image. Write the terminal name to the `/sys/module/kgdboc/parameters/kgdboc` file:

```
# echo ttyS0 > /sys/module/kgdboc/parameters/kgdboc
```

Note that you cannot set the baud rate in this way. If it is the same `tty` as the console, then it is set already. If not, use `stty` or a similar program.

Now you can start GDB on the host, selecting the `vmlinux` file that matches the running kernel:

```
$ cd buildroot
$ output/host/bin/aarch64-buildroot-linux-gnu-gdb output/build/linux-custom/vmlinux
```

GDB loads the symbol table from `vmlinux` and waits for further input.

Next, close any terminal emulator that is attached to the console: you are about to use it for GDB, and if both are active at the same time, some of the debug strings might get corrupted.

Now, you can return to GDB and attempt to connect to `kgdb`. However, you will find that the response you get from the target remote at this time is unhelpful:

```
(gdb) set serial baud 115200
(gdb) target remote /dev/ttyUSB0
Remote debugging using /dev/ttyUSB0

Ignoring packet error, continuing...
warning: unrecognized item "timeout" in "qSupported" response
```

The problem is that `kgdb` is not listening for a connection at this point. You need to interrupt the kernel before you can enter into an interactive GDB session with it. Unfortunately, just typing *Ctrl + C* in GDB, as you would with an application, does not work. You have to force a trap into the kernel by launching another shell on the target, via SSH, for example, and writing g to `/proc/sysrq-trigger` on the target board:

```
# echo g > /proc/sysrq-trigger
```

The target stops dead at this point. Now you can connect to kgdb via the serial device at the host end of the cable:

```
(gdb) target remote /dev/ttyUSB0
Remote debugging using /dev/ttyUSB0

warning: multi-threaded target stopped without sending a thread-id, using
first non-exited thread
[Switching to Thread 4294967294]
arch_kgdb_breakpoint () at ./arch/arm64/include/asm/kgdb.h:21
21              asm ("brk %0" : : "I" (KGDB_COMPILED_DBG_BRK_IMM));
(gdb)
```

At last, GDB is in charge. You can set breakpoints, examine variables, look at backtraces, and so on. As an example, set a break on __sys_accept4:

```
(gdb) break __sys_accept4
Breakpoint 1 at 0xffffffc0089ffe40: file net/socket.c, line 1938.
(gdb) c
Continuing.
```

Now the target comes back to life. Exit out of your SSH session and attempt to reconnect to the target device. Reconnecting calls __sys_accept4 and hits the breakpoint:

```
[New Thread 523]
[Switching to Thread 171]

Thread 79 hit Breakpoint 1, __sys_accept4 (fd=3, upeer_
sockaddr=0x7ffa494848, upeer_addrlen=0x7ffa4946bc, flags=flags@entry=0)
    at net/socket.c:1938
1938    {
(gdb)
```

If you have finished the debug session and want to disable kgdboc, just set the kgdboc terminal to null:

```
# echo "" > /sys/module/kgdboc/parameters/kgdboc
```

Like attaching to a running process with GDB, this technique of trapping the kernel and connecting to kgdb over a serial console works once the kernel is done booting. But what if the kernel never finishes booting because of a bug?

Debugging early code

The preceding example works in cases where the code you are interested in is executed when the system is fully booted. If you need to get in early, you can tell the kernel to wait during boot by adding kgdbwait to the command line, after the kgdboc option:

```
kgdboc=ttyS0,115200 kgdbwait
```

Now, when you boot, you will see this on the console:

```
[ 1.103415] console [ttyS0] enabled
[ 1.108216] kgdb: Registered I/O driver kgdboc.
[ 1.113071] kgdb: Waiting for connection from remote gdb...
```

At this point, you can close the console and connect from GDB in the usual way.

Debugging modules

Debugging kernel modules presents an additional challenge because the code is relocated at run-time, and so you need to find out at what address it resides. The information is presented through sysfs. The relocation addresses for each section of the module are stored in /sys/module/<module name>/sections. Note that since ELF sections begin with a dot (.), they appear as hidden files, and you will have to use ls -a if you want to list them. The important ones are .text, .data, and .bss.

Take as an example a module named mbx:

```
# cat /sys/module/mbx/sections/.text
0xffffffc000cd9000
# cat /sys/module/mbx/sections/.bss
0xffffffc000cdb380
```

Now you can use these numbers in kgdb to load the symbol table for the module at those addresses:

```
(gdb) add-symbol-file /home/frank/buildroot/output/build/mbx-driver-1.0.0/
mbx.ko 0xffffffc000cd9000 -s .bss 0xffffffc000cdb380
add symbol table from file "/home/frank/buildroot/output/build/mbx-
driver-1.0.0/mbx.ko" at
        .text_addr = 0xffffffc000cd9000
        .bss_addr = 0xffffffc000cdb380
(y or n) y
Reading symbols from /home/frank/buildroot/output/build/mbx-driver-1.0.0/
mbx.ko...
```

Everything should now work as normal: you can set breakpoints and inspect global and local variables in the module just as you can in `vmlinux`:

```
(gdb) break mbx_write

Breakpoint 1 at 0xffffffc000cd9280: file /home/frank/buildroot/output/
build/mbx-driver-1.0.0/./mbx.c, line 91.
(gdb) c
Continuing.
```

Then, force the device driver to call `mbx_write`, and it will hit the breakpoint:

```
[New Thread 231]
[Switching to Thread 227]

 Thread 97 hit Breakpoint 1, mbx_write (file=0xffffff8041e83300,
buffer=0x559dae9790 "hello\n", length=6, offset=0xffffffc00a083dc0)
    at /home/frank/buildroot/output/build/mbx-driver-1.0.0/./mbx.c:91
91          {
(gdb)
```

If you already use GDB to debug code in user space, then you should feel right at home debugging kernel code and modules with `kgdb`. Let's look at `kdb` next.

Debugging kernel code with kdb

Although `kdb` does not have the features of `kgdb` and GDB, it does have its uses, and, being selfhosted, there are no external dependencies to worry about. `kdb` has a simple command-line interface that you can use on a serial console. You can use it to inspect memory, registers, process lists, and `dmesg` and even set breakpoints to stop at a certain location.

To configure your kernel so that you can call `kdb` via a serial console, enable `kgdb` as shown previously, and then enable this additional option:

- `CONFIG_KGDB_KDB` in **Kernel hacking | Generic Kernel Debugging Instruments | KGDB: kernel debugger | KGDB_KDB: include kdb frontend for kgdb**

Now, when you force the kernel into a trap, instead of entering into a GDB session, you will see the `kdb` shell on the console:

```
# echo g > /proc/sysrq-trigger
```

```
Entering kdb (current=0xffffff8041b0be00, pid 176) on processor 2 due to
Keyboard Entry
[2]kdb>
```

There are quite a few things you can do in the kdb shell. The help command will print all of the options. Here is an overview:

- **Getting information:**

  - ps: Displays active processes.
  - ps A: Displays all processes.
  - lsmod: Lists modules.
  - dmesg: Displays the kernel log buffer.

- **Breakpoints:**

  - bp: Sets a breakpoint.
  - bl: Lists breakpoints.
  - bc: Clears a breakpoint.
  - bt: Prints a backtrace.
  - go: Continues execution.

- **Inspect memory and registers:**

  - md: Displays memory.
  - rd: Displays registers.

Here is a quick example of setting a breakpoint:

```
[2]kdb> bp __sys_accept4
Instruction(i) BP #0 at 0xffffffc0089ffe40 (__sys_accept4)
    is enabled   addr at ffffffc0089ffe40, hardtype=0 installed=0

[2]kdb> go
```

The kernel returns to life and the console shows the normal shell prompt. If you attempt to re-connect to the target, it hits the breakpoint and enters kdb again:

```
Entering kdb (current=0xffffff8041b05d00, pid 175) on processor 2 due to
Breakpoint @ 0xffffffc0089ffe40
[2]kdb>
```

kdb is not a source-level debugger, so you can't see the source code or single-step. However, you can display a backtrace using the bt command, which is useful for getting an idea of program flow and call hierarchy.

Looking at an Oops

When the kernel performs an invalid memory access or executes an illegal instruction, a kernel **Oops** message is written to the kernel log. The most useful part of this is the backtrace, and I want to show you how to use the information there to locate the line of code that caused the fault. I will also address the problem of preserving Oops messages if they cause the system to crash.

This Oops message was generated by writing to the mailbox driver in MELD/Chapter19/mbx-driver-oops:

```
Unable to handle kernel NULL pointer dereference at virtual address
0000000000000000
Mem abort info:
  ESR = 0x0000000096000005
  EC = 0x25: DABT (current EL), IL = 32 bits
  SET = 0, FnV = 0
  EA = 0, S1PTW = 0
  FSC = 0x05: level 1 translation fault
Data abort info:
  ISV = 0, ISS = 0x00000005
  CM = 0, WnR = 0
user pgtable: 4k pages, 39-bit VAs, pgdp=0000000041fd3000
[0000000000000000] pgd=0000000000000000, p4d=0000000000000000,
pud=0000000000000000
Internal error: Oops: 0000000096000005 [#1] PREEMPT SMP
Modules linked in: mbx(O) ipv6
CPU: 1 PID: 191 Comm: sh Tainted: G           O        6.1.61-v8 #1
Hardware name: Raspberry Pi 4 Model B Rev 1.1 (DT)
pstate: 80000005 (Nzcv daif -PAN -UAO -TCO -DIT -SSBS BTYPE=--)
pc : mbx_write+0x2c/0xf8 [mbx]
lr : vfs_write+0xd8/0x420
sp : ffffffc00a23bcb0
x29: ffffffc00a23bcb0 x28: ffffff8041f89f00 x27: 0000000000000000
x26: 0000000000000000 x25: 0000000000000000 x24: ffffffc00a23bdc0
x23: 000000558cfee770 x22: 0000000000000000 x21: 0000000000000000
```

```
x20: 000000558cfee770 x19: 0000000000000006 x18: 0000000000000000
x17: 0000000000000000 x16: 0000000000000000 x15: 0000000000000000
x14: 0000000000000000 x13: 0000000000000000 x12: 0000000000000000
x11: 0000000000000000 x10: 0000000000000000 x9 : 0000000000000000
x8 : 0000000000000000 x7 : ffffffc00a23c000 x6 : ffffffc00a238000
x5 : ffffffc00a23bda0 x4 : ffffffc000cd9270 x3 : ffffffc00a23bdc0
x2 : 0000000000000006 x1 : 000000558cfee770 x0 : ffffffc008322638
```

The line of the Oops that reads pc is at mbx_write+0x2c/0xf8 [mbx] and tells you most of what you want to know: the last instruction was in the mbx_write function of a kernel module named mbx. Furthermore, it was at offset 0x2c bytes from the start of the function, which is 0xf8 bytes long.

Next, take a look at the backtrace:

```
Call trace:
 mbx_write+0x2c/0xf8 [mbx]
 vfs_write+0xd8/0x420
 ksys_write+0x74/0x100
 __arm64_sys_write+0x24/0x30
 invoke_syscall+0x54/0x120
 el0_svc_common.constprop.3+0x90/0x120
 do_el0_svc+0x3c/0xe0
 el0_svc+0x20/0x60
 el0t_64_sync_handler+0x90/0xc0
 el0t_64_sync+0x15c/0x160
Code: aa0103f4 d503201f f94066b5 f110027f (f94002b6)
---[ end trace 0000000000000000 ]---
```

In this case, we don't learn much more, merely that mbx_write was called from the virtual filesystem function, _vfs_write.

It would be very nice to find the line of code that relates to mbx_write+0x2c, for which we can use the GDB command disassemble with the /s modifier so that it shows source and assembler code together. In this example, the code is in the mbx.ko module, so we load that into gdb:

```
$ output/host/bin/aarch64-buildroot-linux-gnu-gdb output/build/mbx-driver-
oops-1.0.0/mbx.ko
<…>
(gdb) disassemble /s mbx_write
Dump of assembler code for function mbx_write:
```

```
/home/frank/buildroot/output/build/mbx-driver-oops-1.0.0/./mbx.c:
96      {
   0x00000000000002a0 <+0>:      stp      x29, x30, [sp, #-48]!
   0x00000000000002a4 <+4>:      mov      x29, sp
   0x00000000000002a8 <+8>:      stp      x19, x20, [sp, #16]
   0x00000000000002ac <+12>:     stp      x21, x22, [sp, #32]
   0x00000000000002b0 <+16>:     mov      x21, x0
   0x00000000000002b4 <+20>:     mov      x0, x30
   0x00000000000002b8 <+24>:     mov      x19, x2
   0x00000000000002bc <+28>:     mov      x20, x1
   0x00000000000002c0 <+32>:     bl       0x2c0 <mbx_write+32>

97              struct mbx_data *m = (struct mbx_data *)file->private_
data;
   0x00000000000002c4 <+36>:     ldr      x21, [x21, #200]

98
99              if (length > MBX_LEN)
   0x00000000000002c8 <+40>:     cmp      x19, #0x400
   0x00000000000002cc <+44>:     ldr      x22, [x21]
   0x00000000000002d0 <+48>:     b.ls     0x344 <mbx_write+164>  // b.plast

101             m->mbx_len = length;
   0x00000000000002d4 <+52>:     mov      w0, #0x400                          //
#1024
   0x00000000000002d8 <+56>:     mov      x1, #0x7ffffffc00                   //
#549755812864

100                 length = MBX_LEN;
   0x00000000000002dc <+60>:     mov      x19, #0x400                         //
#1024

101             m->mbx_len = length;
   0x00000000000002e0 <+64>:     str      w0, [x21, #8]
<...>
```

You can see from *line 97* that m has the type struct mbx_data *. Here is the place where that structure is defined:

```
#define MBX_LEN 1024
struct mbx_data {
    char mbx[MBX_LEN];
    int mbx_len;
};
```

So, it looks like the m variable is a null pointer, and that is what is causing the Oops. Looking at the code where m is initialized, we can see that there is a line missing. By initializing the pointer, as shown in the following code block, the Oops is eliminated:

```
static int mbx_open(struct inode *inode, struct file *file)
{
    if (MINOR(inode->i_rdev) >= NUM_MAILBOXES) {
        printk("Invalid mbx minor number\n");
        return -ENODEV;
    }
    file->private_data = &mailboxes[MINOR(inode->i_rdev)];   // HERE
    return 0;
}
```

Not every Oops is this easy to pinpoint, especially if it occurs before the contents of the kernel log buffer can be displayed.

Preserving the Oops

Decoding an Oops is only possible if you can capture it in the first place. If the system crashes during boot before the console is enabled, or after a suspend, you won't see it. There are mechanisms to log kernel Oops and messages to an MTD partition or to persistent memory, but here is a simple technique that works in many cases and needs little prior thought.

So long as the contents of memory are not corrupted during a reset (and usually they are not), you can reboot into the bootloader and use it to display memory. You need to know the location of the kernel log buffer, remembering that it is a simple ring buffer of text messages. The symbol is __log_buf. Look this up in System.map for the kernel:

```
$ grep __log_buf output/build/linux-custom/System.map
ffffffc0096ce718 b __log_buf
```

> **IMPORTANT NOTE**
>
> From Linux 3.5 onward, there is a 16-byte binary header for each line in the kernel log buffer that encodes a timestamp, a log level, and other things. There is a discussion about it in the Linux weekly news entitled *Toward more reliable logging*, at `https://lwn.net/Articles/492125/`.

In this section, we examined how kernel code can be debugged at the source level using kgdb. Then we looked at setting breakpoints and printing backtraces inside the kdb shell. Lastly, we learned how to read kernel Oops messages either from a console using dmesg or the U-Boot command line.

Summary

Knowing how to use GDB for interactive debugging is a useful tool in the embedded system developer's tool chest. It is a stable, well-documented, and well-known entity. It has the ability to debug remotely by placing an agent on the target, be it gdbserver for applications or kgdb for kernel code, and although the default command-line user interface takes a while to get used to, there are many alternative frontends. The three I mentioned were TUI, DDD, and Visual Studio Code. Eclipse is another popular frontend that supports debugging with GDB by way of the CDT plugin. I will refer you to the references in the *Further study* section for information on how to configure CDT to work with a cross toolchain and connect to a remote device.

A second and equally important way to approach debugging is to collect crash reports and analyze them offline. In this category, we looked at application core dumps and kernel Oops messages.

However, this is only one way of identifying flaws in programs. In the next chapter, I will talk about profiling and tracing as ways of analyzing and optimizing programs.

Further study

- *The Art of Debugging with GDB, DDD, and Eclipse*, by Norman Matloff and Peter Jay Salzman
- *GDB Pocket Reference*, by Arnold Robbins
- *Python Interpreter in GNU Debugger*, by crazyguitar – `https://www.pythonsheets.com/appendix/python-gdb.html`
- *Extending GDB with Python*, by Lisa Roach – `https://www.youtube.com/watch?v=xt9v5t4_zvE`

- *Getting to grips with Eclipse: cross compiling* – `https://2net.co.uk/tutorial/eclipse-cross-compile`

- *Getting to grips with Eclipse: remote access and debugging* – `https://2net.co.uk/tutorial/eclipse-rse`

20

Profiling and Tracing

Interactive debugging using a source-level debugger, as described in the previous chapter, can give you an insight into the way a program works, but it constrains your view to a small body of code. In this chapter, we will look at the larger picture to see whether the system is performing as intended.

Programmers and system designers are notoriously bad at guessing where bottlenecks are. So, if your system has performance issues, it is wise to start by looking at the full system and then work down, using more sophisticated tools as you go. In this chapter, I'll begin with the well-known top command as a means of getting an overview. Often, the problem can be localized to a single program, which you can analyze using the Linux profiler, perf. If the problem is not so localized and you want to get a broader picture, perf can do that as well. To diagnose problems associated with the kernel, I will describe some trace tools—Ftrace, LTTng, and eBPF—as a means of gathering detailed information.

I will also cover Valgrind, which, because of its sandboxed execution environment, can monitor a program and report on code as it runs. I will complete the chapter with a description of a simple trace tool, strace, which reveals the execution of a program by tracing the system calls it makes.

In this chapter, we will cover the following topics:

- Observer effect
- Beginning to profile
- Profiling with top
- Profiling with GDB
- Introducing perf

- Tracing events
- Introducing Ftrace
- Using LTTng
- Using eBPF
- Using Valgrind
- Using strace

Technical requirements

To follow along with the examples, make sure you have the following:

- An Ubuntu 24.04 or later LTS host system with at least 90 GB of free disk space
- Buildroot 2024.02.6 LTS release
- A microSD card reader and card
- balenaEtcher for Linux
- An Ethernet cable and router with an available port for network connectivity
- Raspberry Pi 4
- A 5 V USB-C power supply capable of delivering 3 A

You should have already installed the 2024.02.6 LTS release of Buildroot in *Chapter 6*. If you have not, then refer to the *System requirements* section of *The Buildroot user manual* (https://buildroot. org/downloads/manual/manual.html) before installing Buildroot on your Linux host according to the instructions from *Chapter 6*.

The code used in this chapter can be found in the chapter folder in this book's GitHub repository: https://github.com/PacktPublishing/Mastering-Embedded-Linux-Development/tree/main/ Chapter20/buildroot.

Observer effect

Before diving into the tools, let's talk about what the tools will show you. As is the case in many fields, measuring a certain property affects the observation itself. Measuring the electric current in a power supply line requires measuring the voltage drop over a small resistor. However, the resistor itself affects the current. The same is true for profiling: every system observation has a cost in CPU cycles, and that resource is no longer spent on the application. Measurement tools also mess up caching behavior, eat memory space, and write to disk, which all make it worse. There is no measurement without overhead.

I've often heard engineers say that the results of a profiling job were totally misleading. That is usually because they were performing the measurements on something not approaching a real situation. Always try to measure on the target, running release builds of the software, with a valid dataset preferably obtained from the field, using as few extra services as possible.

A release build usually implies building fully optimized binaries without debug symbols. These production requirements severely limit the functionality of most profiling tools.

Once our system is up and running, we will hit a problem right away. While it is important to observe the system in its natural state, the tools often need additional information to make sense of the events.

Some tools require special kernel options. For the tools we are examining in this chapter, this applies to perf, Ftrace, LTTng, and eBPF. Therefore, you will probably have to build and deploy a new kernel for these tests.

Debug symbols are very helpful in translating raw program addresses into function names and line numbers in source code. Deploying executables with debug symbols does not change the execution of the code, but it does require that you have copies of the binaries, and a kernel compiled with debug information, at least for the components you want to profile. Some tools work best if you have these installed on the target system: perf, for example. The techniques are the same as for general debugging, as I discussed in *Chapter 19*.

If you want a tool to generate call graphs, you may have to compile with stack frames enabled. If you want the tool to attribute addresses with line numbers in source code accurately, you may need to compile with lower levels of optimization.

Finally, some tools require instrumentation to be inserted into the program to capture samples, so you will have to recompile those components. This applies to Ftrace and LTTng for the kernel.

Be aware that the more you change the system you are observing, the harder it is to relate the measurements you make to the production system.

TIP

It is best to adopt a wait-and-see approach, making changes only when the need is clear, and being mindful that each time you do so, you will change what you are measuring.

Because the results of profiling can be so ambiguous, start with simple, easy-to-use tools that are readily available before reaching for more complex and invasive instruments.

Beginning to profile

When looking at the entire system, a good place to start is with a simple tool such as top, which gives you an overview very quickly. It shows you how much memory is being used, which processes are eating CPU cycles, and how this is spread across different cores and times.

If top shows that a single application is using up all the CPU cycles in user space, then you can profile that application using perf.

If two or more processes have a high CPU usage, there is probably something that is coupling them together, perhaps data communication. If a lot of cycles are spent on system calls or handling interrupts, then there may be an issue with the kernel configuration or with a device driver. In either case, you need to start by taking a profile of the whole system, again using perf.

If you want to find out more about the kernel and the sequencing of events there, use Ftrace, LTTng, or eBPF.

There could be other problems that top will not help you with. If you have multi-threaded code and there are problems with lockups, or if you have random data corruption, then pidstat (part of sysstat) or Valgrind plus the Helgrind plugin might be helpful. Memory leaks also fit into this category; I covered memory-related diagnosis in *Chapter 18*.

Before we get into these more advanced profiling tools, let's start with the most rudimentary one that is found on most systems, including those in production.

Profiling with top

The **top** program is a simple tool that doesn't require any special kernel options or symbol tables. There is a basic version in BusyBox and a more functional version in the procps package, which is available in The Yocto Project and Buildroot. You may also want to consider using htop, which has functionally similar to top but a much nicer user interface.

To begin with, focus on the summary line of top, which is the second line if you are using Busy-Box and the third line if you are using top from procps. Here is an example, using BusyBox's top:

```
Mem: 57044K used, 446172K free, 40K shrd, 3352K buff, 34452K cached
CPU: 58% usr 4% sys 0% nic 0% idle 37% io 0% irq 0% sirq
Load average: 0.24 0.06 0.02 2/51 105
PID PPID USER STAT   VSZ %VSZ %CPU COMMAND
```

```
105  104 root     R 27912    6%  61% ffmpeg -i track2.wav
<...>
```

The summary line shows the percentage of time spent running in various states, as shown in this table:

procps	BusyBox	Description
us	usr	User-space programs with a default nice value
sy	sys	Kernel code
ni	nic	User-space programs with a non-default nice value
id	idle	Idle
wa	io	I/O wait
hi	irq	Hardware interrupts
si	sirq	Software interrupts
st	-	Steal time: only relevant in virtual environments

Table 20.1 – procps top vs. BusyBox top

In the preceding example, almost all of the time (58%) is spent in user mode, with a small amount (4%) in system mode, so this is a system that is CPU-bound in user space. The first line after the summary shows that just one application is responsible: ffmpeg. Any efforts toward reducing CPU usage should be directed there.

Here is another example:

```
Mem: 13128K used, 490088K free, 40K shrd, 0K buff, 2788K cached
CPU: 0% usr 99% sys 0% nic 0% idle 0% io 0% irq 0% sirq
Load average: 0.41 0.11 0.04 2/46 97
PID PPID USER STAT   VSZ %VSZ %CPU COMMAND
 92   82 root     R  2152    0% 100% cat /dev/urandom
<...>
```

This system is spending almost all of the time in kernel space (99% sys), as a result of cat reading from /dev/urandom. In this artificial case, profiling cat by itself would not help, but profiling the kernel functions that cat calls might.

The default view of top shows only processes, so the CPU usage is the total of all the threads in the process. Press *H* to see information for each thread. Likewise, it aggregates the time across all CPUs. If you are using the procps version of top, you can see a summary per CPU by pressing the *1* key.

Once we have singled out the problem process using top, we can attach GDB to it.

Profiling with GDB

You can profile an application just by using **GDB** to stop it at arbitrary intervals to see what it is doing. This is the **poor man's profiler**. It is easy to set up and is one way of gathering profile data.

The procedure is simple:

1. Attach to the process using gdbserver (for a remote debug) or GDB (for a native debug). The process stops.
2. Observe the function it stopped in. You can use the backtrace GDB command to see the call stack.
3. Type continue so that the program resumes.
4. After a while, press *Ctrl + C* to stop it again, and go back to *step 2*.

If you repeat *steps 2* to *4* several times, you will quickly get an idea of whether it is looping or making progress, and if you repeat them often enough, you will get an idea of where the hotspots in the code are.

There is a whole web page dedicated to this idea at https://poormansprofiler.org/, together with scripts that make it a little easier. I have used this technique many times over the years with various operating systems and debuggers.

This is an example of **statistical profiling**, in which you sample the program state at intervals. After a number of samples, you begin to learn the statistical likelihood of the functions being executed. It is surprising how few you really need. Other statistical profilers are perf record, OProfile, and gprof.

Sampling using a debugger is intrusive because the program is stopped for a significant period while you collect the sample. Other tools can sample with less overhead. One such tool is perf.

Introducing perf

perf is an abbreviation of the Linux **performance event counter subsystem**, perf_events, and also the name of the command-line tool for interacting with perf_events. Both have been part of the kernel since Linux 2.6.31. There is plenty of useful information in the Linux source tree in tools/perf/Documentation as well as at https://perfwiki.github.io.

The initial impetus for developing perf was to provide a unified way to access the registers of the **performance measurement unit (PMU)**, which is part of most modern processor cores. Once the API was defined and integrated into Linux, it became logical to extend it to cover other types of performance counters.

At its heart, perf is a collection of event counters with rules about when they actively collect data. By setting the rules, you can capture data from the whole system, just the kernel, or just one process and its children, and do it across all CPUs or just one CPU. It is very flexible. With this one tool, you can start by looking at the whole system, then zero in on a device driver that seems to be causing problems, an application that is running slowly, or a library function that seems to be taking longer to execute than you thought.

The code for the perf command-line tool is part of the kernel, in the tools/perf directory. The tool and the kernel subsystem are developed hand in hand, meaning that they must be from the same version of the kernel. perf can do a lot. In this chapter, I will examine it only as a profiler. For a description of its other capabilities, read the perf man pages and refer to the documentation mentioned at the start of this section.

In addition to debug symbols, there are two configuration options we need to set to fully enable perf in the kernel.

Configuring the kernel for perf

You need a kernel that is configured for perf_events, and you need the perf command cross-compiled to run on the target. The relevant kernel configuration is CONFIG_PERF_EVENTS, present in the **General setup | Kernel Performance Events and Counters** menu.

If you want to profile using tracepoints—more on this subject later—also enable the options described in the section about Ftrace. While you are there, it is worthwhile enabling CONFIG_DEBUG_INFO as well.

The perf command has many dependencies, which makes cross-compiling it quite messy. However, both The Yocto Project and Buildroot have target packages for it.

You will also need debug symbols on the target for the binaries that you are interested in profiling; otherwise, perf will not be able to resolve addresses to meaningful symbols. Ideally, you want debug symbols for the whole system, including the kernel. For the latter, remember that the debug symbols for the kernel are in the vmlinux file.

Building perf with The Yocto Project

If you are using the standard linux-yocto kernel, perf_events is enabled already, so there is nothing more to do.

To build the perf tool, you can add it explicitly to the target image dependencies, or you can add the tools-profile feature. You also want debug symbols on the target image as well as the kernel vmlinux image. In total, this is what you will need in conf/local.conf:

```
EXTRA_IMAGE_FEATURES:append = " tools-profile dbg-pkgs src-pkgs"
IMAGE_INSTALL:append = " kernel-vmlinux binutils"
```

Adding perf to a Buildroot image is more involved for several reasons.

Building perf with Buildroot

Many Buildroot kernel configurations do not include perf_events, so you should begin by checking that your kernel includes the options mentioned in the preceding section.

To cross-compile perf, run the Buildroot menuconfig and select the following:

- BR2_PACKAGE_LINUX_TOOLS_PERF in **Kernel** | **Linux Kernel Tools** | **perf**
- BR2_PACKAGE_LINUX_TOOLS_PERF_TUI in **Kernel** | **Linux Kernel Tools** | **perf** | **Enable perf TUI**

To build binaries with debug information and install them onto the target without stripping, enable the first and disable the second of these two options:

- BR2_ENABLE_DEBUG in **Build options** | **Build packages with debugging symbols**
- BR2_STRIP_strip in **Build options** | **Strip target binaries**

To copy the unstripped vmlinux file to the target image, select the following:

- BR2_LINUX_KERNEL_VMLINUX in **Kernel** | **Kernel binary format** | **vmlinux**
- BR2_LINUX_KERNEL_INSTALL_TARGET in **Kernel** | **Install kernel image to /boot in target**

To increase the size of the root filesystem to accommodate the unstripped binaries and the vmlinux file:

- Select **Filesystem images** | **ext2/3/4 root filesystem** | **Exact size** and enter 960M in the text field.

Then run make clean followed by make.

Once you have built everything, you will have to copy vmlinux to the target image manually.

Profiling with perf

You can use perf to sample the state of a program using one of the event counters and accumulate samples over a period of time to create a profile. This is another example of statistical profiling. The default event counter is called cycles, which is a generic hardware counter that is mapped to a PMU register representing a count of cycles at the core clock frequency.

Creating a profile using perf is a two-stage process: the perf record command captures samples and writes them to a file named perf.data, then perf report analyzes the results. Both commands are run on the target. The samples being collected are filtered for the process and any of its children. Here is an example of profiling a shell script that searches for the linux string:

```
# perf record -a sh -c "find /usr/share | xargs grep linux > /dev/null"
[ perf record: Woken up 1 times to write data ]
[ perf record: Captured and wrote 0.176 MB perf.data (2677 samples) ]
# ls -l perf.data
-rw------- 1 root root 190024 Mar  9 14:28 perf.data
```

Now you can display the results from perf.data using the perf report command.

There are three user interfaces to choose from:

- --stdio: This is a pure-text interface with no user interaction. You will have to launch perf report and annotate for each view of the trace.
- --tui: This is a simple text-based menu interface with traversal between screens.
- --gtk: This is a graphical interface that otherwise acts in the same way as --tui.

The default is TUI, as shown in this example:

```
Samples: 9K of event 'cycles', Event count (approx.): 2006177260
  11.29%    grep  libc-2.20.so        [.] re_search_internal
   8.80%    grep  busybox.nosuid      [.] bb_get_chunk_from_file
   5.55%    grep  libc-2.20.so        [.] _int_malloc
   5.40%    grep  libc-2.20.so        [.] _int_free
   3.74%    grep  libc-2.20.so        [.] realloc
   2.59%    grep  libc-2.20.so        [.] malloc
   2.51%    grep  libc-2.20.so        [.] regexec@@GLIBC_2.4
   1.64%    grep  busybox.nosuid      [.] grep_file
   1.57%    grep  libc-2.20.so        [.] malloc_consolidate
   1.33%    grep  libc-2.20.so        [.] strlen
   1.33%    grep  libc-2.20.so        [.] memset
   1.26%    grep  [kernel.kallsyms]   [k] __copy_to_user_std
   1.20%    grep  libc-2.20.so        [.] free
   1.10%    grep  libc-2.20.so        [.] _int_realloc
   0.95%    grep  libc-2.20.so        [.] re_string_reconstruct
   0.79%    grep  busybox.nosuid      [.] xrealloc
   0.75%    grep  [kernel.kallsyms]   [k] __do_softirq
   0.72%    grep  [kernel.kallsyms]   [k] preempt_count_sub
   0.68%    find  [kernel.kallsyms]   [k] __do_softirq
   0.53%    grep  [kernel.kallsyms]   [k] __dev_queue_xmit
   0.52%    grep  [kernel.kallsyms]   [k] preempt_count_add
   0.47%    grep  [kernel.kallsyms]   [k] finish_task_switch.isra.85
Press '?' for help on key bindings
```

Figure 20.1 – perf report TUI

perf is able to record the kernel functions executed on behalf of the processes because it collects samples in kernel space.

The list is ordered with the most active functions first. In this example, all but one are captured while grep is running. Some are in a library, libc-2.20, some are in a program, busybox.nosuid, and some are in the kernel. We have symbol names for program and library functions because all the binaries have been installed on the target with debug information, and kernel symbols are being read from /boot/vmlinux. If you have vmlinux in a different location, add -k <path> to the perf report command. Rather than storing samples in perf.data, you can save them to a different file using perf record -o <file name> and analyze them using perf report -i <file name>.

By default, perf record samples at a frequency of 1,000 Hz using the cycles counter.

> **TIP**
>
> A sampling frequency of 1,000 Hz may be higher than you really need and may be the cause of the observer effect. Try lower rates; 100 Hz is enough for most cases. You can set the sample frequency using the -F option.

This is still not really making life easy; the functions at the top of the list are mostly low-level memory operations, and you can be fairly sure that they have already been optimized. Fortunately, perf record also gives us the ability to crawl up the call stack and see where these functions are being invoked.

Call graphs

It would be nice to step back and see the surrounding context of these costly functions. You can do that by passing the -g option to perf record to capture the backtrace from each sample.

Now, perf report shows a plus sign (+) where the function is part of a call chain. You can expand the trace to see the functions lower down in the chain:

```
Samples: 10K of event 'cycles', Event count (approx.): 2256721655
-    9.95%    grep   libc-2.20.so        [.] re_search_internal          ◀
  - re_search_internal
        95.96% 0
         3.50% 0x208
+    8.19%    grep   busybox.nosuid      [.] bb_get_chunk_from_file
+    5.07%    grep   libc-2.20.so        [.] _int_free
+    4.76%    grep   libc-2.20.so        [.] _int_malloc
+    3.75%    grep   libc-2.20.so        [.] realloc
+    2.63%    grep   libc-2.20.so        [.] malloc
+    2.04%    grep   libc-2.20.so        [.] regexec@@GLIBC_2.4
+    1.43%    grep   busybox.nosuid      [.] grep_file
+    1.37%    grep   libc-2.20.so        [.] memset
+    1.29%    grep   libc-2.20.so        [.] malloc_consolidate
+    1.22%    grep   libc-2.20.so        [.] _int_realloc
+    1.15%    grep   libc-2.20.so        [.] free
+    1.01%    grep   [kernel.kallsyms]   [k] __copy_to_user_std
+    0.98%    grep   libc-2.20.so        [.] strlen
+    0.89%    grep   libc-2.20.so        [.] re_string_reconstruct
+    0.73%    grep   [kernel.kallsyms]   [k] preempt_count_sub
+    0.68%    grep   [kernel.kallsyms]   [k] finish_task_switch.isra.85
+    0.62%    grep   busybox.nosuid      [.] xrealloc
+    0.57%    grep   [kernel.kallsyms]   [k] __do_softirq
Press '?' for help on key bindings
```

Figure 20.2 – perf report (call graphs)

IMPORTANT NOTE

Generating call graphs relies on the ability to extract call frames from the stack, just like backtraces in GDB. The debug information needed to unwind stacks is encoded in the executables. Call graphs cannot be produced for some combinations of architecture and toolchains because the binaries lack the necessary debug information.

Backtraces are nice, but where is the assembler, or better yet, the source code, for these functions?

perf annotate

Now that you know which functions to look at, it would be nice to step inside and see the code and to have hit counts for each instruction. That is what perf annotate does, by calling down to a copy of objdump installed on the target. You just need to use perf annotate in place of perf report.

perf annotate requires symbol tables for the executables and vmlinux. Here is an example of an annotated function:

```
re_search_internal  /lib/libc-2.20.so
                    cmp     r1,
                    beq     c362c <gai_strerror+0xcaf8>
                    str     r3, [fp, #-40]           ; 0x28
                    b       c3684 <gai_strerror+0xcb50>
        0.65        ldr     ip, [fp, #-256]          ; 0x100
        0.16        ldr     r0, [fp, #-268]          ; 0x10c
        2.44        add     r3,
        4.15        cmp     r0,
        3.91        strle   r3, [fp, #-40]           ; 0x28
                    ble     c3684 <gai_strerror+0xcb50>
        4.72        ldrb    r1, [r2, #1]!
       10.26        ldrb    r1, [ip, r1]
        6.68        cmp     r1,
                    beq     c3660 <gai_strerror+0xcb2c>
        0.90        str     r3, [fp, #-40]           ; 0x28
        2.12        ldr     r3, [fp, #-40]           ; 0x28
        0.08        ldr     r2, [fp, #-268]          ; 0x10c
        0.33        cmp     r2,
                    bne     c3804 <gai_strerror+0xccd0>
        0.08        mov     r3,
                    ldr     r2, [fp, #-280]          ; 0x118
        0.08        cmp     r3,
Press 'h' for help on key bindings
```

Figure 20.3 – perf annotate (assembler)

If you want to see the source code interleaved with the assembler, you can copy the relevant source files to the target device. If you are using The Yocto Project and build with the `src-pkgs` extra image feature or have installed the individual `<package>-src` packages, then the source will have been installed for you in `/usr/src/debug`. Otherwise, you can examine the debug information to see the location of the source code:

```
$ cd ~/buildroot/output
$ host/aarch64-buildroot-linux-gnu/bin/objdump --dwarf target/lib/libc.
so.6 | grep DW_AT_comp_dir | grep libgcc
<41f4dd> DW_AT_comp_dir : (indirect string, offset: 0x2d355): /home/frank/
buildroot/output/build/host-gcc-initial-12.4.0/build/aarch64-buildroot-
linux-gnu/libgcc
```

The path on the target should be *exactly the same* as the path you can see in `DW_AT_comp_dir`.

Here is an example of annotation with the source and assembler code:

```
re_search_internal  /lib/libc-2.20.so
                              ++match_first;
                              goto forward_match_found_start_or_reached_end;

                      case 6:
                        /* Fastmap without translation, match forward.  */
                        while (BE (match_first < right_lim, 1)
  4.15               cmp    r0,
  3.91               strle  r3, [fp, #-40]        ; 0x28
                     ble    c3684 <gai_strerror+0xcb50>
                                  && !fastmap[(unsigned char) string[match_first]])
  4.72               ldrb   r1, [r2, #1]!
 10.26               ldrb   r1, [ip, r1]
  6.68               cmp    r1,
                     beq    c3660 <gai_strerror+0xcb2c>
  0.90               str    r3, [fp, #-40]        ; 0x28
                              ++match_first;

                      forward_match_found_start_or_reached_end:
                        if (BE (match_first == right_lim, 0))
  2.12               ldr    r3, [fp, #-40]        ; 0x28
  0.08               ldr    r2, [fp, #-268]       ; 0x10c
  0.33               cmp    r2,
Press 'h' for help on key bindings
```

Figure 20.4 – perf annotate (source code)

Now we can see the corresponding C source code above `cmp r0` and below the `str r3, [fp, #-40]` instruction.

This concludes our coverage of `perf`. While there are other statistical sampling profilers that pre-date `perf`, like OProfile and gprof, these tools have fallen out of favor in recent years, so I chose to omit them. Next, we will look at event tracers.

Tracing events

The tools we have seen so far all use statistical sampling. You often want to know more about the ordering of events so that you can see them and relate them to each other. Function tracing involves instrumenting the code with tracepoints that capture information about the event, and may include some or all of the following:

- A timestamp
- Context, such as the current PID
- Function parameters and return values
- A call stack

It is more intrusive than statistical profiling and it can generate a large amount of data. The latter problem can be mitigated by applying filters when the sample is captured and, later on, when viewing the trace.

I will cover three trace tools here: the kernel function tracers Ftrace, LTTng, and eBPF.

Introducing Ftrace

The kernel function tracer **Ftrace** evolved from work done by Steven Rostedt and many others as they were tracking down the causes of high scheduling latency in real-time applications. Ftrace appeared in Linux 2.6.27 and has been actively developed since then. There are a number of documents describing kernel tracing in the kernel source in `Documentation/trace`.

Ftrace consists of a number of tracers that can log various types of activity in the kernel. Here, I am going to talk about the `function` and `function_graph` tracers and the event tracepoints. In *Chapter 21*, I will revisit Ftrace when I talk about real-time latencies.

The `function` tracer instruments each kernel function so that calls can be recorded and time-stamped. It compiles the kernel with the -pg switch to inject the instrumentation. The `function_graph` tracer goes further and records both the entry and exit of functions so that it can create a call graph. The event tracepoints feature records parameters associated with the call.

Ftrace has a very embedded-friendly user interface that is entirely implemented through virtual files in the debugfs filesystem, meaning that you do not have to install any tools on the target to make it work. Nevertheless, there are other user interfaces if you prefer: trace-cmd is a command-line tool that records and views traces and is available in Buildroot (BR2_PACKAGE_TRACE_CMD) and The Yocto Project (trace-cmd). There is a graphical trace viewer named **KernelShark** that is available as a package for The Yocto Project.

Like perf, enabling Ftrace requires setting certain kernel configuration options.

Preparing to use Ftrace

Ftrace and its various options are configured in the kernel configuration menu. You will need the following at a minimum:

- CONFIG_FUNCTION_TRACER from the **Kernel hacking** | **Tracers** | **Kernel Function Tracer** menu.

You would be well advised to turn on these options as well:

- CONFIG_FUNCTION_GRAPH_TRACER in the **Kernel hacking** | **Tracers** | **Kernel Function Tracer** | **Kernel Function Graph Tracer** menu
- CONFIG_DYNAMIC_FTRACE in the **Kernel hacking** | **Tracers** | **Kernel Function Tracer** | **Enable/disable function tracing dynamically** menu
- CONFIG_FUNCTION_PROFILER in the **Kernel hacking** | **Tracers** | **Kernel Function Tracer** | **Kernel function profiler** menu

Since the whole thing is hosted in the kernel, there is no user-space configuration to be done.

Using Ftrace

Before you can use Ftrace, you have to mount the debugfs filesystem, which goes in the /sys/kernel/debug directory:

```
# mount -t debugfs none /sys/kernel/debug
```

All the controls for Ftrace are in the /sys/kernel/debug/tracing directory; there is even a mini HOWTO in the README file there.

This is the list of tracers available in the kernel:

```
# cat /sys/kernel/debug/tracing/available_tracers
blk function_graph function nop
```

The active tracer is shown by current_tracer. Initially, it will be the null tracer, nop.

To capture a trace, select the tracer by writing the name of one of the available_tracers to current_tracer. Then, enable tracing for a short while:

```
# echo function > /sys/kernel/debug/tracing/current_tracer
# echo 1 > /sys/kernel/debug/tracing/tracing_on
# sleep 1
# echo 0 > /sys/kernel/debug/tracing/tracing_on
```

In that one second, the trace buffer will have been filled with the details of every function called by the kernel. The format of the trace buffer is plain text, as described in Documentation/trace/ftrace.txt. You can read the trace buffer from the trace file:

```
# cat /sys/kernel/debug/tracing/trace
# tracer: function
#
# entries-in-buffer/entries-written: 40051/40051    #P:1
#
#                    _-----=> irqs-off
#                   / _----=> need-resched
#                  | / _---=> hardirq/softirq
#                  || / _--=> preempt-depth
#                  ||| /     delay
# TASK-PID   CPU#  ||||  TIMESTAMP  FUNCTION
#    | |      |    ||||      |          |
    sh-361   [000] ...1 992.990646: mutex_unlock <-rb_simple_write
    sh-361   [000] ...1 992.990658: __fsnotify_parent <-vfs_write
    sh-361   [000] ...1 992.990661: fsnotify <-vfs_write
    sh-361   [000] ...1 992.990663: __srcu_read_lock <-fsnotify
    sh-361   [000] ...1 992.990666: preempt_count_add <-__srcu_read_lock
    sh-361   [000] ...2 992.990668: preempt_count_sub <-__srcu_read_lock
    sh-361   [000] ...1 992.990670: __srcu_read_unlock <-fsnotify
    sh-361   [000] ...1 992.990672: __sb_end_write <-vfs_write
    sh-361   [000] ...1 992.990674: preempt_count_add <-__sb_end_write
<...>
```

You can capture a large number of data points in just one second—in this case, over 40,000.

As with profilers, it is difficult to make sense of a flat function list like this. If you select the function_graph tracer, Ftrace captures call graphs like this:

```
# tracer: function_graph
#
# CPU    DURATION                  FUNCTION CALLS
# |       |   |                     |   |   |   |
 0) + 63.167 us   |                  } /* cpdma_ctlr_int_ctrl */
 0) + 73.417 us   |                } /* cpsw_intr_disable */
 0)               |                disable_irq_nosync() {
 0)               |                  __disable_irq_nosync() {
 0)               |                    __irq_get_desc_lock() {
 0)   0.541 us    |                      irq_to_desc();
 0)   0.500 us    |                      preempt_count_add();
 0) + 16.000 us   |                    }
 0)               |                    __disable_irq() {
 0)   0.500 us    |                      irq_disable();
 0)   8.208 us    |                    }
 0)               |                    __irq_put_desc_unlock() {
 0)   0.459 us    |                      preempt_count_sub();
 0)   8.000 us    |                    }
 0) + 55.625 us   |                  }
 0) + 63.375 us   |                }
```

Now you can see the nesting of the function calls, delimited by braces, { and }. At the terminating brace, there is a measurement of the time taken in the function, annotated with a plus sign (+) if it takes more than 10 μs and an exclamation mark (!) if it takes more than 100 μs.

You are often only interested in the kernel activity caused by a single process or thread, in which case you can restrict the trace to one thread by writing the thread ID to set_ftrace_pid.

Dynamic Ftrace and trace filters

Enabling CONFIG_DYNAMIC_FTRACE allows Ftrace to modify the function trace sites at runtime, which has a couple of benefits. Firstly, it triggers additional build-time processing of the trace function probes, which allows the Ftrace subsystem to locate them at boot time and overwrite them with nop instructions, thus reducing the overhead of the function trace code to almost nothing. You can then enable Ftrace in production or near-production kernels with no impact on performance.

The second advantage is that you can selectively enable function trace sites rather than tracing everything. The list of functions is put into `available_filter_functions`. You can selectively enable function traces as needed by copying the name from `available_filter_functions` to `set_ftrace_filter`. To stop tracing that function, write its name to `set_ftrace_notrace`. You can also use wildcards and append names to the list. For example, suppose you are interested in `tcp` handling:

```
# cd /sys/kernel/debug/tracing
# echo "tcp*" > set_ftrace_filter
# echo function > current_tracer
# echo 1 > tracing_on
```

Run some tests and then look at `trace`:

```
# cat trace
# tracer: function
#
# entries-in-buffer/entries-written: 590/590    #P:1
#
#                             _-----=> irqs-off
#                            / _----=> need-resched
#                           | / _---=> hardirq/softirq
#                           || / _--=> preempt-depth
#                           ||| /     delay
#   TASK-PID CPU#  ||||   TIMESTAMP  FUNCTION
#      | |     |   ||||      |          |
dropbear-375 [000] ...1 48545.022235: tcp_poll <-sock_poll
dropbear-375 [000] ...1 48545.022372: tcp_poll <-sock_poll
dropbear-375 [000] ...1 48545.022393: tcp_sendmsg <-inet_sendmsg
dropbear-375 [000] ...1 48545.022398: tcp_send_mss <-tcp_sendmsg
dropbear-375 [000] ...1 48545.022400: tcp_current_mss <-tcp_send_mss
<...>
```

The `set_ftrace_filter` function can also contain commands to start and stop tracing when certain functions are executed. There isn't space to go into these details here, but if you want to find out more, read the *Filter commands* section in `Documentation/trace/ftrace.txt`.

Trace events

The `function` and `function_graph` tracers only record the time at which the function was executed. The trace events feature also records parameters associated with the call, making the trace more readable and informative. For example, instead of just recording that the `kmalloc` function has been called, a trace event will record the number of bytes requested and the returned pointer. Trace events are used in `perf` and LTTng as well as Ftrace, but the development of the trace events subsystem was prompted by the LTTng project.

It takes effort from kernel developers to create trace events. They are defined in the source code using the `TRACE_EVENT` macro; there are over a thousand of them now. You can see the list of events available at runtime in `/sys/kernel/debug/tracing/available_events`. They are named `<subsystem>:<function>` (e.g., `kmem:kmalloc`). Each event is also represented by a subdirectory in `tracing/events/<subsystem>/<function>`:

```
# ls events/kmem/kmalloc
enable filter format id trigger
```

The files are:

- `enable`: You write a 1 to this file to enable the event.
- `filter`: This is an expression that must evaluate to `true` for the event to be traced.
- `format`: This is the format of the event and parameters.
- `id`: This is a numeric identifier.
- `trigger`: This is a command that is executed when the event occurs using the syntax defined in the *Filter commands* section of `Documentation/trace/ftrace.txt`.

I will show you a simple example involving `kmalloc` and `kfree`. Event tracing does not depend on the function tracers, so begin by selecting the nop tracer:

```
# echo nop > current_tracer
```

Next, select the events to trace by enabling each one individually:

```
# echo 1 > events/kmem/kmalloc/enable
# echo 1 > events/kmem/kfree/enable
```

You can also write the event names to `set_event`, as shown here:

```
# echo "kmem:kmalloc kmem:kfree" > set_event
```

Now, when you read the trace, you can see the functions and their parameters:

```
# tracer: nop
#
# entries-in-buffer/entries-written: 359/359    #P:1
#
#                              _-----=> irqs-off
#                             / _----=> need-resched
#                            | / _---=> hardirq/softirq
#                            || / _--=> preempt-depth
#                            ||| /     delay
#   TASK-PID    CPU#   ||||    TIMESTAMP  FUNCTION
#      | |       |    ||||       |          |
    cat-382    [000] ...1  2935.586706: kmalloc:call_site=c0554644
ptr=de515a00 bytes_req=384 bytes_alloc=512 gfp_flags=GFP_ATOMIC|GFP_
NOWARN|GFP_NOMEMALLOC
    cat-382    [000] ...1  2935.586718: kfree: call_site=c059c2d8
ptr=(null)
```

Exactly the same trace events are visible in perf as tracepoint events.

Since there is no bloated user-space component to build, Ftrace is well suited for deploying to most embedded targets. Next, we will look at another popular event tracer whose origins predate those of Ftrace.

Using LTTng

The **Linux Trace Toolkit (LTT)** project was started by Karim Yaghmour as a means of tracing kernel activity and was one of the first trace tools generally available for the Linux kernel. Later, Mathieu Desnoyers took up the idea and re-implemented it as a next-generation trace tool, **LTTng**. It was then expanded to cover user-space traces as well as the kernel. The project website is at https://lttng.org/ and contains a comprehensive user manual.

LTTng consists of three components:

- A core session manager
- A kernel tracer implemented as a group of kernel modules
- A user-space tracer implemented as a library

In addition to those, you will need a trace viewer such as **Babeltrace** (https://babeltrace.org/) or the **Eclipse Trace Compass** plugin to display and filter the raw trace data on the host or target.

LTTng requires a kernel configured with `CONFIG_TRACEPOINTS`, which is enabled when you select **Kernel hacking | Tracers | Kernel Function Tracer**.

The description that follows refers to LTTng version 2.13. Other versions may be different.

LTTng and The Yocto Project

You need to add these packages to the target dependencies in `conf/local.conf`:

```
IMAGE_INSTALL:append = " lttng-tools lttng-modules lttng-ust"
```

If you want to run Babeltrace on the target, also append the `babeltrace2` package.

LTTng and Buildroot

You need to enable the following:

- `BR2_PACKAGE_LTTNG_MODULES` in the **Target packages | Debugging, profiling and benchmark | lttng-modules** menu
- `BR2_PACKAGE_LTTNG_TOOLS` in the **Target packages | Debugging, profiling and benchmark | lttng-tools** menu

For user-space trace tracing, enable these:

- `BR2_PACKAGE_UTIL_LINUX_UUIDD` in the **Target packages | System tools | util-linux | uuidd** menu
- `BR2_PACKAGE_LTTNG_LIBUST` in the **Target packages | Libraries | Other | lttng-libust** menu
- `BR2_PACKAGE_HOST_BABELTRACE2` in the **Host utilities | host babeltrace2** menu

There is a package called `babletrace2` for the target. Buildroot installs `babeltrace2` for the host in `output/host/usr/bin/babeltrace2`.

Using LTTng for kernel tracing

LTTng can use the set of Ftrace events described previously as potential tracepoints. Initially, they are disabled.

The control interface for LTTng is the `lttng` command. You can list the kernel probes using the following:

```
# lttng list --kernel
Kernel events:
-------------
writeback_nothread (loglevel: TRACE_EMERG (0)) (type: tracepoint)
```

```
writeback_queue (loglevel: TRACE_EMERG (0)) (type: tracepoint)
writeback_exec (loglevel: TRACE_EMERG (0)) (type: tracepoint)
<…>
```

Traces are captured in the context of a session, which, in this example, is called `test`:

```
# lttng create test
Session test created.
Traces will be written in /home/root/lttng-traces/test20150824-140942
# lttng list
Available tracing sessions:
1) test (/home/root/lttng-traces/test-20150824-140942) [inactive]
```

Now enable a few events in the current session. You can enable all kernel tracepoints using the `--all` option, but remember the warning about generating too much trace data. Let's start with a couple of scheduler-related trace events:

```
# lttng enable-event --kernel sched_switch,sched_process_fork
```

Check that everything is set up:

```
# lttng list test
Tracing session test: [inactive]
    Trace path: /home/root/lttng-traces/test-20150824-140942
    Live timer interval (usec): 0
 === Domain: Kernel ===
 Channels:
 ------------
 - channel0: [enabled]
 Attributes:
       overwrite mode: 0
       subbufers size: 26214
       number of subbufers: 4
       switch timer interval: 0
       read timer interval: 200000
       trace file count: 0
       trace file size (bytes): 0
       output: splice()
 Events:
       sched_process_fork (loglevel: TRACE_EMERG (0)) (type: tracepoint)
```

```
[enabled]
      sched_switch (loglevel: TRACE_EMERG (0)) (type: tracepoint)
[enabled]
```

Now start tracing:

```
# lttng start
```

Run the test load, and then stop tracing:

```
# lttng stop
```

Traces for the session are written to the session directory, lttng-traces/<session>/kernel.

Use the Babeltrace viewer to dump the raw trace data in text format. In this case, I ran it on the host computer:

```
$ babeltrace2 lttng-traces/test-20150824-140942/kernel
```

The output is too verbose to fit on this page, so I will leave it as an exercise for you to capture and display a trace in this way. The text output from Babeltrace has the advantage that it is easy to search for strings using grep and similar commands.

A good choice for a graphical trace viewer is the **Trace Compass** plugin for Eclipse, which is now part of the Eclipse IDE for the C/C++ developer bundle. Importing the trace data into Eclipse is characteristically fiddly. Follow these steps:

1. Open the **Tracing** perspective.
2. Create a new project by selecting **File** | **New** | **Tracing project**.
3. Enter a project name and click on **Finish**.
4. Right-click on the **New Project** option in the **Project Explorer** menu and select **Import**.
5. Expand **Tracing**, and then select **Trace Import**.
6. Browse to the directory containing the traces (e.g., test-20150824-140942), tick the box to indicate which subdirectories you want (might be **kernel**), and click on **Finish**.
7. Expand the project, expand **Traces[1]**, and then double-click on **kernel**.

Now, let's switch gears away from LTTng and jump headfirst into the latest and greatest event tracer for Linux.

Using eBPF

Berkeley Packet Filter (BPF) is a technology that was first introduced in 1992 to capture, filter, and analyze network traffic. In 2013, Alexi Starovoitov undertook a rewrite of BPF with help from Daniel Borkmann. Their work, then known as **eBPF (extended BPF)**, was merged into the kernel in 2014, where it has been available since Linux 3.15. eBPF provides a sandboxed execution environment for running programs inside the Linux kernel. eBPF programs are written in C and are **just-in-time (JIT)** compiled to native code. Before that happens, the intermediate eBPF bytecode must first pass through a series of safety checks so that a program cannot crash the kernel.

Despite its networking origins, eBPF is now a general-purpose virtual machine running inside the Linux kernel. By making it easy to run small programs on specific kernel and application events, eBPF has quickly emerged as the most powerful tracer for Linux. Like what cgroups did for containerized deployments, eBPF has the potential to revolutionize observability by enabling users to fully instrument production systems. Netflix and Facebook make extensive use of eBPF across their microservices and cloud infrastructure for performance analysis and thwarting **distributed denial-of-service (DDoS)** attacks.

The tooling around eBPF is evolving, with **BPF Compiler Collection (BCC)** and **bpftrace** establishing themselves as the two most prominent frontends. Brendan Gregg was deeply involved in both projects and has written about eBPF extensively in his book *BPF Performance Tools: Linux System and Application Observability*. With so many possibilities covering such a vast scope, new technology such as eBPF can seem overwhelming. But much like cgroups, we don't need to understand how eBPF works to start making use of it. BCC comes with several ready-made tools and examples that we can simply run from the command line.

Configuring the kernel for eBPF

A package named **ply** (https://github.com/iovisor/ply) was merged into Buildroot on January 23, 2021, for inclusion in the 2021.02 LTS release of Buildroot. **ply** is a lightweight, dynamic tracer for Linux that leverages eBPF so that probes can be attached to arbitrary points in the kernel. Unlike bpftrace, which depends on BCC, ply does not rely on LLVM and has no required external dependencies aside from libc. This makes it much easier to port to embedded CPU architectures such as arm and powerpc.

Let's begin by configuring an eBPF-enabled kernel for Raspberry Pi 4:

```
$ cd buildroot
$ make clean
$ make raspberrypi4_64_defconfig
$ make linux-configure
```

The make linux-configure command will download and build some host tools before fetching, extracting, and configuring the kernel source code. The raspberrypi4_64_defconfig from the 2024.02.6 LTS release of Buildroot points to a custom 6.1 kernel source tarball from the Raspberry Pi Foundation's GitHub fork. Inspect the contents of your raspberrypi4_64_defconfig to verify what version of the kernel you are on. Once make linux-configure has configured the kernel, we can reconfigure it for eBPF:

```
$ make linux-menuconfig
```

To search for a specific kernel configuration option from the interactive menu, hit / and enter a search string. The search should return a numbered list of matches. Entering a given number takes you directly to that configuration option.

At a minimum, we need to select the following to enable kernel support for eBPF:

```
CONFIG_BPF=y
CONFIG_BPF_SYSCALL=y
```

The following are intended for BCC but there is no harm in adding them:

```
CONFIG_NET_CLS_BPF=m
CONFIG_NET_ACT_BPF=m
CONFIG_BPF_JIT=y
```

Add these so that users can compile and attach eBPF programs to kprobe, uprobe, and tracepoint events:

```
CONFIG_HAVE_EBPF_JIT=y
CONFIG_BPF_EVENTS=y
```

These need to be selected for ply to work:

```
CONFIG_KPROBES=y
CONFIG_TRACEPOINTS=y
CONFIG_FTRACE=y
CONFIG_DYNAMIC_FTRACE=y
```

```
CONFIG_KPROBE_EVENTS_ON_NOTRACE=y
```

Make sure to save your changes when exiting make linux-menuconfig so that they get applied to output/build/linux-custom/.config before building your eBPF-enabled kernel.

Building ply with Buildroot

Let's build ply and install the tool along with some example scripts. The ply scripts are bundled together inside an ebpf package under the MELD/Chapter20/ directory for easy installation. To copy them over to your 2024.02.06 LTS installation of Buildroot:

```
$ cd ~
$ cp -a MELD/Chapter20/buildroot/* buildroot
```

Now build the ply image for Raspberry Pi 4:

```
$ cd buildroot
$ make rpi4_64_ply_defconfig
$ make
```

If your version of Buildroot is 2024.02.06 LTS and you copied the buildroot overlay from MELD/Chapter20 correctly, then the ply image should build successfully. The kernel built for this image is already configured for eBPF so there is no need to perform the previous linux-menuconfig steps. The ply image also automounts debugfs at /sys/kernel/debug so ply is ready to run on boot up.

Insert the finished microSD into your Raspberry Pi 4, plug it into your local network with an Ethernet cable, and power the device up. Use arp-scan to locate your Raspberry Pi 4's IP address and SSH into it as root with the password you set in the previous section. I used temppwd for the root password in the configs/rpi4_64_ply_defconfig that I included with my MELD/Chapter20/ buildroot overlay. Now, we are ready to gain some firsthand experience in experimenting with eBPF.

Using ply

Doing almost anything with eBPF, including running the ply tool and examples, requires root privileges, which is why we enabled root login via SSH. Another prerequisite is mounting debugfs. If there is no debugfs entry in your /etc/fstab, then mount debugfs from the command line:

```
# mount -t debugfs none /sys/kernel/debug
```

Let's start by counting syscalls system-wide by function:

```
# ply 'k:__arm64_sys_* { @syscalls[caller] = count(); }'
^C
```

```
@syscalls:
{ __arm64_sys_ppoll }: 1
{ __arm64_sys_rt_sigaction }: 2
{ __arm64_sys_rt_sigreturn }: 3
{ __arm64_sys_writev }: 12
{ __arm64_sys_brk }: 13
{ __arm64_sys_pselect6 }: 19
{ __arm64_sys_perf_event_open }: 174
{ __arm64_sys_epoll_pwait }: 176
{ __arm64_sys_newfstatat }: 188
{ __arm64_sys_close }: 205
{ __arm64_sys_ioctl }: 247
{ __arm64_sys_read }: 370
{ __arm64_sys_openat }: 383
```

Notice that the ply session terminates, and the trace results are displayed when the user enters *Ctrl + C*. You may need to enter *Ctrl + C* repeatedly until the ply session finally terminates.

The directory where the ply scripts are located is not in the PATH environment variable, so navigate there for easier execution:

```
# cd /root
```

Let's start with a system-wide script that displays read sizes as a histogram:

```
# ./read-dist.ply
^C
@:
{ retsize }:
        [    2,     3]          1 ┤|                                        |
        ...
        [    8,    15]          1 ┤|                                        |
        [   16,    31]          1 ┤|                                        |
        ...
        [  256,   511]        181 ┤███████████████████████████████████████ |
```

The tcp-send-recv.ply script counts TCP I/O by executable and direction:

```
# ./tcp-send-recv.ply &
# redis-cli --latency
```

```
min: 0, max: 1, avg: 0.29 (1033 samples)^C
# fg %1
./tcp-send-recv.ply
^C
@:
{ dropbear       , recv  }: 26
{ redis-cli      , recv  }: 1033
{ redis-cli      , send  }: 1033
{ redis-server   , send  }: 1033
{ redis-server   , recv  }: 1034
{ dropbear       , send  }: 1048
```

In this instance, I am tracing all calls to tcp_sendmsg and tcp_recvmsg while I run a Redis client/ server latency test. I performed the test from an SSH terminal so there is TCP I/O reported for dropbear as well. The number of samples displayed increased from 0 to 1033 over the course of the latency test, which explains the 1048 sends made by dropbear.

The heap-allocs.ply script displays heap allocation counts. I ran an LRU cache simulation of 100,000 keys on Redis:

```
# redis-cli flushall
OK
# ./heap-allocs.ply &
# redis-cli --lru-test 100000
40500 Gets/sec | Hits: 18606 (45.94%) | Misses: 21894 (54.06%)
41000 Gets/sec | Hits: 32880 (80.20%) | Misses: 8120 (19.80%)
40250 Gets/sec | Hits: 35996 (89.43%) | Misses: 4254 (10.57%)
41000 Gets/sec | Hits: 38091 (92.90%) | Misses: 2909 (7.10%)
41000 Gets/sec | Hits: 38766 (94.55%) | Misses: 2234 (5.45%)
41000 Gets/sec | Hits: 39277 (95.80%) | Misses: 1723 (4.20%)
41000 Gets/sec | Hits: 39597 (96.58%) | Misses: 1403 (3.42%)
41000 Gets/sec | Hits: 39807 (97.09%) | Misses: 1193 (2.91%)
41000 Gets/sec | Hits: 39916 (97.36%) | Misses: 1084 (2.64%)
^C
# fg %1
./heap-allocs.ply
^C
@heap_allocs:
{ redis-cli      ,   215 }: 1027
```

Notice that an instance of redis-cli with PID 215 performed 1027 heap allocations. This concludes our coverage of Linux event tracing tools: Ftrace, LTTng, and eBPF. All of them require at least some kernel configuration to work. Valgrind offers more profiling tools that operate entirely from the comfort of user space.

Using Valgrind

I introduced **Valgrind** in *Chapter 18* as a tool for identifying memory problems using the memcheck tool. Valgrind has other useful tools for application profiling. The two I am going to look at here are Callgrind and Helgrind. Since Valgrind works by running the code in a sandbox, it can check the code as it runs and report certain behaviors, which native tracers and profilers cannot do.

Callgrind

Callgrind is a call graph-generating profiler that also collects information about processor cache hit rate and branch prediction. Callgrind is only useful if your bottleneck is CPU-bound. It's not useful if heavy I/O or multiple processes are involved.

Valgrind does not require kernel configuration, but it does need debug symbols. It is available as a target package in both The Yocto Project and Buildroot (BR2_PACKAGE_VALGRIND).

You run Callgrind in Valgrind on the target like so:

```
# valgrind --tool=callgrind <program>
```

This produces a file called callgrind.out.<PID>, which you can copy to the host and analyze with callgrind_annotate.

The default is to capture data for all the threads together in a single file. If you add the --separate-threads=yes option when capturing, there will be profiles for each of the threads in files named callgrind.out.<PID>-<thread id>.

Callgrind can simulate the processor L1/L2 cache and report on cache misses. Capture the trace with the --simulate-cache=yes option. L2 misses are much more expensive than L1 misses, so pay attention to code with high D2mr or D2mw counts.

The raw output from Callgrind can be overwhelming and difficult to untangle. A visualizer such as **KCachegrind** (https://kcachegrind.github.io/html/Home.html) can help you navigate the mountains of data Callgrind collects.

Helgrind

Helgrind is a thread-error detector for detecting synchronization errors in C, C++, and Fortran programs that include POSIX threads.

Helgrind can detect three classes of errors. Firstly, it can detect the incorrect use of the API. Some examples are unlocking a mutex that is already unlocked, unlocking a mutex that was locked by a different thread, or not checking the return value of certain `pthread` functions. Secondly, it monitors the order in which threads acquire locks to detect cycles that may result in deadlocks (also known as the deadly embrace). Finally, it detects data races, which can happen when two threads access a shared memory location without using suitable locks or other synchronization to ensure single-threaded access.

Using Helgrind is simple; you just need this command:

```
# valgrind --tool=helgrind <program>
```

It prints problems and potential problems as it finds them. You can direct these messages to a file by adding `--log-file=<filename>`.

Callgrind and Helgrind rely on Valgrind's virtualization for their profiling and deadlock detection. This heavyweight approach slows down the execution of your programs, increasing the likelihood of the observer effect.

Sometimes the bugs in our programs are so reproducible and easy to isolate that a simpler, less invasive tool is enough to quickly debug them. That tool more often than not is `strace`.

Using strace

I started the chapter with a simple and ubiquitous tool, top, and I will finish with another: **strace**. It is a very simple tracer that captures system calls made by a program and, optionally, its children. You can use it to do the following:

- Learn which system calls a program makes.
- Find those system calls that fail, together with the error code. I find this useful if a program fails to start but doesn't print an error message or if the message is too general.
- Find which files a program opens.
- Find out which `syscalls` a running program is making, for example, to see whether it is stuck in a loop.

There are many more examples online. Just search for strace tips and tricks. Everybody has a favorite strace story, for example, https://alexbilson.dev/plants/technology/debug-a-program-with-strace/.

strace uses the ptrace(2) function to hook calls as they are made from user space to the kernel. If you want to know more about how ptrace works, the manual page is detailed and surprisingly readable.

The simplest way to get a trace is to run the command as a parameter to strace (the listing has been edited for clarity):

```
# strace ./helloworld
execve("./helloworld", ["./helloworld"], [/* 14 vars */]) = 0
brk(0)                                 = 0x11000
uname({sys="Linux", node="beaglebone", ...}) = 0
mmap2(NULL, 4096, PROT_READ|PROT_WRITE, MAP_PRIVATE|MAP_ANONYMOUS, -1, 0)
= 0xb6f40000
access("/etc/ld.so.preload", R_OK)     = -1 ENOENT (No such file or
directory)
open("/etc/ld.so.cache", O_RDONLY|O_CLOEXEC) = 3
fstat64(3, {st_mode=S_IFREG|0644, st_size=8100, ...}) = 0
mmap2(NULL, 8100, PROT_READ, MAP_PRIVATE, 3, 0) = 0xb6f3e000
close(3)                               = 0
open("/lib/tls/v7l/neon/vfp/libc.so.6", O_RDONLY|O_CLOEXEC) = -1
ENOENT (No such file or directory)
<...>
open("/lib/libc.so.6", O_RDONLY|O_CLOEXEC) = 3
read(3, "\177ELF\1\1\1\0\0\0\0\0\0\0\0\0\3\0(\0\1\0\0\0$`\1\0004\0\0\0"...
, 512) = 512
fstat64(3, {st_mode=S_IFREG|0755, st_size=1291884, ...}) = 0
mmap2(NULL, 1328520, PROT_READ|PROT_EXEC, MAP_PRIVATE|MAP_DENYWRITE, 3, 0)
= 0xb6df9000
mprotect(0xb6f30000, 32768, PROT_NONE)  = 0
mmap2(0xb6f38000, 12288, PROT_READ|PROT_WRITE,
MAP_PRIVATE|MAP_FIXED|MAP_DENYWRITE, 3, 0x137000) = 0xb6f38000
mmap2(0xb6f3b000, 9608, PROT_READ|PROT_WRITE,
MAP_PRIVATE|MAP_FIXED|MAP_ANONYMOUS, -1, 0) = 0xb6f3b000
close(3)
<...>
```

```
write(1, "Hello, world!\n", 14Hello, world!)              = 14
exit_group(0)                              = ?
+++ exited with 0 +++
```

Most of the trace shows how the runtime environment is created. In particular, you can see how the library loader hunts for libc.so.6, eventually finding it in /lib. Finally, it gets to running the main() function of the program, which prints its message and exits.

If you want strace to follow any child processes or threads created by the original process, add the -f option.

> **TIP**
>
> If you are using strace to trace a program that creates threads, you almost certainly want to use the -f option. Better still, use -ff and -o <file name> so that the output for each child process or thread is written to a separate file named <filename>.<PID | TID>.

A common use of strace is to discover which files a program tries to open at startup. You can restrict the system calls that are traced through the -e option, and you can write the trace to a file instead of stdout using the -o option:

```
# strace -e open -o ssh-strace.txt ssh localhost
```

This shows the libraries and configuration files ssh opens when it is setting up a connection.

You can even use strace as a basic profile tool. If you use the -c option, it accumulates the time spent in system calls and prints out a summary like this:

```
# strace -c grep linux /usr/lib/* > /dev/null
% time     seconds  usecs/call     calls    errors syscall
------ ----------- ----------- --------- --------- ---------
 78.68    0.012825           1     11098        18 read
 11.03    0.001798           1      3551           write
 10.02    0.001634           8       216        15 open
  0.26    0.000043           0       202           fstat64
  0.00    0.000000           0       201           close
  0.00    0.000000           0         1           execve
  0.00    0.000000           0         1         1 access
  0.00    0.000000           0         3           brk
```

```
    0.00      0.000000         0        199              munmap
    0.00      0.000000         0          1              uname
    0.00      0.000000         0          5              mprotect
    0.00      0.000000         0        207              mmap2
    0.00      0.000000         0         15        15     stat64
    0.00      0.000000         0          1              getuid32
    0.00      0.000000         0          1              set_tls
  ------   ----------   ----------   ---------   ---------   ----------
  100.00     0.016300                15702        49 total
```

strace is extremely versatile. We have only scratched the surface of what the tool can do.

I recommend downloading *Spying on your programs with strace*, a free zine by Julia Evans available at https://wizardzines.com/zines/strace/.

Summary

Nobody can complain that Linux lacks options for profiling and tracing. This chapter has given you an overview of some of the most common ones.

When faced with a system that is not performing as well as you would like, start with top and try to identify the problem. If it proves to be a single application, then you can use perf record/ report to profile it. Bear in mind that you will have to configure the kernel to enable perf and you will need debug symbols for both the binaries and kernel. If the problem is not so well localized, use perf or ply to get a system-wide view.

Ftrace comes into its own when you have specific questions about the behavior of the kernel. The function and function_graph tracers provide a detailed view of the relationship and sequence of function calls. The event tracers allow you to extract more information about functions, including the parameters and return values.

LTTng performs a similar role, making use of the event trace mechanism, and adds high-speed ring buffers to extract large quantities of data from the kernel.

Valgrind has the advantage of running code in a sandbox and can report on errors that are hard to track down in other ways. Using Callgrind, it can generate call graphs and report on processor cache usage, and with Helgrind, it can report on thread-related problems.

Finally, don't forget strace. It is a good standby for finding out which system calls a program is making, from tracking file open calls to finding file pathnames and checking for system wake-ups and incoming signals.

All the while, be aware of, and try to avoid, the observer effect by making sure that your measurements are valid for a production system. In the next chapter, we will delve into the latency tracers that help us quantify the real-time performance of a target system.

Further study

- *Profiling and tracing with perf*, by Julia Evans
- *Systems Performance: Enterprise and the Cloud, Second Edition*, by Brendan Gregg
- *BPF Performance Tools: Linux System and Application Observability*, by Brendan Gregg
- *ply: lightweight eBPF tracing*, by Frank Vasquez: `https://www.youtube.com/watch?v=GuEEJlU9Mr8`
- *Spying on your programs with strace*, by Julia Evans

21

Real-Time Programming

Much of the interaction between a computer system and the real world happens in real time, and so this is an important topic for developers of embedded systems. I have touched on real-time programming in several places so far: in *Chapter 17*, we looked at scheduling policies and priority inversion, and in *Chapter 18*, I described the problems with page faults and the need for memory locking. Now it is time to bring these topics together and look at real-time programming in some depth.

In this chapter, I will begin with a discussion about the characteristics of real-time systems, and then consider the implications for system design, at both the application and kernel levels. I will describe the real-time PREEMPT_RT kernel patch and show how to get it and apply it to a mainline kernel. The final sections will describe how to characterize system latencies using two tools: **cyclictest** and **Ftrace**.

There are other ways to achieve real-time behavior on an embedded Linux device, for instance, using a dedicated microcontroller or a separate real-time kernel alongside the Linux kernel in the way that Xenomai and RTAI do. I am not going to discuss these here because the focus of this book is on using Linux as the core for embedded systems.

In this chapter, we will cover the following topics:

- What is real time?
- Identifying sources of non-determinism
- Understanding scheduling latency
- Kernel preemption
- Preemptible kernel locks

- High-resolution timers
- Avoiding page faults
- Interrupt shielding
- Measuring scheduling latencies

Technical requirements

To follow along with the examples, make sure you have the following:

- An Ubuntu 24.04 or later LTS host system with at least 90 GB of free disk space
- Yocto 5.0 (Scarthgap) LTS release
- A microSD card reader and card
- balenaEtcher for Linux
- An Ethernet cable and router with an available port for network connectivity
- A BeaglePlay
- A 5 V USB-C power supply capable of delivering 3 A

You should have already built the 5.0 (Scarthgap) LTS release of Yocto in *Chapter 6*. If you have not, then please refer to the *Compatible Linux Distribution* and *Build Host Packages* sections of the *Yocto Project Quick Build* guide (https://docs.yoctoproject.org/brief-yoctoprojectqs/) before building Yocto on your Linux host according to the instructions in *Chapter 6*.

What is real time?

The nature of real-time programming is one of the subjects that software engineers love to discuss at length, often giving a range of contradictory definitions. I will begin by setting out what I think is important about real time.

A task is a real-time task if it has to be completed before a certain point in time, known as the **deadline**. The distinction between real-time and non-real-time tasks is shown by considering what happens when you play an audio stream on your computer while compiling the Linux kernel. The first is a real-time task because there is a constant stream of data arriving at the audio driver, and blocks of audio samples have to be written to the audio interface at the playback rate. Meanwhile, the compilation is not real time because there is no deadline. You simply want it to be completed as soon as possible; whether it takes 10 seconds or 10 minutes does not affect the quality of the kernel binaries.

The other important thing to consider is the consequence of missing the deadline, which can range from mild annoyance to system failure or, in the most extreme cases, injury or death. Here are some examples:

- **Playing an audio stream:** There is a deadline in the order of tens of milliseconds. If the audio buffer underruns, you will hear a click, which is annoying, but you will get over it.
- **Moving and clicking a mouse:** The deadline is also in the order of tens of milliseconds. If it is missed, the mouse moves erratically and button clicks will be lost. If the problem persists, the system will become unusable.
- **Printing a piece of paper:** The deadlines for the paper feed are in the millisecond range, which if missed may cause the printer to jam, and somebody will have to go and fix it. Occasional jams are acceptable, but nobody is going to buy a printer that keeps on jamming.
- **Printing sell-by dates on bottles on a production line:** If one bottle is not printed, the whole production line has to be halted, the bottle removed, and the line restarted, which is expensive.
- **Baking a cake:** There is a deadline of 30 minutes or so. If you miss it by a few minutes, the cake might be ruined. If you miss it by a lot, the house may burn down.
- **Power-surge detection system:** If the system detects a surge, a circuit breaker has to be triggered within 2 milliseconds. Failing to do so causes damage to the equipment and may injure or kill someone.

In other words, there are many consequences to missed deadlines. We often talk about these different categories:

- **Soft real-time:** The deadline is desirable but is sometimes missed without the system being considered a failure. The first two examples in the previous list are examples of this.
- **Hard real-time:** Here, missing a deadline has a serious effect. We can further subdivide hard real-time into mission-critical systems, in which there is a cost to missing the deadline, such as the fourth example, and safety-critical systems, in which there is a danger to life and limb, such as the last two examples. I put in the baking example to show that not all hard real-time systems have deadlines measured in milliseconds or microseconds.

Software written for safety-critical systems has to conform to various standards that seek to ensure that it is capable of performing reliably. It is very difficult for a complex operating system such as Linux to meet those requirements.

When it comes to mission-critical systems, it is possible, and common, for Linux to be used for a wide range of control systems. The requirements of the software depend on the combination of the deadline and the confidence level, which can usually be determined through extensive testing.

Therefore, to say that a system is real-time, you have to measure its response times under the maximum anticipated load and show that it meets the deadline for an agreed proportion of the time. As a rule of thumb, a well-configured Linux system using a mainline kernel is good for soft real-time tasks with deadlines down to tens of milliseconds, and a kernel with the PREEMPT_RT patch is good for soft and hard real-time mission-critical systems with deadlines down to several hundreds of microseconds.

The key to creating a real-time system is to reduce the variability in response times so that you have greater confidence that the deadlines will not be missed; in other words, you need to make the system more deterministic. Often, this is done at the expense of performance. For example, caches make systems run faster by making the average time to access an item of data shorter, but the maximum time is longer in the case of a cache miss. Caches make a system faster but less deterministic, which is the opposite of what we want.

> **TIP**
>
> It is a myth of real-time computing that it is fast. This is not so; the more deterministic a system is, the lower the maximum throughput.

The remainder of this chapter is concerned with identifying the causes of latency and the things you can do to reduce it.

Identifying sources of non-determinism

Fundamentally, real-time programming is about making sure that the threads controlling the output in real time are scheduled when needed and so can complete the job before the deadline. Anything that prevents this is a problem. Here are some problem areas:

- **Scheduling**: Real-time threads must be scheduled before others, and so they must have a real-time policy, SCHED_FIFO or SCHED_RR. Additionally, they should have priorities assigned in descending order, starting with the one with the shortest deadline, according to the theory of rate monotonic analysis that I described in *Chapter 17*.

- **Scheduling latency**: The kernel must be able to reschedule as soon as an event such as an interrupt or timer occurs and not be subject to unbounded delays. Reducing scheduling latency is a key topic later on in this chapter.

- **Priority inversion**: This is a consequence of priority-based scheduling, which leads to unbounded delays when a high-priority thread is blocked on a mutex held by a low-priority thread, as I described in *Chapter 17*. User space has priority inheritance and priority ceiling mutexes; in kernel space, we have RT-mutexes, which implement priority inheritance, and I will talk about them in the section on the real-time kernel.

- **Accurate timers**: If you want to manage deadlines in the region of low milliseconds or microseconds, you need timers that match. High-resolution timers are crucial and are a configuration option on almost all kernels.

- **Page faults**: A page fault while executing a critical section of code will upset all timing estimates. You can avoid them by locking memory, as I shall describe later.

- **Interrupts**: They occur at unpredictable times and can result in an unexpected processing overhead if there is a sudden flood of them. There are two ways to avoid this. One is to run interrupts as kernel threads, and the other, on multi-core devices, is to shield one or more CPUs from interrupt handling. I will discuss both possibilities later.

- **Processor caches**: These provide a buffer between the CPU and the main memory and, like all caches, are a source of non-determinism, especially on multi-core devices. Unfortunately, this is beyond the scope of this book, but you may want to refer to the references at the end of the chapter for more details.

- **Memory bus contention**: When peripherals access memory directly through a DMA channel, they use up a slice of memory bus bandwidth, which slows down access from the CPU core (or cores) and so contributes to the non-deterministic execution of the program. However, this is a hardware issue and is also beyond the scope of this book.

I will expand on the most important problems and see what can be done about them in the next sections.

Understanding scheduling latency

Real-time threads need to be scheduled as soon as they have something to do. However, even if there are no other threads of the same or higher priority, there is always a delay from the point at which the wakeup event occurs—an interrupt or system timer—to the time that the thread starts to run. This is called scheduling latency. It can be broken down into several components, as shown in the following diagram:

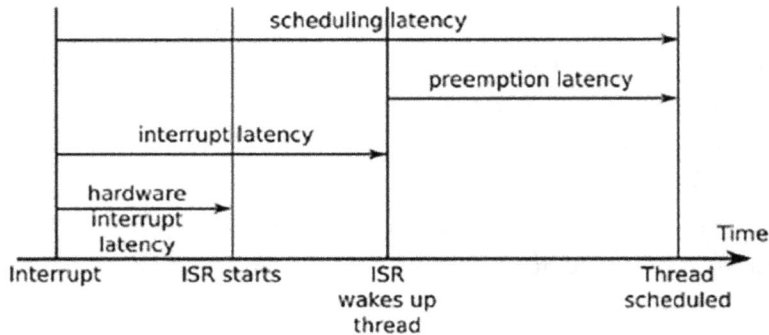

Figure 21.1 – Scheduling latency

Firstly, there is the hardware interrupt latency from the point at which an interrupt is asserted until the **interrupt service routine (ISR)** begins to run. A small part of this is the delay in the interrupt hardware itself, but the biggest problem is due to interrupts being disabled in software. Minimizing this *IRQ off time* is important.

The next is interrupt latency, which is the length of time until the ISR has serviced the interrupt and woken up any threads waiting on this event. It is mostly dependent on the way the ISR was written. Normally, it should take only a short time, measured in microseconds.

The final delay is the preemption latency, which is the time from the point that the kernel is notified that a thread is ready to run to that at which the scheduler actually runs the thread. It is determined by whether the kernel can be preempted or not. If it is running code in a critical section, then the rescheduling will have to wait. The length of the delay is dependent on the configuration of kernel preemption.

Kernel preemption

Preemption latency occurs because it is not always safe or desirable to preempt the current thread of execution and call the scheduler. Mainline Linux has three settings for preemption, selected via the **Kernel Features | Preemption Model** menu:

- `CONFIG_PREEMPT_NONE`: No preemption.
- `CONFIG_PREEMPT_VOLUNTARY`: Enables additional checks for requests for preemption.
- `CONFIG_PREEMPT`: Allows the kernel to be preempted.

With preemption set to none, kernel code will continue without rescheduling until it either returns via a `syscall` back to user space, where preemption is always allowed, or it encounters a sleeping wait that stops the current thread. Since it reduces the number of transitions between the kernel and user space and may reduce the total number of context switches, this option results in the highest throughput at the expense of large preemption latencies. It is the default for servers and some desktop kernels where throughput is more important than responsiveness.

The second option enables explicit preemption points, where the scheduler is called if the need_resched flag is set, which reduces the worst-case preemption latencies at the expense of slightly lower throughput. Some distributions set this option on desktops.

The third option makes the kernel preemptible, meaning that an interrupt can result in an immediate reschedule so long as the kernel is not executing in an atomic context, which I will describe in the following section. This reduces worst-case preemption latencies and, therefore, overall scheduling latencies to something in the order of a few milliseconds on typical embedded hardware.

This is often described as a soft real-time option, and most embedded kernels are configured in this way. Of course, there is a small reduction in overall throughput, but that is usually less important than having more deterministic scheduling for embedded devices.

Real-time Linux kernel (PREEMPT_RT)

There was a long-standing effort to reduce latencies even further that goes by the name of the kernel configuration option for these features, **PREEMPT_RT**. The project was started by Ingo Molnar, Thomas Gleixner, and Steven Rostedt and has had contributions from many more developers over the years. The kernel patches are at https://www.kernel.org/pub/linux/kernel/projects/rt, and there is a wiki at https://wiki.linuxfoundation.org/realtime/start.

IMPORTANT NOTE

PREEMPT_RT was fully merged and enabled in the mainline Linux kernel on September 20, 2024. PREEMPT_RT support for the x86, x86-64, arm64, and riscv architectures was included in the Linux 6.12 LTS release that happened on November 17, 2024.

The central plan was to reduce the amount of time the kernel spends running in an **atomic context**, which is where it is not safe to call the scheduler and switch to a different thread. Typical atomic contexts are when the kernel is in the following states:

- Running an interrupt or trap handler.
- Holding a spin lock or is in an RCU-critical section. Spin locks and RCU are kernel-locking primitives, the details of which are not relevant here.
- Between calls to preempt_disable() and preempt_enable().
- Hardware interrupts are disabled (**IRQs off**).

The changes that comprised PREEMPT_RT had two main goals: one is to reduce the impact of interrupt handlers by turning them into kernel threads, and the other is to make locks preemptible so that a thread can sleep while holding one. It is obvious that there is a large overhead in these changes, which makes average-case interrupt handling slower but much more deterministic, which is what we are striving for.

Threaded interrupt handlers

Not all interrupts are triggers for real-time tasks, but all interrupts steal cycles from real-time tasks. Threaded interrupt handlers allow a priority to be associated with the interrupt and for it to be scheduled at an appropriate time, as shown in the following diagram:

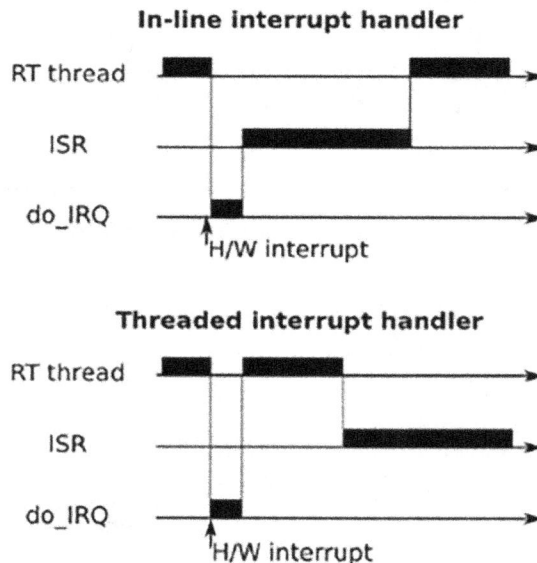

Figure 21.2 – In-line versus threaded interrupt handlers

If the interrupt handler code is run as a kernel thread, there is no reason why it cannot be preempted by a user space thread of higher priority, and so the interrupt handler does not contribute toward scheduling latency of the user space thread. Threaded interrupt handlers have been a feature of mainline Linux since 2.6.30. You can request that an individual interrupt handler be threaded by registering it with `request_threaded_irq()` in place of the normal `request_irq()`. You can make threaded IRQs the default by configuring the kernel with `CONFIG_IRQ_FORCED_THREADING=y`, which makes all handlers into threads unless they have explicitly prevented this by setting the `IRQF_NO_THREAD` flag. When `PREEMPT_RT` is enabled, interrupts are, by default, configured as threads in this way. Here is an example of what you might see:

```
# ps -Leo pid,tid,class,rtprio,stat,comm,wchan | grep FF
  PID   TID CLS RTPRIO STAT COMMAND           WCHAN
   21    21 FF      99 S    migration/0       smpboot_thread_fn
   22    22 FF       1 S    irq_work/0        smpboot_thread_fn
   25    25 FF       1 S    irq_work/1        smpboot_thread_fn
   26    26 FF      99 S    migration/1       smpboot_thread_fn
   32    32 FF       1 S    irq_work/2        smpboot_thread_fn
   33    33 FF      99 S    migration/2       smpboot_thread_fn
   39    39 FF       1 S    irq_work/3        smpboot_thread_fn
   40    40 FF      99 S    migration/3       smpboot_thread_fn
   66    66 FF      50 S    watchdogd         kthread_worker_fn
   78    78 FF      50 S    irq/14-4d000000   irq_thread
<...>
  103   103 FF      50 S    irq/256-8000000   irq_thread
  107   107 FF      50 S    irq/293-xhci-hc   irq_thread
  111   111 FF      50 S    irq/294-mmc0      irq_thread
  112   112 FF      50 S    irq/294-s-mmc0    irq_thread
  119   119 FF      50 S    irq/346-User Ke   irq_thread
  120   120 FF      50 S    irq/476-mmc1      irq_thread
  121   121 FF      50 S    irq/476-s-mmc1    irq_thread
  123   123 FF      50 S    irq/295-mmc2      irq_thread
  124   124 FF      50 S    irq/295-s-mmc2    irq_thread
  127   127 FF      50 S    irq/472-fa00000   irq_thread
```

> **IMPORTANT NOTE**
>
> The interrupt threads have all been given the default SCHED_FIFO policy and a priority of 50. It doesn't make sense to leave them at the defaults, however; now is your chance to assign priorities according to the importance of the interrupts compared to real-time user space threads.

Here is a suggested order of descending thread priorities:

- The POSIX timers thread, posixcputmr, should always have the highest priority.
- Hardware interrupts associated with the highest-priority real-time thread.
- The highest-priority real-time thread.
- Hardware interrupts for the progressively lower-priority real-time threads, followed by the thread itself.
- The next highest priority real-time thread.
- Hardware interrupts for non-real-time interfaces.
- The soft IRQ daemon, ksoftirqd, which on RT kernels is responsible for running delayed interrupt routines and, prior to Linux 3.6, was responsible for running the network stack, the block I/O layer, and other things.

You may need to experiment with different priority levels to achieve a balance. You can change the priorities using the chrt command as part of the boot script with a command like this:

```
# chrt -f -p 90 `pgrep irq/293-xhci-hcd:usb1`
```

The pgrep command is part of the procps package.

Now that we've been introduced to the real-time Linux kernel by way of threaded interrupt handlers, let's dig deeper into its implementation.

Preemptible kernel locks

Making the majority of kernel locks preemptible is the most intrusive change that PREEMPT_RT makes.

The problem occurs with spin locks, which are used for much of the kernel locking. A spin lock is a busy-wait mutex that does not require a context switch in the contended case, and so it is very efficient as long as the lock is held for a short time. Ideally, they should be locked for less than the time it would take to reschedule twice.

The following diagram shows threads running on two different CPUs contending the same spin lock. **CPU 0** gets it first, forcing **CPU 1** to spin, waiting until it is unlocked:

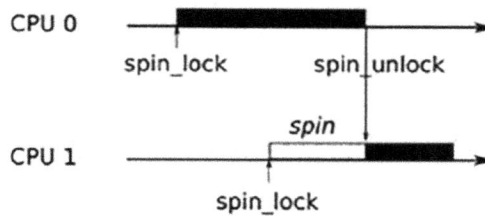

Figure 21.3 – Spin lock

The thread that holds the spin lock cannot be preempted since doing so may make the new thread enter the same code and deadlock when it tries to lock the same spin lock. Consequently, in mainline Linux, locking a spin lock disables kernel preemption, creating an atomic context. This means that a low-priority thread that holds a spin lock can prevent a high-priority thread from being scheduled, a condition otherwise known as **priority inversion**.

> **IMPORTANT NOTE**
>
> The solution adopted by PREEMPT_RT is to replace almost all spin locks with RT-mutexes. A mutex is slower than a spin lock, but it is fully preemptible. Not only that, but RT-mutexes implement priority inheritance and so are not susceptible to priority inversion.

We now have an idea of what's in the PREEMPT_RT patches. So, how do we go about getting them?

Getting the PREEMPT_RT patches

Historically, the RT developers did not create patch sets for every kernel version because of the amount of porting effort involved. On average, they created patches for every other kernel. This practice changed beginning with kernel version 5.9, after which a patch was generated for every kernel version. The most recent kernels that are supported at the time of writing are as follows:

- 6.13-rt
- 6.12-rt
- 6.11-rt
- 6.10-rt
- 6.9-rt

- 6.8-rt
- 6.7-rt
- 6.6-rt
- 6.5-rt
- 6.4-rt
- 6.3-rt
- 6.1-rt

IMPORTANT NOTE

The patches are available at https://www.kernel.org/pub/linux/kernel/projects/rt. From 6.12-rt onward, the patches contain features and optimizations that have yet to be merged into the official kernel.

If you are using The Yocto Project, there is an RT version of the kernel already. Otherwise, it is possible that the place you got your kernel from already has the PREEMPT_RT patch applied. If not, you will have to apply the patch yourself. Firstly, make sure that the PREEMPT_RT patch version and your kernel version match exactly; otherwise, you will not be able to apply the patches cleanly. Then, you apply it in the normal way, as shown in the following command lines. You will then be able to configure the kernel with CONFIG_PREEMPT_RT_FULL:

```
$ cd linux-6.6.74
$ zcat patch-6.6.74-rt48.patch.gz | patch -p1
```

There is a problem in the previous paragraph. The RT patch will only apply if you are using a compatible mainline kernel. You are probably not, because that is the nature of embedded Linux kernels. Therefore, you will have to spend some time looking at failed patches and fixing them and then analyzing the board support for your target and adding any real-time support that is missing. These details are, once again, outside the scope of this book. If you are not sure what to do, you should request support from the kernel vendor that you are using and on kernel developer forums.

The Yocto Project and PREEMPT_RT

The Yocto Project supplies two standard kernel recipes: linux-yocto and linux-yocto-rt with the real-time patches already applied. Assuming that your target is supported by the Yocto kernels, you just need to select linux-yocto-rt as your preferred kernel and declare that your machine is compatible.

Since we are using the `meta-ti-bsp` layer to build a TI kernel for the BeaglePlay, add these two lines to your `conf/local.conf` to build a real-time kernel:

```
PREFERRED_PROVIDER_virtual/kernel = "linux-ti-staging-rt"
COMPATIBLE_MACHINE_beagleplay-ti = "beagleplay-ti"
```

So, now that we know where to get a real-time Linux kernel, let's switch gears and talk about timing.

High-resolution timers

Timer resolution is important if you have precise timing requirements, which is typical for real-time applications. The default timer in Linux is a clock that runs at a configurable rate, typically 100 Hz for embedded systems and 250 Hz for servers and desktops. The interval between two timer ticks is known as a **jiffy** and, in the examples given previously, is 10 milliseconds on an embedded SoC and 4 milliseconds on a server.

Linux gained more accurate timers from the real-time kernel project in version 2.6.18, and now they are available on all platforms, provided that there is a high-resolution timer source and device driver for it—which is almost always the case. You need to configure the kernel with `CONFIG_HIGH_RES_TIMERS=y`.

With this enabled, all the kernel and user space clocks will be accurate down to the granularity of the underlying hardware. Finding the actual clock granularity is difficult. The obvious answer is the value provided by `clock_getres(2)`, but that always claims a resolution of 1 nanosecond.

The `cyclictest` tool has an option to analyze the times reported by the clock to guess the resolution:

```
# cyclictest -R
# /dev/cpu_dma_latency set to 0us
WARN: reported clock resolution: 1 nsec
WARN: measured clock resolution approximately: 60 nsec
```

You can also look at the kernel log messages for clock-related strings like this:

```
# dmesg | grep clock
[    0.000000] clocksource: arch_sys_counter: mask: 0x3ffffffffffffff max_
cycles: 0x2e2049d3e8, max_idle_ns: 440795210634 ns60563 Min:      13 Act:
67 Avg:    67 Max:      241
[    0.000001] sched_clock: 58 bits at 200MHz, resolution 5ns, wraps every
4398046511102ns
```

```
[    0.028415] clocksource: jiffies: mask: 0xffffffff max_cycles:
0xffffffff, max_idle_ns: 1911260446275000 ns
[    0.058173] PTP clock support registered
[    0.060830] clocksource: Switched to clocksource arch_sys_counter
[    0.685471] clk: Disabling unused clocks
```

The two methods provide noticeably different numbers, both of which are below 1 microsecond. Kernel logs show the base resolution of a timer (e.g., jiffies, HPET, TSC) rather than the effective resolution after applying timekeeping adjustments. cyclictest measures actual wakeup latencies, which depend on scheduler wakeup delays, IRQ latencies, and the accuracy of the timer hardware.

High-resolution timers can measure variations in latency with sufficient accuracy. Now, let's look at a couple of ways to mitigate such non-determinism.

Avoiding page faults

A page fault occurs when an application reads or writes to memory that is not committed to physical memory. It is impossible (or very hard) to predict when a page fault will happen, so they are another source of non-determinism in computers.

Fortunately, there is a function that allows you to commit all the memory used by the process and lock it down so that it cannot cause a page fault. It is mlockall(2). These are its two flags:

- MCL_CURRENT: Locks all pages currently mapped.
- MCL_FUTURE: Locks pages that are mapped in later.

You usually call mlockall during the startup of the application with both flags set to lock all current and future memory mappings.

> **TIP**
>
> MCL_FUTURE is not magic, in that there will still be a non-deterministic delay when allocating or freeing heap memory using malloc()/free() or mmap(). Such operations are best done at startup and not in the main control loops.

Memory allocated on the stack is trickier because it is done automatically, and if you call a function that makes the stack deeper than before, you will encounter more memory management delays. A simple fix is to grow the stack to a size larger than you think you will ever need at startup. The code would look like this:

```
#define MAX_STACK (512*1024)
static void stack_grow (void)
{
    char dummy[MAX_STACK];
    memset(dummy, 0, MAX_STACK);
    return;
}
int main(int argc, char* argv[])
{
    <...>
    stack_grow ();
    mlockall(MCL_CURRENT | MCL_FUTURE);
    <...>
```

The stack_grow() function allocates a large variable on the stack and then zeroes it out to force those pages of memory to be committed to this process.

Interrupts are another source of non-determinism we should guard against.

Interrupt shielding

Using threaded interrupt handlers helps mitigate interrupt overhead by running some threads at a higher priority than interrupt handlers that do not impact real-time tasks. If you are using a multi-core processor, you can take a different approach and shield one or more cores from processing interrupts completely, allowing them to be dedicated to real-time tasks instead. This works either with a normal Linux kernel or a PREEMPT_RT kernel.

Achieving this is a question of pinning the real-time threads to one CPU and the interrupt handlers to a different one. You can set the CPU affinity of a thread or process using the taskset command-line tool, or you can use the sched_setaffinity(2) and pthread_setaffinity_np(3) functions.

To set the affinity of an interrupt, first note that there is a subdirectory for each interrupt number in /proc/irq/<IRQ number>. The control files for the interrupt are in there, including a CPU mask in smp_affinity. Write a bitmask to that file with a bit set for each CPU that is allowed to handle that IRQ.

Stack growing and interrupt shielding are nifty techniques for improving responsiveness, but how can you tell whether they are actually working?

Measuring scheduling latencies

All the configuration and tuning you may do will be pointless if you cannot show that your device meets the deadlines. You will need your own benchmarks for the final testing, but I will describe here two important measurement tools: `cyclictest` and `Ftrace`.

cyclictest

`cyclictest` was originally written by Thomas Gleixner and is now available on most platforms in a package named `rt-tests`.

If you are building a Yocto real-time kernel, you can create a target image that includes `rt-tests` by building the real-time image recipe:

```
$ bitbake core-image-rt
```

If you are building a TI real-time kernel for the BeaglePlay, then configure the kernel with `CONFIG_ARM_PSCI_IDLE=y` so that `cyclictest` can write to the `/dev/cpu_dma_latency` socket.

If you are building a TI real-time kernel for the BeaglePlay, then append `rt-tests` to your image by modifying `conf/local.conf`:

```
IMAGE_INSTALL:append = " rt-tests"
```

Build the minimal image recipe to install `rt-tests` onto an image for the BeaglePlay:

```
$ bitbake core-image-minimal
```

If you are using Buildroot, you need to add the `BR2_PACKAGE_RT_TESTS` package in the **Target packages | Debugging, profiling and benchmark | rt-tests** menu.

`cyclictest` measures scheduling latencies by comparing the actual time taken for sleeping to the requested time. If there was no latency, they would be the same, and the reported latency would be 0. `cyclictest` assumes a timer resolution of less than 1 microsecond.

It has a large number of command-line options. To start with, you might try running this command as root on the target:

```
# cyclictest -l 100000 -m -p 99
# /dev/cpu_dma_latency set to 0us
policy: fifo: loadavg: 0.00 0.00 0.00 1/119 430
T: 0 (  422) P:99 I:1000 C: 100000 Min:      5 Act:    7 Avg:    7 Max:
48
```

The options selected are as follows:

- `-l N`: Loops N times (the default is unlimited).
- `-m`: Locks memory with `mlockall`.
- `-p N`: Uses the real-time priority N.

The result line shows the following, reading from left to right:

- `T: 0`: This was thread 0, the only thread in this run. You can set the number of threads with parameter `-t`.
- `( 422)`: This was PID 422.
- `P:99`: The priority was 99.
- `I:1000`: The interval between loops was 1,000 microseconds. You can set the interval with the `-i N` parameter.
- `C:100000`: The final loop count for this thread was 100,000.
- `Min: 5`: The minimum latency was 5 microseconds.
- `Act: 7`: The actual latency was 7 microseconds. The *actual latency* is the most recent latency measurement, which only makes sense if you are watching `cyclictest` as it runs.
- `Avg: 7`: The average latency was 7 microseconds.
- `Max: 48`: The maximum latency was 48 microseconds.

This was obtained on an idle system running a `linux-ti-staging-rt` kernel as a quick demonstration of the tool. To be of real use, you would run tests over a 24-hour period or longer while running a load representative of the maximum you expect. `cyclictest` is a standard metric for scheduling latencies. However, it cannot help you identify and resolve specific problems with kernel latency. To do that, you need Ftrace.

Using Ftrace

The kernel function tracer has tracers to help track down kernel latencies—that is what it was originally written for, after all. These tracers capture the trace for the worst-case latency detected during a run, showing the functions that caused the delay.

The tracers of interest, together with the kernel configuration parameters, are as follows:

- `irqsoff`: `CONFIG_IRQSOFF_TRACER` traces code that disables interrupts, recording the worst case.
- `preemptoff`: `CONFIG_PREEMPT_TRACER` is similar to `irqsoff` but traces the longest time that kernel preemption is disabled (only available on preemptible kernels).

- preemptirqsoff: Combines the previous two traces to record the longest time either irqs and/or preemption are disabled for.

- wakeup: Traces and records the maximum latency that it takes for the highest priority task to get scheduled after it has been woken up.

- wakeup_rt: This is the same as wakeup but only for real-time threads with the SCHED_FIFO, SCHED_RR, or SCHED_DEADLINE policies.

- wakeup_dl: This is the same but only for deadline-scheduled threads with the SCHED_ DEADLINE policy.

Be aware that running Ftrace adds a lot of latency, in the order of tens of milliseconds, every time it captures a new maximum, which Ftrace itself can ignore. However, it skews the results of user space tracers such as cyclictest. In other words, ignore the results of cyclictest if you run it while capturing traces.

Selecting the tracer is the same as for the function tracer we looked at in *Chapter 20*. Here is an example of capturing a trace for the maximum period with preemption disabled for a period of 60 seconds:

```
# echo preemptoff > /sys/kernel/debug/tracing/current_tracer
# echo 0 > /sys/kernel/debug/tracing/tracing_max_latency
# echo 1 > /sys/kernel/debug/tracing/tracing_on
# sleep 60
# echo 0 > /sys/kernel/debug/tracing/tracing_on
```

The resulting trace, heavily edited, looks like this:

```
# cat /sys/kernel/debug/tracing/trace
# tracer: preemptoff
#
# preemptoff latency trace v1.1.5 on 3.14.19-yocto-standard
# --------------------------------------------------------------
# latency: 1160 us, #384/384, CPU#0 | (M:preempt VP:0, KP:0, SP:0 HP:0)
# ---------------
# | task: init-1 (uid:0 nice:0 policy:0 rt_prio:0)
# ---------------
# => started at: ip_finish_output
# => ended at: __local_bh_enable_ip
#
#
```

```
#                  _------=> CPU#
#                 / _-----=> irqs-off
#                | / _----=> need-resched
#                || / _---=> hardirq/softirq
#                ||| / _--=> preempt-depth
#                |||| /      delay
# cmd pid       |||||   time | caller
#    \ /        |||||      \ | /
  init-1    0..s.     1us+: ip_finish_output
  init-1    0d.s2    27us+: preempt_count_add <-cpdma_chan_submit
  init-1    0d.s3    30us+: preempt_count_add <-cpdma_chan_submit
  init-1    0d.s4    37us+: preempt_count_sub <-cpdma_chan_submit
  <...>
  init-1    0d.s2  1152us+: preempt_count_sub <-__local_bh_enable
  init-1    0d..2  1155us+: preempt_count_sub <-__local_bh_enable_ip
  init-1    0d..1  1158us+: __local_bh_enable_ip
  init-1    0d..1  1162us!: trace_preempt_on <-__local_bh_enable_ip
  init-1    0d..1  1340us : <stack trace>
```

Here, you can see that the longest period with kernel preemption disabled while running the trace was 1160 microseconds. This simple fact is available by reading /sys/kernel/debug/tracing/tracing_max_latency, but the previous trace goes further and gives you the sequence of kernel function calls that led up to that measurement. The column marked delay shows the point on the trail where each function was called, ending with the call to trace_preempt_on() at 1162us, at which point kernel preemption is once again enabled. With this information, you can look back through the call chain and (hopefully) work out whether this is a problem or not.

The other tracers mentioned work in the same way.

Combining cyclictest and Ftrace

If cyclictest reports unexpectedly long latencies, you can use the breaktrace option to abort the program and trigger Ftrace to obtain more information.

You invoke breaktrace using -b<N> or --breaktrace=<N>, where N is the number of microseconds of latency that will trigger the trace. You select the Ftrace tracer using -T[tracer name] or one of the following:

- -C: Context switch
- -E: Event

- -f: Function
- -w: Wakeup
- -W: Wakeup-RT

For example, this will trigger the Ftrace function tracer when a latency greater than 100 microseconds is measured:

```
# cyclictest -a -t -p99 -b100
```

We now have two complementary tools for debugging latency issues. `cyclictest` detects the pauses and Ftrace provides the details.

Summary

The term *real-time* is meaningless unless you qualify it with a deadline and an acceptable miss rate. When you have these two pieces of information, you can determine whether or not Linux is a suitable candidate for the operating system and, if so, begin to tune your system to meet the requirements. Tuning Linux and your application to handle real-time events means making it more deterministic so that the real-time threads can meet their deadlines reliably. Determinism usually comes at the price of total throughput, so a real-time system is not going to be able to process as much data as a non-real-time system.

It is not possible to provide mathematical proof that a complex operating system such as Linux will always meet a given deadline, so the only approach is through extensive testing using tools such as `cyclictest` and Ftrace and, more importantly, using your own benchmarks for your own application.

To improve determinism, you need to consider both the application and the kernel. When writing real-time applications, you should follow the guidelines given in this chapter about scheduling, locking, and memory.

The kernel has a large impact on the determinism of your system. Thankfully, there has been a lot of work on this over the years. Enabling kernel preemption is a good first step. If you still find that it is missing deadlines more often than you would like, then you might want to consider PREEMPT_RT. It can certainly produce low latencies, but you may have problems integrating the PREEMPT_RT kernel patch with an older (pre 6.12) vendor kernel for your particular board. You may instead, or in addition, need to embark on the exercise of finding the cause of the latencies using Ftrace and similar tools.

That brings me to the end of this dissection of embedded Linux. Being an engineer of embedded systems requires a very wide range of skills, which includes a low-level knowledge of hardware and how the kernel interacts with it. You need to be an excellent system engineer who can configure user applications and tune them to work in an efficient manner. All of this has to be done with hardware that is, often, only just capable of carrying out the task. There is a quotation that sums this up: *An engineer can do for a dollar what anyone else can do for two.* I hope that you will be able to achieve this with the information I have presented during the course of this book.

Further study

- *Hard Real-Time Computing Systems: Predictable Scheduling Algorithms and Applications*, by Giorgio Buttazzo
- *Multicore Application Programming: for Windows, Linux, and Oracle Solaris*, by Darryl Gove

Join our community on Discord

Join our community's Discord space for discussions with the authors and other readers: https://packt.link/embeddedsystems

‹packt›

Subscribe to our online digital library for full access to over 7,000 books and videos, as well as industry leading tools to help you plan your personal development and advance your career. For more information, please visit our website.

Why subscribe?

- Spend less time learning and more time coding with practical eBooks and Videos from over 4,000 industry professionals
- Improve your learning with Skill Plans built especially for you
- Get a free eBook or video every month
- Fully searchable for easy access to vital information
- Copy and paste, print, and bookmark content

At www.packt.com, you can also read a collection of free technical articles, sign up for a range of free newsletters, and receive exclusive discounts and offers on Packt books and eBooks.

Other Books You May Enjoy

If you enjoyed this book, you may be interested in these other books by Packt:

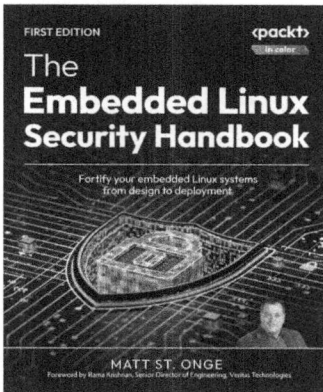

The Embedded Linux Security Handbook

Matt St. Onge

ISBN: 978-1-83588-564-2

- Understand how to determine the optimal hardware platform based on design criteria
- Recognize the importance of security by design in embedded systems
- Implement advanced security measures such as TPM, LUKS encryption, and Secure Boot processes
- Discover best practices for secure life cycle management, including appliance update and upgrade mechanisms
- Create a secure software supply chain efficiently
- Implement childproofing by controlling access and resources on the appliance

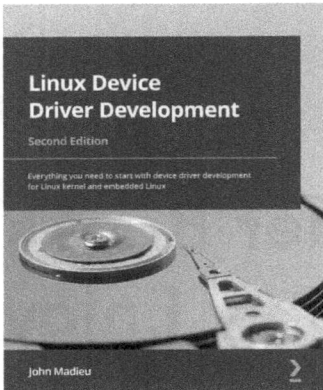

Linux Device Driver Development, Second Edition

John Madieu

ISBN: 978-1-80324-006-0

- Download, configure, build, and tailor the Linux kernel
- Describe the hardware using a device tree
- Write feature-rich platform drivers and leverage I2C and SPI buses
- Get the most out of the new concurrency managed workqueue infrastructure
- Understand the Linux kernel timekeeping mechanism and use time-related APIs
- Use the regmap framework to factor the code and make it generic
- Offload CPU for memory copies using DMA
- Interact with the real world using GPIO, IIO, and input subsystems

Packt is searching for authors like you

If you're interested in becoming an author for Packt, please visit authors.packtpub.com and apply today. We have worked with thousands of developers and tech professionals, just like you, to help them share their insight with the global tech community. You can make a general application, apply for a specific hot topic that we are recruiting an author for, or submit your own idea.

Share your thoughts

Now you've finished *Mastering Embedded Linux Development, Fourth Edition*, we'd love to hear your thoughts! Scan the QR code below to go straight to the Amazon review page for this book and share your feedback or leave a review on the site that you purchased it from.

https://packt.link/r/1803232595

Your review is important to us and the tech community and will help us make sure we're delivering excellent quality content.

Index